D1156740

INTRODUCTION TO PSYCHOLOGY

INTRODUCTION TO PSYCHOLOGY

BY

EDWIN GARRIGUES BORING
Harvard University

HERBERT SIDNEY LANGFELD
Princeton University

HARRY PORTER WELD
Cornell University

AND

COLLABORATORS

NEW YORK
JOHN WILEY & SONS, INC.
LONDON : CHAPMAN & HALL, LIMITED
1939

Printed in U. S. A.

THE HADDON CRAFTSMEN, INC., CAMDEN, N. J.

CONTRIBUTORS

EDWIN GARRIGUES BORING
CHARLES WILLIAM BRAY
HADLEY CANTRIL
LEONARD CARMICHAEL
SHAMMAI FELDMAN
NORMAN FREDERIKSEN
GEORGE HUMPHREY
DANIEL KATZ
CARNEY LANDIS
HERBERT SIDNEY LANGFELD
DONALD WALLACE MACKINNON
ROBERT BRODIE MACLEOD
JOHN ALEXANDER MCGEOCH
CATHARINE COX MILES
DONALD MCLEAN PURDY
MILES ALBERT TINKER
HARRY PORTER WELD
ERNEST GLEN WEVER

JOHN GILBERT BEEBE-CENTER
WARNER BROWN
DWIGHT WESLEY CHAPMAN
KARL M. DALLENBACH
HARRY REGINALD DESILVA
MICHAEL JACOB ZIGLER

The six persons last named contributed to Psychology: A Factual Textbook, *and their contributions have been used in part in the present book.*

PREFACE

In contemplating a revision of our *Psychology: a Factual Textbook*, we turned for criticisms and suggestions to the psychologists who were known to be using the book. Very soon it became evident, with their replies in hand for analysis, that something more than a revision would be necessary to satisfy the needs of many teachers. The older book impressed its users as being conservative and sound. Some few teachers of elementary courses liked it for these reasons; others found it satisfactory for more advanced courses. The majority of the instructors in the elementary courses, however, while speaking generously of our attempt to secure factual accuracy by employing expert authors for the different topics, wanted a more modernistic approach. They were ready, in other words, to leave for special courses the scientific details of those fields which are today richest in established fact—the fields of sensation and perception. Although they wanted the student to know the larger generalities in these subjects, they also wanted him to be informed as fully as possible about reaction, its motivational determinants, and its role in the personality and in social relations. It is this need which we have endeavored to meet. Our aim, therefore, has been to respond to the temper of the times without losing the authority that comes with multiple authorship by experts, and equally without diminishing, we hope, the seriousness of the scientific approach to the problems of psychology.

This new book is so much more than a revision of the old that we have given it a new title. In it we have turned the old book hind part to, beginning with the consideration of conduct and ending with the treatment of perception. The changed order of exposition reflects our final conclusion that, since the student comes to psychology with some knowledge of the functioning of the organism in a social environment, it is best in an elementary course to begin with this knowledge—the problems of conduct, motivation and personality—and to proceed thence analytically to the simpler functions.

The book is considerably enlarged, with some new chapters and some new collaborators. As was the case in the first book, these expert authors have formulated in the first instance the content of the chapters, but thereafter we as editors have freely exercised our right to alter their texts in the interests of unity in the whole.

We list here the specific relations of the new book to the old. The introductory chapter is new. The first portion of the book, devoted to a consideration of conduct, includes new chapters on the social functions of the individual, individual differences (a chapter which takes over some of the old material on statistical measurement), and motivation. The chapter on personality has been so thoroughly revised that it may be considered new. The chapters on response, the response mechanism and emotion have likewise been revised, with the topic of pleasantness and unpleasantness incorporated in the chapter on emotion.

The second portion of the text, which treats of learning, has been considerably expanded and the topic divided into two chapters, one on learning and one on retention. The treatment of the representative functions—recollection, imagination and thought—has also been revised.

The chapter on perception is practically new, and radical alteration has somewhat changed the perspective of the chapter on space perception. The considerations of the perception of time and of movement have been condensed and combined in a single chapter. There is a new chapter on sensation, which, however, includes some of the content of the old chapter on intensity, as well as a treatment of psychophysics which was in the old chapter on mental measurement. The accounts of vision and hearing have been revised, while the old chapters on smell, taste and somesthesis have been condensed and combined into a single chapter.

This preface provides us with a welcome opportunity to express our deep appreciation of the hearty and enthusiastic cooperation of our collaborators, who have at all times during the preparation of this book generously acceded to our plans and wishes. We also thank Miss Katherine Frost for her wise understanding of our problem and her critical emendations of the manuscript and proof.

E. G. B.
January 11, 1939 H. S. L.
H. P. W.

CONTENTS

Chapter 1

THE NATURE OF MAN

What is man?

To this question psychology seeks an answer. Sometimes people think that any person, merely because he is a man, ought to know just what man is; but why should man know what he himself is like? Horses do not know about horses, nor tables about tables; nor is the wisest ape in the world an authority on apes. Man does in fact know a little about himself, but he has not learned it easily, and much of his conduct is determined by motives of which he himself is not aware. Man has to learn about himself, not by sudden insight, but by research, for to "know thyself" means work.

Some of this work is done, however, and the question about the nature of man has a modern answer which is satisfactory, even if not yet final. What is man?

The first thing of importance to say about human life is that it is participated in by persons. The individual is the unit. He acts more or less consistently with himself, although often differently from other individuals, and among the individuals there is a great deal of interaction. They act together in groups; there are families, societies, parties, nations. They communicate with one another by language. They talk as man to man, and also as author to his readers or statesman to his radio audience. With language they incite each other to action; the mother incites her son to be good, the minister of propaganda exhorts his nation to be courageous. Taken in the large, there is a good deal of conflict between individuals and between groups, for the same people get incited in different directions simultaneously. Sometimes they actually get pushed around or made to

---

This chapter was written by Edwin G. Boring of Harvard University.

go where they do not want to go, but mostly the forces of social interaction are expressed by words. Thus the first thing to tell about man is that he is a unit in a complex field of *social* relations, and it is the psychology of these social functions that supplies the details as to how man fits into the social structure and how he adjusts to it or resists it.

The fundamental nature of man does not appear, however, merely in his relation to his fellows. We have also to consider him as a single individual. He turns out to be an active mass of protoplasm which has many fairly persistent consistencies of behavior that make up what is called his *personality*. His particular pattern of behavior may, however, vary greatly from the patterns of other men. He may be introverted or extraverted in relation to his world, ascendant or submissive in relation to his fellows, persistent or volatile in his activities, a radical or a conservative in his thought. He may have a high or a low level of aspiration in his motivation. The number of traits and attitudes which classify these consistencies of mind and conduct is enormous. We ask why men differ in these respects. It is because of their differences in inheritance, in education, in physiological constitution, in past emotional experience, in the secretions of the endocrine glands and in the myriad of lesser variations that are included under these broad terms.

Men *differ* also in many other ways. They differ in intelligence, and with increasing age they change both in intelligence and in motivation. There are two sexes which are unlike in conduct and interests. There are many races which, like the sexes, differ in conduct and interests.

Nevertheless, we have still to get at the essential nature of man. Men differ somewhat and also are somewhat alike, forming groups according to their likenesses. They interact, man with man and group with group. Yet what is man himself? Man is an organism which responds to excitation in accordance with certain of its properties. The organism has necessities for response, which are called man's *needs*. Man has a need for food, and, if you keep a man from food, he will be driven to seek for it until he gets it. In this way a need unsupplied creates a drive. Sex is another fundamental need. Every need leads to a drive which is terminated by the satisfaction of the need. Man has a great capacity for needs. His primary needs become differentiated so that he acquires many new needs. An adult man may need, not only food, but candy; not only love, but fine clothes. Around man's needs and drives centers the psychology of his *motivation*.

Man's *emotions* are closely related to his needs. In his need for self-preservation may arise the emotion of fear. In his sexual need may arise the emotion of love. His emotions, moreover, like his needs, may become differentiated and specific. The fear of insult and the love of music are important, useful, acquired emotions, whereas the fear of mice and the love of liquor are acquired but less useful. We know more about man's emotions than his needs, for in the emotions there are widespread bodily changes that can be studied—changes in the invisible interior of the body and also changes in visible facial expressions and bodily attitudes.

Man, essentially a doer, satisfies his needs by doing something about them. The study of his behavior shows that his action is not fortuitous or spontaneous but that it occurs always as a response to excitation. Why? Because of the *nervous system*. To understand man, the doer, we must understand his nervous system, for upon it his actions depend.

The nervous system connects stimulus with response, making excitation effective. It has simple levels for reflex action that may not even involve the brain. It has complex levels, where action depends upon elaborate connections in the brain. Because no animal that does not respond to stimulation can be said to have a mind, the nervous system is sometimes said to be the organ of man's mind.

Responses develop as the individual grows up. The embryo can squirm as a whole; the infant can clench his fist; the adult can trill a note or say a tongue-twister. Some responses may be primitive and automatic, like winking, whereas others are complex and voluntary in the sense that they are excited by ideas, like going shopping. Still others are complex and learned, yet automatic, like walking. The essential cause of a response may be social pressure, emotion, need, thought, learning, idea or simple stimulation. Indeed, to understand thoroughly the causes of man's responses would be to understand man himself.

Next in importance to the fact that man can respond with movement to excitation is his characteristic of being able to alter his modes of response. He can *learn.* Learning is the establishment of new relations between stimulus and response. Food in man's mouth makes his saliva flow; that is an inherited relationship. Man can, however, learn what food looks like so that his saliva flows at the mere sight of food. His mouth may even learn to water at the sound of a dinner bell. It often happens that a complex response seems entirely new because it is a brand new combination of old response elements, as in the learning of a poem or of a stroke at tennis. Man makes these new *integrations* of responses under the pressure of some need, primitive or sophisticated. He learns to recognize food because he needs to eat to live; and he learns to recognize musical intervals because he needs to play the violin in order to enjoy the life which he lives. Sometimes he perceives a relationship suddenly and acts differently about it ever after: that is *insight.* More often he learns slowly, with many repetitions, a little at a time. Learning is the human capacity that accounts for most of the differences between the adult and the infant. It is so important that some animal psychologists have said that without learning there is no mind, although it is probably more accurate to say that mind exists wherever response exists.

It turns out that learning is not permanent in man. He forgets. In general his *forgetting* goes on continuously in time. His recent memories are more numerous than his old ones. One cause of forgetting is that man has a limited capacity for the acquisition of response-relationships. He cannot learn more than so much at a time and thus generally for complete learning he requires many repetitions. What he succeeds in learning, however, interferes with what he has already learned, so that the new acquisitions cancel some of the old. Perhaps if a man could sleep, without any thinking or learning at all, for a hundred years, he would, like the sleeping beauty, wake up with no forgetfulness and go on just where he had left off.

Next in importance to his capacity for learning is man's capacity for *representation*. He can respond to an absent object because he can learn to let a present object represent it, or because he creates within himself a representative. These internal representatives have been called *images*. Out of sight is not out of mind for man. In terms of his imagery he can recollect and he can think; he can imagine and dream the bizarre dreams of sleep or the wise dreams of creative genius. By images he can solve problems in *thought*. Similarly he can use words, either imaged or spoken, to represent absent objects or abstract generalizations. With them he can think, and create, and solve problems. This great capacity to utilize the symbolic power of words and images is the chief distinction between man and the animals.

Thus the chief properties of man turn out to be his capacities (1) for response, (2) for learning and (3) for symbolization. In addition to these three there is a great deal more that can be said about his capacity (4) for *perception*. Man does not perceive his environment exactly as it is, but alters it in accordance with his needs, for it is too complicated and variable for him to perceive it in all its chaotic changefulness. Needing to simplify it for his own purposes, the first thing that he does to it is to divide it up into objects. Objects are man-made. Perception groups many items of experience together into an object and puts other items outside, so that man, when he sees the world as a collection of objects, has done something to the world in perceiving it. An object must have a certain amount of stability in order that it may seem always to be itself and not to be forever becoming something else. Thus we find man equipped with a set of laws of constancy: seen objects tend to stay the same size, even when they vary in distance; they tend to stay the same shape, even when viewed at different angles; they tend to stay the same brightness and color, even when the intensity and hue of the illumination change.

Since man needs to know where he is and where other things are, we find that he can perceive the localizations and the distances of many objects, as well as their shapes and sizes. From various cues which come to him some of the data of the environment are correctly reconstructed by his nervous system, whereas other data are usefully distorted or ignored in the interests of necessary simplification. The organism is such that in general man gets of the world the picture that he needs.

Although man is, on the whole, successful in reconstructing the all-important external world in perception, still he can never perceive distinctions in that world unless they are transmitted to him by his senses. He has five senses, and about their capacities and limitations we know a great deal—about the ways in which they transform stimulations into color and sound, odor and taste, warmth and cold, pressure and pain. Sensation is the oldest chapter in psychology, the classical field of research where the greatest number of laws have been discovered. For this reason we know much more about tones than needs, more about colors than prejudices. In many cases, moreover, we can see how sensory laws depend upon the nature of the sense organs. The detail with which the facts of man's sensory capacities has been established argues that eventually we shall be able to describe just as fully the laws of his thoughts and motives.

It is thus that our question is answered. What is man?

A man is a mass of protoplasm moving about on the face of the earth. His movements are lawful. He interacts with the other protoplasmic masses in the variety of ways that are discussed by social psychology. The consistencies of his action make up his personality. There is a general law of his behavior that action is always a response to excitation, and there are many specific laws, all of which depend on the properties of his nervous system. We find that the dependence of his response upon excitation can be modified: that is learning. We discover that he can use words and images in place of absent objects: that is recollection and thought. The chief characteristic of man is, however, the fact that all his conduct is dominated by his needs, for it is in order to satisfy needs that he acts, learns, thinks and perceives. And that is what a person is: needy protoplasm with all these properties.

This sketch of man is the outline of modern psychology. The next eighteen chapters supply the details for the complete picture.

CHAPTER 2

SOCIAL FUNCTIONS OF THE INDIVIDUAL

Every individual is born into, and develops within, a social environment. This important though obvious fact is one which the psychologist, particularly, must constantly bear in mind. Man does not live in a vacuum, and if the psychologist is interested in analyzing and explaining the behavior and consciousness of the individual, he must always remember not only that this behavior and this consciousness occur within a social framework but also that to lose sight of this fact is to construct a psychology little related to the problems of real life.

It is necessary to study the social situations to which man reacts, the psychological mechanisms involved in his process of adjusting to the social environment and the interaction of that environment upon his thought and behavior. Such a program means that the psychologist has essentially three related tasks in the understanding of social behavior. First, he must carefully observe the ways of life and the objects that surround both him and the person whom he is studying, in order to determine how these social stimulus-situations have been created or modified because of the fact that other people share the same physical environment. Secondly, he must watch the developing individual that he may discover and describe the particular mental and behavioral processes which make it possible for the human being to react as he does to social stimuli. Finally, to discover the effects of social stimuli upon mental life and overt behavior, he must study the individual both during and after reaction to such stimuli. These are the chief, the general, interests of social psychology.

This chapter was written by Hadley Cantril and Norman Frederiksen of Princeton University.

THE NATURE OF SOCIETY

Social norms. Every individual starts life in a particular culture composed of institutions, laws, fashions, language and objects of all kinds that are characteristic of it. To keep this seemingly obvious fact ever in mind is essential from the outset—essential most of all, indeed, for the psychologist, who is himself one of the people born into a particular culture. If, then, he proposes to study his own culture, he must understand with as much objectivity and perspective as possible the basic assumptions and the predominant modes of thought and behavior that provide the framework for his observation. He must, somehow, jump out of his own skin in order to look at himself and his own kind as he would at his laboratory subject.

For example, suppose an American interested in determining the attitudes of adolescents toward different occupations finds that the banker and the business executive are most highly esteemed, the lawyer and the doctor next, the engineer and the carpenter and the mason last. Can he conclude that there is something about banking or the practice of law that makes its devotees more respectable than would carpentry or brick laying? He should not conclude this, although he often does. What, then, is the fallacy here? Simply that this American is observing within a particular social framework—the United States—a framework within which alone his conclusions are valid. Were he to go to Soviet Russia, he might find his conclusions completely reversed. Or even were he to carry on his study in a small rural community where the local doctor was the outstanding citizen, his findings might likewise be upset. If, however, he decides to compare the vocational ambitions of children in different cultures, then his problem is immediately changed. For instead of asking what the attitudes of children are toward different occupations, the question which he must really ask turns out to be: How does the social framework within which an individual is born determine his attitude toward different vocations? Unless, in other words, an American has this perspective, he will fail to recognize some of the major problems in his field.

Every culture surrounding every individual is, then, more or less specific. In some cases its limits are natural boundaries, such as mountains or oceans; in other cases it is limited by the imaginary lines separating one 'nation' from another; in still other situations, the boundaries are merely those of class, custom, language, income, education, sex or age. Two people living in the same city may, from the point of view of the psychologist, be living in quite different cultures, subjected to quite different social stimulus-situations. To one man may come wealth, prestige, security, while no more than a block away there may live an unskilled laborer, poor, unknown, and unsure of his job. The social frame of reference within which each of these two thinks, feels and acts will turn out to be almost as different as those of an Eskimo and an Australian Bushman—possibly, indeed, even more different. If both the Eskimo and the Bushman happen to be leaders or slaves, their social frames of reference may have a good deal more in common than those of the two neighbors in the city.

There are many assumptions, habits and customs that most people living in the United States at the present time take for granted but that probably would seem queer enough to an outside observer unacquainted with our culture. A few examples are the following:

That a man should have only one wife, a woman only one husband;
That we should eat three times a day, using knives and forks;
That we should regard roast beef and roast pork as delicacies but eschew whales' fins or dried mice;
That most business and professional work should be done by men, and most housework by women;
That we should elect people to govern us;
That we should have a stock exchange.

The term *social norm* is used to describe the standardized social products found in any culture. Such social products include accepted ways of thinking and behaving as well as standardized shapes, sounds, tools and other material objects. Thus, in our culture, they may be represented by such widely different examples as a football game, a skyscraper, democracy, a diatonic scale, or an automobile—all of which may be regarded as social norms, since each has been created and accepted and passed on to the next generation by groups of individuals. In other cultures, on the other hand, certain deviations would be regarded as norms: cricket, igloos, dictatorship, the five-interval scale or jinrikishas.

Social values. Individuals in a culture accept not merely the norms of culture; they accept also the judgments people have already made of these norms. When, for example, we learn about democracy, we also learn that it is a 'good' thing; when we hear about football games, we infer that people 'approve' of them; when we learn about thieves, we are warned that they are 'bad' men. As we shall see later, the fact that we learn how we should judge or evaluate a custom, an institution, a shape or a symbol at the same time that we learn *about* that custom, institution or shape is of the utmost importance if we are to understand social behavior. The term *social value* is used to describe for a culture the norms upon which the majority of the people in the culture have made a judgment. Practically all norms have been so evaluated.

It is these social norms and values that form a large share of the social stimulus-situations to which an individual responds. The individual does not, to be sure, usually react to the abstract norm or value itself, but rather to its concrete representation. We do not stop at a corner because of a vague norm called 'the law,' but because the policeman bars the way, because there is a traffic signal and because we ourselves fear what might happen to us if we did not. We may learn to salute the flag, to sing the Star Spangled Banner, to buy Liberty Bonds and in all these ways learn the abstract value of patriotism. Yet each of these specific objects or modes of behavior must in the end be regarded merely as socially accepted representations of the more generalized ways of thinking or acting approved by our particular society.

PROCESSES OF SOCIALIZATION

The social norms and values may be regarded as forming the superstructure of society into which the individual is born. If he is to live satisfactorily in his society, avoiding jails and insane asylums where the transgressors of norms are isolated, he must as he grows up somehow make these norms and values a part of himself. Most of us have unwittingly incorporated in our conduct the behavior and thought patterns of our particular culture. How was such a process accomplished? What psychological processes made it possible? Of the many factors involved in this development we may select a few of the more important for discussion: imitation, language, suggestion and propaganda.

Imitation. Imitation occurs when a person, having some particular goal in mind, copies the behavior of other people in an effort to learn methods of achieving that goal. The child will imitate a parent's mannerisms in order to feel grown up, just as the uncritical student will imitate the language of his teacher in order to appear sophisticated; likewise the raw recruit in the army will imitate the seasoned veteran in order to avoid the enemy's fire. Probably in the majority of instances in everyday life imitation occurs quite unconsciously. We acquire language, mannerisms, habits or opinions without realizing that what we are actually doing is imitating the language, mannerisms, habits or opinions of some individual or group in our culture.

Although imitation is essentially a kind of learning, the term to be used accurately must not be extended to explain behavior that may be due to other forms of learning. When the raw recruit has himself become a seasoned veteran, then he is no longer imitating. He has learned a mode of response and perhaps a general method of conduct, both of which he can himself apply to new situations. Imitation in this case is merely the first stage of learning. *Imitation is the conscious or unconscious attempt of an individual to reproduce in his thought or behavior the same pattern of thought or behavior that he has perceived in another individual.*

Development of language. The ability to make use of the symbols of language is one of the most conspicuous differences between man and the lower animals. Not only is language indispensable in carrying on abstract thinking; it serves man in countless other ways as well. It enables him to communicate his wishes and his ideas to others, even at a great distance; it permits him to receive impressions from others and to regulate his behavior accordingly; it makes available to him much of the lore and experience of past generations. Through language the child may be trained to become a *social* being, aware of the norms and values of his culture.

The first vocal sound made by an infant, the birth cry, is incidental to the air's being drawn across the vocal cords in breathing. Sounds uttered by the child during its first few weeks are probably simple reflex responses to hunger, cold and pain, and cannot as yet be considered the beginning of language. Very soon, however, the child learns to use these rudimentary sounds for social control. The infant experiences hunger pangs and cries; whereupon the mother comes with a bottle of warm milk. Thus the child, having learned that his cry readily produces satisfactory results, soon tends to intensify his vocal reaction to the hunger situation. In this way it happens that a parent who regularly attempts to pacify a crying child by fondling and caressing teaches the child to make use of crying in order to get more fondling and more attention.

Sometime during the second or third month of the child's life a *babbling* stage of vocalization begins, during which time the child acquires skill in the production of the sounds of speech. In this state the child tends to repeat syllables over and over in various combinations. Actual records of the babblings of children include such sounds as *uggle-uggle*, *a-bah-bah, adu-duddeh, dudde-ooh* and *lul-lul-lah*. Observers report that at this stage a child four months old may actually use all the sounds possible in the English language, as well as a good many others which cannot be spelled with our alphabet.

During the babbling stage of the development of speech the child's vocalizations are, of course, meaningless to an adult. Even by the time the child is a year old, indeed, he is likely to have a comprehensible vocabulary of only two or three words, such as *mama, baby, dada, see* and *bye-bye*. The first word is likely to consist of a reduplicated syllable. At the age of a year and a half, however, approximately one-fourth of the child's vocalizations are comprehensible. At two years, about two-thirds can be understood; at three years, nine-tenths; and at four years more than 99 per cent of the child's speech is comprehensible.

We turn now to a description of the process by which the child acquires his ability to use verbal responses as meaningful symbols representing objects in his environment, and we deal first with the child's tendency to repeat or reduplicate syllables in his vocalization (see pp. 257f.). Such reduplication of sounds may be considered as the first step in the development of language. The child may, for example, by chance articulate the syllable *ma*. Accompanying this vocalization is an auditory experience; the child hears himself say *ma*. Many psychological studies carried out with animals as well as with persons show that, when a sensory experience accompanies a reaction, the experience tends to become in turn a stimulus serving to evoke that reaction. Since, then, the sound of the syllable *ma* uttered by the child becomes associated with the act of producing the sound, he repeats the syllable *ma*. In this manner a circular response is set up, whereby each articulation of the syllable causes the reinstatement of the response, and the child says *ma-ma-ma*, etc., until the circular responses are interrupted by other stimulation or until fatigue of the neural processes involved terminates the response.

Once the circular response is established, it can be set going by sounds uttered by persons other than the child. The mother says the word *mama* to the child, and the baby repeats the syllables. Although this response resembles imitation, actually it is simply the performance of a learned response to an auditory stimulus. Only circular responses that have been acquired by the child will be repeated in this way. One child, for example, responded with the syllable *ba* to the spoken words, *box, bath, bottle, block* and *bye*. Such responses resemble only superficially the process of imitation; at this stage of development there is no voluntary attempt at conscious reproduction of sounds made by others.

When development reaches the stage where the parent can induce the child to repeat syllables, then the growth of meaningful vocabulary begins. In this process, objects present at the time the child repeats the sound become associated, after many repetitions, with that sound itself, until eventually the mere sight of the object is sufficient to evoke the appropriate vocal response. Always when his mother is present the child hears the word *mama*. It finally results, therefore, that his mother's presence alone is sufficient to evoke the response *mama*. In the same way the word *doll*, repeated by the parent while he holds up a doll to the child's gaze, eventually results in an attempt by the child to say the nearest possible equivalent of the word whenever the doll is presented. Thus does the process of acquiring vocabulary proceed.

It appears, therefore, that acquiring a vocabulary is at first a rather mechanical process, one in which the child takes but little spontaneous interest. When the child is somewhere between a year and a half and two years old, however, a change takes place. Beginning apparently to understand the meaning of speech and the fact that everything has a name, he starts to ask the names of objects. During the period immediately following this change, his vocabulary shows a sudden and great increase. It is in this stage, too, that the child first begins to combine words to form sentences. At first the increase in vocabulary consists entirely of nouns; later the child acquires verbs; and last of all does he add the qualifying words and the words denoting relationships.

For Helen Keller, who lost both her sight and her hearing during an illness at the age of nineteen months, the moment of discovery of the meaning of speech occurred with surprising suddenness. She grew up to the age of seven years without acquiring language. At this age her teacher succeeded in teaching her a finger alphabet by touches on the palm of the hand. Although she thereupon built up associations between a few objects and the finger symbols, apparently it was without any realization of the symbolic nature of the signs. Thus her development at this point may be said to correspond to that of the child who says *mama* when his mother is present, simply as a result of association of the verbal response with the presence of the mother.

After about a month of instruction, however, an event occurred which resulted in Helen's sudden realization of the symbolic nature of language. The incident is described by the teacher as follows:

> We went out to the pumphouse, and I made Helen hold her mug under the spout while I pumped. As the cold water gushed forth, filling the mug, I spelled "w-a-t-e-r" in Helen's free hand. The word coming so close upon the sensation of cold water rushing over her hand seemed to startle her. She dropped the mug and stood as one transfixed. A new light came into her face. She spelled "water" several times. Then she dropped on the ground and asked for its name and pointed to the pump and the trellis, and suddenly turning round she asked for my name. I spelled "teacher." Just then the nurse brought Helen's little sister into the pumphouse, and Helen spelled "baby" and pointed to the nurse. All the way back to the house she was highly excited, and learned the name of every object she touched, so that in a few hours she had added thirty new words to her vocabulary.[1]

The vocabulary grows very rapidly after the second year. At one year we have said the child has a vocabulary of only two or three words. At two he uses somewhat fewer than 300 words, at four about 1500 words, at six about 2500 words and at twelve over 7000 words. It is estimated that the average vocabulary of

[1] Helen Keller, *The story of my life,* Doubleday Page, 1903, 316; copyright, 1903, 1931; reprinted by permission of Doubleday, Doran & Co., Inc.

sophomore and junior college students in this country consists of approximately 15,000 non-technical English 'root' words, plus 52,000 derivatives of roots, besides technical words such as are used in science courses and foreign-language vocabularies.

At first the child uses words in too wide a sense; each one denotes far too many objects. The word *daddy* may at first be applied indiscriminately to all men. Not only dogs, but cats, cows and horses may be referred to as *bow-wow*. One child used the word *hat* for anything put on his head, including a comb and brush. For another child all metals were *keys*. Only by increasing experience with objects, by hearing adults use the words correctly and by being corrected himself for their wrong use does the child gradually delimit his notions of the meanings of words.

While the child is overcoming in this way his first overgeneralizations in the use of words, he begins the process of formation of the concept. A concept is an idea which stands for the common properties of the members of a whole class of objects, situations or events. Words provide a tool for cataloguing such a variety of objects or events under a single rubric. Concepts have to be derived gradually from a child's primitive experience. The word *chair*, he learns, is attached to his high chair. Later he finds that the same term is used in connection with lounging chairs, dining-room chairs, rocking chairs, Morris chairs, dentists' chairs and electric chairs. From all these diverse experiences he eventually abstracts the element common to all of them, namely that one may react to them by taking a sitting posture in them. So at length the word *chair* has become for him a symbol which he can use as a tool in thinking. To say "chair" is to utilize a short cut for the enumeration of all the varieties of chairs with which he has had experience. Short cuts such as these are vital to the continuance of abstract thinking. Many of the technical words used in college courses—for example, *energy, wave-length, respiration* and *temperature*—stand for concepts without which abstract thinking would be impossible.

Development of affective value. One usually thinks of words with respect to their substantive or dictionary definitions. In gaining facility in the use of language, the child acquires, however, not only some degree of intellectual understanding of the meaning of the verbal symbol, but also an *affective* value. Some words become disgusting, others are pleasing, some are exciting, still others are fearsome. These affective values may either develop simultaneously with the substantive meanings, or they may come before or after them.

Suppose Bobbie, aged fourteen months, is being wheeled by his nurse in the park, when a large dog trots over, puts his feet on the side of the perambulator and tries to lick Bobbie's face. Frightened, the nurse screams, "Look out for the dog!" Consequently Bobbie is terrified. If that is Bobbie's first experience with a dog, he may acquire on the spot both a substantive meaning and an affective value for the word *dog*. It is possible that thereafter the sound of the word *dog* may, for many years, serve as a stimulus for the partial reinstatement of the fear which occurred in that initial experience.

Affective values of words may be, and probably often are, acquired without actual experience with their objects. The parent who unwisely frightens the child into obedience by saying, "A policeman will get you if you run away," is teaching an emotional response to a verbal symbol, without acquaintance with the object—but one which will, in all likelihood, distort the child's concepts and thinking about policemen for the rest of his life.

The affective connotations of words result in the possibility of a literature emotionally rich and esthetically pleasing. Less fortunate, however, is another result of the affective value of words. It is difficult to think clearly and dispassionately about an issue when all that one reads or hears about the problem is couched in words provocative of emotional reaction rather than of a clear understanding of intellectual concepts. In an attempt to overcome this handicap scientists in their communication with one another devise their own technical vocabulary, where each word is precisely defined in relation to objective reality. Yet even scientific terms that start out as emotionally neutral words sometimes acquire emotional connotations. Most biologists would resent being called 'Lamarckians' (persons who believe in the inheritance of acquired characteristics); nor has 'extra-sensory perception' (the supposed ability to 'perceive' objects without the use of the ordinary senses) remained a neutral term for psychologists.

Reification. There is a second way in which the symbols of language affect abstract thinking. This is the tendency to *reify* concepts, that is to say, to think of subjective phenomena as objective realities. Such words as *gravity*, *electricity, honor* and *justice* are concepts which are often reified. If you ask a man why he wears a necktie, he will probably reply that he wears it because it is the custom. If you question him carefully about the nature of this thing called 'custom,' you will probably find that, superficially at least, he thinks of custom as some sort of force existing outside the people within a given culture, a force which acts upon them, making them behave in a certain way. All he knows, actually, is that under certain circumstances 100 per cent (or nearly that many) of the adult male population may be seen wearing neckties. This concept is a subjective phenomenon, an idea; it is a judgment based on the observation of many specific cases. When such a judgment is given a name and the name is thought of as an entity having actual existence, then the concept has been reified.

A newspaper columnist once wrote, "Destroy the Constitution or ignore it and nothing remains but a government of men." In these words he was reifying the concept of the constitution. He conceived of it evidently as some sort of superindividual entity capable of controlling an individual's behavior, not simply as a written document, a record of the behavior of certain people (called 'The Fathers' by this writer), no different in physical nature from any other such written record of the behavior of legislators. We are all, of course, aware of a difference between the constitution and other laws. The columnist, however, takes advantage of the reification of this concept and thus appeals to the emotions which have become attached to the word.

Modern war would be impossible without the tendency on the part of individuals living within given geographical boundaries to reify the concept of their nation. To them the nation comes to be thought of as a great 'over-person' capable of action and possessing psychological characteristics such as honor and righteousness. The headlines of almost any issue of a daily newspaper will furnish the reader with examples of reification of the concept of the nation, headlines such as "Germany Issues Ultimatum." When an attaché of the American embassy in China was slapped by a Japanese soldier, every American who reified the concept of his nation felt that the honor of the United States had been sullied. Yet when we think more critically about these matters, we realize that the nation itself cannot be an actor, since it exists only as a concept of the interrelationships of many individuals, their leaders, their political behaviors, their geographical boundaries, natural resources and so on. Only *individuals* can sign treaties, slap each other's faces, borrow money or declare war. Without citizens' belief in the reality of their national symbols, without their sensitiveness to national honor, it would be impossible for political leaders to lead millions of people into an aggressive war.

In an investigation of the tendency to reify an institutional concept, each of 1963 fraternity or sorority members at Syracuse University was asked to check the one of the two following statements which more nearly corresponded to his own point of view:

> (*a*) My fraternity is a group standing for high ideals. The active personnel changes from year to year but the fraternity goes on always, upholding the same standards. A disgrace to my fraternity hurts me and reflects on all its members. A high standard of conduct should be required of its members so that the fair name of the fraternity will be upheld.
>
> (*b*) My fraternity is a group of individuals and its ideals are no higher or no lower than those of the individuals. The fraternity and its standards really exist only in the personnel

active at the time. A high standard of conduct should be required of the members because, since they are associated in the fraternity, a disgrace to one may affect the reputation of each of the others.[2]

Statement *a* expresses a reality of the group which is superior to the individuals, a reification of the concept of fraternity as an institution. Statement *b* covers the same points, but bases the matter entirely upon the individuals who are members. Two-thirds of the fraternity members checked *a*, indicating that they tended to reify the concept *fraternity*. One-third checked *b*, indicating that in their more realistic thought about the institution they did not regard it as a super-individual entity existing apart from the members, capable in some way of influencing their behavior.

Use of affective value. Every political orator and every editorial writer knows the power of emotionally toned words and reified concepts in effecting the formation of a desired attitude in his listener or reader. In most cases, indeed, the politician does not desire clear thinking on the part of the potential voter, because of either selfish personal interests or the necessity of fighting fire with fire. Rather, he seeks to bias the individual by deliberately choosing words that distort facts in his own favor.

Some of the newspaper editorials about strikes furnish good examples of the use of such emotionally toned words and reified concepts to influence the thinking of the reader in the desired direction. There was, for instance, a sit-down strike which occurred after the company officials had signed an agreement with the labor union. It was caused by the discharge of a number of union officials, along with other employees, because of a seasonal lag in business. The farmers in the vicinity, having lost the daily market for their milk on account of the strike, marched into town and, reinforced by a number of 'loyal' workers, forcibly evicted the strikers from the building.

[2] D. Katz and F. H. Allport, *Students' attitudes,* Craftsman Press, 1931, 168; reprinted by permission of the publishers.

A few days later an editorial appeared which contained these lines:

> The spirit of militant Americanism which has surged over the town of ———, is the inevitable AMERICAN answer to the challenge of Communist insolence which has foisted the sit-down strike upon this country.[3]

Another paper printed an editorial headed with this caption:

> TYPICAL AMERICAN PATRIOTISM AND SENSE OF JUSTICE MADE QUICK WORK OF STRIKE RACKETEERING AT PHILANTHROPIC PLANT[4]

The deliberate use of disagreeably toned words to describe the strikers ("Communist insolence," "strike racketeering") and of words high in pleasant emotional tone to describe their opponents ("spirit of militant Americanism," "American patriotism and sense of justice," and "philanthropic plant") gives the reader practically nothing in the way of intellectual understanding of the issue, but it does furnish him with stimuli for strong emotional reactions. There is a conscious attempt to identify the actors in the incident with institutions—such as Communism, Americanism, and racketeering—which the average reader regards as real entities over and above the individuals.

Suggestion. One of the most important single concepts in the field of social relations is that of suggestion, for it is largely by means of suggestion that the individual acquires the stereotyped norms of his community, his religion, his politics, his racial prejudices, his ethical and esthetic standards. If the majority of people in this country are Democrats or Republicans, it is not because they have made careful analyses of Anarchism, Socialism, Fascism or the other political points of view found in our modern world, not because they have decided on the basis of their study that the particular principles for which the Democrats or Republicans may stand are superior to those

[3] *New York American,* April 10, 1937.

[4] *New Hope News,* New Hope, Pennsylvania, April 15, 1937.

of other doctrines. On the contrary, they are Democrats or Republicans because they have acquired the particular norms of their culture.

The norms have the advantage of providing us with relatively fixed and limited standards of judgment by means of which we interpret or give meaning to specific events. Without such standards of judgment, which we may call frames of reference, we should be at a loss how to conduct ourselves in a complex world. Since the limits of time and energy forbid our reasoning out an opinion on every issue where we need to have some such opinion, we uncritically accept, instead, the prevailing norms and then try to rationalize them to ourselves.

We may define suggestion as the *acceptance by an individual of a frame of reference without the intervention of critical thought processes.* (For a further analysis of suggestion see pp. 275f.). When a person has no standard of judgment but has a desire for some standard, then he may accept a judgment uncritically. For example, a person who, knowing nothing about music, nevertheless feels that he should know something about it, will accept the critic's judgment of an artist's performance or of a new symphony. At other times an individual may accept a suggestion because it is consistent with some frame of reference which he already possesses. In this latter case, the suggestion merely reinforces his established opinion.

It is largely because of suggestion, of course, that advertising is so successful. Generally the advertiser tries to show how his product will help us attain some desired goal, how vital it is in achieving that end. If we use his soap, we shall all, he tells us, be social successes; if we smoke his cigarette, we shall be athletic; if we serve his whiskey, we shall impress business associates. Frequently the advertiser makes use of what we know as prestige suggestion by telling us of the famous people who use his product. A recent automobile advertisement informs us, "During the past year, for instance, ——— was chosen by 2 members of the English Royal Family, 33 diplomatic representatives of 21 countries, 8 government officials of

Ecuador, a judge of the Supreme Court of China, etc." Such an advertisement not only calls attention to the product; it also provides a highly valued frame of reference (the prestige of the diplomat) by means of which the product may be judged.

The influence of prestige in the acceptance of dogmatic statements has frequently been demonstrated. In one study the experimenter first determined from his subjects what well-known persons they liked best and what ones least. Then he presented the subjects with a questionnaire containing thirty statements, such as the following, with instructions to mark on a five-point scale the degree to which they agreed or disagreed with the statement:

> There is nothing sacred about the American Constitution. If it doesn't serve its purpose, it should be changed as often as necessary.

A third of the subjects were given the impression that the statement had been made by one of the best-liked people (such as Mark Twain, or Woodrow Wilson); another third were given to understand that it had been made by one of the most disliked people (such as Big Bill Thompson or Aimee Semple McPherson); while for the third group the statement was attributed to no one. In this manner the investigators found that statements were in general more likely to be agreed with when attributed to well-liked people than when attributed to disliked persons.

Suggestibility to majority opinion is also common in everyday life. In another experiment a test of attitudes was given to nine hundred people, who were subsequently divided into three groups, A, B and C. One month later the individuals in Group A were told that the majority of people had answered a certain way in the previous test; Group B was told that certain experts had given unanimous opinions in a certain direction; and Group C, used as a control group, was told nothing. When the three groups were retested, it was found that those in Group A had changed their opinion in the direction of the majority about four times as much as the control group, while the people in Group B had changed almost twice as much as those in Group C.

Studies on the conditions of suggestibility have indicated that children are more suggestible than adults, that women are more suggestible than men, that certain primitive peoples are more suggestible than more civilized groups. It would be easy to draw false conclusions from these experiments. There is probably nothing inherent in the child, the female or the primitive to make them more suggestible. These groups have merely had comparatively little experience in certain fields of activity and consequently possess less knowledge concerning the propositions on which tests are usually made. As such differences in training and experience diminish, so will the discrepancy in the acceptance of suggestions. Factors such as fatigue, depression, excitement and fear also increase suggestibility, inhibiting or interfering as they do with maximum critical thought.

Propaganda. No discussion of the processes of socialization would be complete today without at least some mention of propaganda, for the world has never before seen so many propagandas competing for the attention of the bewildered layman—who is influenced by them much more than he suspects. One of the chief reasons for the contemporary barrage of propaganda is the development that has taken place in the media of communication. Newspapers, the radio and the movies are all vehicles of propaganda. In our own culture two of them, the newspaper and the radio, depend for their very existence upon that form of propaganda which we call advertising.

We may define propaganda as *a deliberate attempt by interested individuals or groups to influence opinions or actions of other individuals or groups with reference to predetermined ends.* This definition makes several implications: propaganda is positive, it is well planned, it is selfish, it is one-sided, making use of suggestion and not reason, and, finally, it may be good or bad, depending upon the point of view of the individual judging it.

When the psychologist observes the work of the propagandist, he sees essentially two psychological techniques employed in ingenious ways to influence the actions of people. The first of these is a very simple device, namely that of linking the object or idea to be propagandized with some attitude, symbol or value already known to an individual and already likely to effect emotional reaction. If the propagandist is to use this principle, he must, of course, first of all be thoroughly acquainted with the social values and symbols of the culture in which he works.

The clever propagandist generally tries to join his idea to vague values or symbols which people tend to be for or against, and about which they feel strongly without knowing precisely what the symbols mean. Take, for example, the often-repeated symbols of justice, beauty, liberty, economy, patriotism, security, happiness. To these and other such attitudes we find the propagandist connecting soaps, cigarettes, political campaigns, appeals to join the army or to engage in some crusade. Vague emotionally toned words, such as *Fascist, Communist, Red, atheist, slacker,* are used to arouse us against government officials, labor leaders or any other individuals whom the propagandist thus freely labels. Most people will agree that they either like or dislike these vague words; and that is precisely why the propagandist is careful not to define them. If different individuals or groups should ask what they mean by these terms, they might discover disagreements among themselves. The propagandist, of necessity forced to join the struggle for definition, would lose the following of part of the group. For example, suppose the propagandist appeals to 'liberty' in a campaign. What is meant by the word? Liberty for whom? For workers or for business? For radicals or for conservatives? For Negroes or for whites? For you or for me? Most Americans claim they believe in 'freedom of speech.' Yet almost every week one may find instances where these same Americans protest to a broadcasting company because a Communist or a

Catholic is allowed access to the studios, or criticize a newspaper because it has printed the speech of a C.I.O. organizer, a pacifist or a capitalist.

The simple device of propaganda just described is so commonly employed that most people are by now aware of the trick. Therefore, if the propagandist has some purpose to conceal because it is not socially acceptable, or if he believes he must use more subtle methods, he employs a second principle. He builds up an attitude or value around a product or idea by means of indirect suggestion. The specific use of this principle is so varied and so changing that even the most expert analyst is often fooled unless he knows the selfish interests of the groups conducting the propaganda and carefully scrutinizes all that he reads and hears. In using this technique, for instance, the propagandist frequently gets his propaganda into newspapers as news or as editorial opinion. Another method used to build up an attitude or value for some idea is to disguise propaganda as explanation—explanation which is, however, distorted and incomplete. Since the use of this second principle is so dependent upon the situation in question and upon the tenor of the time, great companies, organizations and governments hire experts in propaganda who call themselves public-relations counsels, whose business it is to feel the public's pulse in all classes and vocations and find out where people are most suggestible. The public-relations counsel, once hired, will work for his client through the newspapers, the radio, the medical journal, the textbook, the cut-out for the kiddies.

If we really want to understand this important force in modern life, however, a knowledge of the techniques of the propagandist is only half the story. For propaganda is always directed at people. As psychologists we must ask ourselves what it is in *us* that makes propaganda possible and effective. Why do the techniques work?

There are several reasons for the success of propaganda. First, as we have already seen, the great majority of the words in our language or any other language are freighted with emotion. Most of the time we do not react to the dictionary meaning of the word, but to a whole complex of feeling that surrounds it. The word *love* can hardly be mentioned without arousing a host of sentiments in every individual. The word *Turk* will arouse in most Americans an unfavorable attitude even though most of these same Americans have never known a Turk. We learn and accept these attitudes toward words, our society's value of words, at the same time that we learn their meaning. Our attitude is determined for us by others.

A second reason why the propagandist is so successful is that most of us are unsure of ourselves. We seek a meaning for those things we do not understand. Since we often have neither the time nor the facilities for studying problems ourselves and since we do not want to appear ignorant on too many questions, we accept the judgment of some authority, of some official, of some newspaper editor, of some columnist or radio commentator. We feel that he must know more about the issue than we do, but we forget that the opinions of such experts are frequently only elaborated rationalizations of their own points of view, rationalizations which seem to us objective, critical analyses. With life becoming more and more specialized, we are depending more and more upon other people for our judgments. The propagandist, then, snatches at the opportunity and gives us *his* meaning. He satisfies our desire for a solution to such questions as what shall I buy, how shall I vote, what shall I believe.

A third reason for his success is that nearly everyone is anxious to preserve his own position in life, to maintain or to enhance his status. A person has, therefore, a tendency to accept the type of propaganda which makes him feel superior to other individuals or makes him feel that his own status is better than the other fellow's. One race will believe itself superior to another race. The rich will think the poor happy or irresponsible. We accept the political philosophy best suited to our interests. That is one reason why most people read a newspaper whose editorials or news slant fits their prejudices, why many people turn off the radio if a speaker's views do not fit their own.

In brief, the propagandist by appeals to the individual's already existing frame of reference leads the individual to extend that frame to include the object or the idea in which he is interested. Or, on the other hand, the propagandist tries to impose on the individual a frame of reference which he will accept because it gives meaning to his environment or because it enables him the better to rationalize his own position in life.

The social determination of attitudes. We have seen that the individual is born into a world containing social norms and values, those standardized social products of all kinds for which groups of men are responsible but which are as real to the individual as the air and the trees of his physical universe. We find that, beyond the ordinary process of learning, imitation and suggestion operate to help the individual assimilate into his own thinking and acting the standards of his culture. Even the language which man learns has subtly embodied in it the social evaluations of society. Much of the process of education may be regarded as a method of teaching the individual to conform. Finally, widespread propaganda surrounds the individual, utilizing his attitudes for specific purposes or building up new attitudes where they are needed, to force some particular action.

The result of these processes of socialization is the formation in individuals of attitudes towards various objects and issues in their social environment. An attitude may be defined as *a mental set which directs an individual's response.* In view of the constant pressure of social stimuli directing the individual's thought and actions into socially prescribed channels, it is not difficult to see why it is generally agreed that the attitudes of the individual are almost entirely socially determined and why very few, if any, of our opinions may be called our 'own' in the sense that we alone are responsible for them. There are at least three different ways by which we obtain our attitudes.

The first and by far the most important and most common method is for the individual to accept an attitude bodily from a culture before he has necessarily had any contact with the specific objects toward which the attitude is later directed. We learn, that is, how we *should* regard things before we see the things themselves. A demonstration of this fact is found in a study of the development of attitudes toward the Negro. The experimenter was interested in determining the differences between the attitudes of northern and southern children toward the Negro. He obtained for his study different groups of children: groups in rural and urban Georgia and Tennessee, children in an all-white school in New York City, children in a mixed school in New York City and children of Communist parents. His results indicate that there are no great differences in the attitudes of rural and urban children in the south; that children in both the north and south have about the same attitudes at about the same age; that children in an all-white school develop the same prejudice as children in a mixed school; and that children of Communist parents do not develop an unfavorable attitude toward the Negro. On the basis of these results, it was concluded that "attitudes toward Negroes are chiefly determined not by contact with Negroes, but by contact with the prevalent attitude toward Negroes." In other words, children accept in toto and uncritically the frame of reference provided in their immediate culture, and this without necessarily having had any experience whatsoever upon which to base the standards they accept.

A second way in which we get our attitudes is the reverse of the first method; we generalize on the basis of our own present or past experience rather than accept a generalization through which to interpret later experience. Experiments indicate that the pattern of behavior which we call 'honesty' is, in our own culture, acquired by the individual only after he has learned to react in specific ways in specific situations. The child will learn not to steal apples, not to copy from his neighbors' arithmetic, not to tell lies. He has, at first, no idea that these specific behaviors are called by society 'dishonest.' But, as he matures, he gradually learns the meaning of the concept 'honesty' so that, by the time he is an adult, he is able to interpret a new possible behavior as honest or dishonest.

A third way in which the individual may evolve an attitude is by means of some intense, traumatic experience. Though this particular method is comparatively rare, it may be of the utmost importance in determining certain attitudes of certain people. It is the method thought most important by Freud and the psychoanalysts. An excellent illustration of the importance of a single experience is found in the autobiography of W. E. Leonard.[5] Leonard as a small child was very badly frightened by a locomotive. Later in life he developed a whole complex of attitudes and behavior which he traced back to this single experience. Now, as a grown man, he is afraid not only of locomotives but also of going more than a few blocks from his home or from a definite point of security. Some persons may develop an attitude toward a certain race because they were once frightened (or imagined they were frightened) by a member of that race; others may change their attitudes toward money because they have suddenly lost or suddenly acquired a fortune.

SOCIAL BEHAVIOR

We have seen how an individual grows from an unsocial infant to a socialized adult with attitudes or frames of reference which have been determined largely by the social stimuli that were applied to him during his lifetime. We turn now to a discussion of the manner in which these socially determined attitudes operate to influence what an individual perceives and how he behaves.

Effects of attitudes. Two observers watching the same event take place may, if they differ in their attitudes toward the stimulating situation, perceive quite different things. An observer's set or readiness to perceive a certain thing, usually the thing that he *wants* to perceive, may modify greatly his interpretation of the situation. Two college students from two different schools watched representatives of their respective institutions engage in a boxing match in a college tournament.

[5] W. E. Leonard, *The locomotive god,* Appleton-Century, 1927.

The fight was the last and deciding bout in a tournament to determine the Intercollegiate Championship. Although the fact was that the two boxers were very closely matched, they did not seem so to the two observers. Observer A thought that the boxer from his school gave his opponent a sound thrashing. His every punch landed with a thud, whereas the blows he himself received were but glancing blows that did not appear to bother him. Observer B thought that his school's representative was making such effective use of his right hand that the other fighter was groggy during the third round. When the judges decreed that A's boxer had won, B went home complaining about the poorly qualified judges. The attitude of each student toward anything identified with the symbol representing his college had determined in part what he would perceive.

Experiments have demonstrated the effect of the attitudes of college students toward artists in their judgments of the esthetic value of pictures. To one large group of college students an experimenter showed eight pictures, to some of which were attached the names of artists known to be great (Raphael, Rubens, Rembrandt, da Vinci) while the others revealed names of little-known artists. The students rated each picture on a five-point scale (1 for 'best,' 2 for 'next-best,' etc.). A second comparable group of students rated the same pictures, with the famous names substituted for the unknown names, and conversely. The students tended to rate the pictures higher when the name of a person who was known to be a great artist was attached. Here the attitude of the observer toward certain artists consisted in part of a readiness to see beauty in a picture—a predisposition which resulted in his seeing what he expected to see. Suggestion by prestige depends on the fact that individuals acquire toward well-known people attitudes which influence favorably the interpretation of their statements.

An experimental study involving suggestion by prestige was made of the effect of attitude on perception with the use of what is called the autokinetic phenomenon. If an observer is taken into a strange room which is in total darkness except for one tiny point of light, and if he watches that light for a time, it will seem to him, although actually stationary, to move. This effect is the autokinetic phenomenon. Because of the darkness and his ignorance of the size of the room, the observer has no visible points of reference which he can use to localize the light. Under these conditions, he may think that the light is either far or near; it may appear first in one position and later in another; and the apparent movement may seem great or small or in any direction (see p. 490). Now it has been found that induced attitudes will affect an observer's perceptions of the supposed movements of such a light. When a naive subject is asked to make judgments as to the amount and direction of the movement after hearing like judgments made by an advanced student in psychology, he tends to follow the sophisticated student in his judgment. An attitude, built up during the time the observer heard judgments being made, determines his perception of the ambiguous stimulus. Moreover, when the subject makes observations during three sessions of one hour each in a group of two or three observers, he tends afterwards when alone to make judgments very similar to the norms established by the group. In this case attitudes or expectancies resulting from the prestige of the group determine the subject's perception of the movement of the light.

The problem of attitudes in relation to behavior is complicated by the fact that a given individual may develop conflicting attitudes toward an issue. A careful study of the people in a small American community disclosed that the residents had two sets of attitudes: public attitudes, which were expressed when there was likelihood of their being circulated throughout the community; and private attitudes, which were expressed only to intimate acquaintances. To illustrate, a majority of the members of the Methodist church in the community expressed the public attitude that games played with face cards were wrong, but that there was no harm in playing with flinch cards; in private, however, a majority of the same individuals expressed the attitude that playing with any kind of cards was not wrong so long as there was no gambling.

These individuals seemed for the most part to behave in accordance with their public attitudes in institutional situations and in accordance with their private attitudes in more informal situations, at home or at a picnic.

Measurement of attitude. The simplest method of measuring attitudes is to count ballots or tabulate answers to a question. This method yields information as to how common an opinion may be in a given population, or what proportion of the population holds opinions representing various degrees of attitude toward some common social issue. One of the most familiar examples of the use of this method is given by the American Institute of Public Opinion, whose most recent polls, it is claimed, are accurate to within 2 per cent. The accuracy of such measurement depends mainly upon the care taken to secure a representative sample. The public-opinion poll does not, of course, measure the *intensity* of opinion of any given individual, but only tells how common a certain opinion may be in a total population. More refined techniques are needed to determine how strongly individuals feel about certain propositions concerning social issues.

The investigators who attempt to measure the intensity of attitude make use of a scale or continuum, one end of which represents the greatest possible amount of favor toward an issue or object, and the other end of which represents the least possible amount of favor. The problem is to formulate general statements about the issue, expressive of various degrees of favor or disfavor toward it, and to let these statements, arranged in order, represent the scale. An individual's attitude is measured by discovering with which of the statements he will agree. The average position on the scale of his agreements is a measure of the intensity of his attitude toward the issue.

Institutions. Institutions are conceived by the ordinary individual as somehow being great over-persons or super-individual entities. A fraternity, as we have seen, is thought to be more than just a collection of individuals behaving in typical ways toward each other and their leaders; it is supposed to be a separate entity existing independently of the members, capable of imposing its standards upon them. Yet to the psychologist, interested primarily in studying the behavior and conscious processes of individuals, the institutions are not entities superior to the individuals and dominating them; rather, individuals contain within their habits of behavior and thinking the system which we call the institution. We are primarily interested in studying, not the ideological concept of institution, which we cannot even see if we look for it, but on the contrary the way individuals conform to situations which we call institutional.

A useful method for studying institutional behavior consists in observation of the behavior of individuals in institutional situations and subsequent classification with respect to the degree in which such behavior satisfies the purpose we ascribe to the institution. These data may then be graphically presented and studied in relation to various factors in the social environment.

In one study of this sort, observers stood where they could watch the behavior of motorists at a sharp turn in the most traveled stretch of road in New York City. There were two lanes for uptown traffic and two lanes for downtown traffic, the lanes being separated by white lines painted on the pavement. Several large signs directed motorists to "KEEP IN LINE." The drivers of motor vehicles had, then, two motives for staying in the proper lane: the presence of the traffic signs and the possibility of accidents resulting from cutting lanes. The observers classified the behavior of the drivers at the sharp turn in four ways, each showing one of four recognizable degrees of conformity to the law regarding keeping in line. *Staying completely in the proper lane* represented the maximum degree of fulfilment of the law. *Crossing the white line less than half the width of the car* was the next recognizable degree; *crossing the white line more than half the width of the car* the next; and finally, *cutting lanes* the fourth, representing no fulfilment whatsoever of the purpose of the traffic law. It was found that 83.3 per cent of the 12,666 motorists whose behavior was observed showed complete conformity by staying in the proper lane; 12.4 per cent crossed the white line less than half the width of the car; 2.2 per cent crossed the white line more than half the width of the car; and 1.7 per cent failed entirely to conform by cutting lanes. A distribution curve plotted from these data is shown in Fig. 1*A*. The shape of the curve, roughly resembling that of a reversed letter J, is called

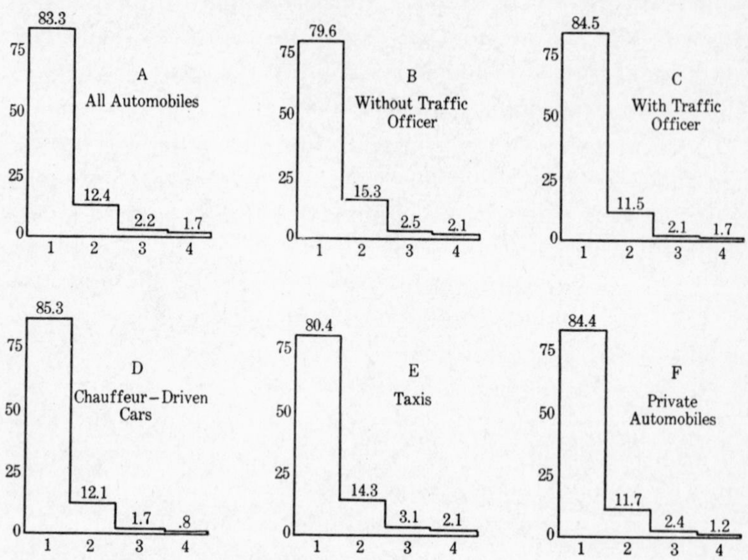

FIG. 1. BEHAVIOR OF MOTORISTS AT A SHARP TURN ON A BUSY HIGHWAY.
Step 1: motorists staying entirely in the proper lane.
Step 2: motorists crossing the white line less than half the width of an automobile.
Step 3: motorists crossing the white line more than half the width of an automobile, but not cutting lanes.
Step 4: motorists cutting lanes.
From N. Frederiksen, G. Frank and H. Freeman, A study of conformity to a traffic regulation, *J. abnorm. soc. Psychol.*, 1939, 34, 120.

a J-curve. Such a curve is thought to be characteristic of institutional behavior.

Studies of the behavior of individuals in other institutional situations yield results which are similar to those in the traffic situation, *i.e.*, they yield J-shaped distribution curves. A study was made of the behavior of pedestrians when confronted with a red traffic light at a street crossing in a city where the law governing pedestrians' behavior at such crossings was enforced. The results were similar to those described above; the mode of the curve came at the point of perfect conformity, and the curve fell off rapidly after the manner of the J-curve. Another study was made of the time-clock records showing the hour of arrival of workmen at a factory. Here complete conformity to the employer's purpose of efficient factory management, the position at the extreme left on the abscissa, was defined as arrival at the factory on time. The other steps on the scale represented various degrees of lateness. The distribution plotted from the obtained data was a J-curve. Other students investigated conformity in religious institutions, including such items of behavior as the degree of participation in the holy-water ceremony or the amount of kneeling in Catholic churches, or the time of arrival at services and the degree of participation in aggregate singing in Protestant churches. When these data were plotted, the distribution curves again approximated the J-curve.

Factors producing conformity. The fact that the majority of individuals conform to institutional requirements is well known; but without careful quantitative studies of the sort just described, we do not know specifically what proportion of people conform. We need to know, moreover, not only about the conformers, but also about the distribution of the non-conformers. Although everyone knows, furthermore, that most people conform to institutional standards, we do not know *why* they conform. By studying the conformity in behavior in relation to various environmental conditions, we may determine what factors are important. It has been suggested that the typical shape of the J-curve is due to the operation of three major factors: the agencies producing conformity, common biological tendencies and the differences in traits of personality.

The agencies which produce conformity include the operation of the processes of socialization already discussed: imitation, suggestion, language and propaganda. We may also mention such methods as physical coercion or threat of coercion, the use of legal or ecclesiastical symbols, the invoking of reified concepts of institution, tradition, custom, and the like and education. As an example of the use of some of these mechanisms of social control the study of the traffic situation may be mentioned again. In this study of the behavior of motorists with respect to their obedience of the regulation to stay in the proper lane, observations were recorded separately during the times when a traffic officer was and was not present at the sharp turn in the highway. When an officer was present, 84.5 per cent of the motorists showed complete conformity; when no policeman was present, but all other conditions were the same, the amount of conformity fell to 79.6 per cent (Fig. 1*B* and 1*C*). The difference, nearly 5 per cent, is statistically significant; that is, it is not due to chance. The fact that nearly 5 per cent more of the motorists conformed completely to the traffic regulation when a policeman was present is clearly the result of an agent tending to produce conformity, namely, the policeman.

The observers in this study also recorded separately the behaviors of taxi-drivers, chauffeurs, and ordinary drivers of passenger cars. It was found that 85.3 per cent of the chauffeurs, 84.4 per cent of the ordinary drivers and 80.4 per cent of the taxi-drivers exhibited complete conformity by staying entirely in the proper lane (Fig. 1*D*, 1*E*, 1*F*). The taxi-drivers showed a considerably greater amount of complete non-conformity than either of the other classes of drivers. The high degree of conformity exhibited by the chauffeurs was probably due to the employer, usually riding in the back seat and acting as a strong conformity-producing agent. Taxi-drivers, on the other hand, are motivated by the desire to discharge their fares as quickly as possible in order to get new ones. Since their cabs are owned by corporations and are insured, the driver is not particularly concerned about inflicting minor damages to the vehicle.

Common biological tendencies determine in part how many individuals will conform to an institutional requirement. If the biological tendency is to do exactly the thing that is required by the institution, the J-curve will be clear-cut. If, however, the biological tendency is to do something different from the institutional requirement, the curve will tend to be more spread out or shifted. For example, no monitor is required to get a group of hungry boys in on time for a noonday meal in their dining hall. Biological tendency and the rule governing time of arrival at the dining room tend to produce behaviors that coincide. But if the meal happens to be early breakfast on a Sunday morning following the night of a dance, the probability is that the J-curve will be missing along with many of the boys. The biological tendency to sleep conflicts with the rule regarding time of arrival at breakfast.

Among the biological needs important in this connection may be mentioned not only the needs for food, water, sleep, exercise and protection from extreme temperatures, but also the tendency toward economy of effort or inertia. An example of the latter is the aversion one may feel toward making the effort required to kneel in church or to stop unnecessarily and shift the gears in a car.

Differences in personality traits tend to lessen the steepness of the J-curve and to spread out the results. Another study of traffic behavior illustrates the importance of this factor. An observer stood at the intersection of two busy streets to record the behavior of the passing motorists. On one of the streets was located a boulevard stop sign. Motorists who entered the intersection from that street had at least two incentives to stop: the presence of the stop sign and the possibility of collision with cross-traffic on the other street. The observer classified the behavior of each motorist who approached the stop sign as showing one of four recognizable degrees of satisfaction of the purpose of the law regarding stopping at a boulevard stop sign. *Stopping completely* represented the maximum degree of fulfilment of the purpose of the law; *slowing down considerably*, but not stopping, was the next recognizable degree; *slowing down slightly* was the third step; and *going ahead without reducing speed* represented no fulfilment of the requirement. The distribution of these behaviors, shown in Fig. 2*A* was the typical J-curve. The boulevard stop sign was the obvious agency producing conformity.

Figure 2*B* shows the behavior of motorists at an intersection which is like that described above in all respects except

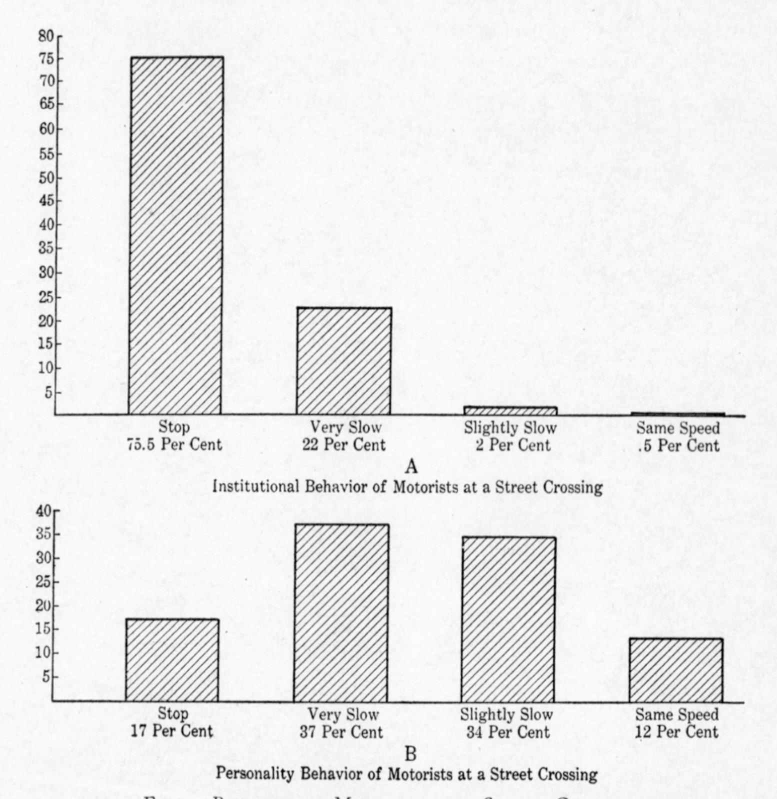

FIG. 2. BEHAVIOR OF MOTORISTS AT A STREET CROSSING.

Modified from F. H. Allport, Social and political problems, in *Psychology at work*, edited by P. S. Achilles; by permission of the McGraw-Hill Book Co.

that there was no stop sign. Under these conditions the more aggressive or reckless individuals are those who cross the intersection without reducing speed. Most individuals show evidence of caution by slowing up to some extent. The more submissive or timid persons stop to let someone else cross ahead of them, so as to avoid all possibility of collision. When the stop sign becomes a part of the situation, all the extremely cautious and most of the individuals in the middle of the personality trait distribution are those who conform. The non-conformers who form the tail of the J are those who were at the 'reckless' end of the curve. Other personality traits which might tend in appropriate situations to produce some degree of non-conformity are tardiness or dilatoriness, radicalism, dishonesty, impiety or intelligence.

Methods of producing conformity. Individuals seldom realize to what extent their behaviors are determined by conformity-producing agencies. Many of these agencies are institutional, controlled by the leaders of such institutions as the state, church or business organization. Others, although not under the direct control of institutional leaders, become effective through suggestion by prestige, the impression of universality or the desire for ego-enhancement, as in the growth of fads and fashions. An individual has surprisingly little opportunity in a modern culture to experience freedom of choice in the manner of expression of his personality. The majority of his acts represent a compromise. He must compromise between choosing ways to satisfy his own personal needs and desires and the necessity of behaving in accordance with the host of social norms which tend to cancel out individual differences and make everyone behave alike. An insoluble dilemma seems thus to result, since the only way to prevent this 'funneling' of diverse personality tendencies into institutional channels of conformity is the entire abandonment of our institutional organization and a return to some kind of primitive handicraft society. For such a sacrifice few people are prepared.

One institution which tends to produce conformity in a certain variety of situations is the *state*. The conformity-producing agency which makes its control especially effective is extreme coercive power through the police, militia and soldiers. In actual practice the coercion is, of course, seldom used. The mere presence of symbols representing that ultimate coercive power has become nearly as effective. Still more effective is the ideology of the state as a reified concept of an entity whose good is greater than individual good. In those states where nationalistic ideology has been developed to its greatest extent and 'blood purges' have been more or less frequent, we should probably find the greatest amount of conformity to the purposes ascribed to the state. Such a state also would be found to influence the behavior of citizens in a wider variety of situations.

Another kind of conforming behavior, which, however, cannot be called institutional, is the behavior resulting in what we are accustomed to call *fashions*. Here the conformity-producing agencies are manipulated for the most part by industrial leaders through the medium of advertising. A variety of styles of wearing apparel originates with designers, milliners and fashions manufacturers. Subsequently certain individuals who have a particular kind of prestige select and wear some of those styles. These individuals are usually wealthy people with a desire to be distinctive. Because the cost of the articles is prohibitive to most people, these styles remain for a time exclusive. During this time fashion 'news' and advertising are educating people as to what is being worn at fashionable resorts. Eventually the styles, copied by other manufacturers, are put on the market at lower prices. Thereupon many individuals of the lower-income groups, already impressed by the advertisers' claims of what 'is being worn,' hasten to identify themselves with the rich and exclusive by imitating their dress. Then that style of apparel becomes the *fashion*; that is to say, there is a considerable amount of conformity with regard to the characteristics of the clothing being worn. When the style is no longer exclusive, the members of the style-setting class hasten to accept a newer mode from the varieties offered by the designers, and the cycle repeats itself.

In the variety of conforming behavior known as the *fad*, the role of advertising is likely to be less important and the importance of the impression of universality greater. "It's all the rage," is the popular way of expressing this impression of universality. Occasionally the appearance of a fad may be traced to some chance occurrence. There was a time when getting a book banned in Boston made its popularity almost certain. When the Prince of Wales came to America and wore double-breasted blue suits, the sales of such suits increased from about 3 per cent to 45 per cent of the total number of men's suits sold. But the reason why certain fads 'click' and assume almost immediate popularity while others fail is still impossible to explain. Music publishers, for example, can make no accurate prediction as to which popular song, the hit of its day, will for a brief time be on everyone's lips.

SOCIAL CHANGE

One of the characteristics of social environment is its constant change. Inventions and new ways of living are continually presenting themselves and as continually being accepted by the individual, who sees his life thus made easier and more efficient. Since these changes occur within the superstructure of the old social norms, there is at first no particular dilemma. Existing patterns of relationship between the individuals and the culture remain intact. Take, for example, the case of a rich man living fifty years ago. Such a man might own a fine carriage, an indication of his status in the community. With the invention of the automobile that same individual would be likely to have the first and best motorcar in his community. When the airplane acquired its usefulness, he might have his private plane, or at least utilize commercial planes for business and recreation. With the carriage, the automobile or the airplane, this individual is still able to keep his particular place in society. Inventions have not upset his norms.

Why then do we get a change of norms in a culture? It is essentially because of the general progress which we know as education — whether it be the formal education of the school system, or the less formal, but perhaps more important, education handed on by the family and the community or other institutional interests. Such education constantly creates new needs and new wants on the part of the large number of individuals within the community. When people see the convenience and comfort provided by the automobile, the desire for automobiles becomes widespread in the culture. It is then that people begin to question those norms which make it impossible for them to own automobiles. There is created what we might call a discrepancy between the superstructure of the old norms and the new needs of the people. This discrepancy is called by the sociologist 'social lag.' Let the discrepancy become apparent to a sufficient number of individuals within the culture, and some change will be demanded. Since the individuals are unwilling to give up their desires, the change must take place on the side of the norms, that is to say, on the side of the laws, customs and mores that are blocking the realization of these desires. Frequently, the change of norms may come about gradually and almost unnoticed; legislators may revise old laws to adjust to the new needs; supreme courts may reinterpret an old decision; a modern minister may reformulate an older creed. By such means the discrepancy between the norms and needs is prevented from becoming so great that individuals are forced to resort to violent methods, such as revolutions, in order to satisfy their needs.

When the norms do not gradually accommodate themselves to the needs of the people, then we find arising mass movements of various kinds, led by individuals who capitalize the wishes of the people and provide new norms that will presumably satisfy them. There are many such mass movements of interest to the psychologist: crowds, revolutions, dictatorships and wars. We may analyze very briefly the crowd situation as an example of such attempted change.

The crowd. We may define a crowd as a *congregate group of individuals who have a common interest and who express a similar emotion.* In order to have crowd behavior, the individuals who come together in a group must possess certain common social values which, for them, have a high feeling tone. The greater the similarity of the pre-established values, the more rapid will be the formation of what we know as crowd behavior. For example, an old-time revival or a modern Holy Roller meeting may express very rapidly the emotional characteristics of crowd behavior, because the individuals who attend such gatherings are already predisposed by the similarity of their values to react in similar ways to such expected stimuli as songs, sermons or symbols. If, on the other hand, values are not already established when the individuals come together in groups, then crowd behavior will be accorded only when a similarity of values is created and is fraught with some emotional meaning. If a revival meeting is filled with students or curiosity seekers, then the revivalist must resort to various tricks in order to build up in the heterogeneous population of the group a common feeling.

The clever leader of a crowd attempts always to create an environment around the group that will be consistent with the social value he advocates. Elaborate techniques are necessary if a heterogeneous group is to be turned into a homogeneous crowd: banners representing broad symbols are necessary; the event must be highly publicized; the audience must be as large as possible to show wavering individuals that other people agree with the leader; the time of day for the gathering must be carefully chosen (the evening seems the best time because then people are tired, non-critical and their full stomachs may dull their mental processes); elaborate uniforms may be employed usefully to symbolize the importance of the event. Once the leader is able to interest the members of his group in a common social value, then he may suggest to them how that value will best achieve the aims of the individuals. The clever leader tries in many ways to make the individual identify himself with the value paramount in the group. He may, to this end, create an enemy if there is not already one. Thus is preserved the solidarity of a single norm and a split within the crowd avoided. The religious leader uses the concept of the devil; the cultural leader may create the symbol of some other race; the political leader may call up the specter of the Red or the economic royalist. The more the crowd hates, the more it will believe in its destiny and the more uncritical will it be of the norms it is accepting.

The individual acceptance of the common norms frequently results in what is called the feeling of universality — the feeling that everybody is doing or thinking as you are. Though this is, of course, true only for the limited psychological world in which the crowd member is temporarily living, the leader enhances the impression by speaking in terms of 'thousands,' 'millions' and 'the multitudes.' Thus the fully developed crowd may be represented as a small world or microcosm within the large world or macrocosm — a microcosm with its own set of norms and values, which may be at odds with the norms and values of the real world outside, but which may, nevertheless, temporarily better satisfy the needs of the individual.

The rise of a revolution, or of a dictatorship, may be interpreted in these terms. Anyone familiar with the American, French or Russian revolutions will see that the basic problem involved is satisfying the needs of the people by a new set of norms. The sequence of the change is usually as follows. Certain individuals, becoming dissatisfied with the conditions under which they are forced to live and with the meager opportunities provided them by the old norms, begin to question these old norms. Perhaps a few clever leaders arise who provide new rationalizations or new norms which will better fit the needs of the dissatisfied persons. By word of mouth, by publicity or by legal or underground propaganda these new norms spread, until a larger and larger number of individuals within the culture become both dissatisfied and aware of the new opportunities that might be afforded if the old standards were eliminated. Usually there follows a period where there is some attempted reform within the existing set of norms. In the French Revolution the finance ministers attempted to ease the lot of the peasants by taxing the nobles and the clergy. In Russia the Kerensky regime attempted to compromise with the old norms. But in both these instances either the individuals in power whose positions depended upon the permanence of the old norms refused to accede to such changes, or the masses found that such changes were only palliatives for their real desires. Hence the compromise with the established norms ceases and there occurs a more drastic and complete overthrow of the old norms, followed eventually by the establishment of the new.

REFERENCES

1. ALLPORT, F. H. *Social psychology.* Cambridge: Houghton Mifflin, 1924.
2. ALLPORT, F. H. *Institutional behavior.* Chapel Hill: University of North Carolina Press, 1933.
3. ALLPORT, F. H. The J-curve hypothesis of conforming behavior. *J. soc. Psychol.,* 1934, 5, 141-183.
4. DOOB, L. *Propaganda, its psychology and technique.* New York: Henry Holt, 1935.
5. HOROWITZ, E. L. The development of attitude toward the Negro. *Arch. Psychol.,* 1936, No. 194.
6. HURLOCK, E. B. *The psychology of dress.* New York: Ronald Press, 1929.
7. KATZ, D., and ALLPORT, F. H. *Students' attitudes.* Syracuse: Craftsman Press, 1931.
8. KATZ, D., and CANTRIL, H. Public opinion polls. *Sociometry,* 1937, 1, 155-179.
9. KATZ, D., and SCHANCK, R. L. *Social psychology.* New York: John Wiley, 1938.
10. MCCARTHY, DOROTHEA. Language development. *A handbook of child psychology.* Worcester, Mass.: Clark University Press, 1931.
11. MURPHY, G., MURPHY, L. B., and NEWCOMB, T. M. *Experimental social psychology.* (Rev. ed.) New York: Harper, 1937.
12. SCHANCK, R. L. A study of a community and its groups and institutions conceived of as behaviors of individuals. *Psychol. Monogr.,* 1932, 43, No. 195.
13. SHERIF, M. *The psychology of social norms.* New York: Harper, 1936.

Chapter 3

PERSONALITY

When we try to understand the drama of social life, we turn naturally to the personalities of the actors in it. A social movement appears on the horizon, and we seek its explanation in the political genius of its leader, the thick-skinned aggressiveness of his lieutenants and the docility of his followers. Thus we make personality a first cause. It seems that, if we only knew the puzzle of individual purpose and the mystery of personality, we should hold the key tc all human problems. This emphasis upon individual essence as the ultimate explanation, however, is more popular than scientific.

THE PROBLEM OF PERSONALITY

To the scientist personality is not a first cause. Since for him people are the products of their environment, personality is something which happens to a biological organism in a social world. The secret of the inner man is readily disclosed once we regard personality as the result of adjustment to biological needs and social barriers. The scientific approach views man as influencing and being influenced in a system of mutually dependent factors. Personality as the dynamic interaction between man and his environment can be seen in clearer perspective if we compare people of our own day in our own society with people of other periods and other cultures.

Modern Western man contrasts strikingly with the Greek of classical times. The orientation towards time and space in the classical period is foreign to the modern mind. Classical man lived completely in the present. The calendar and the

This chapter was written by Daniel Katz of Princeton University.

clock, those dread symbols of the flow of time, did not regulate his life. He had no conception of historical development. So completely did classical writers lack historical feeling, that their fine pieces of history-writing were confined to events occurring within their own memories. Thucydides, it has been said, would have been unable to handle even the Persian Wars, let alone the general history of Greece, while that of Egypt would have utterly confounded him. Likewise the spatial world of classical man was limited to his own narrow experience. Olympus to him represented extreme distance, and even the Gods were no farther away. As against the unhistorical, timeless, spatially restricted mind of the classical Greek stands modern man with his sensitive consciousness of temporal distinctions, his historical perspective, his appreciation of distances beyond his immediate horizon and his orientation to an ever-expanding spatial world.

These differences between classical men and modern men are not to be explained, as some historians have attempted, as the difference between the Apollonian soul and the Faustian soul. Modern man is what he is because he develops in a certain social environment. He grows up in a mechanical world. He learns to adjust his problems by machines which annihilate space. Collective adjustments in a mechanized age call for specialization of labor and synchronization of effort. Trains run according to schedule, factories according to the time-clock and schools open and close their doors by the bell. The pure present of the classical mind becomes transmuted into a finely discriminating time sense which relates each moment as it passes to the future and to the past.

Or consider the personalities of people in primitive societies. The Mountain Arapesh of New Guinea are said to lack egotism. These people are by and large peaceful, friendly, genuine, cooperative, but lacking in foresight and ambition. Among them there is no definite hierarchy of leaders. They recognize no single scale by which success may be socially measured. The admired personality is the all-round man. In contrast to these mild people of New Guinea are the Eskimos of Greenland. The latter are rampant individualists. The cardinal traits of personality in their society are initiative, self-reliance and aggressiveness. Strong development of the ego is the rule rather than the exception.

Again these differences in personality grow out of different conditions of life to which the Arapesh and the Eskimos have been compelled to adjust. The Arapesh occupy a mountainous terrain which guarantees their safety from invasion and which at the same time yields them a dependable though a meager living. They eke out a bare existence through agriculture, trading and hunting. Not menaced by danger from without and not facing actual starvation, the Arapesh have never developed a strong social organization. The tortuous nature of the country with its narrow paths and slippery rocks, moreover, makes standardization of complicated cooperative group-activity difficult. Social relationships are consequently personal in nature. Though common ownership of property is not the usual practice, there are exceptions, such as the communal sharing of food through gifts to friends and the giving of public feasts.

The personality of the Arapesh is the product of these material and social conditions of life. Their enemies are natural forces so much beyond their control that it seems to them useless to work very hard to produce a bumper crop. Their friends are their fellowmen, and they all help one another in the struggle to live. Both the absence of organized pressure upon the individual to spur his competitiveness and the lack of social approval for the aggressive individual make for a mild, unambitious personality.

The Eskimos of Greenland, on the other hand, face such rigorous conditions of life that only strong individuals can survive. Any individual who, through infirmity or other physical handicap, cannot make his economic contribution perishes, commits suicide or is killed. The technology of the group is highly individualistic. Every man hunts for himself and manufactures his own tools and weapons. For open-sea hunting each man uses his own kayak; should he capsize, he must be prepared to right it without help from others. The Eskimo couple is a self-sufficient economic unit. In addition to her other household tasks the wife converts animal skins into clothing and equipment—an arduous procedure.

This type of individualism has grown out of the difficulty of surviving in the frigid zone with the aid of only a very primitive cultural heritage. Simple individual adjustment rather than cooperative group activity is the first adaptation to such a situation. For example, even when a number of families live together in one house during the winter season, each woman cooks the food for her family in her own pot over her own lamp. Communal cooking is impractical, because it would take too long to heat the food for the group over blubber lamps and because it would be difficult to transport from winter to summer quarters a pot large enough for the group.

Personality is thus the result of the way in which individuals have adjusted to the world about them. Every attitude of mind, every habitual way of doing is related to the objective world in which the individual has grown to maturity. Although objective facts often exist to which men fail to adjust, nevertheless men show no patterns of behavior which were not at some time in their lives a function of the environment external to them. The weak ego development among the Arapesh and the strong individualism of the Eskimos have objective reference to the conditions of life in these two societies. This is not to say that all Arapesh fall into one personality type. The impact of environmental forces never strikes all individuals in the same way. But if we compare two groups of people living in two different environments, we are less impressed by the differences between people within either one of the groups than by the differences between the groups. The study of personality for the scientist is thus not the contemplation of esoteric qualities of individuality but the study of how people come to be what they are.

BIOLOGICAL FACTORS AFFECTING DEVELOPMENT OF PERSONALITY

Although the specific patterning of behavior in the individual grows out of his adjustment to his surroundings, the complete story of personality includes more than the objective reference of behavior. Since personality is something which happens to a biological organism in a social world, we need to know about both the biological organism and the social world. In the present section we shall consider the first of these two aspects, the biological factors in the development of personality.

This division of developmental factors into biological and social is like the old opposition between heredity and environment. According to it an individual's attainments, capacity and character were regarded as the result either of nature or of nurture. Whatever could not be ascribed to learning and training was attributed to the genes, the carriers of inheritance. In the old division between heredity and environment, however, certain types of environmental factors were omitted. Such environmental forces as temperature and the chemistry of nutrition contribute to the growth of the nervous system, of the glands and of man's physical structure in general, and to the functioning of these structures. The genes likewise make their contribution, of course, but it is a common error to classify as inherited all those characteristics of man which are not due to learning. The biological factors in personality are, therefore, not so much products of inheritance as of physical structure and the characteristic functioning of physical structure. The strength and quickness of the vigorous child, for example, are not wholly a matter of his good luck in drawing the right pattern of genes. They depend also upon a fortunate interaction of the right genes with favorable environmental forces (see pp. 113-119).

Evidence on this point from anthropological studies is fairly conclusive. The physical measurements of American-born children of southeastern European peoples have been compared with measurements of their parents. East European Hebrews are below the American norms in height and skeletal structure; yet their children, reared in a more favorable environment, deviate from their parents in the direction of the American norms. Even the form of the head undergoes change. The south Italian has an exceedingly long head, but his American-born children are more short-headed. The east European Hebrew has a very round head, but his American-born children are more long-headed. In this country these immigrant groups approach a uniform type with respect to head form.

Likewise fairly constant physiological factors are determined through both inheritance and environment. The onset of puberty occurs earlier in the southern races than in the northern. Italian girls mature more rapidly than American girls. Girls of Italian parentage reared in the United States, however, mature later than did their mothers in their native country.

Since even biological factors are not wholly the effects of inheritance, personality can no longer be considered, as was formerly the case, the progressive unfolding of an innate constitution. The blue-blooded aristocrat does not owe his polished tastes and manners to his chromosomes. Nor does the thief come by his anti-social habits through genes which make for thieving.

The role of biological factors is to set the limits within which the individual will develop. Their influence is general and indirect as compared with the influence of social and psychological forces. This fact will appear more clearly if we consider specific biological factors in development. Three such factors are (1) body chemistry, (2) physique and (3) capacity.

Body chemistry and the endocrine glands. Most of us are aware of differences in mood and behavior due to physical well-being or ill-being. At times we are sluggish and despondent; at other times we feel alert and animated. And we are sometimes correct in attributing these changes to diet, sleep, toxins and infections. In addition, however, the body contains within itself a mechanism of chemical control in its endocrine organs, or glands of internal secretion. These glands release chemical substances, or hormones, into the blood stream, which carries them to all parts of the body. The hormones sensitize or desensitize nervous and muscular tissue, the particular effect depending upon the chemical composition of the hormone. Hence our responses to external objects are facilitated or retarded by the activity of the endocrine organs. Thus, though the primary function of these glands is concerned with the growth and metabolism of the body, they also influence behavior. The various glands of the endocrine system, moreover, have differential effects upon mood and conduct (see pp. 212-217 for a further description of the endocrine system).

The *thyroid gland* is directly related to the metabolism of the body, *i.e.*, the destructive and constructive changes in body tissues. Its hormone acts as a catalyzer to facilitate the breaking down of waste products so that they can be readily eliminated from the body. If the thyroid gland is underactive, partially decomposed proteins are retained in the tissues and further cell destruction diminished. Oxidation is lessened and blood pressure falls. With the metabolic processes slowed up in this manner, the individual becomes lethargic and despondent. Easily fatigued, he often suffers from states of depression. If the thyroid gland is overactive, on the other hand, metabolism is increased and body tissues are overstimulated. An increase in nervous tension follows and the person appears excitable, restless, worried.

The thyroid gland is balanced by the *parathyroids*. An overactive parathyroid tends to quiet and slow down the individual. The mechanism involved is the regulation of the calcium balance of the body; a lowered supply of calcium in the blood stream sensitizes nerves and muscles and makes the individual overexcitable. This supply of calcium is associated with the parathyroid hormone. An excess of the hormone means an excess of calcium salts; a diminution means a lowered calcium supply. The removal of the parathyroids produces muscular tremors, spasms and cramps — an indication that the nervous system is oversensitive. An underactive parathyroid may thus be one determinant of the high-strung temperament.

The *pituitary gland* is important in its contribution to body growth. Impaired functioning of the pituitary in childhood is related to a generally deficient bony structure, weakened skeletal muscles and underdeveloped sex organs. The child thus afflicted lacks aggressiveness, gives up easily, cries readily and is regarded as cowardly. Overactivity of this gland (specifically of its anterior lobe) results in gigantism, thick skin and precocious sex development. The behavior picture in this case is one of aggressiveness and pugnacity.

The development of the secondary sex characteristics is a function of the *gonadal glands*. These secondary characteristics include height, weight, the distribution of hair over the body, subcutaneous fat and the mammary glands. Experimenters have transplanted ovaries from female rats and guinea pigs to castrated male rats and guinea pigs. The result has been that the male animals have taken on the characteristics of the female both in physical and in behavioral traits. Similarly, the transplantation of male interstitial tissue to female animals whose ovaries had been removed, has produced male characteristics. These experiments indicate that the sex hormones may be a contributing factor to masculine and feminine traits of personality.

Extreme instances of glandular malfunctioning have been mentioned to illustrate the importance of the endocrine organs. Normal individuals, however, may vary slightly in either direction from the norm of glandular balance. For example, the sensitivity of the excessively timid child is sometimes a matter of body chemistry. Observations of children show great differences in temperament from infancy which cannot be explained on the basis of experience. In general, however, the endocrines do not have direct effects upon personality. Rather they initiate physiological changes, the final results of which are complicated by habit and experience. Not infrequently the physiological state, produced by abnormal endocrine functioning, seriously affects the individual through his realization of his condition. The depression caused by an underactive thyroid condition is generally accentuated by a knowledge of the deficiency.

Physique and physical health. The most obvious aspects of the individual are his physical characteristics, his height, weight, bodily proportions, coloring and physical beauty. Their importance in the development of personality is generally misconstrued. Since they are easily noticed, they have been unduly emphasized as indicators of personality. We persist in evaluating people according to physical appearance, as if phrenology and related arts of character reading had not been thoroughly discredited. Physical characteristics are not significant as external signs of the internal man, but they do play a part in the development of personality. Their effect is mediated through the social reception accorded to various types of physical appearance. The undersized child, for example, may acquire a feeling of inferiority if both adults and children react differently to him than to his fellows.

Before parents can compare their children with other children on the basis of intellectual attainment, they can and do consult height and weight norms and pronounce judgment accordingly. Their constant attention to physical growth means that the youngster builds up a notion of himself as a normal or an abnormal person physically. This concept of himself is also fostered by the competitive advantage or disadvantage of his size and weight. Most individuals tend to place themselves nearer the desirable norm than they really are. Most men a little under average in height, for example, think of themselves as taller than they are.

Actual deformity handicaps the child both physically and psychologically. Fewer physically handicapped children develop into normal personalities than do physically well-favored children. One study of this problem compared the responses of crippled girls with the responses of normal girls of the same age on a test of emotional stability. The average score for the crippled group was 75 per cent greater in the direction of instability than the score of the normal group.

Sheer size and weight are less important in the development of personality than are strength and agility. It is not so often the undersized child who is pushed around by other children as it is the physically weak youngster. Health and vigor are significant in the formative years, since contacts and competition among children are often on the physical level. Even in adult years the man with a rugged constitution is at an advantage in maintaining an aggressive attitude toward life and in preserving his emotional balance.

The particular way in which a given person is affected by his physical constitution is further shaped by social experience. In general the physically inferior child follows one of two courses of development. If he is pampered and humored at every turn, he *under-reacts* towards his world. He never acquires the ability to solve his own problems. If, however, his inferiority bars him from the center of the stage, he may *over-react* to compensate for his deficiency. It is characteristic of compensation that the individual exceeds the normal person in striving for perfection or for power. One of the most famous track athletes of our time owes his career to an accident in which his legs were badly burned. He persevered in his running to develop the injured leg muscles until he outran all competitors.

Capacity. In addition to body chemistry, physical health and appearance, there is a more specific biological determinant of mental ability, manipulative and motor skills and special talents. *Capacity* is the general term for this factor, which is a function of an attribute or attributes of nervous tissue. In practice it is impossible to distinguish the exact contribution of the biological structure to performance. Training and experience, glandular conditions and temporary situational factors are all involved in what the person does. There is, nevertheless, no gainsaying the fact that a limit is set by the individual's nervous equipment. No amount of special teaching will enable the moron to handle the problems of symbolic logic, nor can musical talent be developed in every child. Similarly with regard to special motor and manipulative skills, every athletic coach knows that certain tricks can be taught and certain techniques perfected, but that motor coordination, speed of reaction time and physical alertness are in good measure determined by the man's own constitution.

Though capacity sets the boundaries beyond which the development of personality cannot go, its influence is frequently exaggerated. Most people never develop their talents as far as their biological equipment permits. Capacity has an effect upon the individual's permanent attitudes in that he compares himself with others. Failure is more important psychologically when others are able to succeed than when no one is successful. Even when a person can succeed by strenuous effort, it is not comforting to see another succeed effortlessly.

SOCIAL FACTORS AFFECTING PERSONALITY

Although biology sets the stage for the drama of personality, the particular play — whether light comedy or heavy tragedy — is determined by the interaction of biological forces with the social environment. The problems to be solved by the growing child are predominantly social and the acceptable solutions socially defined. Specifically, the child's problems consist of questions of relationships with people, of affection in the home, of attention in the school, of approbation in the play group. These problems will be considered in relation to (1) the family, and (2) critical situations in development.

The family. The growing child knows nothing of the abstraction which we call society. His acquaintance with the social is in terms of the specific people in the family grouping. In our culture parents play a dual role. On the one hand, they are a source of security to the child and the main means for the satisfaction of his wants. Thus they become powerful, friendly beings with whom he identifies himself. This affectionate tie greatly facilitates the taking over of the attitudes and actions of the elders by the youngster. On the other hand, the father and mother are also disciplinary agents who enforce rules and regulations which interfere with the child's egoistic pleasures. In this role they may alienate the child and make him turn to substitute social models in the person of the school teacher, or, more likely, the unruly big boy next door.

This contradictory function of the parents frequently produces an ambivalent attitude in children whereby they both love and hate their parents. Such conflict is avoided in many primitive cultures by assigning the disciplinary role to the uncle or to the grandparents. Among the Trobriand Islanders, for example, since the boy belongs to his mother's clan, he is taught his social duties and disciplined by his mother's brother. His relation to his father is solely one of affection and intimacy.

The dual parental role in our society has its best effect on the child's personality when there is balance and integration between the two functions. If the mother avoids all restraint and indulges her child, he will grow up undisciplined, with little respect for any social rules and in the end with little respect for his mother. This *overprotection* in early years leaves the child inadequately prepared to meet the requirements of social living later. If the parent exercises authority in an arbitrary and severe manner, however, the result is either a hardened boy or girl, insensitive to many social demands, or a terrorized youngster lacking the spirit to fight his own battles. Examples of the former effect are furnished by case studies of juvenile delinquents. Many delinquents, guilty of stealing and other offenses, have a home background of repeated, severe punishment. In general, parental care follows neither the extreme of affectionate overindulgence nor the extreme of tyrannical abuse, but seeks some middle ground. If punishment is used objectively and if it is used to direct rather than to repress the child, this middle ground can be a real fusion instead of a compromise.

The objective use of punishment demands that the penalty

be made a function of the situation and not of the changeable temper of the parent. Punishment to direct rather than to repress means that the child's desires are not completely blocked by the imposition of penalties. An acceptable outlet is provided at the same time that the unacceptable expression is penalized. The child, for example, can be punished for playing in the street, but he is not repressed if an adequate playground for him and his companions is provided elsewhere.

For many reasons, the most obvious of which is that he has two parents, the child develops a personality of his own instead of mirroring to a large degree that of a parent. Both father and mother influence the child, as individual personalities and in their relationships to one another. The Freudian theory has it that the boy is more often attached to his mother and the girl to her father. However this may be, studies of the interrelationships of family traits show that in general the mother's personality characteristics are taken over by both boy and girl more often than are the father's characteristics.

Table I reproduces the results found in comparing the scores made by members of the same families on tests of dominance, emotional stability (neuroticism) and self-sufficiency. Mothers affected their daughters more than their sons. Even upon sons, however, the effect of the mother's personality was greater than that of the father. The closest resemblance in intra-family relationships occurred between mother and daughter with respect to emotional stability. Daughters tended to approximate the scores made by their mothers on questions concerning neurotic tendency. Daughters also tended to be dominant or submissive according to the personality of their mothers. Though the father's personality was less effective than the mother's, when it did make itself felt, it influenced the daughter more than the son. One exception to these generalizations should be noted. In the trait of self-sufficiency the personality of the father was more important than that of the mother in affecting the girl.

On the whole, boys are more independent in the development of their characters than are girls. There was only a slight

TABLE I

RESEMBLANCE OF MEMBERS OF THE SAME FAMILY IN PERSONALITY CHARACTERISTICS

(After M. N. Crook, *Psychol. Rec.*, 1937, 1, 488.)

	Number of Pairs	Neuroticism Correlation	Dominance Correlation	Self-Sufficiency Correlation
Brother-brother	50	.25	.09	−.08
Brother-sister	56	.15	.10	.28
Sister-sister	51	.36	.33	.36
Father-son	62	.06	.05	−.03
Father-daughter	64	.24	.26	.39
Mother-son	68	.32	.22	.20
Mother-daughter	73	.63	.43	.13
Husband-wife	79	.07	−.06	.01

(The correlation coefficient is an index of the closeness of relationship between two series of scores. Take, for example, the scores made by brothers on the test of neuroticism. If every boy made the same score as his brother, the correlation would be 1.00. If, however, every boy reversed the score made by his brother, the correlation would be −1.00. But if there were no regularity between the scores of the brothers, the correlation would be 0.00. For a more complete description of the correlation coefficient see pp. 102–104.)

influence of the parents on the boy's character, and this influence was on the side of the mother. Corroborative evidence of the relative independence of the boy is found in the relationships of brothers and sisters. Sisters tend to be more like sisters than brothers like brothers. These results are what one would expect in our society, where the girl is more circumscribed by taboos and where the father is away from home during the day and the rearing of children is left to the mother.

Children also take over the characteristic attitudes of their parents toward life. This influence has been shown in measurements of the attitudes of parents and children toward the church, toward war and toward Communism. For the most part the children showed the same attitudes as did their parents. If the father and mother were strongly pacifistic, so were their children; if they were strongly militaristic, their children were likewise believers in force. Moreover, the more consistent the parents were in their attitudes on related issues, the more consistent were their children.

The economic background of the family is another important

determinant of character. The boy or girl reared in a poor home where there is overcrowding, inadequate medical attention, an overworked mother or a father harassed by economic insecurity, grows up in a world different from that of the youngster raised in a wealthy home where physical want and deprivation are unknown. The significant factors here are not only the direct physical handicaps but also the psychological effects of these handicaps. Economic insecurity leads to parental attitudes of despondency, helplessness and to family disharmony. In one investigation of family disorganization, several hundred children were questioned at length about the peaceful nature of family relations. The children's families were grouped into three classes according to economic status. Their answers showed that the higher the economic level, the greater was the family harmony.

Data concerning the effect of economic background are available in a study of children in two nursery schools. The one school was patronized by parents of professional status, the other by working mothers who left the children to be cared for in their absence from the home. The children in both schools were rated on such behavior as spontaneity of speech, initiative in play, persistence, cooperativeness, poise and self-care. The children from the professional classes were superior to the working-class children on all items save that of self-care. Though other factors besides economic background are involved in these differences, economic status is certainly a significant differential.

Similar results have been discovered among college students. One hundred and twenty-eight undergraduates rated their economic status on a five-point scale. They were also given personality tests for emotional sensitivity, self-confidence and seclusiveness. In general, the lower the economic status the greater was the emotional sensitivity and seclusiveness and the less the self-confidence of the students. The relationship was most marked in the case of emotional sensitivity.

It is customary to emphasize the stimulation to character

development and the spur to achievement provided by adversity. Undoubtedly children from economically handicapped backgrounds who succeed in overcoming these disadvantages often develop into strong personalities. But there is room at the top for only a limited number, and the many who do not scale the height are subject to emotional frustration and inferiority conflict. Moreover, the desperate struggle of parents in the economic battle of life makes of such homes an unfavorable background for the development of well-integrated personalities.

Critical situations in development. The developing child takes on the color of his social environment not only through automatic imitation of the people about him, but also through pressure of parents, teachers and elders who punish him for non-conformity or who show by their attitudes of expectation what they consider proper for a child at a certain age. These social requirements increase in number and change in quality as the child matures. The changes in social expectation produce critical situations for the formation of personality. Although the developmental process is ordinarily gradual, sometimes radically new demands compel revolutionary adjustment. They shock the child into acquiring new attitudes and habits. His old familiar world upon which he has depended seems then to have collapsed. He may adapt to the novel conditions and grow in stature overnight, or he may regress to older infantile habits in an attempt to escape the problem. The psychological shock of the critical situation has been called *traumatic experience* and the resulting revolutionary change in personality sudden *reorientation.*

Traumatic experience is of course related both to the objective situation and to the make-up of the particular child. What is humiliating to one urchin may leave another profoundly unconcerned. In a given society, nevertheless, common crises in development can be found. Attention has been called to certain points in the social demands upon the growing girl or boy which generally compel new adjustment. The following seven situations do not exhaust the list, but they are fairly typical.

1. The arrival of a new baby in the family is an upsetting experience for the child who is displaced when the center of attention shifts to the new arrival. A second phase of this adjustment occurs when the new brother or sister is old enough to compete actively for toys and to compete in the same social roles.

2. Entering school at the age of five or six years is another critical point in the life of the child, who is thus confronted by an unfamiliar world of strange children and strange adults. The protected position he enjoyed at home contrasts with his status on the school playground, where no one mediates between him and the bigger children who dominate the scene.

3. The school child from the age of seven to twelve encounters a new social situation in the demands of his own group. Whether the boy becomes a member of the gang on his street or merely associates with his school friends, in most cases he does enter a group of youngsters of his own age who have their own standards. To win approbation in this group he must show his independence of grown-ups. The youngster who fails to make this adjustment is ridiculed as a 'sissy' and is likely to develop feelings of inferiority.

4. The neglect of sex training in our culture makes puberty a critical period of development, for both boys and girls are inadequately prepared for the physical and psychological changes which occur between twelve and fourteen years. They learn the meaning of puberty not through socially approved channels but through their own groups. Interest in the opposite sex and an awakening of feelings of sex guilt produce an estrangement from parents. This whole period, which is one of a shift from childish aims and ideals to the more realistic values of the adult world, has been called the period of stress and strain. Parents often add to the complexity of the situation by refusing to recognize the fact of the child's growing to maturity. The adolescent, in the eyes of his mother still a child, is treated accordingly. The result may be either thoroughgoing

rebellion or an acquiescence which makes for arrested personality development.

5. In the high school the emphasis upon the social role of the adolescent shifts. On the one hand, more independence is granted him in school work, in the selection of courses and in extra-curricular activities. But on the other hand, greater self-sacrifice in the interests of the group is demanded. Although his individuality is encouraged, it is channelized into group spirit. The boy or girl who will not merge his individual desires into supporting the school team is thrust aside as an outcast.

6. The impact of the economic realities of life hits some adolescents when they leave high school, though for many of them the story is even then an old one. To get a job and become self-supporting is a highly critical experience. Old beliefs crash to the ground. The individual may even modify his whole philosophy of life. Moreover, inability to earn one's living, by intensifying feelings of inadequacy and inferiority, demoralizes personality.

7. Marriage soon comes to accentuate adult responsibilities, both economic and social. Since marriage is usually not a mating of affinities but rather an adjustment of clashing personalities, it brings with it problems of sexual compatibility, problems of the expression of two distinctive individualities in a common way of life and problems of increased necessity for financial success. As a consequence, psychiatrists recruit many of their patients from the ranks of maladjusted husbands and wives. Marriage, on the other hand, is often a steadying influence for otherwise unstable personalities. Affection, companionship and directing of attention from himself to his family may afford the individual a situation in which he finds himself as an effective personality.

The beginnings of personality. The infant in the first few weeks of life is a squirming mass of arms and legs. Diffuse responses rather than specific reactions are the rule as the infant yells, kicks, throws his arms about, clenches and unclenches his hands, writhes, twists and rolls. Satisfaction of his physiological needs quiets this mass-action pattern. Though some specific means for attaining satisfaction are present, in general behavior in early infancy is random, blundering and unrelated to the stimulating situation. Gradually this mass activity is narrowed down to discriminating adjustment.

Such a developmental process is the opening chapter in the formation of personality. Just how soon personality appears is an academic question. Infants naturally are incomplete and unformed personalities. Personality in children is also far from complete development. It is interesting, nevertheless, to find that certain aspects of individuality appear early in life. In this respect a study made of twenty-two babies from birth to two years of age provides relevant data. During the first week of life these babies were observed daily, during the second week every other day. After the first two weeks they were visited in their homes every week during the first year, and every two weeks during the second year. At these times spontaneous behavior was observed and responses to test items recorded in an effort to obtain data on general development, on vocalization and on motor and social traits. During the two-year period the general picture was naturally one of growth and change. Some children, however, retained throughout the period the same relative position they had occupied in the group at two weeks. One child, ranked the highest of all the children in irritability in the first two weeks, remained the most irritable at six months, at one year, at eighteen months and likewise at two years. Most of the children were on the whole fairly consistent in some traits and inconsistent in others. Two youngsters out of the twenty-two were very consistent in almost all traits from babyhood on, whereas two others were consistently inconsistent, varying in all traits from time to time.

TEMPERAMENT

Personality, presenting as it does many facets, may be described from many points of view. Some classificatory scheme is needed to give order to the great number of possible descriptions. Table II attempts such a classification. The five major headings are: (1) capacities, the physical dimension of personality; (2) temperament, the emotional dimension; (3) traits, the behavioral dimension; (4) attitudes, the ideational dimension; and (5) the ego, the depth dimension. With the exception of the first item, capacities, which will be treated at length in the chapter on individual differences, these main aspects of personality will be now considered in some detail in relation to experimental findings.

TABLE II

A Classification of Terms Descriptive of Personality

I. Capacities, the Physical Dimension of Personality
II. Temperament, the Emotional Dimension
  A. Emotional frequency and change
  B. Emotional breadth
  C. Emotional strength
  D. Characteristic mood
  E. Emotional stability
III. Traits, the Behavioral Dimension
  A. Introversion-Extraversion
  B. Ascendance-Submission
  C. Persistence
IV. Attitudes, the Ideational Dimension
  A. Radicalism-Conservatism
  B. General Values
V. The Ego, the Depth Dimension
  A. Aspiration level
  B. Self-understanding

Beginning, then, with the second on the list, we note that characteristic emotional states of the individual are summed up under the general term *temperament.* The word has less objective reference than *sentiment*, which describes emotional organization as related to specific objects or people. Temperament is determined in considerable measure by body chemistry. It will be recalled that in the foregoing discussion of endocrine functioning most of the psychological effects were described in terms of emotional states, such as depression, irritability, despondency and excitability. Similarly toxins and infections affect temperament. In an investigation of the emotionality of nine hundred college students, for example, it was found that those who had suffered from infectious diseases were on the average more irritable and more prone to anger than those who had had a less unfortunate medical history.

Three dimensions of emotional life can be differentiated. One is *emotional frequency and change.* Does the individual maintain the same emotional level for a long period of time? Or does he go through a regular cycle of depression and elation? *Emotional breadth* is another aspect to be considered. How wide a range of stimulating objects calls out emotional reactions in the individual? The sensitive person for whom many and varied situations are emotionally weighted is at a decided disadvantage in adjusting socially in comparison with the person who has himself well under control. *Emotional strength,* the third dimension, is concerned with the depth of feelings. Profundity of emotion is not always related to sensitivity; an individual who is rarely moved may on occasion hate bitterly. There are people, however, whose emotions are so intense and so frequent that "they live at the mercy of their diaphragms."

Characteristic mood should be considered as a qualitative aspect of temperament. Some people are characteristically jolly, others gloomy, others apprehensive and still others irascible. Such habitual moods are maintained in part by their social reflection. If, as is often the case, despair is expected of the gloom-monger, then the man with such a reputation will find it difficult to disappoint the melancholy expectation of his associates.

Research has emphasized the practical problem of *emotional stability.* Normal people differ widely in their tendencies toward nervous breakdown and mental disorder. Granted that repeated crises may destroy the emotional balance of any individual, nevertheless it remains true that some persons succumb to the first genuinely trying situation, whereas others keep their sanity through a veritable series of mental shocks. In order to help the more unstable it is important to know about the relative stability of people.

The measurement of emotional stability had its origin in the

World War, when shell-shock and other forms of nervous disorder were common. The United States Government became interested in a method for selecting recruits who would stand up under the nerve-racking experiences of life at the front. The Woodworth Personal Data Inventory was the result, an inventory which lists in question form a great many symptoms found in the case histories of mentally disordered patients.

Recent research has improved the diagnostic value of the psychoneurotic inventory, or emotional stability test, through the use of which many maladjusted individuals have been found by mental hygiene clinics and personnel offices. In one study of the validity of this test, clinical records of two hundred and fifty subjects were compared with their scores on a psychoneurotic inventory. Persons judged to be serious cases of maladjustment on the basis of clinical observation showed symptom scores in the test far above those made by the average individual.

Though the results of this investigation justify the usefulness of the psychoneurotic inventory as a means of discovering maladjustment, it is a mistake to conclude that because subjects who make high scores are maladjusted, the low scorers are well adjusted. If an individual is on the defensive and determined to make a low neurotic score, it is not difficult for him to do so. The neurotic inventory may be said, then, to serve a useful function in selecting from large groups those individuals in need of psychiatric attention, but it does not select out all such cases.

Emotional maladjustment as measured by the neurotic inventory is not identical with social maladjustment. Failure to adjust socially may of course produce emotional instability if the struggle against the social world is internalized within the individual. If, however, the individual struggles against social barriers external to himself, a neurotic tendency is not the result. Boy tramps, for example, cannot be called socially adjusted; yet an investigation of such a group showed lower neurotic scores than were found among a control group of high-school boys of the same age. The high-school students were troubled by feelings of physical ill-being and of depression; transient boys by feelings of worry about their families.

The relation of emotional instability and neurotic tendency to internal conflict has been demonstrated by a method which consists of recording the involuntary tremors and overt movements of the hand in experimental situations. Given a word as stimulus, the subject responds by simultaneously uttering some associated word and by pressing a pneumatic bulb with his right hand. The activity of the 'idle' left hand is also recorded, though the subject is unaware of the fact. This experimental procedure yields three types of evidence: (1) the nature of verbal response, (2) the time of verbal response, and (3) the shape and regularity of the curves of muscular movement. Hysterical and neurasthenic subjects were differentiated from normal subjects in that the neurotic group showed lack of coordination and diffuse reaction. In the normal subject speech and motor responses were synchronized, there was little fluctuation in the time of speech response and the muscular reactions were regular and coordinated. In the neurotic group, on the contrary, motor control was lacking. These results indicate, therefore, that neuroticism is related to disorganization of behavior, or conflict within the individual.

TRAITS

Traits, which are generalized tendencies toward action, are the typical adjustments which people make to their environment. Though arising as an adjustment to a specific problem, a trait may become so deeply rooted in the personality as to appear in both appropriate and inappropriate situations. Traits are thus qualities of behavior. For example, shyness, talkativeness or introversion are not names for specific acts. They are terms which describe *how* the individual conducts himself in a variety of situations. Of the many traits of personality which might be described we must limit our discussion to three which have been the subject of quantitative study: introversion-extraversion, ascendance-submission, and persistence.

Introversion-extraversion. Many students of personality have been impressed by a trait named by Jung introversion-extraversion, a term which refers to the fundamental orientation of the individual in meeting life's problems. The introverted personality turns from active participation in the objective world to an inner world of thought and phantasy. The extraverted personality, on the contrary, turns from an introspective consideration of his problems to overt action. Such a classification is thus definitely related to the popular discrimination between the practical man of action and the idealistic visionary. Extraversion has also further implications: that a person is thick-skinned and relatively insensitive to criticism, spontaneous in his emotional expression, impersonal in argument, neither deeply affected by his failures, nor much occupied with self-analysis and self-criticism. Introversion, on the other hand, is associated with the opposite tendencies: sensitivity to criticism, inhibition of emotional expression, personalization in discussion, magnification of failures and a preoccupation with self-analysis and self-criticism.

A review of the studies in this field shows that three main aspects of introversion-extraversion have been emphasized by various writers. One emphasis is upon the direction of interest of the individual, that is to say, whether he is self-centered or interested in the world around him. The second conception refers to his ease of social adjustment; the extravert adjusts to social situations more readily than does the introvert. The third notion is concerned with emotionality. Since the introvert expresses his emotion less freely than the extravert, this inhibition or blocking leaves him more sensitive emotionally to a wide range of stimuli. These three characterizations are not mutually exclusive. Rather they supplement one another to make up the final generalization known as introversion-extraversion by describing its intellectual, social and emotional phases. This descriptive analysis has been confirmed in part by the application of statistical methods to tests of introversion-extraversion. Responses made in these tests fall into a number of fairly distinct groupings, the two most important of which correspond with the social and emotional aspects of introversion-extraversion as described above.

Most psychologists do not regard the introverted personality and the extraverted personality as sharply contrasting types into which all human beings can be classed. Rather, they believe that almost all individuals possess both introvertive and extravertive characteristics, a point of view according to which the introvert would be simply one who has many more introvertive than extravertive habits. On the basis of actual studies of the distribution of this trait in large groups of people the majority of individuals turn out to be *ambiverts*, showing a preponderance of neither introvertive nor extravertive mechanisms. The degree to which an individual is introverted or extraverted is a matter of his specific developmental history.

One psychologist has explained introversion-extraversion in relation to the development of behavior in the individual in the following manner. Fairly early in infancy two basic reactions can be observed: *adient* responses and *avoidant* responses. Adient responses give the organism more of the same stimulation that called them forth. Outreaching, inquiring, examining and grasping responses are examples of adient reactions. Avoidant responses, on the other hand, produced by intense or overstrong forms of stimulation, take the organism out of range of the stimuli which originally evoked them.

These two fundamental reactions furnish a clue to extraversion-introversion. The introverted character is the sensitive organism that has developed many avoiding reactions. Extreme introverts shrink or withdraw from stimulation to which the normal person has only adient responses. The extreme extravert (the aggressive character) is characterized by many adient responses. He meets obstacles by a direct frontal attack. When confronted by problems that cannot be demolished by sheer aggression, he is incapable of solving them. For his part the introvert, when he meets problems, falls back upon imaginal processes. Ideas take the place of overt activity. The introvert does not, however, compare his ideas sufficiently with the realities which they symbolize to become an objective thinker; he is more likely to become a poet or an artist. And if his introversion is extreme, he may lose contact completely with reality and think only in terms of the phantasy of the mentally disordered patient.

Whether a stimulus is sufficiently intense to produce an avoidance response depends upon the physiological make-up and experience of the organism. Introverted habits of withdrawal and avoidance may develop in the child through contact with a harsh and rigorous environment with which it is unable to cope. From the blows and scorn of older and stronger children the child may withdraw within himself to construct a dream world of imaginative play. Nutritional and glandular factors which contribute to the structural development of the organism also help to determine the degree of sensitivity of the child to various types of stimulation.

This developmental view of introversion-extraversion helps us to understand the different forms which introversion assumes in different individuals. If the intense stimulation which produces avoidance in the child is predominantly social, like continual parental admonition, the child's subsequent shrinking from stimulation may be largely a withdrawal from social situations. Though, as an adult, he may find difficulty in adjusting himself socially, he will not necessarily be introverted in respect to the non-social environment. Inventors and scientists often represent this type of introversion. Since, however, the non-social and the social environments are so closely related, the more usual occurrence is an avoidance of all reality whether social or non-social.

The results of tests of introversion-extraversion confirm the description of this trait as an avoidant or adient orientation toward one's environment. Physical handicaps have been found by a number of investigators to be more frequently associated with introversion than with extraversion. The partially deaf, we discover, are more introverted than their hearing friends. Introversion tends to follow a poor medical history and present physical handicaps. Not only do physical handicaps hinder the child's exploration and manipulation of his environment, but they grant him special social dispensation to the end that often he does not solve his problems at all but turns in preference to the construction of an inner imaginal world.

Tests of introversion-extraversion reveal also that women tend to make slightly higher scores as introverts than do men. This finding does not establish any innate differences between the sexes, but it reflects the different training of men and women in our civilization. From an early age girls are hedged about with more restrictions than are boys. Coddled more than their brothers, at the same time they are fettered with more taboos. These early inhibitions make women less objective and more personalized than men.

If introversion makes for withdrawal from the real world, we should expect to find that introverts seek activities which bring them into the least possible contact with the harsh realities of existence. Studies of interest, of vocational preferences and of occupational groups bear out this expectation. Students of literature in college make higher introverted scores on tests than do students of science. Introverted students are likely to be interested in journalism, literary pursuits and medicine, whereas extraverted students are interested in engineering, law and architecture. When occupational groups themselves were tested, executives, foremen, policemen and salesgirls were in general on the extraverted side of the scale, with clerical workers, accountants, research engineers and teachers on the opposite introverted side.

An investigation has been made of the reactions of introverted and extraverted children to praise and blame. On the basis of their scores on an introversion inventory, fourth- and fifth-grade pupils from four classes were divided into extraverts and introverts. The four classes then worked on cancellation problems under different conditions of praise and blame.

After the first reproof introverts increased their performance more than extraverts. Repeated application of censure, however, produced a greater increment in performance among extraverts than among introverts. The introverts, being more sensitive, were at first more responsive to criticism, but under continued criticism they tended to give up and withdraw from the problem situation. The first application of praise, on the other hand, improved the performance of the extraverts more than the introverts, whereas repeated praise was more effective for the introverts. Accordingly the use of praise and blame in everyday life must be adjusted to the differing personalities of individuals.

Ascendance-submission. The popular division of mankind into leaders and followers is paralleled in psychology by a description of individuals as ascendant and submissive. Ascendance refers to the domination and control by one individual of his fellows in face-to-face situations. It differs from the concept of leadership in that leadership includes control by means of the cloak of authority and by superior social status as well as non-institutional domination. The trait of ascendance-submission implies much the same behavior as does the trait of introversion-extraversion, except that, whereas the purpose of introversion-extraversion is to characterize individuals in their manner of meeting their problems, the term ascendance-submission emphasizes the way in which individuals deal with their fellows.

Ascendance-submission is so fundamental a behavior relationship that it has been observed among animals as well as people. Within a flock of birds, for example, the hierarchy of rank which reflects this relationship is called the *pecking order*. Observers of various species of birds agree that there is a well-defined rank order with respect to food-getting and other activities. Moreover, a bird low in the pecking order is often a more severe despot over his few subordinates than a bird higher in the pecking order. "It seems," comments one observer, "as if the bird which is a despot over only a few shows its annoyance at the pecks to which it itself is exposed by especially furious pecking, while birds which range high in the pecking order, and so are seldom pecked, are more reasonable."

Other animal species reveal similar phenomena. If a new dog is introduced into the pack, considerable fighting will result until his place in the hierarchy is established. One experiment has concerned itself with the dominance relation among monkeys. A limited food supply was presented to fifteen pairs of previously unacquainted monkeys, and the percentage of food obtained by each animal over a period of thirty such presentations taken as a measure of dominance. Other forms of social behavior were found to be associated with this behavior toward food. Regardless of its sex, the dominant animal played the masculine role in sex activity, initiated fighting and play and was generally more active. The submissive animal played the feminine role in sex activity and responded to the aggressive behavior of the ascendant animal by passivity, cringing or flight.

Ascendance-submission appears among children as soon as they are old enough to play together. In a study of the play activities of nursery-school children, ascendant traits were found consistently in certain children and submissive traits in others. Some of the youthful leaders dominated through physical force and threats of force, others through artful suggestion. The leadership-followership relation, however, was not altogether stable. Changes in the personnel of the group led to shifts in leadership. The submissive child in one group might be the leader in another. The technique of leadership, moreover, was frequently learned through the process of following a forceful leader. The socially independent child, it should be noted, though seldom a follower, was also seldom a leader.

The study just described carries the implication that the strong personality who is impervious to social suggestion stands outside the leadership-followership relation. This implication receives support from observations made on a group of twenty children ranging from three to six and a half years. In this group various children came to the fore from time to time, but, with the exception of one five-year-old boy who stood out as the recognized leader, their leadership never lasted. This boy's plans were generally accepted. The secret of his long rule lay in the fact that his plans summed up the needs of the group so well it seemed as if they had really been made by the group.

The most successful ascendance, therefore, involves conformity with the main tendencies of the group.

Experimental studies demonstrate that ascendant qualities can be strengthened in the child through development of his skill in manipulating objects. One experimenter obtained ratings of ascendance scores by observing, for a five-minute interval, children at play in a sandbox containing three sets of toys. Two children at a time were put in this situation, and in the course of the experiment every child was paired with every other child. On the basis of total records for all pairings the five children with the lowest ascendance scores were selected for special training in the use of the three types of play materials. Subsequently they were paired with ascendant children in the original play situation. As a result of increased familiarity with the play materials, four out of five of the submissive youngsters improved in their ability to compete with other children. A control group which had not been trained showed no appreciable gain in ascendance.

Though leadership is a relationship between the ascendant personality and the submissive individual, characteristics of leaders transcend the specific group relation in which they are found. A study made of leadership in three widely differing groups—criminals, army men and students—illustrates this point. In all three groups leaders were differentiated from followers through higher scores on tests of self-confidence, speed of decision and finality of judgment. Ascendant personalities tend to believe in themselves, to make up their minds quickly, to hold to their decisions.

The directionality of behavior is often indicated by the eyes. We look where we are going, and we show our aggressive or non-aggressive orientation by the degree to which we keep our eyes open and fixed upon our objectives. Ascendance-submission may thus be indicated by eye movement. This fact has been experimentally demonstrated by giving subjects a series of mental additions with instructions to return the fixed gaze of the experimenter. The subjects were selected from a class of 89 students who had been rated for ascendance-submission by their associates. Only the thirteen rated most submissive and the thirteen rated most ascendant were used in the experiment. For the non-aggressive students 72 eye movements were recorded as against 6 for the aggressive group. Not one of the ascendant students averted his gaze from the eyes of the experimenter more than twice during the whole five series of additions. Ten of the thirteen in the submissive group shifted their eyes four times or more.

Is ascendance a consistent trait of an individual, or is it a function of the situation and the individual's attitude at the moment? The studies cited above indicate sufficient constancy in aggressive behavior for us to regard it as a characteristic quality of personality. The situation and the momentary attitude, nevertheless, are contributory factors in most acts of ascendance. Many people who are unaggressive until a genuine interest or a streak of vanity is touched, under such provocation become highly ascendant. Certainly the situation often dictates the qualities which make for successful leadership.

Persistence. The quality of carrying a task through to its completion is another important trait of personality. Although the motivating effects of a particular type of situation affect persistence, if we compare the relative tenacity of people we know in many situations, we shall find a considerable measure of persistence to be characteristic of the same individual.

Persistence has been measured by using a number of tests of endurance under conditions of strongly competitive motivation. Ability to withstand pain has been tested by experimental situations such as pressing an edged instrument against the thumb of the subjects, toasting his hand over an electric toaster, increasing the pressure on a wooden peg placed upon the palm and administering an electric shock. After completing these tests, the subjects were given the dubious privilege of bettering their scores by undergoing further electric shock. The individual tests agreed fairly well with one another in differentiating the subjects. Subjects were also told that they might, if they wished, raise or lower their scores by gambling on the toss of a coin, the object being to discover the relation between persistence and willingness to take a chance.

Although intelligence and persistence, as measured by these tests, appeared to be only slightly related, there was a fairly good correspondence between grades in college courses and persistence scores. The persistent people likewise tended to be ascendant. The more persistent individuals, however, did not take advantage of the opportunity to raise their scores by gambling as often as did the less persistent. The person who would endure pain to attain a high score would not take a chance on the toss of a coin. Moreover the gamblers were lower in intelligence than the non-gamblers.

ATTITUDES

Although no sharp line of demarcation can be drawn between attitudes and personality traits, a practical distinction can be made. Personality traits refer to characteristic forms of behavior; attitudes are mental predispositions for certain kinds of verbal behavior that express a value or judgment. The avoiding behavior of the introvert is an expression of a personality trait, but the verbal affirmation of socialistic ideas is indicative of a radical attitude. Attitudes refer to ideas, traits to overt behavior.

Attitude is not a distinctive concept for personal as against non-personal phenomena. Sometimes attitudes are a lasting function of personality; sometimes they are lightly held and readily discarded when the situation changes. Two important types of attitude that frequently are firmly rooted in the personality are radicalism-conservatism and evaluative attitudes. We shall consider each in order.

Radicalism-conservatism. Radicalism denotes ideas which favor social change of a fundamental sort. Conservatism implies standing pat in order to preserve the status quo. In content, attitudes are radical or conservative only in relation to a particular culture at a particular time, but in form they transcend this specificity. That a radical or conservative outlook on life may be a characteristic of personality is illustrated by the views of Supreme Court justices. These justices often maintain throughout their careers a consistency of interpretation in questions involving social and economic issues.

Although most people have not harmonized their philosophy of life into so integrated a pattern as has a judge of the Supreme Court, it is not difficult to find individuals who maintain a consistently radical or reactionary attitude in many different situations. Such consistency appeared in one study which covered the following social, political and economic issues: birth control, miscegenation, the powers of labor organizations, socialization of medicine, academic freedom, divorce, the protective tariff, the Latin-American policy of the United States and social limitation in mating. Extreme radicalism on one question was more often than not accompanied by extreme radicalism on the other issues. Quantitative study has also confirmed the popular impression that people who accept a radical economic philosophy are generally radical also in their religious views.

Research has confirmed the popular view that in general radicals and conservatives are more emotionally convinced of the correctness of their views than are those who support less extreme doctrines. In addition, radicalism has been found to be associated with independence of thought more often than has conservatism. In one experiment the students, divided into radical and conservative groups according to their views on industrial problems, international relations and domestic politics, were called upon to express also their opinions upon the desirability of certain personal traits. An hour later they were asked to re-evaluate these personal traits. This time, however, they were told how a majority of 1000 college students had voted on the traits. To conform with majority opinion the radicals changed their minds in only 18 instances out of a possible 147 opportunities; the conservatives changed 34 times out of 109.

In another experiment the relationship between radicalism and suggestibility was tested. From a group of 542 students the 50 most conservative and the 50 most radical individuals were selected on the basis of their religious views. The selected groups then took several tests which have been used to measure suggestibility. In one test a picture was presented for a brief period. After its removal the subjects were questioned about its content. Leading questions, suggesting erroneous items, were introduced. The conservatives more often than the radicals remembered seeing things which were not in the picture. In another situation the experimenter gave positive and negative suggestions concerning the difficulty of a task required of the subjects. In response to the suggestion that it was easy the conservatives improved more than the radicals. Still another situation sought to create the illusion of an electric shock. Fewer radicals reported experiencing the shock than conservatives. In all the tests of suggestibility the radicals were relatively more inclined to examine the facts for themselves than blindly to accept the experimenter's suggestion.

Evaluative attitudes. An attempt to portray personality in terms of general interests is Spranger's classification of evaluative attitudes. Spranger describes six basic types of interests which he believes color almost all our mental activities. They are (1) the theoretical, (2) the economic, (3) the esthetic, (4) the social, (5) the political and (6) the religious.

The *theoretical* or intellectual interest is the preoccupation with observation, reason and the discovery of truth. Plato exemplified this attitude when he banished poetry from his ideal philosophic state. And the mathematician revealed the theoretical attitude in his question upon hearing a Beethoven symphony, "Beautiful, but what does it prove?"

The *economic* attitude is the emphasis upon utility as against all other values. Knowledge is evaluated in terms of its direct applications to life's problems. Thus people come to be judged on the basis of their earning capacity. The proverb *Honesty is the best policy* is an example of the practical man's attitude toward ethics. The miser represents the economic interest run wild.

The *esthetic* attitude places its stress upon the life of the imagination. The interest here is upon form, beauty, harmony and proportion. The esthetic aim is one of self-realization and self-fulfilment. The idea of use in regard to an esthetic object, whether technical or moral, is foreign to such an attitude.

The *social* attitude in its highest development is the love of one's fellow men. We find the social attitude in the gregarious tendency to foregather with others for no purpose beyond the pleasure of association. The extremely social individual lives vicariously in the experiences of others. The communistic communities of the Utopians represent the social ideal. Whereas the economic attitude stresses self-preservation, and the esthetic, self-realization, the social interest emphasizes self-sacrifice.

The manipulation of his fellow men is the chief interest of the politician. The *political* value-attitude is not confined to the politician, however, but can be found in all leaders who desire ascendancy over others. The successful leader must be a realistic student of human nature, for he "must take people as they really are, whereas the pedagogue is inclined to see them as they might be."

To fathom the final secret, to understand the ultimate meaning of life, is the goal of the *religious* attitude. Such understanding goes beyond knowledge to rest upon belief and faith. Science deals with the finite and measurable, religion with the infinite.

These six attitudes, Spranger believes, are found in varying degrees in all personalities. To understand people it is necessary to know which interests are dominant in their make-up. A test entitled the *Study of Values* has been devised to determine the relative prominence of these basic interests. In Part I of the test the subject is asked to check one of two alternative answers to statements designed to force a choice of interests. Question 1 from Part I of the test follows:

> The main object of scientific research should be the discovery of pure truth rather than its practical applications.
>
> ...... (*a*) Yes; ...... (*b*) No.

In Part II, one of the four alternative answers is to be chosen to indicate the subject's attitude toward the situation described. For example, Question 14 reads:

> If you should marry, do you prefer a wife who
> ....(*a*) can achieve social prestige, commanding admiration from others;
> ....(*b*) likes to stay at home and keep house;
> ....(*c*) is fundamentally spiritual in her attitude toward life;
> ....(*d*) is gifted along artistic lines.

The whole test contains 120 possible answers, 20 for each of the six values.

The *Study of Values* is a valid means for determining group differences in generalized motives. Although its validity for individual prediction is not perfect, it has been successfully used to differentiate groups of subjects with varying occupational interests. This test has also been compared with the following experimental test of interest. Twenty-two newspaper items were selected from a large number of newspaper clippings by four judges as the clearest representations of Spranger's six types of value. A group of naive subjects glanced over these items and later were given a memory or recognition test for the items. At a subsequent date the subjects were given the *Study of Values* test. The results showed a fairly high correlation (0.71) between the group scores on the *Study of Values* and the recognition of types of news items.

The values of students as measured by the *Study of Values* have been compared with their attitudes as measured by more specific scales. Students who placed a high valuation upon theoretical and scientific interests were opposed to war, opposed to prohibition and opposed to the church, but favorably disposed toward the Negro. Economically and practically minded students were unfavorably disposed toward the Negro and prohibition, but were relatively militaristic. Politically minded students were also militaristic and prejudiced against the Negro.

THE EGO OR SELF

Thus far we have been describing personality from the outside looking in. This objective observation can easily miss a significant aspect of personality which is immediately apparent when we take the point of view of the individual himself. Only then do we become aware of the importance of the ego or self. People not only adjust to external forces, but they also adjust in terms of what they conceive themselves to be. This notion of self is the organized summary of the many experiences which have befallen the individual. Its role in personality will be clarified if we regard it developmentally.

The baby at first has no clearly defined notion of the boundaries between its own body and the external world. It will scratch or strike itself and its crib indiscriminately. The difference between these two experiences provides one of the first sources of self-knowledge. Other actions contribute further to the idea of self. Even moving its own arms and seeing them move become for the child a different experience from pushing an object and seeing it fall. Hearing one's own voice likewise calls into play the attendant sensations of muscular effort not present when someone else speaks.

The child's name, a ready-made symbol standing for his distinctiveness as an individual, pushes still further the organization of the child's personal experiences. Long before the child can utter his own name, he realizes that it is he to whom that name refers. As soon as he is able to vocalize, his name is prefixed to many of the things he does and wants. Both past experiences and present needs are associated with this symbol of self. Immediate specific wants through this association can take on a deeper significance. If a specific want is frustrated, it comes to mean the frustration of the child himself. The hungry child denied a piece of candy may feel this denial not only in terms of hunger pangs but also as a defeat of his ego.

The self early expands to include more than the individual. Personal possessions become an extension of the ego. Cherished toys grow to be part of the child's personality. He takes them to bed at night, and comes to regard an injury to them as an injury to himself. Similarly, the child may identify himself with either parent, thus vicariously enjoying in this manner the superior abilities of the adult. An opposite tendency may also be observed in the restriction of the self. As the individual grows older, he divorces some of his desires and some of his attributes from his central personality. The mature adult generally does not regard his ability at weight-lifting or his skill at foot-racing as an essential part of his ego. On the basis of the above facts, then, we may define the self as a core of emotional experiences associated with the symbol of name or personal pronoun.

Levels of aspiration and expectation. Both consciously and unconsciously the individual sets for himself a certain level of performance to which he aspires. This level is represented not by the impossible desires of the daydream but by what the person in his day-to-day work hopes to be able to do. This is the level of aspiration. Many people also maintain a level of expectation—what they think they can actually accomplish. The relation between the level of expectation and the level of past performance is a relatively permanent characteristic of personality. Some people consistently place their expectations higher than their performance. Some students, for example, always expect to do better in examinations than they really do. Others cautiously underestimate their ability or achievement.

Understanding of self. An interesting aspect of the self is the degree to which it understands itself. People vary consistently from one another in the accuracy with which they can name their own motives and appraise their own abilities. Complete insight is obviously impossible, since the self is at once the source of knowledge and the seat of prejudice. The naive faith persists, even so, that man can know his own mind, that one can find out everything about others merely by bombarding them with questions.

The crassness of a person's rationalizations is one index of insight into the nature of self. Rationalization is the process of giving plausible, acceptable reasons for conduct and desire instead of the actual motivating causes. The child learns to rationalize when his motives and actions are socially disapproved. Thereupon he cloaks over these proscribed activities by a respectable front of approved verbal labels. Since in this process the social prohibitions become part of his own ego, he concludes by deceiving himself with the rationalizations originally formulated for others.

The aspects of the self about which the individual generally has least insight are those which he considers most reprehensible. Characteristics of this sort he is more likely to attribute to other people than to himself. Fraternity members were asked by one investigator to rate one another and themselves on the traits of stinginess, obstinacy, disorderliness and bashfulness, as well as to evaluate the same traits from the point of view of desirability. Insight into the self was measured by a comparison of the individual's rating of himself with the average rating given by his associates. In general, the students with greater insight did not regard the traits of stinginess and obstinacy so blameworthy as did the less insightful students. Moreover, the students poor in self-evaluation on a given trait tended to attribute that trait to their fellows more often than did students who, though possessing the trait in equal measure, had a better knowledge of themselves. The latter, in fact, went to the other extreme and projected traits opposite to their own nature into others. The individuals who were aware of their own stubbornness, for example, were inclined to regard others as pliable and agreeable.

The introverted personality and the extraverted personality show interesting differences in insight into the self. The introvert has far better knowledge of his own mechanisms and motives than has the extravert; his rationalizations are far more subtle. The extravert, on the other hand, has a keener knowledge of his own social abilities than has the introvert. This knowledge of his social ability he derives, of course, from the effects of his personality in social situations, effects which the extravert judges more accurately than does the introvert.

THE INTEGRATION OF PERSONALITY

The problem of the unification or integration of personality poses two separate questions which are often confused. The first query can be formulated thus: Are the separate traits of personality really distinct entities, or are they expressions of a unified pattern which colors everything the individual does? In other words, how thoroughly integrated is the personality? The second question asks: If any relationship does exist among personality traits, how is it to be explained? Here the emphasis is not upon the extent of integration but upon the way in which integration develops.

The traditional concepts concerning the integration of personality and personality types present opposed views. The specificists hold that behavior depends upon the particular situation in which the individual is placed, and upon his specific training with regard to the various elements in that situation. They assert, for example, that the student who walks off with a library book is not necessarily untrustworthy with respect to money. On the other hand, the supporters of the idea of generality assume that responses to varying situations are determined by a general function of personality, fairly independently of the specific nature of the situation. Unfortunately, these traditional concepts have obscured the amount of genuine agreement in the experimental findings on the problem.

The factual evidence concerning the extent of integration of behavior is in essential agreement. Individuals show a high degree of consistency in their behavior, but not a complete consistency.

It will be recalled that a radical or a conservative attitude toward life extends to many areas of social belief. No experimental evidence exists, however, to show that radicalism is a sufficiently generalized attitude to influence all behavior. The measurement of Spranger's six attitudes likewise indicates a spread of the same personal interest over many but not all situations. Subjects who show a practical outlook on life in one problem tend to maintain the same practical attitude in many other problems.

Various expressive movements such as handwriting, walking, drawing and speed of performance are consistently related in the same personality. Tasks performed by the same individual but involving different muscle groups are positively correlated.

The speed of reading and of writing—both handwriting and blackboard writing—is a consistent function of the personality. Though expressive functions are closely related in the individual, they are not so thoroughly unified as to be explicable in terms of one general factor of motility.

Similar results have been found with the various aspects of intelligence. Extensive testing programs have confirmed the popular view that the brilliant individual is generally but not always adept at any type of problem solution, that the dull person is dull in the majority of his responses. To set up different tests of intellectual ability which do not yield some positive correlation is, in fact, difficult. On the basis of experimental findings, therefore, personality should not be regarded as a composite of many unrelated, wholly specific characteristics. At the same time, individuals are too complex, they have too many water-tight compartments in their thinking and acting, to validate the theory of a personality type as a general unitary factor pervading the whole personality. An individual must be understood as possessing not one but a number of generalized functions. Though general types of behavior exist, no one general factor accounts for all the conduct of an individual.

Dissociation and multiple personality. The failure of most people to organize their lives according to a consistent pattern is due to the diversified nature of the world in which they have grown to maturity. An adjustment learned in one type of situation is often useless in another. The respectful obedience to elders which brings approbation in the home is ridiculed in the boy's gang. The moral code which the youngster is taught on Sunday is contradicted by the sharp practices which he meets on Monday. Thus in answer to the conflicting demands of the social environment individuals develop different and even conflicting ways of behaving. Ordinarily from the individual's own point of view these inconsistencies are minor difficulties offering no serious obstacle to his mental poise. Sometimes, however, the discordant adjustments are so incompatible and involve so many actions and ideas that they disturb the continuity of mental life. *Dissociation* is the term used to describe the consequent splitting apart of the stream of consciousness. The conflict between the opposed patterns of activity is temporarily avoided by preventing these antagonists from meeting.

Dissociation of the personality may be simultaneous or successive. An example of simultaneous dissociation is automatic writing, which occurs in hysterical patients and under certain circumstances in normal individuals. The subject is able to write answers to questions written on paper by one person, while carrying on a conversation with another person. Both his conversation and his written answers are sensible and meaningful. Apparently, two habit systems are functioning in the individual at one and the same time with little or no relation between them.

In successive dissociation, the usual activities of the individual are suddenly broken off and replaced by a different mode of life. In his new personality role the individual frequently has no consciousness of his former self. Often he alternates between his two personalities. In such a dual personality, the individual has two major action systems so incompatible with one another that both cannot be given expression at the same time.

One of the first recorded cases of double personality was that of Mary Reynolds. Her friends and relatives knew Miss Reynolds as a reserved, timid, melancholy, even morbid creature. One morning she awoke with all memory of her previous existence gone. She even had to relearn the acts of reading and writing. Her disposition, moreover, had completely changed. She was now fearless, buoyant and gregarious. After five weeks she lapsed back into her first personality with no knowledge of what had befallen her. These alternations from one state to another continued at intervals of varying length for sixteen years, finally leaving her in her second state. Gradually, however, the second personality was modified so that in old age it no longer represented a complete emotional opposition to her first state. Some measure of integration had evidently been achieved.

REFERENCES

1. ALLPORT, G. W. *Personality, a psychological interpretation.* New York: Henry Holt, 1937.
2. ANDERSON, H. H. Domination and integration in the social behavior of young children in an experimental play situation. *Genet. Psychol. Monogr.,* 1937, 19, No. 3.
3. CURTI, M. *Child psychology.* New York: Longmans Green, 1933.
4. FORLANO, G., and AXELROD, H. C. The effect of repeated praise or blame on the performance of introverts and extroverts. *J. educ. Psychol.,* 1937, 28, 92-100.
5. GUILFORD, J. P., and BRALY, K. Extroversion and introversion. *Psychol. Bull.,* 1930, 27, 96-107.
6. HOLT, E. B. *Animal drive and the learning process.* New York: Henry Holt, 1931.
7. JACK, L. M. An experimental study of ascendant behavior in pre-school children. *Univ. Ia Stud. Child Welf.,* 1934, 9, No. 3, Part 1.
8. KATZ, D., and SCHANCK, R. L. *Social psychology.* New York: John Wiley, 1938.
9. LURIA, A. R. *The nature of human conflicts.* New York: Liveright, 1932.
10. MEAD, M. *Cooperation and competition among primitive peoples.* New York: McGraw-Hill, 1937.
11. MURPHY, G., MURPHY, L. B., and NEWCOMB, T. M. *Experimental social psychology.* New York: Harper, 1937.
12. SEARS, R. R. Experimental studies of projection. *J. soc. Psychol.,* 1936, 7, 151-163.
13. SPRANGER, E. *Types of men.* Halle: Niemeyer, 1928.
14. STAGNER, R. *Psychology of personality.* New York: McGraw-Hill, 1937.

CHAPTER 4

INDIVIDUAL DIFFERENCES IN PERSONALITY

In the preceding chapter we have had a qualitative account of personality in terms of biological and social development. In this chapter stress will be placed upon quantitative comparisons of traits and capacities in different individuals. In short, we shall now see in what ways and to what degree people differ in some of the aspects of personality.

Individual differences in psychology are the differences between individuals with respect to specific traits, capacities, skills or interests. People show deviations from the average or from some accepted norm of human performance. Investigation in this field involves largely the collection and interpretation of well-defined measurements of various aspects of behavior.

Our interest in individual human differences is threefold: it may be personal, practical or scientific. The *personal* interest derives from a natural desire to know what one's own capacities are in order to utilize them as effectively as possible for comfortable and successful adjustment to life. A *practical* interest in trait differences has developed from the need for dependable measures in classifying school children. Directed first toward segregating mentally retarded and other problem children, this interest has been extended to include many phases of the psychological appraisal of children in education, as well as of adults in industry and in the social community. *Scientific* interest in individual differences has advanced both the personal and practical aims, the results of pure scientific research having furnished from the beginning the data for personal and

This chapter was written by Catharine Cox Miles of Yale University.

practical applications. This basic scientific interest has been directed toward the solving of two significant problems: one that of defining the range and variety of human abilities and their interrelationships, and the other the problem of the origins of the traits measured, together with the way in which nature and nurture combine to produce them.

The direct and indirect measurement of traits. Physical traits can be measured directly and with a fair degree of precision. In appraising height, for instance, we are not compelled to make elaborate inferences from some other quite different characteristic. Intelligence and skill, on the other hand, have to be measured by just such techniques of inference and deduction; they have to be measured, that is, indirectly through their products—such, for example, as performance in examinations or success in the construction of engineering models. Precision in measurements of this kind can therefore be achieved only when the tasks are objective—extracting the square root of 7, or fitting together a miniature airplane—and the results consequently capable of statement in exact terms. Although in this case experience and familiarity with the materials may differ for two performers, the problems themselves are always the same and the rating standards universal.

In measuring attitudes and personality traits, however, the approach is less direct than in testing intelligence and skill, because now the statement of the test problem may present different meanings to different individuals. Moreover, it is not objective facts but differing social cultures which generally determine the appropriateness of different answers. Thus an affirmative answer to the test question regarding whether you can be optimistic when others about you are greatly depressed may mean any one of three things: that you are young and irresponsible, or that you are self-centered and indifferent, or that you are a supporting pillar of social sanity and courage. Comparisons of scores on tests made up of questions of this kind can therefore be meaningful only where the cultural backgrounds of the tested individuals are similar.

Hence individual differences in attitudes and personality traits, although universally measurable, give scores that are *relative*. They have significance for comparison only within limited groups.

Ways of studying individual differences. There are three methods of measuring individual differences. There is the *chance observation* of friends and relatives. Here neither the selection of the persons to be observed nor the criteria for observation follow any prescribed rules. There is also the *systematic observation* by teachers in classrooms or on the playground or in examinations, by foremen in factories, by physicians, by employers in interviews, by army captains in routine drill or under fire. In the course of such survey large numbers of individuals are observed in a few typical situations where individual differences of practical value are readily noted. The most reliable method of measurement, however, is the *method by test*, for here both the situations and the conditions are controlled and standardized. The test is validated not by hunches or guesses, but by accurate comparisons of large numbers of trial performances under similar conditions. As we proceed, we shall note the nature of some of the standard tests most commonly used.

True differences can be discovered only by the use of tests known to be reliable and valid for the purpose to which they are put. In order to fulfil the criterion of *reliability* the test must give the same results when repeated under standardized conditions on the same individual. For example, the student who scores highest on an intelligence test on entering college should also score very high on the same or a similar test at the end of the same year. In order to meet the criterion of *validity* the results of the test must agree closely with the opinion of observers qualified to judge the traits in question. Thus, the persons who score highest on self-sufficiency must be those whose behavior in daily life is recognized to be highly self-sufficient. For the satisfaction of the two criteria psychology, in common with all other contemporary biological sciences, requires not only an exact standardization of procedure but also satisfactory mathematical units of measurement and an exact statistical treatment of the results.

STATISTICAL UNITS AND METHODS

In order to measure, a science must develop and agree upon certain units and procedures. Thus in the science of anthropology investigators have worked out units and methods for measuring physical height, weight and strength. Similarly, psychologists working in the field of personality have developed units and methods for registering and comparing the elements of behavior.

Units of measurement. Most of the data for the study of individual differences are in the form of individual ratings or *scores* for intelligence, skills or traits. Such scores may be presented in various ways. They may sometimes be in terms of *raw scores* which give in numerical terms the number of right answers in a given test without indicating relative position. A raw score of 8, for example, may be either high or low, depending on its relationship to other scores in a series. More often scores are *converted* into some relative number, or scale index, which shows the position of the individual score in terms of *norms* constructed from series of similar scores of large numbers of people.

In cases where the ratings of the traits or the aptitude scores change characteristically from year to year as physical development takes place, these norms are often arranged in steps on an *age scale*. Intelligence scores, for example, are frequently expressed in age terms. Thus we may say, "John, who is 10, has a mental age of 13." Or the norms may be expressed in terms of *centile ratings* (percentages) which indicate standing in relation to others in a group. On the centile scale the highest score in 100 is the 100th centile, the lowest is the 1st centile. In terms of such norms we may say, accordingly, that John's mechanical skill rates at the 80th centile for 10-year-olds, at the 50th for 13-year-olds, meaning thereby that 20 per cent of the 10-year-olds and 50 per cent of the 13-year-olds have scores higher than John's.

A third kind of norm is based on the *ratio* between the score on an age scale and the actual life-age of the individual. This ratio, obtained by dividing the mental age by the chronological age, is the *quotient* norm most familiar in the intelligence quotient, or IQ scale. In the IQ terminology we may say that John with his mental age of 13 and chronological or life-age of 10 has a quotient (IQ) of 130 (actually 1.30 with the decimal point omitted). For computing the IQ of individuals 16 years of age or older the chronological age of 15 is usually adopted as the constant devisor. This is done because mental-age development does not continue beyond age 15 in terms measurable by tests of general intelligence.

TABLE III

SCORES OF 20 COLLEGE SOPHOMORES IN INTELLIGENCE, VOCABULARY AND PERSONALITY TESTS

		Intelligence Test Scores			Vocabulary Rating Stanford-Binet		Personality Test Centiles		
Age	Name	Otis Speed IQ	Otis 'Power' IQ	Stanford-Binet M. A.	Score	Vocabulary	Neurotic	Self-sufficient	Dominant
17	Barker	133	131	18–10	72	12900	46	45	74
19	Bowles	141	136	20– 7	80	14400	64	21	29
20	Colter	123	124	17–10	87	15660	54	65	38
18	Cooke	127	123	19– 6	80	14400	96	28	11
20	Crane	129	139	18– 2	76	13680	4	84	79
19	Edwards	128	130	19– 7	78	14040	55	49	49
18	Faber	124	125	20– 9	90	16300	41	12	53
17	Fiske	114	110	19– 1	55	9900	22	69	61
18	Foss	134	145	20– 1	74	13320	6	92	82
20	Holman	147	147	22–10	85	15300	11	95	99
20	Kline	143	140	19– 2	70	12600	36	7	57
18	Moore	133	131	18– 0	74	13320	79	75	27
18	Nelson	121	117	18– 7	76	13680	84	3	6
19	Norton	131	129	16–10	63	11340	35	81	85
19	Olsen	139	146	21– 9	77	13860	10	56	43
21	Orcutt	130	135	20– 5	76	13680	88	33	5
19	Sharpe	118	120	19–10	83	14940	78	59	17
20	Ward	130	113	19– 6	81	14580	92	31	94
18	Watson	137	132	20– 3	77	13860	60	17	36
18	Williams	118	127	17– 5	66	11880	25	73	65
18.8	Mean	130	130	19– 6	76	13682 Median	50	52	51

In Table III psychological information about 20 students is presented in the various typical units or scores. The columns of the table include (1) the age of the students, (2) their names (fictitious) and the following scores: (3) speed IQ or intelligence quotient computed from the score in a *timed*, written group test; (4) 'power' IQ or intelligence quotient computed from the age score in an *untimed*, written group test; (5) mental age determined from the score in an individual test orally administered; (6) vocabulary raw score, *i.e.*, number of words correctly defined in a word-definition test; (7) estimated vocabulary or number of root English words that an individual is estimated to possess on the basis of his score (derived by the formula: estimated vocabulary = raw score × 180); and (8, 9, 10) three personality scores (centile ratings) on the neurotic, the self-sufficient and the dominance scales, from a test of personality traits.[1]

Group statistics. Each row of figures in the body of Table III tells us about one individual. As they stand, however, the 20 rows do not furnish us with any single usable rating or index of the group as a whole. To discover a measure or measures of the group we must make use of statistical method.

It would probably occur to almost anyone to take the average of each column of scores as the best approximation to a single measure for the group. And that is exactly what a statistician would advise. In our concrete example we may compute the *average* (or *mean*, as it is better called) by adding together all the items in a column and dividing the total by their number, *N* (also called the population)—in this case 20. The mean values for the ages, intelligence scores and vocabulary scores are entered in the table at the foot of the columns in question. Another kind of average, called the *median*, is sometimes used in preference to the mean when the scores of a series are not concentrated about a central point. The median is the midscore, or middle point in a series of values arranged in order of magnitude. We may use it appropriately

[1] R. G. Bernreuter, *The personality inventory*. Stanford University Press, 1931.

in indicating the midpoint of centiles, as we have done here for the personality ratings.

When a population is large, the procedure for obtaining a mean is somewhat different. If, for example, we had 200 instead of 20 cases, then it would be well to proceed by arranging the scores in a neatly classified form before attempting statistical treatment. Let us suppose that in terms of age our 20 cases are representative of a hypothetical group of 200, *i.e.*, that the larger group has just 10 times as many individuals at each age as the smaller. Then we can write down opposite each age the number of times it occurs in the series of 200—again in the language of statistics, its *frequency*. Adding the customary column headings, X for a measure or score (here age) and f for its frequency, we have Table IV.

TABLE IV

X	f
17	20
18	60
19	70
20	40
21	10
	$N = \Sigma f = 200$

A table of this kind is known as a *frequency distribution*. In constructing this distribution, we have performed one of the elementary processes in statistics, the gathering of data into a form that is compactly represented and easily understood. Here N, the population, can be obtained by adding up the frequencies in the second column. Its value is entered at the bottom of the table, together with its formula, $N = \Sigma f$.

The mean of the ages for the hypothetical 200 cases can now be obtained by multiplying each score by its frequency, adding together these products and dividing their sum by N. The formula for the mean (M) is therefore:

$$M = \frac{\Sigma fX}{N}$$

TABLE V

X	f	fX
17	20	340
18	60	1080
19	70	1330
20	40	800
21	10	210
		$\Sigma fX = 3760$

$$M = \frac{\Sigma fX}{N} = \frac{3760}{200} = 18.8$$

Table V presents the steps in the calculation. The average college sophomore age calculated by this method, one devised for use with large groups, is 18.8, which of course checks with the result obtained by the simple method generally utilized for small numbers.

The computation of average scores makes possible comparisons of one group with another. The score averages of our group of college students may, for example, now be compared with similar averages of other college students, obtained empirically or from published sources, or with averages for preparatory school students or for the general population. In short, meaningful comparisons of groups are made possible by the use of statistical measures.

The normal distribution. Instead of presenting the data in Table IV by means of columns of figures, we might have put them into graphic form. For example, in the case of the students' ages we may draw a horizontal base line (the abscissa), along which at equal intervals we mark off the ages as successive X values. Over these X values we then erect rectangles, each with a unit base and altitude equal to the frequency of the corresponding value of X. This procedure gives us what is known as a *histogram*, as shown in Fig. 3.

If now we connect the center of the top of each rectangle with the next by a continuous line, we have a *frequency curve*. Although such a curve may be of almost any shape, it is an interesting fact that many natural phenomena, when ordered into a frequency distribution according to some measurable characteristic, give a curve that is high in the center and that falls off on either side of its midpoint in a shape resembling the silhouette of a bell. The ideal form of this curve is known as the *normal distribution curve*. It is shown in Fig. 4.

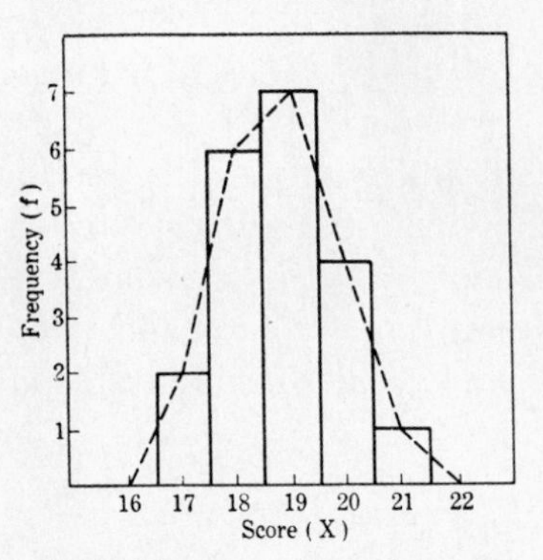

Fig. 3. Histogram (Solid Line) and Frequency Curve (Dotted Line) Representing the Distribution of Scores in Table III.

The normal distribution curve, although it is symmetrical about its midpoint (the mean), may be high and narrow, or low and wide, according as the scores of which it is composed tend to cluster closely about the mean or to lie more widely scattered. Since this clustering (*dispersion*) is a property

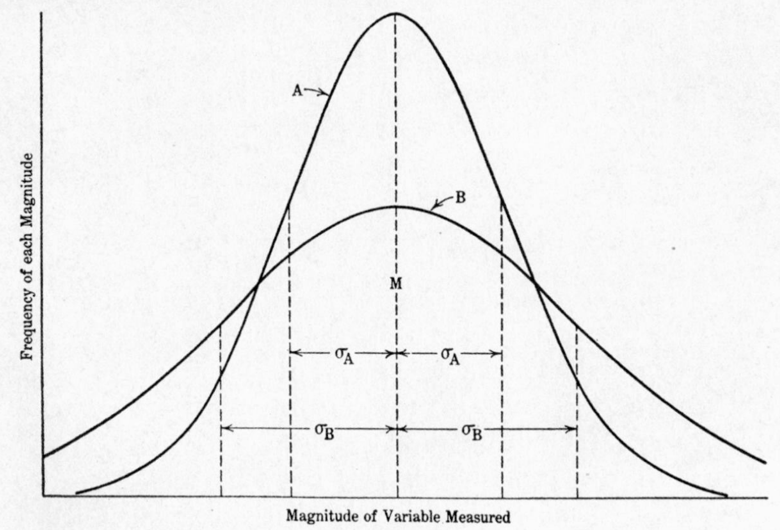

Fig. 4. Two Normal Distribution Curves (*A* and *B*) with Standard Deviations in the Ratio 3:5.

Since the area under the curve between any two verticals represents the proportion of variables having magnitudes between those limits, it is easily seen that σ is a sensitive measure of dispersion.

of distributions which is independent of the values of their means, we must note how it is measured. The most common measure of the scatter of scores about their mean is the *standard deviation*, sometimes abbreviated S.D. but more commonly symbolized by σ (sigma). The standard deviation of a distribution is obtained by rescoring each item as a deviation from the mean, squaring each deviation, adding together these squares, dividing their product by N and taking the square root of the quotient. In other words, if we let x stand for the difference between any score and the mean (that is to say, $x = X - M$), we have the formula for the standard deviation:

$$\sigma = \sqrt{\frac{\Sigma f x^2}{N}}.$$

Table VI shows the actual calculation of σ by this formula as applied to the age distribution in Table III.

TABLE VI

X	f	x	x^2	fx^2
17	2	−1.8	3.24	6.48
18	6	−0.8	0.64	3.84
19	7	0.2	0.04	0.28
20	4	1.2	1.44	5.76
21	1	2.2	4.84	4.84
				$\Sigma fx^2 = 21.20$

$$\sigma = \sqrt{\frac{\Sigma fx^2}{N}} = \sqrt{\frac{21.20}{20}} = \sqrt{1.06} = 1.03$$

The value of σ for any series of scores shows, therefore, in what way the scores tend to be distributed around their mean. If σ is large, it indicates a wide spread of items from the mean outward; if σ is small, the tendency is toward a close clustering about M. Of the practical usefulness of σ, the most common instance may be noted. This is in the comparison of groups where, the smaller the σ's of the distributions, the more dependable, obviously, the difference between the means.

Formulas are known which express the statistical significance of the differences between two means in exact mathematical terms involving directly the values of σ for both distributions. A difference is generally regarded as of doubtful statistical significance unless it is more than three times the standard deviation of the difference. For example, the speed IQ mean of the twenty students of Table III is 130. Suppose now we find that twenty honor students have a mean of 135. The difference is five points, and the question is whether this difference is significant or just due to chance. The standard deviation of the difference in this particular case can be shown to be 2.98, which is over half the difference: 5/2.98. This means that the scores in both groups have such a wide distribution that there is much overlapping of the scores of the two groups. From these results it cannot be said with certainty, therefore, that honor students on the average will have a higher speed IQ than the ordinary run of students.

A second important use of the standard deviation in the study of individual differences is in the calculation of coefficients of correlation to be next described.

Correlation. By *correlation* we understand *mutual dependence*. For example, from our measures of speed and 'power' of intelligence we may expect that an individual with a speed score greater than the average of the group will also generally have a power score greater than the average. If this co-variation occurs, we may speak of speed and power of intelligence as being directly correlated. On the other hand, if through some strange circumstance the fastest intellect proved in the long run to be the least able and the slowest intellect the most able, we should speak of the correlation as inverse (or negative). A third case would be that in which we found no tendency for a given mental speed to be associated with any particular amount of mental power, so that no prediction would be possible from one to the other. This case we should speak of as an example of no correlation, either direct or inverse.

Beside directions of correlation, there are also degrees. If it were discovered that every man with a speed IQ of 130 had a power IQ of 131, and every man with a speed IQ of 131 a power IQ of 132, etc., so that, given a man's speed IQ, we could exactly predict his power IQ, then the two IQ's would be perfectly correlated. But most correlations fall considerably short of perfection. Although mental speed is obviously correlated with mental power, the correlation is not exact.

It would be convenient to be able to rate correlations on a scale running from negative unity (—1.00) through zero to positive unity (1.00). Negative unity would indicate perfect inverse correlation, negative decimals would indicate less perfect negative correlation, zero would indicate utter absence of correlation and positive decimals would show direct degrees of correlation up to perfect direct correlation at positive unity. To make such a rating is precisely what we are enabled to do by means of the correlation coefficient.

The correlation coefficient. The most significant measure of correlation is the so-called product-moment coefficient, for which the symbol r is used.

TABLE VII

Calculation of the Correlation Coefficient r for the Speed and 'Power' IQ's of the First 10 Students in Table III

Name	Speed IQ X	'Power' IQ Y	x	y	xy
Barker	133	131	+ 3	0	+ 3
Bowles	141	136	+11	+ 5	+ 55
Colter	123	124	− 7	− 7	+ 49
Cooke	127	123	− 3	− 8	+ 24
Crane	129	139	− 1	+ 8	− 8
Edwards	128	130	− 2	− 1	+ 2
Faber	124	125	− 6	− 6	+ 36
Fiske	114	110	−16	−21	+336
Foss	134	145	+ 4	+14	+ 56
Holman	147	147	+17	+16	+272
	$M_x = 130$	$M_y = 131$	$\sigma_x = 8.9$	$\sigma_y = 10.6$	$\Sigma xy = 825$

$$r = \frac{\Sigma xy}{N\sigma_x\sigma_y} = \frac{+825}{10 \times 8.9 \times 10.6} = 0.87$$

The correlation coefficient, r, is of doubtful significance unless its value is at least 3 times its probable error, $P.E.$

The coefficient r has the following very convenient properties:

1. It always lies between the limits + 1 and — 1.
2. Its absolute value shows the degree of correlation, from no correlation whatsoever at 0 to perfect correlation at 1.00.
3. It is negative for all degrees of inverse correlation, and positive for all degrees of direct correlation.

The mathematical derivation of r is beyond the compass of this chapter, but its formula and a practical example of its application will serve to introduce this important statistical device. The formula is as follows: $r = \Sigma xy/(N\sigma_x\sigma_y)$, in which the σ's of the two distributions are derived in the manner described above. The xy's are computed as indicated in the example given in Table VII. This table shows the steps in the calculation of the correlation between the speed IQ's and the power IQ's of the first 10 students in Table III. Since these procedures have already been illustrated, the calculation of the means and standard deviations of the two series of scores is not shown. The computation of the quantity Σxy is shown in detail, however, as well as the final calculation of r, the coefficient of correlation.

Since the correlation, when calculated, turns out to be positive and well up toward 1.00, we may conclude that performance on the two intelligence tests is related in such a way that an individual who scores above the average on the one test is very likely to do better than the average on the other.

When two phenomena are found to co-vary consistently, one may hazard a conjecture that they are connected by the possession of some common factor. The determination of correlations, therefore, occasionally results in hypotheses of considerable scientific value. Thus, for example, if tests of motor skill, ability in arithmetic, understanding of verbal relations and memory span are all found to be positively correlated with one another, the indication is that there probably exists some ability or abilities more general than these specific ones and psychologically basic to them. It is precisely on the ground of such findings that psychologists argue for the recognition of one or more general abilities—such as general intelligence—which are basic to many sorts of specific mental performances.

Examples selected from the coefficients of correlation for the various series of scores in Table III illustrate the presence of positive and negative co-variance and its absence (independence). (See Table VIII.) The three measures of intelligence,

TABLE VIII

TRAITS CORRELATED

	r	*P.E.*
Speed IQ and 'power' IQ	+0.79	0.05
Self-sufficiency and dominance	+0.53	0.11
Stanford-Binet and vocabulary	+0.48	0.11
Speed IQ and dominance	+0.32	0.14
Stanford-Binet and dominance	+0.08	0.15
Speed IQ and self-sufficiency	+0.05	0.15
Vocabulary and dominance	−0.16	0.14
Neuroticism and self-sufficiency	−0.54	0.10
Neuroticism and 'power' IQ	−0.54	0.10
Neuroticism and dominance	−0.62	0.09

the two IQ's and the mental ages, are intercorrelated positively. The vocabulary score shows a direct relationship with the Stanford-Binet rating to which it contributes. On the other hand, with the exception of the neuroticism score, which is negatively correlated with the power IQ, the personality scores are unrelated to the measures of intelligence. The self-sufficiency and dominance ratings co-vary and are negatively related to the neurotic series.

Norm charts and individual profiles. In surveying the units for measuring individual differences it was noted that these units were meaningful when expressed in terms of norms. It was noted also that some of the more usual norms were in the form of year scales, of quotients or of centiles. Raw scores, it appeared, would be of value only if expressed in terms of some established norm. It is often useful to make of the measures for a group, as for example the group in Table III, a *norm chart*, or map, on which the norm scales are plotted in parallel lines. In Fig. 5 the scales for Table III are plotted in this way. The scale points for each of the eight measures indicate relative score position in the group. Thus the mean, or median, *M*, is in each case arbitrarily placed at the midpoint of the scale; the upper and lower score limits form the upper and lower boundaries of the chart; and two parallels halfway between the boundaries and the midline give, at their intersections of the eight scales, the respective *quartile* positions. The *upper quartile*, Q_3, marks off the top 25 per cent. The *lower quartile*, Q_1, marks off the lowest 25 per cent. Between Q_1 and Q_3 are the scores of the middle 50 per cent of the group. The distance or value Q_3—Q_1 is called the *interquartile range.*

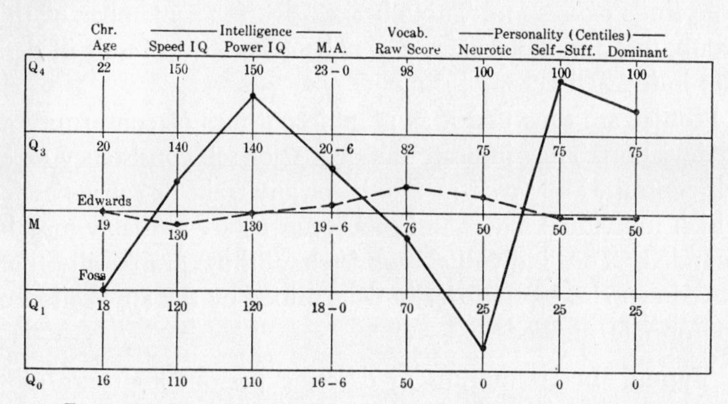

FIG. 5. NORM CHART AND TWO INDIVIDUAL PERSONALITY PROFILES.

If the scores of an individual are now plotted on the chart and lines drawn from point to point on the scale series, we have an *individual profile.* Two such profiles are drawn in Fig. 5. Against the background of the group norms, the profile registers graphically the pattern of abilities and traits of the individuals under consideration. The two profiles given here are in contrast. Edwards, whose scores are within the middle 50 per cent on each of the eight scales, is representative of the group as a whole in every trait. His intelligence ratings show consistent dependability, his vocabulary is fully adequate and his personality trait ratings suggest a balanced and comfortable adjustment. In the college situation we may expect of this student an adequate but undistinguished performance; we may look to him to meet normal demands in a normal way. In contrast, Foss's scores deviate beyond the interquartile range (Q_3—Q_1) on five of the eight scales. Younger than the average, he rates near the middle of the group in speed of intelligence and vocabulary. His Stanford-Binet score is high average in terms of the college norms. His power IQ is above Q_3, indicating intellectual effort and persistence considerably beyond the expectation. The personality trait ratings show high self-sufficiency and high dominance, as well as an absence of neurotic responses. A pressure worker, he is an individual in whose personality traits and intelligence scores a dynamic urge finds expression. Though excessive for a member of this group, this ambitious energy may be expected to result in definite individual accomplishment.

Profiles are thus useful as graphic outlines of conformity or of deviation. They indicate the degree of self-consistency or of self-contrast. Moreover, measures for any traits or capacities for which individual scores and group norms are available may be included. The individual consistency thus graphically portrayed can also be statistically determined by the application of appropriate methods.

Types. In attempting to describe personality traits most people find single or even double descriptive terms useful: they say so-and-so is practical, idealistic, artistic; or beautiful but dumb, strong and silent, a parlor pink, an uncrowned king. Sometimes these designations of personality-pattern can be arranged in contrasting pairs—shy violet and wild rose, sturdy oak and clinging vine, silly guinea pig and wise old owl, straw man and man of iron. Even though certain individuals are aptly designated by terms like these, yet the designation has really the effect of a caricature, for it emphasizes a single trait or trait group as if it were the whole person. To be sure, contrasting groups do exist, such as dwarfs and giants, imbeciles and geniuses, pessimists and optimists, extraverts and introverts, pyknics (Falstaff type) and leptosomes (Cassius type). But appropriate physical or psychological measurements show these to be extremes of normal distributions in terms of height, wit, affective mood, center of motivation and body build. The popular categorical designations are therefore found to possess little or no scientific claim.

Most people prove when measured to be neither dwarfs nor giants, neither imbeciles nor geniuses; nor, in terms of their bodily, mental or emotional characteristics, do they fit precisely (except in the important contrast of male and female) into any pair of opposite types. In every measurable configuration of human traits, with the one exception noted, the individual differences of sufficiently large and representative populations follow a normal distribution curve. This is a *unimodal* curve with a single central tendency or mode, not a *bimodal* or *multimodal* curve.

The concept of types is helpful in individual personality study, in clinical psychology and in psychiatry when used to designate certain trait constellations of more or less frequent occurrence in special groups. And popularly, too, type designations are convenient. The day laborer, the athlete, the musician, the housewife, the business man, the aviatrix, the reformer, the politician, the big shot, are types in this sense. In terms of measurable individual differences and in terms of psychological profiles each of these and similar designations gives the key to behavior tendencies expressed in certain skills, interests and abilities. But actually individuals, however correctly tagged in terms of type, will never exactly coincide with these or any other stereotyped patterns.

INDIVIDUAL DIFFERENCES IN PHYSICAL TRAITS

Differences in stature or in physical strength are psychological data to the extent that they influence mental and emotional development, as was discussed in the previous chapter. In general it is the extremes, the deviates in terms of the norms, for whom such differences have significance as factors consciously or unconsciously motivating behavior. Thus, a certain giantess states that she enjoys going to parties and dancing, but only provided her partners are giants. The deaf find more comfortable social relationships with other deaf people. Children are normally happiest when playing with other children; and the same holds true for the other age groups.

It is sometimes important for industry to be cognizant of individual differences in the forms of special handicaps, like partial color blindness. A defect of this kind may usually be disregarded in the mechanical trades, whereas chemists, bookkeepers and dyemixers find it a serious, unfortunately not always recognized, disability. In general it is found that in the industrial world the necessity for normal social adjustments rules out most of the extreme physical deviates. Exceptional individuals are a problem for themselves or their families, and for psychology, rather than for industry as it is at present organized.

INDIVIDUAL DIFFERENCES IN INTELLIGENCE

Measurement of the important personality factor called intelligence can, as we have already seen illustrated, be made in terms that are objectively meaningful and widely comparable. In any discussion of individual differences, therefore, extended discussion of intelligence tests is in order. Intelligence may be defined as the ability to act adaptively, to benefit by learning, to comprehend cause and effect, to recognize relationships, to discover fallacies, to make critical appraisals, to reason and to deduce laws. The function of intelligence, which is a basic property of the psychophysiological constitution, is dependent upon the character and condition of the nervous system, especially of the higher nerve centers in the cerebral cortex.

Since no adequate means have been devised for directly observing or estimating the amount or kinds of thinking in terms of brain structure or function by any physiological, chemical or electrical measurement, intelligence can be measured only indirectly through motor performance of some kind, most often verbal or manual. For this reason verbal and motor skills are involved in every expression or measurement of intelligence, and the degree of practice in any of the performances or activities through which measurement is made determines in part the nature of the results. If comparisons are to be made between individuals or groups of individuals with respect to native intelligence, therefore, possible differences in motor and verbal skills must be taken into account.

Three important conclusions with reference to intelligence and its measurement emerge from a consideration of the known facts: (1) There is a general capacity of the individual to think and to express his thought in words and actions in such a way that we rate him as bright, average or dull. Not only can this capacity be measured by appropriate tests, but the scores for several varieties of such tests will be correlated among themselves to a high degree. (2) Scores on tests can be improved in a number of ways—by specific coaching in test items, by practice in the exercise of attention, memory, reasoning and other mental functions, by the general improvement in opportunity to learn and to know or by improvement in that general sense of security and well-being which may result from a favorable alteration in the home or school situation. (3) Intelligence-test scores and mental-age ratings, or IQ's based on a reliable composite of mental and motor performances nevertheless show ranges from the poorest to the best that are on the average ten times greater than the amounts of improvement or loss achieved by normal individuals as a result of a change in practice or in environment.

Value of intelligence tests. Intelligence is expressed in daily activity and performance. Objectively minded individuals generally appraise their own capacity and that of their associates in terms of this observed activity. Hence, they know in general and do not need to learn from a test what to expect of themselves in the way of intelligent behavior as compared to others in their group. When, however, the scene is shifted—as in passing from the preparatory school to college, or from college into business—a reappraisal may be needed in terms of the new situation. For employers or school administrators the individual's self-estimate or his family's judgment jotted down on an application blank is often not enough. In order to save time and expense in placement, measurement and comparison with the established standards or norms of performance of the institution in question may be invaluable. Tests thus used serve as a check on misappraisal made on a basis of insufficient evidence or wishful thinking.

Intelligence tests find practical use (1) for the classification of school children; (2) for the classification of college students; and (3) as an aid in the prediction of probable success in school work. They are used further (4) for classification in industry or in other organized group activities where information about intelligence is useful, as in the organization of personnel in police systems involving various types of work and levels of leadership; (5) for vocational guidance in schools, in the civil service and in agencies especially evolved for aiding in placement; and finally (6) for the use of the individual interested in knowing more objectively about his own capacities and powers.

Intelligence tests in schools and in business. Intelligence tests are generally of two kinds: (1) verbal and (2) non-verbal or performance tests. They are administered also in two ways, individually and in groups. Intelligence tests sample such fundamental or primary abilities as memory, verbal fluency, facility with numbers, power of visualization, speed in perceiving and inductive ability. They fulfil their purpose most adequately in tests administered individually under conditions of good rapport and cooperation. When, however, the motivation is adequate (as it is in tests required for candidacy to some desirable position or coveted school admission), almost equally good results can be secured from literate individuals in group tests as in individual tests.

Tests in the Stanford-Binet series for ages 6 and 12 illustrate the types of performance that are found to differentiate intelligence in children (Table IX *A*). The Army Alpha scale illustrates adult tests of the easier type designed to differentiate individuals in the general population (Table IX *B*). The Stanford-Binet and the Thorndike CAVD tests are designed

TABLE IX

Sample Intelligence Test Items

(This table is a compilation of excerpts from *The Stanford-Binet Test*, published by Houghton-Mifflin; *The Army-Alpha Scale*, owned by The Psychological Corporation; and *The Thorndike CAVD Test*, published by Teachers College, Columbia University. All are reprinted by permission of the publishers.)

A. Revised Stanford-Binet (Form L)

Items for age 6.

1. Vocabulary. 5 words defined correctly in simple terms. (Includes words like *straw*, *gown*, *eyelash*.)
2. Copying a bead chain from memory. (7 beads in a pattern alternating square and round beads.)
3. Mutilated pictures. (Indicating what is missing from a wagon minus one wheel, a rabbit minus one ear, etc.)
4. Number concepts. (Selecting correctly numbers of blocks up to 7.)
5. Pictorial likenesses and differences. (Pointing out the one that is unlike in series of 4 simple forms or objects.)
6. Maze tracing. (Tracing shortest path for boy from home to school in simple maze.)

Items for age 12.

1. Vocabulary. 14 words correctly defined. (Includes words like *muzzle*, *haste*, *lecture*.)
2. Verbal absurdities. (Explaining what is foolish after hearing an absurd statement read aloud.)
3. Response to picture. (Giving the significant points regarding a fairly simple dramatic picture.)
4. Repeat 5 digits reversed. (Correct rendering of 1 out of 3 series presented orally in 1 sec. time-rhythm.)
5. Abstract words. (Defining correctly 2 of 5 words like *constant*, *defend*.)
6. Sentence completion. (Writing the missing words in incomplete sentences such as:
   One cannot always be a hero, ________ one can always be a man.)

B. The Army Alpha Scale

Test 1. Directions.

Item 12. If six is more than four, then, cross out the five, unless five is more than seven, in which case draw a line under number six.

1 2 3 4 5 6 7 8 9

Test 2. Arithmetic.

Item 10. If it takes 8 men 2 days to dig a 160-foot drain, how many men are needed to dig it in half a day?

Test 3. Common Sense.

Item 9. Why are warships painted gray? Because gray paint
____ is cheaper than other colors
____ is more durable than other colors
____ makes the ships harder to see

TABLE IX (*Continued*)

Test. 4. Antonyms and Synonyms.

If the two words of a pair mean the same or nearly the same, draw a line under *same.* If they mean the opposite or nearly the opposite, draw a line under *opposite.*

Item 11.	commend	approve	same—opposite
Item 19.	adversary	colleague	same—opposite

Test 5. Sentence Rearrangement.

Think what each of these sentences would say if it were straightened out, but don't write it out. If what it would say is true, draw a line under the word *true;* if what it would say is false, draw a line under the word *false.*

Item 4.	east the in rises sun the	true—false
Item 22.	happiness lists great casualty cause	true—false

C Thorndike CAVD.

Level for college students.

1. Completion of sentences such as the following:

   So far ________ the displeasure of the people by ________ the will of their representatives, a President generally gains ________ by the bold use of his veto power. It conveys the ________ firmness; it shows ________ has a view and does ________ to give effect to it.

2. Arithmetic:

   Rearrange the numbers and signs in the line below to make a true equation as shown in a sample:

   2 2 5 10 70 = × ÷ ( )

3. Vocabulary:

   Check the word that means the same or most nearly the same as the first word in the line.

   largess 1 enormity 2 present 3 monstrosity 4 amiability 5 size

4. Directions:

   In a set of sentences check the two which mean most nearly the same as the sentence underlined.

   Don't count your chickens until they are hatched.

   ____ Don't put all your eggs in one basket.
   ____ There's many a slip 'twixt the cup and the lip.
   ____ Catch the bear before you sell his skin.
   ____ Don't cross the bridge until you come to it.

to measure intelligence from early childhood to adult maturity. The examples from the CAVD scale given in Table IX *C*, in contrast to the Stanford-Binet and the Army Alpha samples, illustrate the harder parts of this test.

HEREDITY AND ENVIRONMENT IN HUMAN TRAITS

In all human traits nature and nurture merge. There is no organism without a heredity, and none that lacks an environment which to some extent can modify its constitutional trends. In studying individual differences we find nature least amenable to alteration in certain physical traits, such as eye color; more amenable in soft tissue development than in bone growth; widely adaptable, especially during childhood, in intellectual functions and skills; and most of all subject to modification in cultural social attitudes.

Nature sets physiological limits within which training and experience may develop maximal or minimal powers and skills. In Carlyle's phrase, nature creates the oaks and the cabbages; nurture decides whether they shall be sturdy and well grown, or stunted.

Heredity. The psychophysiological constitution of every human being is broadly but definitely patterned in the genes. The genes in the germ cells are the trait bearers which heredity selectively contributes in a unique assortment for each individual. Because there are in the world today few pure races, the mixture in organic stock from which each new individual takes his start permits of an enormous number of different permutations and combinations in the quality and kind of genes. Thus races, groups and families may be different with respect to the assortive mixture of the constitutional determiners. Superior and inferior breeds exist as well as average ones. They exhibit their inherent character in the qualities with which they endow their members: physical strength and resistance to disease, energy in motivation, stability in nervous organization and potential effectiveness in intelligence. There seem also to be evidences of special combinations in the material substance that predispose the organism for the appearance of certain more exclusively psychological traits and trends. Just as an individual in a blue-eyed race is blue-eyed, and as the conditioners of potential height, weight and bodily configuration are inherited, so it appears that the degree of emotionality, temperament and certain sensory talents or defects, certain intellectual inclinations and the facilitation of certain motor coordinations are also, in part, predisposed in each human organism.

With reference to psychobiological inheritance three principles are chiefly important. (1) The somatic, or physical substance, is a living continuation of parent stock. (2) The possible reassortments or selections of psychobiological traits, as of others, are so numerous that there is little chance of any two organisms turning out exactly alike. (3) Because there is a level and a certain limitation in assortment of quality and kind in each family and race, members of the same family are more likely to resemble one another than to resemble other people.

Environment. The physical and psychological situations with which the organism comes in contact make up its environment. From the beginning of its existence as an organism onward throughout its entire life, they affect its growth, development and available energy. Nourishment, air, condition of the blood stream, light, warmth, atmospheric pressure, are among the important physical elements of the environment. Comfort, absence of excessive frustration, a sense of security, affection and, later, the mixed domestic and social influence of disapproval and encouragement may be counted among its basic psychological elements. Exposure to objects and people, to relations between them and to ideas about them, constitute the basic materials of formal and informal education.

There are but few persons who have the advantage of the optimal limits of a favorable environmental culture. In general our measurements of individual differences register the average ability or average growth of people of average heredity under average environmental conditions. In these terms the measurements are comparable.

Relation of heredity and environment. Neither the hereditary nor the environmental limits of development are exactly known. Some of them, however, can be estimated and predicted for individuals in a useful way on the basis of studies of individual differences made under conditions where some of the elements of nature and of nurture are definitely known.

Group comparisons reveal a persistent tendency for better stock to produce more able offspring than poorer stock. Individual comparisons show specific differences at every level, differences that persist as personal characteristics throughout life unless illness or injury impairs the organism. Clinical reexaminations from age to age disclose a high degree of conformity of individuals in respect to their development. Thus throughout life the differences between superior, average and inferior intellects continue to be measurable in statistically significant terms.

The character of the parental intellect, moreover, tends to appear in the children; this tendency is demonstrable in spite of the many exceptions that result from hereditary mixture and individual physical or psychological experience. Thus the children of superior parents tend to be above average, those of average parents generally remain average, whereas the children of inferior parents are dull or backward.

Two lines of evidence make untenable an explanation of these results solely or even largely in terms of training and social influence. The first is the tenacious tendency of the individual to manifest his characteristic level of intelligence whatever the circumstances; a tendency for the able to appear and rate as able, no matter what their education and experience may be, and for the inferior to remain inadequate, despite opportunity. This propensity for individual differences to appear, irrespective of environmental circumstances, produces scatter in the educational and familial distributions when otherwise we should find close clustering at certain definite levels of attainment. In the second place it has been demonstrated that there exists an apparent psychophysiological upper limit in all individuals studied, beyond which development as a result of special training cannot go. The occasional appearance of feeble-minded individuals even among persons of superior home training and exceptionally good educational opportunity illustrates this point.

Certain experimental studies drawn from group and individual observation and measurement support these conclusions. They show for groups of differing heredity and similar training that the psychophysiological constitution forms in the personality a kind of irreducible core, which environment can never completely change.

(*a*) Thus, children placed at birth in an institution and reared there together, without home association, nevertheless show differences in intelligence that are correlated with the ratings of family stock. Children of merchants and professional men in these orphan groups rate on the average about 10 IQ points higher than children of laborers, a difference that is statistically significant.

(*b*) Identical twins (those developed from the splitting of a single ovum and hence most alike constitutionally), when reared apart resemble each other more in intelligence than fraternal twins (those developed from two ova) do when reared together. The average interpair difference of the former is 8.2 IQ points, of the latter, 9.9 IQ points (Table X).

TABLE X

AVERAGE PAIR DIFFERENCES IN BINET IQ OF IDENTICAL AND FRATERNAL TWINS, SIBLINGS AND TEST-RETEST DIFFERENCES OF INDIVIDUALS

	Identical Twins* Reared		Fraternal Twins* Reared	Siblings* of Like Sex Reared	Test-Retest† of Same
	Together	Apart	Together	Together	Individual
Average Intra-pair difference.......	5.9	8.2	9.9	9.8	6.7

* Data from H. H. Newman, F. N. Freeman, K. J. Holzinger, *Twins, a study of heredity and environment*, Chicago: University of Chicago Press, 1937. (Table 13, p. 77, and Table 87, opposite p. 335.)

† Datum computed from G. Hildreth, Stanford-Binet retests of 441 school children, *Ped. Sem.*, 1926, 33, 372, Table 3.

(*c*) Identical twins show closer interpair resemblance than fraternal twins when both series have been reared together. In intelligence the differences in this comparison are 5.9 and

9.9 IQ points. These results, when compared in Table X with test-retest scores of a group of people twice tested, show that identical twins tested at approximately the same age resemble each other on the average more closely than people generally resemble their former selves after a year or two has elapsed.

(*d*) Comparison of the correlation coefficients for series of psychophysiological measurements of identical and fraternal twins shows the more marked similarity of the former in all the traits measured (Table XI). In IQ the coefficients for the

TABLE XI

CORRELATION COEFFICIENTS FOR SERIES OF PSYCHOPHYSIOLOGICAL MEASUREMENTS OF TWINS REARED TOGETHER

(Data from K. J. Holzinger, The relative effect of nature and nurture influence on twin differences, *J. educ. Psychol.*, 1929, 20, 242.)

	Identical Twins	Fraternal Twins
Height	.93	.65
Weight	.92	.63
Head length	.91	.58
Binet M. A.	.86	.60
Binet IQ	.88	.63
Educational Age	.89	.70
Woodworth-Matthews Emotional Test	.56	.37
Motor Ability	.69	.38

identical twins of .88 and for the fraternal twins of .63 may be compared with the usual coefficient of approximately .50 for siblings in representative groups. Siblings reared apart in foster homes also show after the period of separation an average correlation of .50 in intelligence.

Parents and children in representative groups resemble one another in intelligence to the extent of .30 to .35. The correlation between the average of the parents' scores (called the mid-parent score) and of the children's scores (mid-child score) is indicated by coefficients of .50 to .70. Representative groups of unrelated individuals (pairs drawn at random) are correlated zero with one another in the same or similar tests.

These data are sufficiently conclusive with reference to the effective energy of hereditary and constitutional factors. On the other side, however, the evidence regarding the effective contributions of environment are equally definite and important. Observation of individuals and groups leaves no doubt of the efficacy of education and experience as modifiers of personal and group behavior.

(*a*) Children from country schools show a gain averaging 5 to 10 or more IQ points after attendance at city schools. The direct interdependence of the IQ and the amount of schooling appears in reports of certain exceptional groups.

(*b*) The coefficients of correlation between children's IQ's and parents' social status range from .20 to .45, with the most frequent coefficient in the .30's. This result supports the natural assumption that the IQ correlation between parents and children is attributable in part to cultural influences.

(*c*) Superiority of achievement as well as high IQ is found with a superior social and economic background. Thus to an extent far exceeding the numerical quota for that class, Terman's gifted children in California come from the families of professional men; and a like situation holds for all other reported groups of superior children.

(*d*) Siblings separated before the age of 5 show a lower degree of correlation in intelligence score (.32) than those separated after the age of 5 (.49). Those separated for less than 7 years show a higher degree of correlation (.41) than those separated for more than 7 years (.27). Those in like homes show a higher degree of correlation (.39) than those in unlike homes (.28). The IQ's of siblings placed in better foster homes average 95, in poorer homes, 86. Children placed in an institution tend to show a slight gain if their IQ's are relatively low, a constant rating or a very slight loss if their IQ's are higher.

(*e*) The correlation between the intelligence scores of foster parents and foster children is about .40. The intelligence of 'own' children, however, has been found on the average to be 8 to 20 IQ points higher than that of the foster children in the same families.

(*f*) Attendance at nursery school has been found to raise the average intelligence scores as much as 10 IQ points. This result is no doubt due chiefly to inequality in training at the preschool level as compared with the more usual equality at school age when universal compulsory education flourishes.

On the basis of series of correlations between related pairs of individuals an index table has been made showing the degrees of genetic resemblance in measures of intellectual traits (Table XII). This hierarchy, we may now conclude, depends in part on environment, in part on heredity. Although neither factor can be eliminated or completely isolated for measurement, each can be brought successively into the focus of attention for estimated measurement. When this is done, it appears that adequate education and experience can improve intelligence-test score, but can never fully equalize diverse native endowments.

TABLE XII

HIERARCHY OF CORRELATION COEFFICIENTS ILLUSTRATING HEREDITARY RELATIONSHIP IN MENTAL MEASURES

(From A. N. Wingfield, *Twins and orphans: the inheritance of intelligence*, London: Dent, 1928; reprinted by permission of the publisher.)

Group	*r*
Physically identical twins	0.90
Like-sex twins	0.82
Fraternal twins	0.70
Unlike-sex twins	0.59
Siblings	0.50
Parent and child	0.31
Cousins	0.27
Grandparent and grandchild	0.16
Unrelated children	0.00

Specific effect of education and coaching. The specific ability of the individual to utilize the test materials adequately can be increased artificially by special coaching. Gains of upwards of 10 IQ points can be obtained by training in the use of materials similar to the test materials; on the average 20 IQ points can be added to the individual score by direct coaching on the test materials themselves. Usually gains made in this way tend to disappear gradually with time, but the rate of loss depends on the age of the children when coached and the nature of the coaching. For practical purposes, if the results are to be used for prediction along with those of others who have had no coaching, IQ or other scores based on coaching have to be discounted, or the individual has to be retested by some test in which his special coaching or information is not effective.

Constancy of the IQ. Intelligence-test ratings of a single individual tend to agree with one another in indicating the general level of intelligence. Intercorrelation of such measures is high. In the same way, test and retest after an interval of time also show high correlation (+ .90). Exceptions occur (1) as a result of individual differences in sustained effort and co-operation, emotionally and intellectually less stable people tending to show relatively greater unevenness in performance; (2) as a result of special handicaps or special abilities, some individuals scoring unevenly on the different test instruments; (3) as a result of gains or losses in scoring ability due to some special experience, or to functional or organic change.

Predictability of performance. Scores obtained from a single test have a moderate predictive value. Clinical psychological studies, however, including a variety of suitable tests, give a basis for a dependable estimate by a psychologist of the probable limits and direction of adult attainment. From average intelligence scores the average attainment of groups can be estimated with a fair degree of certainty. Thus the average attainment of children of 75 IQ will generally not be above the grade-school level; of 100 IQ, not above the high-school level; of 130 IQ, within the college level or its educational equivalent.

Unusual children with IQ's of 140 or above, examined seven years after their first testing, were as markedly accelerated in school as had been predicted earlier from their high intelligence ratings. Among them failures in school work were infrequent, and nearly half of their school marks were A. In a high-school achievement test only 10 per cent of unselected high-school pupils rated as high as these gifted children. In college far more than their numerical share of scholarships, fellowships and other honors fell to the lot of this group. Several had already won distinction beyond college. Not only the intelligence ratings of the group but their personality trait ratings as well continued to be definitely above the average. Its gifted members were as likely to gain non-academic as academic recognition and distinction. With more than 80 per cent reported to have good general health, only 1 per cent were said to have poor health.

Both distinguished contemporaries and historical figures are known to have presaged their mature eminent achievement by youthful performance indicating a high IQ. Among philosophers, Leibnitz and Bentham showed youthful performance entitling them to IQ's over 180; of writers, Goethe and John Stuart Mill reach the 200 IQ mark when rated in terms of their precocious achievements. The kinds of performance that make such high IQ ratings possible for geniuses of the past appear in the following brief accounts of their known early activities.

Leibnitz read Livy by himself and without a dictionary at the age of 8. At 13 he wrote in commendable Latin a poem of 300 hexameters, completing the work between daybreak and noonday. Before he was 15 he had completed a comprehensive course of self-education. Before he was 18 his first printed work appeared, *On the Principle of Individuation,* and at 20 he was awarded the doctor's degree and offered a professorship. At 24, appointed councilor and member of the Supreme Court of the city of Mainz, he advanced a plan, later carried out, for the formation of an alliance of nations. From 20 to 27 he wrote and published pamphlets, theses and books on a diverse assortment of subjects—the book trade, mechanics and mensuration, politics, law, religion and philosophy.

Jeremy Bentham knew the alphabet before he could talk. At 3 he began the study of Latin, of modern languages a little later. His education, independently acquired in the main, included the classics, French, music, chemistry, history and philosophy. He displayed originality in debate. At 15 Oxford granted him the B.A. degree, at 18 the M.A. At 22 he was spoken of as a philosopher, and at 23 his first publications appeared. Called to the bar at 24, he decided that, rather than practice law, he would devote himself to theoretical legal problems. Already a strenuous advocate of constitutional, social and economic reform, he kept at this time careful notes in which are the germs of his major works.

Goethe was distinguished at an early age by his quick understanding and excellent memory. At the age of 8 he performed satisfactorily the school tasks assigned for the senior year in the university preparatory classes. Before he was 10 he had written clever, well-styled, original Latin essays. At 16 he knew the classics in Latin, Greek, Hebrew, French and English, and a year later was recognized at the university as an intellectual leader. His studies included law and medicine as well as literature and philosophy, but he also wrote much verse, achieving thereby both notoriety and praise. Among the lyrics of his early twenties are a number that rank among the finest in all literature. The first version of *Götz von Berlichingen* was written when its author was 23. The publication of *Werther* the following year made the writer's name known throughout the world. "Nothing that he afterward accomplished could outshine the glory which *Werther* laid on his head." When he was 26 there began for him that long career of statesmanship to which the little state of Weimar owed a place of distinction among the governments of Europe.

John Stuart Mill read Greek and history from the age of 4, and before he was 7 had already written a history of Rome. From the age of 10 he read progressively more difficult classical writers, making close marginal notes. At 11 he made a synoptic table of Aristotle's rhetoric. From an early age he was instructed by his father in the ancient languages, history, political economy, philosophy and especially logic. "On these John was a truly precocious youth. His innate aptitudes which must have been great, received the utmost stimulation that it was possible to give." At 17, supported by a group of able, independent young thinkers, he organized the Utilitarian Society. At the same age he entered the service of the East India Company, with which he remained until he was 52. At 18 he was writing regularly for the *Westminster Review*—writing book reviews on history, politics and political economy, or else discussions on special political topics. At 19 he both began the laborious task of editing Bentham's work, *Evidence,* and started the *Parliamentary History and Review.* At 22 he was promoted to the rank of Assistant Examiner in the East India Company. At 24, excited by the French Revolution, he visited Paris, publishing on his return a number of articles on French politics. At 25 he began to outline his logic, developing a distinctive system of terminology and the logical axioms and theory of syllogisms which form the basis of a notable work.

Common tradition to the contrary, great men have usually been precocious children. A group of 300 chosen, not in terms of early brightness, but in terms solely of recognized eminence in the history of thought and of action, was found to have displayed intellectual attainments in childhood which indicate for the group as a whole an IQ average not below 150, and probably as high as 165. Among the distinguished persons popularly supposed to have shown poor mentality in childhood, none when rated psychologically on the whole story of his boyhood activities fell below 130. Of great men sometimes classed as backward in youth, Charles Darwin and Sir Walter Scott were entitled, on the basis of the true record, to IQ's of 165; Lord Byron, 180; Alexander Humboldt, 185.

AGE DIFFERENCES IN PHYSICAL AND MENTAL CAPACITIES

Normal individuals in their development from birth to early adulthood show gradual growth in mental and physical capacities correlated with physiological growth. (See Fig. 6.) The rate of development, greatest at the earliest ages, thereafter follows a decelerating growth rate until a period in early adulthood, when gradually the balance in the process of growth is shifted. Replacement still meets the demands of use and wear, but further development in the form of organic growth does not take place. From this time on, effectiveness in the bodily and mental economy depends no longer on increasing vigor; rather, it is preserved primarily through the maintenance of well-organized habits.

In childhood, growth in intelligence roughly parallels growth in height, and chronological age can be estimated from mental performance as well as from physical appearance in a homogeneous group of children in a grade school. At these early ages

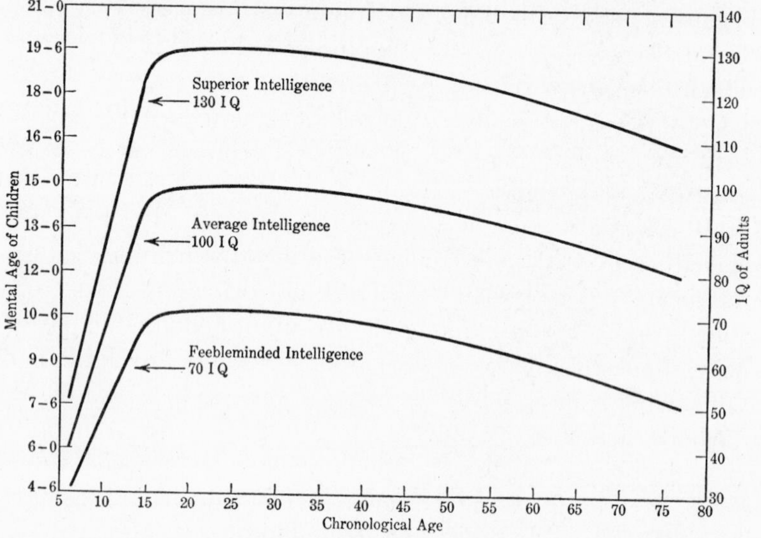

FIG. 6. CURVE OF INTELLIGENCE (AT THREE LEVELS) IN CHILDHOOD, MATURITY AND OLD AGE.

annual gains in mental ability are large, later decreasing gradually at a predictable rate until sometime during the middle or late teens. The chronological age of 15 is now generally regarded as the average age of maturity in intelligence. Those who continue to develop mentally beyond this point do so very slowly and at a rate rapidly approaching zero.

In maturity, from the twenties onward, experience rather than energy or speed accounts for improvement in performance and for the maintenance of intellectual capacity throughout the life span into old age, even after physiological changes may have diminished sensory and motor competence. Habit tends to preserve practiced abilities and acquired skills. Breadth of experience and extent of mental exercise in youth and early maturity, therefore, lay the most satisfactory foundation for psychological longevity.

Positive correlation is the rule between growth functions, such as physical size, height, weight, anatomical age, sensory acuity, perceptual discrimination, motor skill, attention span, memory span, verbal comprehension, logical analysis and synthesis, reasoning and judgment. Similarly, measures of physical and mental defect are correlated positively with mental retardation. During the period of physical and mental growth in childhood and youth, these correlations are fairly large, being all dependent on the general factor of organic development. In maturity, however, the correlations between physical and mental measures in healthy normal people, although still positive, are slight and have little meaning. The physical measures continue to be closely related to one another and similarly the mental measures are intercorrelated to a high degree; but in adulthood it becomes evident that physique and intellect are interdependent only as functions of the total bodily condition. Hence among mature individuals height, weight, perceptual acuity and motor skills no longer afford as in childhood a basis for estimating intelligence and mental age.

In so far as psychological abilities and skills are chiefly dependent on the physical functions of sensory acuity, speed of reaction and bodily strength, they follow a characteristic curve of growth and decline in which an early peak of maximal performance is succeeded by gradual decrement. When, on the other hand, these skills are chiefly dependent on psychological functions, such as the accumulation of experience and practice in mental activity, they tend to reach the peak of performance at a later age, frequently in the thirties and sometimes even in the forties. The contrast between the primarily physiological age curve and the psychological is shown by achievement in various occupations. Thus truck drivers reach maturity in terms of occupational efficiency earlier than do merchants, boxers earlier than sharpshooters, dentists than surgeons, physicists than philosophers. Likewise in the field of interests—occupational, vocational and avocational—there are noticeable age differences that reflect the physical and psychological changes in youth and maturity. The active, adventurous, personal and material preoccupations so typical in youth give way gradually, as age advances, to interests that are sedentary, intellectual, philanthropic and idealistic.

SEX DIFFERENCES

In temperaments, traits, interests and achievements, as well as in bodily structure, the two sexes show marked contrasts. In the first ten years of life the physical differences are relatively slight except in the specific organs of sex. Even at this stage there is, however, some diversity in size and strength and probably also in emotional vigor, as well as in the beginnings of psychosocial differentiation apparent in attitudes, activities and interests. In the level of general intelligence, when representative groups are compared, no real difference in average is found at this age or later. In composite intelligence tests, however, a slight contrasting difference begins to appear even in early childhood between the better verbal facility of the girls and the better mathematical performance of the boys. Here we have a nature-nurture difference which persists and increases with age. In the pre-adolescent period a more rapid physiological growth, which presages earlier maturity in girls, is accompanied by development of a somewhat finer and more sensitive emotional structure.

With adolescence the physical contrast is definitely accentuated. The difference in organic structure and function is moreover accompanied by a divergence in activities and interests, in sports and occupations and by a general patterning of the total behavior in terms of a typically masculine or feminine orientation.

With adulthood the complete picture of sex difference and contrast is established. At this time the fundamental physiological sex structure finally forms a normal distribution for each sex separately, with no essential overlapping in human beings between the two series. There is, to be sure, some overlapping of the two distributions with respect to secondary sex traits, such as distribution of hair and pitch of voice. In tertiary traits, including size, weight, energy, fatigability and emotional balance, there is a large amount of similarity. It frequently happens that in one or more of these traits many men rate higher than the average of the women, and vice versa, without becoming atypical in total general appearance, manner or behavior. A small man may be even more masculine than the average; an untiring woman may be one of the most domestic and feminine of her sex.

Individual differences in adults have most often been studied in populations of college students. At this age of early adulthood, differences in intelligence scores between the sexes are slight if the individuals tested have equal background and training, and if the test materials are selected in terms of equal experience. There is a characteristic masculine mechanical, scientific, problem-solving superiority; a feminine linguistic and general verbal superiority with a correlated rapidity in reading rate. That these differences are nurtural quite as much as natural is indicated by the finding that in any task the lower-scoring sex gains proportionally more through coaching and special practice than the higher-scoring.

Women students are more industrious in academic tasks and more willing to learn assigned lessons. They seem more readily able than men to change the direction of their interests; and by this adaptability they earn their reward in relatively higher social ratings or school grade records. It need hardly be said, of course, that individual differences are far larger than any average sex differences in these respects.

As was noted in the previous chapter there are sex differences in the expression of innumerable personality traits, including humor, self-sufficiency, dominance, introversion and neurotic tendency. According to tests, men seem less subjectively sensitive and reactive in respect to anger, fear and the sense of personal security; they are less inclined to be conservative and to conform to group standards.

Throughout maturity there are four levels of similarity and difference between the sexes. First, there is the level of complete similarity in all forms of behavior involving psychophysiological factors which show no sex differences. Equally able and equally trained brains function, it appears, equally well in terms of adequately balanced intelligence tests. Thus, in six reported comparisons of intelligence tests of 2000 or more individuals, the women are superior as often as the men. In every comparison of intelligence scores similarity between the sexes is more striking than difference. Moreover, difference when present is directly attributable to group selection or test construction. The averages of intelligence-test scores for both men and women from childhood to old age follow the pattern already shown in Fig. 6.

Second in the scale of levels is that of slight intellectual difference where skill is based considerably on experience. Here women excel in verbal, men in mathematical tasks. This contrast is illustrated at the adolescent age in the College Board Entrance Examinations in which the boys exceed the girls in total mathematical score to an extent 15 times the σ of the difference; the girls exceed the boys on the total verbal score to an extent 11 times the σ of the difference (Table XIII).

TABLE XIII

SEX DIFFERENCES IN SCHOLASTIC APTITUDE TEST SCORES

(From C. Brolyer, *Sixth annual report of the Commission on Scholastic Aptitude Tests*, 1931.)

	Boys	Girls	Diff. / σ diff.
Number of cases	4214	3362	
Total verbal score:			
Mean	486.58	512.29	11.3
σ	104.02	92.99	
Total mathematical score:			
Mean	511.15	476.74	15.3
σ	103.40	92.46	

The third is the level of dissimilarity at which the secondary or tertiary sex differences in structure are involved in performance, or where the social factors are important. Here intellectual performance involves (1) physical strength and skill or (2) cultural elements producing diverse motivation. In a study of values women scored significantly higher than men on the esthetic, social and religious scales; men than women on the theoretical, economic and political scales. The largest differences are in the esthetic and the political interests (Fig. 7).

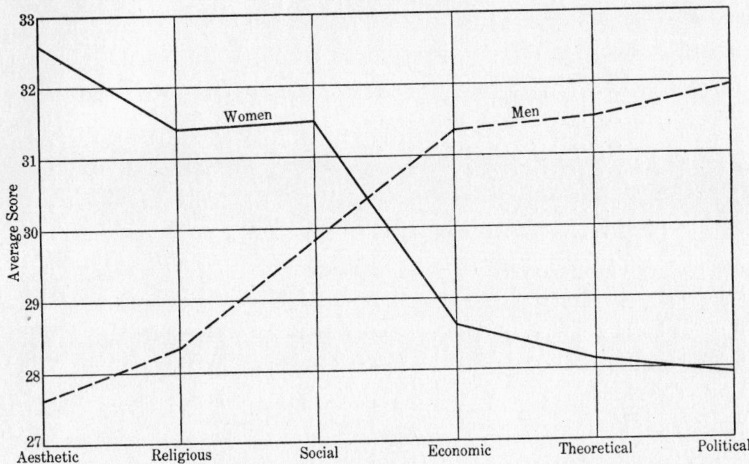

FIG. 7. COMPOSITE PSYCHOGRAPHS OF 463 ADULT MEN AND 313 ADULT WOMEN ON THE ALLPORT-VERNON STUDY OF VALUES.

Adapted from P. E. Vernon and G. W. Allport. A test for personal values, *J. abnorm. soc. Psychol.*, 1931, 26, 246.

The fourth level of psychological divergence between the sexes depends for its large contrasts on the predominance of physical components or of psychological elements directly traceable to sex differences in structure. These include activities with (1) a large strength component available for violent activity (such as playing football or going to war, as contrasted with knitting or rolling bandages); (2) a very large element of social responsibility (presiding as chairman of a large mixed group, as against directing domestic activities); (3) a close relationship to biological function (absorption in vocational pursuits, even to the point of disregarded domestic welfare, versus devotion in the care of children or the sick or old people); or (4) a combination of any of these.

The sex contrast at the fourth level is illustrated by athletic records of men and women. In the table of athletic records (Table XIV) the percentage of decrement, in the last column,

TABLE XIV

THE INTERNATIONAL ATHLETIC RECORDS OF MEN AND WOMEN IN COMPARABLE EVENTS

(From data in the *World Almanac*, 1938, 874; by permission of the publisher.)

Event	Men	Women	Per Cent Decrement
100-meter run	10.3 sec.	11.5 sec.	12
200- " "	20.3 "	23.6 "	16
800- " "	1 m. 49.8 "	2 m. 12.4 "	21
1000- " "	2 " 23.6 "	3 " .6 "	26
400-meter relay	39.8 sec.	46.4 sec.	17
800- " "	1 m. 25.8 "	1 m. 45.8 "	23
Running high jump	2.07 meters	1.65 meters	20
Standing " "	1.67 "	1.32 "	21
Running broad jump	8.13 "	5.98 "	26
Standing " "	3.47 "	2.625 "	24
Discus (two hands)	90.13 "	67.82 "	25
Javelin (best hand)	76.66 "	46.745 "	39
" (two hands)	114.28 "	62.43 "	45
Swimming (free style):			
100 meters	56.4 sec.	1 m. 4.6 sec.	15
300 "	3 m. 21.6 "	3 " 50.4 "	14
500 "	5 " 57.8 "	6 " 45.7 "	13
1000 "	12 " 41.8 "	14 " 44.8 "	16
1500 "	19 " 7.2 "	22 " 36.7 "	18
Swimming (breast stroke):			
100 meters	1 m. 10.0 sec.	1 m. 20.2 sec.	15
400 "	5 " 45.0 "	6 " 24.8 "	12
500 "	7 " 23.8 "	8 " 3.8 "	9
Skating (outdoor records):			
220 yards	18.4 sec.	21.0 sec.	14
1 mile	2 m. 38.2 "	3 m. 15.7 "	24

is a measure of the extent to which strength is a primary factor in the activity. The javelin throw with its dependence on shoulder development and exercise of the arm muscles shows the largest sex difference. Swimming breast stroke, which requires less exertion and more lightness and the protection of the vital organs by body fat, shows the smallest differences.

Further sex differences at this level may be illustrated by reference to adult employment and adult occupations in our present social organization. Table XV, for example, presents an outline of the professional choices of men and women as shown by the classifications of new names listed in a single volume of *Who's Who in America.*

TABLE XV

PROFESSIONAL CHOICES OF MEN AND WOMEN AS SHOWN BY CLASSIFICATION IN *Who's Who in America*

Men		Women	
Business men	22.0	Authors	33.5
Educators	18.0	Educators	17.2
Clergymen	12.7	Newspaper and magazine writers	8.9
Lawyers	7.8	Artists	5.6
Editors	6.5	Lawyers	3.6
Public officials	5.8	Actresses	3.6
Engineers	5.5	Editors	3.1
Writers	5.2	Singers	3.1
Physicians and surgeons	4.0	Librarians	2.7
Artists	3.3	Women in public affairs	1.8
Scientists	2.5	Social workers	1.8
Architects	1.5	Painters	1.7
Army and navy officers	1.2	Club women	1.6
Miscellaneous	4.0	Sculptors	1.5
		Composers	1.2
		College presidents	1.1
		Home economists	1.1
		Illustrators	1.1
		Miscellaneous	5.8

INDIVIDUAL DIFFERENCES IN SPECIAL ABILITIES

Important in the study of individual differences is the problem of special abilities or gifts. It is not impossible that there are very many such abilities. Even so, it is clear that capacity for many if not all kinds of performance depends far more on adequate physical strength, appropriate interest and sufficient general intelligence than on other separately measurable characteristics. Other things being equal, almost any necessary skill can be developed in terms of these three, and achievement along most lines is correlated with the degree of their presence.

Accomplishment in reading and in arithmetic illustrates the relationship between special and general traits. In all representative groups measurements of ability in both these fundamental school skills show high correlation between the two and with intelligence. Nevertheless, there are individuals who deviate, some of them markedly, from the expected score in one of the skills as predicted from that in the other. The deviates, when their general intelligence is sufficient for average or superior occupations, find their happiest adjustment in pursuits where the special skill is useful, the disability no handicap. Thus individuals with relatively high reading capacity, together with a related facility in speech and other language functions, tend to choose clerical occupations or professions involving a direct verbal or even literary element—teaching, journalism and other writing, divinity or law. Those who have special ability in arithmetic with related facility in logical analysis and scientific interest tend to choose either occupations emphasizing mathematical elements—bookkeeping, accounting, buying and selling—or those professions in which scientific accuracy and mathematical precision are involved—among them science teaching, statistics, industrial management, manufacturing and medical or other scientific research.

The theater, the pulpit and the rostrum attract and offer opportunity for a few individuals of exceptional linguistic ability whose other intellectual powers may be relatively less conspicuous. Notable and permanent success in acting, preaching or lecturing is, however, usually dependent not only on special verbal facility but also on general intellectual power of a high order. Among the mathematically talented, rapid calculators with an uncanny arithmetical facility may find a useful place in bookkeeping, accounting or statistical work. But again the special ability must be supported by the presence of superior general intelligence if achievement is to be professionally effective or scientifically noteworthy.

Mechanical ability is related less to intelligence than is reading or arithmetic. It shows no correlation with degree or kind of training, nor with social or other environmental factors. When present it may be developed through appropriate instruction to a high degree of effective expression, but it persists as potential endowment whether or not training is given. It is similar to intelligence in that no amount of training can, in its absence, produce effective results. Distributed in the general population roughly according to the normal curve, it is in most individuals sufficient in amount for ordinary cultural demands. Although present in both sexes, it is generally exercised in boys and men and neglected in girls and women. Test results show the presence of mechanical ability, always expressed in a wide range of skills and aptitudes, in every kind of population.

Special abilities in drawing and in musical expression are, like mechanical ability, little correlated with intelligence. Apparently largely independent of other mental traits, and uncorrelated with amount of special training or other environmental influences, these talents often show a hereditary disposition. Although individuals of low intelligence are as likely to be artistically and musically endowed as are the highly intellectual, yet they do not generally produce notable works of art or compose great music, because these performances involve far more than the special gifts of representative drawing or tonal exposition. Creative expression and interpretation have large intellectual elements. Although exceptionally superior artistic work may be the creation of formally uneducated artists or musicians, such work is never produced by morons.

TESTS OF ADULT CAPACITY

Tests of physical, motor and sensory capacity show age-growth correlation and typically normal score distributions at every age. Among adults vital capacity, strength of grip, quickness and accuracy of movement, steadiness of motor control, visual and auditory acuity, motor discrimination, sensitivity to pain, are all widely variable and yet independent of intelligence and intellectual achievement. Physical equipment and capacity are assets in many types of activity, as vital capacity in running or rowing, visual acuity in marksmanship, quickness and accuracy of movement in telegraphic sending and receiving. Occupational selection, therefore, takes place partly in terms of the elimination of those who are deficient in some motor or sensory respect. The number actually ruled out in this way, however, is very small, and over a certain minimal point the physical factors play a very small role in most kinds of employment.

In contrast individual differences in the *acquisition* of skills are correlated highly with intelligence, on the one hand, and with native ability in the skills on the other. Complex skills depend essentially on individual endowment, intelligence and practice. At every step in the educational ladder there is wide variability in intelligence and close correlation between IQ scores and degree of success.

College learning and advanced professional study require superior intelligence, special endowment in verbal or reasoning functions, or both, and well-developed habits of intellectual work. As individuals proceed from the lower to the higher schools, then to college and finally to the graduate professional schools, comprehension, reasoning and judgment become increasingly important. Whereas in the elementary schools attention, perception, association and memory are equally necessary in determining school success, in high school and college these alone are insufficient. Now they must be organized in complex thinking patterns to be utilized on a basis of well-motivated interest. Because complex thinking rates heavily in the IQ scales, graduate professional students on the average have higher intelligence ratings than undergraduates. So, too, honor students within any group score higher than the general student population at the same academic level. Superior students tend to become distinguished adults, for special educational achievement is correlated with merit in mature performance. Exceptional scientific or literary achievement in college as in later life requires superior intelligence.

Beside the intellectual, other measurable abilities and character traits are involved in educational success. The special verbal and mathematical talents, and many personality traits, such as perseverance, adaptiveness, originality and independence, are correlated only slightly with intellectual capacity. They show wide dispersion at each educational level, and the coefficients of their correlation with educational success are definitely positive.

Whether measured as members of untrained or of skilled groups, older adults show a characteristic normal dispersion of scores of capacity and skill at each age. Among the inexperienced the scores range from near zero well up toward the average for the skilled. In contrast, the experienced show no very low ratings, and in many tasks exhibit a wide diversification of performance through training.

Experience offsets a decline of efficiency with advancing age. Thus, whereas with a cube-assembly construction test there is a gradual decline of score with age in the general population, men engaged in mechanical trades score as well in their fifties and sixties as young men in the same trades. Similarly with a coat-assembly test, women of fifty and sixty years score as well as women in their twenties, whereas men, for whom this is an unfamiliar task, show considerable decrement in score as age increases.

In all tasks there is correlated with age a characteristic rise and decline of efficiency in terms of speed. But the average differences in speed between young adulthood and late maturity are so slight that the individual performance remains the significant point rather than the age decrement. Measures of proneness to accidents and of carefulness in the conservation of materials favor older as compared to younger workers, and the gain in dependability with age equalizes the speed loss in many occupations.

RACE DIFFERENCES

The question of differences in intelligence or other traits in racial groups presents an interesting problem, but one that is difficult of final solution because of the diversity in languages and customs. Significant contrasts in the level of intelligence and measured skill have been scientifically demonstrated in races of diverse cultures, as for instance Aryans and African Bushmen or Orientals and Eskimos. For culturally similar races no appreciable differences in mean scores or in ranges are found when suitable measuring techniques are used. Variability is, of course, large within each group; always individual differences are many times greater than the differences between the racial averages.

Extensive investigations have been made in the United States in which Negro, Indian, Mexican and Oriental children were compared with large groups of native white Americans. These studies show the IQ's of full-blooded Indians clustering around 70, those of southern Negroes around 75, Mexicans 78, northern Negroes 85, Chinese, Japanese and white Americans around 100. The question as to the degree of equality of experience, schooling and social culture is raised by these results. To what extent is the intelligence of the group a function of modifiable environmental influences? When the intelligence of southern Negro school children who moved to New York was measured after various periods of residence, it was found that on school achievement tests the mean score quotient rose from 72 to 94 as the length of residence increased from 1 to 8 years. On the most reliable individual intelligence test (the Stanford-Binet) it rose from 81 to 87. On non-verbal intelligence tests depending on cultural experience it rose 10 points, but on a paper form-board test, which minimizes the influence of school learning and experience, no definite gain was registered.

These and other results suggest that there tends to be a clear gain in ability to score on intelligence tests when the environmental and educational background is improved. Yet such gains are comparatively small when one considers the enduring differences between the more and the less able persons within the same populations.

In every racial group there are superior and inferior individuals. For example, one full-blooded Indian girl's intelligence rated an IQ of 145 on a non-language test, a score 45 points above the white mean, 70 points above the Indian mean. A Mexican boy in an American public school scored at this same high point, or 67 points above the Mexican mean. Negroes and others from groups whose mean scores are lower than the white averages have rated as high or higher. The scores of exceptional children like these are distinguished in any population. From them we learn that whereas group comparisons or group averages may show differences, they do not indicate the superiority or the inferiority of an entire population or race.

Comparisons of the test scores of the racial groups in the United States draft army during the World War afford a basis for racial comparisons among adults. In these studies the recruits born in England, Scotland and Holland scored above average; those from Germany, the Scandinavian countries, Belgium, Ireland and Turkey at the average; whereas the mean for the Russians, Italians and Poles was somewhat lower. When grouped racially the draft men averaged in the following order in terms of one intelligence test: Nordic 13.3, Alpine 11.7, Mediterranean 11.4. But these scores, however significant for the groups in question, told nothing directly respecting the European and other populations from which the immigrants had come. They registered only the composite result produced in large groups of people of undetermined endowment by selective factors of immigration, education and other cultural opportunities. As we should expect, intelligence score was correlated positively with two environmental factors: years of residence in the United States and years of schooling. Yet average differences attributable to either factor are far less than the individual differences in any representative subgroup; and the mean racial difference is far less than the mean gain from ten years of residence.

Studies of the physical traits of immigrant groups in the United States show large differences, partly reflecting the physical character of the home populations. Motor and sensory differences prove to be small. The intellectual and the physical measurements vary independently for these as for other adult groups, and neither is found to be predictable in terms of the other.

The IQ's of American children of immigrant groups from socially and economically homogeneous populations show differences in immigrant stock similar to those demonstrated in the army study. Children of Swedish, English, German, American and Jewish immigrants rate at the average (100 IQ); Canadians, Russians, Poles and Greeks lower (90 IQ); Italians, French Canadians and Portuguese still lower (84 IQ).

Comparisons of the score distributions of diverse national groups in their native countries show similarities rather than differences. The scores in non-language performance tests made in European cities and districts, including Copenhagen, Hanover, the Eastern Pyrenees, Baden, Piedmont, Auverge and Velay, Flanders, Sicily and Rome, have equal ranges and small mean differences of little statistical significance. The three racial groups, Nordic, Alpine and Mediterranean, again rate in the order given, but as before it is the similarity that is significant, the mean differences being small and of doubtful mathematical importance.

Three conclusions may be drawn concerning psychological race differences. First, if they exist, it is probable that in groups of equal culture they are so small as to be practically negligible. Second, environment can exercise a favorable or unfavorable influence upon them, as illustrated among the racial groups in the United States. Third, for any one racial group living within the northern cultures the difference between the most superior and the most deficient individual is much larger than the difference between the means of different racial groups; and it is also larger than the amount that an individual can gain (or lose) through environmental influence.

RANGE OF HUMAN CAPACITIES

Some degree and form of intelligence is characteristic of all living species. Considerable diversification in traits and skills makes its appearance at the mammalian level. In our two domestic animals, the dog and the horse, this fact is particularly well illustrated. In apes some almost human personality traits appear, for these creatures alone beside human beings practice the higher degrees of imitation, cooperation and ideation that make possible complex social and intellectual development. Finally man by virtue of his equipment for symbolic thinking and its expression in language has far outstripped even his nearest associates in the evolutionary scale.

Group range. Among the animals there is no other than the human race that reaches what Galton called the third grade of natural ability. Looking upon social and professional life as a continuous examination or ability test, Galton constructed a *scale of eminence* in human beings corresponding to a scale of ability (Table XVI). First he computed the numbers of those distinguished as leaders of opinion or as creators of original work. In the highest of these, called the illustrious class, he included only one in a million; in the eminent class, about 250 per million, or one in 4000. Using these extreme figures as a guide, he constructed on the basis of the normal curve a classification of men according to their natural gifts. From his own observations and measurements of people and from his statistical studies, he came to the conclusion that for each group above average there is a corresponding group below average, and "that eminently gifted men are raised as much above mediocrity as idiots are depressed below it." By way of comparison he added: "I presume the class F of dogs and others of the more intelligent sort of animals is nearly commensurate with the f of the human race, in respect to memory and powers of reason. Certainly the class G of such

TABLE XVI

GALTON'S CLASSIFICATION OF MEN ACCORDING TO THEIR NATURAL GIFTS

(From F. Galton, *Hereditary genius*, New York: Macmillan, 1892, 30 ff.; reprinted by permission of the publisher.)

Grades of Natural Ability, Separated by Equal Intervals Below Average	Above Average	Proportionate viz. One in	In Each Million of the Same Age	Characterization of Average and Above Average Groups
a	A	4	256,791	Mediocrity, the bulk of the general society
b	B	6	161,279	Upper average
c	C	16	63,563	Abilities a trifle higher than those of the foreman of an ordinary jury
d	D	64	15,696	The mass of men who obtain the ordinary prizes of life
e	E	413	2,423	A stage higher
f	F	4,300	233	The lowest of the eminent classes
g	G	79,000	14	Exceptionally gifted
x	X	1,000,000	1	Illustrious
all grades below g	all grades above G			

animals is far superior to the g of humankind." Modern experimental studies of intelligence have shown Galton's guess to be a good one.

In the United States volunteer and draft army of 1918-1919 groups were differentiated in terms of test and of performance, as shown in Table XVII. A comparison of the army classification with Galton's classes of distinction discloses that the normal distribution curve of one can be superimposed upon the other. Army Class A includes part of Galton's C and all the classes above it. Army Class B includes the remainder of Galton's C and part of B; Army Classes C+ and C contain the remainder of Galton's B and his A and a, etc. Although Galton differentiated more groups than the army classification found essential, the two classifications are thus roughly in agreement. Both illustrate the wide differences in human beings whether viewed in terms of practical organization or of social and economic achievement and distinction. The army classification supports Galton's view that intelligence and

TABLE XVII

PSYCHOLOGISTS' CLASSIFICATION OF MEN IN THE U. S. ARMY ACCORDING TO THEIR INTELLIGENCE TEST SCORES

(From R. M. Yerkes, *Memoirs of National Academy of Sciences*, Vol. XV, 1921, 421–429; reprinted by permission of the publishers.)

Army Alpha Raw Test Scores	Descriptive Term Forming Aptitude Scale		Percentage of Recruits	Description	Estimated IQ Equivalent Revised Stanford-Binet
135–212	Very superior	A	4	High officer type when endowed with leadership and other necessary qualities.	120-up
105–134	Superior	B	10	Commissioned or non-commissioned officer type.	110–119
75-104	High average	C+	19	Usually suitable for non-commissioned officers. With commanding personality, suitable for commissions.	97–109
45–74	Average	C	29	Excellent privates. Some are good enough to become commissioned officers.	86–96
25–44	Low average	C−	22	Good privates, do satisfactory routine work.	78–85
15–24	Inferior	D	9	Fair privates, although they learn slowly, lack initiative and require much supervision.	73–77
0–14	Very inferior	D−	5	Barely fit for regular service.	72 and below
Not fixed	" "	E	2	Cannot make ordinary soldiers. Suitable for development battalion or discharge.	Not fixed

achievement are definitely related, and that in spite of hindrances, men tend to rise to the level of their threefold endowment of "intellectual ability, eagerness to work and power of working." Distinction may occur through achievement along a single line, or it may involve breadth of accomplishment and eminent personal leadership. It involves capacity and zeal, and the combination of these with an adequate power of doing a great deal of laborious work.

In all representative populations, whether of children or of young or older adults, the same classificatory distinctions appear. IQ results for younger and older children conform to this pattern. Measures of adults from 25 to 95 years of age show for each decade a similar distribution. In college students the range of abilities is generally limited to Army Classes A and B with a few of the more vigorous and enterprising members of C+. It has been demonstrated by tests and statistics that persons with IQ's below 100 have little chance of academic success at the college level; whereas those with IQ's of 110 and above can succeed academically if health, interest and effort are adequate. Since students rating below IQ 130 have generally to devote more effort to their studies than do the more gifted, their habits of work, benefiting by this forced zeal, produce in the long run a compensating asset.

In the College Board scholastic aptitude tests, the applicants are rated in classes A to E. Of these, the A's, unlikely to receive college grades below average, rate generally in the upper third of the class. The B's, who are unlikely to fail, rate usually in the upper half of the class. The C's preserve for the most part a low middle course, whereas the D's, who infrequently achieve standing in the upper tenth of the class, are not unlikely to fail and leave college. The E's are usually not admitted to college; if admitted, they usually fail. Scholastic success thus correlates with scholastic aptitude ratings, but not, it is important to note, to the extent of identity. C men in college aptitude terms may achieve highest distinction and may be elected to the academic honor societies. The scores of the best and the poorest students are as far apart as the extremes in the army A and C ratings. Whereas at the lower limit the distribution is cut off by administrative recognition of unfitness, at the upper limit performance may extend with the frequency indicated in Galton's table to his Class G and occasionally to X.

Extra-curricular performance and personality traits are somewhat similarly distributed in college groups, although here the preliminary selection of the human material has been less rigid than along scholastic lines. Hence distinguished achievement—as, for example, in baseball or in social extraversion—may be no greater in the college group than outside it.

Individual abilities. The separate abilities of one person are intercorrelated to about the same extent as the abilities of groups of persons. Thus in a single individual the measures of the traits, skills and performances lie along a normal distribution, with the best measure many times superior to the poorest. Such a distribution resembles the distribution of a single capacity in the population at large where the skill of the best person is many times the skill of the poorest. In planning individual progress the poorer performances may be disregarded after formal education is completed, for the emphasis thereafter is placed on the cultivation of the positive traits and gifts, including those whose exercise gives the greatest satisfaction. By self-analysis or by vocational test, patterns of superiority or clusters of skills and interests may usually be discovered, a careful consideration of which generally serves as a dependable guide to vocational choice.

In scholastic achievement tests the ratio of the poorest to the best score in a class may range from 1.5 to 25 or more. Thus in one group of eighth-grade children the ratio for quality of writing was 1.5; for speed of writing, 1.6; spelling 2; grammar 2.2; reading comprehension 3.5; reading speed 3.7; arithmetic reasoning 8.5; arithmetic addition 15; history 26. The more complex the activity, the larger is the difference between the poorest and the best performance in a single class group.

Similarly in industrial skills the performance ratios are diverse. They are correlated positively with the complexity of the performance in worker groups whose initial competence was equal. It may be concluded that among normal individuals in an average occupation the most able will be somewhere between one and a half and four times as capable as the poorest (Table XVIII).

Test results mathematically treated demonstrate fully the positive interdependence or interrelation of human capacities. Scores for almost all tests and traits show some positive correlation. The most conspicuous exceptions to this rule have been discussed. Ability and achievement are related; capacity is

TABLE XVIII

SHOWING THE RATIO OF THE LEAST EFFICIENT TO THE MOST EFFICIENT INDIVIDUAL ACTUALLY ENGAGED IN A VARIETY OF GAINFUL OCCUPATIONS

(From C. L. Hull, *Aptitude testing*. Yonkers-on-Hudson: World Book Co., 1928; reprinted by permission of the publisher.)

Vocation	Criterion	Ratio of Poorest to Best Worker
Heel trimming (shoes)	No. pairs per day	1:1.4
Loom operation (silk)	Time loom kept in operation	1:1.5
Hosiery maters	Hourly piecework earning	1:1.9
Loom operation (fancy cotton)	Earnings	1:2
Bottom scoring (shoes)	No. pairs per day	1:2
Knitting-machine operators	Pounds of women's hose per hour	1:2.2
Office boys	Weekly salary	1:2.3
Elementary teachers	Ratings of superiors	1:2.5
Polishing spoons	Time per 36 spoons	1:5.1

correlated with skill. But the absence of a one-to-one relationship between available measures is an indication that the structure of human activity is at present by no means completely surveyed in scientific terms. There is still considerable leeway for unmeasured as well as measured motivation, interest and zeal to alter the predicted performance in any given instance. In the period of growth and early maturity the unmeasured

TABLE XIX

AVERAGE IQ LEVELS IN TERMS OF EDUCATIONAL AND OCCUPATIONAL ACHIEVEMENT

IQ		
150	Honors group in graduate professional courses.	
140	Average of college honors group.	American men of science. Ph.D. and M.D. average.
130	Average of college graduates.	Professional adult average.
120	Superior intelligence.	Semi-professional.
110	High average intelligence.	High-school graduates' average. Clerical occupations. Skilled occupations.
100	Average intelligence.	High-school undergraduates' average. Tradesmen. Semi-skilled occupations.
90	Low average intelligence.	Grade-school education. Agricultural workers.
80	Dull intelligence.	Special trade-school education. Unskilled labor.
70	Borderline intelligence.	Special-school education.
60	Feebleminded.	Institutional training.

factors are known to act sometimes with considerable effectiveness. For most individuals who read these words there are many alternative fields in which excellence of performance may be achieved. Although for large groups of people the levels of attainment are predeterminable (see table XIX), for individuals effort and experience may alter predicted performance in many favorable ways.

REFERENCES

1. ANASTASI, A. *Differential psychology.* New York: Macmillan, 1937.
2. BINGHAM, W. V. *Aptitudes and aptitude testing.* New York: Harper, 1937.
3. FREEMAN, F. S. *Individual differences.* New York: Henry Holt, 1934.
4. GILLILAND, A. R., and CLARK, E. L. *Psychology of individual differences.* New York: Prentice-Hall, 1939.
5. GOODENOUGH, F. L. *Developmental psychology.* New York: Appleton-Century, 1934.
6. GUILFORD, J. P. *Psychometric methods.* New York: McGraw-Hill, 1936.
7. MILES, C. C. Intelligence and social adjustment. *Ment. Hyg.*, 1938, 22, 544-566.
8. MILES, C. C. Sex in social psychology. *A handbook of social psychology.* Worcester, Mass.: Clark University Press, 1935.
9. MILES, W. R. Age and human society. *A handbook of social psychology.* Worcester, Mass.: Clark University Press, 1935.
10. PINTNER, R. *Intelligence testing.* New York: Henry Holt, 1931.
11. SCHWESINGER, G. C. *Heredity and environment.* New York: Macmillan, 1933.
12. THORNDIKE, E. L. Mental work and fatigue and individual differences and their causes. *Educational psychology.* Vol. III. New York: Teachers College, 1914.

Chapter 5

MOTIVATION

This chapter is concerned with what the layman usually considers the most important problem of psychology. The question which, above all others, he wants psychology to answer for him is, "Why do people act as they do?" Not satisfied with a mere description of man's behavior, he wants to know the motives back of it. The problem of motivation, narrowly conceived, is the problem of discovering the motives of human beings; but, broadly viewed, it is the problem of determining the forces which impel or incite all living organisms to action.

NEEDS

One cannot long study the behavior of living organisms without observing that they need things; and it is these wants, lacks or needs which have to be investigated if the reasons for their behavior are to be discovered. The things which they need, however, vary greatly, not only from species to species, but also from individual to individual within the same species. Oysters do not need automobiles and men do not need shells; but, if they are to continue to live, oysters and men, like all other living organisms, need to get from their environments a continuous supply of energy and materials. The needs of the amoeba are limited to these vital ones. The needs of man, on the other hand, are ever so much more numerous. He, too, has vital needs. He needs to breathe oxygen, to eat food, to drink water, to eliminate wastes from his body, to maintain a relatively constant body temperature. But in addition to these he has other needs which cannot be considered so vital or so

---

This chapter was written by Donald W. MacKinnon of Bryn Mawr College.

universal. He may need to have more money than anyone else in his town, he may need to be loved by a particular person, he may need to be constantly praised and applauded.

Distinction among needs. There are important respects in which *vital* and *non-vital* needs are different, though in other respects they have much in common.

The vital needs are *primary* and *primitive* in the sense that they are the first needs of the organism. If they remain unsatisfied, the organism does not live to develop non-vital needs as a result of experience. In this sense, non-vital needs are secondary and acquired. This classification does not mean, however, that secondary needs are necessarily weaker or less important than primary ones. The terms primary and secondary apply only to the origins of needs and imply nothing about their relative strengths. The need to possess great wealth may be so much stronger in a man than his needs for food and rest and exercise that, even though he succeeds in amassing great wealth, he may so break his health as to die. In such a case the secondary need for possessions is obviously stronger than the primary vital needs which are frustrated. Furthermore, the distinction between primary and secondary needs does not imply that the latter are always in the service of the former. The example just cited shows that such is not the case. The amassing of great wealth (a secondary need) may be an end in itself and not necessarily a means to the certain and more adequate satisfaction of the need for food or of any other primary need.

There is a sense, then, in which a secondary need may be more vital for the continued existence of an individual than a primary need. It is, for example, not uncommon for a man to commit suicide because he has lost his fortune in a crash of the stock market or because he has lost his honor through becoming involved in a public scandal. For such persons life without money or life without honor is impossible. In a very real sense their secondary needs have become vital ones.

The primary needs are sometimes called *physiological* needs and the secondary ones, *psychological* needs. This does not mean, however, that the secondary psychological needs lack the physiological basis in the body which the primary physiological needs have, although, in general, it is true that we know more about the specific physiological basis of primary than of secondary needs. We know, for example, that the physiological basis of the need for food is a matter, in part, of a reduction of the sugar concentration of the blood and consequent contractions of the smooth muscle of the stomach; and we know at least something about the physiological basis of the other so-called physiological needs. But what the physiological basis of a man's need for superiority may be, or of any other of his so-called psychological needs, we do not know. We assume, however, that they have a physiological basis even though we cannot demonstrate it.

On the other hand, the distinction between physiological and psychological needs does not mean that the psychological needs have a representation in consciousness which is absent in physiological needs. We may be just as much aware of our need for food as we are aware of our need to pass a crucial examination; and we may, at another time, be just as unaware of our need to get even with a person for a slight which he has given us as we are unaware of our need for vitamin B. Physiological and psychological needs are alike in that both may be at certain times known but at other times unrecognized.

The primary needs are sometimes referred to as *biological* needs because they have biological origins. The secondary needs are sometimes called, in contrast, *social* needs because they are the products of social life. Though this is a valid distinction among needs, we must not overlook the fact that social needs are also biological in the sense that they are needs of biological organisms and that biological needs are also social in that the expressions of these needs are to a large extent socially determined. All men need food, but the particular objects which will satisfy this need vary widely from one society or culture to another. Religious taboos and cultural prohibitions limit greatly the number of objects which will satisfy an individual's need for food.

We have seen that needs are of two kinds: first, needs which are *primary, vital, physiological,* and *biological* and, second, needs which are *secondary, non-vital, psychological,* and *social.* But we have seen also that, valid as these distinctions between the two classes of needs are, they are not rigid. All needs have much in common. It is this fact which makes it possible for psychologists to seek the general laws of need regardless of the particular need studied.

Needs, structure and environment. All organisms have the primary need for oxygen, but, although they have this need in common, they satisfy it in different ways. The fish supplied with gills and living in water gets oxygen in one way; man supplied with lungs and living on land gets his in a different manner. The ways in which an organism's needs may be satisfied are determined by its structure as well as by the nature of its environment. This relationship is no less valid for secondary needs. A common need in a highly competitive society is the need to be or to feel superior to others, but it may be satisfied in very different ways. A person skilful in athletics may gain his superiority by excelling in sports; a man of puny body but keen intellect may gain his feeling of superiority by scholastic excellence.

Needs lead to activities which depend upon the following three factors.

1. The *need* itself, conceived of as a want or lack of the organism, involving always a physiological disequilibrium or a tension which tends to discharge in behavior in such a way as to bring about a restoration of the equilibrium which was disturbed by the need. (See pp. 163f. for the definition of need.) Such physiological disequilibria are to be considered the sources of the stimulation which drive the organism to action.

2. The *structure* of the organism, which determines to an important degree not only the needs of the organism but also the manner in which they will be satisfied. Here are to be con-

sidered certain mechanisms—gills as against lungs, the claw of a lobster as against the hand of a man—as well as the sensory organs and nervous system which mediate the perception of needed objects and the muscles and glands which are organized into systems of response.

3. The *environment* of the organism and the objects, present in the environment or absent from it, which are required for the satisfaction of any need. Here both the social and the physical environment have to be considered.

Any concrete case of behavior is determined by the interrelated functioning of all three of these factors; it is only by adopting an analytical attitude that they can be discussed separately. Later we shall consider them in their interrelation.

THE PHYSIOLOGICAL BASIS OF NEEDS

The psychologist has long considered that one of his problems is the determination of the conditions in bodily tissues which release energy and so stimulate the organism to overt activity. He has sought to determine the precise correlation between these known conditions and activity, both general and specific, and having found such correlations he has developed the concept of *drive* defined as *an intra-organic activity or condition of tissue which supplies stimulation for a particular type of behavior.*

Hunger drive. The following facts are known about the physiology of the *hunger drive*. When the sugar concentration of the blood is reduced below a certain level, vigorous contractions of the stomach ensue, these contractions of the smooth muscles of the stomach wall being the physiological concomitants of the conscious pangs of hunger. This latter fact has been demonstrated by having subjects swallow a tube to the end of which a rubber balloon is attached. When the balloon is in the stomach, it is inflated and the tube connected to a recording apparatus so as to give a graphic record of the stomach contractions. If under these conditions subjects are instructed to press a signal key whenever a pang of hunger is experienced, it is found that their stomach contractions and hunger pangs coincide. These experiments have been carried further to determine the relation between stomach contractions and general bodily activity. Subjects were asked to recline on a bed so constructed as to yield a graphic record of their movements—even so slight a movement as that of a single finger. By taking simultaneous records of bodily activity and stomach contractions both when the subjects were asleep and when quietly reading, a very close correlation between the rhythmic contractions of the smooth muscle of the stomach and bodily activity was demonstrated.

Just as the altered chemical state of the blood consequent upon the reduction of its sugar concentration affects the stomach, setting up the vigorous contractions of the smooth muscle, so these contractions in turn set up nervous impulses which make for an increase of bodily activity.

Bodily conditions such as those just described are correlated, however, not only with an increase in general bodily activity, but also with specific activity directed toward the satisfaction of the momentary need. The hungry human being seeks food and eats it when he finds it. The thirsty animal seeks water and drinks it if he gets it.

Although this activity, both general and specific, has been found to be associated with such specific internal conditions as stomach contractions, there are a number of experiments which have demonstrated that the activity may likewise occur in the absence of the usually associated physiological state. Rats in which practically all the contractile tissue of the stomach has been removed are still motivated, when deprived of food, to seek food in a maze. A hungry hen placed before a heap of grain will eat a certain amount and stop, though there is still more food before her. Nevertheless, the hen can be motivated to eat again—this time in the absence of any stomach contractions—if the remaining food is removed and immediately replaced. With some hens this process can be repeated as many as eight times. In the light of such evidence we can hardly assume that stomach contractions are always and necessarily the source of stimulation which motivates the hen to eat. In this case the perception of the food presented is alone sufficient to stimulate eating.

In another experiment the amount of grain that a hen will eat spontaneously after a twenty-four hour fast was determined. The hen was then presented after a similar fast with a heap of grain larger than before. If ordinarily the hen eats 50 grains from a heap of 100 grains of wheat, from a larger heap she will eat from 35 to 50 grains more. Since presumably the chemical state of the blood and the condition of the tissues of the stomach are about the same under both conditions, the increase in eating must be determined not by the stomach contractions but by the increase in the size of the heap and by whatever physiological changes result from the perception of this fact.

Or again, if a hen eats until satisfied and remains motionless in front of a pile of grain, she will begin to eat once more if a hungry hen introduced into the situation starts to eat. And like hens we, too, will start to eat again if, having eaten our fill, we are joined by hungry friends.

Such observations as these indicate how necessary it is to consider, in addition to the internal sources of stimulation in the stomach wall, the environmental factors which may also stimulate the organism to eat. Objects which in the past have been present when physiological hunger has driven the organism to eat, or situations in which eating has occurred, may, because of their connection with previous eating, become adequate in their own right to stimulate the same behavior on later occasions. Thus, we eat when we see others eating; we eat more when more food is presented to us; and we eat, in everyday life, long before we are driven to do so by the goading pangs of hunger. Once we develop habits of eating certain things at certain times and in certain places, the appearance of these things, at these times and in these places, alone suffices to make us eat.

Sex drive. Numerous studies of the *sex drive* in animals have been made. Typical is the study in which female rats were placed in cages with activity wheels, like those provided for the exercise of squirrels, and the activity of the animals measured by determining the revolutions of the wheels per unit of time by means of counters. Rhythmic changes in the amount of general activity (running) of the animals were revealed. Every four or five days there occurred peaks of activity, which were shown to correspond to periods of oestrus (heat) during which females are sexually receptive to the advances of males. That the specific internal condition here involved is the secretion of the hormone of the ovaries seems indicated by the fact that males do not show such rhythms of activity, that females show little activity and no cycles of activity before puberty, that interruption of oestrus rhythm by pregnancy and lactation is accompanied by an interruption of the cycles of activity and that with removal of the ovaries the activity cycle disappears.

Other drives. Many other experiments have confirmed the drive character of endocrine or ductless-gland secretions. Thus, even though the male rat does not show cycles of activity like the female, a great deal of his activity is dependent upon secretions from the gonads (sex glands), for after castration there is a marked reduction in his daily running activity. Likewise the removal of the pituitary, adrenal or thyroid glands in rats, as well as in other animals including men, has been shown to be followed by a reduction in general activity.

Other bodily conditions serving as drives to action are dryness of the mucous lining of the throat in thirst, distention of the bladder or colon, injury to the skin. Such examples could be many times multiplied, but these will suffice.

It is important to point out again, however, that while such physiological conditions as have just been described may be the primary drives to action, nevertheless the environmental situation in which such action occurs may in itself become an effective stimulus for a similar form of behavior in the future.

NEEDS AS DEPENDENT ON THE STRUCTURE OF THE ORGANISM

As we have already seen, the way in which organisms satisfy their needs depends also upon their structures. We cannot understand how an engine runs if we know only that there is steam in the boiler; we must also know the structure of the whole and the relationships among its parts. We have to know as much about living organisms if we are to understand their behavior. The needs of an oyster and of a man are different in large measure because of structural differences. Needs and structures are related. The needs of a blind man are not the same as those of a man who sees, nor those of a bed-ridden cripple the same as those of an athlete. Such individuals may and do have some needs in common, but they will have, in addition, unique needs.

One important respect in which organisms differ is in the extent to which they are able at birth to satisfy their needs. The human infant is absolutely dependent upon others for the gratification of many of his needs; not until years have passed is he able to care for himself alone. He must first learn how to get most of the things he requires. Many animals, such as spiders and the lower insects, on the other hand, are at birth as capable of satisfying their needs as are the adults of the same species. They do not have to learn how to take care of themselves, for they are born with mature structures organized for patterns of action adequate to meet all their needs. Such inborn patterns of response have been called *instincts*, and the behavior resulting from the activation of such patterns, *instinctive*. A fuller description of instinctive behavior is postponed until later (pp. 263-265). Here it is only important to note that, whereas man has to learn through years of experience how he may satisfy his needs, other animals are born with such 'knowledge.'

Most animals are superior to man in the degree to which patterns of response activated by bodily needs operate unconsciously in the satisfaction of these needs. In one experiment hens were fed a diet almost entirely deficient in calcium carbonate. The omission of this important material from the diet soon resulted in a marked thinning of the shells of the eggs and after four days in a cessation of laying. After nine days of this diet deficient in calcium, the hens were divided into two groups. One group was given short pieces of macaroni within which shell had been placed, with the ends of the macaroni so closed that the shell could be neither seen nor tasted. These hens each ate an average of 17 grains of shell. When presented with plain shell a few hours later, each of these hens ate an average of 5 grains more, making 22 grains of shell eaten in all. The other group was first given plain macaroni, but when later presented with plain shell ate on the average 19 grains of shell. Under these dissimilar conditions the hens of both groups ate approximately the same amount of shell. Yet the hens of the first group were guided not by taste or sight but by physicochemical processes within the body.

In a similar experiment hens were offered a choice between three kinds of butter, one high in vitamins A and D, a second high in A but low in D, the third low in both A and D. The result was that the first butter, most adequate for the satisfaction of nutritional needs, was eaten in greatest quantities.

Rats have been shown to have the same ability to choose between suitable and unsuitable diets. Presented with two kinds of food, one containing sufficient and the other insufficient protein for normal growth, they ate both foods, but enough more of the former to maintain normal growth. Given foods varying in vitamin B content, they chose the foods with the richer vitamin content. The same results have been obtained with pigs and cows; these animals have demonstrated under controlled conditions their ability to select a diet adequate to their bodily needs.

Since human adults so frequently and obviously eat an improper diet, it is interesting to note that newly weaned infants, if presented with a variety of foods and allowed complete freedom of choice, have shown an ability from the first to select their food so that their bodily needs are adequately satisfied.

To be sure, they showed definite preferences from time to time for different kinds of food, and these preferences changed in unpredictable ways; yet records of food showed from month to month that, in terms of protein, carbohydrate, fat, calories, acidity and alkalinity, the infants chose an adequate and balanced diet. With such self-feeding the infants gained in weight more than the average for this growth period. Experiments of this sort, however, hardly justify the conclusion that infants and children should be allowed complete freedom in the choice of their food in the situations of everyday life. If a complete and adequate range of foods were always available to children —something which would be most uneconomical—and if the feeding habits of adults were unknown to them, and if, in addition, they were left absolutely free to choose, perhaps they would do as well; but, in the absence of such conditions, they seem to develop specific food preferences and habits of eating which make it difficult, if not impossible, for such unconscious but adequate regulation of diet to continue.

The greater plasticity of man means that he, more than any other animal, has to learn *how* to satisfy his needs. It also means that he learns to need more things than any other animal.

Derived needs. Learned skills and abilities and habits are important in the study of motivation not only because they enable the individual to satisfy his needs, but also because they may themselves become drives to action constituting needs in their own right. The boy who learns boxing in self-defense may find that he wants to box, no longer in self-defense, but just for the fun of boxing; or the girl who learns to sew in order that she may have clothes as attractive as her friends may discover that she wants to sew, even though she needs no more clothes for her few social engagements. It might be argued that the boy who continues to box does so in order to feel superior instead of as formerly merely to protect himself, and that the girl who continues to sew does so in order to feel superior in the exercise of her skill rather than as formerly merely to be attractive. But even so it is in such ways that the number of our specific needs is multiplied many times over in the course of our lives. In general, the greater the patterning of the nervous processes underlying our actions, the greater will be the number of needs which we shall experience.

Such needs, resulting from mechanisms and habits which have become drives in their own right, are called *derived needs.* They are the clearest examples of what at the beginning of this chapter we called secondary needs. Their importance for everyday life lies in the fact that, through their development, objects and activities which earlier were *means* to an end now become *ends* in themselves. Their importance for any theory of motivation lies in the fact that they indicate the complexity of the physiological basis of the behavior which results from need and they reveal the inadequacy of conceiving of drive as simply a matter of a *specific* condition of the tissue in an organ or other restricted part of the body.

Seeing that these secondary needs result from the patterning of the response mechanism, their physiological basis must be in large measure these neural patterns. Since even primary needs are satisfied only when the appropriate patterns of response are activated, and since, as we have seen, these primary needs may be aroused in the absence of the usually associated organic condition, it would seem no less true that their physiological basis is also in large part a matter of patterns in the nervous system. In other words, we are forced to conceive of the physiological basis of all needs, both primary and secondary, as being a matter both of certain organic stimulating conditions (*e.g.,* stomach contractions) and of certain neural states (*e.g.,* neural patterns).

NEEDS AS DEPENDENT ON THE ENVIRONMENT

So important is the role of the environment in determining behavior as an outcome of need that it has been impossible not to mention it in connection with the other two factors already discussed.

A rat confined in an activity cage shows an increase of activity as the time for feeding approaches. In his present environment that is all he can do when driven by hunger. But take him from his cage and put food before him. Then he will no longer run; he will eat. If, on the other hand, you place him in a maze which he has learned, he will run directly to the food box and eat. We may assume in all three cases the same internal state of physiological disequilibrium or drive, so that the differences in behavior would seem to be determined by differences in the rat's environment in the three situations.

Let us observe the same rat just after he has eaten to satiety. A satiated rat remains relatively quiet in his activity cage. If there is food before him, he will ignore it. If placed in a maze, provided it is not a strange one, he will show no active seeking after food. Here, in the same three situations as described above and all quite different from each other, the behavior of the rat is practically identical—a quiet indifference to his environment. Are we, then, to draw from observation of a satiated rat a different conclusion from that we reached by observation of a hungry rat, namely that the similarity of behavior in different environments is determined by the similar internal state of the rat in all three situations?

Relation of environment to needs. Neither conclusion is wholly right nor wholly wrong, and the conflict between them can be resolved if, instead of considering the internal and external factors separately, we see them in relation to each other. The point is that any situation as it exists psychologically for the organism—that is to say, as it is perceived and reacted to—is in large measure dependent upon the needs of the organism; and, since the needs of any organism are constantly changing, this fact means that the same physical environment and objects in it have at different times quite different meanings. When a child is hungry, an apple is something to eat; but when he is angry, it is something to throw at the provoking person. Similarly, a hungry rat is an alert rat, actively seeking in its environment anything that may serve as a means to the satisfaction of its need; but a satiated rat is a sleepy rat, indifferent to many aspects of its environment. Whether food is present or absent is a matter of no consequence, so that environments *physically* unlike may all be the same *psychologically*, in that they are reacted to *as though* they were alike.

It is helpful in distinguishing the physical and psychological environment to call the former the *situation* and the latter the *field*. The physical *situation* is the environment considered as having independent real existence, whereas the psychological *field* is the situation as it exists psychologically for the individual. The psychological field is not to be equated merely to what is consciously perceived or known but rather to everything that at the moment determines the behavior of an individual.

Food in the situation may or may not be food in the field. If there is a need for it, food in the situation is likely to be perceived and reacted to. It then exists in the field and has a positive, attractive value, exciting the hungry person to eat. But, the need for nourishment having been satisfied, the same food may be ignored. Although it may be perceived, it will not excite the individual to activity, for it now has a neutral quality, neither attracting nor repelling him. The presence of others who are hungry and eating may make the food seem slightly attractive so that it is nibbled at. An unpleasant story told at the table may make the food seem unpleasant so that it is pushed away. If, however, for any reason food has been eaten to the point of satiation, especially if this overeating has resulted in any degree of discomfort, the sight and smell of food cease to be neutral and acquire a negative character. The individual experiences a need to push the food out of sight or to remove himself from it.

Incentives. The existence of objects or activities in an individual's field is thus seen to depend to an important degree upon his needs. It is for this reason that objects and activities in the field so often have to be described psychologically as having an attracting, repelling, exhorting, summoning, inviting or demanding character. Things possessing such characteristics are called incentives. An *incentive* may be defined as *an object, a situation or an activity which excites, maintains and directs behavior.* It must be clear, however, that a thing which is an incentive at one moment may not be an incentive at the next moment, or that a thing which is at one time a positive incentive attracting a person may subsequently be a negative incentive repelling the same individual.

Objects or activities offered to an individual may act as incentives to arouse his needs and stir him to action. When a need is very strong, objects to satisfy it will be actively sought even though they are not present in the environment. But, under conditions of a lesser need, an individual may be relatively quiet and contented until something brought into his environment acts as an incentive to arouse that need more actively. A person may not be consciously hungry until he smells the pleasant aroma of food, or he may be little interested in stamp collecting until he hears a lecture on the fascinations of philately. As the advertiser knows, it is possible, within limits, to motivate people to action through a manipulation of their environments; but if this activation is to be wholly successful, it is necessary to know something about the latent needs of those whom one seeks to influence. Otherwise what may seem the most attractive of incentives to the one who offers them may turn out to be no incentives at all for those to whom they are offered.

The social environment, no less than the physical, influences the activities of individuals, causing things to lose or to acquire incentive value for them. It has already been pointed out that a hen which has eaten to satiation will begin to eat again if a hungry second hen is introduced into the situation; and she will eat more if two hungry hens, and still more if three, are brought in. This result occurs, however, only when the hungry hens have been accustomed to tyrannize over the satiated hen in other situations. If instead the satiated hen has habitually tyrannized over the hungry hens, then she will attempt to keep them from eating by pecking at them or chasing them away. The converse experiment has likewise been performed, in which three hens eat to satiation and then are joined by a single hungry hen. Under these conditions the hungry hen begins to peck the grain, but her behavior has no effect upon the group of three, who remain passive or peck only a little.

Other experiments have demonstrated a comparable *social facilitation* of eating in fishes, rats and monkeys, and the same effect is noticeable among persons. The child who does not want his oatmeal may nevertheless eat it eagerly when he sees his brother eating his with relish, just as, in the same way, the eating to excess at an old-fashioned Thanksgiving dinner is a function not only of the increased quantity of food (the same effect as seen in hens, p. 152), but also of the social facilitation supplied by the sight of others eating. The presence of others may, of course, just as well cause objects or activities to become negative incentives as positive, as when, for example, the work one is doing ceases to be interesting because others gather for an evening of fun.

Cultural determination of needs. The importance of the environment in the behavior that is dependent on needs is, however, most clearly seen in the cultural determination of needs. The infant is born into a society in which there are certain social norms of behavior, certain customs which determine to a large extent not only the needs which the members of that society experience, but also the particular means by which these needs may be satisfied. What the norms of his society are is one of the things the infant has to learn. The process of socialization in the developing child is in large measure the incorporation of these norms within himself in order that his general patterns of behavior may coincide with those of his group. In short, he learns that certain ends may be sought, but not others.

The specific nature of the means of satisfying primary needs no less than secondary ones is determined by social norms. The kind of food eaten by people of different cultures varies greatly.

In many societies individuals are not permitted to eat the flesh of certain animals which are believed to be related to them, a relationship which thus renders the idea of eating such flesh abhorrent. In other societies fruits or plants may be prohibited. There is no society in which the entire range of edible objects is included in the diet. Having learned to eat certain things and not others, and having learned to eat them only when prepared in certain ways, one finds it difficult, if not impossible, to change eating habits. It has been found that emigrants frequently find it easier to learn a new language than to learn to like the dishes of their new country. An American may demand a soft mattress and pillow if his need for rest is to be satisfied, a Japanese may demand a hard mat and pillow of wood, and the African native may be able to rest only if he can lie upon the ground. Such differences as these are not racially determined but are rather the effect of social conditions on the needs of individuals in different cultures.

The young of the human species must be cared for if the species is to survive. This fact has led many persons to assume the existence in every mother of a need to care for her offspring, a need so fixed in its expression as to constitute a *maternal instinct.* Yet, actually, there is to be found among different peoples a wide range of norms of behavior in regard to the care and protection of infants. Among the Arapesh an infant is the object of great warmth and affection. Suckled whenever it cries, sleeping in close contact with its mother and carried by her wherever she goes, the Arapesh infant is almost continuously fondled and caressed. In contrast to the Arapesh, the Mundugumor treat their children with little love. The infant is kept in a hard uncomfortable basket, is not suckled unless clearly in need of milk, is not fondled or caressed, is made early to fend for itself and in general is so harshly treated that only the strongest survive. Among the Andaman Islanders adoption of children is so customary that it is rare to find a child more than six or seven years of age living with its parents, for to adopt the child of a friend is an accepted form of expressing friendship and regard. On the Island of Mota, on the other hand, an infant may be sold at birth to the man who pays the midwife at the birth. Although this person is usually the father, it sometimes happens that, in the absence of the father or in the event that he lacks the necessary funds, another man buys the child and becomes its 'father.' In other societies infanticide, at least under certain conditions, is an accepted practice; and the Aztecs sold their children into slavery.

Another form of human behavior which has sometimes been regarded as instinctive is the *aggressive reaction* to frustration. Nevertheless conflict between individuals does not invariably or universally result in the same behavior. Instead of fighting with his fists, the Kwakiutl Indian fights with property in the institution of the "potlatch," in which the more property he can give away or destroy, the more superior he is to his opponent. Eskimos settle their conflicts in a public contest in which each sings abusive songs about the other. When two Indians of Santa Marta quarrel, instead of striking each other they strike a tree or a rock with sticks, and the one first breaking his stick is considered the braver and hence the victor. In other societies aggression is expressed in still other ways; even within the same society there may be a wide range of different socially approved expressions of aggression.

It is now possible to demonstrate a wide range of behavior for any need. In the absence of crucial anthropological knowledge, it was formerly assumed that the needs were in all societies the same as in ours, and therefore instinctive. The fixedness and universality of forms of human behavior, however, turn out to be a myth. Instead, we find that the needs of the individual, as well as the ways in which he is permitted to satisfy them, are determined to a large extent by the social and cultural environment into which he is born and in which he is reared.

THE MEASUREMENT OF NEEDS

Definition of need. The facts reviewed in the preceding sections of this chapter suggest the following definition of need. *A need is a tension within an organism which tends to organize* *the field of the organism with respect to certain incentives or goals and to incite activity directed toward their attainment.* For each need there are certain objects or activities—terminal situations—which, if they are obtained, satisfy the need, thus releasing the tension. It is for this reason that the fullest meaning of any behavior is described only when the final situation toward which it is leading is discovered.

Needs have a qualitative aspect which makes it possible for us to distinguish such primary needs as those for food, sex, thermal constancy, elimination, etc., and such secondary needs as those for superiority, submission, affiliation, freedom, inviolacy, etc. Such terms as these are, of course, generalizations from the specific situations in which the concrete activities of needs end. One does not have a general need to be superior, but rather a need to be superior in a particular way in a specific situation, *e.g.,* to win this race, to get the highest mark on this examination, to know more about a certain field of study than any other person. Yet it is often helpful in the study of certain problems of personality and in the comparison of individuals to conceptualize general needs of which any given activity is but a specific and concrete example.

Needs also have a quantitative aspect which makes it possible by the use of certain techniques to measure their strength. Although, of course, a need cannot be measured directly, an indirect estimate can be obtained by measuring its effect upon consciousness and behavior. Thus by determining the work which the need will do we get an indication of its intensity.

Obstruction method. One technique for the measurement of needs is the obstruction method, by which the strength of a need is measured in terms of the magnitude of an obstacle or the number of times an obstacle of a given magnitude will be overcome in order to obtain a needed object. The obstruction method has been employed most often in the measurement of animal drive, rats having been the subjects most frequently studied.

A diagram of an obstruction box used in such investigations

is shown in Fig. 8. To measure the sex need a female rat is placed in compartment *A*, a male rat (the incentive) in compartment *D*. In order to reach the incentive, the female rat must pass through the alley *B*. The floor of this section is covered with an electric grid which enables the experimenter to give the animal a shock. If she crosses the grid, she steps on *E* which releases door d_2, liberating the male from *D*. It has been found that when a female rat is in heat she crosses the charged grid frequently and with little hesitation, though at other times she scarcely ever crosses it.

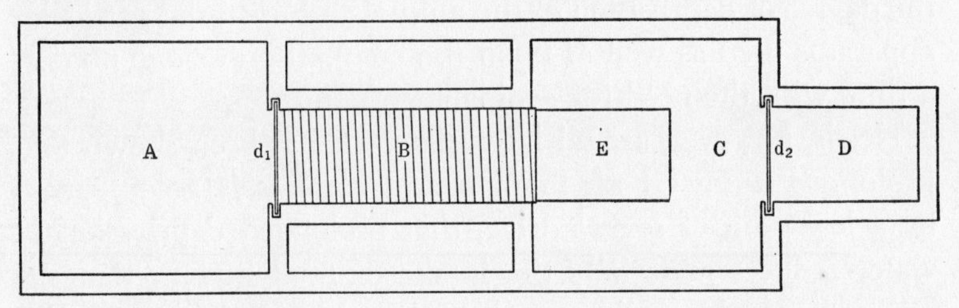

FIG. 8. DIAGRAM OF FLOOR PLAN OF OBSTRUCTION BOX.

A, entrance compartment; *B*, obstruction compartment (electric grid); *C*, *D*, divided incentive compartment; *E*, release plate; d_1, manually operated door between entrance compartment (*A*) and grid (*B*); d_2, automatic door operated by animal's stepping on release plate (*E*). From T. N. Jenkins, L. H. Warner, and C. J. Warden, Standard apparatus for the study of animal motivation, *J. comp. Psychol.*, 1926, 6, 366; reprinted by permission of the Williams & Wilkins Co.

Similar investigations of hunger, thirst, and maternal need have demonstrated that a rat does not repeatedly cross the grid and take a shock in the absence either of a motivating need or of the appropriate incentive.

In the obstruction method not one need is measured, but two which are in conflict. There is the need for food, or water, or whatever other need is being investigated, but there is also the need for avoidance of pain, so that what is actually being measured is the relative strength of the two needs. If, for example, the need for food is stronger than the need for avoidance of pain, the animal will take the shock in order to get the food; and, presumably, the stronger the first need, the more often will the grid be crossed in a given period of time. Since every need is unstable, the measurement of one against another cannot be exact. In evaluating these results we must remember that the animal tends to become accustomed to the electric shock, so that the negative incentive of the physically constant shock decreases in time.

With the use of this method of obstruction attempts have been made to determine the relative strengths of various animal needs. In the most extensive investigations so far recorded, the maternal need has been found to be the strongest. The others in rank order of strength are thirst, hunger, sex and the exploratory need. This order depends, however, upon the degree of deprivation of the animal and upon the particular apparatus used as well as upon the comparison of one need at a time with the need for avoidance of pain.

Needs, however, are all interrelated. It has been shown that prolonged hunger both in man and animals is accompanied by a lessening of sexual drive, that prolonged deprivation of water reduces materially the intake of food in rats, that the brooding of a hen reduces greatly the amount of food she eats, that an increase in the hunger of rats is accompanied by an increase in their need for exploration and that, when sex need is strongest (at the time of oestrus in the female rat), the need for food as measured by its intake is greatly reduced. A similar interrelation can be observed in persons. The need to get good grades may become much less when the student falls in love, the need for food may become secondary to the desire to have a slim figure, and the need of the mother to dress attractively may become negligible when the need to care for her child is great.

Learning method. A second technique for the measurement of needs is the learning method, by which the strength of need is measured in terms of the readiness with which a task is learned under different conditions of motivation. It has long been known that for an organism to learn it must be motivated. This fact makes it possible to vary the factor of motivation and to measure its effect upon the rate of learning. Here again, because animal experimentation is simpler than human, most of the studies have been made with animals, but an analogue of the experimental findings can usually be found in the realm of human behavior.

It has been shown that, within limits, the stronger the motivation the faster the learning. In one experiment which demonstrated this relation the rate of maze learning by three groups of rats differing only in their motivation was investigated. The first group was very hungry and very thirsty, the second was very hungry but only slightly thirsty and the third was very thirsty but only slightly hungry. During the first nine days of the experiment the rats were rewarded with bran mash; during the last nine days they were rewarded with water. In the first half of the experiment the rats motivated both by hunger and thirst learned slightly faster than the animals of the other two groups, a fact which indicates the superiority of two needs over one in motivating learning. In the second half of the experiment, with the shift to water as the reward, the very hungry and thirsty animals were temporarily disturbed by the change. They showed at first an increase in the number of their errors, but at the end of the experiment they were again superior to the other two groups. The effect of the shift in reward upon the other two groups, which had learned at the same rate during the first nine days, was striking. Now rewarded with water, the very thirsty animals speeded up their learning, whereas the very hungry rats showed very little improvement with the inappropriate reward. The second half of the experiment not only confirmed the finding of the first in demonstrating that two needs constitute a more effective condition for learning than one, but it also showed that learning is faster when the need serving as motive is appropriately rewarded.

The needs motivating children for their school work are numerous and varied. Arousing more needs by presenting additional incentives has been shown to increase their accomplishment. In one investigation, the offer of a reward of a chocolate bar raised the performance 52 per cent above the usual level, whereas the introduction of a number of incentives, like candy, a definite goal, rivalry and praise, increased the performance 65 per cent. In human motivation, then, as in animal, it is easy to demonstrate that an increase in motivation leads to an increase of performance.

It has also been shown that the amount of reward offered influences the rate of learning. For instance, chicks who find six grains of boiled rice in the reward box at the end of a simple maze learn the maze more effectively than chicks who are rewarded with only one grain. That the amount of reward offered human beings is not without its effect upon performance is also clear. One will work harder and better for more rather than for less pay. The student works harder for a large scholarship than for a small one.

Not only is the amount of reward important in determining the rate of learning, but also the kind of reward. It has been shown, for example, that of two groups of rats learning a maze, the one rewarded with bran mash will learn the maze more rapidly than the group rewarded with less-preferred sunflower seeds. This finding clearly has its analogue in human behavior.

SOME EFFECTS OF NEED

Effect on perception and imagination. The investigations just reviewed have demonstrated the role of need in learning. They have also shown the effect of need on perception, for all learning involves a reorganization of a field. The maze which a rat has learned is *psychologically* quite different from what it was when first encountered. The keyboard of a typewriter is for the skilled typist quite a different field from what it is for the novice.

A simple example will illustrate that learning involves a *reorganization of a field* as a result of need. Let us take the case of a young child separated from an apple by a fence, as indicated in Fig. 9*a*. If the child is not hungry, but rather is contentedly playing with some toys in the blind alley, he may not even see the apple; or, if he does, he will not be interested in it. If, on the other hand, he is restless, either because he is hungry or because he is tired of playing with his toys, the likelihood is greatly increased that he will see the apple. Under two different conditions of need the field of the child is differently organized. Thus, whether the apple will become a positive incentive depends upon whether it can serve in any way to satisfy a need.

If it does become a positive incentive the very young child will try to get it in the simplest and most direct manner, as indicated in Fig. 9*b*. Since he cannot reach it, or crawl through the fence to it, his need is blocked and his field reorganized until what was previously for him a fence or a row of sticks now looms as a barrier. He may push against this barrier, try

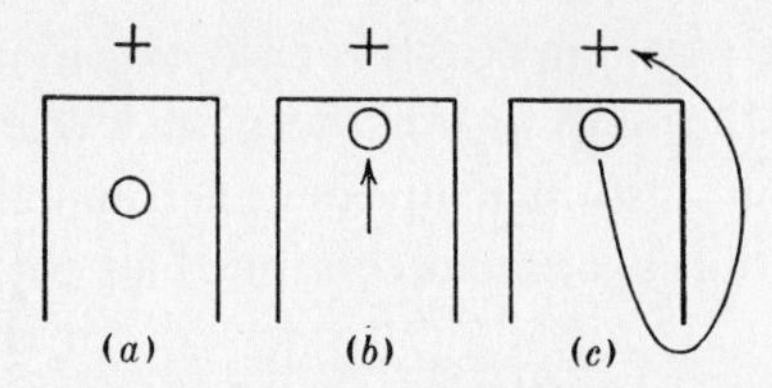

FIG. 9. REPRESENTATION OF STEPS IN THE SOLUTION OF A SIMPLE DETOUR PROBLEM. + = apple. O = child. → = path taken by child.

to crawl under or over it, or reach through it as far as he can, all because the way to the apple is a straight line toward it. Then, blocked and frustrated, he may look around, see the opening, and suddenly run to the apple in the roundabout direction indicated in Fig. 9*c*. Again his field has been reorganized. What was previously either non-existent as a way to the goal, or else a path away from the goal, now becomes the first phase of the path to the goal. If the child is again put back into the blind alley, he will at once take the roundabout way to obtain the apple. He has, in other words, learned the solution of a detour problem (see pp. 304f.). In this case it is clear that learning is the result of a need which reorganizes a field.

When there is no possible solution of a problem, the role of need in reorganizing the field may be even more marked. In an investigation of anger, subjects were given a task for which three different solutions were demanded, although there were only two possible ones. The subject was asked to step within a square outlined upon the floor and, without leaving this area, to obtain a flower which was placed upon a sawhorse four feet outside the square. The two possible solutions were: (1) to place a chair which stood within the square between the square and the horse and, leaning with one hand on the chair, reach the flower with the other hand; and (2) to kneel down (keeping the feet within the square) and reach the flower. Both these solutions were possible only if the subject had perceived the field reorganized in these two ways. After the subjects had arrived at these two solutions, they were asked to demonstrate a third. Since there was no third solution and since the subjects were kept for hours at the task, the mounting tension resulting from the blocking of their need was expressed not only in anger but also in many new perceptual organizations of the field. As the experiment continued all objects came to be seen in relation to the goal—as barriers, disturbances, tools, etc. The greater the tension, the more did objects offer themselves as possible means to the solution. Some rings which had been placed along the side of the square were seen again and again as having something to do with getting the flower. Although they were of no use, they were picked up repeatedly and juggled about in a vain attempt at use. Then they became disturbing factors which the subjects wanted to forget but could not. The subjects were also disturbed by the fact that the back of the square was made of two sticks rather than one, as though this, too, had something to do with the solution.

Such behavior clearly indicates that while a certain degree of need is necessary for that reorganization of a field which constitutes insight and learning, a need in excess of such an optimum may come so to distort the field that it no longer bears any resemblance to the situation. In this experiment, some of the subjects after long periods of frustration revealed momentary fantastic distortions of the field. One person began to act as though she had hypnotic power to draw the flower to her, while another, yielding to fantasy, saw the room filled with water and the horse and flower floating in her direction. Both subjects in their momentary fantasies forgot the harsh realities of their situation. Such a denial of the frustrating realities of a situation is, of course, characteristic of all *fantasy* and *wishful thinking*.

The behavior of these subjects was similar to that of a student who, having endured one frustration after another in his boyhood, was still in college being frustrated both in his scholastic work and in his social relations. But if in reality his needs were frustrated, in fantasy his wishes were fulfilled. He confided that when he sat in a classroom he paid little attention to the lecture, for he found it easier and pleasanter to indulge in the fantasy that he was the head of a large office and that all the other members of the class (so industriously taking notes) were his secretaries and stenographers busily working for him. When he walked from one building to another on the campus, he thought of each as a separate city or town. To his mind he was not merely passing buildings on a campus; he was speeding over the highways from one city to another in a high-powered car. And when, one night, he was, in reality, walking along a country road with two of his friends, it seemed to him in his fantasy that they were a couple of the enemy whom he had captured in a lone raid into no man's land and whom he now was escorting back to his own lines—for which brave action he was soon to be decorated.

The fields of this student deviated far from the objective realities of his everyday situations. Since he found in them a pleasant, vicarious satisfaction of the needs which were in reality frustrated, his fantasies constituted escapes from this reality. We all indulge in such *flights from reality* from time to time, when our needs are excessively frustrated. We return from them frequently with renewed vigor and strength to force the satisfaction of our needs on the level of reality. As a matter of fact, the very distortion that our fields undergo at such times may suggest to us the way in which we can in reality satisfy our needs. There is always the danger, however, that such flights from reality will cease to be momentary or of relatively short duration and will become instead permanent. It is in this sense that the delusions of the insane are merely extreme and lasting distortions of their fields by their needs. The poor man whose need for material things has been enduringly frustrated may end by living in a fantastically distorted field in which he is fabulously wealthy, although in reality he is an inmate of a hospital for the insane.

Less marked and less pathological examples of the organization of a field by a need can be seen in everyday life. When two persons behave differently in the same objective situation, they do so because the situation is for each a different field. Whereas one individual's need for attention may make him see a group of indifferent strangers as an appreciative audience before whom he must show off, another's need for inviolacy may cause him to perceive the members of the same group as hostile critics from whom he must shrink and withdraw. That Napoleon's need for superiority often determined the structure of his fields is revealed in his remark to an attendant prior to the meeting of an Austrian conference. "Carry that chair away before we begin. I have never been able to see a raised chair without wanting to sit in it."

Explorers who have been forced to live on short rations or whose food supplies have become exhausted have often reported their preoccupations at such times with thoughts of food. During the day their conversations have been mostly about food; at night their dreams have been of sumptuous feasts.

In one investigation of the effects of abstinence from food upon imaginal processes, subjects were given, at various intervals after eating, a series of tests in which ambiguous or incomplete material had to be interpreted or completed. With all the tests it was found that, as the interval of time since the last meal increased, the number of interpretations or completions which referred to food also increased. When, for example, the subjects were given a word-association test in which they had to respond to a given word with the first word which came to mind, hungry subjects, more often than others, thought of such words as *spoon, fork, eat, food,* etc. In another test the subjects were asked to tell what was going on in a series of pictures, parts of which had been cut away. In the case of one picture of a child pointing, subjects who were not hungry were likely to interpret this as a child about to strike a key of a typewriter or about to pick up a toy, whereas hungry subjects were inclined to see it as a child about to stick his finger in a pie or in some other way reacting to a food situation.

Under conditions of tension resulting from the frustration of needs other than that for food, tests such as those just described have been used to determine, by an analysis of subjects' responses, something about the relative strength of their needs. Other tests which have been used for the same purpose are: a musical reverie test, in which, while a number of phonograph records are played a subject allows a fantasy to develop which he later reports to the experimenter; an odor imagination test in which, as each of a number of odors is presented, a subject invents some episode or story from the first idea or image which comes to mind upon smelling the odor; and a thematic apperception test in which the subject is presented with a number of pictures and asked to make up a plot or story for which the picture might serve as an illustration. Such tests have been used for the measurement of needs on the assumption that the stronger a need the greater will be its effect in organizing the field. This means that in these tests the stronger needs of the individual determine the content of the fantasies which are evoked and the nature of the interpretations and completions of the material which are made.

Effect on sensitivity. To what extent changes in the field are the result of imagination and to what extent they are the result of changes in the simpler sensory processes is not clear. At least there seems to be some evidence that need may determine an increase in sensitivity. Fasting persons have frequently reported that they are more sensitive to odors and sounds during fasting than at other times, and for such statements there is some experimental confirmation in other sensory fields. In one case it was found that as the fast was prolonged (the fast lasted thirty-one days), the abilities to discriminate two points stimulated tactually on the skin and visually on the retina were increased. Studies of animals and infants, in which the ease of evoking a response is taken as a measure of sensitivity, also indicate an increase of sensitivity to various stimuli under conditions of hunger.

Effect on persistence. If the activity of an individual is interrupted, we should expect, from the definition of need (pp. 163f.), that the residual tension remaining after the interruption would cause the individual to return to the interrupted activity and to attempt again to reach the original goal. A number of experiments have demonstrated precisely this effect.

In one experiment subjects, given a series of simple tasks to perform, were allowed to complete some of them but were interrupted before finishing the others. When, with both completed and interrupted tasks within reach, the subjects were left free to do whatever they desired, it was found that, whereas they almost never took up the completed task again, presumably because their corresponding tensions had been discharged, they resumed the interrupted tasks in about 80 per cent of the cases.

In another investigation subjects were asked to help the experimenter in thinking of words beginning with a certain letter. After writing down as many words as they could think of within the allotted time, some of the subjects were told that they had done unusually well, while others were told that they had done very poorly. The intention of the experiment was to create for some subjects an experience of success and for others an experience of failure. When, two weeks later, the subjects were questioned as to whether they had thought in the interim of words beginning with the assigned letter, there was considerable evidence that they had had great difficulty in keeping their minds off the original task. One subject, who had experienced failure, reported:

> As soon as the experiment was over 'C' words came flooding into my mind. On my way home I felt that I should go insane if I continued to think of them, so I determined to banish them by thinking of other things. At intervals thereafter 'C' words would slip into my thoughts when I was not expecting them, but they gradually ceased coming.[1]

In general the persistence of the activity was greater for those who had felt frustrated in the original experiment, presumably because of the greater unresolved tension which tended to continue the original activity until it was terminated by the fulfilment of the original purpose. We often experience in everyday life the persistence of activities which have failed to reach their goals. Having done poorly in an examination, we continue to think of all the things we should have written but didn't. Worsted in an argument, we can think of nothing but the brilliant things we failed to say.

Experiments such as these, as well as the observation of persisting activities in everyday life, demonstrate that tasks which have been undertaken, like any purpose or intention, set up tendencies within the individual which keep him at work until the goals thus set are attained. It must be noted, however, that in the experiments reported above no conflicting purposes or intentions were aroused, as there might well have been and as there often are in everyday life. These experiments, therefore, offer no guarantee that all human beings will always complete their incompleted tasks if given an opportunity. In some individuals the need for initiating new action may be stronger than the need for finishing work already begun.

Since the residual tensions of incompleted tasks may cause preoccupation with these activities, we should expect to find that incompleted tasks tend to be better remembered than finished ones. This expectation is verified. If subjects are given a series of simple tasks to perform, are allowed to finish one half of them but are interrupted before they have completed

[1] I. Kendig, Studies in perseveration: determining factors in the development of compulsive activity. *J. Psychol.*, 1937, 3, 236.

the other half, and then are asked immediately after the experiment to recall all the tasks which they have attempted, they can recall incompleted tasks almost twice as often as finished ones.

Frustration tolerance. The effects of need upon the behavior and consciousness of the individual depend to a large extent upon the degree of tension in the given case. Some degree of need is necessary for psychobiological adaptation, for otherwise the organism is inert. In order that learning may occur, there must be some degree of tension to reorganize a field, but we have already seen that an excess of tension resulting from a prolonged blocking of a strong need may cause a field to be so grossly distorted, as in the delusions of the insane, that it no longer bears any resemblance to the situation. Tension increased beyond a critical point results in a failure of adjustment of the organism to the requirements of the situation. These facts have suggested the fruitfulness of a concept of *frustration tolerance*, which has been defined as *the amount of frustration which can be borne without a resultant failure in psychobiological adjustment.* The frustration tolerance of an individual is, then, his capacity to stand frustration without distorting his field so that it no longer bears any valid resemblance to the real situation.

The frustration tolerance of an individual is exceeded in all cases in which the increased tension resulting from frustration causes the individual to react inadequately to the situation. If, instead of modifying his behavior in such a way as to effect a satisfaction of his frustrated needs, he reacts with crying, temper tantrums, regression to more primitive behavior or a breakdown of the personality in any of the various forms of mental disorder, the individual's tolerance for frustration has clearly been exceeded.

Just as there is a point beyond which the primary needs, *e.g.*, the need for oxygen, cannot be denied satisfaction without a collapse of the organism, so there is also a point beyond which the secondary needs, *e.g.*, the need for freedom, cannot be frustrated without a breakdown of the individual. One of the important problems of psychology is that of discovering the conditions which determine not only the general frustration tolerance of the individual but also his specific tolerance for the frustration of different needs.

INDIVIDUAL DIFFERENCES IN RESPECT OF NEEDS

The terms with which we characterize individuals are often merely short statements about the need or needs which most often, or at least most obviously, motivate them. When we say of a person, "He's a show-off," we are, in effect, saying that he has a strong need for attention; and when we say of another, "He's a go-getter," we are recognizing in him a strong need for superiority. Such characterizations point to the fact, which we have already noted, that not all the needs of an individual are equally strong, and that the differences among persons are at least in part determined by differences in the relative strength of their needs.

Other differences in personality are determined by differences in the relationships of needs. It is important to know which of an individual's needs are regularly activated in the service of other more important needs. An individual may be motivated to collect rare antiques in order that he may show them off to his friends and thus gain a satisfaction of his needs for attention and superiority. If, however, he does not have the money with which to buy expensive antiques, he may be motivated to gain his goals of attention and superiority in some other way, perhaps by developing and exhibiting athletic skill. We may find at different times different needs serving the dominant need of a given individual. We know, however, a great deal about a person if we know, over a period of time, which needs primarily determine his behavior and which needs are more or less consistently subsidiary to these determinant needs. An important difference among individuals is in respect of the subsidiary relationships which exist among their needs. One person may gain his superiority in one way; another person may gain his superiority in an entirely different way.

There are degrees to which one may be consciously aware of his needs. At one extreme, there may be no awareness of what is needed; one may not even be aware of any tension or uneasiness. At the other extreme one may know precisely what he wants. There are, too, intermediate degrees of awareness where one recognizes that something is lacking, that one is uneasy and dissatisfied, but does not know exactly what is needed. No one is aware of all his needs at all times, but some individuals have much more insight than others in this respect.

A need may fail to be recognized because it is relatively weak in comparison with other needs which for the moment determine the consciousness and behavior of the individual. More important in its consequences for the personality, however, is the failure to recognize a need because it is in conflict with the consciously recognized and accepted needs of the person.

Conflict and repression. Desires and wishes which are felt to be in conflict with the chief aim and accepted goals of the personality are unpleasant and troublesome. Since the satisfaction of such desires results in feelings of guilt and inferiority, one frequently tries to inhibit them. One may do this, not only by denying himself the satisfaction of such needs, but also by doing his best not to think about them at all. Such rejection of impulses felt to be foreign to the personality is known as *repression.* The repression of needs which are in conflict with the accepted and recognized needs of the self does not, however, destroy these needs. Repression merely keeps them from being consciously recognized and satisfied as needs of the personality. They may still continue as tensions which determine the subsequent behavior of the individual. The expression of such repressed needs is not direct, but rather indirect and disguised, an expression the very meaning of which may not be recognized by the person himself.

Some effects of repression. There are many forms of behavior which have come to be recognized as signs of a continued conflict between a repressed need and the repressing forces of the personality. In all such behavior we see the field of the individual excessively distorted from the objective situation. In some cases this distortion is primarily determined by the need which has been repressed, in other cases it is primarily determined by the needs of the personality which have affected the repression, and in still other cases the distortion is determined about equally by the repressed and repressing forces of the personality.

Distortions of the field determined primarily by the indirect and disguised expression of repressed needs may be seen in many aberrations of behavior. The 'old maid' who has repressed all sexual desires may reveal a morbid interest in the love affairs of others, in marriages, in births and especially in all scandals involving sexual misbehavior. Such intense interest in things sexual on the part of one who denies all interest in sex can only be understood as an indirect and disguised expression of repressed sexual desires—"the return of the repressed."

Another common form in which this same need, when repressed, may find indirect and substitute expression is the showering of excessive affection upon some animal—a cat, a dog, a canary. If, on the other hand, the impulses which have been repressed are aggressive and destructive ones, originally aroused by and directed against some person in authority who has frustrated the individual, such impulses may find an indirect and substitute expression in the cruel treatment of some other person or of some animal.

Fantasy, such as that described on p. 171, is another form of behavior in which the tension of a repressed or frustrated need may find indirect and substitute expression. Instead of exciting overt behavior directed to the gaining of an objective superiority, the need excites a fantasy in which the gaining of superiority is subjectively pictured. And similarly other repressed and frustrated needs may find expression and subjective satisfaction in fantasies.

Yet another way in which a repressed or frustrated need

may obtain an indirect and vicarious satisfaction is in the process of *identification*, by means of which an individual through an emotional tie with another person feels and behaves as though he were that person. We tend to identify ourselves with those persons who are obtaining an objective satisfaction of the needs which in us are repressed or frustrated. It is the process of identification which makes us thrill with excitement when Lindbergh flies across the ocean or Byrd across the Pole. In reading and thinking about their exploits we experience a vicarious satisfaction of all those needs which are denied expression in our everyday life. It is through the process of identification that we enter into 'the spirit' of the novel we are reading or the play we are seeing and live for a while in a field which is a flight from reality. In this field we experience a vicarious satisfaction of those needs which in reality are frustrated.

The field of an individual may, however, be determined, not so much by the needs which have been repressed as by the needs which have effected the repression. It often happens that in order to maintain a repression the forces of repression become unduly exaggerated. In such cases we see a marked development of a need and of a trend in the conscious behavior of the individual which is directly opposed to that which has been repressed. Such a development is known as a *reaction formation*. The exaggerated prudishness of the old maid, the overactive, boastful, swaggering behavior of the shy and frightened freshman, and the witty, light-hearted, laughing behavior of the man who has suffered a great sorrow are all examples of reaction formation. The behavior in each case is the result of an exaggerated development of a need which is the opposite of one which has been repressed.

Reaction formations are one type of compensation whereby an individual tries to make up for some lack or defect of the personality. In the development of a reaction formation an individual attempts to defend himself against some need of which he is ashamed and which he has sought to repress, in part, through the development of an opposite need or tendency. Reaction formations may, accordingly, be called *defense compensations.*

Another important type of compensation involves an attempt on the part of an individual to make up for some lack or deficiency. Demosthenes, the stutterer, who in his attempts to master his speech made his task even harder by placing pebbles in his mouth, succeeded finally in becoming one of the world's great orators. Theodore Roosevelt, the sickly child, through hard exercise and rough living became physically strong. Such exaggerated overdevelopment to make up for an initial frustration or insufficiency may be called *deficiency compensation.*

Finally, we must note that some distortions of an individual's field are determined by a continued conflict of repressed and repressing forces of the personality, in which neither the indirect expression of repressed needs nor the overdevelopment of repressing needs primarily determines the distortion.

The clearest example of this type of distortion of a field is seen in what is known as *projection.* In a case of projection a need which is repugnant to the conscious personality and which has consequently been repressed is no longer recognized as one's own but rather is seen as the need or desire of another person. It is as though the need denied in oneself is projected into another. The reformed drunkard who becomes a fanatical prohibitionist sees in others the desire for alcohol which is none other than his own repressed and now projected desire. The old maid who has repressed her erotic desires may complain that men are following her and seeking to abduct her. In such a case it is the person's own repressed desires which are projected into others in whom, in reality, no such desires exist at all.

In cases of projection there is a distortion of an individual's field which serves at one and the same time to satisfy both the repressed and repressing needs. As a result of projection the individual is spared the unpleasantness and self-reproach incidental to recognizing a repugnant need as being his own, while at the same time he is able to feel self-righteous in criticizing and condemning this need in another.

These ways of reacting to conflict and frustration may be observed in the behavior of all of us. Fantasy, reaction formation, projection, etc., are the mechanisms which we all employ in dealing with the persisting tensions of our repressed and frustrated needs. There is nothing abnormal about them, *per se*. It is only when they become exaggerated as the result of tension exceeding the frustration tolerance of the individual that they serve as the basic mechanisms of clearly abnormal behavior.

But whereas these mechanisms are to be found in all individuals they are not present in all in the same degree, and it is seldom that they are all equally important in any one person's reactions to frustration. There is a tendency for some one mechanism to become preferred as a technique for handling tension. Thus, whereas one person may tend to react to frustration with fantasy, another may characteristically react with attempts at compensation. It is upon such preference for one type of reaction in meeting conflict and repression that some of the most interesting differences among individuals are based.

REFERENCES

1. Adams, D. K. A restatement of the problem of learning. *Brit. J. Psychol.* (Gen. Sec.), 1931, 22, 150-178.
2. Katz, D. *Animals and men.* New York: Longmans, Green, 1937.
3. Klineberg, O. *Race differences.* New York: Harper, 1935.
4. Köhler, W. The mentality of apes. New York: Harcourt, Brace, 1925.
5. Lewin, K. *A dynamic theory of personality.* New York: McGraw-Hill, 1935.
6. Mead, M. *Sex and temperament in three primitive societies.* New York: William Morrow, 1935.
7. Murray, H. A., et al. *Explorations in personality.* New York: Oxford University Press, 1938.
8. Rosenzweig, S., et al. Frustration as an experimental problem. *Character & Pers.*, 1938, 7, 126-160.
9. Sherif, M. *The psychology of social norms.* New York: Harper, 1936.
10. Warden, C. J. *Animal motivation.* New York: Columbia University Press, 1931.
11. Young, P. T. *The motivation of behavior.* New York: John Wiley, 1936.

CHAPTER 6

EMOTIONAL AND AFFECTIVE RESPONSES

Emotional behavior, including the affective experience of pleasantness and unpleasantness, forms the basis of human motivation. Accordingly it is understandable that interest in all aspects of emotion is universal. In spite of this interest, however, *scientific knowledge* concerning emotion is neither comprehensive nor overly exact. Since, nevertheless, the more recent developments in psychological methods have been productive of much factual knowledge, emotion is now a rapidly changing and developing chapter in the field of psychology.

NATURE OF EMOTION

Since emotion is a word or a name, there is always the tendency to think that emotion is some *thing*, some discrete, distinct, definable unity. Experiments have uniformly shown that emotion, like perception, cognition and attention, *does not exist as a unique entity*, but that there is a variety of emotional experiences and reactions, just as there is a variety of perceptive experiences, attentive reactions and cognitive experiences. It is also true that such emotions as anger, fear, pity or disgust do not exist in unique independence, but in relation to concrete situations—in such phenomena as fighting reactions or fearfulness, in the experience of pity or of withdrawal from obnoxious objects.

The common characteristics or criteria of emotion are not simple or straightforward. Primarily one thinks of marked or intense pleasantness or unpleasantness (approaching or with-

---

This chapter was written by Carney Landis of the Psychiatric Institute, Columbia University. In it he has incorporated parts of the chapter entitled Pleasantness and Unpleasantness, written by J. G. Beebe-Center for Boring, Langfeld and Weld, *Psychology: a factual textbook*, 1935.

drawing reactions) as pervading emotion, but there are exceptions to this rule. In such a situation as an intense hand-to-hand combat the participant usually experiences neither pleasantness nor unpleasantness during the fight. Reactions under conditions of emotion are commonly not specific but rather involve almost the entire organism. Again there are exceptions. The cautious, well-planned reactions which occur in fearful escapes are narrowly directed upon a particular end. Finally, although emotional experiences or reactions are usually accompanied by some involvement of visceral or organic change, occasional cases occur in which there is a total motor and sensory paralysis below the shoulders, after injury to the spinal cord, with retention of emotional experience and expression. Thus far, in fact, there has been very little experimental verification for a distinct or unique element in any specific portion of the nervous system, nor yet for any particular relationship between nervous impulses which can be labeled as corresponding to the emotional experience.

Thus it seems that emotion can best be characterized as a *relationship existing between many diverse elements of experience and reaction.* This relationship is not well specified, but, generally speaking, it is marked by pleasantness or unpleasantness and by disorganization of usually integrated behavior patterns. An emotion is the total of the experience of an individual during any period of time when marked bodily changes of feeling, surprise or upset occur.

THE DESCRIPTION OF EMOTIONAL BEHAVIOR AND EXPERIENCE

In spite of the great number of literary and dramatic descriptions of emotion that are available, it is not easy to extract material which adequately and accurately pictures emotion. This difficulty is due to the fact that the selection is out of context. *For an emotion to be an emotion it must be part of an entire integrated situation.*

William James has cited many examples of emotional experience drawn from a variety of sources. One which not only describes in small compass the experience of an intense emotion but gives us some insight into the make-up of the emotion itself, runs as follows:

> I remember the night, and almost the very spot on the hilltop, where my soul opened out, as it were, into the Infinite, and there was a rushing together of the two worlds, the inner and the outer. It was deep calling unto deep,—the deep that my own struggle had opened up within being answered by the unfathomable deep without, reaching beyond the stars. I stood alone with Him who had made me, and all the beauty of the world, and love, and sorrow, and even temptation. I did not seek Him, but felt the perfect unison of my spirit with His. The ordinary sense of things around me faded. For the moment nothing but an ineffable joy and exaltation remained. It is impossible fully to describe the experience. It was like the effect of some great orchestra when all the separate notes have melted into one swelling harmony that leaves the listener conscious of nothing save that his soul is being wafted upwards, and almost bursting with its own emotion. The perfect stillness of the night was thrilled by a more solemn silence. The darkness held a presence that was all the more felt because it was not seen.[1]

Another example from the same source, but descriptive of an experience horrible rather than pleasant, is as follows:

> I had such a universal terror that I woke at night with a start, thinking that the Pantheon was tumbling on the Polytechnic school, or that the school was in flames, or that the Seine was pouring into the Catacombs, and that Paris was being swallowed up. And when these impressions were past, all day long without respite I suffered an incurable and intolerable desolation, verging on despair. I thought myself, in fact, rejected by God, lost, damned! I felt something like the suffering of hell. Before that I had never even thought of hell. My mind had never turned in that direction. Neither

[1] W. James, *The varieties of religious experience,* Longmans, Green, 1902, 66; reprinted by permission of the publisher.

> discourses nor reflections had impressed me in that way. I took no account of hell. Now, and all at once, I suffered in a measure what is suffered there.[2]

Another description from a different source is of the emotional outburst of a monkey:

> Sometimes she gazed at the food and at the same time struck the floor with her hand or with a stick. Often she went around touching various objects and at the same time looked up at the food. In case repeated attempts to obtain the food failed, she became more and more affectively disturbed. She went around violently striking the radiator, the floor, or a wooden box, and excitedly uttering a number of sounds. While doing this she again and again looked towards the food. Finally she got into a state of what might be called a 'generalized' affective disturbance, a state in which all reference to the goal was lost. She began throwing things around; she pushed and kicked various objects but she no longer threw them in [the] direction of the goal; she did not even look at the goal. It seemed there was a diffuse discharge of energy instead of one specifically directed towards the goal.[3]

Let us consider certain of the elements with which these examples provide us. In each instance the experience is overwhelming and bewildering. In the human examples the individual finds such difficulty in adequately describing the experience when it is over that usually he resorts to analogy or to terse, exclamatory remarks. His characteristic name for the emotion may be constant, or it may alter diametrically in a very rapid fashion. The experience pervades the entire personality, leaving the individual convinced of its clearness, truth and undeniability. The intensity of the experience is accounted for in part by the total number of elements entering the situation, and in part by the degree to which the individual elements enter. As an entirety the emotional experience is at once overwhelm-

[2] *Ibid.*, 146; reprinted by permission of the publisher.

[3] H. Klüver, *Behavior mechanisms in monkeys,* Univ. of Chicago Press, 1933, 298; reprinted by permission of the publisher.

ing and satisfying, unique and many-in-one, pleasant and unpleasant, integrating and destructive, healthy and unhealthy. It is, however, always a part of an entire situation; never, to the best of our knowledge, does it exist alone or apart in human experience.

EMOTION IN PATHOLOGICAL CONDITIONS

In all disease, but particularly in the various types of nervous and mental disease, we find exaggerations of emotional experience or expression. In *involutional melancholia* or in the depressed phase of the *manic-depressive* insanity, the prevailing affective tone or experience is that of extremely unpleasant depression, unhappiness, anxiety and apprehension. A typical case of acute depression has been described as follows:

> She believed that the world was different; where previously there had been no unhappiness or sin, now all was pervaded by everything horrible and dirty. Food was revolting, dirty, unclean. Her facial expression was one of anxiousness or depression. She agitatedly paced the floor, wringing her hands and vaguely moaned. She believed herself completely changed. Body, mind, and soul were so altered that she was but a weariness to herself. There was nothing to live for, no hope, no joy. It sometimes happened that she would not sleep at all, but would jump in and out of bed, moaning and mumbling about some unpardonable sin. Other nights she would bury her head in the bedclothes refusing to speak, answering questions with a series of pitiful wails. She sometimes spoke somewhat as follows, "Father is dead. He was not my father. The children were all poisoned, my mother was shot. Everyone is good except me—a poor lost sinner. They are waiting to kill me."

Such an individual is experiencing, so far as anyone can tell, a persistent and truly conscious emotional state. The woman herself claims during the period of depression to have a pervasive unpleasant affective feeling; after recovering from one of these periods of depression she will state that her feeling at that time was of the same affective quality as other emotions experienced at other times.

In certain phases of general paralysis of the insane or in the manic episodes of manic-depressive insanity there are periods marked, on the other hand, by a decided sense of well-being (euphoria). When in this condition the patient is unreasonably happy, pervaded with a sense of well-being and buoyant hopefulness, unable to appreciate the depressing events occurring in everyday life. The following is a description of the behavior of such a patient:

> When he arrived at the hospital he said he was leaving Hell and entering Heaven, but he immediately wanted to alter the hospital routine to suit his own desires. He awakened early and sat on the edge of the bed whistling in imitation of the birds outside. When asked by the nurse to be quiet, he sang at the top of his voice, using profane and obscene words in his song. At breakfast he talked continuously, told pointless jokes and got up to dance at intervals. During the morning he hinted by gestures and winks that the nurse was drunk and that he had to watch her very carefully. At lunch he proposed marriage to the waitress, saying that he would divorce his wife and end the gross immoralities of the hospital. He told of his intimate affairs to complete strangers. He maintained that he was the greatest "lady-killer" in the state and went into infinite detail to prove it. He talked of his strength, his wonderful health, his immense wealth. He joked and played silly pranks. It was difficult to get him to go to bed at night since he protested that he was never tired, never needed sleep and that sleep was only for the aged or the ill, whereas he was neither old nor sick.

Except in degree this condition seems to be no different from the normal experience of excessive happiness. In neither the depression nor in the euphoria is there any marked, constant *physiological state* which differentiates this emotional condition from the physiological state of individuals who are not experiencing it.

In *Wilson's disease* the patient shows an uncontrollable laughing or crying. Wilson has thus described such a case:

> Attention was first directed to the emotional change by the fact that when reading of a perfect stranger's death he would begin to weep; with the narration of amusing incidents exaggerated laughing would set in. Under observation bursts of long, uncontrollable, but almost noiseless laughter took place at the veriest trifles. . . . He went off into an apparently interminable series of peculiar hollow laughs, which convulsed the whole ward as well as himself. So facile became the mechanism that he would laugh whenever he began to speak, as though the stimuli of contracting muscles were sufficient to set it off.[4]

Such behavior as this may or may not be accompanied by an appropriate emotional experience. In *Dejerine's disease*, for example, there is frequently an experience of an intense pleasantness or unpleasantness accompanying stimulation applied to an otherwise anesthetic portion of the body. This pleasantness or unpleasantness is referred by the patient to the stimulation, but the experience itself is so unreasonably intense as to be practically unbearable.

These examples of emotional experience and behavior in diseased individuals demonstrate the same relation of emotion to the total personality as was pointed out for normal individuals. In addition, however, several new generalizations are now possible. Emotional experience may be so overwhelming that the patient can judge everything in his surroundings only in terms of his pervading depression or euphoria. Yet even under these conditions the patient himself may be so well aware of the inappropriateness of his expressions that, while outwardly convulsed with laughter, he is inwardly very much embarrassed by his performance. In all these conditions there is latent the possibility that, sooner or later, the patient will recognize how completely the emotion has overwhelmed the rest of his personality. On the heels of such recognition comes a

[4] S. A. K. Wilson, *Modern problems in neurology,* William Wood, 1929, 265; reprinted by permission of the publisher.

tendency for him to speak and think of the experience as though some new and peculiar element had overcome his normal being. All these phenomena indicate that, even though emotion lies at the core of individuality or personality, it is not clearly recognized as such. Thinking back over some emotional crisis, we explain, "It overwhelmed me," characterizing thus the relationship between the emotion and the individual. The emotion, in short, is not thought of as an essential part of the ego. This seeming independence of emotion will appear later in this chapter in other connections.

EXPRESSIVE EMOTIONAL REACTIONS

Since the reactions which occur during emotion are fairly distinct and may be observed and recorded, this portion of the field has invited the greatest amount of experimental investigation. Studies have been made of overt behavior, facial expression, various organic changes and the emotional reactions occurring in disease.

Facial and bodily expression. A number of experimental studies have shown clearly that emotion must be understood and interpreted on the basis of the *total observable material.* Since no emotion, with the exception of startle, has any set pattern of bodily response, a part of the variable pattern is not enough for a correct interpretation of the emotion. The experiments indicate that the more detail there is available, the more accurate the interpretation of the emotion. Concealing the face, the arms or the legs not only modifies the expression which the observer feels is inherent in the posture, but somehow subtracts part of the 'emotion' from the situation.

The most common index of emotion among human beings is facial expression. Indeed, there is a rather well-established, learned language of emotional facial expression. In so many of its aspects is the interpretation of this language universal that it has led many to believe the expressions inherent or inherited. Experimentation has been carried out to establish which, if any, of the patterns of facial or bodily expression are native to all individuals. These studies have shown that, though adults who are acquainted with each other can interpret with relative accuracy the emotional response of their friends and associates, the interpretation of such responses between individuals not known to each other is relatively inaccurate. The most informative work in this respect is that which has been carried out with infants and children.

By means of motion pictures the emotional responses of infants stimulated by hunger, dropping, restraint or pain have been recorded. These pictures of the behavior of the babies were shown first to college students, who named from twelve to twenty-five different emotions as appropriate titles for the reactions to the four situations. When, however, nurses and medical students, familiar with infant behavior, were shown the same photographs, they named only seven or eight emotions. If the films were shown completely, so that the actual stimulation was seen preceding the resultant reaction, there was a great deal more agreement, for the name attached to the response was strongly influenced by a *knowledge of the stimulus*. This same point was evident in another experiment, where the stimulus situations were attached in the films to behavior actually elicited by other situations. These falsified pictures gave rise to interpretations which indicate that the situation preceding the reaction is usually the deciding factor in the name given to the reaction. There is, moreover, little evidence for the belief that anger, fear and love are the three innate patterns of emotional response in infants. Emotional responses vary from child to child as well as from one age level to the next. The important point is that these experiments do *not* show any *innate pattern* of emotional response uniformly apparent in the developing human organism.

In a different experiment the investigator took over twelve hundred photographs of the facial expressions of twenty-five subjects who were exposed to a series of emotional situations. Subsequent analysis of these photographs showed that each individual tended to use certain individual expressions (certain muscles or muscle groups) in practically all his expressive reactions. In these expressions, furthermore, marked individual variations existed. No group of muscles was found to be significantly associated with any single type of stimulation (except surprise), or with any single type of verbal report of emotional experience aroused by the experiment. Smiling, which occurred in one-third of the photographs, was the most common facial reaction. Verbal reports of the emotional experiences indicated that pain, surprise, anger, exasperation, crying, disgust, sex and revolting experiences, in the order named, gave decreasing amounts of expressive movement. The fact that each individual had two or three expressions which appeared in the great majority of his responses to the varying situations and experiences indicates again that the successful interpretation of emotional reactions by an observer must rest in part upon his familiarity with the usual reactions of the subject and in part upon a fairly complete knowledge of the entire situation.

There have been a number of other experimental studies of the conditions and reliability of the interpretation of emotional expression. The findings from these sources indicate that there is, for instance, little agreement among persons asked to interpret the actual crying of infants—to specify, that is, whether they are crying because they are hungry or because they have been dropped or restrained. Nor is there much consistency among the judgments of children who are asked to interpret the emotions conveyed by the sounds of phonograph records of the alphabet recited in tones of fear, anger or happiness. The reliability of such judgments increases with the intelligence of the child making the judgment. In music the vibrato is found almost always to add an emotional coloring to the sound.

Since pronounced emotional reactions are usually accompanied by changes in organic or *visceral* function, many experiments have been conducted in an effort to ascertain the relationship existent between cardiac and circulatory reactions, respiratory responses, the metabolic rate, gastro-intestinal reactions, on the one hand, and emotional experience on the other. Many of these experiments have had as their source the historically famous James-Lange theory of emotion. In brief this theory stated "that *the bodily changes follow directly the perception of the exciting fact, and that our feeling of the same changes as they occur IS the emotion* . . . that we feel sorry because we cry, angry because we strike, afraid because we tremble, and not that we cry, strike, or tremble, because we are sorry, angry, or fearful, as the case may be."[5]

Although there has been a vast amount of experimental research undertaken in the hope of demonstrating a significant relation between visceral change and emotion, positive results have not been clear or frequent. It is true that there is a disturbance of circulation in emotion, but the nature of the circulatory change is neither predictable nor significantly different in different emotions. Admittedly, emotion increases blood pressure; yet the attempts to use this change as an index of emotion or emotionality have proved unreliable. Equally unsatisfactory is the correlation of respiratory changes with emotional states. Again, the rate of metabolism is increased in emotion, but it affords no index by which emotions can be differentiated. Similarly the tone of the gastro-intestinal tract is changed in emotion without the change being specific for particular emotion; in strong emotion gastro-intestinal contractions may even be inhibited. In brief, the visceral changes in emotion lack the specificity which would render them useful in an understanding of the complexities of emotional phenomena.

That these organic responses are very closely interrelated is nevertheless indicated by all studies. Excitement, startle, a mild increase in general activity usually cause an increase in visceral activity. Painful, strong, pronounced stimulation of any variety tends, on the contrary, to interfere with the complicated integration of organic functions. Yet organic responses are generalized, lacking individuality of pattern with respect to the emotion which is being experienced. There are, it is true, pat-

[5] W. James, *Psychology (briefer course)*, Henry Holt, 1892, 375; reprinted by permission of the publisher.

terns of organic response which are peculiar to certain individuals. Certain people manifest one or another pattern of response which is usually associated with one or another emotional experience. Since these are associated, there is a tendency for similar organic reactions in that individual to be interpreted as having a common experiential element. There is, however, no evidence to show any relationship extending from one individual to another with respect to these patterns.

Smiling, laughing and crying. The most clear and well-defined cases of emotional expression are those of smiling, laughing and crying. We uniformly accept the occurrence of this sort of behavior as indicative of emotional experience. Although it is true that this behavior may occur without attendant emotional experience, yet in the ordinary conduct of everyday life smiling, laughing and crying are by common consent regarded as true emotional expressions.

The development of these patterns of response in the infant has been a matter of interest to child psychologists. *Smiling,* for example, is exhibited at a very early age by most children. In the very young infant it is almost invariably brought about by specific stimulation, the response being usually evoked by, or at least exhibited in the presence of, other people. A study of the development of smiling and laughing has shown that originally several varieties of respiratory reactions or compensatory motor mechanisms are elicited by certain situations which the child has not met before and for which he consequently has no immediate appropriate pattern of response. On such occasions a response involving smiling or laughing is approved by the infant's mother or nurse, other respiratory mechanisms disapproved. Since the smiling and laughing are quickly found to be socially acceptable and therefore to lead to reward or comfort, and since they also fill in a certain amount of time during which the infant or child may happen upon some other reaction more appropriate to the situation, the smiling or laughing is 'selected' as socially appropriate. Once they have been socially applied and thus quickly incorporated in the reaction mechanisms of the child—having smoothed over for him some emotional dilemma—this original usage becomes vastly generalized, blending into all the patterns of response which during most of our life we call amusement. Already by the end of the first year of life smiling has become a learned response to an extent which indicates that the smile is now a communicative, adaptive, social reaction rather than a modified respiratory response (see p. 13).

Laughing appears much later in the child's life than smiling, usually after the twentieth week. During the first year of life it is a stereotyped form of behavior. Individual differences between children occur rather in the frequency of smiling or laughing than in the actual form of this behavior.

The behavior of infants during *crying* has been observed experimentally in a series of standard situations. Crying induced by strangers increases in frequency up to about ten months of age. Crying caused by fear or strange situations can be distinguished from other types of response. In the adult, crying, like laughing and smiling, is so bound up with the social reactions of the individual that it is impossible to be certain in a majority of cases whether the response is truly emotional, only partly so, or devoid of emotion.

The observation of adults in situations which produce tears (for example at funerals) shows that tears are usually indicative of a mixed emotional state. Sorrow, dejection, joy and elation, when occurring alone, have but little effect in producing tears. Adult crying occurs in the main only when there is some redeeming feature, followed by pleasant or alleviating stimulation, in an otherwise depressing or unpleasant situation.

Laughter involves a variety of psychological problems. We have the laughter of joy, the laughter of comedy, laughter as a form of social phenomenon, laughter as a release from tension and laughter under pathological, organic or mental conditions. All these involve different psychological elements. The joyful laugh, which is a bubbling over of good humor, is commonly indulged in by children or by adults when in a state of well-being. The comic laugh is directed *at* some joke or ludicrous situation. The entire problem of wit and humor is one which has held the interest of philosophers and psychologists for centuries. There is no one major line of explanation to cover all laughing at the comic. The problem of laughter is a social phenomenon involving many facts of social psychology. We laugh more easily in a group than when alone, for laughter is a variety of gesture language. The act of laughing may be at times a communication of good will and a spirit of fun, at others of pure joy and at still other times of embarrassment.

The laughter which is associated with a relief of tension has been explained on an evolutionary basis. Since the facial musculature is not primarily necessary to the active energetic preservation of life, the excess energy set up by emotional stimulation is drained off by the activity of the facial and respiratory musculature in a way which does not interfere with any activity of the body going on at the time.

Anger and fear. The behavior—of either animals or men—which by common consent is called *anger* and rage is usually agreed upon by observers as a definitely interpretable form of expressive reaction. Actually the expressive reactions of anger and fear are but little different so far as the *bodily responses* are concerned. The real differences between these two presumably opposite emotional states rest in the *total situation* which arouses the states. Reactions occurring during offense, attack and positive movements are usually called anger; those during defense and retreat, fear.

In the child, fear and anger are sometimes studied from the standpoint of the *preparedness of the organism.* Though such preparedness or excitement is originally undifferentiated, it becomes more distinctive and varied as the individual grows older. Finally, partly through maturation and partly through learning, it develops into socialized emotion.

The condition which arouses *anger* in young children is a situation that, instead of being a sudden call for action, is often a more or less sudden stoppage or *interference with action.* Interference with activity, especially activity motivated by the common urges or drives, is an essential criterion of the anger-producing situation. The anger responses in the child are outbursts of impulsive activity—kicking, stamping, slashing about with the arms, and often a prolonged holding of the breath. With increasing age the anger becomes more overtly focused upon a given end. Along with a decrease in the proportion of outbursts consisting of mere displays of undirected energy comes an increase in the frequency of retaliative behavior. The percentage of observable after-reactions, such as resentfulness and sulkiness, increases steadily with advancing age.

The stimuli for *fear* may be regarded as suddenly confronting the individual with certain changes in the total situation, changes requiring a sudden new adjustment which he is unprepared to make. Among the changes which are fear-producing for the very young infant are those which substitute loud sounds or loss of bodily support for his previous quiet, comfortable bodily balance. With the development of the child and the widening of his perceptual life, many things occur to surprise or frighten him, because he perceives that they are new and unusual. Fear arises when so much is known to the individual that he recognizes the potential danger of a situation without, however, having a complete apprehension or control of that situation.

The overt reaction to fear changes with the growth of the child. He comes to substitute a more adequate specific response for his earlier undifferentiated panic. As the child grows older, there is likewise a development of greater variety in response. In place of screaming, crying or rigidity, the child tries running away or partially withdrawing from the fearful situation. At a sudden noise or fall he now substitutes exclamations and laughter. Gradually a more or less indifferent adjustment—one, that is, without accompanying emotion—supersedes the panic.

Both anger and fear responses are easily attached to a new stimulus (see pp. 203-206). The emotional responses thus quickly established may be altered by appropriate training or may persist over long periods of time. Fear, for example, may be counteracted by the appropriate association of a pleasant stimulus with the old fearful stimulus.

Various investigators have shown that the control of anger and fear is closely associated with the development of intelligence. The emotional outbursts indulged in by defective children occur less frequently in higher intellectual levels as measured by intelligence tests.

The nature of adequate stimuli for anger and fear and the form of response are in the adult very diverse, as the following description of the anger responses of college students indicates:

> The causes or stimuli which arouse anger range all the way from a thwarting of a desire to do nothing, to the interference with a desire to do everything. The impulses felt during anger range from a desire to injure, and even kill the offender, to serious self-injury, and from flight to fight. The responses during anger may be dominantly verbal, physiological, psychological, or social in nature, and may range from a pleasant reply to doing violence to the offender. The after-effects range from a very reduced self-feeling to feelings of exalted self-importance.[6]

Love reactions. Under this heading we may consider such diverse manifestations of behavior and experience as the parent-child relationship, the protecting reactions and the appreciation of protection, friendship, attachment between the sexes, attachment to places, to things, to occurrences or to food. According to Freud the central urge or drive of life is the *libido*, this libido being wholly sexual in nature—applying the term sex in its widest sense. If Freud is correct, we have a reasonable explanation for the tremendous resistance to experimental investigation which is found with respect to these reactions. For if life itself is, as he maintains, thus intimately bound up with libidinal reactions, experimental investigation of the subject from a psychological point of view can be compared only to a physiological study of the reactions of the heart by means of human vivisection. It is, moreover, self-evident that these responses are surrounded by an extensive and formidable defense of social custom, law and taboo. That these taboos and

[6] H. Meltzer, Students' adjustments in anger, *J. soc. Psychol.*, 1933, 4, 306.

customs are constantly being broken by the individual and even altered by a whole population has been shown by various studies of the sex life of the normal individual. These investigations reveal that practically every individual experiments with these 'love responses' outside the realm of the so-called socially approved reactions. They also show that, for the most part, these experiments of the individual have but little permanent effect upon the total personality.

Since this general subject is so strongly guarded by social custom, practically all the experimental work in the field has been done upon animals. The studies which have been made on the development of patterns of sex behavior and maternal protection in the rat prove that here, at least, we have a type of very complicated and somewhat varying behavior, appearing spontaneously and without learning, at the time when the animal becomes sexually mature and subsequently when the first litter is born.

Surprise or startle. The one consistent exception to the general statement that there is no fixed, innate pattern of facial or bodily emotional reaction is surprise or the *startle pattern.* If an individual is stimulated by a sudden loud sound, flash of light, intense odor, etc., there occurs a very rapid response pattern. The rapidity of this action suggests that the response is "the bodily change which follows directly the perception of an exciting fact," as the James-Lange theory requires. Unfortunately for the theory, however, all emotions do not portray this characteristic. Many types of reaction which we call emotions cannot be explained in so simple a fashion.

By means of high-speed motion-picture photography the response to the sound of a pistol shot has been intensively studied. Cameras running as fast as 2000 exposures per second have permitted the very exact analysis of this pattern. Figure 10 is a schematic drawing showing the elements of the pattern. The response consists of a sudden movement of the head, blinking of the eyes, a characteristic facial expression, raising and drawing forward of the shoulders, turning inward of the upper arms, bending of the elbows, turning downward of the forearms, flexion of the fingers, forward movement of the trunk, contraction of the abdomen and bending of the knees. Not all these elements occur in every individual every time he is stimulated. Elements in the response which are opposed to any of these reactions, however, rarely if ever occur. Present evidence leads us to believe that, within limits, completeness of appearance of the pattern is closely related to the intensity of the stimulus; mild stimuli give only the eye-blink, intense stimuli the complete pattern.

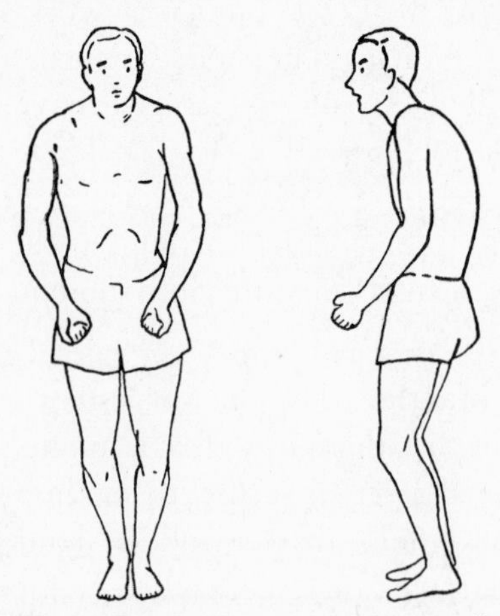

FIG. 10. SCHEMATIC SKETCH OF THE STARTLE PATTERN.

After C. Landis and W. A. Hunt, *The startle pattern,* copyright 1939; reprinted by permission of Farrar & Rinehart, Inc.

It has been shown also that this response becomes habituated rapidly in some individuals and very slowly in others. After a long series of stimuli the eye-blink and certain elements of the facial contortion still persist in practically every individual, although most other elements of the pattern will have dropped out. The pattern, which can be elicited in very early infancy, does not change in its form throughout life. It appears in all the higher animal forms. In certain diseases it is exaggerated, whereas in epilepsy it is totally absent in about one-fifth of the patients.

This startle response is of particular interest in the field of emotion, in that it is probably the initiating element of many emotional reactions of a type fairly widespread but easily seen and described. Since this pattern is usually over in one-half second after it is started, many persons, though certain that they had made some response, are unable, because of its rapidity, to say exactly what it was. Hence, they have insisted that an emotion is somehow innate. If this argument is correct, then the initial portion of the emotion, that is, the startle pattern, is a fixed innate reaction pattern, whereas all the following reactions are so diverse and so modified by learning processes that any close descriptive classification is impossible.

Other emotional reaction patterns. *Pain* is basically a *sensory* phenomenon, yet it sets up many emotional responses. A physical injury with its resultant pain leads to a diversity of responses, all of which are directed either to avoiding, removing or enduring the stimulation. Biologically, the emotional element in pain is probably associated with the complex conscious experiences grouped under the term *self-preservation.* The association of painful stimulation with almost any type of previously neutral stimulation will lead to an associated emotional reaction, which thereupon becomes attached to the stimulus previously neutral in emotional content. For this reason the phenomena of pain, although sensory in quality, complicate practically all the psychological reactions of an individual.

The experiences of *hunger* and *thirst* result from the absence of food and water, respectively. Persistence of these primarily physical sensations leads to a series of responses which may be termed emotional, since they partake in nature of all the criteria which have been used to describe emotional reactions. These responses, diverse in nature, are accompanied by extensive pleasant or unpleasant reactions and by marked changes in the usual visceral rhythms. Since the responses are complicated by a prominent and definite sensory element, they usually have not been regarded as of immediate emotional importance.

Other so-called emotional reaction patterns, such as disgust, contempt, pity, sympathy, jealousy or depression have been listed by various investigators as emotional reactions or as emotions. Little or no evidence exists today which would indicate that there is anything unique psychologically in any of these experiences or responses. In every case it seems that the name is one which is assigned to some particular configuration or type of situation. The elements which can enter into the configurations, however, are extremely varied.

EMOTIONAL EXPRESSION AS A FORM OF LANGUAGE

It was demonstrated many years ago that posed photographs of expressions of emotion can be fairly accurately named. Later investigators have shown that this ability to attach a name to a photograph of an emotional expression increases with the developing mental age of the individual. Still other investigators have pointed out that, whereas some expressions are easily and fairly accurately named, others are very difficult to interpret. A great deal of individual difference has been found among judges making such interpretations. Some people are good judges of emotional expressiveness, others are not.

More recently a study has been made of samples of behavior recorded by means of motion pictures. Various groups of trained and untrained observers were shown the pictures and asked to rate or describe the various aspects of the personality of the individual who had been photographed. These judgments were found to vary in three ways: with the judge, with the subject who had been photographed and with the aspects of the personality or of emotionality that were being judged. Judges who had a strong interest in either art or dramatics were more successful than those with an interest in science and philosophy. As to the subjects, those who were introverted, in the sense of having an aptitude for contemplative observation and for self-analysis, tended to be least accurately judged.

All of this goes to show that behavior and particularly facial expression serve as a method for the communication of feelings or emotion. The whole process, both of conveying the information and of receiving the information, is learned in much the same way that spoken language is acquired. The language of expression is never, however, completely stereotyped or regular so far as any one individual is concerned. Furthermore, just as one person is more fluent in speech than another, so one individual may be much more expressive emotionally (in the sense of language communication) than is another. The actor, either in the spoken drama or in motion pictures, has done much to bring regularity and uniformity into this type of communication. Studies made of Oriental peoples show that, just as spoken Chinese differs from spoken English, so does much of the emotional expressiveness of the native Chinese differ from the corresponding expressiveness of the American.

In understanding and interpreting this variety of communication, the better the subject and judge are acquainted, the more accurate will be the interpretation. Since each individual has a certain set of expressions which he uses to convey emotional feelings and which are not always in common usage, intimate acquaintanceship makes the judgment much more reliable.

Certain of these language expressions are related to some basic muscular organizations which *tend* to accompany real emotion. For example, the facial contortions in physical pain and in mental anguish are much the same. On the other hand, the facial expressions of reverence or awe are completely socialized acquisitions seemingly unrelated to any particular emotional behavior or feeling which might be occasioned by thoughts of the deity or by tremendous respect.

DERIVED EMOTION

In addition to the more conventional systems of emotional response there are several other well-recognized secondary emotional reaction systems or experiences. These *secondary systems* are called *derived emotion.* By this term we mean the response derived from some relatively simple direct primary occurrence that has undergone changes similar to those in the learning process. At some time, some situation has called forth either a very intense or a repetitive emotional response appropriate to that situation. At the same time other secondary elements in the stimulus situation came more or less to the attention of the individual undergoing the experience. In some fashion the emotional elements of the total experience became attached to the secondary elements of the situation. Frequently the fact that such an attachment has taken place is not even consciously perceived by the individual; yet as a result of the changes, the affective or emotional part of the entire experience becomes 'free' from the original primary response and either exists as a *free floating affect* or becomes consciously attached to some new and possibly inappropriate reaction system. Anxieties, phobias, compulsions and obsessions are varieties of derived emotion.

Anxiety is a psychological experience which may be described as ranging from mild worry or apprehension to acute fear. It is distinguished from fear, which is a response to a primary stimulus, by the fact that it is attached to any system of reactions, either appropriate or inappropriate. Anxiety is that pervading worry or apprehension which colors all the emotional life of the individual without seeming to belong to anything in particular. It is the feeling of being worried without anything to worry about.

Anxieties have been produced experimentally only during or after hypnosis. During deep hypnosis it is possible to suggest to the subject that, although he will be unable to remember why it is that he is worrying, he will nevertheless be worried about some very inappropriate fear when he comes out of the hypnosis. Artificial anxiety of this sort corresponds rather closely to the anxieties which we find in pathological cases. Usually anxiety is explained as the persisting in consciousness of some pervasive fear long after the primary cause of that fear has disappeared.

Anxiety very frequently has a profound effect upon the *physiological functions* of the individual. Persistent respiratory, circulatory, digestive or muscular disturbances may occur. Chronic fatigue accompanied by insomnia is also common.

The effect of anxiety on *psychological functions* is to lower the general acuity and completeness of response. Although the individual still reacts, he does so either in a preoccupied fashion, paying attention to only part of what is going on around him, or inadequately, as though he were fatigued or had insufficient energy to meet the demands of the situation. Since anxiety is a rather common human experience, a great deal of medical work has been done in the attempt to control or alleviate it. Generally speaking, if in one way or another the anxious individual can be made to discover the original connection between his anxiety and its primary or original cause, he will be able either to free himself of the anxiety or to control it in a satisfactory fashion.

Phobias differ from anxiety in that they are more intense fear reactions. In anxiety, moreover, the feeling of fear is not attached to anything in particular, whereas in a phobia it has some special reference—a closed room, crossing the street, dislike of certain foods and so on. Phobias, like anxieties, occur without apparent reason. Also like anxieties, phobias can be produced hypnotically.

Generally speaking, the phobias are more difficult to deal with than are anxieties. With the fear thus attached to some point of reference and become so much a part of the individual, it seems unreasonable to him not to be afraid. Very frequently this attachment is of symbolic nature. For example, in the case of an individual unreasonably afraid of crossing streets, prolonged investigation may show that basically this patient has been very much wrought up with the fear of death and has attached the entire emotional experience to the hazards of the pedestrian. Once these intermediate steps have been forgotten, he no longer remembers that originally his fear was a general dread of death rather than a specific, unreasonable fear of crossing an open street.

Compulsions differ from phobias in that they are unreasonable tendencies directed toward some sort of positive action rather than away, as is the case in the negative reaction of fear. Here the individual reacts positively toward some incident or class of incidents which have been emotionally disturbing to him. Even though he may recognize the unreasonableness of his action, he finds it difficult—at times even impossible—to control. For example, if the patient who was afraid of crossing the street reacted by saying that he felt it necessary to puncture the tires of automobiles parked along the side of the street, we would say that he was suffering from a compulsion derived from his phobia.

The derived emotional experience of *apathy* is somewhat different from the other varieties just discussed. In apathy the individual exhibits few adequate or appropriate emotional reactions. We see this condition most clearly in patients suffering from *dementia praecox*. Here the patient fails to respond in any adequate emotional fashion to situations ordinarily productive of fear, anger, love, reward, etc. In any of these situations his responses are shallow and 'silly'; he will giggle or make some foolish statement without giving any evidence of having real feeling about the situation. This loss of emotion is quite as marked as are the euphoria and the depression which we have previously described. A common explanation of these apathies is that the individual protects himself against all varieties of emotional experience by fantasy and daydreaming. He does not attend to conditions that are sufficient to produce emotional reactions in a normal individual. His mind dwells rather upon ideas and thoughts capable of distracting his attention from circumstances which might prove emotional. It can be shown, indeed, that these apathetic individuals will respond emotionally if the stimulation is strong enough to get by their distracting fantasy. Of all the derived emotions, however, the apathetic condition is the most pathological and the most difficult with which to deal.

This discussion of derived emotion indicates that the emotional experience of the individual must be kept integrated with all the other reactions and experiences of that person. Any process which tends to break away emotional reactions from their appropriate system of reference creates difficult problems of psychological adjustment.

PLEASANTNESS AND UNPLEASANTNESS

The pleasant and unpleasant feelings in conscious experiences are called *hedonic tone.* If there is a single psychological characteristic which marks or pervades all emotional life it is this one. Hedonic tone varies in a single continuous scale from unpleasantness through indifference to pleasantness; we regard pleasantness and unpleasantness as being mutually opposed or as excluding each other. It is possible, in fact, to construct a scale from negative unpleasantness to positive pleasantness; for example, very unpleasant is given a value of —3; unpleasant, —2; moderately unpleasant, —1; indifferent, 0; moderately pleasant, + 1; pleasant, + 2; and very pleasant, + 3. Experiments have shown that it is possible for individuals to judge accurately hedonic tone on such a scale.

Hedonic tone can be understood by a study of internal and external conditions which determine it. *Internal conditions* are such factors as learning or motivation; *external conditions* are the situations which set up the pleasantness or the unpleasantness. The study of external conditions has yielded a great deal of factual material in experimental investigations.

In the study of external conditions a distinction is made between primary and secondary stimuli. The *primary stimulus* is that part or aspect of the total situation to which conscious attention is given and which seems to the individual to be the actual stimulus. *Secondary stimuli* refer to all the rest of the effective stimulation. When a green square of paper is said to be the hedonic stimulus, it is usually only the primary stimulus, the immediate object of attention. The secondary stimuli include all the visible surroundings of the square, the preceding visual stimulation and such auditory or tactual stimuli as accompany the primary stimulus.

Hedonic summation. When two simple stimuli are combined as a total perception, the hedonic tone of the combination depends upon the sum of the hedonic tones for each of the two stimuli. For example, if two colors are equally pleasant, their combination is twice as pleasant as either of them. This principle must, however, be limited. It holds only when it can operate without the interference of other hedonic factors such as contrast, and when the relative importance of the different stimuli in the total is demonstrated and taken into account. It does not hold for a rapid succession of stimuli, either visual or auditory, since they become involved in complexities of their own, forming new expressions different from that of the combination.

Intensity as a condition of hedonic tone. Pleasantness and unpleasantness tend to vary with the intensity of the stimu-

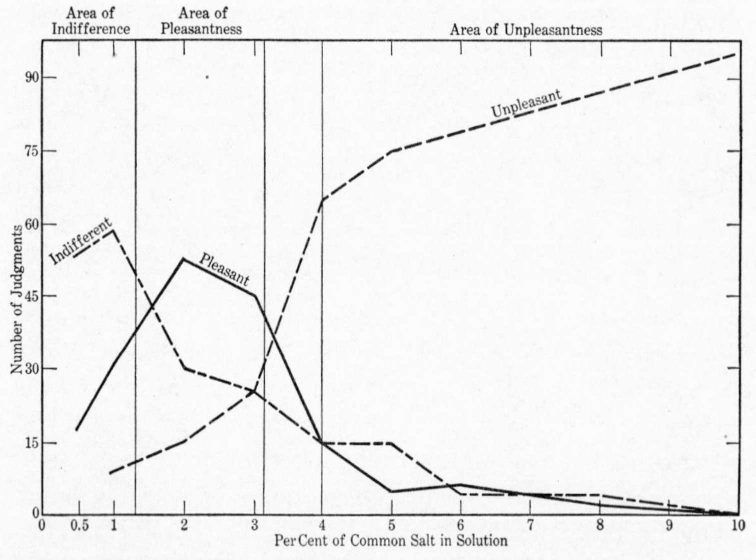

Fig. 11. Hedonic Tone of Common Salt (Sodium Chloride) Solutions as a Function of Strength of Stimulus.

Seven observers in seven sittings. The figure shows also the ideal stimulus-ranges for pleasantness and unpleasantness. After Engel.

lus. As the intensity increases, hedonic tone increases to a maximum of pleasantness, and then decreases, passing through indifference to great unpleasantness for very intense stimuli.

Figure 11 shows this function for stimuli to the primary taste of salt. Similar curves have been obtained for the other taste qualities and in other sense categories. There are occasional exceptions to this rule; sugar at maximal concentration, for example, is not greatly unpleasant. Moreover, certain weak stimuli are unpleasant of themselves. The biological importance of this general rule of intensity is, however, obvious—since intense stimuli tend to be dangerous, unpleasantness acts a warning.

Quality as a condition of hedonic tone. Exact information is lacking concerning the effect of the quality of the stimulus upon pleasantness or unpleasantness because in most of the experiments the intensity of the stimulus has not been adequately controlled. Color, tone, taste, touch and smell, for example, are all altered in different ways, qualitatively, as intensity varies. Generally speaking, saturated colors are preferred to unsaturated; red and blue are considered pleasant, yellow least pleasant. Certain combinations of tones have different affective values, the musical interval of the major third usually being considered the most pleasant and the interval of the minor second the least pleasant. Sweet is almost always called pleasant and bitter unpleasant. Although other types of cutaneous sensibility have differing degrees of hedonic tone, pain is notoriously unpleasant.

Dependence of the hedonic tone upon secondary stimuli. As previously noted, the primary stimulus—the stimulus in the focus of the subject's attention—is not the only stimulus which influences affectivity. When one attends to one of a pair of colors, the hedonic tone of the pair is influenced principally by the color to which he attends, but the other color also has some effect. There is evidence that the pleasantness or unpleasantness of a stimulus may be altered by simultaneous stimulation of even a different sense category. The most striking evidence of the effect of secondary stimulation is the way in which the hedonic tone of a present stimulus depends upon past stimulation.

This is the principle of *hedonic contrast.* The pleasantness of a given stimulus depends upon the hedonic tone of the preceding stimuli. If a stimulus belongs to a certain group of stimuli on one occasion, and to a more pleasant group on another occasion, then this stimulus will be less pleasant on the second occasion. This kind of hedonic contrast exists among colors or odors, but it does not occur from one sense department to another. The mutual effects of stimuli upon one another persist for relatively long intervals of time once such a unitary group is established. A color which in many situations would be only moderately pleasant can be made either more pleasant or less pleasant by grouping it with pleasant or unpleasant combinations—an effect which will continue for several days after the original grouping has been set up.

Hedonic contrast is an example of the general principle of relativity of judgment familiar to everyone. Suppose, for example, a man finds the food at a given restaurant so extremely unpleasant that he declares it the worst food he has ever eaten. But subsequently, if he eats at a cheap boarding house where the food is even worse, it will now seem to him that this present fare is really the worst food he has ever eaten. Should he return to the restaurant under these conditions, the food will seem much better—so long as he does not forget about the food at the boarding house. If, however, he forgets about the boarding house, then the table at the restaurant is likely to become again less and less attractive.

The same relationships work out at the other end of the scale. Our present pleasures fade before still greater ones; nor do the still greater ones remain 'still greater,' but become simply the maximum of which the particular person is capable. This is one of the reasons why wealth does not assure happiness.

Relation of hedonic tone to response. There is a general belief that pleasantness or unpleasantness gives rise to, or is at least associated with, certain muscular movements. In an experiment devised to determine the response to hedonic stimuli under conditions where movement on the part of the subject was not possible, it was found that a pleasant stimulus led to muscular relaxation and an unpleasant one to muscular tension. This situation seems to correspond to the passive enjoyment of pleasant objects and to the restlessness and strain in unpleasant situations where activity is restricted or useless. Under conditions where the subject was left free to move, however, and the stimulus was moving past him, then a pleasant stimulus provoked actual approach and an unpleasant stimulus actual withdrawal.

The entire matter is evidently tied up with the problems which have been raised in the *theories of hedonic action.* Such theories assume that hedonic tone *determines* action. Some hold that present action depends upon the part played by the hedonic tone in the *past* when the action was learned; others hold that present action is directly in accordance with *present* hedonic tone; still others maintain that action is determined with respect to the hedonic tone anticipated in the *future.* All the theories depend on the correspondence of pleasantness with seeking, approach and acquisition; and the correspondence of unpleasantness with avoidance, withdrawal and rejection. There can be little doubt that we are facing here a fundamental fact, although it is complicated and limited in innumerable ways in adult human life.

Dependence of learning upon hedonic tone. Hedonic tone depends upon learning, and conversely, learning, in part, upon hedonic tone. Because pleasantness seems to make learning more permanent, pleasant events are likely to be best remembered. This relationship between learning and hedonic tone is one which has received a great deal of attention in educational psychology. A child who likes candy learns to like the aunt who gives him candy: hedonic tone depends upon learning. Similarly, the child learns the multiplication table because the aunt, whom he now likes, teaches it to him and gives him the pleasure of her approval as a reward: learning depends upon hedonic tone. By such transfers of hedonic value it might be possible to make a lover of candy into a mathematician—provided certain other capacities were available.

Another case of the dependence of pleasantness or unpleasantness upon learning is to be seen in the 'transfer' of emotions and hedonic tone. The classical example from the experimental literature is that of the infant who was accustomed to play happily with a white rat. After the rat and an unpleasant stimulus had been presented simultaneously and repeatedly, however, the child learned to be afraid of his former playmate and to greet the rat with crying and with vigorous movements of avoidance.

There is evidence from the psychological laboratory that pleasantness is conducive to good memory. Pleasant objects and situations are usually more readily recalled than unpleasant ones. Likewise, association experiments show that associations come more rapidly for pleasant than for unpleasant words. Asked to recall the events from some particular period of time, like a summer vacation, people report more pleasant than unpleasant items. Diaries also show that more happy than unhappy events are immediately recorded.

Not only does pleasantness reinforce learning, but unpleasantness hinders learning. For this reason either *reward* or *punishment* may be used in the establishment of a learned response. Experiments with animals show that the task which is followed by the greater reward or by lesser punishment is the task that is learned most rapidly and effectively. Furthermore, the reward or punishment is more effective the more immediate it is (see pp. 292f.).

NEURO-HUMORAL FACTORS IN EMOTIONAL REACTIONS

It has been pointed out previously in this chapter that much research has been reported, in which the relationship between emotional processes and physiological changes has been studied.

The physiological integration of the living organism is dependent on the functional activity of the nervous system and on the chemical interchanges accomplished through the blood and lymph systems. The nervous system is anatomically divided into the *central, peripheral* and *autonomic* divisions. (The central and peripheral divisions will be described in Chapter 7.) The action of the *autonomic* division together with the secretions of the *endocrine* (ductless) glands consti-

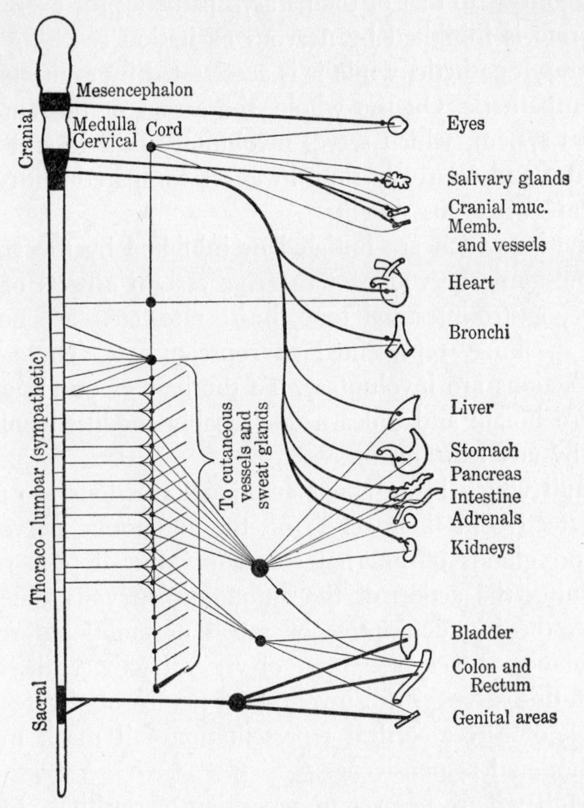

Fig. 12. Schematic Diagram of the Autonomic Nervous System.

tute the neuro-humoral system which, to a large degree, controls the visceral or vegetative functions of the body. It is through the action of this biologically more primitive system that those bodily functions which have to do with the direct physical control of internal bodily integration are maintained.

The autonomic nervous system is essentially a nerve net of interconnections. Anatomically, it is divided into the *sympa-*

thetic and *parasympathetic* divisions. The parasympathetic division is composed of the cranial and sacral sections. A schematic diagram of the interrelations of these divisions and their relationship to the various bodily organs is shown in Fig. 12.

Generally speaking, the activity of the sympathetic division is antagonistic to that of the parasympathetic; for example, the heart rate is inhibited by nervous excitation reaching it over the parasympathetic, while it is accelerated by excitation from the sympathetic. On the whole, the action of the autonomic nervous system, which serves involuntary muscle and glands, is diffuse and relatively slow in effect compared with that of the central nervous system.

Activities which are initiated or inhibited by the action of the autonomic nervous system—*e.g.*, certain aspects of bodily posture, gastro-intestinal tone, heart rate, etc.—are not, generally speaking, represented in consciousness. These actions and reactions are involuntary. To the best of our knowledge they are innate and unlearned, probably modified only indirectly by any learning process.

Stimuli which bring about emotional reactions are particularly effective in their action on the autonomic nervous system and glands of internal secretion. Most of our remarks concerning the action of the autonomic nervous system are, in fact, directly descriptive of much of emotional reaction. The balance or lack of balance of visceral activity, the diffuseness of this activity, the involuntary nature of the responses, the lack of direct cortical representation—all mark much of our emotional responsiveness.

Though we are not yet in a position to say that emotional reactions are uniformly identifiable with the action of the neuro-humoral mechanisms, there is good reason to believe that much of emotion, as it is conceived of in the biological sciences, is mediated particularly by the action of the autonomic nervous system and the endocrine glands.

The endocrine glands are secretory organs or tissues which throw their product directly into the blood stream. The *adrenal glands* are known to be directly involved in the physiological expression of emotion. Two forms of secretion are produced by these glands: that of the *medulla* of the gland, which is called *adrenin*, and that of the *cortex* of the gland, which is called *cortin*. Cortin has, among other things, the function of maintaining the oxygen-carrying power of the blood. It is absolutely necessary for the life of the organism. Emotional stimulation leads to the secretion of adrenin, an excess of which in the blood stream brings about what have been characterized as emergency reactions of biological survival value.

That adrenin is secreted directly into the blood stream during emotional stimulation has been demonstrated by Cannon and his co-workers. An increase in the amount of adrenin in the blood has the following effects upon physiological activity: (1) it increases the tremor in voluntary muscle; (2) it causes relaxation of smooth muscle; (3) it counteracts fatigue in voluntary muscle by affecting the neuromuscular junction; (4) it alters blood distribution; (5) it alters blood pressure; (6) it hastens the rate of clotting of the blood; (7) it relaxes the bronchioles; (8) it causes the liver to release glycogen into the blood stream; and (9) it causes the spleen to secrete or release red blood corpuscles into the blood stream. All these physiological changes brought about by adrenin may be considered emergency reactions which prepare an organism to meet situations calling for the quick and probably prolonged discharge of energy. Although these reactions do not offer specific patterns of response which enable one to differentiate emotions, they do furnish a background for emotion in general.

Several investigators have studied the effect of the direct injection of adrenin into normal and abnormal adults. In many instances they found that the individual reported merely the resultant physiological disturbance, which in those cases seemed devoid of emotional experience. Other persons experienced what has been called a 'cold emotion.' That is to say, they had an experience which they felt was somehow emotional in nature, although no situation to justify the experience was at hand. A few individuals reported true, satisfactory emotional experiences subsequent to the injection of the adrenin. Sometimes the experience was so clearly that of anxiety, apprehension, fear or anger that the subject could detect no difference between his experience and any other emotional experience which he had had.

The *thyroid gland* lies in front of the upper part of the trachea. As we have already learned (see p. 54), its internal secretion is known as *thyroxin*. Although there is no experimental work to show that thyroxin is secreted directly in response to emotional stimulation, it is probable that such secretion does take place. We know that in goiter (a diseased condition of the thyroid gland) a marked emotional instability of the patient occurs. Such patients not only over-react to practically any situation involving pain or an emergency, but are in a state of heightened tension and irritability practically all the time. In other diseased conditions in which the thyroid gland is not functioning at a normal rate we find a marked decrease or absence of emotional expression or responsiveness. The patient is stolid, stuporous or sluggish. It would seem that the thyroid secretion sets up a physiological background for emotional response.

The internal secretion of the *gonads* (sex glands) is known to be directly connected with sexual desire and sexual experiences. Actual experimental work on this subject has, however, never been carried out with human beings. The *pituitary* gland, located at the base of the brain, is the controlling or master gland of internal secretion. Through its mediation the functional activity of all other endocrine glands is believed to be controlled. Undoubtedly diminished function of the pituitary leads to disturbance in the emotional life as well as in the general personality of an individual. Since this gland is so intimately connected with all other glands, as well as the nervous system, it is difficult to isolate its direct function.

On the basis of the studies of the effect of adrenin and the action of the sympathetic nervous system Cannon has proposed an *emergency theory of emotion*. Briefly stated, this theory holds that emotion is essentially a preparatory reaction of the organism, of biological survival value in times of danger. According to this theory all these physiological responses are associated with the biological preservation of the organism and with the defense of the organism against attack.

The role of the thalamus. The unique psychological experience in feeling or emotion has been attributed by various investigators to patterns of response depending upon nervous activity mediated through the *thalamus*. The thalamus is a region in the center of the brain where many pathways are relayed to and out of the central nervous system (see p. 238). Also located in this area are many nuclei involved in the control of the vegetative functions of the organism. The notion is that there is some specific center or combination of centers in the thalamus which may be responsible not only for the facial and bodily expression of emotion, but also for the feelings which accompany affective reactions. We know that when all the brain of a cat above the thalamus is destroyed, any general stimulation leads to an exhibition of 'pseudo-rage.' Likewise, direct stimulation of this area in the thalamus in the intact cat also leads to rage. Human beings suffering from diseases which affect the thalamus occasionally show types of overexpressiveness which we have described above in the discussion of Wilson's disease. All this evidence suggests that certain nervous units in the thalamus have something to do with the organization of emotional expression or emotional experience. The fact that animals other than the cat fail to show this 'pseudo-rage' and the fact that additional clinical observation shows these overexpressive emotional reactions often occurring in cases where there is no involvement of the thalamus lead one to be cautious in generalizing. We may safely conclude that the thalamus is connected with emotional expression and experience. The manner of the connection, however, and the way in which the organization in the nervous system is set up are not at present understood.

MEASUREMENTS OR TESTS OF EMOTION

Much of this work has been centered upon the organic reactions of the circulatory, respiratory or gastro-intestinal systems or metabolic changes.

The galvanic skin response. In 1888 the French scientists, Vigouroux and Féré, called attention to the fact that, when electrodes are placed on the skin and attached to the proper electrical measuring instruments, variations in the electrical properties of the skin appear from time to time. During emotional experience or excitement, they found, there is an increase in these electrical variations. These electrical changes have been named the *galvanic skin response* or *psychogalvanic reflex*, a phenomenon which has been extensively studied by various physiological and psychological investigators. The response was first called prominently to psychological attention by the work of Jung and his pupils, who came to the general conclusion that the galvanic skin response is associated with repressed emotional complexes. Whether this electrical response is associated with physiological and psychological occurrences other than emotion, they did not particularly consider. Their claims were accepted more or less uncritically by many psychologists. More recent critical investigations show, however, that these electrical responses occur not only during emotional experience, but also with practically every other variety of psychological experience. Furthermore, the degree of electrical change does not measure accurately the amount of emotion experienced by the individual.

Electroencephalograms. If electrodes are placed on the head, one over the occiput and the other over any other area, and these electrodes connected through suitable electrical amplifying and recording instruments, records of very rapid electrical changes in the brain may be obtained. Such records are called *electroencephalograms* or *brain-waves* (see Fig. 19, p. 242). The most prominent and regular of these waves is one which can be obtained over the occipital lobes of the brain and which has a frequency of about 10 per second. It appears when the eyes are closed and the subject is in a calm, quiet condition. If emotional stimulation is applied or if the subject thinks of some vivid emotional topic, these 10-per-second waves disappear at the same time that faster and more irregular waves increase. No specific relationship beyond this fact has so far been demonstrated.

Blood pressure changes. The amount of increase, decrease or variability in blood pressure has been used as a measure of emotionality. Perhaps the most extensive use of this type of measurement has been in the detection of falsehood, the so-called 'lie detector' being an instrument to record changes in blood pressure. (Some lie detectors record the galvanic skin response.) Under certain conditions it seems possible on the basis of the changes in the blood pressure record, to determine whether or not an individual has told the truth or has lied—provided the subject is more moved when lying than when telling the truth. It has not been possible to standardize the procedure, since it depends upon so many variables and there are so many different factors which must be considered in the interpretation of the record. For instance, an habitual liar may be quite unmoved about his lies; and there are people who can convince themselves by their lies and become sincere liars.

In a study of blood pressure made on individuals who had suffered severe injury in automobile accidents and upon friends and relatives who were called to the hospital to see the injured, interesting results were obtained. It was found that the injured individuals themselves, who had undoubtedly gone through profound physical and emotional shock, did not show very much alteration in blood pressure. Their friends or relatives, on the other hand, waiting to find out how severely the patients had been injured, showed a tremendous variability in blood pressure. Evidently, then, the rise in blood pressure frequently accompanies the apprehensive state preceding some possible emergency.

Rating scales. The use of rating scales in the measurement of emotion or emotionality has become the most usual and prevalent method of investigation of emotional experience. In this procedure we ask the friends and acquaintances of some person to rate his emotionality or emotional expressiveness. Although this method does not usually give predictive material, nevertheless by statistical manipulation of the data it is possible to obtain some idea of the probable emotional reactivity of an individual in comparison with that of his friends and associates.

Observational and analytic techniques. Several investigations of emotional reactions, particularly with children, have been made by the observational method. One observer watched a large group of children on the playground, following their behavior over a period of several months. All instances of anger, fighting, fear or other emotional reactions were noted. On the basis of such observational studies one can obtain very good descriptions of actual emotional behavior, the stimuli or situations which produced the behavior and the results of the reactions. Although it has been found possible to predict rather accurately the sort of situation which will evoke an emotional reaction in any particular individual, the evidence shows that the same situation is not uniformly effective in producing the same reaction in all individuals or even in the same individual every time.

Psychoanalysis provides a special situation under which emotion can often be observed in adults. In such an analysis, which consists essentially of talking in a free and uninhibited fashion about anything that comes into the mind, very marked emotional reactions sometimes take place. The subject may respond in an intense emotional fashion to his own descriptions of events long past and previously believed forgotten. It is by such methods that we have acquired most of our knowledge concerning the derived emotions.

Questionnaire methods. An entirely different method of measurement and test is the one which makes use of a questionnaire, as, for example, the Pressey X-O, Form B. This test consists of three lists of words. In the first the individual is told to cross out everything he thinks is wrong; in the second list, everything about which he has ever worried; and in the third, everything he likes or is interested in. He is also told to encircle the crossed-out word in each line which he considers to be the worst, the most worrisome or the most interesting, as the case may be. The total number of words crossed out is called a 'score of emotionality,' since, theoretically, the more things a person dislikes, worries about or likes, the more generally emotional he is. The encircled words having been compared with a standard list that gives the most frequently encircled word for each line, the number of encircled words which deviate from this standard list is the 'score of idiosyncrasy.' Various investigators have reported that students who obtain high scores of emotionality and idiosyncrasy tend to have more than the usual number of emotional conflicts in school.

REFERENCES

1. Bard, P. Emotion: I. The neuro-humoral basis of emotional reactions. *A handbook of general experimental psychology.* Worcester, Mass.: Clark University Press, 1934. Chap. 6.
2. Beebe-Center, J. G. *The psychology of pleasantness and unpleasantness.* New York: D. Van Nostrand, 1932.
3. Cannon, W. B. *Bodily changes in pain, hunger, fear and rage.* (2nd ed.) New York: Appleton, 1929.
4. Dickinson, R. L. and Beam, L. *A thousand marriages.* Baltimore: Williams & Wilkins, 1931.
5. Freud, S. *Introductory lectures on psychoanalysis.* New York: Boni & Liveright, 1923.
6. Freud, S. *New introductory lectures on psychoanalysis.* New York: Norton, 1933.
7. Goodenough, F. L. *Anger in young children.* Minneapolis, Minn.: University of Minnesota Press, 1931.
8. Hamilton, G. V. *A research in marriage.* New York: Boni, 1929.
9. Henderson, D. K., and Gillespie, R. D. *A text-book of psychiatry.* (3rd ed.) New York: Oxford University Press, 1932.
10. Jones, M. C. Emotional development. *A handbook of child psychology.* (2nd ed.) Worcester, Mass.: Clark Universitv Press, 1933. Chap. 6.

11. Landis, C. Emotion: The expressions of emotion. *A handbook of general experimental psychology.* Worcester, Mass.: Clark University Press, 1934. Chap. 7.

12. Landis, C., and Hunt, W. A. *The startle pattern.* New York: Farrar & Rinehart, 1939.

13. Ruckmick, C. A. *The psychology of feeling and emotion.* New York: McGraw-Hill, 1936.

Chapter 7

THE RESPONSE MECHANISM

The preceding chapters have made it clear that a knowledge of the structure and function of the living organism is important for a correct understanding of the conditions under which behavior and conscious experience occur. For most of the purposes of scientific psychology, however, what may be termed the *response mechanism* may be studied without specific reference to the other systems of the living body, such, for example, as those concerned in the circulation of the blood and in digestion.

The response mechanism in man and in the higher animals includes: the sense organs or *receptors*, which are organized to receive stimulation and to start processes of excitation in the living individual; the *nervous system*, which is specialized for the propagation of excitation; and the muscles and glands or *effectors*, which are specially developed to make response possible. It is largely by means of this highly complex mechanism that the living organism itself is given a functional unity, so that the individual responds to those physical energies of the environment which effectively stimulate it.

DEVELOPMENT OF THE RESPONSE MECHANISM

Evolution of the response mechanism in the animal series. This responsive relationship between the adult living human being and the physical energies of his environment may be made clearer by a consideration of the gradual evolution of the response mechanism. Even the simplest organisms respond to environmental energies. The word *stimulus* is used

This chapter was written by Leonard Carmichael of Tufts College.

to describe any change in the energies external to a receptor which is responsible for so altering the physico-chemical make-up of the receptor that excitation may be said to have been initiated. The characteristics of a stimulus are described in the quantitative units employed in the sciences of physics and chemistry. A unicellular animal, such as an amoeba, has obviously no specialized receptors or organs for the reception of stimuli, for the transmission of excitation or for the effecting of response. Yet the amoeba may be considered to be a self-contained, living system of energies which may be acted upon and dynamically changed by many of the same physical stimuli which are significant in determining the behavior adjustments and, indeed, the whole psychological life of man. Radiant energy, vibrations in material media, chemical and other energies act upon the amoeba and initiate processes in its single cell. As a result of the processes so initiated, the total orientation of the organism in relation to its environment may be changed. Thus the amoeba responds to its environment (Fig. 13, I).

In the evolutionary development of the more complex multicellular organisms, the progressive improvement of the response mechanism may be considered as involving a number of stages. First came the specialization of effector cells without special receptors or central nervous system, such effectors being primitive muscle cells which respond when directly stimulated. This stage is exemplified in the so-called *independent effectors* in the sponge (Fig. 13, II). Next came the establishment of specialized receptors related to effectors by a diffuse *nerve-net* system, a *receptor-effector* system seen typically in the sea-anemone (Fig. 13, III). Finally, in forms such as the worms came the development of a true central nervous or *receptor-adjustor-effector system*, as it has been called (Fig. 13, IV and V). The receptor-adjustor-effector mechanism is seen in increasing effectiveness in the series of mammals and finally in man.

The central nervous system or adjustor mechanism makes possible the different connections between incoming and outgoing impulses. The possibility of this switchboard-like action is in part related to the fact that the continuity of the nervous

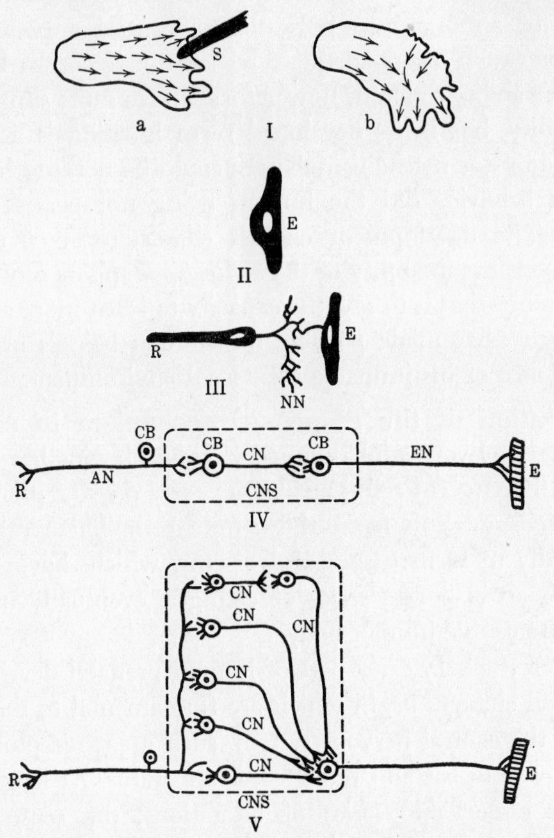

FIG. 13. STAGES IN PHYLOGENETIC DEVELOPMENT OF THE RESPONSIVE MECHANISM. I. Amoeba. (*a*) Just stimulated by glass rod (*S*); (*b*) change of flow of protoplasm and response of amoeba to such stimulation. II. Independent effector cell. III. Receptor-effector mechanism, with some indication of nerve net (*NN*). IV. Simple receptor-adjustor-effector mechanism or reflex arc. V. More complex receptor-adjustor-effector mechanism. Abbreviations: *S* = stimulus, *E* = effector, *R* = receptor, *NN* = nerve net, *AN* = afferent neuron, *CB* = cell body of neuron, *CN* = connector neuron, *CNS* = central nervous system, *EN* = efferent neuron.

system, as seen in the old nerve-net stage, has given place in the receptor-adjustor-effector system to relatively independent nerve cells or *neurons*. In understanding the functions of the human nervous system a clear knowledge of the structure, function, independence and, indeed, the interdependence of neurons is important (see Fig. 14).

Among the many characteristics which distinguish the behavior of an organism possessing a central nervous system from one with a less adequate response mechanism is the organism's ability to learn. Lower forms have some simple learning ability, but in its developed form learning is a function of the adjustor mechanism. There could be nothing like adult human behavior did the human being not possess this capacity. The development of this characteristic of relatively permanent modifiability of the *central ganglia* or central nervous system—that is to say, the capacity to learn more and more effectively—has made possible the human being's unique independence of his immediate external environment.

Evolution of the response mechanism in each individual. Every adult living individual begins life as a single fertilized germ cell. During the early days of prenatal life other cells develop from this single cell. These cells come eventually to form tissues and organs, which, having passed through an elaborate series of changes, eventually constitute the recognizable human body.

During the very early part of human prenatal development, structural changes begin which are fundamental to the formation of the central nervous system, such great receptor organs as the eye and ear and the effector apparatus. At length, after a most remarkable series of alterations, the sense organs, nervous system and muscles of the yet unborn child begin to work in such fashion that the stimulation of receptors leads to effector response. Usually such true responses begin more than five months before normal birth. From this time on until birth, patterns of response, as released by internal and such external stimuli as are present, develop. The outcome of this course of change in prenatal behavior is that the young organism is increasingly able to respond adaptively to the stimuli of its environment. In other words, as the normal maturation of the response mechanism and especially of the adjustor mechanism goes on in the human infant, more and more precise and discriminative responses to the physical energies of the environment become possible. What is usually called *growth* and what is usually called *learning* cooperate in bringing about those changes in the response mechanism which underlie this development.

Thus, both in the animal series and in the individual, the story of the development of the response mechanism is the story of the evolution of a greater and greater capacity on the part of the organism to respond *differentially* and, from the standpoint of the welfare of the organism, *adaptively* to the physical energies of the external world.

Role of the receptors in the response mechanism. At all stages in the development of the organism effective stimuli may be described as physical energies. In the higher organic forms such energies usually act on specialized receptors. Some of these receptors are at the surface of the body, so located that they may be easily affected by external environmental forces. These, called *exteroceptors*, are exemplified by the receptor cells of the eye. Some receptors, on the other hand, are imbedded in the bodily substance itself. Typical of such receptor cells are the sensory cells of the muscles, which are stimulated by the movement of the muscle substance. Such receptors are called *proprioceptors*. There are also receptors associated with the lining of the digestive tract, sometimes characterized as *interoceptors* (see Fig. 21). The exteroceptors, proprioceptors and interoceptors alike are associated with the peripheral endings of *afferent* neuron fibers. These fibers pass from the periphery to the central nervous system. From the central nervous system *efferent* neurons in turn pass out to effectors. This total path from receptor to effector, involving all the great divisions of the response mechanism, is called a *reflex* or *response arc*. (Two diagrammatic forms of such arcs are shown in Fig. 13, IV and V.)

The total living organism may be conceived of, not only as an anatomical entity, but also as a complex system of energies. The essential process of receptor action may be described in terms of the manner in which an external physical energy is able to bring about a change in specific subsystems of energy in the organism. Stimulation thus initiates processes in the

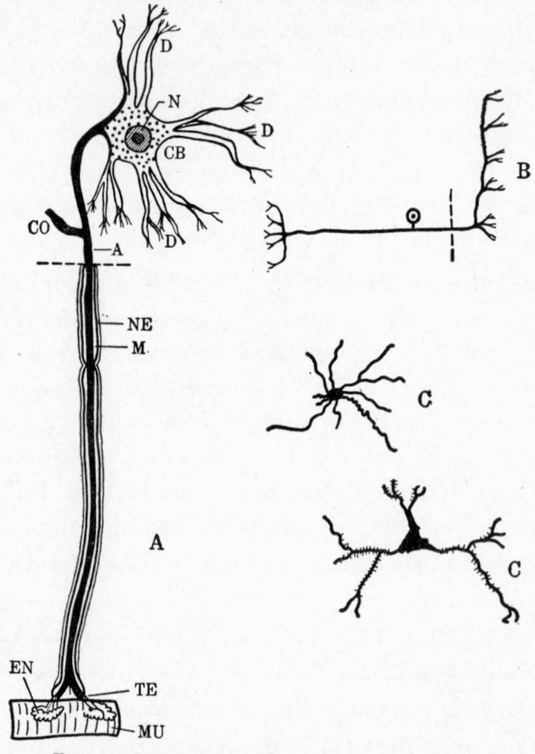

Fig. 14. Structure of Some Typical Neurons.

A. A typical efferent (motor) neuron. *B*. A typical afferent (sensory) neuron (in less detail than *A*). *C*. Typical central (connector) neurons (in less detail than *A*). Abbreviations: *D* = dendrites, *N* = nucleus, *CB* = cell body, *CO* = collateral, *A* = axon, *NE* = neurilemma sheath, *M* = myelin (medullary sheath), *MU* = muscle, *EN* = motor end plate, *TE* = terminal arborization or end brush.

animal which usually lead in the course of time to effector response and a change of orientation of the individual in relation to its environment. Stimulation is in some respects analogous to the finger pressure on the trigger which initiates the release of energy in the gunpowder in a cartridge, and thus leads to the expulsion of a bullet from a gun. Obviously in the cartridge the explosion of the stored energy, and not the movement of the finger, drives the bullet. In the same way the release (by stimulation) of energy stored in the receptor does not propel matter through space, but it does truly initiate a *progressive release of energy.* That is to say, the physical energy of the stimulus does not itself go through the receptor; it merely sets off certain energies of the organism located in the receptor, whereupon other progressive releases of energy follow.

In the higher animals not all receptors are alike in the work they do. The main function of a specialized receptor is to be easily 'set off' by one sort of physical energy and at the same time to be stimulated with difficulty or not at all by any other form of energy. Technically the energy for which a receptor is specialized is called, in relation to that receptor, *adequate.* All other energies, even though they may set the receptor in action, are called *inadequate.* From one point of view, however, the end result of receptor stimulation, *i.e.*, the initiation of a *nerve impulse*, is in each case similar in certain respects. For example, if radiant energy from the so-called visible spectrum stimulates the receptors of the retina, we have adequate stimulation of the eye, for processes are started which are correlated with the experience of light. But pressure on the eye may inadequately stimulate the receptors of the retina so that the subject reports that he sees light even though he may be in a completely dark room.

GENERAL STRUCTURE AND FUNCTION OF THE NERVOUS SYSTEM

We have just seen that, as a result of the stimulation of a receptor by external physical energies, a certain energy change is initiated in the receptor. This energy change involves a spread of a chemical and electrical disturbance in the living cell which is activated. In the simplest cases in the human body the receptor is itself merely the free ending of an *afferent neuron of the peripheral nervous system.* Usually the receptor is a specialized cell associated with such a neuron. The afferent peripheral neuron itself is typically a continuous protoplasmic thread connecting a receptor with the neurons of the central nervous system. The peripheral fiber of a single neuron may thus be several feet long, for it is unbroken from receptor to central nervous system, but it is microscopic in diameter. In most cases each such neuron fiber is insulated by special sheaths. A great many such insulated fibers are ordinarily held together by non-neural tissue to form a cable called a *peripheral nerve.* Such nerves usually contain, at least for certain distances, many independent fibers, of which some may be afferent and others efferent.

The chemical and electrical disturbances which are set up in the receptors as a result of stimulation in turn initiate similar processes in the protoplasmic threads of the afferent neurons. These 'disturbances' spread along the fibers. Such *propagated regions of increased activity* are called *nervous impulses.* From the standpoint of a knowledge of the response mechanism as a whole, an understanding of the nature of these impulses is most important, because the brain and the muscles, unlike the receptors, do not respond directly to external energies—those so-called 'properties of external things'—but to differences in nerve impulses alone.

Nature of the neural excitation. When the stimulated receptor starts a process of activity in the afferent peripheral neuron, the receptor does not pour something into the neuron. Instead, by a trigger mechanism, the energy of the active receptor upsets the energy balance of the neuron and thus in turn initiates a further disturbance in the afferent fiber. This disturbance is thereupon propagated along the axon. Experiment shows that, if a single neuron is excited in this way at all, it is excited to its maximum extent, a generalization known as *the all-or-none law*. This law may be stated more formally as follows: The magnitude of the activity in any single neural functional unit is as great as it can be in that unit at that time and is independent of the magnitude of the energy exciting it, provided only that the stimulating energy is sufficiently strong to excite the neuron at all. A crude analogue of this characteristic of nerve activity may be found in a burning trail of gunpowder, or indeed a simple burning string. The energy which is released and the characteristics of the moving flame are not dependent on the quantity of energy of the match that ignites the train; rather, the combustion is locally determined as each point in the train is successively burned. Careful experimental work has shown that the characteristics of the nervous impulse at any point on a neuron fiber are determined by that part of the fiber, and not by the energy which in the first place started the impulse.

One fundamental change which may be studied in determining the nature of the propagated disturbance in the neuron is an electrical phenomenon, the *action potential* or *action current.* The active region of the neuron fiber is electrically negative in relation to the unexcited portion of the same fiber. Figure 15 shows how such a propagated region of negativity may be recorded on a galvanometer. Though this impulse, or region of excitation, travels in mammalian neurons at very varying speeds, a speed of approximately 100 meters a second may be taken as typical. Such a speed, though relatively fast, is, of course, in no way comparable to the speed of light or to the speed of an electric impulse in a wire.

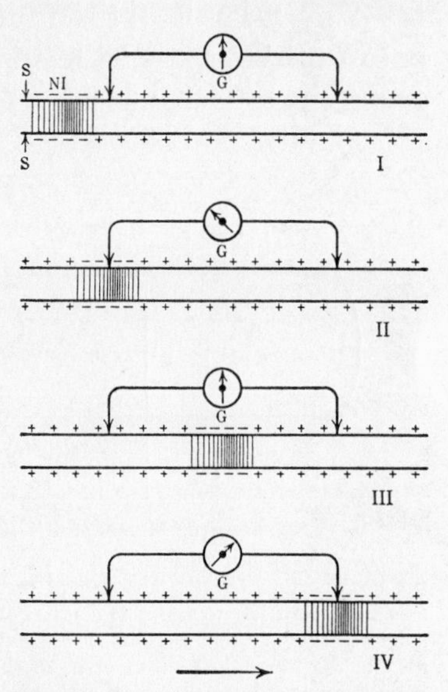

FIG. 15. PROPAGATION OF AN ELECTRICAL DISTURBANCE ALONG A NEURON FIBER.

I, II, III, IV show successive time intervals as the impulse passes from left to right. The galvanometer deflection is indicated in each case. It will be noticed that the impulse is marked by a negative deflection. Abbreviations: S = stimulus, NI = nerve impulse, G = galvanometer.

If we return to the analogue of the burning trail of gunpowder, we may say that, once the gunpowder trail has been burned, it cannot be ignited again until new energy in the form of a new trail of gunpowder has once more been laid. In the nerve, careful study of time relations in stimulation has shown a process which is roughly comparable to this need for replenishing combustible material before re-ignition can occur. Likewise, it has been shown that there is a period immediately following the peak of activity in a neuron during which it cannot be activated again, no matter how strong the stimulus.

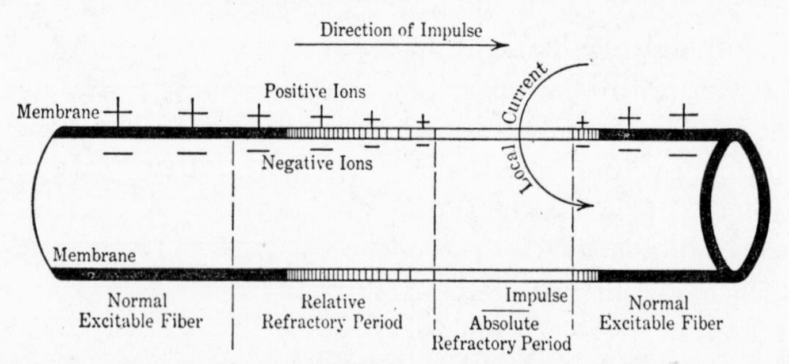

FIG. 16. MEMBRANE THEORY OF NERVE CONDUCTION.

Hypothetical and schematic. The semipermeable membrane is shown in black with the positive ions on the outside and the negative ions on the inside. The impulse is traveling from left to right. It consists of a local current as the positive and negative ions unite when the membrane becomes permeable, and this current renders permeable the membrane ahead of it, so that the impulse continues on. The permeable membrane is shown in white, and the membrane which is being restored after the passage of the impulse is shaded. Thus the diagram also shows the refractory periods. Adapted from Boring.

Technically such a time interval is known as the *absolute refractory period*. Following this period there is an interval during which the neuron may indeed be stimulated, but only provided the stimulus is stronger than the minimal stimulus which would have been effective in starting an impulse in that neuron when it was normal or resting. This second interval is called the *relative refractory period*. Immediately after the relative refractory period the neuron may be thought of as having recovered, and thus as being ready again for activation by a stimulus of normal magnitude. It has even been demonstrated that, at least under certain laboratory conditions, immediately following the relative refractory period, a stimulus of an intensity lower than that required to excite the resting nerve may be effective. The time during which this phenomenon is possible has been called the supernormal period. Characteristic time relations of these processes are shown in Fig. 16. Careful experimental work has also demonstrated that the events involved in the passage of a nerve impulse produce a measurable amount of heat; and that in this activity, moreover, oxygen is used up and carbon dioxide given off.

A short intense stimulus has been found to set up processes in the receptor which outlast the short duration of the stimulus. The time of the cessation of this effect has been found to be related to the intensity of the exciting stimulus. Thus, nerve impulses which are *periodic* in character, because of the refractory periods of the tissues involved, may follow for a short time from an excited receptor after the receptor itself is no longer being activated by an outside energy.

Experimental study of the relative refractory periods of the receptor and the individual fiber has also shown that it is possible for an intense stimulus to excite such a mechanism into a relatively rapid series of successive impulses, while a weak stimulus acting upon the same mechanism may produce a less rapid series. The rate of discharge in a peripheral fiber thus becomes greater the more intense the physical energy of the stimulus applied to its receptor. The total limits of this frequency are, it can be seen, always determined by the time limits of the relative and absolute refractory periods of the activated cells in question. This increase in frequency of discharge in relation to the increased intensity of stimulation has been shown to occur experimentally where but a single receptor and a single neuron are involved.

In any consideration of the correlation between the stimulus and the nervous impulse, it must not be forgotten that in many sense fields the receptors present a surface of 'receptive points.' In excitation by a physical stimulus having area, or in certain cases, it may be, by the spread of excitation from a strong single point of stimulation, a number of fibers may be activated. In some receptor fields, such as the retina, the relationship between receptors and associated neurons is most complicated. The complications in the retina, which in reality is embryologically part of the central nervous system, cannot be considered in detail here, but some of the results of its complex structure and function are discussed in detail in Chapter 17. It is altogether probable, however, that the various sensory cells in any typical receptor field may *differ* with respect to the *lower thresholds of excitation*; that is to say, a stimulus of a particular physical intensity may call into action some, but not all, such receptors. In a condition of this sort, it might well be that the boundary and, indeed, the surface area of the nonpunctate stimulus would be approximately represented by the excited receptors, without necessarily involving the activation of all the receptors within the area covered by the stimulus. The number of receptors involved in any given stimulated area at a specific degree of stimulus intensity has been spoken of as the *density* of stimulation.

The diameter of different fibers determines different rates of conduction within the neurons. It has recently been suggested that in a typical motor or efferent nerve there may be neurons which conduct impulses at about 100 meters per second and other neurons which conduct at, for example, 60, 40, 25, 10 and 2 meters per second.

None of these facts related to the multiple-receptor and multiple-fiber mechanism must be forgotten in working out the relationship between the measured characteristics of the physical stimulus and the physiological events of the activated nervous system. For example, from what has just been said it will be obvious that with stimuli which affect an areal receptor surface it may be possible that, as the intensity of the stimulus increases, an increasing number of individual receptors will be stimulated, each fiber reacting in an all-or-none manner. At the same time intense stimulation may also lead to more frequent impulses, in that it can reactivate the neuron before the recovery process of the relative refractory phase is complete. It thus seems that an increase in the intensity of stimuli may be correlated, in the peripheral nervous system, with an increase in *number of units* affected as well as with an increase in the *number of impulses* per second in each fiber involved. The part played by these two factors in determining the neural correlate of stimulus intensity is considered later (pp. 507f.).

It has become clear that the characteristics of the propagated excitation which occurs in the fibers composing a peripheral nerve may differ in a number of ways, of which the following seem to be most important. (1) The frequency of impulse may vary in any given fiber. (2) The frequency of impulse may vary from fiber to fiber. (3) The total number of fibers excited may vary as the total area of excitation in the receptor field is changed. (4) In two equal areas the total number of fibers excited may vary in relation to the strength of stimulation. (5) The duration of activity may vary. (6) The form and speed of what may be called the energy gradient of the active portion of the neuron, the 'impulse,' may vary from neuron to neuron.

The most important theory that has been developed to account for the chemical and physical processes underlying neuron excitation is the *membrane hypothesis of nerve conduction.* According to this view each threadlike fiber of a neuron is physiologically as well as anatomically complex. In its resting state such a fiber may be thought of as a cylinder, the walls of which consist of a semipermeable membrane. The wall is called semipermeable for the reason that it forms a differential barrier to the passage of chemical or electrical elements. In the living neuron this membrane is electrically polarized: positive ions are on its outside and negative ions are on its inside surface. In terms of this theory the action current is a local change in such polarization. The action current is therefore related to the establishment, by a process of depolarization, of a new electrical potential difference on the outer surface of the membrane between an inactive and positive region and the now active and negative region. This electric change causes a local reorganization of ions on the surface, involving also to some extent the membrane ahead of it. In this way the part just beyond the excited region in turn becomes permeable, and thus a spread of depolarization is brought about. Although the spread may occur in either direction in the peripheral fiber, yet, once established, it can move in but one way. This directionality is due to the fact that the disturbance of the ions accompanying activity is such as to require time, as explained above, for an elaborate process of restoration of resting polarity in the recently active region (see Fig. 16).

We have now considered something of the nature of the organism's activities resultant from external stimulation as they appear in the receptor and in the peripheral nerve. Next we must follow the progressive release of energy into the central nervous system and consider the special phenomena which are related to the spread of such excitation in the brain and spinal cord.

Structure of the central nervous system. The central nervous system in man is made up of the spinal cord and the brain (Fig. 17). The *spinal cord* is the part of the nervous system that is enclosed in the jointed bony case of the vertebral column. It is connected with receptors and effectors by more than thirty pairs of spinal peripheral nerves. The spinal cord is primarily to be thought of as a cable, by means of which impulses initiated at the receptors of the body may be transmitted to and from the higher centers of the brain. Yet the cord is also in its own right a center for the correlation and adjustment of relatively simple reflex arcs.

Continuous with the spinal cord and protected by the bony case of the skull is a very complex system of nerve centers and communication tracts known as the brain. Immediately above the cord and in continuity with it is located the *medulla oblongata*. Like the cord the medulla is an important adjustment center in its own right, but it is primarily—again like the cord—to be thought of as a great cable of fibers connecting the spinal system below with the higher brain centers above. Situated dorsally to the medulla and, as it were, off the main track of the central nervous system are the two hemispheres of the *cerebellum*, which functions in the coordination of bodily movements. Below the cerebellum there is a large structure, the *pons*, made up of fiber tracts and specialized adjustment centers. Above the cerebellum and pons is found an elaborate

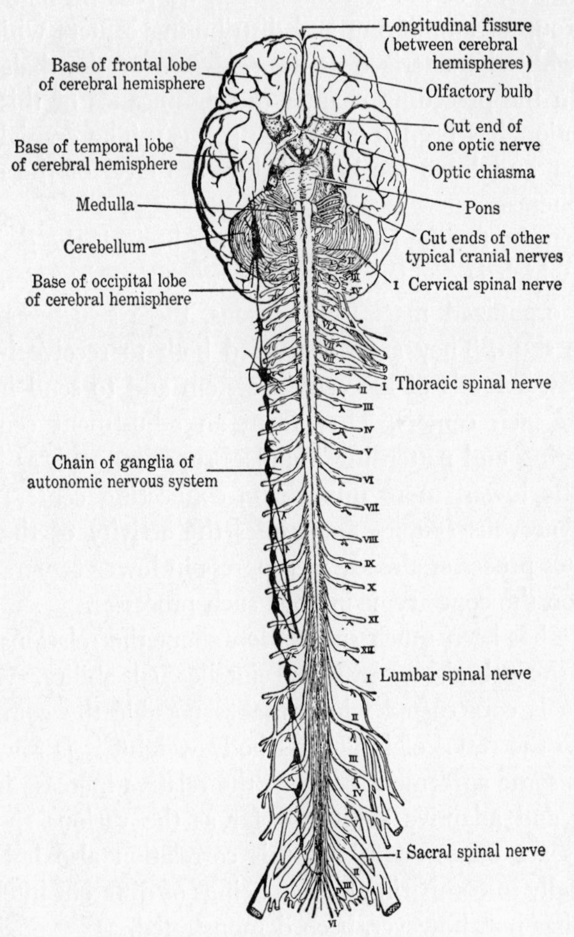

FIG. 17. BASE OF BRAIN AND SPINAL CORD.

Heavy black structure at left of cord indicates part of autonomic nervous system. Adapted from C. J. Herrick, *An introduction to neurology,* 1931; by permission of the W. B. Saunders Co.

series of special connecting centers, all of which play an important part in the adjustment of impulses and in the adaptation of the organism to its environment. Much is known concerning these centers, and much is still to be discovered. It is impossible here to review the anatomical relationships of these centers. It is important to note, nevertheless, that, before we reach the level of the cerebral cortex, we pass through a complex group of amplifying and distributing centers which may be roughly characterized as the *thalamus* or the thalamic region. In the preceding chapter the significance of this region in emotion has been treated (see p. 217). The cranial nerves all enter and leave the brain below the level of the cerebral hemispheres.

In man by far the largest part of the brain is the great *cerebrum*, which is divided into two *cerebral hemispheres*. Large, closely organized masses of neurons, these structures almost fill the skull. They are constructed both to receive impulses from lower levels of the central system and to send impulses back to such centers. They form an adjustment center for recircuiting and patterning impulses superimposed, as it were, upon the lower, more immediate, connecting centers of the central nervous system. Sometimes the activity of the cortex facilitates processes already in progress in lower centers; sometimes, on the contrary, it inhibits such processes.

There has been much speculation about the relationship between sheer brain weight and intellectual ability. When a formula is constructed which makes possible the comparison between the ratios of brain and body weight, it is found that there is some agreement between the relative increase in brain weight and adaptive ability, so far as the various species of animals are concerned. That this correlation also holds true statistically in comparing human beings of different intellectual ability has not, however, been demonstrated.

General functions of the central nervous system. In any consideration of the central nervous system one may well remember that, no matter what the complications of this system may be, it is possible to look at it as basically organized for the purpose of making connections between incoming and outgoing nerve impulses possible. The mechanism of these connections is, of course, more than a simple transmission. Sherrington, one of the most thorough students of this field, has said of the central nervous system that it is "an organ of reflex reinforcements and interferences, and of refractory phases, and shifts of connective pattern; that it is, in short, an *organ of coordination* in which from a concourse of multitudinous excitations there result orderly acts, reactions adapted to the needs of the organism, and that these reactions occur in arrangements (*patterns*) marked by absence of confusion and proceed in *sequences* likewise free from confusion."[1]

Biologists have calculated that there are approximately twelve thousand million nerve cells in the central nervous system. At first this inconceivable complexity almost seems to balk any hope of understanding central-nervous-system activity. The conception of the response arc, however, provides a key to at least some basic central-nervous-system processes. In the central portion of each such arc lie the spinal cord and brain. In regard to that part of the arc which is in the central nervous system, it will be seen from Fig. 18 that some of the paths from a receptor to an effector are relatively short, simple and direct, whereas others are longer and more intricate (see also Fig. 13, V).

Some of the fundamental properties of the central nervous system may be attributed to the *synapses* or points of physiological junction between neurons in the system of neural arcs. Anatomically it is probable that there is protoplasmic discontinuity at such junctures. This judgment is based upon direct microscopic study and upon the fact that when one neuron dies, the consequent degeneration does not ordinarily pass the point of juncture. On physiological grounds many other characteristics are attributed to the synaptic regions. Such inferences are indirect; nevertheless, there is evidence that the following special properties of the central nervous system are in part at least referable to synaptic regions. (1) *Speed:* the rate of transmission of a nervous impulse is slower in the central nerv-

[1] C. S. Sherrington, *The integrative action of the nervous system,* Yale University Press, 1906, 313.

ous system than in the peripheral fiber. The delay is attributed to the synapse. (2) *Irreversibility:* nerve impulses travel in only one direction in the total neural arc. Such one-way conduction is attributed to the valvelike action of the synapses. (3) *Susceptibility to drugs:* the central nervous system with its many synapses is much more susceptible to drugs than is the periph-

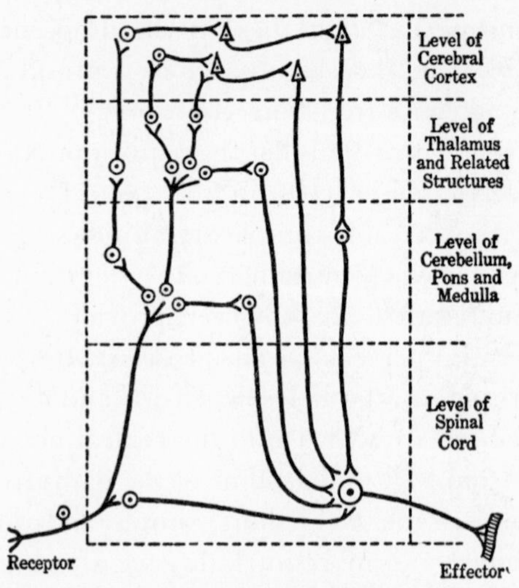

FIG. 18. SCHEMATIC DIAGRAM TO SHOW ALTERNATE LOOPS AT VARIOUS LEVELS OF THE CENTRAL NERVOUS SYSTEM.

Many other schemes of levels in the nervous system have been proposed. The diagram here given is not intended to represent a final view of the hierarchy of governing centers, but merely to emphasize the fact that there are levels in the brain and that they influence each other. Adapted from W. M. Bayliss, *Principles of general physiology,* 1927; by permission of Longmans, Green & Co.

eral nervous system. This tendency is true both of the abolishing of functional activity by anesthetics and the heightening of such activity by strychnine. (4) *Variability of physiological action:* this variability, as seen in *reinforcement* (the augmenting of one process by another), in *inhibition* (the partial or complete extinguishing of one functional activity by another) and in *summation* (the cumulative effect of repeated action), may be thought of as brought about in the central nervous system at its synaptic junctures. (5) *Fatigue:* the fact that the central nervous system is more subject to fatigue on continued activity than is the peripheral system may be attributed to changes that take place in the synapses.

There are certain general problems of the central nervous system in which the student of mental phenomena must always be keenly interested. The first of these is the question of the alleged localization of various psychological functions in the cerebral hemispheres, and the second is the problem of the anatomical and physiological basis of learning. In order to deal with these problems, however, we must consider the methods by which the detailed function of the brain may be studied. These methods all show how a change in the brain or central nervous system affects behavior and experience. The principal ones are as follows:

1. The method of experimental destruction of tissue, or, in other words, of extirpation or ablation.
2. The method of studying accidental destruction of tissue.
3. The method of studying pathological changes.
4. The method of direct electrical stimulation of the brain.
5. The method of local application of drugs on the cortex.
6. The methods of the histology and embryology of the brain in relation to known facts of behavior and experience.
7. The general physiological methods of brain study.

Under the latter category, for example, changes of brain volume may be studied in relation to various behavior characteristics of the individual; or electrical potentials may be led off from the intact brain or from various areas of the brain and from subcortical centers, and an effort made to correlate the characteristics of these currents with other specific activities.

One of the most interesting developments in this last field is the study of the electrical output of the normal intact human brain. Following the pioneer work of Berger, it has been demonstrated that, when the adult human subject is in a relatively relaxed condition, his brain cells are sending out a more or less regular series of electrical oscillations. Typically these pulsations, called the Alpha rhythm or Berger rhythm, appear at about 10 cycles per second. The galvanometer deflections making up this rhythm are characteristically less than 100 microvolts (millionths of a volt).

It is generally considered that the electrical activity correlated with this rhythm is related to a 'spontaneous rhythm' of the activity of the brain cells. Such spontaneous activity of nervous centers has been studied in other connections. One gets an inkling of how complex may be the relations between

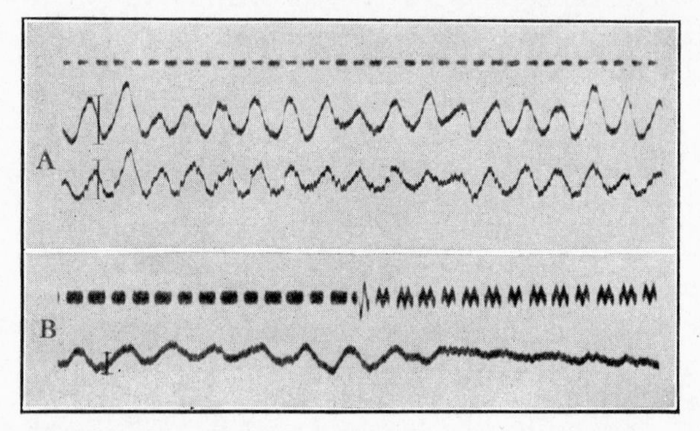

FIG. 19. ELECTROENCEPHALOGRAMS OF A COLLEGE STUDENT.

The records shown above are a sample of Berger-rhythm records made by the author of this chapter. In both records time in 1/20-of-a-second intervals is shown by the dotted line. The small upright bars in each record indicate the same voltage, namely 50 microvolts. The parallel records in *A* show the rhythms as recorded simultaneously from the two cerebral hemispheres. In both cases the recording was made from bipolar leads, one at the back of the head (occipital cortex) and the other on top (precentral gyrus). The upper of the two lines is from the right hemisphere, the lower from the left. *B* shows the dropping out of the large Alpha rhythm following stimulating of the eyes by light. The delay in the action of the light stimulus in this record is shown by the delay of the saw-toothed record in the time-line. In all cases the electrodes were attached to the scalp.

afferent and efferent nerve impulses and hence between stimulation and response, when one realizes that the connecting centers are themselves often independently and rhythmically active. Thus it happens that many factors—for example, stimulation of the eye by light, concentration such as that required in mental arithmetic—depress this spontaneous activity of the Berger rhythm. Figure 19 shows a record of such change.

The central nervous system and learning. The work of Lashley may be taken as typical of controlled scientific study of learning in its dependence on the central nervous system.

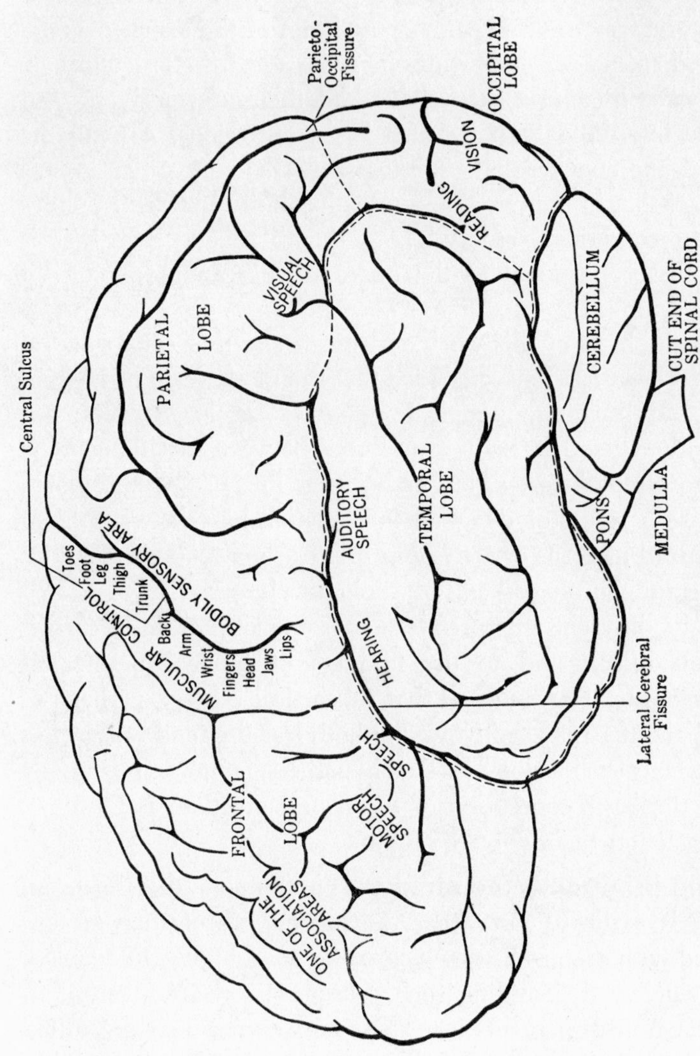

Fig. 20. Schematic Diagram of the Left Aspect of the Cerebral Cortex.

Some of the so-called motor and sensory areas shown by labeling. Great caution must be used in interpreting such maps. Adapted from various sources.

This physiological psychologist has trained animals in a variety of different situations to perform definite and quantifiable tasks. Then, in order to note the changes in behavior which result, he has removed parts of the brain of the experimentally trained animals. Subsequently he has studied the process of re-education in animals that have had their previously learned habits interfered with by such brain operations. Among the significant conclusions resulting from these investigations is the fact that in the rat, at any rate, the ability to learn is, under certain conditions, reduced in a quantitative degree that is roughly proportional to the quantitative amount of cortical tissue removed.

On the basis of this work and much else that cannot be reviewed here, Lashley concluded that the mechanism of integration and learning, though to some extent localized, is not basically dependent upon connections between specific neurons in the cerebral cortex, but rather that integration and learning are a result of dynamic interrelationships between large organized patterns of activity in the neurons of the brain.

Certain neurologists and psychologists, however, have given a slightly different interpretation to some of Lashley's experimental results and to the findings of other experimental neurologists. They suggest that subcortical centers, perhaps in the thalamus, may be involved in both learning and re-learning in animals such as the rat. This hypothesis is more in harmony with the basic conception of the neural arc than is Lashley's "mass-action theory" of the brain.

The brain and 'the mind.' Throughout this book an effort is made to show that the mental life of man is concerned with the processes which make possible human adaptive behavior, even including such processes as those involved in language and mathematics. Those processes which are called conscious occur only when the response mechanism is active. Because 'mind' depends upon brain, the brain surgeon can sometimes bring about mental recovery by removing a tumor. Drugs that act on the brain can change the character of sensation and other conscious processes. The complex details of the relationship of conscious events to activities of the brain and other parts of the nervous system have, however, not yet been worked out.

The efferent peripheral nervous system and the effector organs. We have seen that in the central nervous system the results of sensory peripheral activity may spread over many alternate paths and possibly involve specialized functions characteristic of the total masses of cells in certain parts of the brain. Eventually, as a result of such activity, *efferent* or *motor* neurons must be activated, the central end of the motor neural mechanism being called the beginning of the *final common path.* This final common path is the sole avenue which all impulses, no matter whence they come, must travel if they are to act on muscle fibers or glands and bring about response. Thus activities in various parts of the brain and spinal cord, which have resulted, it may be, from exteroceptive stimulation, can be brought into relation with impulses from other parts of the central nervous system which have themselves originated, for example, in the proprioceptors of certain muscles. Some of these impulses may mutually strengthen or *facilitate* one another; some may act in such a way as to lead to mutual extinction or *inhibition.* In the normal individual, however, the outcome of such complex activity of adjustment is the finely graded and precisely timed effector response. In such a way do activities occur which make up adaptive, intelligent behavior.

In a complete consideration of the motor aspects of the response mechanism it would be necessary to deal with the facts of the so-called autonomic nervous system, a motor nervous system which enjoys a measure of independence from the great peripheral and central systems already considered. In this book, however, an outline of these facts in regard to the autonomic nervous system has already been presented in the chapter on emotion (see pp. 212-217).

By means of peripheral efferent fibers and special fibers of the autonomic nervous system, impulses reach effector mechanisms. All muscle—be it *smooth* (that typical of the walls of the intestines), *skeletal* (that typical of the arm and leg muscles) or, like heart muscle, midway between these two types—is specialized for one function. That function is *contraction*. Contraction alone makes the response possible by means of which the stimulated organism *behaves*, that is, readjusts itself in its environment. As we shall see in the next chapter, the property of contraction is the basic function around which all specialization in the neuro-muscular mechanism has been built. (For a diagrammatic schema of the relationship between the various subsystems of the response mechanism see Fig. 21.)

The contraction of typical muscle cells is accompanied by an electrical disturbance possible to record and study by means not unlike those employed in the study of the electrical phenomena of nerve. The electrical changes of the nerve initiate the essential physical and chemical events which lead to the release of stored energy in the muscle and thus to the *work* and *heat* characteristics of activated living muscle.

The secretion of the *glands* is typically a simple and direct response. Stimulation of a nerve passing to a gland reveals a positive relationship between the strength of the stimulus and the amount of secretion of the gland. The complex mechanism by means of which a typical salivary gland may secrete its own weight in saliva in five minutes involves marked changes in the blood supply to the gland and in the gland itself. These changes are accompanied by electrical phenomena probably associated in their inception with the electrical phenomena of the nerve which initiates the activity.

Glands may be variously classified. The two most significant groups are ordinarily thought of as those which pour the product of secretion through a tube into a cavity of the body or out upon the body surface. Such glands are characterized as *duct* or *exocrine* glands. There are other glands in the body, of which the thyroid and the adrenal medulla are typical, which have no duct, but which pour their secretions directly into the blood stream. They are called *endocrine* glands. For a complete understanding of the response mechanism, the physiological effects of endocrine substances which are carried in the blood stream must be taken into consideration (see pp. 214-217).

Chemical mediators are also of direct importance in the function of the response mechanism itself. When an efferent nerve impulse activates a skeletal muscle, it is now believed

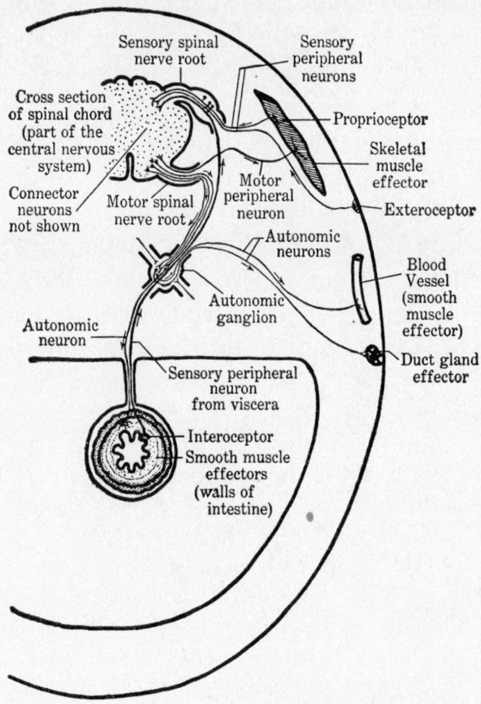

FIG. 21. RELATIONSHIP BETWEEN THE VARIOUS CLASSES OF RECEPTORS, THE NERVOUS SYSTEM AND THE EFFECTORS.

A diagram to show the relationship of exteroceptors, proprioceptors, and interoceptors to the peripheral, central and autonomic nervous systems, and to the muscular and glandular effectors of the body. Adapted from various sources.

that the transmission involves the liberation of a chemical called *acetylcholine*. This substance, liberated by the nerve impulse, then initiates the process of contraction. The same chemical plays an important part in the activity of certain of the peripheral ganglia of the autonomic nervous system. In certain effector organs the effect of the released acetylcholine is opposed by the release of another chemical, adrenine. It now seems clear that these chemical mediators perform many functions in the response mechanism which were previously little understood and which were very hard to explain in terms of the known characteristics of nerve impulses.

Thus by means of effector response, neurally and chemically mediated, the behavior of the living organism is made possible. To the extent that the receptors, effectors and especially the adjustor mechanisms of the activated organism are adequate to the task of selective response, this behavior is appropriate to the stimulating energies of the environment. In the animal series such capacity becomes more and more specific in the long line of development from the amoeba to man. So too in the life history of the individual human being, the specificity of behavior becomes more and more precise during that long series of changes which extend from the first squirm of the fetus to the adaptive discriminative choices of the intelligent adult man.

REFERENCES

I. **On the history of the development of the relationship between psychology and neurology:**

1. Boring, E. G. *A history of experimental psychology.* New York: Century, 1929.
2. Fulton, J. F. *Selected readings in the history of physiology.* Springfield, Ill.: C. C. Thomas, 1930. Esp. pp. 181-295.

II. **On the general significance of the response mechanism:**

3. Child, C. M. *Physiological foundations of behavior.* New York: Henry Holt, 1924.
4. Crozier, W. J., and Hoagland, H. The study of living organisms. *A handbook of general experimental psychology.* Worcester, Mass.: Clark University Press, 1934. Pp. 3-23.
5. Herrick, C. J. *An introduction to neurology.* (5th ed.) Philadelphia: W. B. Saunders, 1931.

III. **On the evolution of the response mechanism in the animal series:**

6. Herrick, C. J. *Brains of rats and men.* Chicago: University of Chicago Press, 1926.
7. Parker, G. H. *The elementary nervous system.* Philadelphia: J. B. Lippincott, 1919.

IV. **On the evolution of the response mechanism in each individual:**

8. Carmichael, L. Origin and prenatal growth of behavior. *A handbook of child psychology.* (2nd ed.) Worcester, Mass.: Clark University Press, 1933. Pp. 31-159.
9. Child, C. M. *The origin and development of the nervous system from a physiological viewpoint.* Chicago: University of Chicago Press, 1921.

V. **On the general structure and function of the nervous system:**

10. Forbes, A. The mechanism of reaction. *A handbook of general experimental psychology.* Worcester, Mass.: Clark University Press, 1934. Pp. 155-203.
11. Kappers, C. V. A., Huber, G. C., and Crosby, E. C. *The comparative anatomy of the nervous system of vertebrates including man.* 2 vols. New York: Macmillan, 1936.
12. Papez, J. W. *Comparative neurology.* New York: Thomas Y. Crowell, 1929.

VI. **On the nature of the neural excitation:**

13. Adrian, E. D. *The mechanism of nervous action: electrical studies of the neuron.* Philadelphia: University of Pennsylvania Press, 1932.
14. Cannon, W. B., and Rosenblueth, A. *Autonomic neuro-effector systems.* New York: Macmillan, 1937.
15. Erlanger, J., and Gasser, H. S. *Electrical signs of nervous activity.* Philadelphia: University of Pennsylvania Press, 1937.
16. Lillie, R. S. *Protoplasmic action and nervous action.* (2nd ed.) Chicago: University of Chicago Press, 1932.

VII. **On the efferent peripheral nervous system and the effector organs:**

17. Creed, R. S., Denny-Brown, D., Eccles, J. C., Liddell, E. G. T., and Sherrington, C. S. *Reflex activity of the spinal cord.* Oxford: Clarendon Press, 1932.
18. Fulton, J. F. *Muscular contraction and the reflex control of movement.* Baltimore: Williams and Wilkins, 1926.
19. Hill, A. V. *Muscular activity.* Baltimore: Williams and Wilkins, 1926.
20. Sherrington, C. S. *The integrative action of the nervous system.* New Haven: Yale University Press, 1906.

Chapter 8

RESPONSE

Man is seldom, if ever, quiet in his waking moments, nor is he very tranquil in sleep. In response to stimulation he is constantly making movements, though often they are hardly noticeable. There are the incipient movements of his vocal organs and other muscles while he is thinking, the ever-present eye-wink, the shifting of his limbs, the restless movements of his body, the frequent turning of his head, and the more co-ordinated activities such as walking, talking, piano-playing and tennis. We are dealing here with behavior directed primarily toward a manipulation and understanding of things of the external world. This behavior, which is dependent for the most part on the striped muscles, is chiefly the concern of the psychologist. There is, in addition, the action of the smooth muscles, such as those connected with the function of nutrition and of reproduction, but these movements are mainly of interest to the physiologist.

The importance of the behavior which the psychologist studies need hardly be emphasized. If we may judge from the lower forms of life, such as the sponge, whose muscles are stimulated by direct contact only, behavior was present in the evolution of life even before the development of a nervous system. It is the means by which the organism, in order to survive, becomes adapted to the ever-changing external situation. We have seen in the previous chapter what are the anatomical and physiological conditions for the various responses of the organism. Our present task is to explain the characteristics of these responses and how they are initiated and developed.

This chapter was written by Herbert S. Langfeld of Princeton University.

DEVELOPMENT OF ACTION

Mass movement versus specific response. In order to understand the nature of behavior in adult life and to be able to form an intelligent opinion of the relative importance of *inheritance* and *experience*, it is necessary to know something of the development of behavior before and immediately after birth.

The most general question for us to consider is this. Does behavior start with units of discrete and unrelated reflexes which later combine into complex patterns of response, or is there a general pattern of response out of which specific behavior develops? The results of Coghill's experiments upon the salamander help us to answer this question. He found that the first movement of the salamander is a bending of the head either to the right or to the left, a movement which is produced by the contraction of the muscles behind the head. With the bending of the head there is the start of a muscular contraction which extends rapidly towards the tail and involves finally the whole animal, causing it to assume a C-shape. A movement of the head in the direction opposite to its first movement follows before the movement caused by the initial bending of the head has been completed. The animal thus assumes an S-shape, and this S-shaped movement, when speeded up, becomes the typical swimming movement. The successive stages of the development of this movement are shown in the three pictures of Fig. 22. This movement of the whole body is an integrated *mass movement.*

The limbs of the salamander appear after the swimming reaction has developed. At first both sets of its limbs move with its trunk; only gradually do they acquire independent movement. When a limb begins to move independently, it first moves as a whole; then the movement at the elbow appears, and finally movements of the wrist and digits gain independence. From these observations Coghill concluded that there is at first a total pattern or integrated unit of behavior and that it is from this pattern through *individuation* that finer responses emerge as relatively independent units.

Coghill's theory lies as far to the one extreme as does the reflex theory to the other. Experiments upon the fetuses of guinea-pigs, rats, cats and other animals have produced results

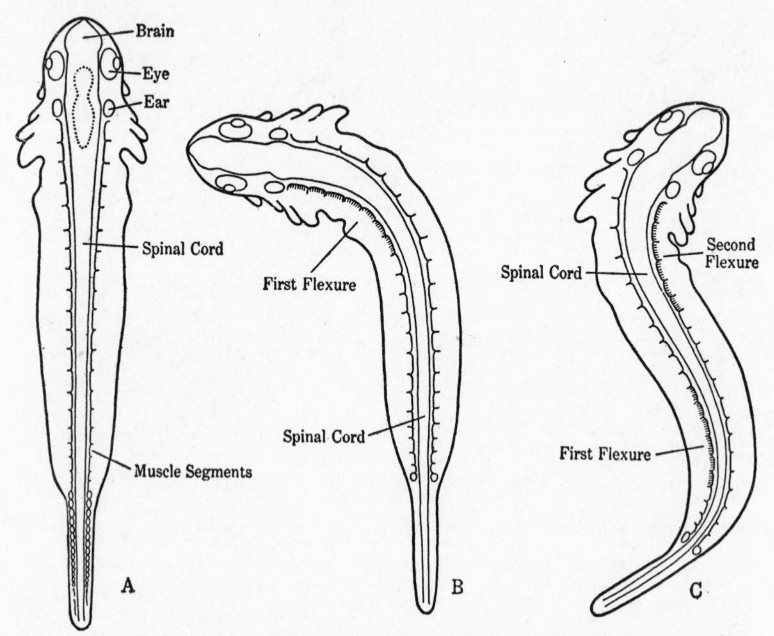

FIG. 22. SWIMMING DEVELOPMENT OF THE SALAMANDER.

A, stage without evidence of muscle contraction. *B*, beginning of swimming. C-shaped movement. Flexure is produced by contraction of anterior muscle segments, indicated by cross-hatching. *C*, S-shaped swimming movement. The first flexure has progressed toward the tail; the second flexure has started in the region of the head. Muscle contractions are indicated by cross-hatching. After G. E. Coghill, *Anatomy and the problem of behavior;* reprinted by permission of the Macmillan Company.

which seem only in part to substantiate Coghill's view. Experiments on the fetal behavior of the guinea-pig, for example, showed both mass activity and simple reflexes. Although the first activities were of the 'spontaneous' type, stimulation of the various receptors by the experimenters soon aroused a large variety of responses from the simplest type to complex behavior. Stimulation of the nose, for instance, caused the raising of a forepaw, the winking of the closed eyelids and numerous other reflexes. Experiments upon the human fetus indicate that there is at first a general tendency for neural impulse to spread, causing mass movements, but that gradually during the developmental process various individual responses appear, becoming more or less specific according to their nature and circumstances. Frequently these mass movements are termed 'random' from the fact that, as yet, they do not seem to have any particular goal—as, for example, the uncoordinated movements of the arms and legs that occur when various parts of the skin are stimulated. It is interesting to note in this connection that even the adult, under painful stimulation, frequently reverts to this primitive form of response. He 'writhes in agony.' It would be incorrect to suppose, however, that, even in the first stages of development, stimuli always produce a general movement of all muscle groups, as if the human nervous system were in the beginning similar in action to the nerve net of the sea-anemone. We must, therefore, conclude that there is merely a tendency at first for the neural impulse to spread and for it later to be restricted to more definite forms of response.

Heredity and environment. The earliest movements of the human embryo take place in the second month of fetal life and consist of slow uncoordinated movements of the trunk and limbs. Though reflexes are reported to occur in the third month, it is difficult to decide whether they are true reflexes. At the end of the third or the beginning of the fourth month, however, a response of the toes may be produced by stimulation of the sole of the foot. During the fourth month many responses become more specific and more intense. In the sixth month certain tendon reflexes are known to occur, and in the seventh month the knee jerk. From this time on, the increase of specific responses is marked. On the basis of experimental evidence one may conclude that the proprioceptors likewise function early in fetal development, thus initiating impulses for muscular contraction. In short, at the time of birth the human fetus already has an elaborately coordinated and organized response mechanism, one which forms the basis for the fundamental behavior of its later years.

Prenatal development of behavior is in the first place dependent upon *maturation,* the growth or ripening of the organism. Maturation consists in structural changes which are mainly hereditary, *i.e.,* which have their origin in the chromosome of the fertilized ovum, but which are also in part a product of the interaction of the organism with its environment.

The influence of maturation in conjunction with environmental conditions on the development of behavior is shown in the results of extensive studies on several thousand embryo chicks. By chipping off a piece of the shell of the egg and coating the exposed membrane with vaseline to make it transparent, it was possible to observe the movements of the developing embryo. Typical examples of the coincidence of structural and behavioral changes may be cited. The forelimbs of the chick first move in a headward-tailward direction, but on about the eighth day of life they start a sidewise flapping movement which disappears a day or two later. This alteration in movement coincides with the growth of a winglike structure on the forelimbs which crowds the limb against the shell wall. About the twelfth day the bending, straightening and lateral twisting movements of the trunk are replaced by jerkings and wrigglings. Because the growth of the organism has left insufficient space for any other kind of activity, these latter types of movement are now the only ones possible. From these and similar coincidences it is evident that the alteration in the activity of the organism is in large part determined by a combination of changes in its bodily structure and environmental conditions.

Before birth all organisms accumulate a considerable fund of experience. Learning commences at the time of the first movement, and from then until death the process of establishing more or less fixed patterns of response is continuous.

The relative importance of these factors of development is very difficult to determine, since it is through their constant interaction that the development takes place. No doubt exists, however, that, at least in lower forms of animal life, there are situations in which maturation plays a dominant role and where the environmental influences are at a minimum. Experiments have been conducted where the animal was rendered incapable of overt action, and could therefore gain no experience of such movement. Embryos of the frog and salamander, for example, were placed in an anesthetic long before they had reached the stage at which movement can be observed. As a check the experimenter placed other embryos in fresh water. At the time when these latter were swimming freely about, the anesthetized organisms were still inactive. When, however, the anesthetized embryos were placed in fresh water, they too soon showed signs of movement upon stimulation. It is difficult to observe these first movements, but the experimenter described them as twitching movements of the head or tail, such as one is accustomed to call 'random.' In a few minutes the embryos were swimming so perfectly that they could not be distinguished from individuals of the control group.

These results show that, at least in such lower forms of life, the neuro-muscular mechanism can develop normally without any apparent external stimulation and without response; when it has sufficiently matured, it will produce relatively integrated movements almost the first time it is appropriately stimulated. We apparently have here an example of the minimum amount of environmental influence compatible with normal development. Studies of various other forms of life, however, seem clearly to indicate, not a decrease in the effect of heredity, but an increasing influence from the environment in the progression from the lower to the higher forms of life. When one comes to man, the environmental influence is at a maximum.

Behavioral development at birth. Just as they differ in physical maturity, animals differ greatly in the degree of their behavioral development at birth. The hairless, new-born rat is scarcely able to crawl. It lies with its litter mates, a helpless limp form, almost entirely dependent upon its mother. The kitten, though not quite so helpless or so immature physically, does not walk perfectly until its fourth week. The guinea-pig, on the other hand, is born with an adequate coat of fur and walks and runs almost at once. The colt and the calf also have well-developed forms of response at birth and are able to stand and walk almost immediately. A class of animals that shows one form of unusually early development of behavior is the marsupial, to which the opossum and the kangaroo belong. These animals are born in a condition which may be considered that of a very immature fetus and are cared for by their mother in a pouch where the nipples are situated. Entirely unaided by the mother they travel from the vulva to the pouch and, in spite of their early stage of embryonic development, attach themselves to the teats. The opossum, when it makes this journey, is only ten days removed from an unfertilized ovum.

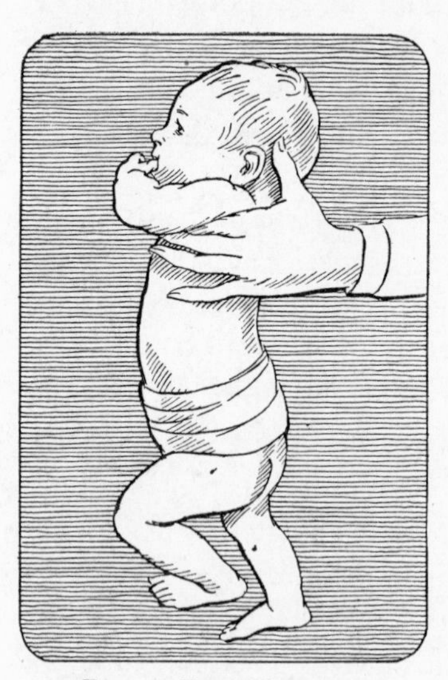

Fig. 23. Early Stepping Movements.

Infants a few hours old when supported under the arms frequently make prancing steps which are probably the early stages of walking. Sketch of a photograph from M. B. McGraw, From reflex to muscular control in the assumption of an erect posture and ambulation in the human infant, *Child Development,* 1932, 3, 295; by permission of the Williams & Wilkins Co.

So far as its actions are concerned, the human infant at birth does not rank very high. Only gradually, in fact, does it develop those habits which will make it independent of its mother. Yet, as we have seen, it already has a great many simple modes of response which have developed during the prenatal state, and which are the basis of the more complex behavior to follow. Able to make elementary movements of its arms and legs and trunk, it is soon capable of lifting its head and rear quarters. It stretches by bending the head and extending the hands above the head. It makes 'startled' responses in which the arms are moved apart, fingers spread, the legs extended and the head thrown backward. Smiling may occur on the first day of life if the infant is tickled under the chin. Crying, which occurs at birth, is often accompanied by activity of the arms and legs. It may be caused by various stimuli—hunger, a bright light, a loud noise, falling, cold, heat or pain. A pin prick on the hand will cause a withdrawal of the arm, whereas a slight push on the sole of the foot is sufficient to cause an extensor thrust of the leg, often strong enough to support the infant's weight.

There are in addition more highly coordinated movements at birth. When the infant is placed prone, the arms and legs are drawn under the body; frequently each pair makes reciprocal movements, as in creeping. When it is held upright with its feet touching the floor, it makes stepping movements (Fig. 23). The grasping reflex is also present at birth. If a stick is placed on the palm of an infant's hand, its fingers will curl about the stick and hold on with considerable strength. Indeed, shortly after birth one is able to raise an infant from the ground by its hold on the stick. Some of these early reactions remain and develop further; some disappear. The stepping movements of infancy later become well coordinated walking responses. In contrast to these are the swimming movements of the breast-stroke style which an infant makes when first placed in water; unless encouraged by instruction to continue its efforts, it soon loses this seemingly innate response.

QUALITATIVE DEVELOPMENT OF ACTION

These responses which appear at birth are, as we have seen, not entirely due to inherited factors. Holt's explanation of the development of such activities as the grasping reflex is based on the principle of the *reflex circle*. It is the contention of this theory that, when a movement occurs, the stimulation of the proprioceptors caused by this movement produces a sensory impulse, which has a tendency to excite again the motor pathway of the original movement, thus reactivating the original movement. The reason the incoming impulse takes this particular motor pathway is that the pathway is still in a state of excitation. It is through this mechanism of a reflex circle that a response is sustained. For example, if an infant utters the sound *ah*, this sound stimulus affects its ear and an impulse travels along the auditory nerve. Since the muscles of the vocal organs are the ones that have just moved, this motor path is reactivated by the impulse from the auditory nerve, and again the infant says *ah*. It is clear that until there is a break in this circle, the infant will continue to utter the sound.

Even in older children this phenomenon is frequently observed. They seem to delight in repeating sounds to the annoyance of their parents, who think the children do it purposely to irritate them. One boy of eight was known to bleat like a sheep on various occasions until, with difficulty, he was made to stop. Similar habits are seen in the field of movement. There is the case of a mental defective who sat in a corner, hitting his two index fingers together and murmuring "Beelzebub" day in and day out. But obviously the phenomenon is not restricted to children and the abnormal. The adult has many such continuous circular responses—such as chewing gum, or twisting a lock of hair, or turning a coat button while thinking.

Specialization of response. In the development of behavior there is, as we have seen, a marked tendency for responses to become increasingly *specific*; the organism, in other words, tends to become more delicately and adequately adjusted to varying situations. This adjustment can take place in several ways. The stimulus may become more specific, the area of stimulation may become more restricted or the response may become more specific. All three directions of specificity are generally involved in the course of an adjustment.

By a study of the *conditioned response* which was first experimentally demonstrated by the famous Russian physiologist Pavlov, it is possible to observe the development of specificity of stimulus and of locality of stimulation. Pavlov stimulated a dog with the sound of a bell for a brief period, and then gave it food and measured the resulting flow of saliva. After a considerable number of such pairings of bell with food, the sound of the bell alone would call forth salivation in somewhat the same manner as had the food; that is to say, the bell had taken the place of the food as a stimulus to salivation. Pavlov called this fact a conditioned reflex, but because later work has shown that many other responses than reflexes alone can be conditioned in a similar manner, the phenomenon has come to be known as the conditioned response. For further description of the conditioned response see pp. 296-301.

Now the point for our present purpose is that, in the early stages of training, there is likely to be a salivary response, not only to the tone used in the experiment, but also to tones differing considerably in pitch from the original tone. Eventually, however, the salivary response occurs only to the tone used in the conditioning process or to one differing but slightly from this tone. Here we have plainly obtained a specificity of stimulus. A common example of such specificity is the tendency of a mother to awaken only to the voice of her own child, although, as in a large city, she may be fairly bombarded by the sound of crying and shouting children.

The development of specific localization of stimulation is shown in the experiment in which a dog is touched on a certain spot on the side and immediately afterward given an electric shock on the leg sufficiently intense to cause a flexion of that member. After a number of trials, touching the side alone without the electric shock will produce a flexion of the leg. In the early stages of conditioning, one may obtain the leg movement by stimulating any point of the skin within a certain area around the point originally stimulated. With repetition, however, this area becomes increasingly restricted, until finally the response of the limb is elicited only when the originally conditioned spot is stimulated.

The progress toward greater specificity in the response of the organism is evidently present in all learning. The rat, in learning to run through a maze, gradually eliminates useless movements into blind alleys until it can reach the goal without errors. The typist at first makes many false finger movements, later becomes expert. In the early stages of learning to play golf, one is likely to move more than the specific muscles necessary for the swing, especially when an unusual effort is intended. Although these unnecessary movements are later eliminated, there is a tendency for them to reappear, even after long practice, especially when one becomes fatigued—as is shown by the moving of the head and swaying of the body.

Generalization of response. Although these fixed modes of response to definite environmental situations are necessary if the organism is to become properly adjusted, obviously this process of specialization alone would produce mere automatism. Man soon learns also to vary his response to a stimulus according to the total situation.

Generalization parallels specialization in all but the lowest forms of intelligence. In order to realize the truth of this statement, we may consider what usually happens when one learns to drive an automobile. A man learns first to operate his own car. In this case a definite pattern of stimuli sets off definite forms of response. Soon he is able to manage any car of a like make even though not of the same year, and finally he is capable of driving almost any make of car without preliminary instruction. In the development of his ability as a driver his responses have become generalized to changed but similar situations. It is this generalized form of response which is fundamental to intelligence according to the definition of intelligence as ability to meet new situations on the basis of past experience. When such response is absent, there is a stereotyped behavior, which is observed in persons of low-grade intelligence. Such persons can be taught simple tasks, but they will continue to act in a fixed and rigid manner even when the situation is no longer appropriate to the act; as, for instance, the moron who was given the job of painting a fence around the four sides of a garden, and who, instead of stopping when he had finished the four sides, continued round and round for hours.

Reflex action. If liquid gets into the throat of an infant, its swallowing muscles respond; if there is too much liquid, it chokes. It begins breathing at birth. Its eyelids close at a loud noise or when something moves rapidly toward its eyes. Its glands commence functioning even during the fetal period. There are many other responses of this nature in the human repertoire. They are called *reflexes* and may be defined as involuntary and prompt responses of the striped or of the smooth muscles.

The simplest form of reflex would require a receptor, sensory neuron, motor neuron and effector. Such a simple neural arc, however, is not found isolated functionally from all other parts of the nervous system in a mature human organism. Take, for instance, the following example of a spinal reflex. If one pinches the paw of an animal whose cord has been cut just below the medulla, one can still obtain a withdrawal or flexion of the paw accompanied by a forward thrust of the other paw. A relatively simple neural arc is involved in the flexion of the paw, but even here more than one motor neuron is necessary to bend the leg; and, besides, there must be a connection in the cord between the sensory neuron and the motor neuron going to the opposite leg to produce the thrust of that leg. There are also connections between these arcs and many more remote reflexes, which, if stimulated at the same time, may exert either an inhibitory or facilitating effect upon the first reflex. Furthermore, if the central nervous system is intact, the legs may be moved voluntarily, a fact which means that there are connections between the spinal reflex arc and the cerebrum. This brief sketch of the physiology of the *reflex arc* is given to emphasize once more the fact that a simple form of response involves a very complicated neural and muscular pattern.

For the most part, although there is a question whether some stimulation is not always necessary for their development, reflexes are in the broad sense of the term unlearned. Certainly in the case of such reflexes as that of grasping, which has been explained by the principle of the reflex circle (see pp.

257f.), there appears to be a developmental history involving more than maturation. After the reflexes are once firmly established, they are stable and predictable, many of them invariably found in organisms of the same species.

That reflexes as such are *involuntary* does not imply that they are always *unconscious.* Many of our reflex actions, it is true, do occur without our being aware of them, as for example, the reflexes connected with the functioning of the internal organs. Many others, which are usually unconscious, such as breathing and eye-winking, may become fully conscious if we attend to them. Of others such as the knee jerk or the rapid withdrawal of the hand from an electric shock, we are perhaps always conscious. Moreover, some reflexes, although ordinarily involuntary, can at times be voluntarily initiated or inhibited; others cannot be. The reflexes which are always unconscious are for practical purposes beyond our power to regulate, but we can stop breathing or change its rate; we can wink voluntarily and can frequently prevent winking. We can indirectly even change the heart rate by voluntarily recalling some scene highly tinged with emotion. Who cannot, for example, cause his heart to palpitate by voluntarily imagining himself charging over the top in battle or by recalling some harrowing experience such as a serious automobile accident?

By the method of conditioning it is even possible to obtain voluntary control of what is for most persons always an involuntary reflex. In certain experiments of this nature, the pupil of the eye was trained to contract at command. In the first stage of the training, a bell was rung immediately before a light was shone in the eyes. After some trials the sound of the bell alone caused the pupil to contract. Then the subject was instructed to close and open the circuit for both bell and light by closing and opening his hand at the verbal command of the experimenter. The verbal command was thus connected through the hand movements and the bell to the pupillary reflex. The next step in the experiment was to eliminate the hand movements and the bell. This left only the vocal instruction of the experimenter as the conditioned stimulus to which the pupil now contracted. The last stage was the repetition by the subject himself of the verbal instructions, first aloud, then by whispering and finally subvocally. All these forms of stimuli, it was found, became the conditions for the contraction of the pupil. The subject could, in short, now command his pupillary reflex, and this ability was still present after fifteen days without further conditioning in the meantime.

Instinct. Reflex action is frequently termed instinctive because it is, in the first instance, an unlearned response depending upon innate connections in the nervous system. Under this category also fall the *primary responses* to the internal drives of the organism, such as hunger and sex. More complicated responses are called instinctive when they involve innate reflexes in their response patterns, and when organic needs or drives are their immediate causes. These complicated responses, however, owe their development to experience as well as to innate connections, and it is the interest of the psychologist to endeavor to determine by observation and experimentation how much may be rightly classed as instinctive and innate and how much is acquired. It is for this purpose that observation and analysis are made of the various forms of both prenatal and infantile behavior. Much study has also been given to the adaptive behavior of animals.

An interesting form of behavior, which is in part instinctive, is the pecking response of chicks. Shortly before the chick is hatched, its whole body may be seen to move violently in the shell. The movements of its head take on the form essential to pecking, while its legs thrust upward against the shell. It is during one of these agitated movements that the shell cracks open and the chick emerges. The chick's action in breaking out of the shell is instinctive in the sense that it is caused by the internal development of the organism, but not in the more popular sense that the *idea* of getting out of the shell at the right time was inherited by the chick. After the chick is thus released, it gradually learns to eat. At first it often misses the grain of corn that it strikes at. It may strike the corn but not seize it, or it may seize it but not swallow it. Only after some days does it peck accurately and eat with the proficiency of the adult hen. If some of the chicks are fed artificially for several days and not allowed to peck during that time, they will nevertheless very soon learn to peck as accurately as the chicks who had started 'practicing' earlier. Thus we see, even in this relatively simple response of pecking, that both instinctive response and learning play a part.

Many animals build nests according to a pattern which varies little within the species. In some instances the offspring have had no opportunity to learn from their progenitors. There must, therefore, be at least some innate tendency running through the activity. That such behavior, however, cannot possibly be an instinct in the sense in which an instinct is sometimes defined (*i.e.,* a series of chained reflexes whose connections are innate and determined) is evident from the fact that the animal must change the nature and sequence of its responses in order to fit its behavior to the particular surroundings in which it finds itself and to the kind of material immediately available for its purpose.

In other cases so-called instincts, both in animals and man, are undoubtedly learned behavior. Naturalists frequently have reported, for example, that the wild animals they have met were not 'instinctively' either afraid of man or inclined to attack him until they had had unpleasant experiences with him. Hunters in Africa have frequently been able to approach by automobile within a few yards of a lion without the lion's paying particular attention to them.

When a child touches a hot radiator, it instinctively pulls its hand away—instinctively because the strong stimulus causes a withdrawal response in the muscles without previous training. When later, at sight of the radiator the child avoids the painful contact, it is evident that its behavior is a learned response and that it can no longer, therefore, be legitimately called instinctive even though it is immediate and unreflecting. From such observations we learn that it is a wise and prudent principle when explaining behavior to endeavor first to determine all the factors of experience that could possibly have been operative in the development of such behavior before concluding that the behavior is innate.

Differences between reflex, conditioned response and voluntary acts. In many instances of human behavior there is no difficulty in distinguishing a simple reflex from the more complicated conditioned response or from a voluntary response. One knows, for example, whether he has winked voluntarily or whether the eyelid reflex has been caused by some sudden stimulus. In the conditioned patellar reflex, when the knee jerk is conditioned to a bell, one can distinguish the movement of his leg at the sound of the bell from the movement which is caused by a rap on the knee, or one that is produced voluntarily. In these cases the person making the movement draws his inference primarily from the nature of the antecedents to the movement.

When it is necessary to decide merely on the basis of the overt or observable behavior to what type of action a response belongs, a judgment is more difficult to make. In the case of the conditioned knee jerk, for example, the investigator cannot always tell whether the movement caused by the bell alone is involuntary or whether the subject is 'faking' results by voluntarily moving his leg when he hears the bell.

Numerous experiments have been devised to obtain some objective criterion for the differentiation of these three forms of response. It has been found that the reflex is, on the average, more rapid than either the conditioned response or the voluntary response. Experiments in which the pupillary light reflex was conditioned showed that the average *latency* (the time between the presentation of the stimulus and the onset of the response) of the conditioned dilation of the pupil was 1.56 sec. and of the conditioned contraction 2.29 sec., whereas the simple reflex to light is generally from 0.2 to 0.5 sec. The *duration* of the conditioned dilation response was 8.24 sec. and of the conditioned contraction response 10.93 sec.; the duration of the simple reflex to light is usually from 1 to 4 sec. There may be overlapping, however, in the speed of these different forms of response. In the case of the eyelid response it was found that, through practice in opening the eyes as quickly as possible immediately after the eyes had closed, the speed of such voluntary opening increased above the speed of the reflex response. Yet this result does not mean that the voluntary response has developed into a reflex.

The conditioned response, moreover, usually differs qualitatively from the unconditioned. The conditioned knee jerk is not quite the same as the reflex knee jerk, nor is the conditioned wink response identical with the reflex eye-wink. Under most experimental conditions the conditioned response is seldom as great in magnitude as the unconditioned.

In regard to the objective differentiation of the reflex from the voluntary response, if the total time of the wink is analyzed into the time of opening and the time of closing the eye, it is found for the reflex that as the time of closing decreases, the time of opening also decreases. In voluntary response this relationship is changed. Another difference is that voluntary response is more readily modified by instruction than is the reflex. At times the change of the reflex is opposite in direction from that of voluntary response. For example, subjects were told to relax as much as possible during both voluntary and reflex action. When the records of the lid movements were analyzed, it was found that the latency of response was generally slightly decreased for the reflex. The latency of the voluntary response, on the other hand, is known to increase under relaxation. These last results are readily understood. The football player has to be 'keyed up' to start immediately upon the snapping of the ball. If he relaxes for a moment, he will be caught off his guard. The reflex, on the other hand, seems to work best when one is caught off guard. If one's attention is concentrated on the appearance of the stimulus for, let us say, the knee jerk, there is likely to be a slight tendency to inhibit the reflex.

Experiments have also been made to determine whether any differences between reflex and voluntary activity can be discovered in the action currents from the nerves involved. The results indicate that the pattern of the action current is more stereotyped in the reflex, a discovery which is in accord with the conception of a reflex as a *fixed* form of response as compared with the *variability* of voluntary response.

Voluntary and semivoluntary acts. Although most of our movements in the early stages of life are of the reflex type, the voluntary, semivoluntary and automatic acts soon assume the ascendancy. A voluntary act is a fully conscious one. It is an act in which one knows both what he desires to do and how to make at least a beginning toward that end. When one starts to learn some difficult movement, such as a new kind of dive, he has an idea of the form of movement that he wishes to make, and especially is he conscious of the first movements involved in the spring from the board. If he is being taught, it is quite probable that he will repeat the instructions to himself subvocally as he stands on the board. During the dive he will be aware to a certain extent of the position of his limbs, and after the completion of the dive he will have a memory of what he has done, accompanied by a certain consciousness of the amount of success attained. Or in learning to play the piano, one at first thinks of the finger movements connected with the note and the position of the key before making the necessary movement. Although we need not, in this place, describe the learning process, we must note how fully conscious we are of what we do immediately preceding, during and after acts which we try to perform for the first time.

This type of voluntary action may appear not only at the beginning of learning, but also during the process, especially when a person makes a mistake—when, for example, he presses the wrong key in learning to use the typewriter. In such a case, even though he may be already fairly proficient, he is likely to revert to the first stage of the learning process and to become conscious of the direction in which he should move his finger. The interruption in the smooth sequence of movement brings the movement again to consciousness. The reverse is also true.

Let a person become suddenly fully conscious of what he is doing, while he is performing some well-coordinated response, and there is likely to be an interference in the smoothness of the response. When he is very eager not to make a mistake in the letter he is typing, he is almost sure to do something wrong. If he thinks of voluntarily moving his legs when going rapidly upstairs, he is likely to trip. This change from an automatic response to a voluntary act throws the individual back to the initial stages in the development of the habit.

Obviously no one is completely conscious of the acts performed in the round of daily duty. A pitcher, when he throws a ball, does not have to think of the movements he is going to make. The act is voluntary in the sense that he intends to pitch the ball, but, as he starts the swing of his arm, he is probably looking at the plate, his mind occupied with little else than the corner of the plate he wishes to 'cut.' Even during the act of throwing he is hardly aware of what his arm is doing, for his attention is still focused on the batter and the plate. It is evident that we cannot call such an action fully voluntary in the sense that we should apply the term to the same pitcher's acts when as a boy he first learned to pitch a ball.

One of the most common examples of an act which is even more involuntary is speech. Seldom are we conscious of the movements of our vocal organs while talking, nor are we often conscious of how we are going to move them before we start. For the most part we are occupied with the direction of the thought, the effect we are making and to some slight degree with the sound of our voices. That we are usually unconscious of the way we talk is made clear by contrast when we hesitate before a foreign word which is difficult to pronounce. We are even more unconscious of our actual vocal movements when we read an uninteresting book aloud to a friend, while we think at the same time of something quite different. In fact, we are almost unaware, not only of our motor responses, but even of the meaning of what we are reading. Through long training the words on the page (the visual stimuli) set off the appropriate action patterns and we read quite intelligently with a minimum of attention—a minimum of intention, in fact.

A day is replete with such semivoluntary acts, acts that hardly touch the conscious level. Even while one writes with concentration at his desk these incidental actions intrude and pass. One looks up for an instant while pondering a difficult problem and his eyes rest upon his pipe. His hand reaches out for it, puts it in his mouth, and the writing goes on with scarcely a break.

Automatic acts. It is possible in situations like the preceding for the individual to be totally unconscious of what he has done. An act in which the person is thus unaware of his performance is called *automatic*. Automatic acts, like semivoluntary ones, are very common. We curl a strand of hair, bite our pencil tip, tap on the floor, rattle a bunch of keys, entirely unaware that we are doing anything. While walking with a friend we engage in animated conversation, completely unconscious of the action of our legs. Automatic acts can be as complex and can involve as highly an integrated set of reactions as any fully voluntary response. This fact is well demonstrated by instances of automatic writing, where a person writes the answers to questions put to him without the slightest idea of what he has written. Since it seems evident in such cases that the hand has been guided by subconscious processes, the method is often used to discover what lies below the level of consciously controlled behavior.

The examples which we have examined in these last sections illustrate the various forms of action, from the fully voluntary through the different degrees of semivoluntary behavior to unconscious automatic acts. Such a classification, however, is by no means clear cut. Although we can have acts that are entirely automatic and unconscious, almost all voluntary acts contain some automatic process. In fact, such acts as piano-playing, when performed by a proficient person, contain so much automatic response that it is customary to use the word automatic rather than voluntary in regard to them. Here action has become so well established a habit that correct response follows immediately upon stimulus, whether the musician is using the score or playing from memory, that is to say, whether the stimuli are the musical notations and the preceding finger movements, or the latter alone. It is, indeed, frequently difficult to say whether an action is entirely automatic or not, as when the musician plays softly over the keys while conversing with a friend, or when a telegraph operator taps SOS on the desk with his finger while he is reading an engrossing detective story. The important point is that most of our responses are a mixture of the two types, automatic and voluntary.

Voluntary control of movement. What do we have to do in order to gain voluntary control of a response? It was at one time supposed that, if we could call to mind how the muscles would feel when moved in a certain way—in other words, if we had a clear memory of the *kinesthetic* sensations produced by the movement (see pp. 618-620)—we could then move those muscles appropriately. It was even sometimes supposed that such a memory of a movement must necessarily precede the movement which we desire to make. That this assumption is not true follows from the fact that voluntary control of a reflex can be obtained by the method of conditioning (pp. 262f.). Not only, however, is kinesthesis not necessary, but research has also shown that kinesthesis alone—or even when combined with a visual image of what the movement should be—is not a sufficient preliminary process to produce at will a movement never before voluntarily initiated.

In certain experiments, persons who could not move their ears voluntarily had the ear muscles stimulated electrically so as to produce the movement. These persons felt the movement and saw it in a mirror; still they could not move their ears voluntarily. In attempting to move them, they had the same sense of helplessness which they had experienced before the electrical stimulation. In their attempts, however, they moved the voluntarily controlled muscles of the brow, jaw and cheek, in such a way that the muscles of the ear were accidentally moved with them. Thus the ear muscles were brought into the reaction pattern, with the result that there occurred both efferent impulses to the muscles and proprioceptor stimulation from their contraction. It was only then that the appropriate kinesthesis, by becoming a link in the reflex circle, helped to develop full voluntary control of the ear. The role of kinesthesis in voluntary response is discussed further in the next section on ideo-motor action.

There is a method of re-educating paralytics which throws additional light upon the subject of muscular control. The paralysis in question is usually caused by injury to the cerebral motor area concerned with the particular movements. Though the person may try earnestly to move the limb, no movement results; nor does it usually help him to gain control of the limb if someone else moves it for him, any more than the electric shock is an aid in learning to move the ear. When he makes an unusually great effort, however, he may move unimpaired muscles, and that movement involves the paralyzed muscles. Gradually in this way, probably because of the formation of new nervous connections, he slowly learns to make the desired movement. Recovery may be hastened by encouraging the patient to play athletic games, since he is thus placed in a situation where he is likely to make strong muscular efforts.

These facts give us a picture of the origin and development of voluntary movement. It is clear from them that the *first movements* of our muscle groups are *unconscious* and *involuntary* and that they come under conscious voluntary control only later, after the muscles have been 'accidentally' innervated. The fact that conscious habits tend to develop into automatic action has in the past given rise to the opposite notion that all movement is at first conscious, but this view is no longer tenable.

Ideo-motor action. After a response has become voluntary, one often calls to mind kinesthetic images of the intended movement before making the response, especially when learning difficult tasks. Kinesthetic imagery, however, is not necessary as a preliminary to a voluntary act. The idea may be merely the verbal instruction to move in a certain way. In fact, it may be any kind of imagery even remotely connected with the act to be performed. The idea of the actual movement to be executed, however, whatever may be the imaginal terms in which it is carried, seems to be the most compelling antecedent to action. A response which thus follows directly the thought of the act is called ideo-motor action.

In the following experiment this form of response is clearly shown. If a recording instrument is placed on a person's head so that a graphic record of his head movements can be obtained, it is found that when, with his eyes closed, he merely thinks of his head moving to the right, the record shows that his head has actually made a slight movement in that direction. When he thinks of moving his head to the left, the record indicates that such a movement has been made. Yet the person himself is unlikely at any time during the experiment to realize that he has made an actual movement.

The feat of muscle reading, a form of 'mind reading,' is based on this fact of action following the thought of it. The performer takes the hand of an individual and tells him to think as hard as possible of what he wants him to do. If the individual wishes him to go toward the window, his hand will make a slight movement in that direction, which the performer, who is supersensitive to such weak muscular responses, will immediately feel and use as a cue. Animals are particularly acute in noticing unconscious movements. A trained dog may be able to pick out the correct one of a series of playing cards spread on the floor if persons who know the correct card are nearby. In thinking of the card, these onlookers are likely unconsciously to turn their eyes for a fraction of a second toward the card in question, a hint which is not lost on the dog.

Ideo-motor action is also illustrated in the dislike of some persons for high places. The idea of jumping comes so strongly to mind that they fear it will break over into action. Nearly everyone has had at some time so vivid an idea of the act of jumping out of the window at which he was standing that he has wished to withdraw from the spot in order to avoid the danger. Another example is the desire to knock off the top hat of a fellow traveler, an idea which, once brought to mind, may prove almost irresistible. Advertising has made good use of the principle of ideo-motor action. The tired tennis player is portrayed in the act of smoking a certain brand of cigarette, so that the reader will be induced by the idea to do likewise. Innumerable examples of a similar nature could be taken from daily life, for ideo-motor action is a very common experience.

Empathy. Still more frequent, however, are the incipient movements, sometimes too slight to be readily detected, at other times quite noticeable, which are aroused in us by movements in our environment. An obvious example may be observed at a football game where the home team, let us say, is holding on the one-yard line. An enthusiastic and partisan spectator may push actively and urgently with the players, until suddenly he realizes that he is actually pushing his neighbor. Or again, when spectators watch an acrobat climb to the top of a pole balanced on the head of a colleague and swing back and forth with the tottering pole, the whole crowd sways in unison. An example of empathy is presented in Fig. 24.

In looking at statues and buildings and pictures, or in listening to music, this sort of movement likewise occurs. We may feel the thrust of the foot or the tension of the outstretched hand of a statue, the weight of the arch on its column or the rise of the column itself, and the direction of the lines and weight of the represented mass in the picture. Listening to music, we often find ourselves following the rhythm with some part of our bodies. Even the rhythmical click of the car wheel over the rail may arouse a motor response. Since we are occupied with the perception of the object, we are for the most part not conscious of these movements in ourselves. Nevertheless our responses, though unconscious as such, give dynamic quality to these perceptions. The lines of the picture become lines of force, the represented mass has weight, the rhythm of the music seems to flow smoothly, the curves of the architecture appear to have the grace of a moving object.

Gracefulness is indeed a very interesting example of the manner in which movements influence perceptions. Herbert Spencer rightly defined gracefulness as the characteristic of movement which is produced with the minimum amount of effort. The accomplished ballet dancer tries to conceal any movements of face or body which would suggest strain or effort to the observer. The more successful the performer in achiev-

FIG. 24. EMPATHY.
Blind Bill Kelley clearing the pole, with his trainer, Peter Bennett, watching. Notice the empathic response of the trainer. By permission of Pictures, Inc.

ing this end, the more graceful the dance appears. Her face is usually placid or even smiling; she whirls and springs with apparent ease. Inasmuch as little feeling of strain is aroused in us as we watch, she therefore seems to move in the air with the lightness of a leaf blown by the wind.

Now we do not think of these responses, but rather of the characteristics they produce for us in the objective world. It is as if we had projected our own experience into the object of our perception. This sort of projection has been termed *empathy*, or a feeling of ourselves into the object of regard. Empathy is an important factor, especially in much of our esthetic experience, that side of our life concerned with the beauty of things.

Suggestion. In the broad sense of the term, suggestion plays a large role in our lives of action. The immediate perception of an object most frequently leads to some response which depends upon previous experience with the object. The flame suggests withdrawal of the hand. The sight of a half-read book suggests continuing the story; without any intervening thought the student picks it up, when he had fully intended to settle down to study. The sleight-of-hand performer, by a movement of the other hand, suggests a shift of the attention of the audience away from the hand that is doing the trick. In the empathic perception of lines and mass there is the direct suggestion of some motor response. The individuals of a mob are extremely suggestible to the actions of one or more of their companions. Although the term suggestion is used legitimately in all these instances, it is usually restricted to that action which is brought about by a verbal instruction. One acts through suggestion when he responds to the written or spoken word *uncritically*. In most instances such a response is immediate, but it may on occasions be delayed. Children, being obviously less critical then adults, are more suggestible; as a consequence, their testimony is particularly untrustworthy. This trait may be easily demonstrated. The child is asked to place his hand on an electric heater and told to say when he feels the warmth. After the experimenter has made the motion of turning on the current (without actually throwing the switch) the child will soon report that he feels the heat.

On occasion, however, adults can be just as suggestible as children. Given the proper emotional setting, they will imagine the impossible. An excellent example is what occurred in the autumn of 1938 when the story of the Martians came over the radio. Many persons actually smelt the poisoned fumes which the Martians were supposed to have spread.

A person is said to be highly suggestible when he lacks firm convictions of his own. Though most of us can act through suggestion a thousand times a day without losing individuality, there are the extreme cases where a person has so few firm convictions of his own that no counter argument enters his mind when he is presented with an important course of action. Conversely, there is the negatively suggestible person. He almost invariably has some reason for not doing what is desired of him. The first type cuts out the coupon of the advertisement at once and mails it. The second type immediately throws the advertisement in the waste-basket. It is thus that attitudes toward suggestion determine action in the large as well as the small affairs of life. Degree of suggestibility is an essential feature of personality.

Hypnotism. The hypnotic trance and its manifestations are the result of an extreme state of suggestibility, but one which may be induced in varying degrees in most normal persons who are willing to cooperate with the hypnotist. Except that he can respond adequately to external stimulation when the hypnotist suggests it, the person who has been hypnotized is in a condition resembling sleep. If the subject's mind is free from the ordinary inhibitions and resistance, he readily carries out the instructions given him by the hypnotist, provided that the task does not conflict with his most fundamental convictions. He will commit an artificially arranged crime but, contrary to popular belief, he cannot easily be induced to commit an offense if it really contravenes strong tendencies of ethical conduct.

It has been supposed that under hypnosis a person's senses are keener and his strength greater than normal. Experiments, however, have shown that this is not the case. There is little if any difference in his threshold of sensitivity, and the feats of strength he performs under hypnosis he can also do in his normal state if he is willing to make great effort. It has also been found experimentally that persons who acted through hypnotic suggestion as if they could not see, actually had normal vision. Moreover, the hypnotic removal of pain does not affect the changes in the small blood vessels which accompany pain.

An interesting phenomenon of the hypnotic state is *post-hypnotic suggestion*, an extreme form of delayed response. For example, if a person under hypnosis is told by the hypnotizer to drink a glass of water at a specified time after coming out of the hypnosis, he will obey the instruction accurately. If asked why he took a drink, he will probably reply that he was thirsty, since he will have no recollection of the initial cause of his action. (For a further example see p. 389.)

QUANTITATIVE DESCRIPTION OF RESPONSE

Reaction time. The preceding sections have dealt principally with the qualitative aspects of volitional acts. It is now necessary to consider in more detail the speed of response and the conditions which determine the speed. The problem of the reaction time arose in 1796, when a certain astronomer at the Greenwich Observatory in England dismissed his assistant because the latter's observations of the time at which stars cross a cross-hair in the field of the telescope were almost a second later than his own. Twenty years later it was discovered by checking the observations of different astronomers that the discrepancies were due to more fundamental differences in the manner of reaction than would be produced by mere carelessness. The conclusion was reached that these measurements, which depend upon the speed of reaction of the observer, were affected by what was then called the personal equation, that is to say, constant individual differences in reaction time. When the first psychological laboratory was established in Leipzig in 1879, experiments on reaction times were undertaken. Ever since, reaction times have represented an important technique in experimental psychology.

One of the most accurate arrangements for the measurement of human response is illustrated in Fig. 25. Its main feature is a chronoscope or timing device, consisting of a synchronous motor and a dial whose hand is attached to a magnetic clutch. Two telegraph keys are wired to the instrument in such a way that when one key is pressed the clutch engages with the motor and when the other key is pressed the motor is released. In the simplest experiment the subject is seated at one key and the experimenter at the other, and the motor is started. The experimenter presses his key, which gives the desired stimulus to the subject and engages the clutch so that the hand on the dial revolves. As quickly as possible

FIG. 25. INSTRUMENT FOR TIMING REACTIONS.

A, bulb for response key; *B,* voice keys; *C,* light stimulus; *D,* relay for touch stimulus; *E,* chronoscope; *F,* relay for sound stimulus; *G,* tuning-fork for time control; *H,* stimulus keys. Courtesy of the C. H. Stoelting Company of Chicago.

upon perceiving the appropriate signal the subject presses his key, thereby releasing the clutch, so that the hand on the dial stops. The revolutions of the hand are recorded on the dial. As the speed of revolution is already known, the time that elapsed between the pressing of the two keys—in short, between stimulus and response—may be read from the dial in milliseconds.

Various stimuli and types of response may be used. For example, the experimenter may signal by means of a clicking sound produced by a relay, or he may give a tactual stimulus by means of a magnetic contrivance that presses on the subject's hand. He may flash an electric lamp as a visual stimulus; or, if a 'choice reaction' is desired, he may illuminate in haphazard order either a green or red lamp. For word reactions he uses a voice-key containing a thin diaphragm which vibrates when spoken against, thus temporarily breaking the electric circuit. The experimenter may speak into one voice-key, starting the clock, and the subject may speak into the other key, stopping it. There are other possible arrangements, but in each of them the clock is started and stopped automatically and reaction times are obtained which are accurate within a few milliseconds.

Simple reactions. In the *simple* reaction experiment, the subject is generally instructed to respond by pressing a telegraph key as quickly as possible after the signal is given by the experimenter. Not only do individuals vary among themselves in speed of reaction, but also the reaction time of the same individual varies according to the *sense organ stimulated.* The following table will give an idea of the approximate range of the reaction times in milliseconds for the different senses:

Kind of Stimulation	Reaction Times
Visual	150 to 225 ms.
Auditory	120 to 185 ms.
Tactual	115 to 190 ms.
Olfactory	200 to 800 ms.
Gustatory	305 to 1080 ms.
Pain	400 to 1000 ms.
Cold	150 ms.
Warm	180 ms.

The reaction times to painful stimuli are especially long, due in part to the fact that there is a considerable lag between the application of a stimulus and the consciousness of pain. The reaction times for warmth and cold vary according to the manner of application of the stimuli. The reaction to taste varies with the part of the tongue stimulated and the kind of stimulus; the time is shortest for salt and longest for bitter. The time for touch varies according to the part of the body stimulated and to the limb making the response. The reaction time for a stimulus applied to the forehead is longer than for one applied to the hand. The reaction of the right hand to a tactual stimulus applied to the same hand is quicker than to a stimulus applied to the opposite hand. The reaction to light is faster when the light falls on the fovea (the area of clearest vision near the center of the retina, which is the sensitive inner layer of the eye) than when it falls on an eccentric part of the retina, the time increasing continuously with the distance of stimulation from the fovea. Reaction is more rapid to binocular than to monocular stimulation.

In most experiments upon reaction time, a preparatory signal is given before the presentation of the stimulus. It is found that the reaction time varies with the *length of the interval* between the preparatory signal and reaction signal. Constant intervals between 2 and 4 sec. give the shortest times. If the preparatory signal is varied within a series, so that the subject never knows exactly how long he will have to wait for the reaction signal, the optimal interval ranges between 12 and 16 sec. The act of preparation seems to be the chief factor involved in these results. If the interval is too short, the subject has not sufficient time to 'get set' and the stimulus may come before he is quite ready. If he has to wait more than 4 sec., the interval becomes too monotonous for him to hold his attention entirely on the task. If the interval is varied, he is unable to assume a constant attitude of expectation and therefore requires a longer interval for his quickest reaction than when the interval is constant.

Distraction usually lengthens reaction time, but sometimes the supposedly distracting stimulus acts as a spur and decreases the time. This paradoxical effect, which has been found in other experiments where concentration is necessary, is explained by the fact that some persons use more effort to concentrate when there is an obstacle to overcome. City dwellers become so accustomed to concentration 'in spite of' the noise of the street that they often have difficulty at first in working efficiently when they go into the country.

Reaction times to all kinds of stimuli decrease with an increase in the *intensity* of the stimulus. This decrease in time is most marked in the range of weak intensities.

Although an individual's reaction time varies according to the nature of the stimulus, the question arises whether, if he is quicker than his fellows in his response to visual stimuli, he will also respond more quickly to auditory and tactual stimuli. In other words, is there a speed characteristic of response that runs through all of a person's motor reactions? In a series of experiments it was found that the correlation of simple visual, auditory and tactual reaction times was 0.86 in one experiment and 0.72 in a second experiment. These results indicate that if a person excels in speed of reaction to one kind of stimulus, there is a good chance that he will also be quick in his reactions to other kinds.

Sensory and motor reactions. If a runner starts sooner than his rival at the crack of the pistol, it is due in part to the difference in attitude of the contestants. It has been shown in the laboratory that there are two types of reaction; *sensory* and *motor*. In the sensory type, the subject's attention is directed by the instruction to the stimulus, and in the motor type to the response which he is to make. In the extreme form of sensory reaction, the attention of the subject is directed almost exclusively to the coming stimulus, often with a steady fixation in the direction of its appearance. In the extreme motor reaction the idea of the movement to be performed in terms of kinesthesis is dominant. If the subject is allowed to react 'naturally,' there is usually an attitude midway between these two forms, or an alternation of the two.

These differences in attitude cause differences in reaction time. When the reaction tends toward the sensory type, the time is longer than when it tends toward the motor type. In the table on reaction times, page 279, visual reactions range from 150 ms. to 225 ms. It is probable that the time 150 ms. was obtained under a motor set and the 225 ms. under a sensory attitude. With practice one tends to become increasingly motor until the reaction becomes practically automatic;

then the finger movements occur with little conscious intention as soon as a signal is given. With this extreme motor attitude, however, premature reactions are not infrequent, as one finds not only in the laboratory but also in such situations as racing. A runner who is of the extreme motor type often makes a false start. Some runners, however, prefer to be sure of the signal, even though they are a little late. These different types are found among people in general; there are those who are slow, safe and sure, and those who go off 'half-cocked.'

Discrimination and choice reactions. Most of our reactions in life are not like the simple reaction experiments. It is seldom in everyday life that we can be so sure of what is going to happen as to set ourselves to react automatically at maximum speed. The runner who is not alert may, for example, start at the sound of an automobile back-firing instead of at the pistol shot. Consequently some *discrimination* is generally necessary for a correct response.

In the laboratory this complicated situation is produced by varying the stimuli. The subject may be instructed to react only to a red light, when both red and green signals are used in haphazard order. It is obvious that this problem is similar to that confronting the locomotive engineer and the automobile driver. The necessity of recognizing the correct signal increases the average reaction time above the time of the simple reaction; and, the more motor the set of the subject is, the more likely he is to react to the wrong light. This situation may be further complicated by requiring a *choice* between two or more reactions as well as a discrimination between stimuli. The subject may, for example, be instructed to respond with the right hand if the light is red and with the left hand if the light is green, or with the right hand if the red light appears on the right of the green and with the left hand if the stimuli are reversed. The greater the complications, the longer the reaction time.

In the discrimination experiment it is found that the more

the stimuli resemble each other, the longer are the reaction times. If black and white are used as stimuli, the reactions are quickest. Red and green come next, then red and blue, followed by red and yellow, and finally red and orange. If tones are used, the reaction to tones differing by 16 cycles is quicker than to tones differing by 12 cycles, and much quicker than to tones only 4 cycles apart. When lines differing in length are the stimuli, the less the difference between the lines, the longer are the reactions. The reaction time is, for example, shorter for discrimination between lines of 10 mm. and 13 mm. than for 10 mm. and 12 mm.

Word reactions. The commonest reactions in life are *verbal*. To determine the nature and speed of such responses numerous experiments have been devised. The usual method is to present a word visually or vocally, the subject being told to respond as quickly as possible with the word that is suggested by the stimulus word. The time, which may be taken by a stop watch or by means of voice-keys and a chronoscope, indicates the speed of the association of ideas for the individual tested. If the subject is told to respond with the first word that occurs to him, the association is termed 'free.' Frequently, however, the instructions are more limited. For example, a general term indicating a class, such as *animal*, is given and the subject is required to reply with the name of a member of this class, such as *bear*; or he is instructed to respond with a word opposite in meaning to the stimulus word. Many other variations in instruction may be given. These associations, being partially determined from the start, are called controlled associations. Experiments of this nature have been extensively employed in investigations of the nature of the thought process.

Practical use of reaction experiments. An individual's ability in practical affairs depends in part upon his speed of reaction. It is therefore frequently of value to know both his speed of reaction in a given situation and how he compares with other individuals under similar circumstances. It is also of interest to know how much he may improve his speed and accuracy by practice as well as under the incentive of increased interest in the task.

Reaction time is an important factor both in vocational selection and in determining the individual's aptitudes as a basis for vocational advice. For example, in the selection of telephone switchboard operators speed of response and relative freedom from errors are essential requirements. A consideration of the same characteristics is necessary in the selection of chauffeurs and machine operators. According to the results of tests of taxi drivers, those men with the greatest number of accidents have the slowest reaction times. Those who have the fastest reaction times have also many accidents, perhaps because they are overconfident and take chances. It is therefore desirable to select drivers from the group whose reaction times are neither very fast nor very slow.

The association-reaction experiments have been used with some success to determine guilt. Words are selected which are related to the crime and these interspersed with 'neutral' words. The words of this combined list are read to the subject, who must answer as rapidly as possible to each one with any word he can think of. Anyone knows from his own experience that when he is faced with an embarrassing situation—one that is emotionally toned—he is liable to hesitate and often to reply foolishly or irrelevantly. In the 'crime' experiment there is exactly such an embarrassing situation for the guilty person. Therefore the tendency is for the reaction time to the relevant words to be unusually long, or at least to vary more than the reaction times to the neutral words; in addition, the meaningful reference of the words is often different in the two cases.

This same method is used to discover suppressed complexes—the memory of painful experiences which, held in a subconscious state, often give rise to abnormal mental conditions. Owing to the fact that such complexes are, like the concealed knowledge of the guilty subject, highly emotional in nature, the two test situations are very similar.

THE NATURE OF THE WILL

The will. A person decides to go to town. He walks down the stairs, puts on his coat and hat, opens the door, gets into his car and starts the engine. Common sense says that he has willed to do these various acts. Or again someone is trying to read a difficult passage in a textbook. His mind continues to wander from the book to irrelevant matters, until finally with great effort he succeeds in concentrating on the work at hand. It is usual to say that he has had to use his will power. No fault can be found with such an expression in ordinary speech, but the psychologist desires to know what is this conscious experience, and, further, what is the general process that one calls 'will.'

In voluntary action, as we have seen, there is frequently some idea of the movement or thought of the instruction preliminary to the movement itself. Many such descriptions of the period antecedent to action have been obtained. An example may be taken from the experiments on reaction time. If the response is to be made with the right hand to a red light and with the left hand to a green light, the subject of the experiment may at first repeat the instructions to himself. He may also associate in his mind his right hand with the red light and his left hand with the green light. He will probably in addition feel some tension in his arms. In such terms as these the task or problem will be represented in the subject's mind before a reaction takes place. This attitude of the subject is called the *set* toward the task. As the experimental series progresses, the set will become increasingly motor in nature, so that eventually the movement will occur immediately upon the appearance of the stimulus without any intervening mental state. This set may be either positive or negative. In the experiment with the red and green lights, the set for the right hand may be positive toward the red light and negative or inhibitory toward the green light.

An experiment can be arranged to investigate the motor set

by placing a rubber bulb or tambour on the reaction key in order to measure the amount of pressure of the finger. By such means it has been found that the finger frequently makes an actual anticipatory movement of downward pressure on the key before the real movement is carried out. A good example of motor set is that of the football player who has in mind just what to do in answer to the play of his opponents. Off-side play is frequently due to an overintensified set similar to the set in the experiment just described, when the finger made an anticipatory movement. In another experiment it has been shown that there is greater effort as recorded in preliminary tension when the task is difficult than when it is easy. In the daily acts such as those cited in the beginning of this section, the sequence of events follows so rapidly and one is so little given to observing his own action that the essential attitudes escape attention. They can be observed, however, especially when the task is difficult.

The second phase of the voluntary act is its execution. Here the set or attitude carries through as a directive mechanism called the *determining tendency*. (For its description in relation to thought see pp. 389-391.) It is this directive tendency which makes an act more than a rigid mechanical sequence of events, such as is found in the movements of a machine. The determining tendency, formed by the preliminary set, causes the subject to respond correctly with the right hand instead of the left on the appearance of a red light. It is likewise responsible for the selection of the correct words of a sentence.

In a voluntary act there is no special force that can be called the 'will.' What is felt in an experience of 'will power' is the muscular tension involved—tension in the arms, for instance, in acts like the reaction experiments where movement is involved, or tension in the muscles of the forehead when the brow is wrinkled in an effort to concentrate on a mental task. It has been argued that, since a person paralyzed in one leg experiences an effort of will when he tries to move the inert limb and yet does not move it, the will experience obviously cannot come from these muscles. But what actually happens is that unknowingly he moves the other limbs or some other member, and it is this movement that gives him the impression of will power. The will, then, so far as experience is concerned, turns out to be the preliminary attitude and the experience of movement plus the knowledge that the movement follows directly on the attitude and has not been caused by any external force. We *know* that we have made the movement. It is unfortunate that 'will' is a noun, for it implies some agent, faculty or special kind of energy. There is *'willing' but not a 'will.' Willing is a process which one calls a voluntary act.*

Abulia. Everyone at times finds it hard to get down to work, especially if the task is difficult or if there has been a long interruption such as a summer vacation. Under such circumstances he invents all sorts of excuses to postpone action. A person in this condition is not inactive or lazy, for he will perform such useless acts as repeatedly washing his hands or cleaning his glasses or going down to the cellar every few minutes to see if he closed the furnace door. He may get up in the morning full of energy and resolution only to find himself caught in the toils of petty activities directly he has finished his breakfast. This state of vacillation and procrastination gives him a sense of inferiority which aggravates the situation. Such behavior is a mild form of what in its more pronounced manifestations is called *abulia.*

Sometimes, where there is inability to act or to make a decision, abulia is simply deficient impulsion; sometimes it represents a positive conflict in which the individual remains unable to bring himself to do what he nevertheless strongly desires to do. The failure of a student to undertake necessary study may be an abulia of either kind.

Authorities believe that abulia is due either to lowered vitality or to repressed unconscious wishes, which, being impossible of fulfilment under existing conditions, cause fear and anxiety with an accompanying tendency to retreat from reality.

Abulia may be either general or specific. In the former case there is general apathy, indecision and lack of attention accompanied by unusual docility and suggestibility. An hysterical patient, for example, will hesitate before initiating some new activity. Although he will make futile, spasmodic efforts to do what he is told to do, he will soon fail. Another type of patient will go through the mechanical act of reading, but will not understand the content until someone explains the meaning to him. In the specific type of abulia there is an abnormal weakness of some particular form of behavior, probably due to a mental complex. An example of the suppression of action by a conflicting motive is seen in a certain instance of multiple personality. The patient often came to her doctor for the purpose of telling him something which was of importance to her welfare, but which happened to conflict with the favorite scheme of another of her personalities which was for the moment suppressed. Under such circumstances, after vain efforts to speak, she would give up with the remark, "Well, it doesn't matter."

In mild cases of abulia the patient, though able eventually to perform his ordinary duties, finds it necessary to exert great effort to accomplish the simplest task. He feels himself subject to some mysterious fatigue neither produced by overwork nor relieved by sleep. In the more serious cases all activity progresses at a slow pace and much work is left unfinished. The patient moves with dragging feet, speaks in a weak voice and lounges about. In one instance a girl patient remained for hours in front of a door which she wanted to enter without being able to bring herself to turn the knob. In the most extreme cases the patient is incapable of doing anything. He lies helplessly upon his back, cannot speak, and cannot even eat without assistance.

REFERENCES

1. Bair, J. H. Development of voluntary control. *Psychol. Rev.*, 1901, 8, 474-510.
2. Bridges, J. W. *Outline of abnormal psychology.* (2nd ed.) Columbus, Ohio: R. G. Adams, 1921. Pp. 98-99.

3. Carmichael, L. Origin and prenatal growth of behavior. *A handbook of child psychology.* (2nd ed.) Worcester, Mass.: Clark University Press, 1933. Chap. 2.
4. Carmichael, L. The development of behavior in vertebrates experimentally removed from the influence of external stimulation. *Psychol. Rev.,* 1926, 33, 51-58.
5. Coghill, G. E. *Anatomy and the problem of behavior.* New York: Macmillan, 1929.
6. Fearing, F. *Reflex action.* Baltimore: Williams & Wilkins, 1930.
7. Garrett, H. *Great experiments in psychology.* New York: Appleton-Century, 1930. Chap. 9.
8. Holt, E. B. *Animal drive and the learning process.* New York: Henry Holt, 1931.
9. Hudgins, C. V. Conditioning and the voluntary control of the pupillary light reflex. *J. gen. Psychol.,* 1933, 8, 3-51.
10. Kuo, Z. Y. Ontogeny of embryonic behavior in aves. *Psychol. Rev.,* 1932, 39, 499-515.
11. Lanier, L. H. The interrelations of speed of reaction measurements. *J. exper. Psychol.,* 1934, 17, 371-399.
12. Lewin, K. Environmental forces. *A handbook of child psychology.* (2nd ed.) Worcester, Mass.: Clark University Press, 1933. Chap. 14.
13. Peak, H. Modification of the lid-reflex by voluntarily induced sets. *Psychol. Monogr.,* 1931, 42, No. 188.
14. Tolman, E. C. *Purposive behavior.* New York: Century, 1932.
15. Travis, L. E., and Patterson, M. Rate and direction of the contraction wave in muscle during voluntary and reflex movement. *J. exper. Psychol.,* 1933, 16, 208-220.

Chapter 9

LEARNING

The psychology of learning is divided into two large topics: *learning* and *retention*. Each of these is a name given to a different aspect either of experience or of behavior. Most of the experimental work has, however, to do with behavior.

LEARNING AND RETENTION

Because human beings learn from birth to death, perhaps even before birth, the act of learning is so common that it goes almost unremarked. When we notice it at all, we think of it in rough, unanalytic terms. The careful laboratory analysis of learning, on the other hand, requires the use of materials, methods and concepts which at first appear to be strange and divorced from the learning of everyday life. Yet we should remember that learning in the laboratory is the same in kind as the learning which pervades everyday life; what the laboratory does is simply to provide an analysis of the learning process.

The importance of learning in the life of man can be appreciated more fully if we think of the number and complexity of the things which any one of us has learned. Each of us began life as an organism which was capable of only a few simple responses. From birth until this moment the changes in performance which are the marks of learning have gone progressively onward to bring us to whatever complexity of performance we have now reached. We have learned to walk, to eat the things we eat in the ways we eat them, to respond as we do to other people and—the crowning achievement of the human being—to use language. We have

This chapter was written by John A. McGeoch of the University of Iowa.

learned not only to use language for communication but to use it also to control the behavior of other people and to satisfy our needs. Nor is learning only intellectualistic. Likes and dislikes, emotional responses, most of the complex panoply of reactions which we call personality, all have been learned. Most of this learning has occurred informally in the give and take of daily life; learning is not necessarily formal learning. Although many things learned in practical life cannot be transferred to the laboratory and studied there, there is reason to believe that the fundamental principles which we discover in the laboratory are applicable to everyday life.

Learning and retention are measured by discovering how large is the change in some performance in the direction of satisfying some motive during a certain period of time or on account of a certain expenditure of effort. *Learning* means improvement in the satisfaction of some need, whether it be a rat seeking food in a maze or a laboratory subject seeking the approval of the experimenter. Learning depends upon *practice*, the occurrence and usually the continued recurrence of the situation that involves the need. Thus learning is often measured by the number of *repetitions* of the situation that are required before some *criterion* of perfection is reached.

Often typewriting is used as a performance for the study of learning. Learning in this case is measured by the increase in the number of words typed per minute or by the decrease in the number of errors. The need is present in the subject's desire to learn, either because he wants to cooperate in an experiment or because he wants to learn typewriting. If the subject repeatedly retypes a given material, then the number of his repetitions can be counted until he reaches some predetermined criterion of excellence, such as three errorless performances in succession.

Retention is the persistence of learning, and *forgetting* is the loss of learning. One of these functions is the inverse of the other. Since ordinarily there is a loss in retention with the lapse of time, the measurement of retention is often the observation of the amount of depreciation of an original learning as time passes. As we shall see later, what goes on during the time elapsed is fully as important as the time.

Retention is, of course, continuously present during learning. A second repetition of a situation advances learning only because there is some retention of the effect of the first repetition. Forgetting, on the other hand, is also constantly operative during learning. The effect of a repetition always diminishes in time as subsequent events work upon it. One learns always against forgetting, and in spite of forgetting.

CONDITIONS OF LEARNING

The existence of an organism which practices and of a performance which is practiced is necessary if learning is to occur at all, but besides these minimal essentials there are a few general conditions of the utmost importance. In describing these conditions we shall use the word *association* to denote the fact that, when a given phenomenon appears, a certain other phenomenon will follow it. Association means that when you hear the question, "In what year did Columbus discover America?" you reply, "1492"; that, when you sit at your typewriter, your fingers execute the movements necessary to type the copy or words which express your ideas; or that, when you are faced with a thought problem, such as solving an alegbraic formula, relevant data come to mind and are used. The initial situation in all these cases is 'associated with' the phenomena which follow it.

Motive and effect. Practice assumes a motive or need in the subject; otherwise he would not practice. These needs are complex, including many not controlled by the experimenter, but for the purpose of the present discussion the important thing is that they are present (see pp. 166-168). It is extremely improbable that there is any learning at all in the absence of motives to learn. Certainly such motives are necessary for sustained practice, and they are probably necessary for any learning whatever.

Motivation alone, however, is not sufficient for learning. The subject needs to know the consequences of his responses. Such a knowledge of results, whether it be in terms of factual information, of pleasantness or unpleasantness, or of some other psychological product, is called the *effect* of activity, and its influence has been formulated in the *law of effect*. This law reads: *Other things being equal, those acts leading to consequences which satisfy a need are selected and learned, whereas those leading to consequences which do not satisfy a need are eliminated or inhibited.* The influence of effect is fundamental in accounting for the selection of some acts and the elimination of others in such cases as the learning of skills and the solution of problems.

The everyday learning of our lives is pervaded by the action of the law of effect. The responses which are successful in getting us what we want, *i.e.,* in satisfying a need, are the ones we learn. Responses which bring us praise or some desired reward, even if no more than the avoidance of pain, become fixed: "The burned child dreads the fire."

Few of the needs which enter into our learning as adults are fundamental biological ones. Most of them are, as they stand, learned motives. We do not seek praise or money or social approval under the influence of a directly biological need, but rather in response to a complex organization of acquired needs. (See the discussion of derived needs, pp. 156f.)

Because of the complexity of motives, and especially of those which the experimenter is unable to control or measure, it is often difficult to specify in a given instance of learning what need has been satisfied. Sometimes *incidental learning*—the learning of casually observed items, such as a chance remark, or of casually performed acts—seems to be unmotivated, but the lack of motivation is probably more seeming than actual. The law of effect has broad scope, and trivial incidents connected with a successful act may be remembered on that account. Undoubtedly some cases of apparently unmotivated incidental learning are to be explained in this manner.

Associative spread. Every new instance of learning is influenced by what has been learned in the past and retained until the present. It is hardly possible for an adult, or even a child, to be faced with so novel a problem of learning that it has no relation to any of his past learning. Thus the already existent organization of his past spreads and carries over to the new material. The new material is fitted into the old. During practice there is a mutual interaction between old and new, until finally the new becomes assimilated. Though this interaction sometimes makes the new material easier to learn and sometimes makes it harder, the balance is usually on the side of making it easier. If every learning were entirely independent of all others, if there were no spread of the old to influence the new, learning as we know it would not occur.

The fact of associative spread lies at the basis of the transfer of practice from an earlier to a later learning—a phenomenon which we shall discuss later on. Associative spread is illustrated whenever we deal with a new situation, whenever we perceive similarities and for that matter whenever we perceive or learn anything at all. By means of it the new is assimilated and the complex integration of new and old made possible.

Temporal relations of learned events. A certain degree of temporal proximity is necessary for the formation of an association between two items or events. Neither simultaneity nor immediate succession is, however, necessary. Associations may be formed between terms which are separated by an interval at least as long as several seconds and sometimes by a much longer time. The fact that a certain degree of temporal proximity is nevertheless a necessary condition of association is known as *the law of contiguity.*

Frequency. The things which human beings learn, if of any degree of complexity, require at least several repetitions; everything learned at all, however simple, requires at least one. It has often been assumed that frequency of repetition, in and of itself, selects and fixates learning. This conception deserves critical examination.

1. The concept has usually implied that successive repetitions of any act are repetitions of the same thing. Actually, however, successive repetitions are far from being identical.

When a rat learns a maze, each run from start to goal may have different spatial and temporal characteristics, and, even after the errors have been eliminated and the true path selected and fixed, successive correct runs are not identical. The rat may go down one side of the path on one run, down the other side on the next and may cross from one side to the other in the middle of a section on the third. Variability of performance throughout learning is the rule. The pattern to be learned is approached by a series of successive approximations. This being the case, what is repeated? The attempt to get from start to goal, or to carry through whatever the conditions demand, is the only thing repeated. The specific performances whereby this attempt is carried out may vary widely. There can be, therefore, no stamping-in of specific neural paths by repetition, as older 'frequency theories' have assumed.

2. Repetition does not necessarily select and fix. It may also inhibit and eliminate. The making of an error in learning a maze or in solving a rational problem aids in the final elimination of the error if elimination satisfies the prevailing motivation. It is thus that errors in typing, among other things, are inhibited by repetition when repetition is used intentionally; for it has been found that, if one intentionally repeats an error over and over again, knowing all the while that it is an error, this repetition may favor the elimination of the error. In typing, for example, the habitual error of writing *hte* for *the* may be removed by typing many lines of *hte's*, thinking all the time: "This is an error which I will not make again." Elimination by this means brings directly to bear upon the error the motivation to be rid of it; it provides punishment because it is a nuisance to have to type the wrong spelling; and by tying up the error with other learning it makes use of associative spread. By this means, likewise, nail-biting, stuttering and kindred bad habits have sometimes been eliminated.

3. In many experiments, it has been shown that mere frequency of a connection or act, even when successive repetitions are as alike as possible, yields little if any learning. When to frequency is added a factor which has been called *belonging-*

ness (*i.e.*, the frequently connected terms seem to the learner naturally or rightly to go together), somewhat more evidence of learning appears, although not much. Belongingness involves transfer or spread of effect from prior learning and perhaps also from needs other than those supposedly aroused by the experimental situation. Thus it means going beyond mere frequency as a condition for learning. That frequency by itself ever determines learning is very doubtful.

Our conclusion therefore must be that, although it is certainly practice that makes perfect, improvement in performance cannot be referred to repetition itself. Practice works because of *effect*, to which repetition leads, and because of the associative *spread* which repetition allows. Frequency acts as a carrier of *effect* and *spread*.

CONDITIONED RESPONSES

The phenomena of the conditioned response, since they are among the simpler phenomena of learning, provide an introduction to the field. Although the fact of conditioning itself had been established long before Pavlov, nevertheless his work in connection with it has become so well known that the conditioned response is commonly associated with his name. In the previous chapter, in connection with the specialization of response, the nature of his experiments has already been described. In the present chapter we turn rather to the bearing of Pavlov's experiments and of others like them upon the problem of learning. In this discussion it is important to keep in mind the distinction between the primary or unconditioned stimulus, the unconditioned response, the secondary or conditioned stimulus and the conditioned response (see pp. 258-259).

The stimulus which will elicit the measured response prior to the beginning of the conditioning experiment is called the *unconditioned stimulus* and the resulting response the *unconditioned response*. The stimulus which, when paired with the unconditioned one, comes to elicit a similar response is called the *conditioned stimulus* and the response to it a *conditioned response.* Sometimes too the unconditioned stimulus is called the *primary stimulus* and the conditioned stimulus the *secondary stimulus.*

A large number of reflexes may be conditioned in both animals and men. Among these reflexes, in addition to the salivary reflex with which Pavlov worked, are the knee jerk, the pupillary reflex, winking, breathing and the galvanic skin response. Conditioning is not, however, confined to reflexes; it occurs with voluntary reactions as well. The range of stimuli which may become conditioned stimuli is indefinitely wide; the range of responses which can be conditioned is equally wide.

By no means is the occurrence of conditioned responses confined to the laboratory. When our mouths 'water' at the sight or description of food, we are displaying the phenomenon of conditioned salivary response; the emotional response to sudden danger is conditioned emotional behavior; in fact, the phenomena of conditioning pervade life.

Characteristics of the conditioned response. Early in the course of establishment of conditioned responses there appears the phenomenon of *irradiation*: other stimuli, but usually others from the same sense department as the conditioned stimulus, will also elicit the response. If the conditioned stimulus is a bell, other sounds, like tones or noises, will also call forth the response which is in process of being conditioned to the bell. As conditioning continues, the response gradually becomes specific to the conditioned stimulus (see pp. 258f.).

It was Pavlov's initial conclusion with regard to *temporal sequence* that the conditioned stimulus must precede or be simultaneous with the unconditioned stimulus if a conditioned response is to be set up. More recent work, however, has revealed that conditioning can occur when the conditioned stimulus follows the unconditioned stimulus, though usually rate of conditioning is slower. The graph in Fig. 26 shows the percentage of conditioning at each of several different time relations between the two stimuli. The unconditioned stimulus here was an electric shock which produced finger withdrawal, and the conditioned stimulus was a harmless auditory one. In this case the optimal time interval was a half second, with the conditioned stimulus preceding the unconditioned stimulus. It will be noted that the order, unconditioned-conditioned, reverses the order of actual functioning, since the response to which the conditioned stimulus is being connected will already have started before the conditioned stimulus appears.

There are various ways in which a conditioned response

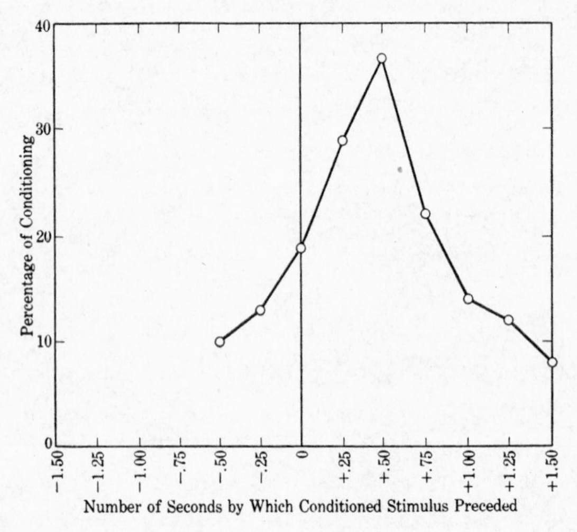

FIG. 26. GRAPH SHOWING THE RATE OF CONDITIONING WITH DIFFERENT TIME RELATIONS BETWEEN THE CONDITIONED AND THE UNCONDITIONED STIMULUS.

After Wolfle, from C. L. Hull, *Handbook of general experimental psychology,* 420; by permission of the Clark University Press.

may be inhibited, and in which the inhibition may also be itself inhibited, restoring the response. The introduction of an additional extraneous stimulus, such as the presence of a stranger in the room, may inhibit a conditioned response. That is called *external inhibition*. Pavlov's students often found that, having set up a conditioned response in a dog, they could not exhibit it to Pavlov because his presence in the room inhibited it. In the same way, recently acquired acts of skill may be disintegrated by a distraction. When one has just mastered a difficult passage on the piano, the appearance of a stranger may prevent its execution. Furthermore, conditioned responses undergo *extinction*—a kind of 'internal inhibition' —when they are continuously repeated without the unconditioned stimulus. The dog no longer salivates at the sound of the bell after the bell has been rung a certain number of times without food. Similarly the threat of punishment loses its force if punishment never follows. These laboratory extinctions of conditioned responses are, however, not necessarily permanent. A response that has lapsed today may be found intact tomorrow, a case of *spontaneous recovery*. An extraneous stimulus may not only inhibit a response; it may also inhibit the inhibition of a response, *i.e.*, abolish the extinction. This phenomenon is called *disinhibition*. Thus the unexpected presence of a stranger in the experimental room may work in either of two ways: it may extinguish a recently acquired conditioned response or it may revive a recently extinguished response. Disinhibition is seen also when distraction or embarrassment—'external stimulation'—revives extinct habits. The man who has at last learned never to say, "It don't," may find this old response revived—'disinhibited'—when he is plunged unexpectedly into the making of an after-dinner speech.

The straightforward conditioning thus far described is not the only form in which the phenomenon will occur. Suppose that the conditioned stimulus, a bell or tone, is given continuously for several minutes and that only toward the end of this period is the unconditioned stimulus introduced. When the conditioned response has been established in this manner, the response may begin to appear only some time after the beginning of the conditioned stimulus, although the latter is still acting. Such responses are known as *delayed conditioned responses*; the delay is an effective part of the stimulus. There is another form of conditioning, related to this, which is called a *trace conditioned response*. A conditioned stimulus acts for a time and stops; then after an interval the unconditioned stimulus is presented. Again the interval becomes an essential part of the stimulus. The delay depends upon the length of the interval and may be even as long as half an hour.

Conditioned emotional responses. Many of the characteristics of conditioning are illustrated in conditioned emotional responses. When, for example, a child who already shows startle and other so-called fear responses to loud sounds but not to animals is presented with a loud sound and a rabbit, he becomes conditioned in a very few trials so that the presence of the rabbit alone will elicit startle, crying or related behavior. The fears which both children and adults have of harmless objects are often such conditioned responses. In the case above, for instance, once the conditioned response to a rabbit has been established, it may be elicited likewise by other hairy or furry objects; that is to say, the child will show the effects of irradiation. Similarly, extinction and disinhibition are principles that apply to emotional responses.

Anticipatory function of conditioned responses. Although it is typical of conditioning that a new stimulus becomes attached to a given response and has the power to call it forth, there is more to conditioning than this new stimulus-response connection. As the connection becomes established, the response to the conditioned stimulus occurs before the unconditioned stimulus. Salivation takes place before the food is eaten, the knee jerks before the hammer falls against the patellar tendon, the eye-wink occurs before the puff of air strikes the eyeball, the finger is removed from the electrode before the shock is received. It will be recognized that here the conditioned response anticipates the unconditioned stimulus and in many cases obviates its occurrence.

This anticipatory character of the conditioned response pervades all learning. We are able, because of having learned, to respond in a way which looks to the future. We can learn to avoid harmful stimuli before they strike the receptors. The child, once burned, avoids the stove. The animal, having received strong electric shock in a given room, may be afraid of the very sight of that room. The results of such learning pyramid greatly. The word *danger* may be enough to warn us from a region where noxious stimuli are probable; words of all kinds acquire the power to guide behavior anticipatorily. From the simplest forms of learning to the most complex this anticipatory function, whereby we prepare for the future, is continuous.

SERIAL LEARNING AND ACTS OF SKILL

Serial learning. Much of human learning is a matter of fixing a series of items so that they can be recited one after the other in response to a single cue or stimulus. The items may be words or they may be movements of the fingers, limbs and body, but much of the experimental work has been done with verbal series.

One of the most widely used forms of verbal materials is the *nonsense syllable*, first described and used experimentally by Ebbinghaus in 1885. The nonsense syllable consists of three letters, two consonants with a vowel between them, such as *BAP, ZOF* or *TUD*. The use of these nonsense syllables has certain advantages. Large numbers of them can be constructed with the twenty-six letters of the alphabet; they are relatively new to all subjects; and they offer an excellent opportunity for constructing different series of equivalent difficulty. Many other materials—such as poems, pictures and the ideational content of prose—have also been employed in studying serial learning. These materials, presented to the learner in the form in which he is to learn them, offer comparatively little opportunity for the making of errors. The subject is either all right or all wrong.

Acts of skill. Unlike such serial learning, on the other hand, are most acts of skill—such as dancing, typing or rifle shooting—which involve the fixation of certain responses and sometimes of a definite series of them. Acts of this kind differ from verbal series in that the correct responses must first be discovered by the subject and the wrong responses eliminated, until the right ones, whatever they may be, are finally established. The subject is more often partly right than all right or all wrong.

The stylus maze is one of the most commonly used instruments for studying the acquisition of skill. Such a maze is a winding path from a starting point to a goal, with blind alleys branching off from it at a number of points (see Fig. 27). Without the aid of vision the subject is to find the true path by feeling his way with a stylus. He must go from starting point to goal without error. In finding the true path he

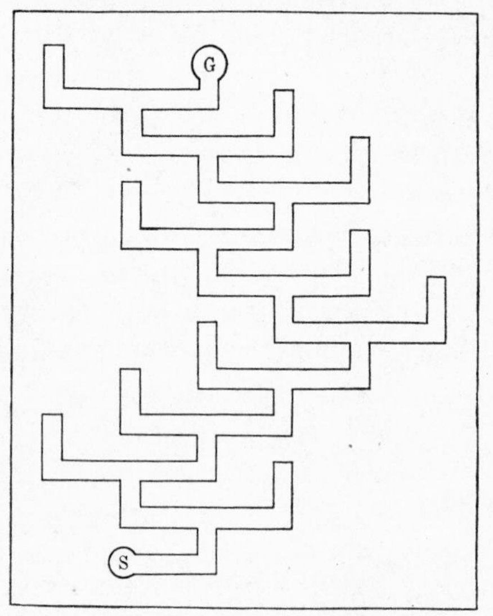

Fig. 27. A Typical Stylus-Maze Pattern.
From C. J. Warden, *J. exper. Psychol.*, 1924, 7, 101.

has to resort to trial-and-error behavior, which will be described presently. His progress is measured in time, trials and errors.

The pursuitmeter is another instrument requiring the learning of a serial movement. By means of this apparatus the subject is presented with a rotating platform, like that of a victrola, in which, flush with the surface and near the periphery, is set a small metal disk. While the platform revolves rapidly, the subject is required to pursue the disk with a metal stylus and to learn to maintain constant contact with it. His performance is measured by the number of contacts he makes with the disk in a given length of time, or by the total amount of time he requires to learn to remain constantly in contact with the disk for a given number of revolutions.

In such experiments the subject acts under some definite instruction in an effort to reach some predetermined level of performance which has been established as the *criterion* of learning (see p. 291). Told about the goal, he is left to find out for himself the exact means of reaching it. He must discover the right movements, and he must also eliminate the wrong ones.

The learning of many acts of skill involves an organization of simpler acts into a hierarchy of successively more complex ones. Thus, in learning to type or to send and receive in the telegraphic language, a subject commonly responds at first to each letter individually, *i.e.*, he types *the* as t-h-e. With further practice, however, sight or thought of the word elicits the smoothly flowing unitary response *the*. At this stage the subject may for a time respond to most words as individual units, but with further practice he passes to a higher level in the hierarchy of habits and types several words, phrases, clauses or complete sentences each as a single smooth response.

PROBLEM SOLVING

To the subjects most acts of skill—and perhaps all of them—represent problems to be solved. There are other activities, however, less obviously classifiable as acts of skill but even more clearly illustrative of problem solution as the layman understands the term. These activities involve the use of ideas somewhat more than do most acts of skill. We shall begin with a relatively simple example.

Learning of relationships. Many of the activities which we have been discussing may be described as responses to specific individual stimuli. There are numerous instances, however, in which the subject learns to respond to relationships. When an animal has been taught, for example, to go always to the darker of two gray surfaces for food, he will continue to choose the darker of any pair that is presented to him, even though the darker surface in the second pair may be the identical surface which was lighter in the first pair. It is plain that he is not choosing a particular stimulus when he prefers one stimulus one time and rejects it another, according to its relation to the other stimulus with which it is combined. It seems that the animal has, in this case, learned to respond favorably to the *relation* 'darker than.' This acquisition of response to relations of all sorts has been demonstrated by many different experimental operations and with many different species. The relations to which the human being may be trained to respond are, of course, subtle and far-reaching.

Detour learning. Let either an animal or a human subject be presented with food or any other incentive, but let the direct path to the goal be blocked in some manner. The immediate response, except for the experienced subject, is an attempt to crawl, climb or batter a way over or through the obstruction. When the direct attack proves impossible, a period of variable behavior usually ensues, until, if the situation is not too difficult, the subject eventually perceives that an indirect route will permit him to obtain the desired object. He may then go directly away from the desired object until he has passed around the obstruction, or he may achieve his goal by some other indirect route. Suppose a young child sees and desires a piece of chocolate on the other side of a bench. Unable to go to it directly, he must either go indirectly around the bench which obstructs his path or must take some still more roundabout route. Children have to learn to make such detours; and the solution of the problem is the more difficult the more the subject must move in a direction away from the desired object (see pp. 169f. and Fig. 9).

A great deal of our problem solving is done by means of this detour behavior, much of which is complex. The elimination of errors in the learning of an act of skill is in one sense a detour phenomenon, an arrival at a goal by a roundabout path. The 'defense reactions' by which people avoid the feeling of inferiority are forms of detour behavior. A man, convicted of error, may make the *argumentum ad hominem* to his accuser; he may say, "Who are *you* to accuse *me*?" and thus, by a detour into the personality of his antagonist, arrive at the sense of superiority from which he at first seemed definitely barred by the accusation.

Learning by insight. When an individual 'sees into' the way in which a learning problem may be solved, puts different features of a situation together and understands what to do, when he understands that "to make this happen this must be done," and grasps the essential features of a solution or part of a solution, he is said to exhibit insightful behavior. In an experiment upon chimpanzees, for example, one of the animals, which had already learned to pull in a banana through a fence by using a stick, was given two sticks, each alone too short to reach the banana, but arranged like a fishing rod so that one end of one would fit into one end of the other. The animal tried to obtain the food with each stick separately, but failed. Finally he happened to hold one stick in either hand with the appropriate ends pointing toward each other. Recognizing suddenly that the two would go together, he inserted one in the other and at once used the new stick of double length as a tool for getting the food. The 'seeing' that the two would go together is an instance of insight.

Learning with multiple choice. An experiment often performed with either animals or persons is one in which the subject is presented with a certain number of possible choices, such as a number of doors, and asked to find which one of these multiple choices is correct. When he has learned to make the right choice, he is next presented with a different number of doors and again asked to find the correct one. The right choice always follows a definite principle. With animals it may be simple—*the one at the left* or *the second from the right.* With human subjects the rule may be much more difficult, as *second from the right, first at the left, then the middle one.* The subject must begin by trial and error and work out the principle which will allow him always to make the right choice, regardless of the number of possible choices available to him.

This kind of experiment has much in common with the experiments on the learning of relations and with those on insightful behavior. In all these experiments, if he is to solve the problem, the subject must discover certain relations and must comprehend or 'see into' them.

METHODS OF PROBLEM SOLVING

Trial and error. Whenever a learner is presented with a problem to which he must discover the solution, he has several possible methods of procedure. Dominant among these is the method of trial and error. Consider, as an example of this method, the behavior of a cat in a puzzle box. The cat, which is hungry when it is placed in the box, can see food outside; consequently, by climbing along the wire ceiling and by various other maneuvers it indulges in a vigorous series of unsuccessful efforts to get the food through the meshes of the wire sides. Finally it happens to pull the string which releases the door catch, thus letting itself out to get the food. The next time the cat is put in the box, although it goes through a similar set of trial-and-error movements, it concentrates them somewhat more in the region of the string. Eventually, after a number of trials, the cat learns to go immediately to the string, put its paws through the loop, pull and get out to the food.

A considerable amount of misunderstanding has grown up around this concept of trial and error, and it requires, therefore, some elaboration.

1. *Trial and error* is a descriptive term, not an explanatory one. It describes the behavior exhibited by the learner in attacking a problem, but it does not state the conditions necessary for final mastery.

2. Trial-and-error behavior is not purely random. The subject proceeds under some instruction, either given to him by the

experimenter or imposed by himself—an instruction which limits and to some extent controls his behavior. A further control to prevent random responses is provided by the learner's own previous training and structural characteristics, which determine that certain responses shall be elicited by the learning situation, others not. The cat in the puzzle box, for example, even during the first trial, concentrates his responses on the side toward the food. There is always some such internal guidance of behavior; the only purely random or chance aspect of trial and error lies in the fact that neither subject nor experimenter can predict before the practice begins the time at which the goal will be reached or the number of errors which will be made in reaching it. *The behavior itself is variable but not at random.* As practice goes on, variability becomes less, until it is finally reduced to small changes in the way in which the right response is made.

Nor does the right response always mean the best possible response. Experiments in trials and errors of animals in puzzle boxes have shown that, if the animal happens by chance to hit the release mechanism with some 'inappropriate' part of his body such as his rear quarters, he may continue to use this method to get his release. All of us frequently resort to equally inappropriate solutions. We use the first method that seems to work, even though it is not the most economical in time and energy. It is such 'awkward' habits that the efficiency engineer is endeavoring to eliminate in industrial operation.

To some degree everyone employs the method of trial and error. The student can grasp even more clearly what it involves by recalling his own behavior in trying for the first time to solve a puzzle, to open a box with a hidden catch or to find his way to a given address in a strange city when only the general location is known. It is a method employed in reasoning, as well as in problems where the response is more overt (see pp. 391f.).

Other methods. Often the trials and errors take place in terms of ideas, even in the acquisition of a muscular skill, so that to an outside observer there seems to be no trial and error. When this ideational trial and error occurs, and when the correct relations are also perceived in ideational terms, then the solution may seem to have been hit upon suddenly. Though it may not really come suddenly, it seems sudden to an observer who does not know what has been going on in the subject's mind. When the relationships necessary to successful performance are thus perceived without overt trial-and-error behavior, the solution is said to have been achieved by *insight*.

Still other modes of solution may occur. Guidance—help from someone else or from some external source, such as definite instructions—is one such method. Imitation of someone else may be a form of guidance.

GENERALITY OF CONDITIONS OF LEARNING

We may pause here to review the general conditions of learning, as we first understood them, in relation to their direct application to the forms of learning with which we have just been dealing.

1. First we see that for all those forms of learning motivation is essential. The subject cannot form a conditioned response if he is not 'pointed' in some way toward the stimuli and responses involved, nor will he read over a serial list, run a maze, practice a pursuitmeter, seek the relations necessary for a solution, make a detour or invite insight unless he is motivated.

2. There is in all learning an associative spread from the subject's already existent organization acquired through previous learning. Since he brings to conditioning many acquired modes of response, the phenomenon of irradiation may be regarded as an associative spread on the stimulus side of the connection. Even a nonsense syllable has some meaning and can be given more. To the learning of a list of meaningful words one brings a huge amount of associative context for each word. In learning an act of skill there is a carrying over both from what one has heard about that skill and from one's own already learned skills. To the solution of problems of all sorts are

brought ideas and modes of attack which one has learned in dealing with related things.

3. The temporal relations between the events to be associated are a factor in all the forms of learning. Items contiguous in time are most easily related in learning. As an illustration of this principle with the conditioned response see Fig. 26.

4. Because it favors the operation of the law of effect, frequency of connections enters as a condition into all these forms of learning. Under sufficiently favorable conditions, on the other hand, a connection can be established with a single presentation of the items.

LEARNING CURVES

Representative curves. The first question to arise, when we turn from a description of things learned to the conditions of their being learned, is the influence of successive amounts of practice. Few acts or materials can be acquired at a single trial or single brief moment of time. Most of them require several repetitions and considerable time, so that with succeeding repetitions varying increments of performance appear. We wish to know the relation between successive units of practice and the performance which practice brings. This relation can be seen most clearly if we plot performance against repetitions and connect the plotted points. The resulting graph is called a *learning curve.*

Learning curves may show a general rise or a general fall depending upon the way performance is measured. If measurement is in terms of time or of errors, the curve will fall; if in terms of amount accomplished, like number of words learned, it will rise. The curves for individual subjects will show in either case a considerable fluctuation, as in the curve of Fig. 28, which represents the number of nonsense syllables recalled at each successive presentation of a ten-syllable list. These fluctuations, which are a result of variable factors in the stimulating conditions and in the subject's response to them, are inevitable features of performance during learning.

Sometimes fluctuations may continue for a relatively long time without showing any trend toward further increments. This region of no definite change in performance is called a plateau (Fig. 29) and is of considerable interest because of its departure from the general trend of the functions and, as well, because of the discouragement which it causes the learner.

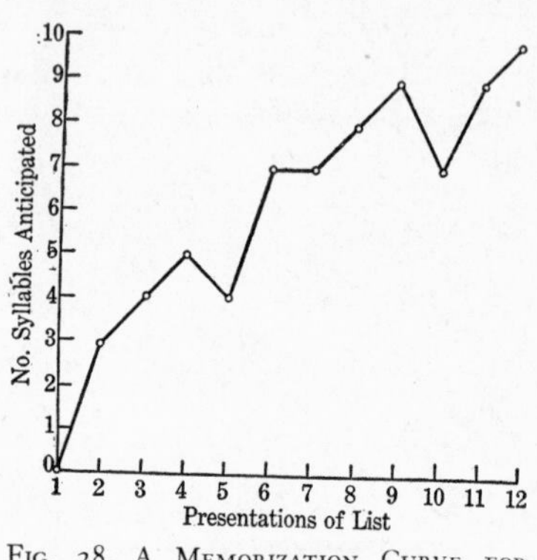

FIG. 28. A MEMORIZATION CURVE FOR ONE SUBJECT.

Plateaus are not to be accounted for by any single condition. They may be produced by a diminution in the subject's motivation and in the vigor with which he practices, by interference between the different parts of the reactions which are being learned, by the fixation of errors or by any condition which will for a time retard performance. They are not necessary features of the relation between practice and performance.

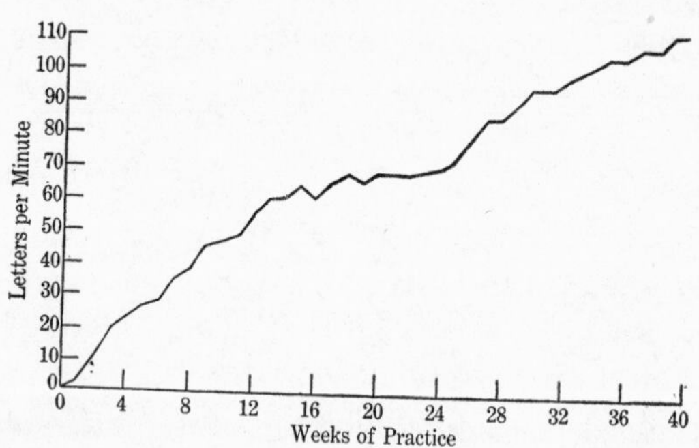

FIG. 29. A PERFORMANCE CURVE FOR ONE SUBJECT IN LEARNING TO RECEIVE IN THE TELEGRAPHIC LANGUAGE.

"This is a curve of sample performance. The region of very little or no progress toward the middle of the curve is a plateau." From W. L. Bryan, and N. Harter, *Psychol. Rev.*, 1897, 4, 49.

When the functions of a large number of subjects are combined, the fluctuations which typically occur in the curves for individual subjects average out to give a smooth composite curve. Both irregular individual curves and the smoother composite ones usually approximate one of the three characteristic forms of Fig. 30. There are, however, as many specific curves as there are conditions under which learning is done, and the three given are only general modes with respect to which the variety of empirical curves may be classified and described. There is, therefore, no curve which may be called *the* curve of learning, none which represents learning as a whole or in general.

The chief problem of description in the present case is the statement of conditions under which a given curve-form appears. Negatively accelerated curves of Type A show that the increments of performance are relatively large during the early stages of practice and relatively small during the later ones. Curves of this form are most often obtained (1) when motivation is high at first and decreases as practice continues; (2) when interference within the materials being learned increases as practice goes on; (3) when the subject has had previous practice, and the effects of practice transfer to the early repetitions of the material being learned or to the learning method employed; and (4) when measurement is in terms of errors or time rather than of positive increments of performance.

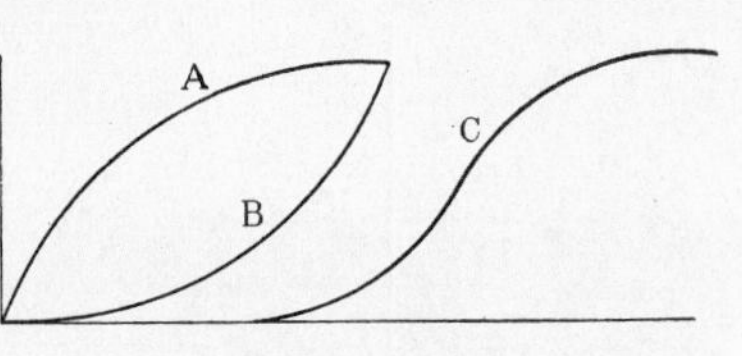

FIG. 30. REPRESENTATIVE LEARNING CURVES.

Curves *A* and *B* are from H. A. Carr, *Psychology: a study of mental activity,* 218; reprinted by permission of Longmans, Green & Co.

Positively accelerated curves of Type B represent increments which, relatively small during the early part of practice, increase in magnitude with continued practice. We seldom find curves which are positively accelerated throughout (they appear only when the limit is some arbitrarily selected criterion). The positively accelerated curve in Fig. 31 is for the establishment of a conditioned salivary response.

More commonly we find an initial positive acceleration,

which may continue for some time but which is followed by negative acceleration. In this case the total curve is an S-shaped curve of the kind shown as Type C (Fig. 30).

Curves of Type B and C most often appear (1) when the subject has had very little prior practice, the effects of which transfer to the initial repetitions of activities concerned; (2) when the subjects are relatively young, either in years or mentality; (3) when the acts learned are, for any reason other than

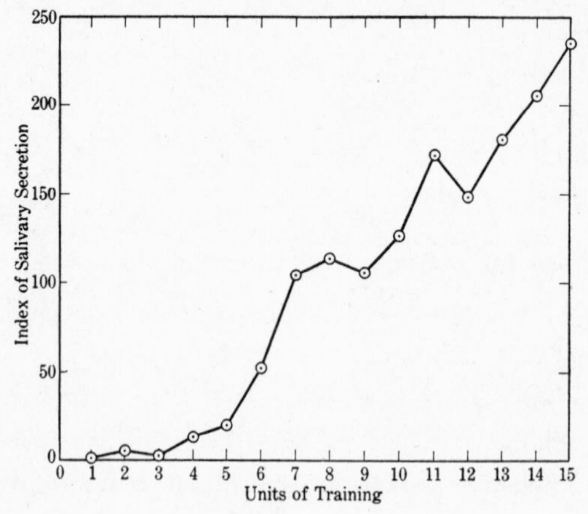

FIG. 31. COMPOSITE CURVE FOR THE ACQUISITION OF A SALIVARY CONDITIONED RESPONSE BY FOUR DOGS.

From data of Kleitman and Crisler, *Amer. J. Physiol.*, as plotted by C. L. Hull, *Handbook of general experimental psychology*, 425; by permission of the Clark University Press.

those already mentioned, relatively difficult for the learner; and (4) when scoring is in terms of positive attainment rather than in terms of time or errors.

Sometimes, under conditions which permit learning by insight, the curve of learning will change abruptly, and will approach its limit suddenly. Because here the acceleration is too rapid to allow the measurement of many successive increments, such a curve obviously does not resemble those of Fig. 30. There is no indication, however, that the process measured differs in nature from the cases of slow, measurable acceleration.

Physiological limits. A consideration of learning curves leads directly to the question whether—or how rapidly—learners reach a physiological limit, *i.e.,* the level of performance beyond which, by reason of the physical limitations of their organisms, they cannot go. Since under ordinary laboratory conditions subjects seldom approach such an extreme limit of performance, one must rely for an answer to this question upon fragmentary evidence.

It has been found that years of practice at such skills as telegraphy or typesetting do not commonly bring a man to his maximal performance. The introduction of a special incentive may increase the performance of long-practiced workers by remarkable amounts. In a printing house, for example, where a special bonus was introduced for output beyond a certain level, and where the hand compositors had been working at their trade for an average of about ten years, performance rose steadily for at least twenty weeks, following a negatively accelerated course. The increased output resulted from elimination of ineffective habits of work and the acquisition of better ones. It occurred both with the less experienced men and the more experienced. Analogous results have been obtained with other kinds of work. Some investigators who studied the learning of telegraphers laid down the general rule: "It is intense effort that educates." Given that, physiological limits are indefinitely remote.

The fact that in athletics and in other skills records are repeatedly broken under standard conditions is best interpreted as an indication of the practical remoteness of a physiological limit. It has, likewise, been found repeatedly in the laboratory that, after a subject has reached a relatively high level of performance, increased motivation or better methods will produce further substantial increments. The conclusion is probable that in normal persons a physiological limit is not reached by ordinary amounts of practice and, indeed, may not be reached even by prolonged practice under favorable conditions.

LEARNING AS A FUNCTION OF THE LEARNER

The speed with which a given level of performance is reached offers a problem entirely distinct from that of the correlation between successive increments of performance and successive units of practice. Whether the criterial level is attained in five trials or in twenty, the form of the curve might be the same in either case. The general problem involved in studying speed of learning apart from the form of the curve is the problem of the conditions which determine speed; or, when stated in experimental terms, it becomes the problem of the measurement of either the amount of increment in a given number of practice units or the number of practice units required to attain a given level of performance. The conditions determining a given rate may be roughly classified into those which vary with or are a function of the learner and those which vary with or are a function of the material learned and the conditions of its presentation. We shall deal in this section with the conditions in the first group.

Chronological age. Under normal conditions, rate of learning increases as actual age increases; such an increase is characteristic from the earliest age at which adequate measurements can be made up to some point in the teens or early twenties. The form of the curve obtained by plotting performance against age varies with a number of conditions, as does the point at which further increases in age cease to be accompanied by increases in rate; but the fact of the increase in rate from an early age to some later one remains unaffected by a very wide range of conditions. The curve for card sorting shown in Fig. 32 is an example.

Only within recent years has the question of the form of the curve beyond early maturity received extensive experimental attack. In the learning of most of the activities studied, increases with age have ceased to appear by the age of twenty or soon thereafter. The evidence which is now available indicates a gradual decline from the early twenties onward to old age. Representative of this decline is the curve given in Fig. 33 for code learning (see also Fig. 6, p. 124).

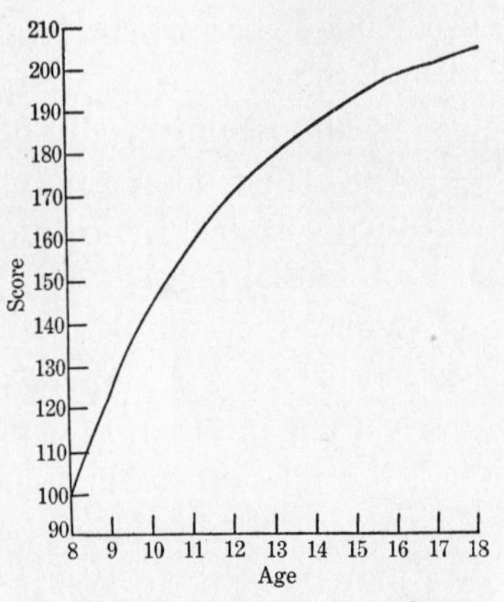

Fig. 32. A Smoothed Curve Showing Change with Age in Performance During Practice at Card Sorting.

From W. H. Pyle, *Nature and development of learning capacity*, 19; reprinted by permission of Warwick and York.

Although learning in most activities probably decreases gradually with age from early maturity onward, this fact does not mean that the older person cannot learn, nor need it be interpreted to mean that he is seriously handicapped. Rather, it means that he learns less readily than he did at the peak of his performance. In code learning, for example, the average person of sixty learned as rapidly as the average child of eleven, and the eleven-year-old is not usually considered an ineffective learner. In a few activities and under a few conditions, moreover, it seems that the age curve shows either no later decrement or shows it only very late in

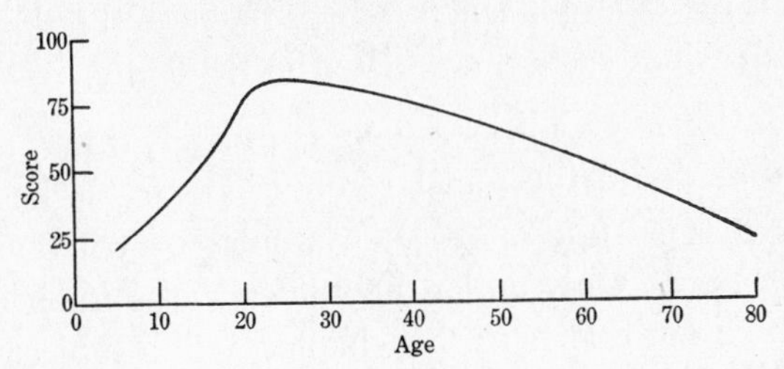

Fig. 33. The Trend of Mean Performance in Digit-Symbol Substitution with Age.

From R. R. Willoughby, *J. educ. Psychol.*, 1929, 20, 678; reprinted by permission of Warwick and York.

life. The acquisition and manipulation of ideas, particularly if they are related to fields of knowledge with which one has been actively engaged, offer a case in point.

Intelligence. One might well expect, on the ground of common observation, a high correlation between intelligence and learning. When, however, intelligence-test scores and measurements of performance upon specific learning tasks are correlated, the coefficients are seldom high. The relation is, nevertheless, almost universally positive. When, moreover, measures of performance upon a number of learning tasks are combined and then correlated with intelligence-test scores, the coefficient is a substantial one ($r = 0.60$, for example).

Evidence is accumulating to prove that the magnitude of the relation between intelligence and learning is a function of the task learned and that, as we pass from simple tasks to complex ones, the relation becomes increasingly high. The highest coefficients yet obtained have been with rational problems, where they may reach the 0.80's. It has been shown, further, that the influence of practice upon the differences in performance between groups of different intelligence is a function of the task. The learning curves for card sorting converge with continued practice, those for code substitution remain parallel, whereas those for the learning of abstract relations diverge.

We may conclude that speed of learning and intelligence are, over a wide range of things learned, positively related, that the magnitude of the relation is a function of the learning task and is much larger when records for several tasks are combined than when each is correlated individually.

Motivation. Conditions such as hunger, thirst, avoidance of pain and desire for social recognition are, as has already been shown (see pp. 146-163), examples of what are called motives or needs. Only under the influence of some need, as we have pointed out earlier in this chapter, will a subject practice. The acts he attempts to learn, *i.e.,* the 'right' acts, are distinguished from the 'wrong' ones by whether or not they satisfy his needs. We shall use the term *need* in this discussion to mean *any condition of the organism which points it toward the practice of a given task and which defines the satisfactory completion of that task.* The term *incentive* means an object perceived as potentially satisfying a given need. Hunger is a need; the sight of food is an incentive.

In experiments upon the learning of human subjects the needs are complex. A college student may practice a maze habit under the influence of a need to please the experimenter, to make a record which he himself will consider good, to excel over other subjects or to find out what maze learning is like. Any one or all of these may be operating in a single subject, and we may add to them, in a given experiment, the need to escape an electric shock administered whenever a blind alley is entered or to receive some specific reward when the maze is learned.

The form which the problem has commonly taken in experimentation has been a comparison between learning for whatever need is present (as when a subject is merely asked by an experimenter to learn a given task) and learning for this condition plus some special need like that set up by reward or punishment. The introduction of such special needs almost uniformly accelerates learning, and the extent of the acceleration is sometimes large. In one experiment, for example, an electric shock of 27 volts, administered at the end of each blind alley of a stylus maze, decreased the number of trials required to reach the criterion by 50 per cent and decreased the various kinds of errors by 30 to 60 per cent. Competition and rivalry, praise and blame, or other special conditions of a similar nature designed to arouse special needs, likewise exert a definite facilitating effect. There is no doubt that over a wide range of special needs this result may be expected.

A concrete case of the influence of a special incentive upon learning has already been cited in discussing physiological limits. Although they were already far along in their learning of this activity, the hand compositors who were offered a bonus for performance beyond a given level adopted better methods of work and eliminated ineffective habits.

The general problem of motivation has also been studied, especially with verbal and observational materials, in relation to the influence of intention to learn. A subject may observe or repeat a material passively or he may assume toward it an active attitude and attempt to learn it. The experimental results show that, whereas mere passive repetition is either without influence or is relatively ineffective, active noting and reacting to the material are necessary for learning. At least a part of the effectiveness of need is referable to the intent to learn which it produces.

That most human beings learn fewer things than they could learn, and learn even those at a much slower rate than they easily might if their needs were greater, is so probable as to be practically certain. What we take to be a physiological limit may often be only a point beyond which we are not sufficiently motivated to go.

Recitation during learning. A subject may practice by repeating the activity or the material as it comes to him; or he may attempt to recite or rehearse it during the learning with such prompting as is necessary. Thus, during the running of a maze he may verbally rehearse to himself the turns which he has just made, while at the same time he is going forward through other sections. During the memorizing of a list of words he may try to repeat the list without the copy. Table XX presents data upon the influence of varying amounts of recitation. Lists of nonsense syllables and short biographies were practiced either by repeated reading until learned or by reading followed by recitations with prompting whenever necessary. The table gives the percentages recalled immediately at the close of the learning period.

These results show that direct repetition plus recitation yields larger increments of performance than time spent only in direct repetition, and that the increments vary directly in magnitude with the proportion of the total learning time spent in recitation. The advantage of recitation is greater with the nonsense syllables than with the biographies, probably because a considerable amount of organization of meanings is progressively going on during the repetition of meaningful material even when there is no overt attempt at recitation. By other

TABLE XX

THE INFLUENCE OF DIFFERENT AMOUNTS OF RECITATION UPON LEARNING

(From Gates, *Arch. Psychol.*, 1917, 4, 36 and 41.)

Per Cent of Total Time Spent		Material Learned	
In Reading	In Recitation	Syllables	Biographies
100	0	65.4	87.8
80	20	92.2	94.6
60	40	99.7	105.0
40	60	105.5	105.5
20	80	137.3	106.8

(The figures are for subjects in Grade VIII and have been obtained by computing the percentage which the amount learned by each method is of the average of all methods.)

investigators it has been found that more favorable results are obtained when readings and recitations are interspersed than when they are grouped together.

The superiority of reading-plus-recitation over reading alone results from several independent conditions. (1) The recitation arouses a more active attitude on the part of the subject. (2) During recitation the subject is practicing the recall of the material in the way in which he is to use it on the test. (3) The recitation yields progressive information about both errors and right responses, thereby permitting the correction of the errors through prompting from the copy, and providing increased motivation.

Guidance. The usual procedure in the learning of acts of skill and of rational problems is to allow the subject to discover and fix the solution by his own methods. Unless the problem and his past training on similar problems furnish enough preparation to permit insight to occur, he must, therefore, proceed by the trial-and-error method. It is possible, however, in a great many tasks for the experimenter to give the subject aid during discovery and fixation. This aid, designated as *guidance* or *tuition*, is distinguished from the guidance provided by such factors as the subject's self-instructions and the effect of his past training in that it is external; in other words, it is more directly imposed by the experimenter, whereas self-instruction is internal and a function of the learner. A series of studies of external guidance has been made, using both stylus mazes and rational problems. In the case of the maze, the subject may, for example, be guided a certain number of times through the true path, may be prevented from making errors by blocks inserted in the blind alleys or may be given verbal information. When rational problems are used, the fundamental principles required for solution may be stated, or the subject may be given information designed to aid him in finding those principles.

In a majority of the maze experiments some guidance has proved to be more effective than an equivalent amount of unguided practice, although occasionally guidance is ineffective or even detrimental. The greatest possible effect is obtained when small amounts of tuition are given early in practice. Large amounts of tuition and amounts introduced late in practice have usually only a very small positive influence or prove actually harmful. In experiments upon rational learning, information leading to the principle involved in the solution, if given early in practice, may act to hasten learning.

Individual cues and modes of attack. We have been dealing thus far with motor performance and its conditions, but the experience of the subject should also be considered. The reports of the subjective accompaniments of improvement in performance do not, however, provide us with a point-for-point subjective parallel to the course of learning. A wisp of imagery, a faint imaginal schema, intermittent flashes of subvocal speech, a fluctuating series of muscular strains—these, among other things, are what the subjects report. Of so little significance are these phenomena for an understanding of learning that their importance is difficult to assess.

One form of investigation has, however, yielded a definite relation between measured performance and subjective report. Subjects who had learned a maze were asked to describe their modes of attack and the subjective means which they used in learning. Their reports can be grouped in three divisions: (1) verbal methods, in which the turns and other moves are remembered in words, so that the subject guides himself through the maze by saying, "First turn to the right, then straight ahead," etc.; (2) motor methods, in which the cues employed are dominantly motor and the subject "follows the lead of his hand" without consciously organizing his movements; and (3) visual methods, in which attempts are made to construct visual images of the maze pattern. The frequencies with which the three methods are used decrease in the order just given, with the visual methods appearing infrequently. The learning curves of subjects using the different methods show a clear superiority for the verbal method over the other two, and, usually, a superiority of visual over motor. Table XXI

TABLE XXI

PERFORMANCE SCORES MADE BY SUBJECTS USING DIFFERENT MODES OF ATTACK

(Data from R. W. Husband, *J. genet. Psychol.*, 1931, 39, 258–277.)

Mode of Attack	Trials	Score (errors)	Time (seconds)
Verbal	10.1	20	358
Visual	15.0	29	505
Motor	25.8	23	802

gives a sample set of results for one section of a high-relief finger maze which the subject learns to trace with one finger. Results of a similar tendency have been found with stylus mazes, where it has been observed also that the more intelligent subjects are the more likely to adopt the verbal method.

The pronounced superiority of the verbal method over the motor in the learning of a motor problem is significant. It shows that the motor problem as actually learned by most subjects is learned as a pattern with both verbal and motor constituents, that so-called 'motor' learning is not, therefore, of necessity completely motor, that the trials and errors may be in part ideationally controlled and that the learning proceeds much more rapidly when ideational factors are employed. These facts support the generalization that there is no clean-cut division between different kinds of materials with respect to the activities which they require.

Individual differences. Wide differences are found among the learning records of different individuals when all are practicing under the same external conditions. Differences still appear when the subjects are of the same age and sex, in the same class in college, and of equivalent prior training in the activity practiced. In one experiment in which these conditions were fulfilled, the fastest learner required 8 trials to learn a list of 8 nonsense syllables and the slowest required 37—more than 4 times as many. Likewise, the fastest learner mastered a maze of considerable difficulty in 19 trials, whereas the slowest took 78. Ranges still wider than these are often found. When the records of a large group of subjects are plotted, the resulting distribution curve often approximates a normal bell-shaped curve (pp. 98f.).

CHARACTERISTICS OF THE MATERIALS OF LEARNING

We shall be concerned in this section with the influence upon rate of learning exercised by conditions which are primarily functions of the things learned and of the way in which they are presented to the subject. Learner and thing learned are not, of course, as sharply divided from each other as this classification makes them seem to be. What is learned is something perceived by the subject; it will vary as the subject varies. When, however, we systematically vary the characteristics of the material, while maintaining a chance distribution of subjects, we are able to treat the material as a major variable and to study its influence.

Meaningfulness of the material. If we adopt for the moment a common-sense view of meaning, it is possible to rank a large number of verbal materials from low to high with respect to their meaningfulness. On such a scale, nonsense syllables are placed well toward the lower end, single words are higher, poetry and prose are still higher. Since an almost perfect correlation is found between meaningfulness and ease of learning, it may be said that, over a wide range of materials, rate of learning is a direct function of the meaningfulness of the material. Meaningfulness is a function of the subject's prior learning of related things, so that in one sense the generalization just made could be stated: The rate of learning is a direct function of the amount of transfer which takes place from the learner's already existent knowledge to the particular performance at hand. This factor of meaning has a much greater influence on learning than do such physical features of the material as the size of the letters and the color of printing or background. Even though these latter conditions may sometimes affect rate of learning, the magnitude of their effect is almost negligible compared to that of meaning.

The significance of meaning becomes still clearer when we consider the learning of relations and insightful behavior. When a relation has once been grasped in a single set of material, it can be applied to a wide range of other materials. Given the right conditions, insight may come quickly.

The factor of meaning may also be approached from the side of the activity of the learner. A subject may study a list of words or a paragraph of prose in verbatim fashion, attempting to connect each word with the following one, or he may try to weave the words into a meaningful pattern in which the interrelations either aid in fixing the words or take entire precedence over them. The two methods are usually referred to as the *verbatim* and the *logical* methods of memorizing, and in the majority of cases the latter yields the more rapid learning.

Amount of material. The question of the relation between the time required for learning and the length or amount of the material learned has received considerable study. The common result has been that material becomes disproportionately more difficult to master as it increases in length. One investigator found, for example, that he could learn a list of 12 nonsense syllables in 1.5 min., a list of 24 in 5 min. and a list of 72 in 25 min. If time had been proportional to length, the corresponding figures would have been 1.5, 3.0 and 9.0 min. This generalization has been found to hold for a large number of verbal materials and at least partially for maze patterns.

The disproportionate increase in difficulty with increasing length may be accounted for by the operation of several factors which vary with length. As length increases, the opportunities for interference between different parts of the material and for consequent forgetting increase. Some parts of a material, learned early in practice, are unnecessarily repeated during all later trials; the shorter the material, the less will there be of such repetition. The attitude of the subject toward the practice is also more favorable when the amount of work before him is relatively small.

Distributed vs. massed practice. The trials required to bring performance up to a given level may be taken in immediate succession—in short, the practice may be *massed*—or intervals of no practice may be inserted at any desired points to give a *distributed* practice. Massed practice involves continuous presentation of the material. Distributed practice involves intermittent presentation.

The two chief variables in distributing practice are (1) the number of trials (or amount of time) per practice period and (2) the length of the interval of rest, *i.e.,* of no practice, between practice periods. In experiments upon the influence of the first variable a constant rest interval is used, and various numbers of trials are taken before each introduction of the interval. A comparison of 1, 3, 5 and 7 trials before each rest interval of 24 hours is an example. In experiments upon the second variable, on the other hand, the number of trials is kept constant and varying lengths of rest interval are compared. Thus, intervals of 1, 12, 24 and 48 hours could be inserted after each practice period of 3 trials.

The conclusion is well established that, over a wide range of conditions, some form of positive distribution is a more favorable condition of learning than is no distribution, or massed practice. The curve shown in Fig. 34 is one illustration of this fact in the case of an interval as short as one minute.

The differences between performance under massed and distributed practice are commonly greater than are those between any two modes of distribution thus far considered. These statements refer, of course, to comparisons of amounts of time actually spent in practice. The total time covered by the experiment will almost always be greater under distribution because of the addition of the rest periods.

Since the relative effects of various numbers of trials and various lengths of rest intervals are functions of a number of conditions, generalizations concerning them can be understood only in terms of those conditions. A few of the most general results may, however, be stated without a detailed analysis of the related conditions. (1) The influence of the number of trials per period is a function of the length of the rest interval between periods; but when an advantageous interval is used, the fewer the trials per period the more rapid is the learning likely to be. (2) Relatively short intervals are more often advantageous; relatively long ones are more often detrimental. Very long ones, particularly those which are longer than a few days, are nearly always detrimental. The longer the practice period, the longer may the effective interval be. (3) For many activities, distribution is most effective during the early practice periods; whereas for some, a progressive decrease in practice period with increasing length of rest interval is, as practice continues, more effective than an unchanging series.

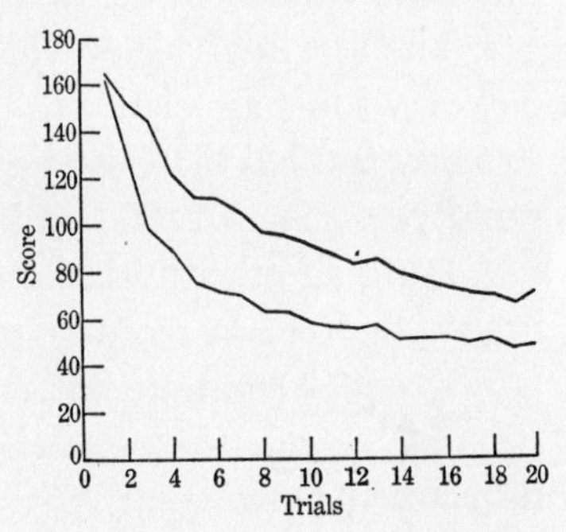

FIG. 34. LEARNING CURVES FOR MIRROR DRAWING WHEN PRACTICE IS MASSED AND WHEN A REST INTERVAL OF ONE MINUTE IS INTRODUCED AFTER EACH TRIAL.

From I. Lorge, *Teach. Coll. Contr. Educ.*, 1930, No. 438, 38.

The primary conditions which determine the facts of distributed practice offer an interesting problem, the more so in view of the fact that an interval of no practice is commonly accompanied by forgetting. The efficacy of distribution flies in the face, as it were, of the falling retention curve which is usually found when an interval of no practice has elapsed. It has been demonstrated that rehearsal during the rest periods of distributed practice will not account for the results. Probably no single factor accounts for this phenomenon, which may be determined by various conditions, not all of which operate in every case.

Some of the more important of the conditions which determine the efficacy of distributed practice are noted here.

1. The rest intervals provide an opportunity for the dropping out of wrong associations. These associations, commonly less strongly formed than the right ones, are hence forgotten more rapidly.

2. Long ago there was formulated the hypothesis, which has been supported in recent experiments, that, if two associations are of equal strength but of different age, a new repetition strengthens the older association more than the younger. In distributed practice all associations will have a greater age at all practice periods after the first than at the corresponding repetitions under massed practice; consequently they will be strengthened more by succeeding repetitions.

3. In some cases motivation may be higher and the subject's set more favorable to learning when the practice periods are relatively shorter, as they are under distributed practice. It is conceivable that this factor also may reduce to the dropping out of wrong associations with time.

4. It has recently been found that associative processes exhibit a phenomenon of refractory period, analogous to that of nerve and muscle (see pp. 232f.), in which an associative response, once made, tends not to be repeated at once. There seems to be a barrier against immediate repetition. This fact favors distribution, but it is doubtful if such refractoriness is a major factor here.

Other conditions. There are many other conditions which affect speed of learning and which merit brief comment.

When the variables of motivation and transfer are equated in the two sexes, sex differences in learning are negligible. Large differences in favor of males have been found when the materials to be learned were interesting to the men and of a kind familiar to them; conversely, large differences in favor of females have been found when the materials lay within their sphere of experience.

Rhythm aids learning importantly, a fact which in part accounts for its being easier to learn poetry verbatim than to learn equal amounts of prose.

Voluntary muscular contraction during learning frequently has a positive effect, although too much muscular tension may disrupt the acquisition of a pattern of response.

The sense department to which the material is presented has little effect upon rate of learning. One may become accustomed to learning verbal materials by visual or by auditory presentation and may find learning easier through whichever sense he habitually uses the more, but when practice is a constant there is no advantage for any sense.

One may practice a material in parts—a stanza of poetry at a time—connecting the parts later, or one may practice the entire material as a whole. Sometimes one method is more effective, sometimes the other. The conditions are so complex that no single generalization is possible.

RELATIONS WITHIN SERIES

Serial position. Many of the things learned under laboratory conditions and in life are arranged in series of more or less equivalent units. It is a well-established fact, however, that items in some parts of the series are learned more rapidly than items in other parts. The data of Table XXII represent the usual relation between serial position and learning. Items in the early and late positions are learned most rapidly, whereas those in the intermediate positions are learned more slowly. The least advantageous positions are those just past the middle of the list. The alleys of a maze show a similar relation. The superiority of the early and late positions is known as the *primacy-finality effect.* When such measurements as those in Table XXII are plotted, they yield a curve which is highest at

TABLE XXII

PERCENTAGE OF CORRECT ANTICIPATIONS AT EACH SERIAL POSITION DURING 10 PRESENTATIONS OF A LIST OF 10 ADJECTIVES

Position	1	2	3	4	5	6	7	8	9	10
Percentage correct anticipations	71	63	58	53	47	43	47	45	51	68

the ends and dips to a low point just past the middle of the list. This function was well characterized by a student who, learning a list of words in the laboratory and noticing the greater difficulty of the intermediate words, remarked disgustedly, "Confound it, my mind sags in the middle." It is probable that the primacy-finality effect is largely a function of the greater freedom of the first and last parts of the list from interference of a kind which we shall discuss in the next chapter under the name of associative and retroactive inhibition.

Remote forward and backward association. The direction of practice upon serial activities is forward. It is, however, a question of great importance whether the learning is entirely in a forward direction—a matter of connecting or associating adjacent terms only—or whether backward associations and associations between serially remote or non-adjacent items are also formed. The experimental work on the problem has shown clearly that associations are formed in the backward direction as well as in the forward and that a considerable number of remote associations are formed in both directions. This relation has already been illustrated for conditioned responses by Fig. 26. The largest number of associations is between adjacent items, however, and the frequency of the remote connections declines in most cases with increasing degree of remoteness. These facts mean that the members of a series are complexly interconnected to form a much more highly organized whole than serial connection alone could give.

The possibility at once presents itself that these remote associations were formed by direct practice in the sense that the subject could react to spatially remote items in direct temporal succession. He could recall a remote item while any other given item was present in perception. The best evidence available, however, indicates that this explanation will not account for all cases, that there are, indeed, conditions where it will account for no more than a few. Remote associations may, apparently, be formed indirectly and across the time gap filled by the subject's reaction to intervening items.

REFERENCES

1. Bird, C. *Effective study habits.* New York: Appleton-Century, 1931.
2. Hull, C. L. The factor of the conditioned reflex. *A handbook of general experimental psychology.* Worcester, Mass.: Clark University Press, 1934. Chap. 9.
3. Hunter, W. S. Experimental studies of learning. *A handbook of general experimental psychology.* Worcester, Mass.: Clark University Press. 1934. Chap. 11.
4. Köhler, W. *Gestalt psychology.* New York: Liveright, 1929. Chaps. 8 and 10.
5. Peterson, J. Learning in children. *A handbook of child psychology.* Worcester, Mass.: Clark University Press, 1933. Chap. 10.
6. Robinson, E. S. *Association theory today.* New York: Appleton-Century, 1932.
7. Thorndike, E. L. *Human learning.* New York: Appleton-Century, 1931.

CHAPTER 10

RETENTION

All learning involves retention. To have learned is to have retained the effects of previous events. In the preceding chapter on *learning* we considered the early events in learning and retention—the way in which ideas and skills are organized and prepared for persistence. In the present chapter we have to do with *retention* as the subsequent history of learning—the decay of the effects of learning over long periods of time, the effect of subsequent activities upon the persistence of learning and other related phenomena. A chapter on retention is a chapter on the persistence of learning.

TRANSFER OF LEARNING

When earlier learning affects later learning, there is said to be *transfer* from the earlier to the later. Often the earlier aids the later, so that it appears as if some of the first learning were directly transferred to the second; that is called *positive transfer*. Sometimes, however, the first learning actually interferes with the second, or else some established association or habit has to be unlearned before the second can be perfected; then we have *negative transfer*. When there is no effect of the earlier learning on the later, or when these two influences cancel each other, we say that there is *zero transfer*.

Doctrine of formal discipline. The doctrine of formal discipline asserts that there is positive transfer from certain studies that have disciplinary value to a wide range of other mental activities. The doctrine was forged in the practical context of school curricula. It was held that certain subjects, like

This chapter was written by John A. McGeoch of the University of Iowa.

Latin, Greek and mathematics, provide 'mental discipline' and thus enable the mind, being disciplined, to function with increased efficiency in other intellectual endeavors. Originally this doctrine received support from the now discredited conception of mental faculties. So long as the mind was supposed to be divisible into such independent faculties as memory, reason and perception, the training of one faculty in any subject matter would be so much gain for that faculty in every other subject matter. Nowadays we know that there are no faculties of this sort that admit of practice or of separate development, that formal discipline can work only if and when it provides the conditions for positive transfer from the learning of one subject to the learning of another. It is, then, to the facts of transfer that we must turn, remembering that transfer may be negative as well as positive, that 'disciplinary' learning may be disadvantageous as well as advantageous.

Transfer within the same class. Practice upon one sample of a given material—one maze, for instance, or one list of words—may result not only in the learning of that sample but also in a facilitation of the learning of other samples of that specific material. Practice effects of this kind, which are not specific to the sample learned, are one form of what is called *transfer of learning*. Often large, they occur within most materials, probably within all. The data of Table XXIII illustrate such transfer. They relate to the learning of a problem in which the subject has first to discover the correct responses and then to fix them, using the information gained at successive responses to avoid later errors. It will be seen that by all the measures there is a marked change in the direction of faster learning with prior practice at similar problems. In a certain maze experiment, likewise, the number of trials decreased from 17 to 6 after practice upon two other mazes, time decreased from 676 sec. to 127, and errors from 194 to 35. With continued practice at successive samples, the increments in rate of learning still continue to appear after a relatively larger number of samples but at a negatively accelerated rate.

This transfer from one sample to another of the same class can ordinarily be described by a curve which is like a learning curve for a single material. It is, indeed, a learning curve which shows continuous improvement with successively different materials instead of with repetitions of the same material. Such a curve represents the only way in which a person can learn to learn.

TABLE XXIII

THE INFLUENCE OF PRACTICE AT ONE AND AT TWO PRIOR RATIONAL LEARNING PROBLEMS

(From J. A. McGeoch and V. J. Oberschelp, *J. gen. Psychol.*, 1930, 4, 164.)

Number of Prior Problems	Pairs Presented	Time (minutes)	Errors		
			Logical	Perseverative	Unclassified
0	112.50	32.32	104.62	24.25	121.75
1	75.00	18.33	44.62	14.75	74.25
2	58.50	10.66	22.75	2.00	63.37

(The Peterson Rational Learning Problem consists of a series of pairs of letters and numbers such as $\begin{matrix}A & B & C & D & E & F\\ 4 & 1 & 5 & 3 & 6 & 2\end{matrix}$ When the experimenter calls out the first letter, the subject is to guess which number between 1 and 6 goes with that letter, and so on to the end. A number once correctly given cannot logically be used again, nor can the same wrong guess be repeated. The subject must learn to make the correct pairings without error.)

Analogous to these cases is the transfer of relations, whereby a subject always chooses the darker of two surfaces, regardless of his specific training upon either (see p. 303). There the subject is dealing with successive perceptual situations and, having learned that a certain relation works successfully with some of them, he carries that relation over to others. In learning by insight he also often seems to transfer responses which fitted earlier behavior to present behavior situations of the same kind.

Bilateral transfer. Bilateral transfer, or cross-education, a second form of transfer of learning, is the facilitation of the learning of responses on one side of the body by the learning of responses made on the other side.

The procedure used in experimenting upon bilateral transfer and, indeed, upon all transfer from one class of material to another is shown in Table XXIV. *L* (learning) in the table stands for any number of practice trials. There is an experimental group of subjects and a control group, the two groups being equated as nearly as possible at the beginning. A brief introductory practice, L_1, provides a test of performance prior to training. Then, while one group receives no further practice, the other is given training, L_2, in responses made on the other side of the body or on some other class of material. Finally, both groups are tested by continuing practice, L_1, at the responses first tested. If the training given the experimental group is transferred, the performance of this group on the final test will be better than that of the control.

TABLE XXIV

Experimental Procedure in Studying Transfer

Group	Initial Test	Training	Final Test
Control	L_1	No further training	L_1 (continued)
Experimental	L_1	L_2	L_1 (continued)

Bilateral transfer has been found in a large number of acts, among them drawing in a mirror, rapid tapping on a tapping board, tossing a ball at a target, running a maze and following a pursuitmeter. The amount of transfer varies from a small percentage to as much as 50 per cent. Tactual discrimination of the Braille alphabet by subjects with normal vision has been found to transfer completely in some cases from one hand to the other; in such cases there is a positive transfer of 100 per cent. Conditioned responses established on one side of the body have been found to appear on the other side with a consistency almost equal to that shown on the trained side. There is, as well, a great deal of similarity between bilateral transfer and the irradiation characteristic of conditioned responses.

In our own common behavior bilateral transfer may be observed frequently enough. Having learned to shift the gears of an automobile with one hand, we can do it nearly as well with the other. Analogous transfer may be seen in the free shift from one hand to the other in the manipulation of the settings of a radio or in the handling of a telephone. The transfer is seldom complete at the beginning, but the learning is so rapid that the originally untrained side very quickly reaches the level of performance which the originally trained side required long practice to attain.

Transfer from one class to another. The next question, the one which is basic in the problem of formal discipline, is whether practice upon one or more samples of one class will facilitate the learning of samples of a different class. Will practice at maze learning facilitate mirror drawing; will practice at learning nonsense syllables transfer to learning poetry; or will studying Latin help English usage? Would the 'formal discipline' of learning to make multiple choices help a rat to run mazes better?

To this question experimental psychology answers that any one of the three possibilities may take place. Transfer may be (1) positive, (2) zero or (3) negative. Although positive transfer is by far the most common in experimental work and probably also in everyday life, zero and negative transfer occur in both. It can safely be said that *every instance of learning is influenced in some way by the already existent associative organization of the learner.* Even zero transfer may be the result of a balance of positive and negative influences.

Thus the experimental problem is narrowed to the discovery of the conditions determining transfer—which aspects of the learner's acquired organization will transfer and in what amounts, and whether the transfer will be positive or negative. The specific conditions of the present situation in relation to already existent organization yield the answers to these questions.

Determining conditions of transfer. There are two important and similar theories of the transfer of learning: the theory of identical elements and the theory of generalization. The theory of *identical elements* states that transfer occurs between two activities which contain common elements. Thus, learning addition will make easier the learning of multiplication, because addition is involved in multiplication; in the same way, learning algebra will not only aid the learning of calculus, but also prove essential to it, because calculus uses algebra. Aims, methods and general principles, being nearly always common elements in many different tasks, thus assure transfer from one to another. The theory of *generalization* differs from the theory of identical elements only in that it limits the common items which transfer to general principles and relations. In any case, then, it is clear that transfer between two activities depends upon the community between them.

The nature of this community becomes obvious from an examination of some of the familiar instances where transfer can take place. Knowing addition helps the learning of multiplication. Knowing the Latin roots helps the learning of French. There is a transfer when there is similarity of meaning, as from the study of history to the study of economics, from algebra to geometry, from logic to law. There is a transfer when there is similarity of form or of relations, as from choosing the lighter of two dark grays to choosing the lighter of two light grays, or as from solving one quadratic equation to solving another, as—Newton's contribution—in understanding the moon's motion in relation to the earth by understanding the apple's motion in relation to the earth. A great deal of scientific invention is similarly dependent upon the transfer of a familiar relation to a novel situation.

Relations that transfer may belong not only to the things learned, but also to the conditions of learning. When one learns a second maze more rapidly than a first, the chief vehicles of transfer are the modes of attack which, having been learned on the first maze, are now applied to the second. Also carried over, of course, is the knowledge of what a maze is like and of what to expect in a maze. A great deal of the transfer value of general education lies in this acquisition of methods of work.

Transfer in terms of general principles and methods of work is not automatic and inevitable. If it were, learning would be easier. For a general principle to transfer, it must usually be learned as one which is applicable to more than one situation. Otherwise it is unlikely to transfer. Witness the scientist who, a consistent adherent of the scientific method in his own field, forsakes it completely when he deals with philosophical or social or theological problems. Or consider the man who accepts the doctrine of evolution in biology but fails to realize its applicability to society. If transfer is to be assured, a general principle or any general relations must be learned *as general*, as reaching beyond the specific field in which they are learned.

Associative inhibition. One of the conditions of negative transfer is stated in a law which reads thus: *When any two items, as A and B, have been associated, it is more difficult to form an association between either one and a third item, K.* The inhibition of *A-K* by the prior learning of *A-B* is more pronounced when *A-B* has been learned to only a moderate degree. An example of this phenomenon of associative inhibition is afforded by the greater difficulty of learning that Jones' telephone number is 4916 when one has learned only fairly well his last year's number, 8921. This gross fact is illustrated, also, by many phenomena of *habit interference*, such as are found in changing to a car with a different gear shift or in learning a maze in which the correct turns are the opposite of those in a maze previously learned.

RETENTION AS A FUNCTION OF TIME

We have been dealing thus far with the course of the learning process and with the conditions which affect it. This learning, as we have already seen, necessarily involves a progressive retention throughout its course. If learning were not retained, there could be no transfer of learning. Experimentally, however, we speak of measuring retention only when we measure learned performance at some time after a given criterial level has been reached. We then inquire how much of the criterial performance will appear in measurement after the interval. Experimentally we define retention as performance under certain conditions when compared with performance prior to the elapsed interval.

There are four principal ways in which retention may be measured. (1) The method of *reproduction* is that whereby the subject is placed again in the original stimulating situation, confronted with the same problem (or given the same cue) and asked to perform as nearly as possible as he did at the criterial level. (2) In the method of *saving*, we require the subject again to reach the criterial level obtained during learning, and then compute the difference between the saving in the relearning over the original learning. Thus, if one originally takes 20 trials to learn and after an interval of a week relearns in 5 trials, he has saved 75 per cent. (3) In the method of *recognition*, the subject, confronted with the material learned, mixed at random with similar items, is asked to indicate those items which had been in the original material. (4) In the method of *reconstruction*, the material learned is presented in a new arrangement, and the subject is required to arrange it in the order in which it was learned.

Retention curves. In general we wish to know how much of any given performance is retained, not only after a single

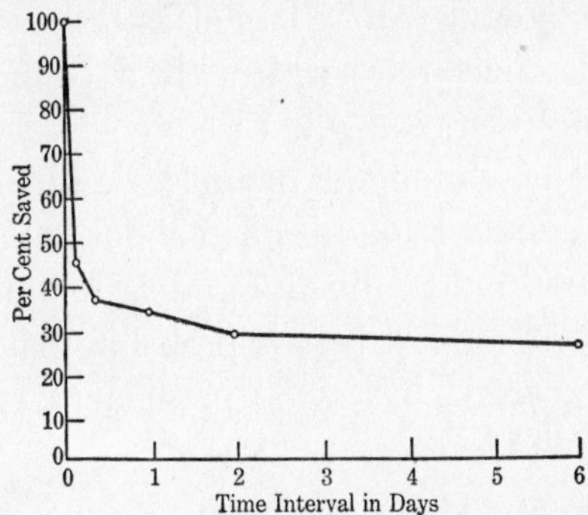

FIG. 35. EBBINGHAUS CURVE OF RETENTION AS MEASURED BY THE SAVING METHOD. From H. Ebbinghaus, *Memory* (tr. Ruger and Bussenius), New York: Teachers College, 1913, 76. The curve is plotted from the data given there.

interval, but also after as many different intervals as possible. By taking the proper measurements of performance after a number of intervals, we obtain the data for a curve of retention. This measurement was made first in 1885 by Ebbinghaus, whose work is one of the classics in the field of learning. Employing the method of saving with nonsense syllables learned to a criterion of two perfect repetitions, he obtained the curve shown in Fig. 35. This curve has a negatively accelerated form, falling rapidly at first and then at a steadily decreasing rate. Most curves for serial materials and short intervals have this general form. Though the specific amounts retained vary with a number of conditions presently to be discussed, under most conditions retention decreases rapidly during the time immediately after learning and thereafter at a decreasing rate.

Curves of retention approach zero as a limit, but they seldom reach it. Most of the measurements from which such curves are plotted are the averages for a group. Some of the subjects may reach a zero point in measured retention; yet other conditions and methods of measuring might reveal for them some degree of retention even after considerable intervals of time. It has been found that activities once learned may be retained for long periods. One subject, for example, lost only a third of his typing skill in terms of words typed per hour after an interval of 2 years and 35 days. Meaningful materials have been retained after 120 days with a loss of as little as 12.2 per cent, and similar materials relearned with a considerable saving after as long as 5 years—in one case after 46 years. Studies of the adult recall of childhood memories and of the recall of long past events under hypnosis or in abnormal conditions support the conclusion that much more is retained for a long time than is often supposed. It is probable that most of what has once been learned has some permanent effect upon the organization of the learner.

Reminiscence. There are certain striking exceptions to the rule of the decrease in retention during the period immediately following practice. When the appropriate measurements are made, it is found that under some conditions recall is greater after an interval than immediately at the close of practice. This phenomenon of improvement in retention after practice is called *reminiscence*. It occurs under two sets of conditions: first, when recall is measured at intervals of a few minutes after practice; and second, when the measurements are spaced over longer intervals of hours or days. The curve in Fig. 36 is an example of the results obtained under the first-named set of conditions. In the experiment which yielded this curve, retention was also measured in terms of the number of trials needed to relearn (saving), the curve for which shows in even more pronounced form the phenomenon of reminiscence. The curves which show reminiscence after longer intervals rise from the end of practice to a point one or two days later and then fall.

It will be evident upon a little thought that there can be no reminiscence, as shown by the method of reproduction, unless

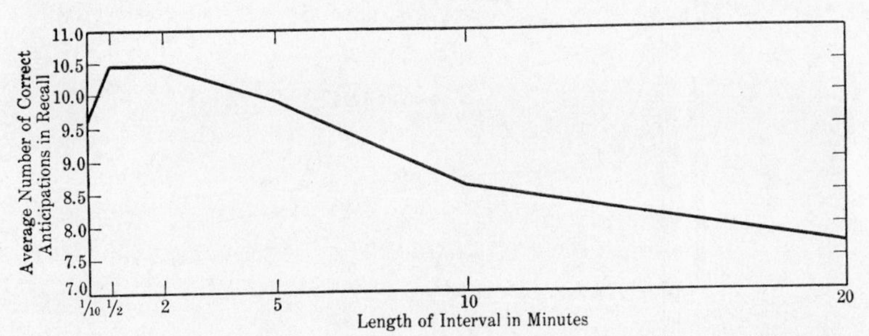

FIG. 36. CURVE SHOWING REMINISCENCE AFTER SHORT INTERVALS (LISTS OF NONSENSE SYLLABLES).

From L. B. Ward, Reminiscence and rote learning, *Psychol. Monogr.*, 1937, 49, No. 220, 17.

the material has been incompletely learned. If the recall at the close of practice is complete, no later recall can be greater, so that there is no opportunity for reminiscence to show itself.

The determining conditions of reminiscence are as yet incompletely understood. It has been established that reminiscence is not produced, as it might well be, by rehearsal during the interval. Sometimes a second recall is better than a first because the first acts as an additional recitation, but not all cases admit of this explanation. At present the best hypothesis is that the interferences among the parts of the material, since they are less strong than the correct associations, drop out faster, disinhibiting the correct associations. This explanation unifies the data for distribution of practice and for reminiscence in that it offers a common basis for the two.

CONDITIONS OF RETENTION

The relative amounts of retention are a function of the method by which the measurement is made. In general, the indicated amount of retention is greatest by the recognition method, less by the reconstruction method and least by the reproduction method. The saving method commonly yields relatively smaller amounts of retention than do some of the others after short intervals and relatively larger amounts after

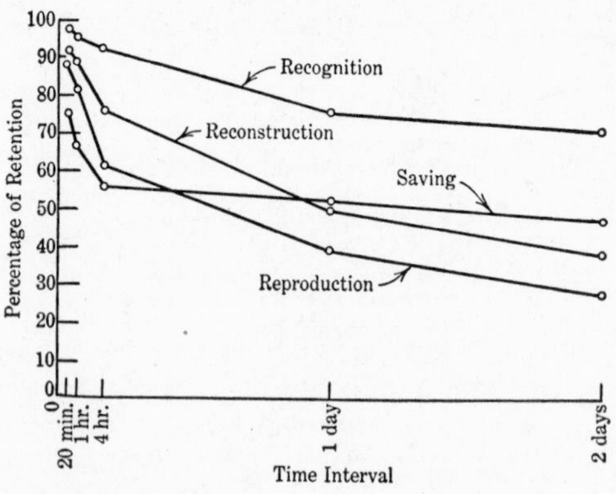

FIG. 37. RETENTION CURVES YIELDED BY DIFFERENT METHODS OF MEASUREMENT. From C. W. Luh, *Psychol. Monogr.*, 1922, 31, No. 142, 22.

longer intervals. These facts are represented in the curves of Fig. 37. Although each of these methods measures what we call retention, each one provides a different stimulating and instructional context with consequent differences in results. Thus generalizations about retention are, necessarily, specific to the operations by which performance has been measured.

Retention as a function of the learner. Since retention so completely pervades learning, we should, other things being equal, expect various conditions to affect retention after an interval in essentially the same way as they affect it during learning, and to affect relearning as they do learning. To a large extent this expectation is justified. (1) Measurements of retention yield an age-curve which resembles in form the age-curve for learning. (2) Absolute amounts retained are positively correlated with intelligence. (3) Learning with intent to remember indefinitely has a favorable influence upon retention. (4) Recitation during learning leads to an absolutely higher degree of retention. (5) The range of individual differences for retention is of the same order as the range for learning.

Retention as a function of the materials. (1) Meaningful material is much better retained than non-meaningful. A comparison of Figs. 35 and 38 will illustrate this fact. (2) Retention increases within fairly wide limits with the amount of the material learned. (3) For retention as well as for learning, distribution of practice during learning is superior to massed practice; moreover, the duration of the practice periods has been shown with some materials to be a more important variable for retention than is length of rest interval. (4) Although measurements of degree of learning and retention are necessarily functions of specific methods of measurement, in general we may say that retention increases as does degree of learning until a considerable degree of overlearning is reached; after that, additional repetitions of material already mastered may have an inhibitory effect.

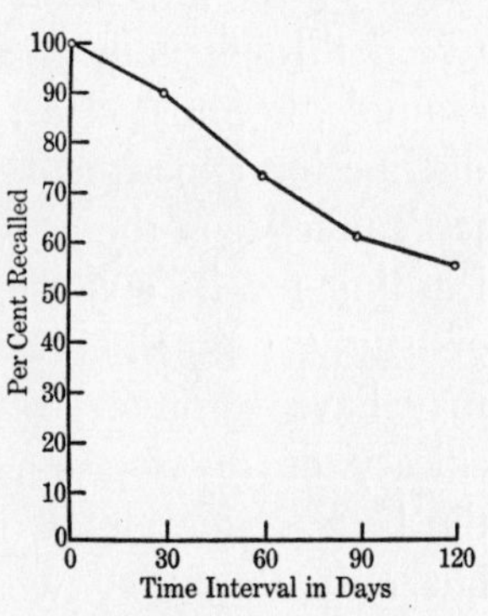

FIG. 38. A CURVE OF RETENTION FOR MATERIAL (OBJECTS) BRIEFLY OBSERVED.

From J. A. McGeoch, and P. L. Whitely, *J. educ. Psychol.*, 1926, 17, 422; reprinted by permission of Warwick and York.

Retention of completed and uncompleted tasks. The effect of motivation upon retention is shown by the fact that uncompleted tasks are generally retained better than completed ones. Let subjects be given a large number of tasks to do at a continuous sitting and permitted to finish only half of them, being interrupted on some plausible pretext before each task of the other half has been completed. At the close of the session, let the subjects be asked to name as many of the tasks as they can, without, in the meantime, having been told that the interruption is an integral part of the experiment. The results will show, for a wide variety of conditions, better recall of the tasks which have been interrupted.

This advantage of interrupted tasks over completed tasks has been demonstrated clearly only for the recall of the names of the tasks. We cannot yet be sure that the same relation will appear for a total act such as a maze tracing, although there is some indication that it may. If it does, the relation between this phenomenon and that of distributed practice, for example, becomes clear. The introduction of a rest interval in distribution experiments represents an interruption of the subject's practice at the activity. Reminiscence requires incomplete learning for its appearance, and, to the extent that cessation of study represents an interruption, the two phenomena may have common conditions. This is not to say that the efficacy of distribution, the advantage of reminiscence and the better retention of interrupted tasks are the same thing, but only that they would appear to have common conditions.

Exceptional memorizing. Occasionally, because of remarkable performance at memorizing and retaining, an individual attracts popular attention and sometimes even scientific study. Persons who can learn a list of 200 digits in 9 minutes, and retain it for some time, or who can repeat the numbers of every car in a long freight train to a total which fills several pages in the conductor's notebook are cases in point. The question at once arises whether such performances are a result of some special native ability or of intensive practice. Certainly these performances do not require high intelligence. One man, for example, who could somewhat slowly recall a huge assortment of the populations of large cities, had an IQ of 74. The conclusion which emerges from the available data on these exceptional memorizers is that their performances are a result of special practice. The ability is usually limited to narrow classes of materials, such as dates, numbers and other disparate items.

The exceptional memorizer is highly motivated to relate and recall the materials with which he works. He groups the items, uses them whenever possible and utilizes many of the methods of learning and recalling already discussed. With sufficient motivation almost anyone could do as well. In one experiment the feat of a memory expert was duplicated with relatively little practice by a group of college students. This expert could recall the order of a 52-card deck of shuffled cards after 20 minutes of study. The college students were able to duplicate this performance after an average of 5.25 practice periods of 20 minutes each. Two students did it at the first sitting and twelve at the third.

Dependence of retention on speed of learning. The problem of the relation between the measure of learning and the measure of retention after an elapsed interval has commonly been stated in the form of the question: Is the rapid learner a good retainer? The critical student will recognize that this question is a partial and inadequate formulation of a more general problem, the answer to which is beset with many difficulties of method. If retention is measured by relearning, for example, the conditions which determine each subject's learning will also condition his relearning, quite aside from the amount which he has forgotten, and the correlation will be too high. There are other difficulties, but when they are surmounted, there remains a high positive relation between measures of learning and retention. The 'slow' learner gains no retentive advantage from his slowness, and the 'fast' learner suffers no disadvantage from his fastness. There is here no benign law of compensation.

Retroactive inhibition. Early in the history of research on learning it was demonstrated that learning another sample of the same material during the interval between the end of practice and the measurement of retention produced a decrement in retention. The phenomenon has since been found under a large number of conditions. The name *retroactive inhibition* is used to designate it and to refer to any decrement in retention produced by activity interpolated between the end of practice and the measurement of retention.

The experimental procedure employed in studying retroactive inhibition is of the general form shown in Table XXV, where the numbers 1 and 2 stand for two distinct learning materials. The difference between the two retentions under these two conditions is the gross amount of inhibition.

TABLE XXV

EXPERIMENTAL PROCEDURE IN STUDYING RETROACTIVE INHIBITION

Condition	Original Activity	Interpolated Activity	Final Test
Rest	Learn (1)	Rest	Measure retention (1)
Work	Learn (1)	Learn (2)	Measure retention (1)

If a subject recalls 10 words of a list after rest and only 6 words after work, he shows a gross interference effect of 4 words and a relative interference of 40 per cent from the interpolated activity. The two conditions are arranged so that they differ importantly only in respect of the interpolated activity (rest or learning) between the original learning and the measurement of its retention.

The experimentally obtained decrements from interpolated learning vary in amount from nearly zero to nearly 100 per cent. The amounts which appear are a function of several conditions. Over a considerable range of similarity, degree of inhibition varies directly with the degree of similarity between the original activity and the interpolated. When, for example, the original material consists of lists of adjectives and the interpolated material of lists of synonyms of these adjectives, the amount of inhibition is great (in one experiment as high as 72 per cent), the percentage of inhibition decreasing for antonyms, unrelated adjectives, nonsense syllables and three-place numbers, in that order.

Meaningful material is less susceptible to retroactive inhibition than are lists of disconnected items. The longer the material and the more difficult to learn, the less susceptible it

ıibition. Inhibition may also be decreased by instruc
the subject to try to avoid interference from the inter
learning. Moreover, if the learning of the interpolate
is held constant, inhibition will decrease in the even

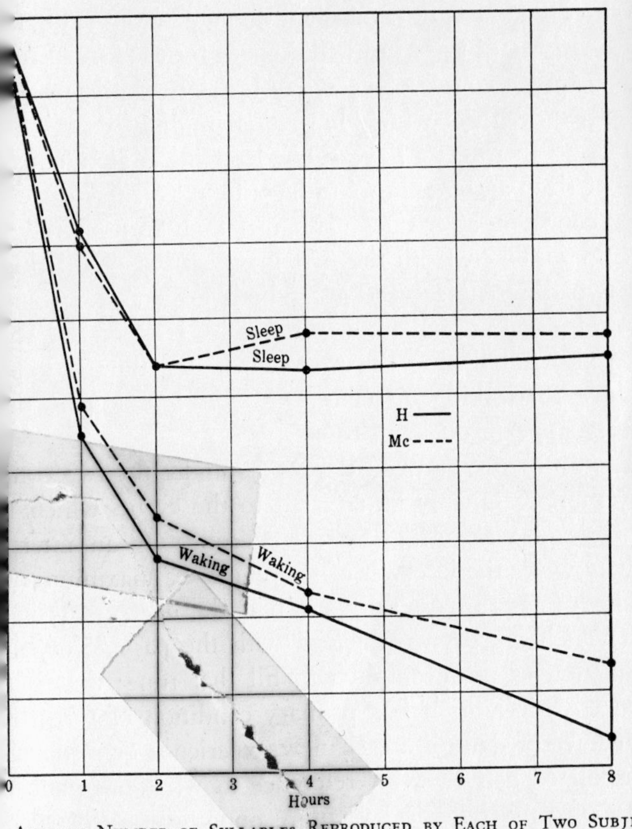

AVERAGE NUMBER OF SYLLABLES REPRODUCED BY EACH OF TWO SUBJEC
AFTER VARIOUS TIME-INTERVALS OF SLEEP AND WAKING.

reased learning of the original activity. When these con
ıs are reversed and the degree of interpolated learning
l, inhibition increases with degree of interpolated learn
t first, but, as complete mastery is approached, addition
nents of interpolated learning cease to increase the amoun
hibition, finally even decreasing it.

5

12-7

The experimental data upon the inhibitory effects o
olated learning show that a large decrement in retent
produced by such interpolation. They imply, also, th
ecrements are a matter, not of passive decay or disint
ith time, but of active blocking of one performa
nother. The facts thus far cited do not, however, dem
at blocking of this kind will account for the forgetting
curs in the course of everyday life. There are, never
her experiments which have this implication.

These experiments have studied retention after equa
ls of sleep and waking and have found a superiority
eep condition after intervals longer than an hour. The
Fig. 39, taken from the first investigation of this ki
r two different subjects after both sleep and wakin
rves for waking fall at a negatively accelerated rate. Th
eep also fall during the first two hours, though not
those for waking. After the first two hours no furth
tting appears during sleep.

The difference between the results under the two con
ay most reasonably be referred to the events which f
tervals of waking. These events constitute an interp
tivity while the intervals of sleeping are a maximum of
These facts support the view that the decrements in
on which we commonly find with the passage of tim
function of the events which fill that time; that is t
troactive inhibition is a primary condition of forgetti
e course of daily life each new experience or response
terpolated activity with reference to what has gone b
ort of a psychological vacuum, opportunities for such
tion cannot be escaped. A large amount of decremen
avoided only by a favorable operation of all the f
hich determine the degree of inhibition.

There remains a question as to the fundamental natu
troactive inhibition. The best evidence shows it to be a
negative transfer. The original and interpolated mat
t, as it were, mixed up. That is why the inhibition is g
t for similar materials. Whenever one gets two sets of r

rial confused, as when in learning elementary languages one mixes French words with German rules, the negative transfer phenomenon of retroactive inhibition is taking place.

Context and set. Everything which the human being learns has, during practice, a complex context which is a part of the total stimulus situation. We may call it the stimulational context, and it may be subdivided into three parts. One kind of context consists of the stimulation from the external environment, such as the furniture of the room, the experimenter and the apparatus. A second kind is the stimulation from the interoceptors which make up the feeling of the body, and a third is the ideational context which constitutes the unessential content of consciousness. These factors may be, and many of them are, connected with the material learned. They alter with time, and the alteration creates a situation in which, although the intent to recall may be present, the necessary eliciting stimuli are not. An example of this situation is one's failure to recall the name of a person seen in a new environment, although the name may be reproduced readily enough in the usual environment.

Some stimulus is always necessary to elicit a learned performance. It is probable that the failure of a previously learned performance to appear may often be referred to the fact that the stimulational context necessary to elicit it is not present. This condition, together with the inhibitory effect of interpolated activities, offers our most reasonable explanation of the phenomena of forgetting. In order to remember an engagement at five o'clock we are wholly dependent upon the chance that the environment will produce some cue to turn our minds in the right direction. It is only because the environment so constantly suggests the time of day that so few engagements are missed.

It is probable, although the experimental evidence in support of it is not yet conclusive, that forgetting also depends upon set or determining tendency. That interest or set in a given direction has a selective influence on recall is well known; if the set is in an incorrect direction, recall may fail, even though with a correct set it may occur. Thus if, seeking to recall a name, one insists incorrectly that the name is Scotch, the search will be confined to Scotch names to the neglect of others, and it will seem that the name has been forgotten. Similarly, if interest is strongly directed in other channels, one may note the time but still forget the engagement.

Why we forget. The conditions just discussed are the conditions which explain forgetting. In time we forget, but it is not time which produces forgetting. The three major conditions of forgetting are (1) the interference from interpolated activity, (2) altered stimulating context and (3) altered set. When one considers the prevalence of these three, the wonder is not that we forget but that we remember anything at all. When we remember, it is because of favorable conditions which reduce the influence of these three conditions. Retroactive inhibition may be reduced, for example, by learning material thoroughly, or by learning in sequence materials which are as dissimilar as possible. Failure of recall from altered stimulating contexts may be decreased by intensive learning or by connecting what is being learned with many different stimulating cues and things already well known. By the same means the influence of altered set may be lessened.

HOW TO STUDY

The researches of the psychological laboratory have direct application to the problem of college study; there are good and bad methods of study. The student must note at the outset, however, that, no matter how much he may be told about effective methods of studying, the use of these methods depends entirely upon him. There is no sugar-coated technique to relieve him of effort. If, nevertheless, he will apply what is known about learning, he will find that the effectiveness of his study time will be greatly increased.

Motivation is a first essential to learning. A student must be motivated to study or what passes for study will be little more than exposure to the material. Although there is no simple rule for acquiring a missing motivation, it may be said that motivation is aided by thought about what is to be gained by the studying. If the material to be learned is not interesting in its own right, it will usually become interesting after something is known about it. One device is, therefore, to force oneself to learn something about a subject, knowing that the knowledge will then become, as it were, a motive for further knowledge.

Closely connected with motivation is the importance of taking an *active attitude* toward the material. React to it, study it with intent to remember indefinitely. Recall the material as you read it and prompt yourself when you cannot recall. This procedure, which will serve as a check on what has not been learned or on what has been incorrectly learned, will yield large results in effective learning. Try at the same time to relate the meanings of the different parts of what is being studied to each other, to other parts of the same subject, to other things you already know and to the activities of your everyday life. In this way knowledge becomes organized and assimilated, made a permanent part of your repertoire.

Wherever possible employ *distributed practice.* In ordinary studying one cannot resort to lengthy schedules of study and rest periods, but one can come back to the material at least once after a rest interval and recall as much as possible, prompting oneself when recall fails. This is one of the best ways to insure learning for permanent retention. To this end use what has been learned whenever possible. Think about it, talk about it, write about it.

People often speak of a good memory or a poor memory, as if a given performance in learning and retaining were the result of a basic organic capacity which one either has or does not have. On the contrary, in persons of the intelligence of college students, a good memory is almost entirely a matter of the habits of study and thinking which have been acquired and which can be used. It is not a mysterious power which has been born with us. That we can learn and retain at all is mysterious enough, but the extent to which we learn and retain is a matter of the methods we employ.

Much has been written and said about *memory systems*, and there are many of them advertised and sold. The core of these systems is some artificial association scheme into which the learner must fit the new material to be learned. Usually there are key words which, first learned by rote, are later used as associative cues or as anchors for the new. There is nothing pernicious about most of these systems, but it is far easier and more economical to utilize the principles already described than it is to learn an artificial set of cues which have nothing to do with the material itself. Unless one practices long, the cues are likely to be themselves forgotten and the connected material along with them. Make your own memory system by organizing the material to be learned both within itself and with reference to what you already know. Sometimes, of course, an artificial system works because it provides motivation; what one has paid for, one wants to use! In any case, it works only by bringing into use the principles already described.

It will often help to remember that methods of study are themselves matters of habit and that the physiological limits in their application are indefinitely remote. We do nothing uninfluenced by our already existent organization. What we have already learned will work to help or hinder each instance of new learning. Positive and negative transfer are always operating. For this reason, efficient study always tries to fit the new into the already known.

REFERENCES

See the references cited for *Learning* at the end of the preceding chapter, p. 329.

Chapter 11

RECOLLECTION AND IMAGINATION

After a person has had repeated experience in learning a list of words or in running through a maze, his behavior always changes; he can repeat the list or run through the maze more accurately. This change, however, is not the only effect of past experience. Suppose one meets a friend on the street; afterward, one remembers the events of the meeting, recalls the appearance of the friend, the sound of his voice and the grip of his hand. If there has been an argument, one may remember its topic, some of the specific words spoken and the emotional reactions of both parties. One may also think of the things that should have been said and done at that past meeting, of other things that one would like to say and do at the next. Thus, in addition to the effects of past experience on the efficiency of behavior, there are conscious effects, which, as we experience them in everyday life, seem to underlie and explain the changes in behavior. These conscious processes have two aspects. On the one hand, we relive our past, review the road we have been traveling, noting our successes and failures; we *recollect* the real events of the past. On the other hand, we think of things that might have been, and of the application of past experience to our present and future needs; we *imagine* ideal events of the past and future.

Recollection and imagination are complementary processes. When our thoughts refer to the *real past* we usually describe them as recollections; when they refer to events which *have not actually occurred*, then we use the term imagination. But nearly always there is some imagination in recollection. The unreal is introduced into the real past; and, conversely, the

This chapter was written by C. W. Bray of Princeton University.

materials of imagination are recollections. The unreal is created from the real.

RECOLLECTION

Kinds. Recollections appear in consciousness in at least two fairly distinct forms, or in combinations of the two. On the one hand, our reactions to previous situations may be recalled in much the same form as the original experiences. After an automobile ride it is possible to see in the 'mind's eye' the appearance of the car, to hear again the sound of its horn and feel the draft of cold air from its open window. Or we may experience once more the exhilaration of speed and the fear of accident. These conscious memories, which *partially reproduce the experiences of the past*, are known as *images.*

Many memories, on the other hand, do not involve the reproduction of the actual experiences but merely refer to the events of the past. After the ride in the car, we may simply recall that we felt cold, heard a horn or were afraid. Though the actual feeling of coldness does not recur, we remember that we were cold. Sometimes this knowledge about the past occurs in *verbal* terms. At other times, however, it appears in a way which defies accurate description but which is called, for lack of a better term, a *conscious attitude*. An example, common to nearly everyone, is the impression, experienced just before speaking of a past event, that we know what to say, even though no actual words and no images are present. Students frequently experience in examinations this impression of knowing the subject even when, to their sorrow, no words come to mind in which to state their knowledge. It is believed that these conscious attitudes, or 'nut-shell' recollections with little conscious content, play an important though frequently unrecognized role in the thought processes.

Recollections make up a large part of our mental life. Throughout popular and scientific literature, therefore, one finds references to them. William James stated that a student of his who often learned poetry by heart, could, after memorizing a page, see a visual image of the first words of each line. As an example he gave the following from a poem by La Fontaine:

> Étant fait. . . .
> Tous. . . .
> A des. . . .
> Que fit. . . .
> Céres. . . .
>   Avec. . . .
> Une fleur. . . .
>   Comme. . . .

When he thought of the poem, this individual could see these words in visual imagery. The words at the beginning of the indented lines were less clear than the others in the image.

Beethoven would seem to illustrate the same point—but in another sense department. Since he composed several long symphonies after he was completely deaf, it is reasonable to suppose that he must have had vivid auditory imagery, by means of which, even though he could not hear the notes, he could play over the score of his composition and get the sound of the music. In making such inferences about famous men, however, one has to be cautious. Although this probably was indeed the method Beethoven used, it is seldom safe to draw conclusions about imagery from casual accounts of the achievements of great men.

The term image is likely to suggest that reproductions of past experiences are complete, as in photographic pictures of scenes, and that images are always visual. Neither supposition is true. Images are seldom exact copies of past experience. Even in relatively complete images some details are almost certain to be omitted or false details added. It may be said that all recollection is *creative* rather than imitative; it is influenced by the person's interests and attitudes and by past experiences. In this respect recollection is like perception, which, as will be pointed out in a later chapter, consists not of the passive reception of stimuli but of an active integrating reaction. Just as a perception is never a mere copy of a stimulus, so an image is never an exact copy of a past experience. An example of change in a recollection is shown in Fig. 40. The drawing at the left with the caption below it was shown to a person; the drawing and caption at the right is his reproduction of it made a few minutes later.

It is also a mistake to suppose that imagery is always visual in character. Although visual imagery is prominent in mental life, auditory, tactual, organic and other images are experienced as well; it is safe to say that all the senses contribute to recollection. Most recollections, indeed, are composite, involving components from many senses simultaneously. The dominant or clearest component serves to classify a recollection as of visual, auditory or other sense-modality.

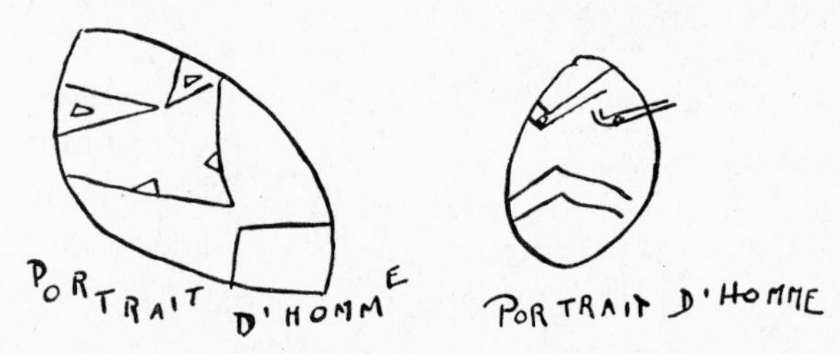

FIG. 40. PERCEPTION AND IMAGE.

The drawing at the left was observed by a certain person at a certain time and reproduced by him 15-30 min. later as on the right. Thus the figure at the left represents the stimulus, and the figure on the right the change in the subsequent recall. From F. C. Bartlett, *Remembering*, Cambridge: University Press, 1932, 178.

Use of motor imagery. Memories of movement, like the other forms of imagery, often involve a partial reinstatement of the previous activity. In this case, partial reinstatement means that the movement itself is reinstated. Occasionally the movements are strong enough to be seen; the golfer, remembering his fine shot, executes a turn or two of his wrist. Usually, of course, the reinstatement is only partial and the movements are so weak that they pass unobserved.

Motor imagery is most readily observed in recollections involving language, where it frequently involves movements of the vocal muscles in the throat and mouth. Since the movements are very weak and no sound is made, they usually pass unobserved unless attention is directed to them. These movements are known as *vocal-motor activity*.

A person may, in vocal-motor activity, remember not only his own words but also the words of others. Even music or mere noises may likewise be recalled in this manner. Owing to the fact that generally when one speaks one also hears the sound of one's voice, there is a close connection between speech and hearing. Consequently, auditory memories often involve both vocal-motor activity and auditory imagery.

Knowledge about the past, as distinct from reproduction of the past, is usually also expressed in terms of vocal-motor activity. A traveler, describing his home from memory, frequently has no visual image of that home, nor does he describe it in the precise terms in which he has previously heard it described. Here again the creative and imaginative aspect of memory should be stressed. There is brought into play a new pattern of words, expressive of the style of architecture, the size of the house, its landscaping and outlook—invented on the spot to meet the needs of description.

Memory, we have seen, can be expressed in imagery and in conscious attitude. It can also be expressed in overt movement. This difference in the ways of expression is excellently illustrated in an account by a lecturer of his methods of reading to himself and lecturing to a class. In reading he found that the printed words were spoken subvocally, *i.e.,* the sight of the words gave rise to vocal-motor activity. Though the movements of articulation were brief and reduced to a minimum, yet prolonged reading, on occasion, made his throat begin to feel stiff as with too much talking. In lecturing, on the other hand, he observed that, when he wished to follow a set procedure or definite organization of the material to be given, he would refer to a visual image of the manuscript or outline of the lecture. The image helped to orient him and to keep the material in its proper place in the lecture. At other times, when the subject matter was difficult, he tended to think ahead to the coming words. These he experienced in auditory imagery.

(Other people might experience here only the conscious attitude or knowledge of the coming topic.) While saying certain words aloud, he was at the same time imagining others. This procedure, as he pointed out, sounds confusing, and yet is not actually so. When the material was easy and familiar to him, he let his voice take care of itself, while he gave his attention to blackboard illustrations and the like.

The systematic study of recollection has been carried out in a variety of ways. One approach has been to compare the characteristics of the image with the characteristics of the experience (usually the perception) which is reproduced. A second procedure has been to study those inaccuracies of recollection which arise from a distortion of the facts remembered. The methods used in this latter type of study are essentially similar to the methods for the study of retention described in the previous chapter; only the emphasis is not on the amounts retained or forgotten but rather on the accuracy of what is remembered. The results of the two methods together give a basis for classifying recollections into different forms—particularly the recollections which are expressed in imagery.

The characteristics of images. We must note, in the first place, that images are usually *limited in detail.* If one calls up an image of some past experience, say the appearance of one's room on awakening in the morning, only a few of the details that were actually perceived will be reproduced in the image, and some of them may be erroneous. Perhaps the appearance of the clothes chest, with one or two objects standing on it, may be the only phase of the original perception that occurs in the image. In the perception one might have grasped many more details: the toilet articles on top of the chest, certain drawers left open and others closed, the mirror with reflections in it and the play of light and shadow on the wall.

In addition to being readily susceptible to loss and change of detail, images are less *stable* than perceptions. They come and go, change and are modified with great rapidity. The fleeting character of the image makes difficult its study, for no sooner does one observe it than it changes.

Images are seldom as *clear* as perceptions. Such details as are present in the image are usually blurred, without sharp edges and of indefinite shape. Sometimes, in a visual image, there will be only an irregular dark gray spot in the place where we know an object to be. Though this vague spot is known to represent the object, it does not necessarily resemble it.

Even very detailed, stable and clear images are seldom as *intense* or, if colored, of as good *saturation* as the original perception. The memory image of thunder does not approach the loudness of real thunder. The memory image of the glare of the sun or of an electric light bulb is seldom as bright as the original. In comparison to the vividness of an original perception, the imaginal color of a red evening gown seems washed out and faded.

These modifications in the structure of the image are all *changes of degree*. Compared with the structure of the perception, the image suffers a loss of a quantitative sort only. Since no differences of kind exist between them, and since perceptions may be as limited in detail or quite as faint as vivid images, it is sometimes impossible to distinguish between them. This confusion between perception and image is likely to occur in everyday life, particularly when stimuli are weak or fleeting. It may be hard, for example, to decide by listening whether a clock is running or not, for our image of the sound of its tick may be very nearly as intense as the perception would be. At twilight or at night one may 'see' objects moving about which turn out to be apparitions. These objects are our own images, projected into outer space and mistaken for perceptions of real objects.

An ingenious experiment has been devised to demonstrate the possibility of confusion between image and perception. The subjects of the experiment, some of them practiced in introspection and familiar with imagery, were asked to project images of such common objects as a banana or a knife on a ground-glass screen. The screen was situated in the wall between two rooms and, unknown to the subjects, a lantern slide projector was placed so as to throw pictures on the screen from behind the wall. While the subjects were trying to call up an adequate image, a very dim picture of the object was thrown on the screen and gradually increased in illumination. Its edges blurred, it was made to vibrate gently. The subjects, mistaking this picture for an image, signaled that they had successfully projected an image on the screen. When the picture was gradually removed, the subjects continued to see an image on the screen; whether the projector was turned on or off, this image remained.

In psychological experiments, the lack of distinction between perception and image frequently causes difficulty. If one is testing a person's ability to hear weak tones or see small objects, images of the stimulus tone or object interfere with the experiment. It is only by rigorous control of the stimulus and by repeated tests that the experimenter can tell whether the subject is actually perceiving or only imagining the stimulus.

These experiences in which *images are mistaken for perceptions* are known as *hallucinations.* Although hallucinatory images occur to everyone, nevertheless when they are frequent and occur in the absence of confusing circumstances they are symptoms of mental abnormality. Abnormal individuals suffer greatly from images of voices and sounds, pressures and movements of the body. These images, regarded by such individuals as perceptions, sometimes contribute to a disastrous dislocation of the life of the person afflicted by them.

In many toxic or poisonous conditions and in states produced by drugs, hallucinations and vivid imagery are common. The hallucinations of the alcoholic are notorious. The patient under an anesthetic has clear and intense dreams. A drug from the plant mescal produces vivid dreams or hallucinations of brilliant, saturated colors; and other drugs have similar effects.

Accuracy of recollection. The accuracy with which past events are recalled clearly depends not merely on the quantitative losses in detail, stability, clarity, etc., described above, but also on qualitative changes in the character of the memory. That past events can be remembered in considerable detail and vividness, yet with very great inaccuracy, is common knowledge. It is clear that the factors, discussed in the previous chapter, which influence the amount of material retained in memory must influence the accuracy of memory as well. Those factors which merit particular emphasis here are repetition of the experience, the intention to remember it, and the meaning of the experience.

The first two factors are of considerable importance in practical life because many situations which must be recalled later *are not repeated, and frequently no effort is made to remember them.* Memory under these conditions is *incidental* to other activities. Most legal testimony by witnesses of accidents and crimes is based on these incidental memories. Thus gross inaccuracies are likely to appear in the testimony, a fact which should be kept in mind by those involved in a legal trial.

Many experiments have been devised to study the accuracy of incidental memory. For example, a feigned quarrel or crime is staged before a group of subjects who are unprepared for anything of the sort, and who after the event are asked to describe what they saw. Later a motion-picture record of the scene is compared with the descriptions. Obviously the trustworthiness of a subject's report depends in part upon the recollections that occur to him.

The accuracy of the report varies considerably with the nature of the event. Statements about objects and persons and their activities are more accurate than statements about characteristics of objects and persons. Statements about time and distance are quite inaccurate. The most frequent errors consist in omissions of detail. The insertion or substitution of erroneous detail is, however, only slightly less frequent. Questioning the subject leads to a more complete report but also to more errors, and the number of errors depends in great part on the character of the suggestion involved in the questions. It is generally found that if the testimony is limited to those details of which the subject is certain, it will be somewhat more accurate. Allowing the subject to repeat his testimony increases his feeling of certainty without, however, increasing his accuracy. It is clear that many of the errors are due to imperfect perception resulting from emotional activity, the attitude of the perceiver, etc.

The omission of detail and the insertion of erroneous detail in recollection depend also on the meaning of the situation recalled. The process is illustrated in experiments in which geometrical figures and outline drawings of objects are observed and then at later periods reproduced from memory. The results of the experiments show that much more than a simple decay of memory takes place with the passage of time. Rather, memories of the figures are *reorganized* until they come to resemble objects suggested by the original figure rather than the figure itself. An example of this reorganization has already been given in Fig. 40 of this chapter.

Some of the results of similar experiments are shown in Fig. 41. A number of drawings of relatively meaningless geometrical shapes, exposed in succession for two seconds each, were shown to a group of subjects. In the first column of Fig. 41 some of the stimulus drawings used in this and a related experiment are shown. To the right of each stimulus there appear a few of the reproductions of it. The reproductions of the first stimulus drawing illustrate the factor of change toward the shape of suggested objects, or *object assimilation* as it is called. To different people this stimulus suggested different objects; reproductions were given by subjects who saw it (1) as a woman's torso, (2) as a "footprint on the sands of time," (3) as a dumb-bell, (4) as a violin and (5) as a dumb-bell.

In the second and third lines of the illustration are shown the results of a related type of modification. In these, the stimuli have been *analyzed verbally* into several parts, as indicated in the legend of the figure. Verbal analysis and object assimilation can be produced experimentally by a remark of the experimenter as a figure is shown, "This figure resembles. . . ." In the fourth and fifth lines of the figure are given some of the results of such an experiment.

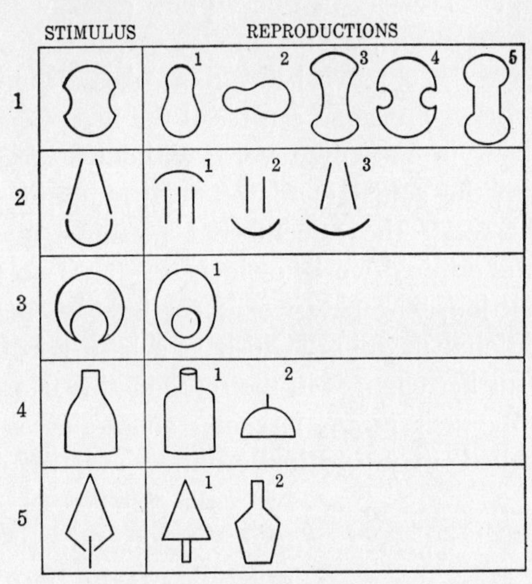

FIG. 41. DEPENDENCE OF RECOLLECTION ON MEANING.

The figures in the stimulus column were shown, among a number of others, to a group of subjects. Their reproductions of these stimuli, made from memory, varied according to the meaning suggested by the figures. Thus stimulus 1 suggested (1) a woman's torso; (2) a "footprint on the sands of time"; (3) a dumb-bell; (4) a violin; (5) a dumb-bell. Stimulus 2 received the names (1) pillars with curve; (2) pillars with curve (same subject as (1) but after a second exposure of the figure); (3) megaphone in a bowl. Stimulus 3 was named (1) one circle inside another. The experimenter gave different names to stimulus 4 as he showed it to different individuals. Their reproductions varied according to the name: (1) bottle; (2) stirrup. Stimulus 5 was treated like stimulus 4. The names were (1) pine tree; (2) trowel. After J. J. Gibson, The reproduction of visually perceived forms, *J. exper. Psychol.*, 1929, 12, 15 and 19; and L. Carmichael, H. P. Hogan and A. A. Walter, An experimental study of the effect of language on the reproduction of visually perceived form, *J. exper. Psychol.*, 1932, 15, 75 and 80.

Other changes than those illustrated also occur. Figures are assimilated to one another, so that the reproduction contains features of each. With the passage of time, some features of the memory are emphasized and others disappear. Often these changes are the results of imperfect or faulty perception; in other cases the change occurs after correct perception has been demonstrated by a good reproduction.

Many of the changes in the detail of images may be related to the influence of meaning on perception and memory. Every new object is perceived in the light of the meaning it evokes. Subsequently those details which are essential to the meaning of the object are preserved and even new details added, to the end that the meaning may be emphasized. It is probable that the meaning of the object is better remembered than its physical characteristics. Thus one can recall the meaning of a paragraph in a book in one's own words without being able to repeat verbatim the actual words of the paragraph. This very fact—that in recall the remembered meaning may call up other than the original words or images—may result in a mistaken recollection. The new words (or images) may in turn suggest additional meanings which at a later recall will contribute still further changes in the reproduction of the original experience. By such means it comes about that a story frequently recalled may eventually differ radically from the original.

Amnesia. There are certain conditions under which a whole group of interrelated experiences cannot be consciously recalled at all. The relatively permanent loss of such a group of recollections is known as *amnesia.* One kind of amnesia is a loss of the events preceding or following a shock or an intense emotional experience. After a fall while ice-skating one individual was unable to recall either the circumstances of the fall itself or his actions immediately thereafter, though the latter included skating, talking to a friend and driving himself home in a car. Or, for another example, one might cite the case of a man who was knocked unconscious by a car while walking home from work. After he regained consciousness he was able to recall the events of the earlier part of the day, but had a complete blank for the events which took place from the time of leaving his office until consciousness returned.

Amnesia following intense emotional experiences seems often to be related to the wish to forget. Abnormal psychology contains many an instance of inability in a deranged patient to remember any of the events following an incident which that patient seems determined to ignore. Thus for a period of ten years a widow remembered none of the events following the death of her husband. Throughout this period she believed him to be alive. A girl, overcome by discouragement and despair, went to sleep suggesting to herself that if she "could forget everything—name and everything else," she could escape her troubles. On answering the telephone after she awoke the next day, she found she could not remember her name. The condition persisted for three days. Such forgetting is, as Freud suggests, closely similar to the common tendency of us all to forget the names of well-known people whom we dislike, or to forget the unpleasant appointments we have made.

The experiences which apparently disappear in amnesia are probably not entirely lost. Without question some of them are represented in the person's behavior. A man, for example, who had learned shorthand during a period for which he later became completely amnesic was still able to use shorthand even though he could recall nothing of how he had learned it. Similarly, our adult skills and tastes, like walking and eating, reflect the events of early childhood for which we are all relatively amnesic.

Spontaneous recovery from abnormal states of amnesia sometimes occurs, the circumstances being often reminiscent of those observed in the normal recall of temporarily forgotten material. In brief, some event indirectly associated with that which is forgotten reminds us of a part of it. This cue, in turn, leads us to more and more of the forgotten episode. It is believed, however, that if the wish to forget is involved, it must be eliminated before recovery can occur. Sometimes its elimination is achieved by suggestion, sometimes by deliberate change of the circumstances surrounding the patient and sometimes by the course of events, such as the end of a war.

The after-image. The forms of imagery, in the order of their similarity to the original perception, are the after-image (after-sensation), eidetic image, memory image and imagination image. The after-image is most, and the imagination image least, like the perception. Since these forms are closely related to one another, no hard and fast lines can be drawn between them, except perhaps between the after-image and the others. In practice, therefore, it is often difficult to classify an image.

Various facts point to the *perceptual character of after-images.* They outlast the physical stimulus for only a few seconds or minutes, whereas the other images may recur long after, even years after, the perception. Visual after-images change their location with a change in the direction of regard; other images, on the contrary, are relatively unaffected by movement of the eyes. Finally, the after-image, in contrast to other forms of imagery, varies in size in accordance with the distance to which it is projected. This fact is known as Emmert's law, which states that the size of the after-image is directly proportional to the relation between the projection distance and the original stimulus distance. Thus if a spot of color 1 cm. square in size is fixated at a distance of 50 cm., its after-image will be 2 cm. square if it is projected 100 cm. away; 1 cm. square if projected 50 cm.; and ½ cm. square if projected only 25 cm. If the difference between projection distance and fixation distance is too great, the law breaks down, but for smaller differences it holds very well. It is thought that after-images result from a physiological persistence of the perceptual processes after the physical stimulus has ceased; that they are, in truth, after-sensations.

Eidetic imagery. Those more permanent images which resemble perceptions very closely, containing as they do many vivid and clear details, are known as *eidetic images* or primary memory images. Among adults their occurrence is rare. Children, however, frequently have them, and investigations of imagery in children have, of late years, centered around this phenomenon.

Eidetic images, when they occur, resemble perceptions so closely that they are sometimes described as pseudo-perceptual.

Except that the subject knows the experience to be one of memory and does not mistake it for a perception, the images are analogous to hallucinations.

Eidetic images are experimentally studied by exposing a complicated picture, such as that shown in Fig. 42, to a child.

FIG. 42. PICTURE USED FOR EIDETIC IMAGERY.

This picture was shown to a number of English school children for 35 sec. From an image of the picture the children were later able to describe accurately a very great many details, including, in some cases, the long German word over the entrance of the building. Used by G. W. Allport, Eidetic imagery, *Brit. J. Psychol.*, 1924, 15, 99-120.

The exposure time is brief, from 10 to 40 sec. The subject of the experiment does not fixate a particular spot or keep his gaze steady, as he must to obtain an after-image, but lets his eyes roam over the picture at will. At the conclusion of the exposure the subject shifts his gaze to a gray screen and projects an image of the picture on it. Thereupon he is asked to describe his image, stating what he can see in it and describing the character of the details seen.

When Fig. 42 was shown to 30 English school children especially selected for their clear imagery, some of the children demonstrated an amazing ability to reproduce the picture or parts of it. They were able to recall in the image many obscure details in addition to those more prominent. Some of them, for example, were able to spell out the long German word *Gartenwirthschaft* from their image, although they did not know German. Three out of the 30 children were able to spell it correctly not only in the forward direction but backward as well. Seven more could spell it in either direction with no more than two mistakes—and the mistakes were the same in either direction of spelling. All these children could give still other details of the picture.

It is this amazing fidelity of reproduction of the eidetic image that marks it out for special consideration. Yet the eidetic image, like the other forms of imagery, is seldom if ever a complete copy of the original. Details may be unclear or even lacking. In a picture showing a boy leading a dog by a rope, one of the two figures was seen with great clarity while the other was only a blur or dark spot in the image. Erroneous details, furthermore, are sometimes inserted into the image. In these changes, interest plays a large part. Indeed an uninteresting picture may evoke no eidetic image at all, although, for the same child, an interesting picture will give rise to a very clear image. A picture of a house, for example, failed to stimulate any image, whereas a picture of a monkey called out a very good one.

Eidetic images are not only clearer and richer in detail but they are also more intense and of better quality than memory images. Scientists sometimes find that some hours after having looked intently through a microscope they have a very bright image of the contents of the field. Many people report spontaneous eidetic images which occur after an evening of reading or card playing. As they go to sleep, they experience clear and bright images of the book or the playing cards.

Similarly, there are often very clear and intense auditory eidetic images. The tune that runs through one's head with great persistence for several hours or days is an eidetic image. Likewise, after a conversation or argument has ceased, one may hear a sentence from it very clearly and distinctly.

Memory images. The *memory image* differs from the eidetic image in many respects. It is less stable, not so vivid, has fewer details and consequently is a less accurate representation of the original event. Of more frequent occurrence than the eidetic image, it may have a personal reference which is lacking in the latter. The personal aspect of the memory image is indicated by such verbal expressions as, "It is *my* recollection," "*My* memory is—," "*I* dreamed last night"; it is likely to appear in the recollection of emotional occurrences, or of one's own movements in response to the situation, provided the movements were not so habitual as to escape notice. A locomotive engineer, for example, may not be certain whether on a particular day he blew the whistle as usual for a crossing, unless there was some special incident to call his attention to it.

An important part of the personal aspect of recollection is the tendency to localize the past event in time and space. Memories, usually, contain a reference to one's own past. This personal reference may be of all degrees of specificity, ranging from the quite definite, as when one says, "On my trip to New York on April 14th, I met so-and-so," to the highly indefinite reference which merely indicates that the event actually occurred in one's past. The very indefinite reference corresponds to the phrase, "Once upon a time."

There appear, however, to be at least two types of exception to this tendency to refer recollections to one's own personal past. One of these is the rare, but impressive, occasion when a past event is so completely reproduced that the distinction between past and present is lost. An example is the nightmare dream of a terrifying event of the recent past, fairly common among children. During and following a war it is also frequently reported by soldiers. Similar but more extreme instances are occasionally observed in abnormal individuals. Occasionally, too, a past experience may be so completely relived that the person not only dreams the events but carries out the actions previously made. In one instance, famous in the history of abnormal psychology, a patient repeatedly entered a trancelike state—or *somnambulism* as it is technically called—in which all the events relating to the death of her mother were so vividly recalled that the patient felt and acted as if the mother were dying before her. An example of a similar state occurs in the sleep-walking scene of Shakespeare's *Macbeth.*

A second type of loss of reference to the personal past occurs, sometimes rather strikingly, with recollections of objects that have been frequently perceived. If one attempts to recall the appearance of one's mother or a very close friend, the recollection may seem to have little or no reference to one's past. Such a person has been perceived in so many situations and in so many relations that no single reference remains. Correspondingly, the recollection itself frequently becomes highly schematic, until only a very few details remain and these not at all clear.

As is well known, reference to one's past is often false. Children particularly seem to find difficulty in distinguishing between recollection and imagination; a child is often accused of lying because he recounts vivid details of imaginary events as if he had actually had a part in them. Though the distinction between the real and the imagined apparently increases with age and experience, the danger of false reference to the past is never entirely lost. The mere fact of telling a story in the first person makes the events of the narrative seem true, particularly if the story adds prestige or gives other values to the story-teller. A false reference to the past is also found in perception when, for example, one faces a scene that he knows to be new, but nevertheless has the feeling that it is familiar.

IMAGINATION

The structure of imagination is like the structure of recollection. When imagination takes the form of imagery, we speak of the *imagination image*. As experienced, these images do not differ from eidetic and memory images in any way except that more often than the latter they have no reference to the past of the person concerned. Sometimes, as when we anticipate an event, the imagination image has a future reference. Sometimes also we know that the object or event imagined is new. But occasionally in both imagination and recollection we are mistaken about the temporal reference; we not infrequently take an imagined event to be a recollection, while what is really a recollection may seem to be new. We cannot, therefore, always distinguish recollection and imagination by their temporal reference.

FIG. 43. A PRODUCT OF IMAGINATION.
Elements of past experience with apes are combined with elements of past experience with human beings to produce an image unlike either ape or human. After R. M. and A. W. Yerkes, *The great apes*, 1932; by permission of the Yale University Press.

The close relation between recollection and imagination is more clearly seen when we study the materials of imagination. Imagination images are always a reorganization of a number of recollections (or of recollections and perceptions present at the time). Thus imagination is always limited by what we know of the real world. Except by way of hints derived from other senses, those persons who are born blind cannot imagine what it is like to see. Imagination about life on other planets, or about life after death, is based upon what we know about life on our own planet. Illustrations of the materials of imagination are found in imaginary animals such as the centaur, the mermaid, and the creature shown in Fig. 43. This figure is an animal combining the features of ape and man. The early explorers of Africa, impressed by the similarity of the ape to man, emphasized in their pictures of the ape its human qualities, even though they retained some of the outstanding features of the ape such as its hairy body and long arms. The result, consisting as it does of parts of several experiences put together in new relationships, does not resemble any single perception.

There is, for all this, something new in imagination. The materials from recollection and perception are reorganized into a pattern which differs from any previous experience. When a Bach in imagination integrates the familiar notes of the musical scale into a new musical composition, it is clear that one very important aspect of the process would be ignored if we stressed only the familiarity of the notes. Even our fantasies and dreams are usually new constructions. When we 'visualize' a tale of adventure we are reading, or a symphony we are hearing, we are, when not recollecting, creating something new. Finally, as will be seen in the next chapter, creations like these are, in addition to familiar materials, utilized by the poet, the novelist, the inventor, the scientist as he thinks out the solution of his problem.

INDIVIDUAL DIFFERENCES IN RECOLLECTION AND IMAGINATION

The modes of expression of imagination and recollection are not found to the same degree among all people. There are great individual differences in imagery, for some people recall the past in terms of all the senses, whereas others are limited primarily to memories based on one or a few senses. The majority of people fall between these extremes. Most individuals, then, are *versatile* rather than specialized in their recollections.

Likewise there are differences between individuals in the clarity and completeness of their imagery. At one extreme are a few people with highly developed imagery from one or more senses. We hear of many instances of apparently phenomenal accomplishments based on just such clear and accurate images; for instance, the feat of a boy who was able to give the day of the week for every date in the years 1920-1927 from eidetic images of the calendar. Professional memory-artists and lightning calculators often have exceptionally good visual or auditory imagery. It is probable that by well-directed practice many people could develop similar abilities (see pp. 342f.).

At the other extreme are those individuals who are quite limited in the clarity and accuracy of their imagery. Many of them claim that they think almost entirely in terms of words or in terms of conscious attitudes alone.

Number forms. Some individuals show a tendency to organize series of related objects into spatial forms. Among the most common of these are number forms. The numbers in common use are imagined as occupying a position in space. *Each number has its own position* in relation to the head, a position which is thought of whenever the number comes to mind. The numbers of a series are arranged in some more or less orderly and regular progression from low to high. Though the numbers themselves are not necessarily present in imaginal form, each position in space represents or means its own number. This phenomenon may be analogous to the common experience of remembering the position of words on a printed page without the words themselves actually being present in imagery.

The shape of number forms differs greatly from person to person. An example of a number form is shown in Fig. 44. It will be noticed that certain numbers—those in common use, 1, 10, 20, 30, etc., and also 12—occupy prominent positions, coming at breaks in the spatial sequence or at curves in the form. The higher numbers are usually less accurately localized than the lower, more common ones, and the number form tapers off to an indefinite end. Similar to number forms are month, year and alphabet forms, examples of which are also shown in Fig. 44.

Color associations. Many individuals constantly experience colors, rather than spatial locations, in association with numbers and letters. One person studied by Galton saw 1 as black; 2, yellow; 3, pale brick-red; 4, brown; 5, blackish gray; 6, reddish brown; 7, green; 8, bluish; 9, reddish brown (like

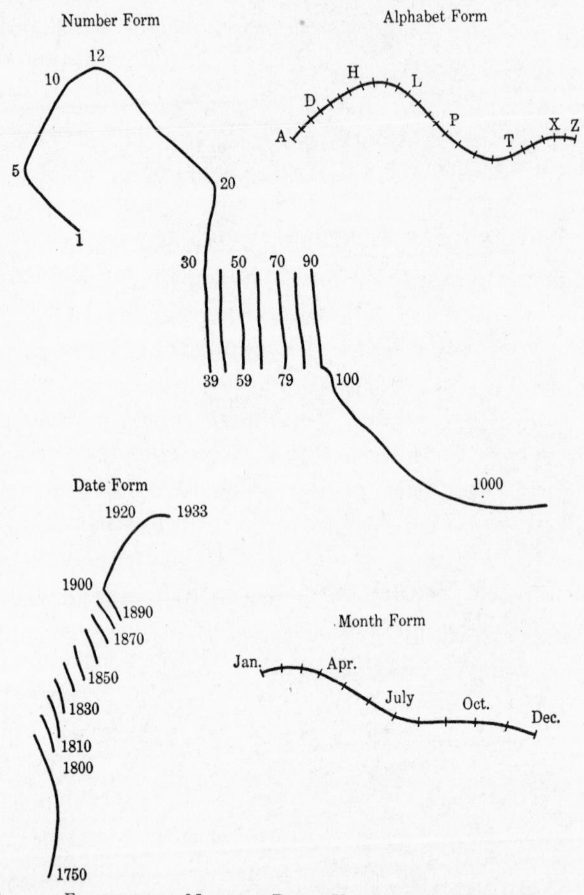

FIG. 44. EXAMPLES OF NUMBER, DATE, YEAR AND ALPHABET FORMS.

The person whose number form is shown thinks of a point directly in front of his eyes when the number 1 comes to mind. 12 is farther away and slightly higher than 1. 39 is back of the right elbow, and the number form tapers off to the right of his body. Dates, years and the letters of the alphabet are also arranged in forms in his thinking. Courtesy of C. C. Pratt.

6). Whenever numbers were involved, the associations literally colored his thoughts. The events of the century 1700-1799 were imagined as occurring on a greenish background from the color association for 7. Color associations and number forms remain quite constant from year to year. Those who experience them say they have always experienced numbers and letters in that way.

Synesthesia. Closely related to the phenomena of color associations are those of synesthesia. Synesthesia is the tendency *to experience definite images of one sense quality when another sense is stimulated*. The best-known type is colored hearing or chromesthesia. In this case the notes of the musical scale (and other sounds) give rise to images of colors. Each note has its particular color, but notes an octave apart often stimulate the same or similar colors. In Table XXVI is a report on a case of chromesthesia investigated twice with an interval of 7½ years between investigations. The constancy of the images, as shown in the table, is striking.

The individual whose synesthesia is summarized in this table experienced a fusion of colors when two notes were sounded together. The fusion followed the laws of color mixture, and this despite the fact that the individual was ignorant of those laws. The tones *g* (blue) and *a* (cold yellow) gave a hazy gray mist, although at times either blue or yellow predominated. The tones *c* (red) and *f#* (blue-green) gave an indefinite light verging on gray.

Other forms of synesthesia, such as colored odors and colored tastes, are frequently found. A peculiar form of synesthesia was accidentally discovered during an investigation of sensitivity to cold. It was found that, when certain cold spots of the arm were stimulated, one of the subjects experienced light, transient, pressure sensations in and around the teeth and cheeks. Another peculiar case of synesthesia is that of a certain psychologist who, blind since the age of 11, experiences colors in conjunction with the stimuli of all the senses. These imaginary colors give meaning to the words and other stimuli which arouse them.

The origin of synesthetic images and of number forms being obscure, there is, at present, no satisfactory explanation of

TABLE XXVI

A Case of Chromesthesia Investigated in 1905 and Again in 1912

The notes of the musical scale are associated with images of very constant colors. (From H. S. Langfeld, *Psychol. Bull.*, 1914, 11, 113.)

	1905	1912
c	Red	Red
d♭	Purple	Lavender
d	Violet	Violet
e♭	Soft blue	Thick blue
e	Golden yellow	Sunlight
f	Pink	Pink, apple blossoms
f♯	Green blue	Blue green
g♭	Greener blue	Greener blue
g	Clear blue	Clear sky blue
a	Cold yellow	Clear yellow, hard, not warm
b♭	Orange	Verges on orange
b	Very brilliant coppery	Very brilliant coppery

them. Many of these constant associations of certain images and sensations are undoubtedly due to early experience. Whether experience can explain all of them or whether, in some cases, innate connections are the cause of the associations is still a matter of doubt.

THE CONDITIONS OF RECOLLECTION AND IMAGINATION

Studies of recollection and imagination show that these processes are of little importance when stimuli lead us to direct action. When response is unimpeded, few images are experienced and consciousness is largely limited to perceptual activity. Conversely, when movement is difficult or when the situation does not call for action, recollection and imagination become prominent in mental life.

A flood of imagery arises when an individual is faced with a *problem*, that is to say, with a relatively new situation for which he has no habitual response. Let stimuli call out conflicting reactions, and doubt arise as to a course of action, and thereupon many images will be experienced. These images represent possible ways of solving the problem. They symbolize modes of action or facts previously learned and now of possible use in a new situation.

It is partly by means of images that past experience is brought to bear on the situation. Thus in walking home over a very familiar road no imagery of the route occurs; but in walking over a somewhat unfamiliar road, images of landmarks, of familiar objects seen a moment before, and of one's own previous movements furnish clues for orientation. One thinks of going toward a building, of turning right or left, of retracing his footsteps. These are tentative, mental solutions of the problem of finding one's way. Mental trial and error precedes overt trial and error, and the probable success or failure of any trial is weighed consciously before it is undertaken (see pp. 306-308). In this process each trial and its probable consequences, so far as they can be determined from past experience, may be partly represented in imagery.

Although images are prominent in the mental life of most individuals when problems or conflicts occur, it does not follow that in all individuals they are necessary to the solution of problems. Some people say that, except perhaps for the motor imagery of subvocal speech, they have never experienced imagery of any sort. These individuals may even attain considerable success in fields where it would seem that the possession of imagery would almost be a necessity. Thus, there are the cases of a painter and of a geometrician, each said to have been quite successful in his field, neither of whom ever experienced visual imagery. Likewise there have been musicians with so little auditory imagery that they have had to compose by trying out successions of notes on an instrument.

Experimental investigations of the role of imagery in the solution of problems have been carried out by giving individuals problems to be solved mentally. After completing the task, the subjects describe the nature of the imagery used. With some problems it is apparent that clear imagery, if suited to the task, aids considerably in the solution. The following problem, for instance, is most readily solved by those having a clear visual image.

Imagine a 3-in. cube painted on all sides. If this cube were divided into smaller cubes of 1 in. each, how many would have paint on three sides; how many on two sides; how many on one; and how many on none of the sides?

In this problem a clear visual image of the large cube and its subdivisions is of great value. Motor imagery also helps some subjects, who in imagination pick up the smaller cubes and turn them over, looking at each side. Subjects with scanty visual imagery are slower in solving the problem. On the other hand, the problem can be solved entirely by the verbal formulas of mathematics. Some individuals find, furthermore, that at times a clear visual image unsuited to the problem may arise and block its solution. The image of yesterday's football game, for example, may come between one and one's work.

In this type of mental work experience is an important factor. This fact is implied in the statement that the image must be suited to the task if it is to aid in the solution. The effect of practice is shown if, after solving the 3-in.-cube problem mentioned above, one tries to solve the related, but more difficult, problem of dividing a 4-in. cube into 1-in. cubes and calculating the number of painted sides on each.

The role of recollection in the solution of problems is often seen even in idle fancies, imaginative play, daydreams and the dreams of sleep, where no problem is apparent to the person experiencing the imagery. Children who are left too much alone invent imaginary playmates to help fill their solitary hours, even though they do not realize their need for companionship. When they are mistreated by a servant or teacher, the images of their dreams and daydreams represent ways of getting rid of the offending person. Often the only way to obtain insight into the needs of children is to analyze carefully the meaning of the imaginative states in which they indulge.

In the daydreams and fancies of the adult the same tendency is sometimes seen. Castles in Spain, dreams of riches or of superlative skill in work or play, are imaginary solutions of the problems of everyday life. Even the bizarre images of dreams, as will be shown below, can sometimes be related to the unfulfilled desires of the dreamer.

Fantasy, in which the play of recollection and imagination is relatively independent of the present situation, occurs most commonly when the situation *does not call for action* or when such action as does occur is highly habituated. Thus, for many people the drowsy period just preceding sleep is especially rich in imagery. Vivid, lifelike faces, landscapes and events arise. Not only do these images usually appear without any effort to call them up, but they even occur sometimes despite one's will. Frequently they appear so real, perhaps as a result of their great vividness and seeming independence, that they approach or attain the character of hallucinations.

Likewise if one studies the effects of different kinds of literature on imagination, one finds that some books—the thriller or the detective story, for example—stimulate one to read rapidly and to move toward the end with increasing muscular tension. Little imagination is involved in such reading. Other books, in which, perhaps, the element of suspense is less important, suggest memories of the past, fantasy and daydreams. One relaxes, and the meaning of the printed words is slowly developed by a rich series of references to one's own experience. Similar differences are found in the effects of different kinds of music.

Dreams. Dreams, of course, furnish the clearest illustrations of the fact that imagination is at its height when action is at a minimum. The imagery of dreams ranges from fairly accurate reproductions of past events to the most grotesque and distorted experiences.

Dreams are studied in various ways. In order to determine the *influence of external stimuli,* a sleeping person may be subjected to sounds, touches, removal of the covers and other forms of stimulation. To interpret the *meaning* of dreams, that is to say, their relation to the past experiences of the dreamer, dreams are written down immediately on awakening and subsequently analyzed in relation to the life of the dreamer. A more complex method of studying the meaning of dreams is that of *psychoanalysis.* The individual starts from one of the events of a dream and allows his thoughts to wander freely. Each idea in the chain of associations that follow is noted down without reservation or omission. When this procedure has been completed for all the events of a dream, the trains of thought are analyzed in an effort to interpret the meaning of the dream.

In experiments to determine the effect of *stimuli* it is found that a touch on the forehead may be followed by a dream of being bitten by a spider, of a headache or of being struck on the face in a quarrel. A cold stimulus applied by uncovering parts of the body may evoke a dream of climbing mountains, of wading in a stream or of nakedness. It is also known from common observation that internal stimuli arising from cramped muscles, indigestion, worry and organic conditions frequently evoke dreaming.

It is found that dreams are related to the *recent life* of the dreamer. Dreams are most frequently drawn from the experiences of the previous day, particularly from the intense, vivid experiences. Often a train of thought concerning past events or plans for the future is continued from the waking state into the dream state. This too occurs most frequently when the train of thought is vivid or characterized by emotion and excitement. Remote events are seldom *directly* represented in dreams, although dreams can be related to long-past events and even to some experiences apparently forgotten and in waking life incapable of recall.

In addition to stimulation and past experience, the *unsatisfied desires* of an individual play a part in his dreams. Freud has shown that many dreams are *wish fulfilments.* An example of this fact is the dream of a child who, having been allowed but one piece of candy, awoke the next morning exclaiming that she had eaten the whole dishful during the night. Another example is the common dream of adults, so comforting on a cold morning, of being up, dressed and at breakfast. In these dreams unsatisfied desires are fulfilled in imagination.

Freud believes that unsatisfied desires play a part in fantastic and apparently meaningless dreams. As a result of studies by the method of psychoanalysis he has come to the conclusion that dreams in their distortion and grotesqueness symbolize the satisfaction of repressed desires. Repressed desires are those which are so unpleasant, painful or shameful that the individual tries to thrust them out of mind, hiding them from himself and others. Refusing to think about a desire does not, however, eliminate it. The desire, persisting as the latent content of the dream, is able to get by what has been called the censor by appearing in distorted form as the manifest content of the dream. The dream is a disguised symbol of the desire and of the ways of satisfying it. The disguise or distortion results from the repression.

The Freudian theory holds that only the sexual desires are repressed and, consequently, that all distorted dreams symbolize sexual repressions. The term 'sex' is used in the broad sense of affection. The theory has, nevertheless, been severely criticized on this point, and it is now generally believed that any unpleasant desire or fear may be repressed and direct the course of our dreams.

The role of intense, emotionally toned, personal desires and fears is clearly seen in another aspect of imagination, the field of belief. Certain forms of abnormality are characterized by highly integrated or systematized, false beliefs, which are called *paranoid delusions.* The paranoid person perceives and recalls the commonplace events of everyday life as fraught with significance for his personal and emotional life. Thus a janitor in a university dormitory saw, in the pattern of the rugs he swept, the symbol of the Masonic order and believed that the presence of the symbol forecast a continuation of the 'persecution' which he felt was directed at him. Patients in mental hospitals find evidence in their past and present lives to support their 'delusions of grandeur'; they believe, despite obvious evidence to the contrary, that they are famous or highly distinguished persons, or even God. We have here clear indication of the tendency to select evidence from perception and memory to support a previously established, imaginative pattern of belief.

REFERENCES

1. Allport, G. W. Eidetic imagery. *Brit. J. Psychol.*, 1924, 15, 99-120.
2. Bartlett, F. C. *Remembering.* Cambridge, England: University Press, 1932.
3. Davis, F. C. The functional significance of imagery differences. *J. exper. Psychol.*, 1932, 15, 630-661.
4. De Sanctis, S., and Neyroz, U. (translated by H. C. Warren). Experimental investigations concerning the depth of sleep. *Psychol. Rev.*, 1902, 9, 254-282.
5. Fox, C. The conditions which arouse mental images in thought. *Brit. J. Psychol.*, 1914, 6, 420-431.
6. Freud, S. *The interpretation of dreams* (translated by A. A. Brill). New York: Macmillan, 1913.
7. Galton, F. *Inquiries into human faculty and its development* [1883]. (2nd ed.) New York: Dutton, 1907. Pp. 57-128.
8. Klüver, H. Mescal visions and eidetic vision. *Amer. J. Psychol.*, 1926, 37, 502-515.
9. Perky, C. W. An experimental study of imagination. *Amer. J. Psychol.*, 1910, 21, 422-452.
10. Stern, W. *General Psychology* (translated by H. D. Spoerl). New York: Macmillan, 1938. Pp. 188-267.
11. Titchener, E. B. *Lectures on the experimental psychology of the thought processes.* New York: Macmillan, 1909. Pp. 3-37.
12. Wheeler, R. H. and Cutsforth, T. D. Synaesthesia and meaning. *Amer. J. Psychol.*, 1922, 33, 361-384.

Chapter 12

THOUGHT

When a human being meets, recognizes and solves a problem, he is usually said to think or reason. The general nature of the processes involved may be illustrated by the behavior of two boys observed by the writer on the top of a Roman tower.

The boys were discussing the height of the structure. They walked round the platform, leaned over the rail, looked at the ground. Something like the following conversation took place:

"How high do you think it is?"

"It looks about seventy feet."

"How do you know?"

The first speaker looked over the side again. The other answered, "We're more than twice as far up as that house. That's about thirty feet."

The first replied, "You can't tell from that. Let's count the steps or something."

There was a short silence after which the first boy shouted triumphantly, "Let's drop something and time it!"

A coin was produced and dropped, and the fall timed by a watch. Apparently the fall took about two and a half seconds. The sum was worked out with a pen and paper, and the announcement made, with considerable satisfaction, that the height was a hundred feet.

Several points in this conversation are worth noting.

1. There is a specific *problem*, in the form of the question: How high is the platform?

2. There are successive *steps* or ideas—the first estimation of seventy feet, the questioning of this figure, the statement concerning the house, and so on.

This chapter was written by George Humphrey of Queen's University.

3. These steps are not irrelevant, but are related to the problem; that is to say, they are *directed* towards the solution. The boys look for a coin in order to drop it.

4. The final solution is achieved by trying out first one scheme then another until a satisfactory one is found. The guess of seventy feet was rejected, and also the methods of comparison with the house and of counting the steps. The procedure is one of *trial and error*.

5. There is much *action*. The boys are continually walking about the platform, bending over the edge, looking at objects on the ground. They search for the coin, one takes his watch from his pocket, they write their calculations and so on.

6. In particular, action of a very specialized kind—*speech*—is going on nearly all the time.

7. Not only are the boys acting, but they are actively *perceiving*, and their perceptions make possible the process of solving the problem. They look over the side to make the first estimation of height. They look at the house. One feels for his watch. They listen for the coin to drop. They look at the hands of the watch.

8. All these actions, ideas, provisional solutions, spoken sentences and perceptions are part of a single, joint attempt to solve the problem. Beginning with the perception of the problem and ending with the announcement of the solution we have a series of activities bound together by the fact that all of them are directed towards the same end.

Although the present example concerns two human beings, very much the same process goes on when a single person is trying to solve a problem, except that in this case much of what is happening cannot be seen by an outsider. The individual faces the problem situation. A train of thought and action follows. 'Ideas,' action, lines of attack are tried, some of them rejected, others accepted. In this way a series of steps is directed towards the solution. The process involves many different activities. Perception is active, in grasping the problem and also often during the taking of the various steps. Language is at work, mostly in the form of *internal speech*, the vocal-motor imagery in which the person 'talks' to himself rather than aloud. In addition, there is much mental imagery of other kinds, visual, auditory, and so on. *All these different activities form part of a single, unified, or,* as it is called, *integrative attack on the problem. A train of mental processes thus directed towards an end is known as directive thinking.*

Some of these features may be absent in any particular case. There may perhaps be no internal speech; or a simple problem may be solved without intermediate steps. But the general plan holds good for a surprisingly large number of cases, especially where somewhat difficult problems are involved.

Stated in the simplest form we have then a diagram of this kind.

$$\text{Problem } (\rightarrow X \rightarrow X \rightarrow X \rightarrow X \rightarrow X \rightarrow) \text{ Solution.}$$

Faced with the problem, the individual initiates successive thoughts and actions, represented by the row of *X*'s. The intermediate processes, directed towards the solution, may be considered as parts of the total response to the problem situation.

Many points in the preceding account must now be made clearer.

Integration and thought. We have said that thought is integrative, meaning that it combines many diverse data and experiences into a single line of action and thinking. Integrative action is found wherever life is found, from the single-celled amoeba up. If the organism is to live, it must meet the diversities of the outside world with a unified set of reactions. Further, a human being has one mind, not many minds. Except possibly in abnormal cases, each of us is one personality, not many personalities. We coordinate experiences into experience. Integration takes place on the side of thought as well as on the side of action.

The integrative action of thinking may be seen in what is known in logic as the syllogism. Here there are two premises from which a single conclusion is reached. Thus, a man wishes to buy an electric kettle at a department store.

"What voltage?" he is asked.

"I don't know. I live in Maryville."

"(*a*) *All voltages in York county are 250;* (*b*) *Maryville is in York county;* (*c*) *So your voltage will be 250.*"

(*a*), (*b*) and (*c*) constitute a syllogism. Since (*c*) is obtained by combining (*a*) and (*b*), the process of thought is therefore an integrative one. The conclusion might of course have been obtained equally well by *reading* the premises (*a*) and (*b*).

In order that such integration of thought may take place, a very complicated integration of action must first have occurred. Apart from the immensely complex processes that unify the working of the rest of the body, the act of reading itself implies integration of a high order. Studies of eye movements show that whereas a first-grade child often makes a separate movement for nearly every letter, a college student normally telescopes these reactions by shifting the eye only once for a whole group of words. Thus a single reaction is made to a number of separate letters.

But more than this. Thought and action are in turn parts of the single activity of 'reading.' Indeed it is often very difficult to say where action ends and thought begins. Thinking and acting are themselves integrated, fused into a unity. The process of deducing the conclusion of the syllogism therefore presents a complex process of unification, involving integration both of thought and of action. The same relation could easily be seen to hold for any other act of directive thinking. *Thinking directed towards an end is the conscious side of the complicated process of integration of experience and action that goes on when an individual meets and solves a problem.* When a man is solving a problem, he is forging a single line of thought-and-action to meet a diverse situation in the world without. The various stages through which his thought passes are parts of this total integrative process.

The problem situation. When considering the boys on the tower we saw that the situation constituted a problem. We must now ask the meaning of this statement. What sort of a situation is a *problem* situation? The specific situation which the boys face is the spoken question—how high is it?—taken in its total context.

Now many situations of everyday life clearly do not constitute problems at all. Such are those to which we respond by habit. It is no problem for the ordinary person to lace up his shoes or to dress himself. These actions call for integrative processes of a very complex kind, the existence of which in everyday life we are, however, likely to overlook. Again, it is no problem for the educated adult to read his newspaper; once more, the complex integrative processes necessary for this response are accomplished so readily that we need experiment to tell us they are there. For a foreigner to read the same paper, on the other hand, may constitute a real problem. If a man knows only a few words of the language, highly complex mental activities will be consciously involved in effecting the unifying activity of piecing together a single paragraph.

It can now be seen that the term problem is a relative one. What may be a problem for one may not be so for another. We may say that a problem is a difficult situation, one which, for some reason or another, appreciably holds up the action of the organism until the necessary integrative processes have been effected. Such a situation often comprises elements which, to the particular organism in question, are apparently incompatible, so that a conflict is involved. The organism must then painfully match one element of the diverse situation against another in the way called reasoning.

In a certain experiment a basket containing bananas was hung on a tree out of reach of a chimpanzee. For a while the animal moved restlessly about. Then it suddenly ran to the tree, climbed up, shook and ultimately broke the rope, and thus spilled the bananas to the ground.

For the ape, the situation clearly contained incompatible elements, a conflict. The animal was impelled towards the bananas, but at the same time physical conditions were not such that he could obtain them directly. The result was that he remained on the spot, held by a need which he was unable to satisfy. The solution came by an appropriate insight. When the tree, the branch and the rope were seen combining into a means to obtain the fruit, action followed.

Yet it is not the situation in itself that constitutes the problem, but rather the animal's relation to it. To a man coming into the enclosure the situation would have presented no problem, no conflict. The necessary integration would have been effected automatically, that is to say, the human being would not have had to reason. Many people would say that the animal did reason. Thus we reach the paradoxical conclusion that reasoning may be a mark of stupidity. The animal, perhaps, or the young child may have to reason a thing out; the adult, on the other hand, may be gifted enough to see the solution at a glance. In the same way, one may see patients at the institutions for the feeble-minded struggling heroically to thread a white bootlace in a black frame when they have been taught only to thread a black lace in a white frame. The situation presents a problem to them because they are stupid. They are reasoning on an elementary plane.

We may summarize this discussion as follows. The term *problem* is one of convenience only. It describes a situation where for some reason or other the organism is held up while integration is being effected. The words *reason* and *reasoning* are conveniently used to describe the conscious processes that take place while a human being or an animal is recognizing and responding to such a situation. In practice the term is often limited to cases in which emphasis is laid on the directively ordered character of the whole process, and on the original diversity and the newness of the situation.

It is sometimes said that reasoning occurs only when a new problem is met. But every problem and every situation is a blend of new and old. Thus the banana situation would present certain new features to both man and animal, namely the position of the banana relative to the tree and the ground. On the other hand, both chimpanzee and man have seen trees and bananas many times, though the chimpanzee is more familiar with the tree in question. If anything, the situation is newer for the man, who does not reason.

Thus reason is not, as it was once said to be, a special faculty that distinguishes man from animals. It is not a mark of unique intelligence. One might, in fact, imagine a superior being pitying our scientists because they stupidly have to puzzle out, by mathematical reasoning, things that to a higher mind would be obvious at a glance.

The determination of thought. The stages between the problem and the solution are in general *relevant*. When the boys were trying to find the height of the platform, what they said was to the point. They did not begin a discussion on the merits of cars or the values of postage stamps, but canvassed only the possibilities for obtaining the height—by comparison with the house, counting the steps, using the formula. This relevance of the intermediate processes to the solution gives direction or determination to thought. We have already assigned the term 'directive' to such thinking, which is thereby contrasted with so-called 'free thought' such as is found in daydreaming.

As to the fact of direction in thought, there can be no doubt. Its explanation is another matter. The problem is: What causes one mental process to follow another, relevantly to the point at issue? A schoolboy in the examination room finds printed on his paper:

$$\text{Solve the equation: } x^2 - 7x = 60 \qquad (1)$$

The boy writes something like the following:

$$x^2 - 7x - 60 = 0 \qquad (2)$$
$$(x - 12)(x + 5) = 0 \qquad (3)$$
$$x = 12, \text{ or } x = -5 \qquad (4)$$

It is assumed that this is the first time the boy has faced this particular equation, although he has had quadratic equations in his course. Thus the situation characteristically presents new and familiar elements. Since it is a new equation, its solution can hardly be said to be mere memory, as it would be if the boy had learned these four lines by heart. The boy is thinking, though in a comparatively routine way. The problem is a real one to him.

Why does line (2) follow from line (1), and so on?

The simplest explanation, and one which seems to have the support of what may be called psychological common sense, refers the process to association of some kind. This may be association of mental elements, or it may involve stimuli leading to action by means of the conditioned reflex or otherwise. According to this theory, the boy's training has been planned for the very purpose of giving him the necessary habits of thought and action. Many a time at school he has said, "Five twelves are sixty," and "Five from twelve is seven," or whatever the approved formula may be. The sight of the letters and the figures on the examination paper lets loose a chain of successive responses. All the figures are put on one side, the numbers 12 and 5 written down, and so on, by means of sheer association derived from training.

There is no doubt that memory is active when we are thinking, but whether it operates in so simple a manner is another question. The difficulty has always been to explain why, out of all the associations clinging to a given stimulus, the appropriate one should be released in the solution of any specific problem. According to the context the figures $\genfrac{}{}{0pt}{}{9}{5}$ may be followed by the response 4, 14 or 45. Though it is not impossible to explain by an associational scheme how this result may come about, the explanation becomes somewhat complicated. Perhaps the most widely accepted alternative explanation is the one proposed by the Würzburg psychologists who, in the first decade of this century, undertook a systematic examination of the whole process of thought.

The mental processes examined were of various degrees of complexity. They ranged from such simple processes as prearranged reactions to cards of various kinds or the comparison of different weights to more complex activities, such as the naming of a part of a specified object. For example, the word *man* might be given, and the word *leg* spoken in response.

Very difficult problems of a verbal type were also solved, such as "Can our thought understand the nature of thought?" and "Is this true? To give each man his due would be to will justice and to achieve chaos."

The work of the Würzburg school placed psychology in possession of a new concept of great value: the *determining tendency*.

It was found that, when a subject is confronted with a problem, his behavior and thought are determined not only by the associations which past experience has attached to the problem, but also by what we now call a need that springs from the task the subject has set himself. It is these needs that give mental life its ordered and directed character, even though we are not *conscious* of them as such. They are called *determining tendencies*.

A good illustration of determining tendency is found in an experiment with hypnosis. After a subject was hypnotized, the suggestion was made that, after waking, he would be shown two cards with two digits on each. To the first he was to give the sum, and to the second the difference of the digits. On his waking from the hypnotic state a card was shown on which were written the digits 6/2. The subject immediately said "8." When the second card was shown, with 4/2, the same subject said "2." He had no memory of the suggestion, and could give no explanation of what he had said. Nor did it occur to him that 8 was the sum of 2 and 6, or that 2 was the difference of 4 and 2.

The determining tendencies fix the course of thought by favoring certain 'associations' that spring from the immediate situation, and by inhibiting others. Thus they introduce directive order into the chaos of competing possibilities. They enable an answer to be given to the question of why a particular possibility is realized rather than any other. Why does the boy in solving the equation which is given on page 387 regard the numbers 60 and 7 as requiring him to find the digits 12 and 5 rather than the number 67? He was clearly unconscious of this alternative, which was eliminated by the determining tendency—that guiding, selective and inhibitory influence which springs from the task expressed in the words, "Solve the equation."

Later experiment has shown other ways in which the determining tendency gives mental life its ordered character. Thus it may function so as to complete already established patterns of thought. Suppose a student perceives in an examination paper this item: "The junctions between neurons are called ————"; and then correctly completes the sentence. He has been faced with a problem, possibly an entirely new one, since he may never before have had to express that bit of knowledge. By keeping him on the job until the completion of the sentence, the determining tendency has solved the problem for him. In the same way, a person presented with the word *month* and the task to find a superordinate concept would think *year*, even though he had never solved that problem before; or, if the task were to find a rhyme, he might even complete the incomplete pattern under the action of a determining tendency by thinking of the only rhyme that there is for *month*: $(n + 1)$th.

A determining tendency is, then, really such a need as is set up by an unsolved problem. The fact that a determining tendency reinforces old associations, thus causing an individual to complete uncompleted patterns, does not mean, however, that it never produces any brand-new result. On the contrary, the production of the novel is the chief business of the determining tendency, for a problem remains a problem only so long as it is new. Familiar problems, like tying a bow or solving a quadratic equation, are to an adult not really problems any more; their solutions having once been learned, they are solved rather by memory than by thought.

Consider the experiment in which the subjects were asked to devise a method of showing how much and where a metal ball was compressed when it was bounced on a hard surface. All five of the subjects completed this incomplete situation by finding the solution, although three of them had to be prompted by such hints as "think of footprints in the snow." The simplest solution is to paint the surface on which the ball is to be dropped and then drop the ball while the paint is still wet. The task here was to find the solution. There was, under the determining tendency which the task set up, a great deal of hunting around, or mental trial and error, until the solution that resolved the need appeared. With the satisfactory solution in mind, the need disappeared, just as in the reaction experiment the need to move the finger is abolished when the finger is moved.

There is an element of newness and an element of familiarity in all thought, as in all situations and responses. No adult can ever go through a process of thought that is entirely new; the terms of thought are contributed by past experience. On the other hand, it is fully as unlikely that a train of thought would ever be exactly duplicated as it is that a meal or a walk would repeat itself in all its minutiae. There are always slight differences. Both thought and response contain an almost inextricable blend of the old and the new.

Trial and error in thinking. Of the different steps between problem and solution, it has been seen that some are recognized as mistakes, some accepted as correct. The boys rejected the guess of seventy feet and the methods of comparison with the height of the house and of counting the steps, but accepted as correct that of timing the coin's fall. We have already called this procedure of rejection and acceptance *trial and error* (see pp. 306f.).

This fact, that certain steps or part solutions are accepted and others rejected, has been noted whenever the thought process has been carefully examined. Children engaged in solving problems—perhaps building with blocks—may be observed to try out first one solution and then another. Experiments on tracing geometrical figures seen in a mirror show adult human beings feeling their way by trial and error until, finally, the right path is taken quite easily. Both mentally and in actual random manipulation adult subjects solving mechanical puzzles use the same process. In fact, an elaborate examination of the method by which subjects learned to play a 'reasoning' game with matches or beads led to the conclusion that trial and error appear to be the invariable method in learning to solve a problem.

The attempt has indeed been made to *explain* all thought on this principle. According to the trial-and-error theory of thought, the animal learns by trying one action after another until the successful one is reached. In the same way, it is pointed out, human beings may actually try out responses until success is attained, although it is more usual for them to test the possibilities mentally, thus saving time and energy. In either case the fundamental fact in thinking is the trial of possibilities which are accepted or rejected until the final solution is reached.

Let us return for a moment to the boy in the examination room (p. 387). Before finally deciding that line 3 follows line 2, he will probably try out and discard more than one pair of numbers. In particular, he will probably have to make a trial before he can decide whether line 3 shall read $(x + 12)(x - 5)$ or whether the signs shall be reversed as printed. The trial may take place in his head, or he may actually write the figures down.

It must be realized, however, that the statement that thinking proceeds by trial and error is a description, not an explanation. All are agreed that some solutions are rejected, others accepted. The problem still remains why this or that particular solution was tried and rejected, while another is accepted. Trial and error undoubtedly take place, for they are a striking feature of all complex thinking. They constitute, however, one aspect only of the total process. The fact of trial and error should be carefully distinguished from the trial-and-error theory.

Thought and imagery. Up to the present we have concerned ourselves mainly with what may be called the mechanism of thought, namely the process by which one step follows another. We now have to consider the problem of the materials of thought. What is it that is present in consciousness when we think? What are the items represented by the *X*'s in the diagram (p. 383)? Careful observation reveals that processes of bewildering complexity are involved, about which there has been considerable disagreement. Certain striking features are, however, obvious. First of all, of course, perceptions are present, as already stated. In addition, it is generally easy to detect both images and feelings of pleasantness and unpleasantness, though the latter are not usually considered to be part of the real thought process.

The imagery may be visual, auditory, motor (kinesthetic) or the vocal-motor imagery of words and fragments of words (see pp. 352-355). Usually more than one kind of imagery is present. Motor imagery, though often difficult to detect, is present in a large number of cases. When asked to multiply 12 by 13 in his head, one subject reported the visual image of a blackboard, with his own arm writing. At the same time, he had motor imagery as of the arm being moved.

Where the nature of the problem allows, successive steps will often be marked by observable action, as happened with the boys on the tower. On the conscious side, definite steps are often accomplished by a more or less complete word or sentence spoken internally, like the sentences in the boys' conversation. One might say to oneself: "I'll drop something." Or there may be more or less complete visual imagery which serves as a starting point for further thought or for the solution.

Thus, it was reported of a subject who was given a mechanical puzzle to solve: "The solution later flashed upon him by means of an involuntary analysis of the image." Such visual imagery has been recorded for a lightning calculator who could give the sum of fifteen digits at a glance. The imagery was here apparently of an eidetic type (see pp. 364-367); it appeared as though written in chalk on a freshly washed blackboard in the calculator's own handwriting. The calculator could, so to speak, turn to one or another imaged item. Thus we see that an image may serve as a conscious nucleus around which thought may crystallize. The appearance of the image in the solving of the puzzle, its establishment in the course of the 'lightning' calculation, furnished a center for the organization of thought, and thus marked a stage in the total process.

Between the thinking of one person and that of another there is an enormous individual variation both in quantity and quality of imagery. Thus to the problem, "How long will it take to fill a pit 4 ft. × 3 ft. × 2 ft. at the rate of a cubic foot a minute?" most adults will give the same answer, using much the same method; yet the imagery involved will show extreme variability from person to person.

Thought and consciousness. Many workers have stressed the fact that conscious experience is not enough to explain what goes on during thinking. It will be remembered that the Würzburg investigators maintained that the determining tendencies work unconsciously. Many a time in these and other experimental reports we find such statements as: "The word flashed suddenly into my mind. I do not know how it got there." Such sudden *insights* without knowledge of certain intervening steps are, as a matter of fact, common in our mental processes. It was upon just such situations that the doctrine of insight was based (see p. 305). Though we may puzzle about the explanation, we must nevertheless accept the fact that we are unconscious of many of the processes which govern our thinking.

There exists, indeed, an intricate mechanism which is functioning during the process of thought, but which has no conscious counterpart. This fact is well brought out in an experiment where the subject was required to tie together two hanging ropes which were too short to reach each other except by special manipulation. One rope had first to be swung, and then caught on the rebound while the other was held at a slant. The experimenter sometimes gave a hint by swinging one rope, with the result that the subject then solved the problem. The subject might afterwards insist that the hint had not been noticed. In other words, he might be quite unconscious of the function of the nucleus round which the solution was organized. The solution usually appeared without his being able to describe the process of its formation, for he was unconscious of the basic mechanism involved.

To speak of an unconscious directive or basic mechanism of thought does not of course necessitate belief in any of the more elaborate theories of the unconscious or subconscious mind. It implies only that, during thinking, unconscious processes are ordinarily, perhaps always, involved. There is no reason to believe that such processes are necessarily different in quality from those of which we are conscious.

Thus we have a picture of directive thought as proceeding from a problem, as moving by successive steps, successful and unsuccessful, to a solution, as crystallizing around nuclei of whose function we may or may not be conscious and as largely regulated by processes of which we are normally quite unconscious.

Thought and action. At the beginning of this chapter, we noted that thought is intimately related to action. It will be remembered that the boys on the tower were engaged in activity which persisted until the problem was solved. A series of actions which aims at a definite end is known as *directive action*, the end being usually called the *goal*. To represent the process we may use a diagram similar to the previous one (p. 383).

Immediate situation ($\rightarrow X \rightarrow X \rightarrow X \rightarrow X \rightarrow X \rightarrow$) Goal.

Wishing to attain a goal, the individual finds himself in a specific situation. He must then 'take steps' to attain the end. The *X*'s stand for *actions leading to the goal*. Just as the trains of thought are directed towards a solution, so these actions are directed towards the goal. A man is on the street when it starts to rain. His goal is to get home. Finding no taxicab, he runs to a public telephone, only to discover it in use. Thereupon he waits till the telephone is free, eventually reaches the taxicab company, and so he continues until he finally arrives home. All these actions are controlled by the fact that a goal is to be reached. The man does not perform irrelevant actions; when the storm begins, he does not take a newspaper out of his pocket and read in the rain.

It is important to remember, however, that conscious processes are going on at the same time as this train of actions. In fact, we have here what may be called a train of thought acted out. Although observable action is not always so prominent in our thinking, it is almost always present, even where the simplest trains of directive thought are concerned. This fact is to be expected if we remember that directive thought is what goes on in consciousness during the process of integrative response to a situation of a certain type. Thought cannot be understood unless its intimate relation to action is continually kept in mind.

Recession of the response. It would, however, be a mistake to assume that every train of integrative thought necessarily and invariably issues in observable action. This fact may be seen by considering the evolution of thinking. Organic life gradually increases in complexity from the simplest forms up to human kind. As we come towards the top of the scale, the period that may elapse between the situation and the response to it lengthens out, while at the same time the intermediate processes become more and more important and complex. With the human being these intermediate processes are often so elaborate as to dwarf everything else; as a result, we are likely to forget that reasoning is initiated by a situation and normally leads towards observable response. The mathematician may work for weeks on a difficult problem, and finally write down the solution in half an hour. Or he may never write it down. However it is in human nature to do something about solutions as well as problems—even abstract mathematical solutions. Thought is, in short, ordinarily associated with observable action, though the stage of final response is sometimes omitted.

Thought and muscle. Since thought is so intimately related to response, it will not be surprising to find that during the process of thinking there are occurring widespread bodily changes of a sort which cannot be observed. In fact, one should envisage thinking and its physiological accompaniments as a series of events involving the whole organism, both physically and mentally. "We think with our muscles," it has been said. Change of muscular tension during thought is a matter of common observance. The brows are wrinkled; the posture is often intent. Even the chimpanzee may scratch his head when confronted with a difficult problem.

Considerable attention has lately been devoted to processes occurring in the muscles during thinking. The ultimate point at issue touches very closely the motor theory of consciousness, that is to say, the theory that consciousness, and therefore thought experience, *is* response. Into that theory we shall enter only as it involves the question of how *thought* and response are related.

A number of subjects were trained in a highly elaborate method of physical relaxation. It is claimed that, by practice, not only can the postural muscles be relaxed to a degree previously unattained, but also the internal and external muscles of the eyes, the muscles of the larynx and the tongue involved in speech, and those connected with the activity of breathing. There is evidence that during such complete relaxation, tension of smooth or involuntary muscles may also be diminished. When these trained subjects were in a state of complete relaxation, they reported that thought did not take place. The experience of muscular tenseness was apparently a necessary part of attention and the thought process.

In order to check these introspective reports, an apparatus was developed to detect and measure the slight electrical changes that occur in nerves and muscles during mental activity. The results were striking and fully confirmatory of the introspective reports; for the records showed that, during visual imagination and during recollection and imagination of muscular actions, there was muscular activity in the eyes and the other parts of the body concerned.

Many other workers have corroborated this general result. Recognizable differences have been found in the degree of tension of various muscles when subjects are preparing for tasks of different degrees of difficulty. When a subject is doing mental arithmetic, the tension of the muscles has been shown to be in a continual state of change. No *complete* correspondence has been found, however, between thought processes and the *pattern* of such implicit muscular responses, as they are termed.

LANGUAGE

An outstanding instance of directive organic response, one that stands in peculiarly close relation to thought, is the activity known as speech or language. Speech is behavior of a most complex and highly adaptive type. Though the chief characteristic that distinguishes it from most other action is the fact that it serves the purpose of communication, it is distinguished also by the fact that it is symbolic. It is, in fact, social behavior of a very highly specialized kind.

Language and thought. Language, both written and spoken, exhibits many of the characteristics we have attributed to directive thought. To begin with, it is plainly directive. Words and sentences do not follow at haphazard; they have a more or less direct relation to the situation—generally a social one—to which response is being made. The process of control is more particularly evident in prepared speeches and literary productions, where words and sentences are often carefully pruned, eliminated, restored, changed and so on.

Another point of similarity between speech and thought lies in the fact that in speech trial and error are often prominent. Most writers have had the experience of cutting out or changing a word or phrase, restoring the original word and then cutting it out or changing it back again.

To say that speech is directive is, furthermore, to imply that it is unitary or integrative. So much insistence is laid upon unity by teachers of oral and written composition that there is hardly need to emphasize the fact once more. The sentence, the paragraph, the story, essay or speech are all units. We know, again, from experimental researches that the word and the letter are units. This highly complex elaboration of unities within unities is effected by the integrative functioning of the organism, which is meeting a diverse situation with a unitary response.

Again, in speech as in thought new and old are very subtly intermixed. We have a standard system of letters to form words. These letters are common to many modern languages. The words which they form are, for the most part, peculiar to one language. Each language has a standard system of word arrangement—rules of syntax. Much the same thing is true for spoken language, where, from about thirty elementary sounds, we fashion standard words which must be used in accordance with the grammar and idiom of the language we are speaking. Thus the raw material of language is already in our possession in a relatively fixed form before we speak or write. It is by no means new.

But the factor of newness is no less apparent. New combinations of words, newly coined words, new uses for old words, as well as such things as intonation, rhythm, emotional and affective factors, personality traits—all these operate to make of speech a living, ceaselessly changing thing rather than a collection of stereotyped sounds. If any speaker repeated a sentence of any considerable length in *exactly* the same way, the duplication would be laid to coincidence. So important is this contrast between the new and the old in spoken communication that it has been proposed to apply the name language to the relatively static dictionary and grammar element, and to reserve the term speech for the adaptable, living drama of actual communication.

All these characteristics which language possesses in common with thought have been experimentally illustrated in the case of telegraphic messages. Telegraphy is of course essentially a language. Its primary elements, corresponding to phonetic or alphabetical elements, are the dot and dash, with intervals of time between them. The use and understanding of such language constitute an integrative process. A letter containing four to six elements is first perceived as a unity. Then such letters are grouped into words, which later are perceived as unities in their turn. Still later, larger language units are integrated. There is, further, a constant element in all sending and receiving of telegraphic messages, namely the identity of sounds as heard and the motions of the sender's hand. Yet there is constant intentional variation in the spacing of these sounds by the operator. The more expert the operator, the greater this momentary variation, which corresponds to inflection in speech. A telegraphic message, then, is a subtle blend of new and old. Thus language, whether spoken, written or telegraphic, exhibits striking similarities to directive thought.

This intimate relation between thought and language is again brought out in the studies of aphasia, which is an inability to speak because of injury to a certain part of the brain.

It would seem that, in order that speech may take place, a further process is necessary, in addition to the fundamental process of integration. This process, which is the one affected in aphasia, has been called "symbolic formulation and expression." Formulation is the process of making a formula which is of more or less general validity; expression is the act of fitting words to it. Although the two may be distinguished by introspection, they are intimately blended in a single inclusive activity.

A patient is told to copy the examiner's movements. Facing his patient, the examiner raises his right hand. The aphasic person of a certain type cannot repeat the movement. The examiner goes behind the patient, and both look into a mirror. The patient can now copy the movements without difficulty. A possible explanation is that in the first situation it is necessary to go through the special process of making some kind of verbal formula such as "right equals left," or "change sides." Such a special process, which appears to be fundamental for ordinary speech, is beyond the powers of the aphasic person. It depends on the ability to make a *suitable* formula out of the experience provided by the past and to fit the proper words to it, a process in which thought and language are joined in a unitary psychological activity.

Are thought and language identical? They are very closely related—so closely, in fact, that it has been held at many different times that the one *is* the other. To support this claim many have identified with speech those movements of throat and tongue which sometimes occur when thought is carried on by unspoken verbal symbols. But experiment shows that this 'internal speech,' as it is called, is not simply audible speech reduced to so small a scale that it becomes inaudible. Even if it were, it would not mean that thought and language are identical, for thought processes can apparently be carried on in non-linguistic terms. The essential thing is symbols. It is obvious, therefore, that thought cannot be language, because there are other symbols than words which can be used. We have all had the experience of thought for which we cannot find the words. Furthermore, animals cannot speak; yet, we shall see, it is extremely probable that they think. To equate thought and language is not justified by experimental fact. Language is, in fact, but one form of the general response activity with which thought is so closely related.

The function of verbalization. Language does, however, occupy a unique place among our reactions. Thinking and talking have grown up together and should be considered as two aspects of the same phase of mental development. By language, as by no other means, thought is clarified, sharpened and made exact. The very foundation of modern science depends on mathematical analysis, which is but a special development of language. Even on an elementary plane, a science of chemistry would be impossible without the ability to name the elements and compounds, and a science of astronomy equally helpless without the ability to name the stars. Indeed, it is evident that language, the most highly organized system of response we possess, is of the greatest advantage in our attempts to understand and dominate our environment.

The experiments described in the chapter on imagery (pp.

360f.) are instructive in this regard. There it was found that the reproduction of figures is easier if they are given names of objects. In fact, when the figures were of unusual shape or relatively meaningless, they could be retained in memory *only* if they were named. It is true that the subjects differed in the name they assigned to a given object. Thus the same figure was called by different subjects a violin, a dumb-bell, etc., as shown in Fig. 41. The point is, however, that a name was necessary if some resemblance to the figure was to be held in mind. A practical parallel to the experiments is shown when a student beginning a subject such as botany or anatomy is told what the various structures 'look like'—a procedure which is later of material help in remembering the details. One who has been told that the *cochlea* of the ear is like a snail-shell, and has been shown a model, will find it difficult to forget the shape of that structure.

Other experiments have been performed from somewhat different angles. For instance, it is found that the blindfolded tracing of a maze with a pencil may be improved by verbalization. A memory pattern of the maze is formed in words, by means of which many details may be recalled later. The subject may say to himself, "Turn to the left, once to the right, twice to the left, double the distance, then goal." (See pp. 320f.)

Rules for reasoning. The following instructions, preceded by a 20-minute lecture on them, doubled the number of successes in solving a difficult problem. (1) Locate a difficulty and try to overcome it. If you fail, get it completely out of your mind and seek an entirely different difficulty. (2) Do not be a creature of habit and stay in a rut. Keep your mind open for new meanings. (3) The solution pattern appears suddenly. You cannot force it. Keep your mind open for new combinations and do not waste your time on unsuccessful attempts. "Reasoning," said the investigator, "is at least in part the overcoming . . . of habitual responses."

MEANING AND CONCEPTS

Mental processes and meaning. Language is symbolic. It has meaning. We talk and think *about* something.

A telegrapher is taking a message. If we are to understand what is happening, we must take into account not only the metallic sounds which a stranger hears, but their meaning to the operator. In other words, for a psychological understanding of what happens to the telegrapher, we must put the sounds which he hears into some form of context. They cannot be understood by themselves, as mere sounds. In the operator's mind they *refer* to something.

A railway telegrapher hears the series of sounds that signal his station. He leaves the window at which he is selling a ticket, goes to the instrument, signals "MQ" (wait ten minutes) and returns. What is the *meaning* of the sounds he heard? For a subjective or introspective account we must start with the *primary sensory experience* of the receiving telegrapher. It is of auditory quality and includes two sounds repeated at different intervals, making a group of perhaps eight sounds altogether. The meaning of this total set of experiences is, then, its context in consciousness. There is perhaps a verbal image of the name of the station calling, or the fleeting visual picture of the man making the call, kinesthetic imagery of various kinds, or verbal imagery of the words "must answer him."

The meaning of the group of *stimuli* according to an objective description is what the station agent does about it at the moment; he interrupts his conversation, walks over and makes certain movements on the telegraph key. Although these responses may vary somewhat according to the actions on which the telegrapher is engaged when he hears the signal, yet in all such different responses to the group of stimuli in question there is something similar. It is this similarity which causes us to say that the stimuli have a definite meaning.

Objectively the meaning of the light-stimulus in a conditioned reflex may be the *response* which the dog makes to food.

Introspectively the meaning of the light-experience would be the idea of food. It is context that is involved in each case, but context of a different kind.

It is well known that human thinking makes very large use of signs. They enormously enhance our ability to analyze and control the environment, and at the same time very greatly economize our observable actions. Often we lose sight entirely of the thing signified by the symbol, be it a mathematical sign or a word. It is largely to the highly developed use of symbols that human thought owes its astonishing efficiency. On the other hand, as we have seen, the use of symbols sometimes leads to ineffectual thinking. There is always the danger that, through constant use of a given symbol, we may lose sight of the real meaning for which the symbol stands and endow the symbol uncritically with significance far beyond that of its original context (see pp. 19-22).

Generalization and abstraction. One feature of human thinking has captured the imagination of observers from the time of the Greek philosophers to the present. It is the fact that thought processes initiated in a concrete situation may have reference to many situations other than the original one. A concrete thought may take on the quality of *general* validity.

A well-known experiment in physics shows that, if two weights are suspended one at each end of a uniform lever, they will balance if the products of the weights and their respective distances from the fulcrum are equal. After this fact is demonstrated for a number of particular cases, ultimately we recognize the features that are common to them all. Somehow we have abstracted from the particular cases and see that the formula is universal. The foundations of science are built upon this ability to abstract and to generalize, to recognize common features in a variable world.

When we generalize, we are learning to respond specifically to a situational feature or set of features, irrespective of the particular circumstances in which it may be found. Such a response is often, though not necessarily, a verbal one. On the conscious side, we are said to form a concept. *By the accompanying process of abstraction we learn to disregard the irrelevant details* (see p. 417).

For example, when a child has learned to distinguish horses from other animals, it attaches the same verbal response 'horse' to all horses, regardless of their differences. It has generalized. On the conscious side it is said to have acquired a concept, sometimes called a general idea. At the same time it has learned to disregard irrelevant detail—size, color and so on. This is abstraction. Later, the child learns that "the three angles of a triangle are equal to two right angles." This verbal statement is made, not of any particular triangle as such, but of those features which any triangle shares with others. It is a general statement, the product of generalization. By the process of abstraction the pupil has learned to disregard irrelevancies, such as the size or color of any particular triangle. He has developed a concept of triangle.

Many experiments have been directed upon the processes both of generalization and abstraction. We shall first consider an investigation of *abstraction*.

A group of five geometrical figures was shown to a subject for a quarter of a second, and was then replaced by a second group, and so on up to twenty-five exposures. All the groups had one figure in common (see Fig. 45). The subject was told to watch for repetition. As soon as he was sure he had seen some figure twice, he was to turn a switch which stopped the exposures. The recognition of the common figure in a group might require any number of exposures from five to twenty-five.

The process of abstraction was initiated by breaking up the group of figures. While the common element was accentuated, the others faded from consciousness. The irrelevant figures were "not merely neglected, but . . . positively cast aside and swept more or less completely from the field of consciousness." Thus the process of abstraction was twofold. There was a positive accentuation of the figure abstracted, and an equally positive thrusting away of irrelevants.

This dual nature of abstraction points to a practical danger in everyday life. By the nature of his work the professional specialist is obliged to concentrate on certain aspects of the people with whom he is dealing. Such concentration tends to make him shut his eyes to other, equally important, aspects. The business man, treating people all day solely as 'customers,' often finds it difficult to remember that they are human beings. "The lawyer," said Schopenhauer, "sees mankind in all its

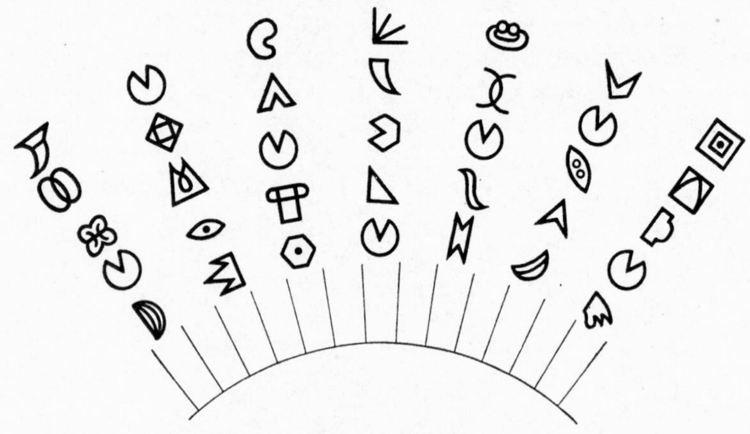

Fig. 45. Designs Used for a Study of Abstraction.
From T. V. Moore, The process of abstraction, *Univ. Calif. Publ. Psychol.*, 1910, 1, No. 2, 123; reprinted by permission of the University of California Press.

wickedness, the doctor in all its weakness." There is no doubt that this 'professional abstraction' helps to determine the attitude of professional men towards other people.

The process of abstraction in the experiment in question was a gradual one. The subject had first only a general idea that a figure was being repeated, a vague notion which gradually gave way to clearer and clearer recognition of just what it was that had been repeated. This characteristic has many examples in everyday life.

In order to study the process of *generalization*, an experimenter required his subjects to repeat the names (invented) of Chinese characters, those characters which had a part in common being given the same name. Gradually the subject learned to associate the common element with the common name, until finally he could give the name even when the common element appeared in an entirely new context. Thus the subject learned to give a specific verbal response to a feature irrespective of the particular circumstances in which it was found. In other words, he had generalized.

Another investigator worked with colored geometrical designs which were also named. Thus a *vec* was the name of an equilateral triangle bisected by a line drawn from an angle to the opposite side. A *dax* was a circle and two dots, one dot being inside, the other outside, the circle. The designs might be of any color, shape or position, provided only that the defining conditions were observed. Different varieties of the designs were exposed, and the subject told, for example: "Each of these drawings is a *dax*." He was then tested by being asked to define a *dax*, by being asked to draw one and by a test series in which he indicated whether or not a given figure was a *dax*. The same was done for the other figures. The subject learned to respond specifically to a single set of features irrespective of any particular setting and to neglect irrelevant details. He learned to generalize and abstract. It will be noticed that this experiment does not employ identical elements in the different settings, but, instead, common features of a more complex nature.

It is important to observe that certain subjects could complete correctly the task set in the test series without being able to give a verbal definition of the concept. A further result of this experiment was that the ability to acquire a concept was found to be correlated with intelligence.

Through all experiments the fact emerges that final generalization takes time to develop. Psychologically speaking, we evolve our concepts; they are not immutable. We realize that this must be so when we remember that 'generalization' and 'abstraction' are but special cases of learning. They are akin to the maze behavior of the rat which, by gradually learning to disregard the wrong passages, develops a uniform and correct response to the maze situation.

COMPARATIVE PSYCHOLOGY OF THOUGHT

Levels of thought. Published scientific work probably represents the expression of the most highly logical and socialized thought. The scientist, dealing with abstract situations, must put his results into such a form that others can understand and repeat his experiments. He starts his investigation where his predecessors left off. In his earlier life he has acquired a general education, in school and out, in a social environment. His thought, like that of the writer, the musician and the pictorial artist, is socially derived and socially directed. Science is a symbolic drama which the investigator plays to an audience of fellow workers.

In contrast to scientific thinking there are many thought processes, both of adults and children, which are neither 'logical' nor couched in a form suitable for communication. Children of six and seven years of age, it has been found, often are unable to understand one another, a fact which stamps the child's thinking as relatively non-logical; but it has also been shown that college students, when they attempt to deal with material somewhat beyond their scope, are subject to the same limitations. Children and adults think logically and in communicable form when their knowledge and experience allow, and when their thought is not warped by prejudice or special predilection.

Thought and animals. The question whether animals think has been variously answered. For one who believes that thinking is internal speech, thought in animals is impossible. If one includes obscure manual (manipulative) and visceral activity in his account of thinking, he may assign thinking of a simple kind to animals even though he does not allow them 'ideas.' At one time the question seemed to have been settled by the theory that an animal in a new situation does not think, but struggles blindly until by chance it hits on a satisfactory response. Recent investigators, however, have challenged this interpretation. Some animals apparently solve problems by means which indicate an insight into the situation. Thus we have seen how a chimpanzee, given two bamboo canes of which neither is long enough to reach a coveted banana, may by accident fit the two canes together in the manner of a fishing rod, jump up and at once draw the banana towards him with this double stick (p. 305). Such evidence of insight in animals is evidence of thought.

The experimental work which has made possible this change of expert opinion is so extensive that it cannot even be summarized here. It belongs primarily to the field of learning, which is closely related to the problem of thought. The statement may be made, however, that certain modern experimentalists now believe that animals show in their behavior many of the characteristics of human thought. If this supposition is true, we must believe that animals think mainly through the medium of observable action, with some power of analysis and synthesis, while they talk not at all; and that they act largely on the spur of the moment. Observable action in man, on the other hand, is often shrunk to a minimum through the economy of symbolic operations, with the result that response is separated from situation by processes of prodigious complexity.

The neurologist, Herrick, says: "The human brain can fabricate symbols and abstractions; it can use language, numbers and equations, design machines, bridges, telescopes and use them. The chimpanzee does not know the meaning of $y^2 = 2px$, *and he can never find out.*"[1]

REFERENCES

1. DUNCKER, K. A qualitative (experimental and theoretical) study of productive thinking (solving of comprehensible problems). *Ped. Sem.*, 1926, 33, 642-708.
2. GARDINER, A. H. *The theory of speech and language.* Oxford: Oxford University Press, 1932.
3. HEAD, H. Disorders of symbolic thinking and expression. *Brit. J. Psychol.*, 1921, 11, 179-193.

[1] C. J. Herrick, *Brains of rats and men,* University of Chicago Press, 1926, 290; reprinted by permission of the publisher.

4. HEAD, H. *Aphasia and kindred disorders of speech.* Cambridge, England: Cambridge University Press, 1926. Vol. I.
5. HERRICK, C. J . *Brains of rats and men.* Chicago: University of Chicago Press, 1926.
6. KÖHLER, W. *The mentality of apes.* New York: Harcourt, Brace, 1925.
7. LAMBERT, J. F., and EWERT, P. H. The effect of verbal instructions upon stylus maze learning. *J. gen. Psychol.,* 1932, 6, 377-399.
8. MOORE, T. V. The process of abstraction. *Univ. Calif. Publ. Psychol.,* 1910, 1, 73-197.
9. PETERSON, J. C. The higher mental processes in learning. *Psychol. Monogr.,* 1920, 28, No. 129.
10. PIAGET, J. *The language and thought of the child.* New York: Harcourt, Brace, 1926.
11. RUGER, H. A. The psychology of efficiency. *Arch. Psychol.,* 1910, 2, No. 15.
12. SMOKE, K. L. An objective study of concept formation. *Psychol. Monogr.,* 1932, 42, No. 191.
13. TITCHENER, E. B. *Experimental psychology of the thought processes.* New York: Macmillan, 1909.
14. WEISENBURG, T., and MCBRIDE, K. *Aphasia.* New York: The Commonwealth Fund, 1935.

Chapter 13

PERCEPTION

Perception is the apprehension of immediately present objects and events. Whenever we read a book, watch a football game, listen to music, heft a tennis racquet, smell a rose, taste an apple or feel dizzy we are perceiving. Its limitation to the present is what distinguishes perception from recollection and imagination. Perception is the primary activity, whereas recollection and imagination extend our knowledge of the world beyond the immediate present.

The fundamental aspects of perceived objects are spatial and temporal. The hunter who suddenly sees game identifies it in part by its shape and size; as he aims at his target, he needs also to take into account its direction and distance. The apprehension of these properties is called spatial perception, a topic discussed in the next chapter. When the hunter perceives that he has time for a careful shot, when he times his shot to the movement of his target, when he notes that the afternoon is nearly gone or when he hears a prearranged signal of three shots in rapid succession—then he apprehends aspects of objects and events that belong to temporal perception, another topic treated in Chapter 15. In subsequent chapters are considered the individual roles played in perception by the several senses—vision, hearing and so on. The intent of the present chapter is to prepare the way by giving an account of certain general features of perception.

EQUIPMENT FOR PERCEPTION

For the most part we shall be concerned with perception in man, whose perceptions differ from those of other animals

This chapter was written by S. Feldman and H. P. Weld of Cornell University.

principally because he has a more complex and a more versatile equipment for perceiving. How, then, is an organism equipped for the perception of itself, of other objects and of events? The first requisite is that the object or event shall affect in some way the body's sense organs. In the case of events in the body (such as the stomach's contractions in hunger) the requirement is easily met, since the body interior (including the walls of the stomach) is provided with sense organs. As for objects and events outside the body, these must somehow send out changes of energy (light, air disturbance, chemical diffusion, pressure) that are capable of stimulating an accessible sense organ. The first requirement for perception, then, is the *stimulation* of one or more sense organs.

A second requisite for perception is *neural activity*. Such activity includes not only the functioning of the nerve fibers connected with the sense organs, but also the distinctive contributions of the various levels of the central nervous system, up to and including the cortex. It is impossible to explain perception solely in terms of what happens in the sense organs or in the afferent nerves. The relevance of the brain to perception will be evident if we consider but two points: the cooperation of the senses and certain fundamental equivalences among the senses.

It is the unitary functioning of the nervous system, of nerves and brain as a whole, that makes it possible for the several senses to *cooperate* in perception. When, for example, a buzzing bee alights on a person's hand, he may see, hear and feel the bee in the same place. Again, touch and vision are integrated when a piece of cloth is examined with eyes and fingers together. The perception of a sizzling steak may, in addition to sight and touch, call for the cooperation of hearing, smell and taste.

Over and above their separate and cooperative contributions, the several senses also make many *similar* contributions. For example, roughness, smoothness and softness are properties common to vision, touch and hearing. Everyone knows that roughness can be both felt and seen, *e.g.,* in sandpaper; but roughness can also be heard. Certain sounds are definitely rough; others are just as definitely smooth. Colors are sometimes perceived as warm, cold or heavy. Other properties, such as brightness and dullness, are common to all the senses. Not only do colors differ in brightness, but also sounds, pressures and even odors and tastes. These common attributes point to a unity of the senses induced by processes in the brain.

Our equipment for perception includes, thirdly, the *motor apparatus* of the body. Bodily movement serves perception by facilitating sensory cooperation; it also facilitates stimulation. Thus head movements are of assistance both to vision and to hearing. Visual stimulation is further facilitated by eye movement; the eyes are motor, as well as sensory, organs. When a touch or a sound causes a person to turn his head and eyes and look at the stimulating object, vision is superimposed upon touch or hearing. If he then approaches, reaches for and handles the object, touch supplements vision and vision itself is facilitated. Oral manipulation (as in eating) brings touch, taste and smell together. In such ways does movement—manipulation of objects with mouth and hands, orientation of head and eyes, reaching and locomotion—contribute to perception.

From the embryonic period onward, the bodily activities and structures involved in perception undergo development in the individual organism. Growth, maturation, practice and learning are as essential for perception as for other psychological functions. Consequently perception is different in the infant and in the more mature individual. Differences in perceiving among various orders of animal life, furthermore, point to a long evolutionary history of this activity.

ATTENTION: THE CONTROL OF PERCEPTION

Often we fail to perceive objects and events under conditions of stimulation that at other times are quite adequate for perception. One example is the body and its states. Although the body is always with us, is active in a variety of ways and constantly providing internal sources of stimulation, it does not always enter into perception. No one, that is to say, is aware of his body at every moment. Such bodily events as walking, breathing, movements of tongue or eyes, and all sorts of pulls and pressures pass unnoticed unless attention is called to them. If we undertake a methodical examination of ourselves, proceeding from the head down and keeping alert to anything that may turn up, we discover all sorts of tensions and pressures that we failed to perceive previously. The same limitation applies to the perception of many outside objects and events. The pressure of our clothing, the pressure of our shoes against the ground, the prevailing temperature, scents and sounds, the furnishings of a room, objects outdoors—all these may remain unperceived.

This failure to perceive when stimulation is present—let us call it *imperception*—is also evidenced in such bits of conversation as: "What did you say? I am sorry, I was not listening"; or, "Why don't you look where you are going?" Only when one is told: "There is Mr. Andrews," or asked: "Is the soup salty?" "Do you smell smoke?" "How is the pain today?"—only then does one see Mr. Andrews, taste the salt, smell the smoke or feel the pain.

Imperception is in its way as useful as perception. The advertiser, the hawker, the person on promenade may wish to attract attention; but the retiring person, the burglar, the detective, the spy, the soldier at the front want to avoid attention, to be inconspicuous or imperceived. The puzzle-picture maker skilfully conceals the hidden object. We shall see that imperception has many other uses.

Obviously, then, stimuli do not always induce perception. In fact, stimulation becomes effective for perception only (1) when it represents a change from the established level of stimulation or (2) when the individual is already prepared or primed to perceive.

Stimulus level. We try to wake the sleeper by nudging, by making sounds or by flashing a light. When a person is preoccupied, similar means are useful for eliciting perception:

knocking at the door, calling or whistling, waving one's hand or handkerchief. Bells, whistles, flashing lights, waving flags are thus used in factories, in lighthouses, in the army and at street and railway crossings. These stimuli are rendered more effective by increasing their *intensity*. The sleeper is nudged more vigorously, the voice is raised. Bright lights are more effective than faint lights. Another way of enhancing the action of a stimulus is through *movement*; hence the waving of flags, the moving signs of the advertiser. Efficacy is also enhanced through *repetition*. The nudge, the call, the waving or flashing is continued. Bells, telephones, alarm clocks, flash signals are constructed to provide repetitive stimulation.

Ultimately, however, repetition may result in *imperception*. We become used to noises in the home, in the office and in the factory. The ticking clock, the blaring radio, the rushing waterfall, the familiar automobile sounds may not be heard at all. What happens is that *we adjust ourselves to the level of stimulation*.

When we are so adjusted, perception fails unless there is a change in the stimulus. Thus we may fail to hear the ticking of a clock, yet notice when the clock stops. We begin to listen again when the lecturer changes to a new pitch level or alters his tempo. The driver readily perceives a new sound in his car, even if it is a faint sound. So, also, it is the unusual bodily event that is likely to enter into perception, as when a leg goes lame, or when the contractions of the stomach become excessively vigorous or when heart action and breathing alter considerably under excitement and emotion.

Although animals ordinarily escape notice through immobility, there is a certain bird, living among swaying reeds, that stands on its long legs and sways with the reeds and thus remains unperceived; standing stock-still, it would be very noticeable. Again, *checkered patterns* in fabrics and in road signs are common means of attracting attention. Yet the checkered pattern of many animals, merging perfectly with their gaudy surroundings, renders them invisible. *Novelty* too, is one of the conditions of attention. Yet a *familiar* object catches the attention when in a strange place. In all these cases it is the *change* in stimulus that governs perception.

Priming. Perception is also governed by the business of the moment. One's day is filled with the undertaking of various tasks, tasks of action and thought. *When* one perceives and *how* one perceives are determined in an important way by the requirements of the situation. The situation induces the individual to search, to expect, to anticipate, to make an effort, to concentrate. In this way he is primed, prepared to perceive certain things and not others, and to perceive them in a certain way. All sorts of things that ordinarily remain unnoticed may come to be perceived if the occasion or a suggestion induces a state of preparedness.

In the army, the command "attention!" serves to induce preparation. In the classroom, the entrance of the lecturer or the sound of his voice serves a similar purpose. The automobile driver is prepared to perceive the road and traffic signals. The hunter is primed to see and hear. The piano tuner is set to hear, and the tea taster to taste. The lookout, the explorer, the observer in the laboratory are primed to observe. In experiments which seek to ascertain the minimal energy of stimulation that is effective for perception, the subject has to be brought into a suitable state of preparedness in order to perceive, and that state must be maintained as constant as possible. This principle of priming is also evident in animal behavior. Not only men but also rats when hungry are more sensitive to smell.

The state of the individual, his priming at the moment, may also be responsible for imperception and for pseudo-perception or hallucination (see pp. 357f.). When we do not want to see a person, we may actually fail to see him; yet, on the other hand, a person expecting a visitor may hear hallucinatory footsteps. In hysterical blindness and anesthesia the person is primed not to perceive. The hypnotized person may fail to see or feel if blindness or anesthesia is suggested to him, or he may have an hallucination if he is so instructed.

The influence of priming is demonstrated likewise in the following experiments.

1. *Bell-pointer experiment.* The observer faces a clock mechanism which is adjusted so that a bell rings when the hand of the clock, moving rapidly, has reached a certain position. If the observer *pays attention to the hand or pointer*, he will hear the bell at a *later* position of the hand, whereas, if he *pays attention to the bell*, he will hear it at an *earlier* position. Perception alters with the observer's attitude. The perception of the sound arises more quickly when the observer is primed for it.

2. *Suggestion.* In an experiment on color mixture, the observer was told that the amount of blue in a purple would be gradually increased and the red diminished. Although the experimenter then proceeded to do exactly the opposite, the observer nevertheless saw the purple as turning bluer. He was prepared by suggestion.

3. *Abstraction.* In still another experiment, groups of letters differing in color and arrangement were shown for 1/8 sec. In certain observations the subject was instructed to note the number of letters, in others their colors, in still others their arrangement or their individual character. It turned out that he generally perceived only what he was set to perceive and that he failed to perceive anything else. After observing the colors of the letters, for example, he was often totally unable to tell, when asked, the names of the letters or their arrangement. What happens in this experiment is usually called abstraction. A few items only are abstracted from the total situation. In this sense, *perception is always abstractive.* We never perceive at one glance all we can, even of a single object. New features always emerge when observation is continued, although for most purposes the first impression suffices.

4. *Range of perception.* This abstractive character is also evident in the limited range of perception. How many separate items can be perceived 'at once'? The top limit varies both with one's priming and also with the character of the objects and their arrangement or grouping. The range of perception has been measured in various ways. In one method, the method of

testimony, a scene is presented on a screen for a moment. The observer lists the items he saw, and his list is compared with the detailed list made out by the experimenter.

In another method, letters, words or forms are exposed for less than 1/10 sec. through the window of a tachistoscope, an apparatus for rapid exposure. The results of such an experiment are given in Table XXVII. The different columns indicate the results obtained when the subjects are primed with different instructions. The three observers were required to report in separate experiments the number of forms, the names of letters, the names of forms, and the number, name and color of forms.

TABLE XXVII

Average Number of Items Reported by Three Observers under Four Different Instructions

Observers	Number of Forms	Names of Letters	Names of Forms	Number, Name and Color of Forms
A	11.3	7.9	4.3	3.3
B	6.2	6.9	3.2	3.0
C	9.2	5.9	3.9	3.3

It will be seen that the limit of correct report, or the range of perception, varies with the difficulty of the task; the values are smallest in the last column because then the observers had three things to report. These results represent the limits of perception only when it is directed in a very specific manner, for obviously we can take in with one look more objects than we can correctly number, name or describe. We can see thousands of people at once on a bathing beach.

Such methods measure the extent of perception in a small span of time. As perception is continued, or repeated, the amount perceived may increase. The practiced observer takes in more details at a glance than the unpracticed observer. What is observed always depends upon the character and degree of preparation. In legal testimony a distinction is made between incidental and deliberate observation; also between uninformed and informed observation. The scientist observes, at least in his own province, both with deliberation and with information. On the other hand, spectators observing the magician, and not knowing what to look for, find their observation easily misdirected by his patter and misleading movements.

Priming and preparation in the past. The state of preparation, so far considered, immediately precedes perception. Indeed it may be regarded as the initial, preliminary stage of perception. It is this first stage that prepares the way for the immediately following stage of perception proper. The preparation, however, is often established earlier. On leaving the house one puts a letter in his pocket with the intention of mailing it. This intention favors the perception of the letter-box on the corner when it is reached, whereas without such priming no notice would have been taken of it. *Perception is governed by 'unfinished business.'* In the same way, a resolution to wake early favors the hearing of the alarm clock.

Interests. After seeing a new word or name for the first time, this word or name is likely to stand out on the page in one's later reading. The interest aroused at an earlier time always gives a special advantage to subsequent perception. Long standing, as well as recent, interests govern perception. The mother is tuned to the baby's cry; the nurse to the patient's call; the physician to the ringing of the telephone; the operator to the click of the instrument; the ornithologist to the flitting bird.

On the other hand, one may become habituated in *im*perception. Routine perception is notoriously abbreviated and foreshortened, becoming in extreme cases chronic imperception and absent-mindedness. We perceive very little of a familiar person, garment, room or scene. We learn to perceive, and also not to perceive. In so far as this practice makes for economy, it represents another way in which imperception may be useful.

Perception and learning. Antecedent priming, as in learning and in the formation of habits, also determines *how* objects are perceived. In a substitution test, for instance, the subject is given a sheet with circles, triangles, stars, squares and other geometrical forms, and he is required to inscribe different numerals in the forms according to an assigned key. Before long the circle, for example, comes to be perceived at once as that "5" thing. In fact, the numeral is sometimes seen as image in the circle.

Sir Francis Galton, an inveterate experimenter, set up the figure of Punch as an idol and practiced towards it genuflection, prayer and reverence. After a time he noted that he had 'acquired the habit.' He found himself perceiving the figure as a divine being at moments when he did not plan to do so. The character of divinity stuck to the object.

This sort of priming makes for economy also. We learn to *see* ice as cold. We judge the weight of an object by the mere sound of its fall or by the groaning of its bearer. We identify a person by his voice, gait or the slope of his shoulders. We perceive a melody by the printed score. In all these instances a reduced stimulus becomes as effective as the more inclusive stimulus. When one turns in the financial section of a newspaper to the chart that mimics, by an arrangement of lines, the ups and downs of the prices of stocks over a period of years, one perceives at a glance a very long series of events. In this case spatial perception is put to temporal ends.

It has been shown that perception operates under the combined control of stimulation and the individual's priming. This dual manner of control is useful because it means that we make use of perception as the business of the moment requires and yet are able to turn to anything out of the way that may be of importance.

OBJECT CONSTANCY

Circumstances make a difference in the way in which an object is perceived. We know that our opinion of a person's actions depends upon the circumstances. Circumstances, we say, alter cases. What is true in the realm of opinion is also true of perception.

Objects and circumstances. One and the same object may be perceived under a variety of circumstances. A sound may be near or far. An object too may be near or far, facing us directly or at an angle, brightly illuminated or shaded. When these circumstances vary, so likewise does the stimulation of the sense organs vary. Stimulation decreases in intensity with the distance of the sound. Intensity of stimulation is less when an object stands in shadow, or is poorly illuminated, than when it is free from shadow or is examined in a good light. Stimulation of the retina of the eye decreases, in strength and in area, with the distance of the object. When an object is seen at an angle, the pattern of retinal stimulation is distorted.

All these changes in stimulation do, as is to be expected, affect perception. Distant noises sound faint, distant objects look faint and small. That such changes in perception are the exception rather than the rule is, however, a point one is likely to overlook. The rule is that *objects are perceived in a fairly constant manner.* That is to say, objects may change but little in size and shape when seen from different positions. Object brightness similarly tends toward constancy at different distances and in different illuminations. For example, the distant snow seen at night still looks white.

It is easy to see that if this were not the rule, the identification of objects would be practically impossible. A person would look so different when seen from different positions, or in different illuminations, that we could not recognize him. Constancy is obviously useful. But how does it come about? What object constancy means is that *our perception of objects takes the circumstances into account* and compensates accordingly for the variability of the stimulus. This principle also explains such exceptions to constancy as do occur. For the degree of constancy depends upon our sensitivity to the circumstances. It is only, for example, when an object is so far away that our appreciation of its distance is defective that the object begins to shrink in size. Circumstances still make a difference, but in an unexpectedly useful way.

The rule that objects remain constant for perception, *as long as the accompanying circumstances actually register,* will be demonstrated here by a consideration of the role of shadows and of illumination. The following chapter on spatial perception will deal with the constancy of object size, position and shape.

The role of shadows. Shadows play several distinct roles in the visual perception of objects. Without shadows, for one thing, objects would lose much of their solid appearance; they would look flat (see p. 454). Shadows are perceived in a number of ways: (1) as mere modifications of the object's sur-

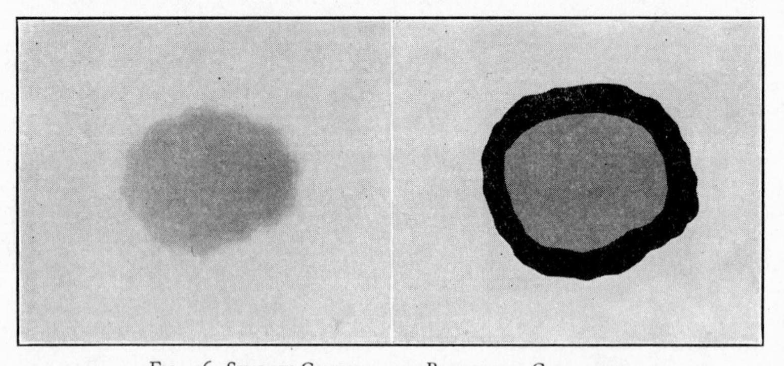

Fig. 46. Shadow-Contour and Brightness Constancy.

Two photographs of a shadow. The one on the right has the penumbra covered by the heavy black line.

face (giving the surface a somewhat filmy appearance), (2) as clinging to the surface or (3) as detached, tridimensional, space-filling shadows. The great painter, Leonardo da Vinci, thus distinguished fused shadows, clinging shadows and detached shadows.

The characteristic of a shadow *which makes it appear to be a shadow* is its fuzzy edge or penumbra. This fact makes possible the following experiments.

1. The first experiment is illustrated in Fig. 46. A shadow is cast on a white surface. Then the penumbra of the shadow is covered with a broad black line. As soon as this is done, the shaded area turns darker, while the shadow flattens and hardens so that, instead of a shaded white, one sees a dark area and no shadow at all.

The fact that the shaded area is no longer seen in shadow proves, as has been said, that the perception of shadow requires the presence of the penumbra. The other fact, that the shaded area turns darker, shows that a shadow exerts its full darkening effect only in the absence of the penumbra, *i.e.*, when the shadow as such is not perceived. Conversely a shadowed object tends to retain its normal brightness so long as the shadow is perceived as shadow.

2. The influence of the penumbra can be demonstrated also as follows. By suspending a circular object between a white disk and the source of illumination it is possible to cast a shadow on the disk so that shadow and disk coincide. Such a fitting of the shadow to the disk causes the sharp contour of the disk to prevail over the soft contour of the shadow. The white disk then turns dark, and no shadow is seen. If, however, the shadow-casting object is moved slightly to one side, so that the shadow no longer coincides precisely with the disk, the shadow becomes visible and the disk resumes its normal brightness.

A black disk may, in turn, be lightened by projecting upon it a cone of light that coincides with the circular area of the disk. The black appearance of the disk can then be restored by moving the projection lantern so that the light no longer exactly coincides with the area of the disk. The perception of high light, like the perception of shadow, depends upon the contour. Thus it comes about that, whenever we see an object in shadow or examine it in the light of a desk lamp, our perception of its brightness is influenced by its special illumination, whether shadow or high light.

3. The observer (*O*) faces two disks (*A* and *B* in Fig. 47, I) that are illuminated from a window (*W*). Between the disks is a screen (*S*) that casts a shadow on the white disk *A*. On disk *B* (the comparison disk) are sectors of white and black which are adjusted so that, when the disk is rotated, the observer will see an unshadowed white that *matches* the shadowed white of the other disk. Such a match is photographed

in Part I of Fig. 48. The disks, of course, do not match for the camera because reflection is less from the shadowed than from the unshadowed disk.

In front of the two disks a *reduction screen* (*R*) is then placed. The screen has two holes, so placed that only part of one disk is seen through each opening (Fig. 47, II). Since the screen reduces the perception by eliminating the cues for shadow, one no longer sees the shadow as shadow; hence

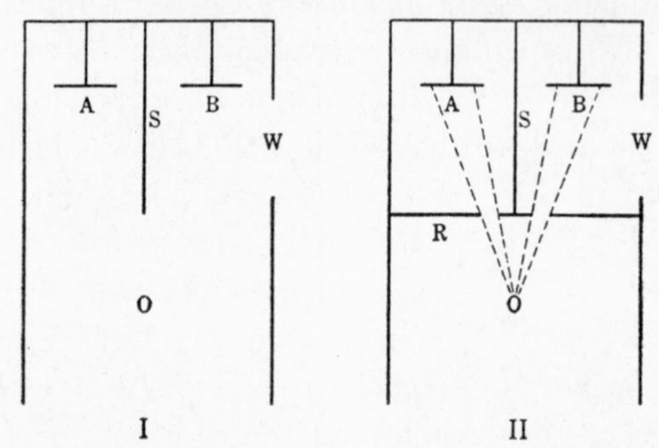

FIG. 47. PLAN OF AN EXPERIMENT IN BRIGHTNESS CONSTANCY.

As seen from above. The meaning of the symbols is given in the text. In No. I there is no reduction screen. The dotted lines in No. II show the parts of the disks that can be seen through the holes in the reduction screen (R). After D. Katz, *Aufbau der Farbwelt,* 2nd ed., Leipzig: J. A. Barth, 1930, 210; by permission of the publisher.

disk *A*, observed through the opening, is seen not as a shadowed white but as an unshadowed dark area. This change in brightness is confirmed by again matching the two disks. Part II of Fig. 48 shows the second match photographed. Since this time reflection is equal for the two disks, the matched disks now also match for the camera.

The phenomenon of constancy presents a problem for painters. "Every painter represents a white object in shadow by means of *gray* pigment and, if he has correctly imitated nature, it appears pure white."

We may then sum up our discussion of shadowed objects by saying that our sensitivity to shadows exerts a direct and useful effect upon the perception of object-brightness. By making for brightness constancy it enables us to identify objects observed under different circumstances, in shadow and out of shadow.

The role of general illumination. Our sensitivity to

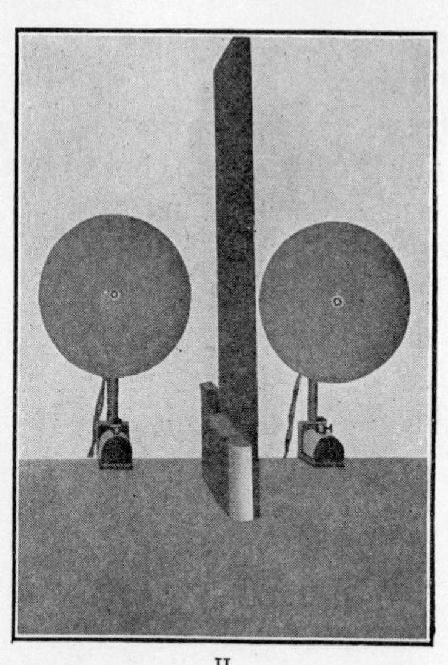

I II

Fig. 48. Two Photographs Showing Brightness Constancy.

The light comes from a window (not shown) on the right. The disks on the left in both pictures are white, and both stand in shadows cast by the vertical screens. Each of the disks on the right contains sectors of black and white adjusted to match the shadowed surface of the left-hand disk. No. I shows the match made without, and No. II the match made with the reduction screen. After D. Katz, *Aufbau der Farbwelt,* 2nd ed., Leipzig: J. A. Barth, 1930, 211; by permission of the publisher.

the general illumination makes for brightness constancy also. In moonlight as well as in sunlight, a white wall looks whitish; that is to say, the object appears the same under different illuminations. This fact becomes puzzling as soon as we realize that the amounts of light reflected into the eye differ enormously. How great that difference may be is brought home to us by the estimate that sunlight is *800,000* times as strong as full moonlight. If, instead of being more or less constant, the brightness of objects varied directly with the amount of light they reflect, we should find life very confusing. The white wall, for example, in moonlight would look black. Up to noon, when sunlight is most intense, all objects would grow whiter;

and from noon on, they would gradually turn blacker. Similarly, the paper of this book would look white near the window, but dark gray at the other end of the room.

Brightness constancy in general illumination can be illustrated in yet another way. Under any illumination, the best white paper reflects only 60 times as much light as the deepest black paper. Consequently, by placing the black paper in an illumination that is but 60 times greater than that of the white paper, one can make the two surfaces—black and white—reflect into the eye the *same amount of light* and thus stimulate the retina with equal intensity. We know, nevertheless, that the two surfaces will not look alike. The black surface will be seen as a black in high illumination, the other as a white in a lower illumination. Nor does it make any difference in this experiment whether or not the observer knows beforehand that the papers are black and white.

That we are sensitive to the *total* stimulation of the retina is shown by the fact that we can perceive an illuminated field without objects. Thus in a certain disease of the eye, the light entering the pupil, instead of being concentrated by the lens so as to form a sharp image, scatters over the entire retina with the result that stimulation is homogeneous, all of a kind. In such a case the visual field is a diffuse bright or dark mass. The brightness of the mass varies, of course, with the intensity of the light entering the eye, so that a perception of the prevailing illumination is possible. The visual field also takes on this character even to the normal eye when a person is surrounded by heavy mist, looks out from the window of a bathysphere or enters a room inside a glacier. The only light that enters the room comes through the ice and is a uniform blue. Since stimulation is homogeneous, the person inside the glacier does not see the walls at all but only a field of blue illumination.

When we close our eyes or enter a lightless room, we say that we see nothing. What we mean is that we see no objects. Only the truly blind, who lack retinal stimulation altogether, see literally nothing at any time. Normally, the retina is active even in the absence of light, for there is a source of stimulation in the eye itself. It is because local differences of stimulation are lacking that one does not see objects in the dark. One does, however, see a dark field—an objectless space. This seemingly futile form of perceiving depends upon the uniform stimulation of the retina as a whole.

Color constancy. Color constancy is just like brightness constancy in that colorless objects tend to remain colorless even under colored illumination. As every photographer knows, the white photographic film seen in the dark room under red illumination looks not red but white. When the conditions are right, colored objects too retain their color under different colored illuminations. Seen through the reduction screen, a green disk in red illumination looks practically colorless; yet in ordinary illumination it retains much of its greenish appearance.

Constancy in animal perception. The aspect of perception with which we are dealing here is not solely a human achievement. Both brightness and color constancy have been demonstrated in certain animal species. Chickens, for instance, were trained to peck food from the lighter of two sheets of paper. Then, in the decisive or critical experiment, the darker paper was placed under direct sunlight in such a way that it reflected considerably more light than the lighter paper. Yet the chickens continued to feed from the same paper as before. The papers remained, for the chickens, constant in brightness despite the change of illumination.

In another experiment, chickens were trained to eat only ordinary white rice and to ignore colored rice. Somewhat later white rice was placed under colored illumination alongside colored rice in ordinary illumination. The experimenter could not tell them apart when he looked at them through the reduction screen. But the chickens were not fooled. They could still tell which rice was white even under colored illumination.

CONTOUR PERCEPTION

In the last section we met with a peculiar case of imperception: the disappearance of a shadow when its penumbra is modified, when its characteristic contour is changed. We shall now discover that *contours* are in fact fundamental to both perception and imperception.

Contour perception, we shall also see, includes more than the perception of the outline of objects. It takes many forms, of which but three will be considered here: first, the *perception of object and background* ('figure and ground'), and then *surface perception* and *contour in touch.*

The perception of object and background. In 1912 a Danish psychologist was puzzled by the behavior of his sub-

FIG. 49. REVERSAL OF OBJECT AND BACKGROUND.
From E. Rubin, *Visuell wahrgenommene Figuren,* Copenhagen: Gyldendalske Boghandel, 1921, Abb. 3; by permission of the publisher.

jects in an experiment in learning. He had cut irregular holes in squares of cardboard in order, by means of a lantern, to project the silhouettes on a screen. At the second showing of the silhouettes he tested the subjects for recognition. Although recognition is the simplest task of learning, in this experiment it turned out to be more difficult than was expected.

The difficulty, it was discovered, lay in a peculiarity of contouring, a peculiarity exemplified in Fig. 49.

This figure shows a white vase against a black background, and that is what one is likely to see at first glance. As one continues to look, however, the vase disappears. Instead one sees two faces in profile, black and white. As observation is continued further, the profiles too vanish and the vase reappears. This fluctuation or reversal will go on so long as the figure remains under observation.

We have assumed that the vase will be seen first because it is in the center of the figure, and a central position favors the perception of a thing as foreground-object (or *figure*) rather than as background (or *ground*). Some individuals, on the other hand, see the profiles first; perhaps for them the factor of sociality outweighs that of centrality. Now what happened in the recognition experiment mentioned above was that the silhouettes, seen by the observers first in one way, reversed themselves on the second showing and so became quite unrecognizable. Obviously, a man who had seen a vase an hour before but now sees two profiles would declare that the figure is entirely new.

FIG. 50. REVERSAL OF OBJECT AND BACKGROUND.
From E. C. Sanford, *A course in experimental psychology,* 1898, 254; reprinted by permission of D. C. Heath & Co.

Similar reversals of object and background may be observed in an outline map; the bodies of water are sometimes mistaken for land masses, with the result that objects and background are reversed. So, too, when one is examining a puzzle picture or an inverted painting, reversal is likely to occur. The same observation can be made in Figs. 50, 51 and 52. *Such fluctuation is not a matter of attention.* It cannot be prevented by concentrating. When the vase disappears, in Fig. 49, it does not simply become less clear, or less obvious. It is, on the contrary, not perceived at all; its place is taken by background. Here is an excellent illustration of imperception. Contour, we see, determines both perception and imperception. So in camouflage,

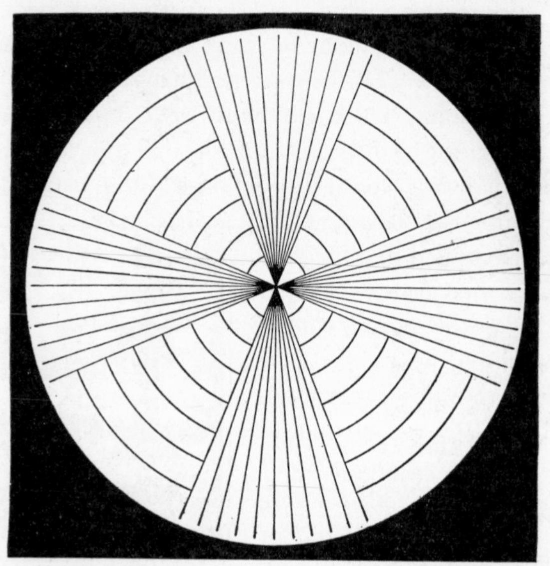

Fig. 51. Reversal of Object and Background.
From E. Rubin, *Visuell wahrgenommene Figuren,* Copenhagen: Gyldendalske Boghandel, 1921, Abb. 5; by permission of the publisher.

Fig. 52. A Hidden Square.
From F. Schumann, *Zsch. f. Psychol.,* 1900, 23, 13.

both human and animal, imperception is achieved by breaking up contours.

Of special interest in these reversals is the behavior of the boundary or contour that separates the object from the background. Observing the line of separation between the white and black areas in Fig. 49, we note that the contour is *unilateral*; it acts in only one direction. When the vase is seen, the contour bounds and shapes the white area. The black area, on the other hand, seems to continue uninterrupted behind the white. The contour has no effect upon the background; it neither limits nor shapes it. When the profiles appear, the contour turns the other way. Now it limits and defines the black area, while the white area continues behind the black. Again the contour bounds the object or figure without limiting or shaping the background. This feature of contour, its one-sided action, is fundamental to the discrimination of objects.

The perception of surface. The term contour may be extended to include both surface and outline. A surface, like an outline, serves to bound or delimit the object. The perception of surface is the perception of surface boundary or surface contour, whereas the perception of outline is the perception of outline contour.

That surface and outline undergo parallel changes under certain conditions is made evident in the following experiments.

1. *Adaptation.* If an object is observed steadily, without eye movement, its outline becomes blurred, fuzzy and irregular. Let fixation be continued long enough, and the object may disappear entirely, merging indistinguishably with the background. Along with the breaking down of the outline, the object's surface disintegrates also; it becomes soft, fluffy, thick, shadowy, filmy. The object is *de-surfaced.*

2. *Peripheral vision.* Such parallel changes in outline and in surface occur also in peripheral vision, that is to say, when one is observing a thing out of the corner of the eye. We all know how under those circumstances both outline and surface become blurred, fuzzy and filmy.

3. *Faint and distant objects.* The same changes may be observed in faint and distant objects. If a faint light projected

from behind on a translucent screen is gradually made brighter, both outline and surface, indefinite at first, end by becoming firm and definite.

4. *Reduction screen.* De-surfacing is strikingly demonstrated by use of the reduction-screen. The screen, which has a small hole in the center, is placed in front of an object in such a way that the object's outline is invisible through the hole. When seen in this way *the object appears de-surfaced.* Seen through the screen-hole, it is simply a mass of color; a finger or pencil inserted into the hole seems to *penetrate and become immersed in the color mass.*

5. *Complete loss of surface-vision.* The preceding account of de-surfaced vision, reported just before the World War, proved unexpectedly useful. There was, for example, a soldier, hospitalized with a gunshot wound in the back of the head, who exhibited certain peculiarities of behavior. Frequently he stumbled on the stairs or dropped his cup on the table, excusing himself by saying that things did not seem to be where they were. The routine tests of vision revealed no explanation. Then it was that a psychologist who was assisting the hospital physicians recalled the phenomenon of de-surfaced vision. He tested the patient by asking him to bring his finger just up to the object. *The patient's finger stopped an inch or more from the surface.* When, upon request, he moved his finger until he *felt* the surface, the finger seemed to him to penetrate the object! The distance of penetration he estimated to be one or two inches in the case of white objects, and *from six to eight inches* in the case of black objects; *i.e.,* dark surfaces looked nearer and thicker than light surfaces. His own dark hair seen in the mirror, and his black military boots, looked to him startlingly thick and massive.

Along with this de-surfaced vision went certain accompanying peculiarities in outline-vision. Asked to point to the edge of an object, the soldier again stopped before touching it. When finger and edge were brought into contact, the penetration-effect was repeated. The object swelled laterally as well as forward; both surface and outline were out of bounds. Once more it is evident that surface perception and outline perception go together.

Contour in touch. In touch, the typical contour discriminates two contact-surfaces: body-surface and object-surface. When, for example, the finger is touched with a pencil, two objects—finger and pencil—are discriminated. *Yet stimulation is single.* Lay the hand on the table. Two object-surfaces are discriminated: the cool, hard, flat table-surface, and the warm, soft, somewhat curved surface of the palm. The same duality may be observed in touching the forehead with the hand, but in this case stimulation is itself dual.

When the table-surface is felt through a cloth, three objects are discriminated: finger, cloth and table. The cloth in this case becomes a medium through which the table is felt, a fact which means that there is 'transparency' in touch as well as in vision. Other instances of 'transparent' touch are the feeling of objects through gloves, the ground through shoes or walking stick, ice through skates, the billiard ball through the cue, a weight through the string or handle by which it is lifted, a piece of wood through the saw, a bone through the skin, the curb through the wheel of the automobile. In this manner objects may become extensions of the body. To poke at an object with a stick is to make the stick into an elongated finger. Similarly a tall hat or a large coat or even an automobile may extend the perceptual radius of its owner—they make us feel bigger.

FLUCTUATION

Cases of perceptual instability, where perception changes although the stimulating object does not itself alter, are of especial interest for the way they point to internal conditions of perception.

We are already familiar with fluctuations in perception, one type of instability, which we encountered when observing the reversal of object and background in Figs. 49, 50, 51 and 52. Fluctuations of all sorts are common enough in ordinary perception. In poor illumination or at a distance, indeed, we often find it difficult to tell what an object is. Now it seems to be one thing, now another. We experience the same difficulty when a person addressing us speaks indistinctly, or with an unfamiliar pronounciation.

What is called retinal rivalry furnishes interesting examples

FIG. 53. AN EQUIVOCAL STIMULUS.
Reproduced by permission of Winter Thomas Advertising Company, Ltd.

of fluctuation. If, for example, two diagrams differing in shape are presented separately to the two eyes in a stereoscope, it is difficult to get a composite view; perception fluctuates from one of the single views to the other (see p. 459). Fluctuation is likely to occur also when one is listening to a series of equal metronome beats. Even without any rhythmical intention on the part of the listener, the beats fall now into one rhythm, now into another. Faint stimuli are inherently subject to fluctuation; a faint sound, for example, is heard only intermittently.

Often a simple change in external conditions serves to stabilize a fluctuating perception. The object may be approached more closely or brought into a better light. We ask a person to repeat what he has said, hoping that he will speak more distinctly. Or we prevail upon him to write out what he wants to say—although, on the other hand, nothing is so subject to annoying fluctuation as badly written words. In the same way, though fluctuation is likely to go on indefinitely in the vase-profiles (Fig. 49), the figure will stay put if proper shading is introduced.

Although fluctuation may be thus averted by improving the stimulus conditions, stabilization is essentially a process of *internal readjustment.* Fig. 53, for example, is seen at first glance as a mess of streaks. As one continues to look, the figure suddenly takes on the appearance of a man smoking a cigarette. Here, however, fluctuation does *not* continue. Once the facial contours establish themselves, perception remains stable; there is no fluctuation. It is practically impossible to see the figure again as a haphazard collection of ink smears.

GROUPING

Certain designs are hard on the eyes. Looking at a sheet of paper filled with equally spaced small dots may give one a dizzy feeling. Fluctuation is the reason for this phenomenon. The dots try, as it were, to arrange themselves in one grouping and then in another, but stable grouping is never achieved; fluctuation is incessant.

Law of similarity. An obvious way of introducing stable grouping in the dot-design is to introduce variety, either in the dots themselves or in the spacing between the dots. Making some of them of a different color (as is done in tests for color blindness) or, better still, giving them different shapes and sizes will allow the *similar* objects to be grouped together. When we look at three persons standing near a lamp post, we do not see a foursome, but rather a grouping into three persons and one lamp post. Similarity is the basis of the grouping. That birds of a feather flock together is a law of perception.

Law of spacing. Unequal *spacing*, too, will permit stable group formation. Objects close together are grouped together. Because of their spacing the stars in the sky group themselves into constellations. This same spacing factor is responsible also for the illusion of the 'magnetic eye.' Particles of chalk scattered over a mirror-surface arrange themselves into what look like magnetic lines of force—even though there is no magnet. The mirror, by reflection, doubles the chalk-particles, and the closer spacing thus produced favors the grouping of the particles into lines.

ADAPTATION

One variety of instability and internal readjustment that lends itself to direct observation is the process of adaptation and its negative after-effect.

Size adaptation. As one looks in a magnifying mirror, one's face, at first enormous and brobdingnagian, is perceived as gradually diminishing to normal size. A process of readjustment or adaptation is taking place. Thereafter, if one looks in an ordinary mirror, the face seems small and lilliputian. Likewise, the puppets in a puppet show soon grow in stature, until immediately after the show human actors on the same stage look like giants.

Directional adaptation. The perception of direction shows similar changes. A curved line, when observation is continued, gradually grows less curved. If a straight line is then substituted, it will appear curved in the opposite direction.

The following incident may illustrate such change in curvature. In the upper story of an old university building the wooden stairs are hollowed out with use. After one has walked down this flight of stairs, the remaining stairs, which have a new and even surface, are felt as being bumpy, as curved *upward*. So compelling is the impression that one automatically adjusts one's manner of walking to the illusory bumps.

This sort of negative after-effect is especially pronounced in the perception of movement. After looking at a waterfall, or undergoing rotation, one perceives movement in a contrary direction (see pp. 488, 625).

The after-effect has also been observed in stationary objects. If the head is kept turned to the *right* for a time and then brought back, a line directly in front will be seen as displaced to the *left*.

Utility of contrast. The negative after-effects just described exhibit the process of readjustment in exaggerated form. Milder instances—and they, of course, are the rule—are generally useful in that the negative after-effect serves, by contrast, to enhance or emphasize differences. A dessert tastes sweeter after a salad, and the sour is in turn enhanced after the neutral savor of the roast. Sunshine is brighter after cloudy days. The relaxed ease of a vacation is greater after long-sustained labor. Variety, it is said, is the spice of life, and perceptual contrast heightens variety. By this same principle of contrast the artist's work is freshened and accented. The architect relieves a monotonous space with a bit of decoration. The painter creates a focal point of interest by toning down everything else. The musician, composing his symphony, contrasts the andante with a scherzo. Perceptual contrast emphasizes these objective differences.

REFERENCES

1. Ellis, W. D. *A source book of Gestalt psychology.* New York: Harcourt, Brace, 1938. Esp. pp. 1-263.
2. Gibson, J. J. Adaptation, after-effect, and contrast in the perception of curved lines. *J. exper. Psychol.,* 1933, 16, 1-32.
3. Katz, D. *The world of color.* London: Kegan Paul, 1935.
4. MacLeod, R. B. An experimental investigation of brightness constancy. *Arch. Psychol.,* 1932, 135, 1-102.
5. Metzger, W. *Gesetze des Sehens.* Frankfurt: Kramer, 1936.

6. THOULESS, R. H. Phenomenal regression to the real object. *Brit. J. Psychol.,* 1931, 21, 339-359; 22, 1-30.
7. VERNON, M. D. *Visual perception.* Cambridge, England: University Press, 1937.
8. WOODWORTH, R. S. *Experimental psychology.* New York: Henry Holt, 1938. Chaps. 24 and 25.

Chapter 14

SPATIAL PERCEPTION

Nearly all animals are capable of locomotion and other types of movement. When an animal moves, he brings his own characteristic motor apparatus into adjustment with the spatial features of his surroundings—an adjustment which is achieved by the cooperation of several agencies. External receptors of the animal register spatial changes in his surroundings; internal receptors register spatial changes produced by his own movements; and the upper levels of the nervous system do the adjusting.

The following spatial features, dependent upon the characteristic structure of a person and his geographical surroundings, are of particular significance in the perception of space. (1) We are capable, first of all, of perception of the vertical, a perception related to the maintenance of upright position. (2) Then there is, in addition, the perception of bodily orientation; in other words, a person perceives the position in which his body happens to be at the moment, whether he is standing upright, lying horizontally or in some other position. (3) An individual is also able to distinguish between free space which permits locomotion or other movement, and objects which offer resistance to movement. (4) He perceives space itself as tridimensional—as extending in distance and in all directions. The principal directions in space are for him: front and back, right and left, up and down. The perception of the vertical, however, has unique status, for the momentary position of the body is always perceived relative to the vertical, or as a deviation from the vertical. (5) Then, too, we perceive

---

This chapter, written by Robert B. MacLeod of Swarthmore College and H. P. Weld of Cornell University, is based upon a similar chapter by Warner Brown in Boring, Langfeld and Weld, *Psychology: A factual textbook*, 1935.

the position of objects in space, a capacity which we call localization. An object or a sound may be perceived as at a certain distance in front of or behind the body, as to the right or to the left, above or below the body. Objects may also be perceived as touching one part or another of the body itself, or, in addition, as localized in relation to each other. One building may be perceived as to the right of another building, to the left of it, in front of it, or behind it. One picture may be perceived as above or below another. Localization, then, includes both the perception of direction and of distance; moreover, it always involves at least two objects, one of which acts as a point of reference for the other. Since, therefore, the position of an object or a sound is perceived in relation to the body or to some other object, position is always relative. (6) Relative position, however, is only one of the spatial properties which we observe in objects, for we also perceive their orientation—whether for example, a stick is in a horizontal position, or vertical, or extending away from us in depth, or in some other position. (7) In addition, we take into account an object's shape, and size, and other spatial details.

Spatial perception has many aspects. We shall deal more or less separately with *direction* (direction in space, orientation of the body, orientation of other objects), *localization* (relative direction and distance of the body and other objects from each other), *size* and *shape*, even though perception is unitary, and we do not ordinarily perceive place, shape, size and other spatial features separately. Perception at any moment generally includes a whole array of objects and, more or less prominently, one's own body and the surrounding medium.

SOMESTHETIC SPACE PERCEPTION

To the seeing person vision is of such primary importance for the perceiving of the positions, shapes and sizes of objects that he is likely to forget how adequate spatial perception can be without benefit of vision. The predominance of vision even makes it difficult for the seeing person to get a clear idea of what spatial perception of the non-visual sort is like; how, for example, it feels to grope one's way about in an unfamiliar room in the dark. In such a case the individual is guided, not by visual stimulation, but by touch and by the perceptions of his own movements. Such perceptions are called *somesthetic* (see pp. 505f., 618-620).

Perception of free space. In achieving some inkling of the space perception that is somesthetic, we may be helped by recalling our own experiences while walking in the dark or swimming under water with closed eyes. We may remember, in the first place, what it is like to feel the body move unimpeded through space or water. At such times we perceive the medium about us, and ourselves as moving through it. Specifically, the medium is perceived as a region of possible locomotion or movement. Let us call such a region, whether empty or aqueous, *free space*.

But we may recall, secondly, a time when, groping our way through the dark or stroking through the water, the hand or some other part of the body comes into contact with an obstruction, an obstacle, some resistance to movement. The obstacle is at once perceived as an object, as a thing that impedes one's movement A moment's consideration of this experience will help us to realize the difference between free space and an object. Nor are detached objects the only obstacles; the ground upon which we walk, or which we may touch while swimming, is likewise an object offering resistance.

Perception of direction. In the dark or under water we also perceive direction. Even under water the normal person can tell when he is swimming to the bottom or to the surface. No one with normal sense organs has ever drowned by swimming to the bottom when he intended to come to the surface. For some deaf people, on the other hand, swimming under water is dangerous, because they lose their sense of direction. The reason for this loss is a type of injury to the ear which affects not only the organ of hearing but also the adjacent organs of equilibrium (see pp. 621-625) so important in the perception of direction.

The fact that the normal person can distinguish between swimming up and down means that he relates the momentary posture of his body to certain fixed directions of space. These fixed directions act as a frame of reference for the perception of body posture. It is by relating his posture to this frame of reference that each of us perceives himself as standing upright, as lying horizontally, as swimming in an inclined position or as keeling over. When one stands upright he perceives the posture of his body as coinciding with the vertical dimension of space. *Up* in that case means the same thing as the direction of the head. If, however, one lies in a horizontal position and is asked to point up, he does not point to his head but up. We distinguish between the momentary posture of the body and the fixed directions of space.

Under certain circumstances our perception of direction changes. With it, consequently, the perception of body posture changes also. People who ride on a merry-go-round lean inwards as the speed of rotation increases; they shift their postures to avoid flying off at a tangent. Provided, however, that their eyes are closed, the riders think that they are sitting upright, for their perception of the vertical has changed. When a person with a defect of his organs of equilibrium is placed on the merry-go-round with eyes closed, he sits upright. If he is asked to hold up a stick vertically, he will hold it almost vertically, but a normal man will hold it at a decided slant. Like body posture, the direction of other objects is perceived by relating it to the directions of space.

The accuracy of our perception of direction has been measured. A person strapped to a tilting board and blindfolded is likely to make an error of about 5° in his perception of the vertical as he is tilted, and a larger error in his perception of the horizontal. In judging the direction of a stick held in his hand he makes corresponding errors.

Somesthetic localization. When a person operates in familiar surroundings, localization is easy. He can close his eyes while sitting at his desk, and then reach accurately toward the bookcase on the right. The child can point to his nose. Anyone can run up a familiar staircase in the dark with confidence. Such localization is obviously a product of learning. Through learning we have acquired a spatial schema of the parts of the body, and of our surroundings. Any individual part of the body, or any environmental object, is then localized with reference to this schema.

When we find ourselves in unfamiliar surroundings, however, the environmental portion of our acquired schema becomes inadequate. Left with only a body schema—one's knowledge of his own body and its parts—we use this guide alone in localizing objects. We localize objects thus when groping about in a dark unfamiliar place, or when playing blindman's buff or when swimming under water. A jagged rock encountered under water is localized as being at the foot or at the fingers, or at the elbow—in short, at whatever part of the body that is touched.

This type of localization, exclusively by reference to the body, has been studied experimentally. In experiments on the accuracy of cutaneous localization, the subject, touched while his eyes are closed, is required to point to the part of the body touched or to a drawn model of it. That a person always carries with him a schema of his body is shown by the fact that he can localize the spot as well upon a drawn model as upon the body itself.

Precision of localization varies greatly from one part of the body to another. If we blindfold an observer and touch him lightly on the finger tip, he can usually localize the point with an error of less than 2 mm. On the lips the error is even smaller; but on the back of the hand it may average 5 mm., and on the thigh or back it may be as great as several centimeters. In general, localization is best on those parts of the body which move, such as hands, feet and lips.

Localization of objects in the mouth is in principle no different from localization on the body surface. Whether the object tastes or is tasteless seems to make no difference.

Pressure, pain and temperature aroused by internal stimulation, on the contrary, are at best only vaguely localized in a general region of the body, and may in some cases seem to be far from their point of origin. Clinical studies of internally aroused pain show that aches and dull pains are referred to an internal region, sharp pains to the surface of the body. Similarly, pressure in the mid-regions of the esophagus may be localized at regions just above or just below the breast bone.

In pathological cases resulting from brain disorders the body schema may be seriously disrupted, with corresponding disturbances of localization. In the extreme case the patient is helpless when he is asked to indicate various parts of his body. A more common case is that in which the patient, confusing right and left, feels a touch on the right arm, for instance, at a corresponding position on the left arm. There are on record several cases in which the patient, paralyzed on one side of the body, has behaved as though that side were nonexistent, feeling all touches in corresponding places on the unparalyzed side. It is as though the functionally useless part of the body were ignored, and the body schema appropriately reconstructed. An opposite type of observation is made in cases of amputation. In spite of the loss of the leg, for instance, the body schema may remain intact, with the missing leg replaced by a 'phantom' leg in which clearly localized pains and pressures may be felt. With the passage of time the phantom limb gradually diminishes in size and finally, though sometimes only after many years, disappears.

Spatial perception of the blind. The spatial perception of the blind is like the spatial perception we have been discussing. A blind person distinguishes between free space and objects. He perceives, too, the fixed directions of space, by reference to which he knows his own posture and the postures of other objects. Like the seeing, the blind person acquires a schema of his surroundings, a schema composed of the familiar chairs and tables of his room or the familiar houses, fences and lamp posts of the street in which he walks. On familiar ground he moves more confidently than the blindfolded normal person, practiced as he is in somesthetic localization.

What is known as the 'warning sense' of the blind—his perception of the presence of an object in his near neighborhood—seems to be due to changes in temperature, or in the pressure of air, occasioned by the object. This 'sense,' which is referred by the blind to the face, has been called 'facial vision,' as if the blind man could train his skin to see. The fact that the blind are guided thus by changes in temperature is interesting in that it shows they have an equivalent for the seeing person's perception of shadow. A building, we might say, casts a temperature shadow. On windy days even persons of normal vision notice this fact, seeking shelter from the blustering gale in the lee of a building. The blind use such temperature differences as a matter of course.

Tactual perception of size and shape. Most of our knowledge of tactual size derives from experiments with two-point stimulation. When two points on the skin are simultaneously stimulated, they will, unless separated by a sufficient distance, feel like a single point. The amount of this separation is known as the 'two-point threshold.' Different separations are found for different parts of the body, and the amounts themselves, like all threshold values, are averages of

TABLE XXVIII

Representative Values of the Two-Point Threshold

	Mm.
Tip of the tongue	1
Palmar side of the last phalanx of the finger	2
Red part of the lips	5
Palmar side of the second and dorsal side of the third phalanx of the finger	7
White of the lips, and metacarpus of the thumb	9
Cheek, and plantar side of the last phalanx of the great toe	11
Dorsal side of the first phalanx of the finger	16
Skin on the back part of cheek-bone, and forehead	23
Back of the hand	31
Kneepan, and surrounding region	36
Forearm, lower leg	40
Back of foot, neck, chest	54
Middle of the back, and of the upper arm and leg	68

a variable sensitivity. Table XXVIII gives values representative of the relative magnitudes of two-point thresholds.

The two-point threshold is usually considered as a measure of cutaneous acuity. It has further significance, however, in that it furnishes us with information about the conditions of tactual shape and size. When the distance between the two stimuli is less than the two-point threshold, the observer may report a continuous pattern on his skin—an elongated bar, an ellipse or a dumb-bell. In other words, one perceives continuity when adjacent receptors are stimulated. There is some evidence that tactual size varies inversely with the magnitude of the two-point threshold; for example, a stimulus pattern is felt as smaller on the back, where discrimination is poor, than on the finger or tongue, where discrimination is good.

Ordinarily, however, tactual perceptions of objects are based not on passive stimulation—as when objects are placed on the skin—but on active or exploratory stimulation—as when the hand moves over the object. The latter method reduces the two-point threshold considerably, increasing at the same time the accuracy of tactual perceptions of size. Yet the superiority of active over passive touch is not necessarily to be explained in terms of kinesthesis, since movement of an object over the surface of the skin is almost as effective as movement of the hand or tongue over the object. When, furthermore, tactual stimuli are eliminated by means of cutaneous anesthesia, even active exploration gives a poor impression of the size of an object. It is active touch, too, that brings us our clearest impressions of tridimensionality. As the fingers or the hands close about an object, we know it for a solid object, not simply an array of pressures on the surface of the skin.

As in the case of visual perception, the tactual size of an object may be influenced by changes in the immediately surrounding conditions. Relationships of contrast and such 'illusions' as those in Fig. 69 are as pronounced in the tactual as in the visual field, and are perceived even by people who have been blind from birth.

VISUAL AND SOMESTHETIC SPACE PERCEPTION

Vision and somesthesis may, in many instances, be used independently as equivalents. Either one gives us the distinction between objects and free space. The blind man localizes an object by touching it with his fingers or with his cane; the seeing person can, in addition, localize by vision. In solving a jigsaw puzzle the seeing person uses his eyes in finding the pieces of the right size and shape; but he could, if he tried, do the same thing by touch.

To be sure, the parallel use of the two senses sometimes yields results that are not quite equivalent. To the tongue a cavity in a tooth seems enormous, whereas to the eye it seems minute. Tongue and eye thus seem to use different scales in the assessment of size. A blindfolded person who identifies an object placed in his hands may, on removing the blindfold, find the object to be quite different from what he had described.

It would be a mistake, however, to suppose that the two senses always function separately. In fact, they usually function together. Normally they develop together, and in the course of development they interact with each other. We shall, therefore, not be surprised to find important relations between the two.

VISUAL PERCEPTION OF DIRECTION

The eyes are like two cameras set on a movable support, to the end that they may command a view in all directions. A person may note what is ahead of him and also what is behind him; what is above, below, to the right of and to the left of him. As he turns, the eye cameras swing with him and one retinal image follows another.

The retinal image itself provides no indication of *the direction* in which one is looking. That one is looking now ahead, now to the side, and now behind is known on the basis of somesthesis. Visual perception, then, works in conjunction with somesthesis. Eye and body cooperate.

Neither does the retina alone determine the orientation of an object; the position of the body is always taken into account. Suppose that at high noon one looks at the face of a clock on a wall. Standing with head erect, one sees the hands of the clock to be vertical; both point upward. They will, however, continue to be seen as vertical whether one turns his head to the one side or the other, whether one peers at the clock while lying down or while standing on his head. With every different position of the head, nevertheless, different receptors in the retina are stimulated. Direction in visual perception is determined, therefore, by reference to the body. We have here another case of constancy similar to that discussed in the previous chapter. Despite retinal displacement stationary objects in the visual field are seen in a fixed position, because the observer takes into account those movements of his own body which are responsible for the displacement.

These relations between vision and somesthesis provide a reliable basis for movements of localization. One reaches with confidence for his hat or for a friend's outstretched hand. Under certain circumstances, however, the normal relations between vision and somesthesis are altered. When, for example, one looks in a mirror, he sees the right-left direction reversed; a mole on the right cheek is seen as on the left. Movements that are guided by the mirror-images are at first confused. The correct movements have to be learned; yet once learned they are as sure and precise as in situations without mirroring. At the same time, the perceived relations in the mirror remain reversed—the mole is still seen on the wrong side. This fact, that perceived reversal persists though our movements readjust themselves, has been demonstrated in a striking manner.

In normal vision the retinal image is upside down, like the image on the film in a camera. It is possible, however, by placing a suitable system of lenses in front of the eyes, to obtain an upright retinal image. This experiment has actually been tried. The experimenter, who wore an extra set of lenses for several days, saw the entire landscape upside down, the sky below the horizon, and the ground above. Whenever he wanted to make a turn or to reach for things, naturally he got into difficulty. He would reach for his shoe and find his hat. By the end of eight days, however, his movements had become adjusted to the new relations to such an extent that he was able to find his way about with a fairly high degree of confidence. Yet the retinal field of excitation remained reversed.

The relation between eye and body in determining visual direction has also been shown in a number of other experiments. In a dark room an observer, strapped to a board in a vertical position, is tipped sidewise from the vertical. If the board is moved slowly and without jerks, the observer fails to notice the tipping; he still perceives himself as in a vertical position. Thereupon a dim vertical line is shown in the dark room. Under these conditions the line may be perceived as tipped. In short, the direction of the seen line is determined by the actual position of the body.

Under other conditions vision influences the perception of the vertical. If the dark room is slightly illuminated, the line is perceived as vertical despite the inclined position of the observer's body. Likewise, when the blindfold is removed from the rider on the merry-go-round, he at once perceives the inclined position of both his own body and the stick in his hand. In these cases the presence of other vertical lines in the visual field are the conditioning factors.

Conditions may be arranged in such fashion that there is a conflict between the eye and the body. Let an observer be seated in a lighted room so constructed that it can be rotated about him, and, even though the body is stationary, a slight tipping of the room will be felt as in the body, not as in the room. If then the room is tipped still farther, a point will be reached at which there is a sudden reversal, whereupon the observer will feel himself as upright and the room as changing its position. If, however, the room is moved rapidly, the observer will lose his bearings; the change once again will be referred to his own body, and he may feel himself turning somersaults in space. Similarly a person sitting on the deck of a ship in a surging sea may first see the horizon rise and fall, and then suddenly see the horizon as stationary and feel himself as rising and sinking.

Mutual adjustment of eye and body. There is some evidence that when normal visual directions are changed, the organism seeks to readjust its perception to the new situation. In one experiment a mirror was tilted in such a way as to make everything in it look askew, with people walking on a tilted floor, objects dropping obliquely, etc. The observer looked through a tube which excluded everything but the mirror-image. After a few minutes of continuous observation the room tended gradually to right itself, until both the objects and the people in it came to look normal and behave in a normal way. For some observers the adjustment was complete; for others the room or objects never completely righted themselves, though the field became less strikingly tilted or the tilting was "less noticed." Evidence of readjustment is more pronounced in simpler situations. If a line that is not quite perpendicular to the floor on which the observer stands is fixated steadily for a few moments, it swings back gradually until it appears to be perfectly vertical; and a similar observation can be made with horizontal lines. Immediately after such a period of fixation, a vertical or horizontal line will appear correspondingly tipped in the opposite direction.

Lines of reference in the visual field. A vertical object in the visual field may serve as reference for the direction of another object in the same field. Thus by reference to the window frame or the bookcase we see that a picture on the wall is not hanging straight; or, when we plant a tree and want it to stand upright, we bring it into line with the vertical of the gate post or the side of the house. There may be in the visual field two different points of possible reference which will give different perceptions. A person on a railway train which is going up an incline may glance out of the window and note with astonishment that the telegraph poles are tipped away from the vertical. If then he thrusts his head out of the window, he perceives the poles as emerging vertically from the hillside. In the first case the window was the point of reference, in the second the landscape.

VISUAL PERCEPTION OF DISTANCE

In both visual and non-visual perception we perceive that space extends in the third dimension, and we localize objects at a distance. Vision, however, extends the range of distance enormously.

In principle, we can see objects at any distance away from us provided they are large enough and send enough light to the eye. A glance at the starry sky at night shows this observation to be true. The fact, however, that we see the moon, the planets and the stars at about the same distances means that our discrimination of different distances declines with the increasing distance of the objects.

In principle, again, we could, if it were not for the earth's curvature and for one object getting in the way of another, see sufficiently large objects at any distance *on* the earth. Even as it is, on a clear day we can see mountains many miles away. But, here again, distant mountain ranges that we know to be far apart are seen pushed together as on a theater curtain. Our discrimination of distance fails. For objects that are too close to the eyes the discrimination of distance is also defective. Under ordinary conditions, however, there are a number of ways in which we can tell that one object is farther away than another.

Interposition of objects. An object whose complete outline can be seen is perceived as in front of another object whose outline is broken by it (see Fig. 54).

Linear perspective. Whenever the retinal image of an object decreases in size, we tend to perceive the distance of the object as increasing, even though the perceived size of the object may not be altered. If a number of objects of the same size are distributed in front of and at different distances from the observer and their sides connected with each other by lines, these lines, as the objects appear smaller and smaller, appear to converge in the remote distance. In the same way when we look down a highway, parallel lines are perceived as converging to a point. If these lines are crossed by other lines, angles are formed in accordance with simple geometric

Fig. 54. Interposition.

principles. Thus, the right angles which are formed by the wires and cross-arms of the telegraph line are represented in Fig. 55 as a series of oblique angles but are perceived as right angles. Linear perspective is employed as one of the most reliable means of representing distance in pictures.

Fig. 55. Linear Perspective.

Aerial perspective. Remote objects are less distinct than near objects. Since dust or smoke or mist in the air reduces the distinctness with which objects can be seen, hazy objects are perceived as more distant than distinct objects (see Fig. 56). When an object, moreover, is seen as at a considerable distance, the sizes of the smaller parts—the details of the object—become so minute that they are no longer visible. The absence of detail is then taken as a sign of distance. If, on the contrary, the distant object is viewed through a telescope, so that the image is magnified and details not visible to the naked eye are seen, the magnified object appears to be nearer, not only because it occupies a larger part of the retina (according to the principles of linear perspective) but also because its

Fig. 56. Aerial Perspective.

details are more distinctly seen, as in Fig. 57. Irrespective of difference in detail, the brightness and color of an object may also be a sign of distance. Other things being equal, the brighter the object the closer it is perceived to be. Dim stars seem farther away than bright stars; when automobile lights grow brighter they are seen to approach; and objects with dull colors tend to seem farther away.

In regions where low humidity and lack of smoke leave the atmosphere very clear, it is extremely difficult for the inexperienced individual to estimate the distances of remote objects. Hills which seem only a few miles off may prove to be many times that distance away. As the very clear atmosphere reveals details of form, it frequently happens that large trees in the distance are seen as bushes, or large rock formations as much smaller ones. What appear to be small bushes on the remote hill in Fig. 58 are really trees like the one in the insert.

Fig. 57.

Fig. 58.

Light and shade. Since light normally falls from above downward upon the objects we see, it follows that the shadows of objects fall in characteristic patterns. That shadow pattern

Fig. 59. The Influence of Light and Shade.

The effect of reversing the relation of light and shade may be seen by turning the figure upside down. Reproduced by permission of Western Air Express Corp.

is an important factor in determining the relation of foreground and background may be seen by turning Fig. 59 upside down, thus reversing the relations of light and shadow.

Even when the light falls from one side or from below, the presence of shadows brings out relief.

Accommodation. In addition to the above ways of telling distance—ways that are used by every painter of landscapes—there are still others that derive from the muscular mechanism of the eyes by means of which the eyes are turned and focused on the object. Accommodation, for example, is the process whereby the rays of light reflected from an object are brought into focus on the retina. Near-accommodation is effected by a contraction in the ciliary muscles (see Fig. 60

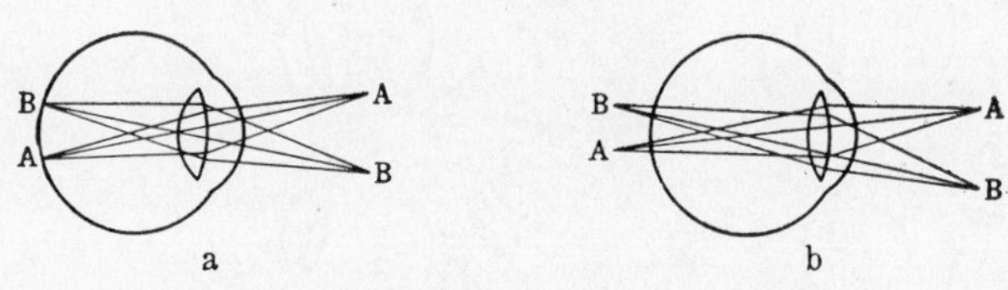

FIG. 60. THE ACCOMMODATION OF THE EYE.

In *a*, with more convex lens, the images are in focus on the retina. In *b* the focus lies behind the retina so that the images intercepted by the retina are out of focus.

and Fig. 82, p. 520) which allows an increase in the convexity of the lens. When the ciliary muscles are relaxed, the normal eye is, for all practical purposes, accommodated for any distance greater than 2 meters, although small muscular adjustments may take place up to distances of 6 meters. In this condition the eye has a universal focus analogous to that of a box camera with the lens at a fixed distance from a sensitive plate. Thus, beyond approximately 2 meters, accommodation cannot have any appreciable effect on the perception of distance. Within this region, however, any displacement of the fixated object toward or away from the eye results in a blurring of the image on the retina, and consequently an immediate readjustment of the lens in the direction of greater clarity.

For the perception of sharp contours and of surfaces, accommodation is particularly important. The eye constantly adjusts itself so as to preserve the greatest possible clarity of surface detail. If a surface is beyond the range of accommodation, then it will, other things being equal, appear filmy and indefinitely localized. If, on the other hand, the surface is in focus, its small irregularities will be clearly perceived. Under these circumstances the object will be sharply differentiated from its background and more definitely localized. Within a short range, therefore, accommodation plays a part in localization.

Convergence. The mechanism for convergence governs the cooperation of the two eyes. Normally the muscular sys-

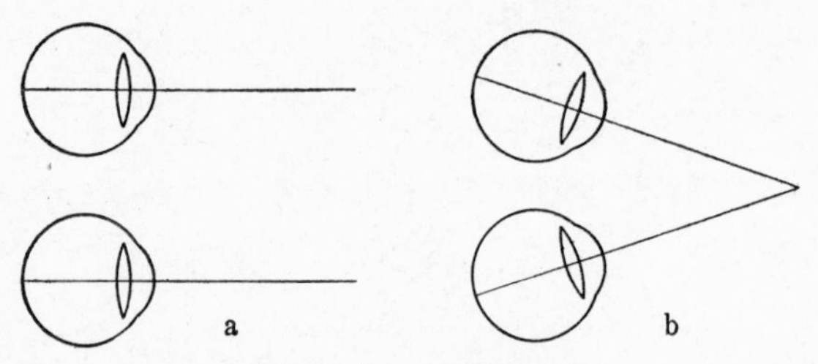

Fig. 61. Lines of Sight.

In *a* of the figure, the lines of sight are directed to the horizon. In *b*, they are converged upon a near object.

tems of the eyes are so adjusted that when an object is observed at the horizon the two lines of sight are parallel (Fig. 61, *a*). When the object is near, however, the muscles cause a movement by means of which the lines of sight converge upon the object (Fig. 61, *b*). In each eye, when the proper convergence has been accomplished, the image of the object which is being observed falls upon the region of clearest vision at the center of the retina (the fovea). When such objects are seen entirely as single, their images are said to fall upon *corresponding* or *identical points* of the two retinas, like the images of *A* and *F* in Fig. 62. The images of objects farther or nearer than the point of fixation upon which the eyes are

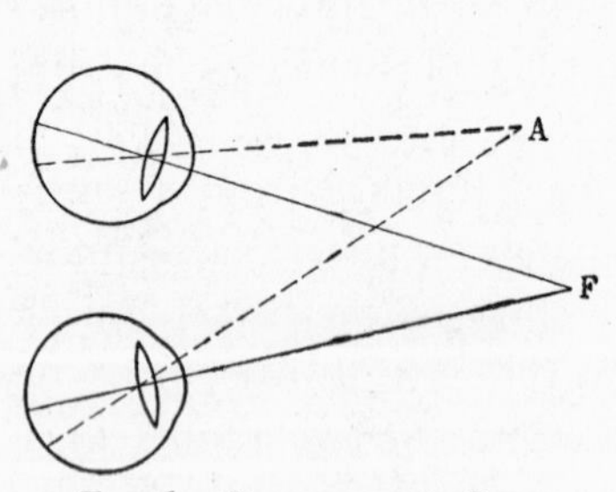

Fig. 62. Corresponding Points.

converged cannot, however, fall on corresponding points. The points upon which they fall are called *non-corresponding*; if, without changing the point of fixation, we attend to such objects we may see them double. The images of points nearer (Fig. 63, *a*) or farther (Fig. 63, *b*) than the point of fixation are called *double images*. When they belong to a *nearer* point, they are said to be *crossed*, because the image in the *right* eye (observed by closing the left eye) lies to the *left* of *X* (Fig. 63, *a*), and *vice versa*. When the double images represent an object farther than *X* (Fig. 63, *b*) they are said to be

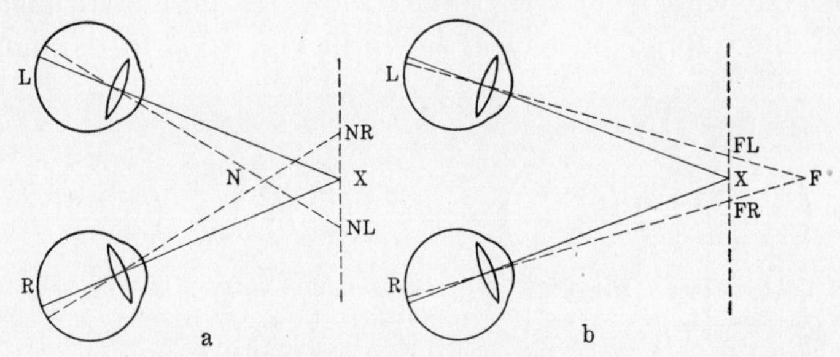

FIG. 63. DOUBLE IMAGES.

In *a* the images of *N*, a point nearer than the point of fixation, *X*, are seen at *NR* and *NL*. In *b* the images of *F*, a point farther than *X*, are seen at *FR* and *FL*.

uncrossed, i.e., the *right* eye's image is on the *right* of *X* and the left eye's image is on the left.

Thus the function of convergence seems to be that of regulating the patterns of stimuli on the two retinas in such a way that those representing the fixated object fall on corresponding points, so as to avoid double imagery. As in the case of accommodation, the action of convergence is more or less automatic, but unlike accommodation it functions up to a limit of approximately 16 to 20 meters. Under ordinary circumstances the two mechanisms work together. If, for instance, a card is held in front of one eye while the other accommodates for a near object, it will be found, when the card is removed, that the two eyes are properly converged upon the object.

Retinal disparity. The discussion of convergence leads, however, to a more fundamental question. Why do we perceive distance so much more precisely with two eyes than with one; and, more particularly, why in binocular vision is the tridimensional character of objects apprehended so much more clearly than in monocular vision? The answer lies partly in the fact of retinal disparity. Since the two eyes are not in exactly the same place, it is evident that a solid object will produce slightly different patterns of stimulation on the two retinas, a difference which will increase as the object is brought closer to the eyes. If a small truncated cone made of paper is placed with its base against the wall directly in front of the observer, with its exterior surface showing, the retinal images will differ approximately as shown in Fig. 64, *a*. In the figure

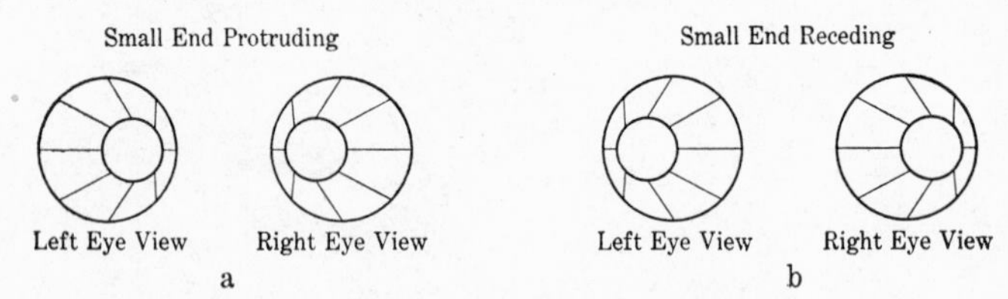

FIG. 64. A TRUNCATED CONE AS SEEN BY EACH EYE SEPARATELY.

The small circles represent the small end of the cone, the large circles the large end, the straight lines the sides. In *a* the disparity is such as to bring the small end nearer the observer, whereas in *b* it is such as to bring the larger end nearer.

the base and top of the cone are represented by circles, and the surface of the cone by straight lines. If the cone is attached to the wall by its small truncated end, the respective stimulus patterns will be approximately as in Fig. 64, *b*. In spite of the inequalities of retinal pattern, however, the observer will see in each case a single tridimensional figure jutting out from the wall, the first with the small end nearer and the second with the large end nearer. Evidently the eyes cooperate in such a way as to produce an effect suggestive of vision with a single eye located in the center of the forehead.

The problems of retinal disparity can be studied best with the aid of a *stereoscope*, an instrument for presenting simultaneously two disparate pictures, one to each eye. It has two essential features: (*a*) there must be a partition so that neither eye can see the picture intended for the other, and (*b*) there must be a device to adjust the retinal images of the two pictures to the places on the retinas that would be occupied by the images of a real object if the two eyes were seeing it. In the common Brewster stereoscope this adjustment is obtained by means of prisms which project the images onto the retinal areas upon which they would fall if the eyes were looking along parallel lines, as at distant objects, while actually the eyes remain converged upon the cards in the instrument (see Fig. 65).

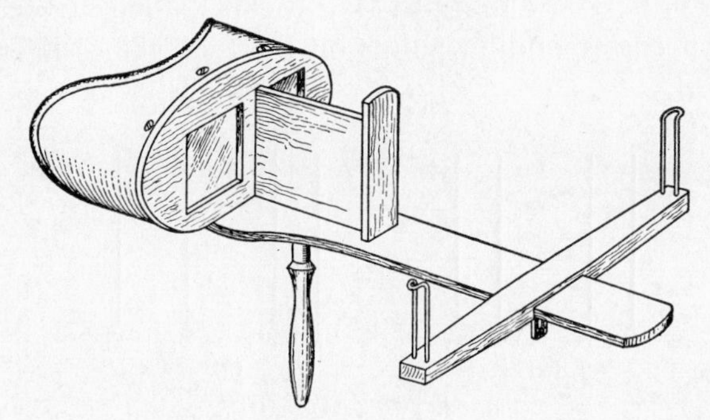

Fig. 65. Brewster Stereoscope.

The pictures used in the stereoscope can be made by a camera with two lenses usually separated by about the distance between the two eyes; in other words, two pictures are taken of the same object at different angles. When two such slightly different pictures are presented in the stereoscope and the proper adjustment made, we see only one picture, wherein the objects are clearly localized at different distances, just as they would be under the ordinary conditions of binocular vision. When the difference between the two pictures is increased by taking them with lenses still farther apart, the effect of distance is enhanced. If, moreover, the two pictures of a simple object like a mask are interchanged, left for right, the depth may actually be reversed from convex to concave. A change in retinal disparity produces a change in perceived distance, and its reversal a reversal of relative distance.

We have noted the fact that the effect of convergence is to

project images of a fixated object on corresponding areas of the two retinas, and that, when there is a lack of correspondence between the points simultaneously stimulated, we may have double imagery. What is the nature of this correspondence? If two vertical lines, freely suspended in space, are presented stereoscopically, one to each eye, we have no difficulty in adjusting our eyes so that the lines appear as one. If instead of single lines we present two equal pairs, as in Fig. 66, *a*, they can just as easily be seen as one pair, X_1 fusing with X, and Y_1 with Y. It is customary to say, in explanation of these two cases, that corresponding points on the two retinas have been stimulated.

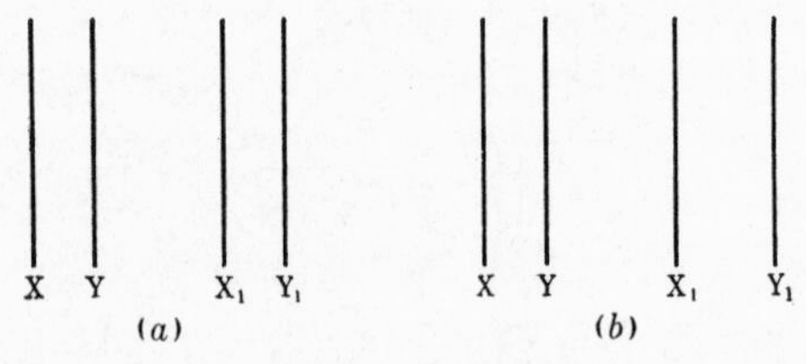

Fig. 66. Two Stereograms.

Let us, however, increase the distance between the two lines in one of the pairs, as in Fig. 66, *b*, and observe the result through the stereoscope. In terms of a strictly anatomical definition of correspondence we must say that Y and Y_1 fall on non-corresponding points. We still, nevertheless, have a single pair, although in this case line Y is seen somewhat behind line X. If the distance between lines X_1 and Y_1 is increased still more, we find a corresponding increase in the depth, and eventually, if they are separated enough, we no longer see a single pair in relief, but rather three lines, X, Y and Y_1, all in one plane, or even perhaps all four lines.

Such an experiment demonstrates the fact that the 'corresponding' points in the two eyes cannot be exactly fixed. Not only may the stimulation of points that do not exactly correspond result in the perception of depth or of tridimensionality, but the distance between such points is exceedingly variable, depending on other conditions. It has been found, for example, that the greater the detail of the drawings or photographs, the readier the tridimensionality of the perception.

Parallax. If the head is moved at a time when there are in the field of view objects at varying distances—some near and some far—the nearest objects seem to move across the field with respect to the more remote ones. The motion of the nearer object is in the direction opposite to that of the head; when the head is moved to the right, the object seems to move to the left. If, on the other hand, an object in the foreground is fixated, all objects in the background seem to move—and to move in the same direction as the head. Such displacement of objects when the position of the observer is changed is an instance of parallax; it is called *monocular parallax* because only one eye may be used, being thus in contrast with *binocular parallax*, which depends upon the difference in position of the two eyes with respect to each other.

The direction of the apparent motion establishes a very clear relief of foreground against background. When all other signs fail, one may, by shifting the position of the head, determine this fundamental spatial relation. The speed of the apparent movement due to parallax depends upon the distance of the objects. With a movement of the head there is a relatively slow, and small, apparent movement of remote objects and a relatively rapid, and large, apparent movement of near objects. It follows that the speed and amount of the perceived motion afford an indication of the *relative* distance of objects. Since the retina is extremely sensitive to those changes which signify motion, parallax seems at times as an extremely useful guide in estimating distance. In moving pictures, furthermore, the principle of monocular parallax may give an excellent stereoscopic effect. Such an effect is the result of a sudden short movement on the part of the camera at the time when the pictures were being photographed.

Summary. We have listed eight ways in which the eyes register distance. Some of them are effective in one situation, others in another. It is obvious that when one eye is used, binocular disparity drops out. When on the other hand, the eyes are stationary, monocular parallax drops out. On a cloudy day there are no shadows. The effect of accommodation, whether by way of the relative distinctness of the object or by the stimulation from the ciliary muscles, is limited to short distances. The influence of convergence, whether from double images or from muscular stimulations, is probably not useful beyond fifty or sixty feet. Though in theory retinal disparity may be effective for a distance of a mile or more, in practice it may operate for perhaps only half that distance.

Although experiments have been devised to determine the relative influence of the various factors that enter into the perception of depth, it cannot be asserted that the results give a true indication of their relative effect under normal conditions. In any given situation the brain takes whatever stimulation may be effective and integrates it for the perception.

VISUAL PERCEPTION OF SIZE

The most obvious determinant of visually perceived size is, of course, the size of the retinal image, which stands in a fixed

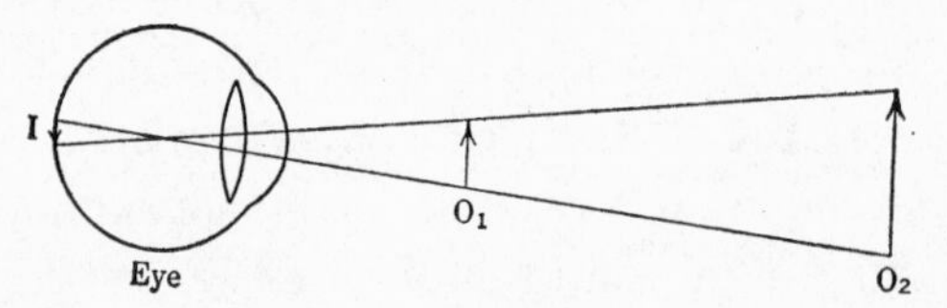

FIG. 67. THE VISUAL ANGLE.

relation to the size and distance of the object. It is customary to state this relation in terms of visual angle (see Fig. 67). With a constant visual angle, the linear extension of the object subtended varies directly as the distance of the object from the eye. With an object of constant size, the size of the visual angle (and consequently of the retinal image) varies inversely as the distance of the object. Thus, from a knowledge of the physical size of an object and of its distance from the eye, we can calculate the approximate size of the image which it produces on the retina; and, on the basis of this rule, we could predict how large the object ought to look at any given distance *if* its size were determined solely by visual angle.

Visual size and perceived distance. Under ordinary conditions, however, the perception of size deviates from the law. A negative after-image, for instance, though it subtends a constant visual angle (see p. 364), nevertheless looks correspondingly larger with each increase in the distance at which the after-image is projected; its size is determined not by the visual angle but by the perceived distance of the projected surface. Conversely, if we look at two objects of the same physical size, one at a distance of 2 meters and the other at a distance of 4 meters from the eye, the nearer object produces a retinal image four times as large as that of the farther object; *yet they do not look correspondingly different in size.* Within very wide limits the size of a seen object remains approximately constant in spite of variations in its distance from the eye and consequently in the size of its retinal image.

This is the principle of *size constancy*, analogous to the principle of brightness constancy. If, however, we view two objects monocularly through holes in a reduction screen (see pp. 432f.), cut in such a way that the conditions for the perception of distance have been eliminated, we find that the object which produces the smaller retinal image will also appear as smaller. Apparently, then, the constancy of size is a special case of the relationship between perceived size and perceived distance. It is as though the organism made an automatic adjustment of perceived size to allow for changes in perceived distance.

The rule of size constancy does not hold at all distances. It fails for small objects—such as a coin—when held within a few centimeters of the eye, and for large objects at great distances. A familiar object will, other things being equal, remain constant in size over a greater range of distances than will an unfamiliar object. In general, therefore, the rule holds for a middle range of distances, within which range the relative familiarity of the object is a factor.

The relation between perceived size and perceived distance is strikingly illustrated in the familiar moon illusion. The moon at the horizon usually looks about twice as large in diameter as the moon at its culmination, and sometimes even larger. The traditional explanation in terms of atmospheric refraction has been definitely disproved. Nor can the illusion be explained in terms of comparison with such neighboring objects as trees and houses, because the effect is destroyed if one inverts his head and looks at the moon between his legs. The illusion is reversed, furthermore, when the observer lies on his back and looks over his head at the horizon moon, and then later up at the moon in culmination.

The same illusion has been obtained under experimental conditions in a dark room. For this purpose a standard luminous circle is projected directly overhead by a lantern, and a second circle, capable of being varied in size, projected at the same distance in the horizontal direction. For an erect observer the latter circle has to be decreased in diameter by about 50 per cent before it appears equal to the circle overhead. When the overhead circle is brought down toward the horizon, without change of distance from the observer, the difference in size between the two circles gradually decreases.

The moon illusion shows that the direction of observation, whether horizontal or vertical, is an important determinant of apparent size. It would appear, then, that the moon on the horizon is apprehended as at a greater distance from the observer than the moon in culmination, and that, in keeping with the size-distance relationship, the horizon moon is thus seen as correspondingly larger. Since the retinal size of the two moons is the same, variations in perceived distance are accompanied by corresponding variations in perceived size. If the horizon moon is viewed in an ordinary mirror it looks small. The observer, seeing the frame and glass of the mirror, adjusts his vision as if the moon were much nearer, as if it had shifted from the horizon toward the mirror.

Visual size and surrounding objects. The relationship between size and distance is one of many instances in which specific properties of things are determined by their situations. If an object appears at a *great* distance, as in the case of a perspective drawing (see Fig. 55), its size corresponds approximately to that distance.

The principle holds also, however, for bidimensional situations. The line *AX* in Fig. 68, *a,* appears longer than the line *AY*; the former is apprehended as the diagonal of a larger,

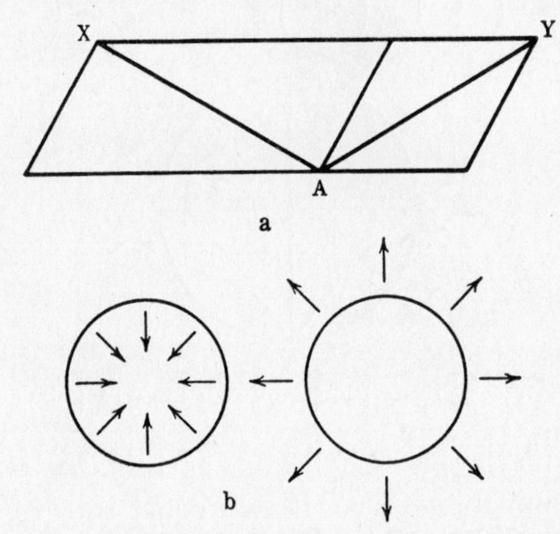

Fig. 68. Influence of Linear Figure Taken as a Whole upon the Size of One of Its Parts.

and the latter as the diagonal of a smaller parallelogram. Similarly in Fig. 68, *b,* the difference in size between the two circles must be referred to the influence of the included and excluded lines. In the familiar arrowhead illusion, Fig. 69, *a,* the line *c* appears longer than *d* because it is a part of a larger area suggested by the direction of the arrowheads. Similarly in Fig. 69, *b,* it is almost impossible to see the distance between the outer limits of circles *A* and *B* as equal to the distance between the right extreme of *B* and the left extreme of *A.* The perception of the circles as *objects* constrains us to perceive the distance as between circle and circle rather than as between point and point. In Fig. 70 the lower object looks smaller than the upper object, possibly because of a contrast between the short upper line of the lower figure and the long lower line of the upper figure, possibly because of a perspective effect induced by the convergence of the straight lines at the two extremes.

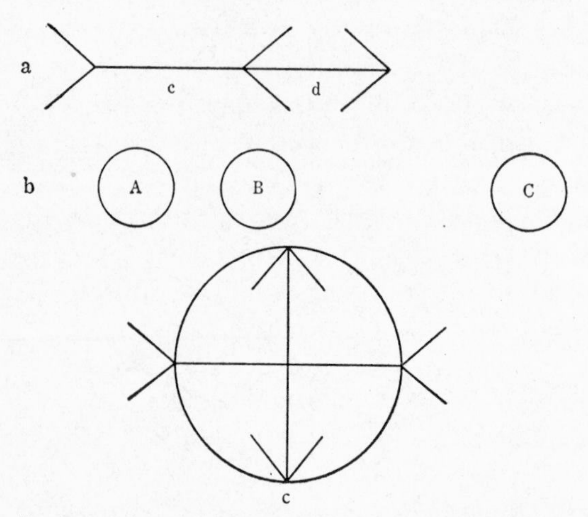

FIG. 69. EFFECT OF A TOTAL FIGURE UPON AN ISOLATED LINEAR DISTANCE.

Within limits even such factors as brightness may function as determinants of size. If two equal squares, one black and one white, are placed side by side against a gray ground, the white will usually appear larger than the black. It may be that the more intense stimulation coming from the white object produces an irradiation of excitation of the retina, and consequently an actually larger stimulus pattern. This, however, cannot be the only determining factor. Suppose we place side by side against a gray ground a number of equal squares, ranging in color from white through various shades of gray to black. The white square, it is true, appears larger than the black, but the black itself appears larger than the grays, which approach in brightness the color of the background. Apparently the degree to which an object stands out clearly from its

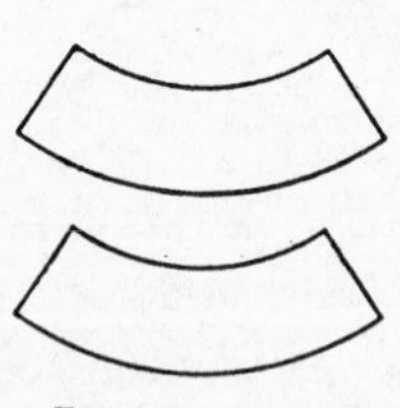

FIG. 70. SPATIAL CONTRAST.

background is important. Differences in hue may also have an effect on apparent size. To most people a red object will appear slightly larger, and nearer, than an equally bright blue object; and in some pathological cases such differences become pronounced.

Thresholds in visual size perception. The smallest object that can be seen depends upon several variables. A white spot on a black ground in sunlight can just be seen when the angle subtended is about 10 or 12 sec.; a black spot on a white ground in diffuse daylight requires an angle of 25-36 sec. Similar values have been determined for the smallest perceptible degree of separation between two objects, a determination which depends upon a number of different factors. The separation of two vertical *lines* placed end to end may be perceived when the ends are separated by a visual angle of only 5 sec. The separation between *points* in space must, however, be larger in order to be perceived. In a well-lighted room two black dots can just be seen as two when they subtend an angle of 60 sec. In abnormally high or abnormally low illuminations the angle must be increased, as also if lines are substituted for the dots and the separation is apprehended as a gap in an otherwise complete figure. The threshold of 60 sec. for just noticeable separation has been accepted by the oculist as the standard for normal vision. If the eye can see a letter the distance between whose parts—*e.g.,* the horizontal bars of an **E**—subtends an angle of 60 sec., it is in that respect considered normal. If, on the other hand, the angle subtended by the parts of the letter must be, say, 120 sec. before the letter can be distinctly seen, visual acuity is said to be one-half normal. The test letters are, of course, always shown under good illumination.

VISUAL PERCEPTION OF SHAPE

Visual shape and retinal pattern. Under highly controlled conditions of vision, when simple designs are presented in the frontal plane squarely in front of the individual and the stimulus patterns are focused on the fovea, there is a fairly direct correspondence between the shape of the retinal pattern and the shape of the perceived object. Under ordinary conditions of vision, however, the stimulus conditions are seldom so simple. In the first place, most of the objects we see, being tridimensional in character, cannot be represented as such on a bidimensional retina. In the second place, the retinal image of even a bidimensional object changes its shape with every change in the position of the object or of the eyes. The book on the table, although it looks rectangular, is represented on the retina by a trapezoid which changes in shape with every shift of the eyes; and the table top itself, which looks square, could be represented by a square retinal image only if we were to tip the table on its side or if we were to look directly at it from a point above it. We have a problem here analogous to the problem of size constancy: namely, how to account for the fact that objects tend to retain their essential shape in spite of variations in the shapes of the retinal stimulus patterns they produce. As in the case of the size problem, the answer lies principally in the relationship between the object and the surrounding visual field.

Constancy of visual shape and perceived orientation. If we fixate a circle directly in front of us, and then project the resulting after-image on a surface that is inclined forward or backward from the perpendicular, the after-image will appear as an ellipse, the shape of which can be predicted fairly accurately on the basis of elementary geometry. Every change in the orientation of the projection surface produces a corresponding change in the shape of the after-image. If, however, we tip the circle itself away from the frontal-parallel plane, it tends to be perceived as circular; in no case does it appear to be as elliptical as is the retinal stimulus pattern which corresponds to it. The constancy of shape is strongest when some such factor as the character of the surface of the screen or its contour is clearly perceived, so that the tilted screen is perceived as tilted. The use of a reduction screen, because it destroys the surface character and hides the contour of the tilted screen, greatly weakens the constancy of shape or destroys it altogether. Thus the apparent shape, like the apparent size, of an object is dependent in an important way on the surrounding visual field.

Preferred shapes. The organism seems to prefer some shapes to others. An ellipse which is tipped slightly away from the frontal-parallel plane will tend to appear as a circle tipped still farther away. Similarly, an ellipse exposed for a very short interval will appear rounder; a slightly acute or a slightly obtuse angle will be perceived as a right angle; an irregular quadrilateral will be seen as a square; and nearly parallel lines will become parallel. In a word, when the stimulus conditions permit, certain simple geometrical forms are more readily perceived than similar, slightly different forms. The preferred shapes, as a rule, are simple, symmetrical and well proportioned.

Illusions of shape. The tendency toward preferred shapes is not always realized. Sometimes two preferred figures con-

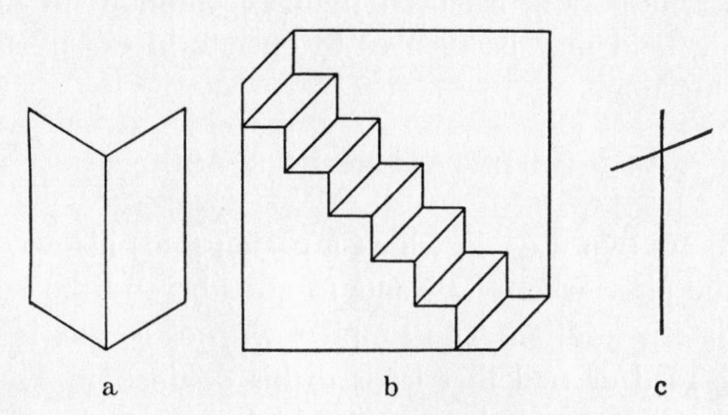

FIG. 71. ILLUSIONS OF REVERSIBLE PERSPECTIVE.

flict with each other; at other times the field surrounding the figure contains other factors which conflict with the tendency toward the preferred shape. In such cases either the cues are equally balanced and the figure is ambiguous, or else the stronger wins. Instances of the former are the reversible perspectives in Figs. 71 and 72. In 71, *c,* for example, the simple figure with acute and obtuse angles conflicts with the tendency to see these angles as right angles and consequently to see the figure as a drawing in perspective.

Examples of the influence of the surrounding field are seen in Fig. 73. The transverse lines in *b* and *c*, for instance, appear parallel when the rest of the field is blocked out. Their perceived curvature has been explained as a result of the tendency toward the overestimation of acute and the underestimation of obtuse angles. But this tendency is itself probably a special case of the more general preference for right angles which takes place whenever the surrounding field permits. In Fig. 73, *f,* the preferred circle appears distorted when placed on an angular ground, and in Fig. 69, *c,* the circle responds to the same cues as those which produce the arrowhead illusion. Thus, in spite of the organism's preference for simple, symmetrical, balanced figures, conditions in the surrounding field may be such as to operate in exactly the opposite direction.

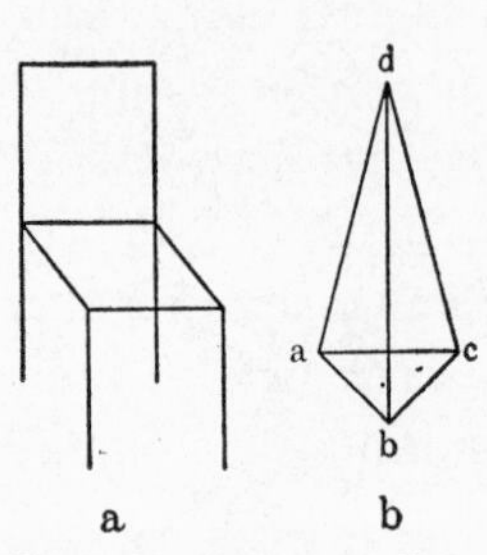

FIG. 72. AMBIGUOUS PERSPECTIVE.

ORIENTATION IN SPACE

There are two ways in which a person finds his way about when the place where he wants to go is beyond the reach of immediate perception. The simplest way, of course, is to follow the road or trail that leads to his destination. Thus one goes where the road signs of the highway point, where the cairns of the mountain side or the tree blazes of the forest direct, or the map or the lodestar leads. Just so the dog, for his part, follows a trail of scent.

The other method is to learn one's way about. In familiar surroundings a directional schema is developed, made up of a network of directions and places. The schema may be somesthetic—as it is for the blind man—or it may be visual, or a mixture of the two. In this schema the places where one goes

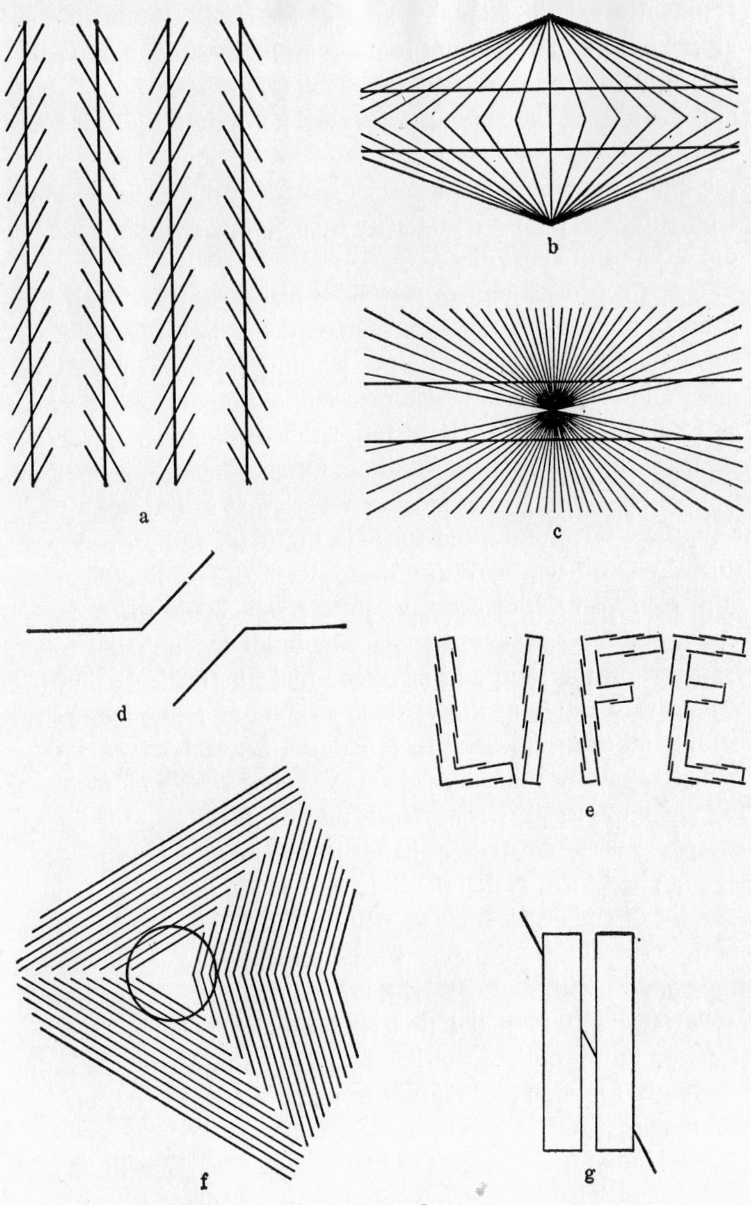

FIG. 73. ANGLE ILLUSION.

frequently are directional points of reference. When, for example, we go to the dining room or to the post office, we go in the right direction without taking thought. The dining room and the library and the post office are not only places; they are also directions. Familiar places too become points of reference for the directions of less familiar objects in the vicinity. Thus, a bookstore or even a remote city may, in our schema, have the direction of the post office.

When a person goes to a strange place, he takes with him parts of his old schema, which may, depending upon the circumstances, aid or hinder him in learning the new directions—*i.e.,* in developing a new schema. The old one is an aid when, as frequently happens, it includes the cardinal points of the compass and fits the new situation. Often, however, it does not fit because, although the journey was started in the right direction, there were unnoticed turns in the road, and a conflict results. "When I was in Wilkinsburg, Pa.," a psychologist writes, "the trolleys for the eastern suburbs ran north through the town, but the east-bound trains ran south through the town. I arrived on the train and of course took the trolley going the wrong way to get to the west. My frame of reference was in conflict all that summer." In learning a new schema, one may be led astray by the assumed directions of streets or paths. If the assumption is wrong and the road, instead of going straight, runs at an angle or bends in its course or even makes a right-angled turn, and if these deviations are not noticed, one's sense of direction becomes utterly confused. The Boston Common is surrounded by five streets which make approximate right angles with each other. Some of these streets are bowed inward enough to make this circumstance possible, but the stranger rarely notices the bends. Hence those who take the Common as point of reference may often be 90° out of reckoning.

Some individuals are said to have a better 'sense of direction' than others. The difference, really in the first place a difference in directional schemas, is secondly based upon the habit of noticing directions. The person who drives an automobile or who lives in wide spaces like the sea or the plains is more likely to notice directions than the person who rides in a car as passenger or who merely follows the signs at the junctions of city streets.

The orientation of the lower animals offers problems which are not entirely solved. Though some animals are guided by smell, others, like the fishes, may follow gradations in the specific gravity of the water as they swim from salt to fresh water, or changes in the temperature of the water, or again the direction of the current in a stream. The migrations of birds are probably oriented by a food supply or changes in temperature.

Sometimes animals seem to have a sense of direction, a directional schema. Experiments with birds and also with dogs have shown that, even when the ordinary sensory cues are controlled, so that following a trail becomes impossible, such creatures are still able to find their way.

REFERENCES

1. Boring, E. G. *The physical dimensions of consciousness.* New York: Century, 1933. Chap. 4.
2. Carr, H. A. *An introduction to space perception.* New York: Longmans, Green, 1935.
3. Ellis, W. D. *A source book of Gestalt psychology.* New York: Harcourt, Brace, 1938. Esp. pp. 193-263, 315-369.
4. Katz, D. *Animals and men.* London: Longmans, Green, 1937.
5. Koffka, K. *Principles of Gestalt psychology.* New York: Harcourt Brace, 1935. Chaps. 3 to 7.
6. Schilder, P. *The image and appearance of the human body.* London: Kegan Paul, 1935.
7. Vernon, M. D. *Visual perception.* Cambridge: University Press, 1937.
8. Villey, P. *The world of the blind.* New York: Macmillan, 1930.
9. Werner, H. Dynamics in binocular depth-perception. *Psychol. Monogr.*, 1937, No. 218.
10. Woodworth, R. C. *Experimental psychology.* New York: Henry Holt, 1938. Chaps. 25 and 26.

Chapter 15

PERCEPTION OF TIME AND MOVEMENT

Just as we may be oriented in space, so also we may be oriented in time. Furthermore, just as we perceive objects with spatial properties and localized in space, so also we perceive events with temporal properties and localized in time. Every perception has, of course, both spatial and temporal aspects; it is only by attention that we separate them. In the perception of movement the two aspects are so closely integrated that they normally are observed in the same perceptual pattern—as, for example, when we stand on the curb and wait while an automobile rushes past a street intersection at a rapid rate. But even in the perception of movement there are these two aspects: we may be primarily interested in its temporal character—*e.g.,* the slow *rate* at which the object moves; or in its spatial aspect—the *direction* in which the object moves.

Both temporal perception and perception of movement are based upon integrations of events into perceptual patterns. The present chapter considers the psychological principles underlying these integrations.

PERCEPTION OF TIME

A prime characteristic of integrations of successively occurring events into temporal perception is the continuous nature of the events. They have a beginning and an end, to be sure; nevertheless, once begun they last until the end is reached.

Temporal perceptions also have an important functional aspect; that is to say, successive events act together as parts of

This chapter was written by M. A. Tinker of the University of Minnesota. In it he has incorporated parts of the chapter on movement written by H. R. DeSilva for Boring, Langfeld and Weld, *Psychology: a factual textbook,* 1935.

some single whole, as they do in memory or in a situation which is the occasion for action or thought. Thus a melody is an integration in time; the first few notes of a measure mean the whole measure and indeed almost inevitably lead to its completion in thought. The significance of the separate notes depends upon the context of the preceding and succeeding notes. The solution of a simple problem such as adding 7 and 9 is a similar temporal integration, for it has a definite temporal structure. These two characteristics, the durative nature of experience and the integration of a number of successive events into a single whole, are the basic conditions of five principal types of temporal perception: the perception of continuity, the perception of succession, the perception of temporal length, temporal orientation and the perception of rhythm.

Perception of continuity. The perception of continuity occurs under two different circumstances. In the one an experience is running its course without appreciable qualitative or intensitive change; in the other the experience is itself perceived as changing. With the former we tend to ignore the durative character of the experience until some change occurs in the total situation; until, for example, a steadily burning lamp begins to flicker, until the pressure of our clothing gets uncomfortable, until a sound is lasting longer than we expected, or we fear a particularly pleasant experience may cease, or we wish a toothache would stop, or until we wonder, as we listen to Niagara, if its roar will ever be stilled. In all such cases we perceive what otherwise escapes our notice, that the experience of the moment is continuously going on even though no change in the experience is observable.

The perception of continuity is much more obvious, however, when the experience of the moment is itself changing; when, for example, the colors of a sunset slowly fade, when a whistle rises or falls in pitch or grows louder or softer in intensity, when the strain of effort increases or diminishes. In all these instances we perceive a continuous change in quality or intensity. We may also perceive a similar change in the position or in the size of an object, as happens when a bird flies across the field of vision, or when we see an object growing larger or shrinking without change of distance, as objects sometimes do in animated cartoons.

Perception of succession. In the perception of succession, stimuli are presented at a rapid rate, and qualities or events perceived as discrete and as following one another in time. The rate of presentation, however, must not be too rapid, for then the qualities will fuse into a single continuous impression. If, for example, black and white sectors on a color wheel succeed each other too rapidly in rotation, one perceives either a smooth gray, or else, if the rate is a bit slower, a continuous flicker. With auditory stimuli and a rate that is too rapid one perceives either a continuous noise, or else, if the rate is slower, a harsh, rough noise. These phenomena, from discrete clicks to a continuous noise, may be demonstrated by drawing the thumb nail at different rates along the teeth of a comb. The rate, however, must not be too slow, for in that case the perception of the interval between the qualities or events tends to intrude, even to become the characteristic feature of the perception, in which case succession as such becomes difficult to perceive.

If one takes his pencil and taps on a hard surface, at first as rapidly as possible and then slowly with about 1 sec. between taps, he will notice that with the rapid rate the sounds follow each other like beads on a string. With this rate it is not only impossible clearly to perceive an interval between the successive sounds, but also the sounds themselves appear to belong together. It is just this belonging together of a series of discrete impressions—this temporal organization of discrete impressions—that constitutes the essential character of the perception of succession. Let the rate be slow, on the other hand, and the intervals between taps become the objects of attention, with the taps themselves serving merely as marks of the beginning and end of the interval between them.

The intervals between stimuli which permit perception of

succession have been measured objectively, the important rates being those that determine the upper and lower limits of the perception. The upper limit is the shortest possible time that will yield the perception of succession; this we shall call the *threshold of discontinuity*. The most important factor which conditions its magnitude is the kind of stimuli employed. Auditory succession is experienced with the shortest period between stimuli (about 50 ms.).

As the rate with which stimuli succeed each other becomes slower, the perception of succession becomes more difficult, tending of course to break up. When the time between the stimuli approaches about ½ to ¾ sec., perception of succession is replaced by perception of intervals bounded by stimuli. Since, however, the rate at which the change occurs is influenced by the attitude of the observer, it is not fixed but variable.

Perception of temporal length. Duration is a length of time with a beginning and an end. Tap twice with your foot or pencil, leaving an interval of about 1 sec. between taps. The two sounds mark the beginning and the end of a definite stretch of time; taken together with the interval, they constitute a pattern. The duration of the interval itself is the dominant characteristic, the two taps serving as contours to mark the beginning and the end, much as an outline drawing on white paper separates the white space inside the figure from its background. We may also, of course, perceive a stretch of a continuous quality or event as, for example, a musical note. Here the beginning and the end of the sound itself are the contours of the pattern, in the way that the round edge or border of the full moon separates the disk from its background. Intervals of the first kind, those marked off by taps or flashes of light, are technically called 'empty time'; whereas intervals of the second kind, consisting of continuous sounds or pressures, are called 'filled time.' The so-called empty interval is, of course, not empty but has an indeterminate conscious content, quite different from the definite visual, auditory or tactual qualities of filled intervals.

All this is true of relatively short intervals, say of less than 5 sec. in length. Yet we also experience the duration of much longer intervals—minutes, hours or days. In most of the work on perception of long intervals, however, times varying from 10 sec. to a few minutes have been used. Although we may perceive such intervals as long or short, as passing slowly or swiftly, the integrated pattern of the perception is different from that of 'small' intervals. In either instance, to be sure, the interval has a beginning in some event and an end in another; so far the patterns of long and short intervals are similar. The long interval, however, is filled with a number of other events, many of which may have no relation to each other or to the 'end.' The experimental investigations of the perception of temporal length, therefore, fall into two groups according as they are directed to the 'short' or to the 'long' intervals.

EXPERIMENTS ON TEMPORAL PERCEPTION

The principal method employed in the study of short intervals has been the method of comparison. In a single observation, two *stimulus intervals* are given and the observer is asked to say whether the second is perceived as longer than, shorter than, or equal to the first. The problem is to determine by measurement the just noticeable difference, or the differential threshold, between two intervals (see pp. 509-511). Another method, one frequently used with long intervals, is the method of *estimation*. After an interval has elapsed the observer estimates its duration in seconds or some other temporal unit.

The *length* of the interval employed determines to some degree the accuracy of time perception. Relatively small times tend to be perceived as greater (positive constant error) and relatively long times as smaller (negative constant error) than they actually are. On the average the critical interval where the subject tends to have as many negative as positive errors is characterized by little or no constant error. This interval, which is perceived with maximum accuracy, is termed the *indifference point.* Above and below this point, errors of perception increase in size. The most accurately determined value for the indifference interval is approximately 0.60 sec.

Perception of short intervals is influenced by a variety of special experimental conditions:

1. The perception of the temporal length of *filled* intervals is partly determined by the quality of the stimulus. Because of the persistence of the after-sensation in touch and vision, those intervals which are tactually and visually filled are perceived as longer than sounds of the same length.

2. A *filled* interval tends to be perceived as longer than an *empty* interval of the same length, whether the filling is from a continuous or an intermittent stimulation.

3. The *empty* interval whose delimiting sounds possess the more striking characteristics will be perceived as longer than an interval with indifferent boundaries. This difference is due to the fact that the apparent duration of the delimiting sounds is added to the interval itself, resulting in a unitary pattern which is the basis of the perception.

In an effort to determine the influence of variation in the type of filling upon the perception of time, several experiments have been devised. Results obtained by comparison, it turns out, depend less upon the number of separate presentations in the interval than upon the attitude of the observer toward them. The more the observer notices or becomes interested in the filling, the shorter will he estimate the intervals to be. Words, for example, are shorter than noises, and meaningful sentences are shorter than a series of nonsense syllables of the same objective length. Results obtained by estimation reveal a similar tendency. The more engrossing the contents, the shorter is the interval judged to be.

Temporal estimation is influenced also by certain factors which modify the internal state of the body. Thus a rise in temperature produced by fever may result in faster tapping and counting; in other words, a rise in temperature may make temporal intervals seem shorter than they really are, may make time pass more quickly. Similarly, thyroxin and caffeine make intervals seem shorter; quinine and alcohol make them seem longer.

Orientation in time. If, instead of asking which of two temporal intervals is longer than the other, or how much time has elapsed since the beginning of an event, we ask what the time is now, we are posing a question in temporal orientation; we are asking where in the course of time the individual perceives himself to be. The point of reference may, but need not, be the position of the hour and minute hands of the clock. It may be only in terms of morning or evening, bedtime or mealtime, or some other similar time mark. Nor is it necessary to pose or verbally to answer a definite question: "What time is it?" It may merely occur suddenly to the individual that 'it is time to go,' or he may simply turn up at mealtime. We may for convenience call the latter phenomenon 'personal-time' in order to distinguish it from clock-time. There may be a wide variation between the two, but there may also be a remarkable coincidence. There is, we are told, the case of an idiot girl who screamed for her dinner at exactly the same time each day. There is another case of an adult who could almost invariably give the time of day within a few minutes, without reference to his watch and apparently without noting the sun or other external conditions; on dark and cloudy nights his guessing was just as accurate as during the bright daylight. Other similar examples have been reported. On the basis of such observations some writers infer that this accurate timing is made possible by a unique ability, a 'time sense.' It should be noted, however, that the observations cited were not controlled by the elimination of environmental cues and that accuracy of guessing was frequently affected by practice. The ability, at any rate, is apparently possessed by relatively few people. Most of the persons reported upon have cultivated the guessing of time as a hobby.

Estimation of the time after sleep is related to the time guessing discussed above. Many instances are reported of individuals who can wake very close to a predetermined time. One investigator could, on the average, awake within 10 min. of the set hour. Most of the awakenings came, however, between 6 and 10 A.M., when ample environmental cues were available. Since this method of awakening had been employed for a year prior to the investigation, the influence of practice seems obvious. In another experiment the subjects estimated the time and recorded the conscious basis of their estimates on being awakened between midnight and 5 A.M. The average error of their estimates was about 50 min. Cues which formed the basis for this temporal estimation included degree of fatigue, degree of restlessness, sensations from stomach and bladder, closeness of thought to the topic in mind on retiring and amount of dreams recalled. It would appear, then, that the temporal frame of reference in guessing time, either during the day or upon waking, includes a great variety of auditory, visual and organic sensory processes supported by memory images. Practice in interpreting these cues, especially the extra-organic ones, apparently improves the accuracy of estimation.

Estimation of clock-time is not, however, necessary for temporal orientation. In one experiment two observers were shut up in a sound-proof room, one for two, the other for three days. All extra-organic cues were eliminated. They could obtain sleep and food as they desired, and, except for occasional reports to the experimenter through a speaking tube, they had no personal or social obligations to perform. It was found that clock-time soon gave way to a personal-time. The frame of reference was the day from the time of awaking until retiring. Although the length of this day was fairly constant at 13 or 14 hours for the two subjects, within the day mealtimes were variable, depending upon the time of awaking, but still spaced with some regularity. If, for example, breakfast was at 5:15 A.M., luncheon was at 9:30 and dinner at 4:30 P.M.; if breakfast was at 12:04 P.M., luncheon was at 3:38 P.M. and dinner at 9:30 P.M. Orientation in personal-time seems to be based either on habitual physiological rhythms or else upon some non-observable physiological mechanism whose nature is unknown.

The former possibility is supported by the temporal orientation of certain animals.

It is reported, for instance, that fish in a stream adjacent to a railroad station assembled at the time scheduled for the arrival of the trains, when they were fed by the passengers. To trains arriving at other than the regular time the fish made no response. Certain animals, like hermit crabs and marine snails, show specific phototropic reactions that correspond in time to the oscillations of the tide. When these animals are removed to an aquarium or a laboratory, they continue to give the same reactions to light at the hours of high and low tide, even though, of course, the stimulation from the tidal changes is entirely absent.

Various observers have noted that bees will come for honey at the specific hours when this food is available. Although this temporal orientation operates day or night, independent of the alternation of light and dark, and of weather changes, it appears, nevertheless, to be bound up with a 24-hour rhythm. Similarly, ants and termites have been trained to go to a feeding position according to rhythms of 3, 21, 24 and 27 hours.

In an isolated laboratory room a dog was given food regularly every thirtieth minute. After several repetitions a single feeding was omitted. At approximately the thirtieth minute, however, there occurred a secretion of saliva which had previously happened only when food was present.

These reactions of animals are understandable in terms of *physiological rhythms.* Through many repetitions the reactions have become organized as part of the animals' physiological processes. When internal organic changes continue for the length of time which usually elapses between succeeding exposures to the rhythmic stimulation, the customary response appears in the absence of the original stimulus. Temporal orientation has become part of an integrated pattern in the physiological rhythms of the animal.

Perception of rhythm. If, without counting, one gives attention to the movements of the body and limbs while dancing, walking rapidly or running, he will readily perceive a fairly consistent recurrent pattern of movements. Similarly the uniform puffs of a locomotive seem naturally to fall into rhythmical groups of two or of four puffs. Rhythm is the perception of groups or patterns of successive impressions, the members of which are perceived to be consistently different in some quantitative aspect, usually in relative intensity and duration. With this variation come subordination and synthesis of the elements into groups. Rhythmical perception of this kind occurs in the auditory, tactual, motor and visual fields. Auditory rhythm, however, appears to arise most readily.

For the perception of rhythm repetition is an essential. Although rhythm never arises from the presentation of a single rhythmical unit, it may appear promptly with the first recurrence of that unit.

Besides repetition, rhythm also requires a periodic accentuation of certain elements in the series of sensory impressions. When a series of identical and equally intense stimuli is presented at a constant rate and is attended to with a passive attitude, there appears a periodic change in the intensity of some of the sounds which divides the series into groups usually of two but sometimes of three or more sounds. The result is a *subjective accentuation* of the first member of each group, an accentuation which produces also an apparent lengthening of the intervals between successive groups. To some individuals a perception of subjective rhythm comes more readily than to others.

The number of stimuli integrated into subjective unit groups varies considerably. Groupings that may be classed as natural, easy or pleasurable have 2, 3, 4, 6 or 8 elements. The 2-group and the 4-group occur most frequently. The larger groups of 4, 6 and 8 elements tend to divide into subgroups of 2, 3 or 4 elements each. Although subjective accentuation may be altered to some degree voluntarily, odd groups of 5 to 7 are difficult either to obtain or to maintain without extended practice.

In a series of sensory impressions, any regularly recurrent

impression which is more intense or longer than the rest subordinates the other impressions to it, with the result that grouping occurs. Such rhythm, which is *objective*, is well illustrated by rhythm in dance music or in recited poetry.

For the perception of rhythm the rate with which the stimuli recur must be neither too slow nor too fast. No subjective rhythm occurs with rates faster than about 8 per sec., or slower than about 1.5 sec. between stimuli. Ordinarily the 2-group appears first with the slow rates. As the speed is increased, the 3- and 4-groups appear, finally the 6- and 8-groups. At slow rates where rhythm just appears, the integration of the successive groups is weak. As the rate increases, the definition of the rhythmic form becomes more precise; the apparent intervals between succeeding groups grow larger, the accentuation within each group more pronounced.

The maximum integration of successive groups which may be perceived as a whole has been termed the *temporal range of consciousness*. In this case apprehension of the whole must occur, of course, without counting. If the rate of the succession is advantageous, a comparatively long series of impressions, such as equally spaced clicks, may be perceived as a united cluster. One investigator found that the most favorable rate for apprehending audible strokes in groups was about 3 to 5 per sec. Under these conditions as many as 40 strokes, heard as five subgroups of 8, could be distinguished from 39 or 41 strokes without counting.

Rhythmical integration has a direct bearing upon musical and poetical practice. Small groups of impressions may recombine into larger groups. It is this kind of organization that produces musical phrases and poetical lines, as well as their subsequent organization into still higher units. Neither the phrase nor the line contains more than six measures, or feet, respectively. Even the larger musical groups and the poetical stanza, furthermore, seldom comprise more than six phrases or six lines. Thus they too would seem ordinarily to lie within the range of immediate apprehension.

In general a kinesthetic theory seems satisfactory to explain rhythm. Observation reveals that the motor factor is almost always present in rhythm. Apparently, therefore, *kinesthesis is sufficient for the establishment of rhythmical perception.* For the most part the evidence indicates that the perception of rhythmical groups as wholes is due to sensations of movement or strain accompanying the qualities which are grouped. One makes a series of clicks into a rhythm by barely tapping with his toe or barely nodding his head, or—when the more overt movements are lacking—by accenting the clicks by ear strain, *i.e.,* the kinesthesis of listening that arises in the muscles of the middle ear. The kinesthetic sensations give rise to a perceived change in the intensity or quality of certain members of a series of impressions, whereupon grouping results.

PERCEPTION OF MOVEMENT

When we look fixedly at the minute hand of a watch we see no movement; but if, after a brief interval, we look at the watch once more, we observe the hand in a new position. In this case we perceive a change in position but not a continuous change. When we see an athlete doing a standing broad jump, on the contrary, we see him—as we saw the hand of the watch—first in one place, then later at another place; but in addition we see him moving or changing his position from one place to another. It is the perception of this continuous change in position of an object that is called the perception of movement.

General conditions for the perception of movement. Variations in brightness, intensity, distinctness and size are especially significant for the perception of movement in the near-far direction. Thus, we may perceive auditorially an approaching or receding locomotive by a continuous increase or decrease in the volume and intensity of its noise, or perceive visually an approaching or receding automobile by the change in its size and distinctness in the daytime and by the change in the brightness and size of its lights at night.

In any but the near-far direction successive stimulation of sensory receptors is the most important condition for perception of movement. This succession is possible in the visual and tactual fields where the receptors are spatially distinct from one another and distributed in a mosaic (see pp. 521-23, 609-11).

The change which determines the perceptions of these movements is a *successive stimulation of the receptors* at a rate rapid enough and slow enough to provide for the *continuity* of the movement. When an insect crawls on the skin, for example, it successively stimulates pressure receptors. If the insect should fly across the field of vision, the retinal image will move across the retina, and the receptors that lie in its path be successively stimulated. When the forearm is moved by bending the arm at the elbow joint, the surfaces in the joint rub against each other with the result that the receptors are again stimulated successively. A certain rate of stimulation (not too fast and not too slow) is necessary, however, in order to obtain continuity of movement with the successive stimulation of discrete points.

When a person is in passive motion as, for example, when riding in a street car or on a merry-go-round, the perception of motion is complicated. Here stimulation from the proprioceptors is added to visual stimulation. Frequently too, in such a case, there are accessory cues from the change in speed and from the jolting and swaying of the vehicle in which he is riding. In certain situations in which some aspect of the stimulus pattern is strongly emphasized, the perception is modified. When, for example, one takes off in an airplane, he frequently sees the earth as receding from him instead of perceiving the change of altitude of his own body. In this case it is the change in size of the retinal image which is dominant and decides the outcome.

Head and eye movements also furnish aids to the perception of moving objects. When a visually fixated object, such as a fly, approaches or recedes, the eyes continue to follow the object with changes in convergence; but if a fixated object like a flying bird or an automobile moves across the landscape, following or pursuit movements of the eyes occur. Head movements also frequently accompany these eye movements. The head movements are readily noticed, but neither the convergence nor the pursuit movements of the eyes are clearly apprehended. All, however, furnish cues to the perception of movement of the fixated object.

We have, then, a triple set of cues for the perception of visual movement: the displacement of retinal images, the stimulation from the moving body as a whole and cues from head and eye movements. At times some one, or a pair, of these cues determines the perception of movement. When a bird flies across our field of vision and the eyes are stationary, the retina is successively stimulated at different places (retinal images) and we see the movement. But if the bird is stationary, the head and eyes may be moved in such a way that the same retinal places are stimulated as were stimulated by the flying bird. The bird, nevertheless, is usually perceived as stationary (movements of the head and eyes). Furthermore, the eye may follow a moving object so that only one place on the retina is stimulated and yet the object may be seen as moving (movement of the eyes overcomes the cue from the retinal image). Or, finally, if while fixating a stationary object the position of the eyeball is displaced by pressure upon it with the finger, the object may be seen to move (displacement of the retinal image).

If we recall what in the previous chapter has been said about the variability of the points of reference in the visual field (see pp. 448-451), it will be apparent that the relative effectiveness of the cues for the perception of movement depends upon a shift from one point of reference to another. When the moon and moving clouds are seen against a background of sky, the clouds are perceived as moving when the moon is taken as the point of reference; but when the clouds are taken as point of reference, they become stationary and the moon is perceived as moving. The same principle holds for the more complicated situations just described. It is as if we inferred that the bird moves because we (or other objects in the field, perhaps our bodies, or our heads or eyes) are standing still; or we infer that our eyes move both because we feel their movement and because some other object in the field is standing still. Consciously, of course, we make no such inferences, nor are we always aware of the shift in reference. Our brains automatically turn the trick for us; or, what amounts to the same thing, we are already disposed by our past experience to perceive immediately.

After-images of movement. If we look fixedly for fifteen or twenty seconds at a slowly rotating white disk upon which has been drawn a heavy black spiral line, the disk will seem to contract or expand, depending upon the direction of rotation of the spiral. If we then turn our eyes away and fixate a person's face, the face too will appear to expand or shrink depending upon the direction of rotation of the spiral. Similarly, if we look for a minute or so at a waterfall or at a flowing stream, and then glance away at the landscape, the latter will appear to flow in the opposite direction. Or, if we are riding on the rear platform of a train which suddenly stops, we notice that the formerly shrinking and receding objects appear to broaden or come nearer. In short, under certain conditions a movement produces an after-effect which manifests itself as a movement in the opposite direction. The velocity of the after-image of movement corresponds roughly but by no means exactly to the relative velocity of the moving object.

Movement with a moving stimulus. Thus far we have been concerned with the *nature* of the perception of movement and its *general* conditions. We now turn to the more special results of the experimental investigation of the perception.

A stimulus must travel a minimal distance before movement is perceived, a distance depending in part on the rate at which the stimulus travels. It depends also upon other conditions, such as the part of the retina or skin that is stimulated. Three things may be noted about the distance traveled by a stimulus before perception occurs. (1) In the case of vision it is always larger than the extent of the involuntary tremors of the eye that occur whenever we try to keep the eyes still. (2) Except in the center of the retina it is always smaller than the threshold for the perception of the separation of two points. Thus movements on the periphery of the retina and on the skin may be perceived distinctly when objects are indistinct. (3) The magnitude of the threshold for movement varies with the spatial acuity of the retina and of the cutaneous surface. On the periphery of the retina the decrease in sensitivity to movement is, however, not proportional to the decrease in visual acuity. Thus at the center of the retina the two thresholds are approximately the same, but at a distance of 20° from the center the threshold for acuity is four times as large as that for movement. When we look directly at a moving automobile, for example, we can see the automobile as distinctly as we can see its movement. When we look out of the corner of our eyes, on the contrary, though we cannot see either one as well as we could in direct vision, we still can see the *movement* of the automobile before we can see the automobile *itself*.

What are the limiting rates of stimulation that will arouse the perception of movement? In vision under optimal conditions and at a distance of 2 meters an object must move about 0.2 cm. per sec. before it is perceived as moving. When the rate becomes about 150 cm. per sec. the stimulus will at the same distance be perceived as a flicker or a blur. The minute hand of a watch would have to move some five or six times faster than it does to be seen as moving. From the point of view of our everyday experiences the rate of 150 cm. per sec. seems slow, for it is only about 3 miles per hour, and we can perceive objects moving at several times this rate. If, however, one were looking at the ground 2 meters away through a peep-hole in a board fence, and a mouse running at the rate of 3 miles per hour passed through the restricted field of vision, it would undoubtedly be seen as a blur rather than as an object moving.

The remoteness of a moving object decreases the *perceived rate of movement*. At a distance of a few yards an automobile traveling at 60 miles per hour will appear to be moving rapidly, but at a distance of a few miles only slowly. A ship on the horizon is not perceived as moving at all. The decrease in rate is not, however, proportional to the distance. The tendency for objects to maintain their size with increasing distance (size constancy, see pp. 463f.) tends to keep constant the apparent rate as distance increases. For example, if one backs away from a revolving barber's sign, it will not appear to decrease in rate of rotation as much as it would if it decreased proportionately in perceived size.

Autokinetic movement. Under certain conditions a single stationary stimulus is perceived to move. It is a common observation that a single star in the dark sky appears to move about when steadily fixated. This phenomenon, as produced in the laboratory, is called the *autokinetic movement.* One has only to fixate a small spot of light in a dark room to observe that it tends after a few seconds to move at a rather slow rate irregularly toward the periphery (usually upward). The extent of the movement is seldom more than 40°. For this effect there is no accepted explanation. The one condition for its appearance is that there must be no objects of reference in the visual field for the observer to use as a point of reference for definite localization.

Movement with discontinuous displacement of stimulus. Since the perception of movement usually results from the successive stimulation of different receptors, there would seem to be no fundamental necessity for the stimulus itself to be moving. A series of *discontinuous stimuli* that would successively stimulate different receptors should also produce the perception of movement, provided the rate of succession were adequate. This is exactly what happens in what is termed stroboscopic or *apparent movement,* of which there are many examples in everyday experiences. The simplest situation is at railroad crossings where two lights, placed side by side, light up alternately when a train is near. With continued fixation the light seems to move from one position to the other in succession. Everyone is familiar with the motion seen in electric signs before theaters, stores, hotels and on billboards. There is, of course, no actual movement present. The lights are turned on and off in proper sequence and with proper timing.

The most interesting example, perhaps, is to see the movies themselves move. In the cinema the stimuli are a series of still photographs projected on the screen. Every one of the photographs represents a slightly different snapshot of an object which was moving when the pictures were taken. When the series is projected on the screen in the proper order and at the proper rate—usually 24 per second—normal movement is perceived. The quality of the movement changes with the rate of projection. If this rate is very slow, one sees a succession of static pictures. If the rate is increased, the movement becomes first a flicker, then normal and finally jerky and blurry. Beyond this stage all movement disappears and one has only an impression of a filmy surface, such as that seen in looking at a rapidly revolving color wheel or electric fan.

One of the disadvantages of having an upper threshold of speed is that we cannot observe the details of many ordinary everyday happenings—how a golf ball responds to a blow, how a piece of china breaks or how a sleight-of-hand performer fools us. By the use of a mercury-vapor-tube stroboscope this human limitation is now being circumvented.

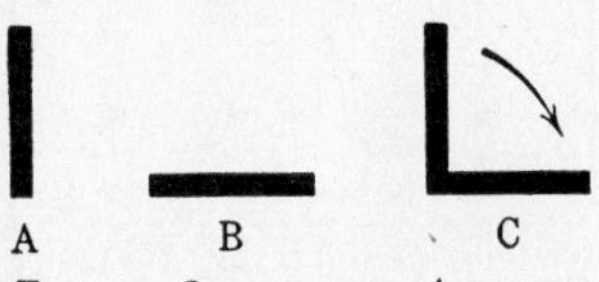

FIG. 74. STIMULI FOR APPARENT MOVEMENT.

Used in a dark room this lamp illuminates a moving object, such as a moving golf club, several hundred times per second, so that a very rapid moving-picture camera may take still pictures of various stages of the rapid movement. After development the film is run at a rate sufficiently slow for one to observe the smallest details of how the golf ball is deformed when it is hit and how it regains its roundness as it moves away.

A situation for the perception of apparent movement with two successive stationary stimuli at different places is shown in Fig. 74. If a vertical line *A* is presented and then immediately after an interval of 60 ms. a horizontal line *B* is presented, the vertical line will be seen to rotate clockwise from the 12 o'clock to the 3 o'clock position as in *C* of the figure. Should the interval of exposure of the two lines be shortened to about 20 ms., the two lines would appear simultaneously and form a right angle. If, on the other hand, the interval between the exposures were lengthened to 200 ms., the two lines would be seen successively with no movement at all.

Exposing the two lines a short distance apart always produces a better perception of movement than exposing them farther apart. The motion-picture cartoonist, recognizing this fact, makes sure that the difference between his successive drawings is very slight. The less the displacement between successive drawings, the more lifelike and complete the movements of the figures.

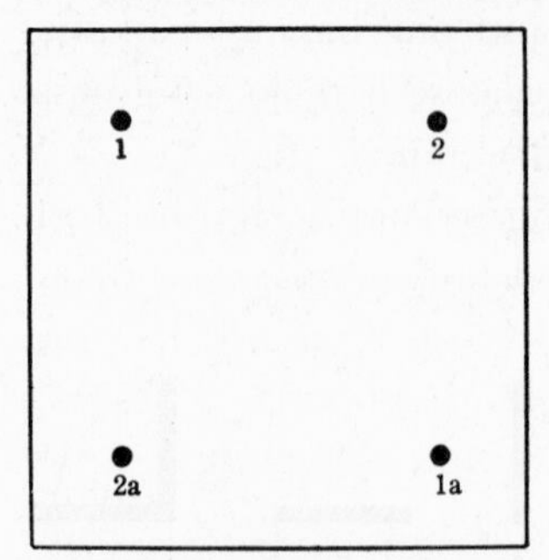

FIG. 75. STIMULI FOR APPARENT MOVEMENT.

When dots 1-1a and 2-2a are shown successively with a fraction of a second between presentations, movement may be seen in the up-down, right-left, clockwise or counter-clockwise directions.

Exposing both stimuli briefly gives an impression of swifter movement, whereas lengthening the exposure time slows down the movement and makes it jerky. Similarly, small stimuli tend to produce smooth movement and large stimuli jerky movement. Thus we reject the front seats in the movies to avoid jerkiness and flicker.

The *attitude of the observer* often determines the direction of the movement. Suppose a subject observes successively appearing lines going from left to right for a number of presentations, whereupon, without his knowledge the direction of the stimulus movement is suddenly reversed; the subject will nevertheless continue to see the lines moving from left to right for three or four presentations. If in Fig. 75 dots in the position 1, 1*a* are succeeded by dots in the position 2, 2*a* the observer may get a left-right, right-left movement, or an up-down, down-up movement, or a clockwise or counterclockwise spinning movement. Many an observer can at will, by changing his point of regard or by suggestion, get any one of these four different kinds of movement.

When one point is applied to the skin, and shortly after another point is applied at a neighboring place, an observer sometimes gets the impression of tactual movement from the first to the second position. In about half the cases, however, even with optimal conditions of stimulation, the observers do not get a good experience of movement. *Apparent tactual movement* is thus not nearly so compulsory as apparent visual movement.

Conditions of movement. The perception of movement occurs, as we have seen, under a wide variety of circumstances. In so far as the perception involves locality, its conditions are those of localization and need not be further discussed here (see pp. 488f.). In so far as the perception involves continuous change in position, however, its conditions are those of spatial continuity. The distribution of receptors in both the retina and the skin is punctiform. Although a moving stimulus excites these receptors successively, nevertheless, if the rate of succession is adequate, we perceive not a succession of impressions in different places but a continuous change in position. The experiments in apparent movement show that the receptors may be widely separated and still, if the other conditions are realized, movement results. Apparent movement is, therefore, a limiting case of the perception of movement at large. The problem of movement is the problem of how perceived continuity issues out of discreteness in the stimulus.

REFERENCES

1. Boring, E. G. *The physical dimensions of consciousness.* New York: Appleton-Century, 1933, 127-149.
2. Brown, J. F. The visual perception of velocity. *Psychol. Forsch.*, 1931, 14, 199-232.
3. De Silva, H. R. An analysis of the visual perception of movement. *Brit. J. Psychol.*, 1929, 19, 268-305.
4. Ellis, W. D. *A source book of Gestalt psychology.* New York: Harcourt, Brace, 1938, esp. 149-191.
5. Hulin, W. S. An experimental study of apparent tactual movement. *J. exper. Psychol.*, 1927, 10, 293-320.

6. MacDougall, R. The structure of simple rhythm forms. *Psychol. Monogr.*, 1903, 4, 309-411.

7. MacLeod, R. B., and Roff, M. F. An experiment in temporal disorientation. *Acta Psychol.*, 1936, 1, 381-423.

8. Ruckmick, C. A. The rhythmical experience from the systematic point of view. *Amer. J. Psychol.*, 1927, 39, 356-366.

9. Vernon, M. D. *Visual perception.* Cambridge: Cambridge University Press, 1937, 157-177.

10. Woodrow, H. Individual differences in the reproduction of temporal intervals. *Amer. J. Psychol.*, 1933, 45, 271-281.

Chapter 16

SENSATION

The chief business of the living organism is adaptation to its ever-changing environment. The protozoan, swimming along near the muddy floor of a pond, turns aside from the sharp cold of a fresh current and moves toward a safer region. Man's problems and man's responses may be more complicated than the protozoan's, yet man, crossing the street in traffic, dodging taxicabs in the five-o'clock rush hour, solves similar problems of avoidance in similar ways. Both cases involve perception: the protozoan perceives cold and the man perceives the oncoming rush of steel and glass and screaming brakes which is the taxicab. Both organisms, protozoan and man, preserve themselves in a careless universe by a knowledge of the external world which comes to them through their sensory mechanisms.

The preceding chapters have dealt with problems of perception. In perception the organism does all it can to get the best possible information about the external world. A piece of coal in the sunshine may reflect more light than a piece of note-paper in the shade; yet we see the coal as black and the paper as white. The constancy phenomenon has come into play here, because it is important for us to recognize these and other objects in a way which has most meaning for us. A lump of whiteness and a sheet of blackness make less sense to us than do coal and paper. So too the organism gets the third visual dimension out of the relations between a considerable number of muscular and retinal data that it receives from the two eyes (accommodation, convergence, binocular parallax and the other cues to depth); it sees that a mountain or a trolley car has, not only height and width, but also depth. As it 'inter-

This chapter was written by Edwin G. Boring of Harvard University.

prets' the data from its two eyes, so also the organism 'interprets' the data from its two ears, not merely hearing a sound—the horn of the taxicab—but knowing also the direction from which it came. In short, in one way or another the organism musters all its resources to the end that it may get the most valuable information about its environment; and this process we call *perception*. To know coal from paper is, in nine cases out of ten, more important for man than to perceive nuances of light and shade. The constancy principle, brought into play in such a case, is only one of many which see to it that man gets, in general, the 'best' information.

Sensation is the core of perception. It is what the organism would perceive if it had only the nature of the stimulus and the stimulated sense organ to go upon. We know a great deal more about the way stimuli affect the sense organs—how light acts on the retina and sound on the inner ear—than we do about the manner in which these sensory data are worked over by the nervous system in perception. The remaining chapters of this book are devoted to these more specific perceptual problems about which there is such a great amount of exactly determined experimental fact.

STIMULUS AND ATTRIBUTES

Stimulus. *A stimulus is any event that activates a sense organ and its receptors.* It is a stimulus only when it stimulates. Light is not a stimulus to a totally blind person, nor are the radio waves that fill the air a direct stimulus to any organism. Many phenomena of nature, because they affect no sense organs in any organism, come to our attention only indirectly by their effects or by the elaborate inferences of science. The important classes of stimuli in the world—the kinds of events that indicate the state of the organism's environment by affecting its sense organs—are mechanical, thermal, acoustic, chemical and photic.

The simplest forms of animals respond to all these classes of stimuli except the acoustic. Their responses, which occur automatically with very little variation, are called *tropisms*, and the list of tropisms is a catalogue of the kinds of stimulation that are effective. In higher vertebrates and man, whose responses to stimulation are ever so much more varied, we do not call the behavior tropistic. The higher animal forms have much greater sensory capacity than the lower. Not only do they perceive sound and all the classes of stimuli that the lower forms perceive; they are also sensitive to much smaller differences in excitation.

Man himself reacts to many kinds of *mechanical* stimulation. He has the tactual sense of his skin, by which he appreciates the presence, size and shape of the objects with which he comes in contact. He can feel pain, which warns him of violent or dangerous contact. He perceives his own posture by means of the proprioceptive organs that lie in his muscles and joints. By their use and by vision he maintains his erect position. He perceives rotation of his own body with great accuracy because rotation stimulates certain specialized organs in his inner ear. He perceives certain contractions of his stomach and calls them hunger. He perceives dryness in his mouth and throat and calls it thirst. These instances are samples of the wide variety of mechanical events which can act as stimuli in man.

Thermal stimulation is also effective for man. He must keep the temperature of his body constant. If it varies a little, he is ill; if it varies much, he dies. Although his body is equipped with a remarkable system for automatic thermostatic control, he needs also to help out by conscious adaptive behavior. The thermal sense tells him when to put on warmer or cooler clothes, when to start the electric fan, when to turn on the radiator.

All animals that live in the air can hear. *Sound,* which shares with vision the important function of giving information about distant stimuli, is a very important and highly developed sense. The stone deaf, deprived of speech and music, seem to suffer even more from their deficiency than do the blind.

Taste and smell are *chemical* senses, the direct descendants of the chemical sense of fishes. Taste is a water sense; it is stimulated only by substances in solution. Smell is an air sense; it is activated by small particles of substance diffused in the air. Although a highly developed sense, smell is little used by man, who, with his erect posture, keeps his nose away from the ground where most of the smells lie. The dog, nose to ground, finds how extremely informative olfactory stimuli can be.

Vision is the *photic* sense and light man's most important stimulus, even though the other senses may, in the blind, become remarkably effective substitutes for vision. Whereas the lower animals sense only the intensity of light, man and some of the higher vertebrates can discriminate its wave-length as well; that is to say, they can see hues as well as brightnesses. Probably this sensitivity to difference in the wave-length of light is one of man's most recent sensory acquisitions, for the development of color vision is still incomplete in that an appreciable portion of the population is color blind.

Attributes of sensation. Since there are many ways in which a sensation can change, an observer, experiencing a sensation, describes it completely only when he has specified its value with respect to every possible dimension of change. These possible dimensions constitute the attributes of sensation.

Suppose a congenitally blind man were suddenly given perfect vision and shown a red square. This single experience would not teach him anything about the attributes of visual sensation, but we could soon show him what some of them are. First, we could change the square in *quality* by altering its hue toward orange or purple, telling the man that this sort of change is a change in the qualitative attribute of hue. Then we could change it in *intensity* or saturation by making the red square fade out toward gray without any change of hue, so that the man would come to recognize a second sensory attribute. To change the square in size would be to teach him about an attribute of *extension*. To change the time of its exposure would be to exhibit *duration* to him. In this way we could demonstrate at least four attributes, four dimensions of visual experience, but the man would not have been able to understand them until he had seen them change independently of one another. Just so have all of us in the casual experience of living learned about sensory attributes.

FIG. 76. DISCRIMINATION OF SHAPE.

The subject was trained to choose the triangle in pair *S*. Then the experiment was arranged to discover whether he would choose, without further training, the triangle in each of the pairs *A* to *G*. The stimuli were large and presented with the triangle as often at the right as at the left. A child learned to discriminate 'pure triangularity' in this way; a chimpanzee almost, but not quite, succeeded. From L. W. Gellerman, *J. genetic Psychol.*, 1933, 42, 14.

It is conventional to classify the sensory attributes under four main heads: *quality, intensity, extension* and *duration*. There can be, however, many more than four sensory attributes. There are just as many attributes as there are possible modes of variation of sensation. In his course in psychology the college student often discovers attributes that are new to him—for most people do not know, until they are taught, that colors have the three attributes of hue, brightness and saturation, or that tones have volume as well as pitch and loudness. Perhaps there are some sensory attributes which the psychologist himself has not yet discovered.

The problem of attributes comes up for animals as well as persons. For instance, size is an extensitive attribute. Can a rat perceive *size*? Yes, because he can learn to choose, for a reward, the larger of two circles, a judgment which he can, although only with difficulty, learn to make independently of the relative brightness of the two circles. Can a rat perceive *shape* as such, independently of all the other spatial properties of visual stimuli? Probably not. Fig. 76 shows the stimuli of an experiment which was arranged to test the capacity of human and animal subjects to perceive triangularity as such. The subject was first trained to choose the triangle and avoid the square in the standard pair of stimuli, *S*. He was then tested to see whether he would choose the triangle instead of the other figure in each of the other seven pairs of stimuli, *A* to *G*. If he chose the triangle in preference to the square in *S* because it was a triangle, then he should choose the triangle instead of the circle in *A* and the inverted triangle in *B*; he should choose the triangle instead of the rotated square, without regard to the rotation of the triangle, in *C* to *F*; and he should prefer the dark triangle to the dark square in *G*. Since each pair of figures is equated in total area and thus in total brightness and since the triangle was shown as often on the right as on the left, it can be argued that shape—not brightness, angular position or size—must have been the basis for the original discrimination in *S*. The general problem has proved, however, too hard for the rat. A chimpanzee almost succeeded in it, and a child did succeed. Thus it is apparent that a person may be able to analyze a perception more specifically into its attributes than can a rat or even a chimpanzee.

Another interesting case of attributive analysis turns up with human subjects in the perception of tones. The observer who has learned about tonal attributes can distinguish in any pure tone at least three aspects: pitch, loudness and volume. Everyone knows what is meant by pitch and loudness, but to most persons the idea that tones have volume is entirely new. The fact is that low tones tend to appear big and high tones small; also that loud tones tend to appear big and soft tones small. This relationship holds so exactly that it is possible to find a loud high tone that seems just the same size as a weak low tone. The relation of these three attributes of tonal perception to the frequency and intensity of the tonal stimulus is shown in Fig. 77. Here the mid-point (0, 0) marks the frequency and intensity of some standard tone. The lines drawn through it show the values of frequency and intensity for which pitch, loudness and volume, respectively, would remain unchanged. Many persons think that the *pitch* of a tone and the frequency of its stimulus are the same thing, but that is not true. The fact that the line for pitch is not strictly vertical in Fig. 77 shows that pitch may change a little with intensity when frequency is constant. Nor is the *loudness* of a tone the same thing as the intensity of its stimulus. A given amount of energy produces the loudest sensations in the middle of the range of audible frequencies; at the two ends of the musical scale the energy must be greatly

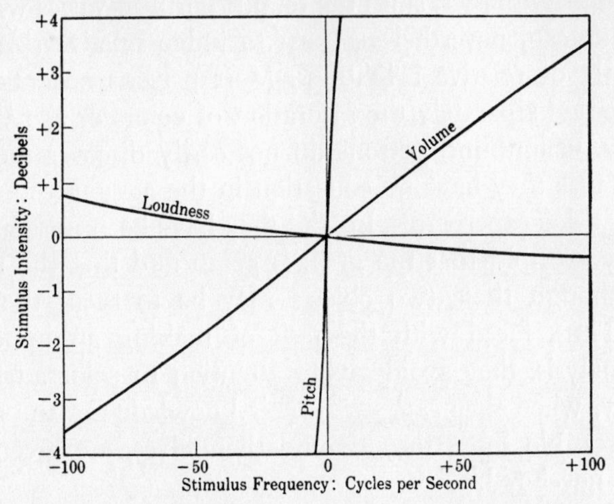

FIG. 77. CONSTANCY LINES FOR THE ATTRIBUTES OF TONE.

The three lines are loci for constant pitch, loudness and volume, equal respectively to the pitch, loudness and volume of the standard tone represented by the frequency and intensity of the point at the middle of the diagram. The lines are called 'contours' because they resemble contour lines of a topograhic map: there is a whole set of lines of constant pitch, one for every different pitch, a set of lines for all the loudnesses, and a third set for the different volumes. Some psychologists think that there is a fourth attribute, density, whose contours cut across this figure from the upper left region to the lower right. In this case the standard has a frequency of 500 cycles per sec. and an intensity of 60 db. For other standards the curves are different. From S. S. Stevens, *Proc. nat. Acad. Sci.*, 1934, 20, 458.

increased to keep the sounds equally loud. *Volume,* of course, becomes a third attribute of tone, one which like the others depends on both the frequency and the intensity of the stimulus. Thus we see that two attributes of a stimulus can give rise to three attributes in a perception, all depending upon the way in which the stimulus affects the organism and its sense organs. That is why the chapters on sensation make so much of the nature of the sense organ, for what we perceive is, in the first instance, dependent upon its properties.

It is important to realize that a person has to learn about particular attributes before he can describe experience in respect of them. People learn readily enough to distinguish between size and brightness, but animals may not. Rats, for instance, do not easily learn this distinction. They usually discriminate a larger white object from a smaller on the basis of the total brightnesses, since the total brightness varies with the size. Rats can, nevertheless, learn to judge relative size independently of relative brightness. Most persons need training to recognize separately the saturation of colors or the volume of tones. Color-blind persons do not easily discover their defect because they have no education in the attributive analysis of their color experiences. Instead they have been miseducated, for they are told that the grass is green and that the rose is red, although these two objects may be to them the same color. Thus, faced with the task of making an impossible color analysis, they avoid giving attention to color attributes, and rely, when they can, upon their knowledge of the nature of objects. No roses, they remind themselves, are green, and grass is never red.

QUALITY

Primary qualities. All the senses but hearing seem to be based upon a few *primary qualities*, which may unite in fusions to give other secondary qualities.

In *vision* the six primary qualities are red, yellow, green, blue, white and black. Perhaps gray should be added as a seventh. All other colors occur as blends of the primary hues (see pp. 527-530). In *smell* the primary qualities are flowery, fruity, spicy, resinous, burned and putrid, and a huge number of intermediates that fit in between these six (see p. 602). In *taste* the primary qualities are sweet, saline, sour and bitter, and for these, too, there are intermediates (see p. 606). In *somesthesis*, the body sense, the primary qualities are pressure, pain, warmth and cold. There are also a great many complex patterns of these four qualities, like hunger, dizziness and itch (see pp. 595f.). *Hearing* is the one sense that cannot be reduced to a few primary qualities. The tones form a continuous series of qualities from the lowest pitch to the highest. Instead of a mere four or seven primary qualities we have in hearing over a thousand.

There is almost no satisfactory physiological theory of sensory quality. All we know about quality is that the fibers for each of the five senses lead to a particular part of the cerebral cortex. It seems probable that of the four primary qualities of touch each has its special fibers; that, in hearing, although a given tone excites many fibers, its quality may be dependent upon the excitation of one particular fiber more than the others. In vision it seems likely that there are only three kinds of fibers in the optic nerve, that the six or seven primary colors are not differentiated physiologically from the others until the excitation has reached the brain. Though all this is pretty vague, it means essentially that, when an organism is making a qualitative discrimination, it is distinguishing between the excitation of one system of nerve fibers and another system. That is why quality seems to be more fundamental than the other attributes, why we talk about the loudness of a pitch but not the pitch of a loudness, about the duration of a red but not the redness of a duration. Quality indicates *what* neural system is functioning. Intensity, extension and duration merely tell *how* the system is functioning.

Qualitative fusions and patterns. In every sense the primary qualities can fuse or combine to form new secondary qualities resembling the components, or mixtures in which the components still retain their identities, or spatial and temporal patterns. Let us examine the five senses for instances of these fusions and patterns.

1. In *vision* all the secondary qualities between the primary colors are perfect fusions. Orange is a fusion of red and yellow. Pink is a fusion of red and white. Brown is a fusion of black and orange, that is to say, of black and red and yellow. There is no such color as a reddish green because red and green are complementary and do not fuse.

Another sort of combination occurs when, according to the

constancy principle, we perceive two brightnesses in the same place, as, for example, when we see a black piece of coal illuminated by sunshine. Although the coal in sunshine is physically the proper stimulus for a light gray, we see it as black, and then we perceive in addition the bright sunshine illuminating it.

2. In *hearing* the best fusion occurs for the tones that make up a musical note. The note is a combination of a fundamental tone and its overtones. As the different overtones vary in their relative intensities, we get different 'musical qualities' or timbres for the note, the sort of difference that distinguishes one voice from another or one musical instrument from another. It is easy to recognize these differences in timbre, although difficult to distinguish the component overtones that determine the timbre.

It is also well known that the pairs of notes in *musical intervals* fuse in different degrees. The octave (*c-c′*) is the best fusion, so smooth and unitary that sometimes observers mistake the two notes for a single one. The musical intervals of the fifth (*c-g*) and the fourth (*c-f*) are not such good fusions; the third (*c-e*) and the sixth (*c-a*) are poorer; the second (*c-d*) and the seventh (*c-b*) are the poorest of all. It is probable that these differences come about because the overtones, present in every musical note, coincide most for the octave and least for the second and seventh. For the octave there is actually a fusion of the notes because all the overtones of the higher component are also overtones of the lower component; and these coincidences diminish in the order in which the different intervals have just been listed.

In a sense *noises* can also be regarded as fusions. They are extremely complex combinations of tones that are for the most part irregularly initiated and interrupted.

3. In *smell* and *taste* the secondary qualities between the primary qualities exhibit various degrees of intimacy in their fusions. Sometimes the components are obvious to the observer; sometimes the sensation seems unitary but has certain clear

resemblances to two or more of the primary qualities. The odor of thyme is spicy-flowery; the odor of geranium is fruity-flowery; the characteristic odor of an ape is burned-putrid; cedar has resemblances to four primary classes—flowery, fruity, spicy and resinous. So it is with the tastes, except that the analysis of the tastes into their components is easier. Potassium iodide is saline-bitter; acetone is bitter-sweet; lead acetate is sour-sweet.

Taste and smell constantly fuse with each other in the production of *flavors*. The 'taste' of food is mostly smell with some taste mixed with it. So close are these fusions that it is almost impossible for an observer, without experimental aids, to distinguish all the smell and taste qualities in the flavor of a complicated food.

4. In *somesthesis*, the body sense, there seem to be, with the possible exception of the experience of heat (see p. 617), no perfect fusions which give intermediates between primary qualities. There are, however, many imperfect fusions and patterns which account for such perceptions as wet, dry, hard, soft, smooth, rough, dull, sharp, oily, sticky, clammy, slimy, mushy, soggy, doughy and spongy. A few of these perceptions have been experimentally analyzed. *Wetness* is a blend of the qualities of pressure and cold; a thin dry rubber bag full of water and cracked ice feels wet. *Oiliness* is a fusion of warmth and light pressure. *Roughness* is an areal pattern which depends on movement. *Clamminess* seems to be a mixture of cold, softness (itself a blend) and certain imaginal components.

It is customary to speak of the 'sensations' of hunger, thirst, nausea, sex, stuffiness, suffocation, dizziness and similar organic experiences connected with digestion or other bodily functions. These perceptions are all *somesthetic patterns* of pressure, pain, warmth and cold. They depend upon no new qualities, but merely on the special patterning of the old. *Hunger*—not the desire for food that makes us eat desserts but the sensory pangs that one feels in the region of the stomach when fasting—depends upon the occurrence of those slow rhythmic contractions of the stomach which are the immediate stimulus to the hunger perception. Qualitatively hunger is a mixture of dull pressure and dull pain, which follows the rhythmic waxing and waning of the stomachic contractions. *Nausea*, also involving dull pain, is sometimes in its incipient stages actually confused with hunger. *Thirst* is a pattern of pressure and pain or warmth, a pattern which we call 'dryness of the mouth.'

INTENSITY

Intensitive stimulation. Usually the intensity of a sensation increases when the energy of its stimulus is increased. A paperweight makes more noise if it drops from the desk to the floor than if it drops only a few inches. On the other hand, intensity of sensation also varies with the sensitivity of the sense organ. In hearing, for instance, sensitivity is greatest in the middle of the musical scale. A tone in this region, therefore, requires less energy than a low tone which sounds equally loud. Perceived sensory intensity is really a measure of the strength with which the stimulus activates the sense organ.

Both vision and hearing are senses tuned to respond to certain limited ranges of a continuous stimulus. The electromagnetic waves, which we sometimes call light, extend through a long range; yet the retina responds to only a limited range of these wave-lengths. The long infra-red waves and the short ultra-violet waves are invisible under all circumstances. For visible light the retina is least sensitive at the two extremes of the spectrum and most sensitive in the middle (see pp. 537-539). Similarly the ear responds to only a limited range of tonal frequencies, being completely deaf to very low and very high frequencies and most sensitive to the middle frequencies of the musical range (see pp. 570-572). Thus it is plain that, if we wish to predict the intensity of a sensation, we must know all about its stimulus, its frequency as well as its energy.

The sensitivity of the organism to a given stimulus is just as important as the energy of the stimulus.

Physiology of intensity. The discovery of the all-or-none principle of nerve conduction raised a difficulty with respect to the physiology of sensory intensity. Previously it had been supposed that an afferent nerve fiber, linking a receptor with the central nervous system, would function for a single quality with various degrees of excitation, thus giving rise to

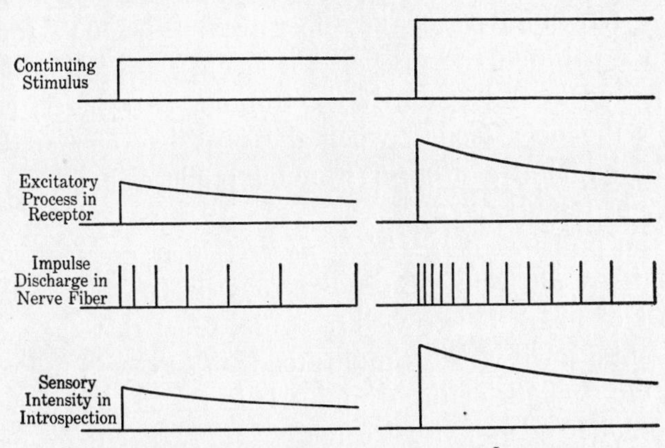

FIG. 78. FREQUENCY PRINCIPLE OF SENSORY INTENSITY.

The figure shows four successive phases in the stimulation of sensory intensity, for a weak stimulus at the left and a strong stimulus at the right. The excitatory process in the receptor diminishes in strength as it is continued, and its diminution is reflected in the decrease of the frequency of the impulses and of the resultant sensory intensity. All nerve impulses are of equal strength under the all-or-none law, but greater stimulus strength means greater frequency in the nerve. Adapted from E. D. Adrian, *The basis of sensation*, 1928; by permission of W. W. Norton & Co.

corresponding degrees of sensory intensity. When, however, it became known that a single fiber responds only with one magnitude of excitation, a need for a special physiological explanation of intensity arose.

There are two principles by means of which the intensity of a stimulus gets represented in the central nervous system of an organism. The two complement each other, and it is doubtful whether either ever acts entirely alone without the concurrence of the other (see pp. 232-235).

1. The *frequency* principle is represented in Fig. 78. A con-

tinuous stimulus gives rise to a series of impulses along the excited fiber, the rate of these impulses being increased when the stimulus is stronger. A brief stimulus will also act in the same way when its effect persists in the receptor long enough to set up a number of successive impulses. It is easy to see how this result comes about when we remember the facts of the refractory period in nervous excitation (see Fig. 16, p. 232). The stimulus discharges the fiber. The fiber becomes refractory, and the stimulus is ineffective. At some point in its relative refractory period the fiber recovers enough for the continuing stimulus to discharge it again, a process which is repeated again and again. If the stimulus is stronger, it discharges the fiber sooner, when the fiber has recovered less completely. Thus a stronger stimulus produces a greater frequency of impulses.

2. The principle of *multiple fibers* is that greater sensory intensities result from the simultaneous excitation of a larger number of fibers. It is a well-recognized fact that the excitation from a small visual stimulus tends to spread in the retina when the strength of the stimulus is increased; and it seems probable that a large visual stimulus also excites more retinal receptors as its strength increases—for a weak stimulus would excite only the most sensitive receptors within a given area, whereas a very strong stimulus might stimulate all (see pp. 556-558). Likewise the effects of mechanical and thermal stimuli spread farther as intensity increases, with the result, of course, that the farther they spread the more receptors they affect. Similarly an intense tone stimulates more receptors in the inner ear than a weak tone (see pp. 595-597).

In brief, then, the intensity of a sensation—its brightness, its loudness, the strength of a tactual quality, an odor or a taste—depends on the total neural excitation that the stimulus arouses. As intensity increases, the number of fibers excited increases, along with the frequency of impulses in each of the excited fibers. Somewhere in the brain there must be an integration of all these impulses when the organism responds to the total excitation as such.

PSYCHOPHYSICS

Thresholds. The *absolute threshold* is the value of a stimulus at which the sensation is (on the average) just noticeable. It marks the beginning or end of a sensory series. For *intensity* the absolute threshold is that amount of the stimulus which is (on the average) just strong enough to elicit the sensation; the smaller the threshold, the greater is the sensitivity of the organism (see pp. 514-516). *Qualitative* series are limited at both ends by absolute thresholds. The visible spectrum lies between the first just noticeable wave-length at the red end and the last just noticeable wave-length at the violet end. Similarly the tonal series lies between the lowest and the highest audible frequencies. There are also such things as a least perceptible *extent* and a least perceptible *duration*.

The *differential threshold* is that difference between two stimuli for which the two sensations are (on the average) just noticeably different. So important is this just noticeable difference that it is abbreviated as j.n.d. The more j.n.d.'s in a given range of stimulus, the greater is the differential sensitivity. The differential threshold is, however, by no means the same in all parts of the same sensory scale. The next section considers how the differential threshold for intensity varies with the intensive level at which it is determined. There are also differential thresholds for quality; one can determine the number of j.n.d.'s of color in the spectrum or of j.n.d.'s of pitch in the tonal series. So too j.n.d.'s can be found for other perceptions, such as length, area, angle, depth, duration and speed.

A threshold represents the determination of a critical point in a sensory series. Since the sensitivity of the organism varies from instant to instant, it is always, however, an *average* point. Sometimes the value of a threshold is discovered by changing the stimulus very slowly until the sensation (or the difference between two sensations) just appears or disappears. Sometimes the experimenter gives the subject various stimuli in haphazard order so that he may find out with what frequency the sensation (or the difference between two sensations) is experienced for each stimulus. In this case the threshold is con-

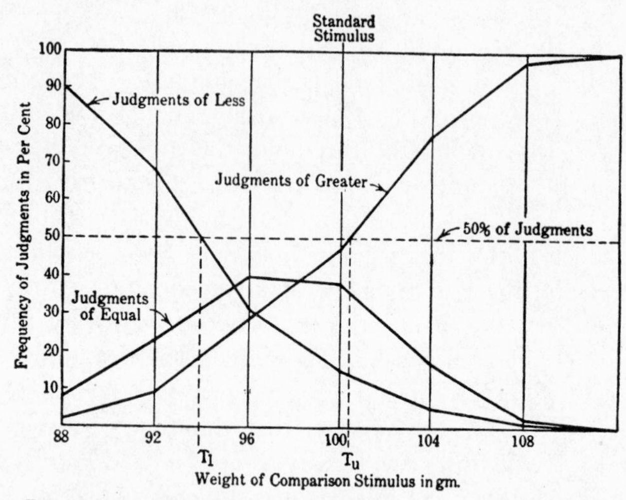

FIG. 79. PSYCHOMETRIC FUNCTIONS FOR DIFFERENTIAL THRESHOLDS.

The figure is a graphical representation of the data of Table XXIX. It shows the three psychometric functions for a case of differential sensitivity to weight and the upper and lower differential thresholds (T_u and T_l). The asymmetrical distribution of the function about the standard weight (100 gm.) results from the fact that the standard stimulus was always presented to the subject before the comparison stimulus, so that the effect of the standard diminished somewhat before the comparison came. In this case the 100 gm. was worth only about 97 gm. by the time the comparison weight arrived.

sidered to be the point at which the sensation (or difference) occurs just as often as it does not. The following example for a differential threshold will make this procedure clear.

TABLE XXIX

Weight of comparison stimulus in grams	88	92	96	100	104	108	112
Number of times judged *greater*	2	9	29	47	78	97	100
Number of times judged *equal*	8	23	40	38	17	2	0
Number of times judged *less*	90	68	31	15	5	1	0
Total judgments	100	100	100	100	100	100	100

Table XXIX gives the data for the determination of the differential thresholds for lifted weights at an intensity of 100 gm.; *i.e.*, the standard weight was 100 gm. Seven other weights were compared with this standard; they varied by 4-gm. steps from 88 to 112 gm. In every case the subject was required to say whether the comparison weight was perceived as greater than the standard, equal to it, or less than it. The table gives these resultant frequencies. Twice in a hundred judgments 88 gm. was felt as heavier than 100 gm., and 90 times as lighter, whereas 112 gm. was always felt as heavier. These three sets of frequencies have been plotted as the three curves of Fig. 79, curves which are called *psychometric functions.* Each psychometric function shows how the frequency of a particular judgment changes with the magnitude of the stimulus. Figure 79 shows that there are two differential thresholds. The lower threshold (T_l) occurs at 92 gm. where the psychometric function for judgments of *less* crosses the 50 per cent line; or, in other words, this subject is just as likely as not to perceive 92 gm. as less than 100 gm. The upper threshold (T_u) is at 100.5 gm.: the subject is just as likely as not to perceive 100.5 gm. greater than 100 gm. The difference between these two thresholds is 8.5 gm., a quantity that measures the sensitivity of discrimination at 100 gm.

The Weber function. When the strength of a stimulus is increased, the resultant sensory intensity follows a law of diminishing returns. If to two lighted candles in a room a third is added, there is a greater increase in the sensed illumination than there would be if a twenty-first candle were added to twenty. The additional light has more effect when added to a lesser illumination. A cough counts for more in church than in the subway. In other words, the differential threshold for intensity gets larger as the intensity gets greater.

It is usual to measure sensitivity by taking the ratio of the differential threshold—let us call it ΔI—to the total intensity at which the threshold was obtained, which we may call I. This ratio, $\Delta I/I$, is called the Weber ratio or the Weber fraction, because a century ago the physiologist, E. H. Weber, thought that it remained constant at different intensities. Modern re-

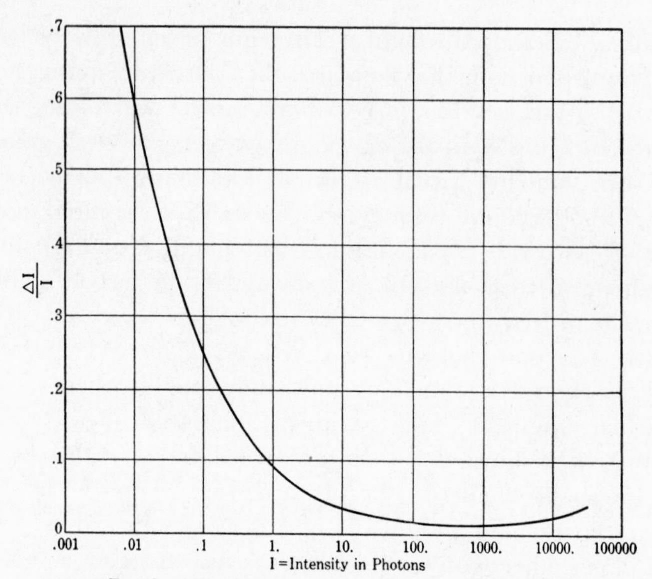

FIG. 80. WEBER FUNCTION FOR VISUAL BRIGHTNESS.

I = retinal illumination in photons of white light. ΔI = differential threshold, the average for the eyes of König and Brodhun in their classical experiment. Maximal sensitivity ($\Delta I/I = 0.016$) is at about 1000 photons.

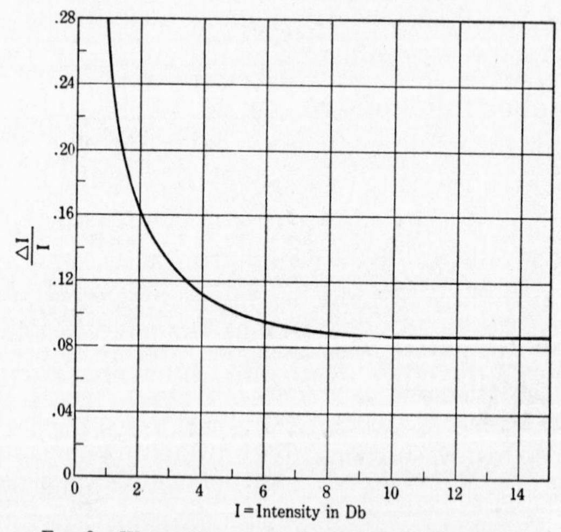

FIG. 81. WEBER FUNCTION FOR LOUDNESS OF TONES.

I = intensity of tone in decibels above the absolute threshold. ΔI = differential threshold. The Weber fraction is constant and minimal ($\Delta I/I = 0.088$) above 60 db, and practically so above 36 db. The curve does not rise at the greatest intensities (see Fig. 80), but perhaps it would if it could be continued further without injury to the ear.

search has corrected his view. The true form of the Weber function is shown in Figs. 80 and 81. Although Weber held that such a function would be a horizontal straight line, actually the function is, as the figures show, a curve. The value of the Weber fraction first decreases rapidly as the intensity increases, and then more slowly until it reaches a minimal value. Thereafter it may remain constant, as for tone (Fig. 81); or it may again increase slightly, as for visual brightness (Fig. 80).

TABLE XXX

MINIMAL WEBER FRACTIONS

For all cases below, except tones and smells, the Weber fraction has a minimal value in the middle range of intensities, for sensitivity is less at both extremes, as in Fig. 80. The minimal values for tone and smell are for the maximal intensities after the Weber function has leveled off, as in Fig. 81. While each of the different values would be somewhat altered by a different choice of experimental conditions, still the difference between 1/77 and 1/5 is so very great that there can be no doubt about the general fact that different sensory mechanisms differ significantly in sensitivity.

	Weber Ratio	Weber Fraction
Deep pressure, from skin and subcutaneous tissue, at about 400 gm.	0.013	1/77
Visual brightness, at about 1000 photons	0.016	1/62
Lifted weights, at about 300 gm.	0.019	1/53
Tone, for 1000 cycles per sec., at about 100 db above the absolute threshold	0.088	1/11
Smell, for rubber, at about 200 olfacties	0.104	1/10
Cutaneous pressure, on an isolated spot, at about 5 gm. per mm.	0.136	1/7
Taste, for saline solution, at about 3 moles per liter concentration	0.200	1/5

In terms of the Weber fractions it is possible to compare one sense with another in respect of sensitivity. Since the fraction varies within a single sense, we must choose for each sense some one representative value, and it is obvious that the minimal fractions best lend themselves to comparison, since each shows the maximal sensitivity of which that sense is capable. In Table XXX these minimal values are listed for seven well-established cases. It is true that these figures apply only to particular experimental conditions; nevertheless, the general relation of the senses is clear. Tonal sensitivity is less than visual. The skin is not so sensitive to a difference in pressure as are the muscles to a difference of lifted weight.

In all this discussion of fractions and curves and minima we must not lose sight of the fact that the Weber function is a general statement that *relativity* is approximated in the world of sensory intensities. The principle of relativity signifies that a little thing means more to another little thing than it does to a big thing. A dollar means more in poverty than it does in wealth, whereas an error of an inch in the length of the equator matters less than an error of an inch in a fountain pen. Just so the Weber function means that differences that are noticeable or even large at small intensities become quite unnoticeable at large intensities.

SENSITIVITY

Absolute sensitivity. Under optimal conditions the energy required to excite sensation is surprisingly small. The absolute intensitive thresholds are quite low as compared with most of the stimulus magnitudes that the human organism constantly meets and takes into account.

The threshold for visual brightness, at the center of the eye and in the dark, is about 0.275 microwatt per square meter of illuminated surface. A microwatt is a millionth of a watt; it is the power required to raise a weight of 1 gm. a distance of 0.01 cm. in 1 sec.—a very small amount of power. Nevertheless, the threshold in the outer regions of the retina is still smaller; it is only about one thousandth as large as the threshold at the center.

Very small stimuli, like the stars, reveal an even greater retinal sensitivity. The power of a faint star, just visible out of the corner of the eye, is about 10^{-8} microwatt (100 million millionths of a watt). Such a star would have to shine on the retina for forty years to deliver one erg of energy to it. If the star can be perceived in a fifth of a second, as seems probable, then the retina is some 30,000 times as sensitive as that very sensitive instrument, the radiometer, which the physicists use for measuring radiant energy.

For tone the absolute intensitive threshold varies greatly with pitch. It is least for frequencies in the region of 2000 to

4000 cycles per second, where it is approximately 4×10^{-9} microwatt. This value is about half as large as the figure given for visual brightness in the preceding paragraph, in spite of the common belief that the retina can be excited by less energy than can excite the ear. The safest generalization, however, is that the sensitivities of the eye and the ear are, under optimal conditions, of the same order. Certain investigators have computed that, if the minimal auditory threshold were only 6 decibels lower, the ear could detect as sound the movement of the molecules of the air.

The energy required to reach the threshold increases tremendously toward the limits of hearing. For the lowest audible tones it is about six million times as great as in the most sensitive middle region, whereas for the highest audible tones it is about six billion times as great as in the middle region. Beyond these limits no energy that it is safe to deliver to the ear will elicit tone.

Absolute thresholds for cutaneous pressures may vary from 0.02 gm. to 0.10 gm. One investigator has estimated that the minimal stimulus for pressure involves about 0.0001 erg, a small value, yet one that is about 10,000 times as large as the threshold values for light and tone.

Olfactory sensitivity is great, although, since the intensitive stimulus cannot be measured in terms of energy, olfaction cannot be directly compared with vision and audition. The putrid-smelling mercaptan creates a vile stench when the solution of the stimulus is only one in three hundred million parts of air, and the threshold for mercaptan is represented by a dilution of approximately one part in fifty thousand million. A single breath of this just noticeable stimulus would contain about 0.000,000,000,002 gm. of mercaptan, which is less than one three hundredth of the smallest amount of matter (sodium) that can be detected by the spectroscope. Still we are not anywhere near the limits of a subdivision of a compound, for this threshold stimulus would contain about twenty-one thousand million molecules of mercaptan, a very great many of which would come into contact with the olfactory organ.

The absolute thresholds for taste are expressed in no such minute quantities of substance. About 0.005 gm. of sugar per cc. of water, or 0.000,01 gm. of saccharine, is just noticeably sweet. It takes only about 0.000,000,5 gm. of quinine per cc. of water to be just noticeably bitter. Bitter seems most often to be aroused by a very low concentration of stimulus, but there is no general rule among the tastes.

Differential sensitivity. Differential sensitivity is not so great as absolute sensitivity. The absolute threshold may be very small, and yet the number of j.n.d.'s above it may not be large. The Weber function explains this seeming disparity. Consider, for instance, a tone of 2048 cycles per sec., for which the absolute threshold is about 0.000,000,000,4 microwatt. If the differential thresholds were constant and as small as the absolute threshold—that is to say, if we could distinguish at any loudness an intensitive difference of 0.000,000,000,4 microwatt—then we should be able to distinguish about twelve million different intensities between the faintest audible tone and the tone which is so loud that it begins to hurt. Actually, because the differential threshold becomes so much larger at the higher intensities, there are only about 366 discriminably different intensities in this range.

Ordinary speech does not approach either of the intensitive extremes. A very soft whisper has a power of about 0.001 microwatt. A faint voice may drop to about 0.1 microwatt without becoming a whisper. A very loud shout would be about 1000 microwatts. The power involved in ordinary speech is about 10 microwatts, under which conditions the air particles move only about 0.01 mm. It would require a million persons all talking at once to produce the power necessary to light a small electric lamp. Factory and city noises may be much louder than speech, so loud that a shout cannot be heard. One noise survey found Sixth Avenue at Thirty-fourth Street the noisiest place in New York City. The power of that noise was 1,000,000 microwatts.

The best figures for the differential thresholds of visual

brightness show 572 steps from no illumination at all up to the maximal brilliance that the eye can stand. Again we can see how the number of discriminable differences is reduced in accordance with the Weber function. The illumination of the disk of the sun is about sixty million million times the illumination of a white disk that is just perceptible in the dark, and the illumination of white paper in direct sunlight is about sixty thousand million times the absolute threshold. These great brightnesses, however, injure the eyes. The stimuli for ordinary good vision lie between two million and two hundred million times the absolute threshold.

If we consider the total number of possible sensations within a given sense, then we have to take account of the qualitative, as well as the intensitive, differential thresholds. In vision there are in the spectrum 128 j.n.d.'s in hue, and to them must be added 28 j.n.d.'s in the purples which lie outside the spectrum—156 hues in all. The spectral hues exhibit from 16 to 23 j.n.d.'s of saturation, that is to say, there are about 20 steps from the richest spectral color to pure gray. From black to white there are, as we have noted, 572 brightnesses. We cannot multiply these three values together to get the number of discriminably different colors, because the different dimensions of color are interrelated: there are, for example, fewer discriminable hues and saturations among the very bright and the very dark colors (see pp. 530f.). However, approximations which take these relationships into account indicate that the number of discriminably different colors is of the order of 300,000.

The same problem comes up with the tones. The number of j.n.d.'s for pitch, at the intensity where the j.n.d.'s for pitch are most numerous, is about 1500. Although there are not many discriminable intensities at the two extremes of pitch, the total number of tones that differ either in pitch or in loudness has been estimated as somewhat over 300,000. In a sense there are, speaking very generally, about as many tones as colors.

REFERENCES

1. ADRIAN, E. D. *The basis of sensation.* New York: W. W. Norton, 1928.
2. ADRIAN, E. D. *The mechanism of nervous action.* Philadelphia: University of Pennsylvania Press, 1932. Chaps. 1 and 2.
3. BORING, E. G. *The physical dimensions of consciousness.* New York: D. Appleton-Century, 1933. Chaps. 2, 3 and 6.
4. GUILFORD, J. P. *Psychometric methods.* New York: McGraw-Hill, 1936. Chaps. 2 and 6.
5. *Handbook of general experimental psychology.* Worcester, Mass.: Clark University Press, 1934. Chaps. 3, 13-20.
6. HOLWAY, A. H., and PRATT, C. C. The Weber-ratio for intensitive discrimination. *Psychol. Rev.,* 1936, 43, 322-340.
7. STEVENS, S. S., and DAVIS, H. *Hearing: its psychology and physiology.* New York: John Wiley, 1938. Chaps. 2-5.
8. TROLAND, L. T. *The principles of psychophysiology.* New York: D. Van Nostrand, 1930. Vol. 2, esp. sections 53, 54 and 61.

CHAPTER 17

VISION

The study of vision, in the most limited sense, is the study of *color-discriminations*, with particular attention to the way in which discrimination depends upon the receptors in the eye. It is with this problem that we are concerned in the present chapter.

THE ORGAN OF VISION

The eye. The eye is only partly a system of light-sensitive receptors; in large part it is an apparatus like a photographic camera, serving to produce an optical image of the world in front of it. Like a camera, it forms that image upon a sensitive film at the back. This film, which is called the *retina*, contains the receptor cells.

When one says that the eye or the camera forms an 'optical image' on its film, what one means is that the light-waves coming from any particular point in front of the apparatus are made to come together at a corresponding special point on the film. In the case of the eye this image-formation, or focusing of the light, makes certain that waves coming from different parts of the outer world shall fall on different receptors.

Figure 82 shows the gross structure of the eye. Light entering it passes first through the transparent *cornea*, then through a watery fluid, the *aqueous humor*, then through the *lens* and finally through a gelatinous substance, the *vitreous humor*, before reaching the retina. Not only the lens, but also the cornea and the two humors play a part in focusing the light.

Just in front of the lens is the *iris*, the familiar 'colored part' of the eye. The iris is a muscular ring containing a cir-

This chapter was written by D. M. Purdy of Mills College.

cular opening, the *pupil*, which is automatically changed in size when the stimulation of the retina becomes weaker or stronger. The action of the iris tends to prevent the light in the retinal image from becoming too strong or too weak.

The lens can be focused for near or far objects. The change in focus (or the *accommodation*) of the eye is brought about by an automatic change in the curvature of the lens. The lens

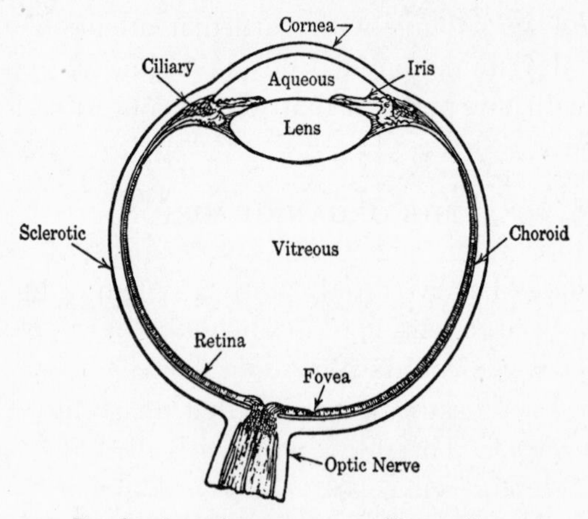

FIG. 82. CROSS-SECTION OF THE HUMAN EYE.

This figure represents a cross-section of the right eye, as viewed from above. After L. T. Troland, *The principles of psychophysiology,* 1930, II, 98; by permission of D. Van Nostrand Co.

has elasticity, which tends to make it bulge; but it is held under tension by a ring of radial fibers encircling it. The tension of these fibers is in turn controlled by an outlying ring of muscular tissue, the *ciliary muscle*. When we look at a nearby object, the ciliary muscle contracts, the tension on the lens is removed and the lens bulges. When we transfer our gaze to a distant object, the ciliary muscle relaxes, and the lens is pulled out so that its front surface flattens.

The whole eyeball is enclosed in a leathery casing, the *sclerotic coat*, which at the front of the eye has a transparent part, the cornea. The sclerotic coat, but not the cornea, is lined by a dark-colored membrane, the *choroid coat*. Within the choroid, in turn, is the thin membrane which is called the *retina.*

The retina. The retina (Fig. 83) has a very complex microscopic structure. It contains two sorts of nerve cells or

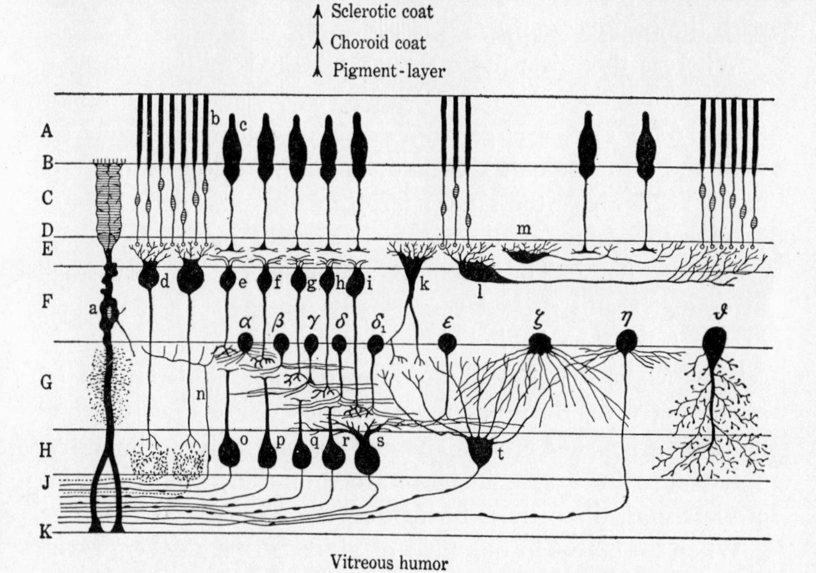

FIG. 83. SCHEMATIC CROSS-SECTION OF THE HUMAN RETINA.

b = a rod.
c = a cone.
d, e, f, g, h, i = bipolar cells.
o, p, q, r, s, t = optic-nerve cells.
k, l, m = lateral neurons (horizontal cells).
$\alpha, \beta, \gamma, \delta, \epsilon, \zeta, \eta, \vartheta$ = lateral neurons (amacrine cells).
After Kallius; based on the work of Ramón y Cajal.

neurons: the receptors and a system of neurons for the transmission of nervous impulses from them.

The receptors are of two types, the *rods* and *cones,* so named after their typical shapes. Curiously enough, the rods and cones are placed behind the layers of conducting neurons, so that the light must first go through these layers (which are almost perfectly transparent) before it can act upon the receptors.

The rods and cones are connected, by way of synapses, to short conducting neurons called *bipolar cells*. The bipolar cells in turn make synaptic connection with a second set of conducting neurons, the *cells of the optic nerve*. The cells of the optic nerve have very long axons, and these axons are the individual fibers of the *optic nerve* that connects the retina with the brain (see Fig. 14, p. 228).

Whereas there are more than a hundred million receptors in the retina, the optic nerve contains only about half a million fibers. As a rule, a large number of receptors are connected with the same bipolar cell, and, in turn, a large number of bipolar cells share the same neuron in the optic nerve.

Near the center of the retina is a small pit or depression called the *fovea*. The receptors at this place are very small in diameter and packed very closely together. Each receptor in the fovea has its individual bipolar cell and optic-nerve cell, which it shares with no other receptor. This central region, therefore, furnishes more distinct vision than the outlying or *peripheral* retina. The eye is admittedly an imperfect optical instrument; the images formed on the peripheral retina are less sharp than those formed on the central area.

When an object in our field of vision attracts us, we involuntarily turn our eyes so that the retinal image in each eye falls on the fovea and the object is seen with maximum distinctness. Such an adjustment of the eyes is called *fixation*.

The rods and cones have a characteristic distribution on the retina. The fovea and its immediate surroundings contain only cones; they make up the central *rod-free area* of the retina. Just outside this area, a few rods are intermingled with the cones, but the rods become more and more numerous as the edges of the retina are approached. Finally, the extreme periphery contains an overwhelmingly large percentage of rods, although even this area is not quite free of cones.

The fibers of the optic nerve pass from all parts of the retina towards a common meeting place, where they form themselves into a bundle, the optic nerve. The place of exit of the optic nerve is called the *optic disk* or *blind spot*; the optic disk of each eye is situated on the inner or nasal side of the retina. Under ordinary conditions the optic disk is blind, as one would expect if it consisted entirely of nerve tissue and contained no rods or cones. There are experiments to show, however, that the optic disk responds when very strong light is thrown upon it. It seems likely, therefore, that this region contains a few receptor cells.

In addition to the bipolar and optic-nerve cells, which form a direct line of conduction between the receptors and the brain, there are also *lateral neurons* which connect one part of the retina with another (Fig. 83, *k, l, m*).

Most of the theories about the processes that take place in the receptors are hypotheses based upon the psychological facts of color perception rather than upon direct physiological study of the receptors themselves. The processes in the receptors are complicated and difficult to unravel by direct physiological methods. It is well established, even so, that light acts on the receptors by producing *chemical* effects in them. Here we have one more point of resemblance between the eye and a camera, for the action of light on a photographic film is also chemical.

There is, as we shall see later, one very firmly established fact about the working of the receptors: the two kinds of receptors, the rods and the cones, have different functions.

THE EXPERIENCE OF COLOR

Colors *vs.* light-waves. To understand the problems of vision one must always be clearly aware of the difference between *colors*, such as blue, yellow, white and gray, and *light-waves*, which are the stimuli acting on the eye. Colors are psychological facts; light-waves are facts of physics.

When light-waves stimulate the receptors, which in turn transmit a physiological effect to the brain, we see a color, but whether we see red, blue or gray depends upon the nature of the waves. Yet the color does not exist in the light-waves, nor does it travel along the optic nerve. It does not come into being until physiological processes have been aroused in the nervous system. Light-waves are *responsible* for our seeing the color; they are not themselves the color.

Here is a striking example of the difference between light-waves and colors. There are four *primary hues*: red, yellow, green and blue. One might expect that perhaps there would be four species of light-waves to correspond to these hues; but there are not. Light-waves differ from each other in that some have longer and others shorter wave-length, and in that some have high and others low energy; but they are in no way differentiated into *types.* The existence of the four outstanding hues is a property of the seeing organism and not of the light-waves as such.

Brightness, hue and saturation. Colors as they occur in normal perception have various modes of appearance; there are *surface-colors, film-colors and transparent colors* (pp. 431f., 426f.). When we see surface-colors, we may at the same time perceive separately the illumination upon them, whereas with the film-colors, such as are seen in a spectroscope or through the hole of a reduction screen (p. 432), and the transparent colors we make no distinction between color of object and color of illumination. In daily life most of the colors that are important for us are surface-colors, the colors of objects. Object-colors, as we have seen, show approximate 'constancy' even though the light-waves that the object reflects into the eye undergo great changes. We shall now consider the three characteristics that apply to any color—no matter whether it is surface, film or transparent bulk, or the color of an illumination. These characteristics are brightness, hue and saturation.

We begin with *brightness.* Consider the brightness of surface-colors: a sheet of snow is brighter than a piece of gray cloth that stands in the same illumination, and the cloth in turn is brighter than a piece of coal. Or, consider the illumination on such a surface-color: a sheet of snow appears more brightly illuminated at noonday than at twilight. Film-colors also have different degrees of brightness: the blue vault of the noonday sky is brighter than the heavens at twilight. The same holds true for transparent colors.

All colors, without exception, have brightness; whereas some, but not all, have the additional property of *hue*. Hue is what we have in mind when we speak of a color as yellow, as violet, as bluish green and so on.

The colors that possess hue are called *chromatic*; those without hue are called *neutral* (or *achromatic*). Snow, gray cloth and coal have neutral surface-color; normal daylight is a neutral illumination.

Any chromatic color can be matched with some particular neutral color in regard to brightness. This matching may not be easy, especially if the chromatic color is a rich one; but it can always be done at least roughly. Suppose, for instance, we have a series of neutral surface-colors—let us say bits of paper ranging in an orderly series by small steps from white through light grays and dark grays to black. If we are now given some chromatic surface-color, perhaps a piece of red paper, we can find some member of our neutral series that has the same lightness or darkness as the red. Or, to turn from surface to illumination colors, we find that two illuminations can appear equally bright even though one is neutral daylight and the other is reddish.

Not only do chromatic colors have brightness and hue, but also a third attribute called *saturation*, or richness. Though two reds may be exactly alike in both brightness and hue, yet the one may be a rich, full red and the other merely tinged with reddishness, barely distinguishable from a neutral color. The saturation of any chromatic color may be defined as its degree of difference from a neutral color of equal brightness. We can think of a neutral color as a color of zero saturation; it is a limiting point that chromatic colors approach as they become less and less saturated.

Brightness vision and chromatic vision. Brightness, as we have seen, is a property of all colors, whether chromatic or neutral. A neutral color is, so to speak, a mere brightness, whereas a chromatic color is something *more* than a mere brightness; and the higher its saturation, the more pronounced is this 'something more.'

A person who never experienced any *brightness* would be blind; but one to whom all objects appeared as having brightness alone, without any hue or saturation, would by no means be blind. As a matter of fact, when the light is dim or when the objects are at the extreme edge of the field of vision, all normal people have neutral vision, seeing only brightnesses. There are, moreover, abnormal individuals in whom this type of vision is present at all times. 'Total color blindness' is the common name for this defect.

According to certain evolutionary theories, the simpler animals have nothing but brightness vision, chromatic vision having evolved or become differentiated more or less gradually out of this more primitive kind of function. It ought to be remarked, however, that animals as low in the evolutionary scale as the bee and the minnow have an elaborate sort of chromatic vision, albeit unlike that of man. On the other hand, an animal as high in the scale as the dog has, according to some investigators, only very weak chromatic vision, or, according to others, none at all.

From the point of view of biological usefulness, it is far more important that an animal have brightness vision, *i.e.,* the fundamental ability to *see*, than that it have the added capacity of chromatic vision. Yet it is also true, of course, that hue and saturation often serve as valuable aids to the recognition and identification of objects, as, for instance, when we recognize a house or a book or a traffic signal by its color. It is true too that richly saturated colors often give an object an impressiveness which makes it stand out from its background. In spite of all this, brightness remains fundamental, the principal means by which objects are set off from their surroundings.

Thus, in certain experiments dealing with this question, a finely detailed pattern of one hue was placed on a background of another hue of exactly equal brightness. It was found that, in the absence of any brightness difference, the details of the pattern tended to 'swim together' and become very diffuse. The implication is that in our field of vision differences in hue do not contribute nearly so much to the formation of sharp contours as differences of brightness.

Another question is this: Given black details on white, like the letters on a printed page, what kind of *illumination* is best for sharp vision? Experiments show that, at any given brightness, neutral sunlight is better than any chromatic illumination. Yellow proves to be the best of the chromatic illuminations; but the less saturated the yellow, the better it is.

INTERRELATIONS OF COLORS

The spectrum and the hue circle. Our discussion of the three properties of colors—brightness, hue and saturation—is not yet complete; we have not finished with hue.

There is a curious fact about hue as compared with the other two attributes. Brightness and saturation vary by mere degrees; they vary, so to speak, along a simple straight line. The variation of hue, however, is *circular*; in other words, if one starts at any point in the series of hues and continues along the series, he finally comes back to the starting point.

In this circular series we shall also find that there are four primary hues, yellow, green, blue and red, which are singular or primary (see p. 502). In this respect, too, hue is unlike brightness or saturation. Besides black and white there are no primary brightnesses or saturations that stand out as unique. Consider, for instance, how difficult it is to hold in one's memory any particular brightness or saturation, as compared with the ease of remembering and recognizing yellow, green, blue and red.

A convenient object with which to begin our study of the hue circle is the band of colors called the *spectrum*. Since the spectrum plays an important part in our whole study of vision, we shall consider not only what it looks like, but also how it originates.

To begin with, we must note that most of the colors with

which we have to do in daily life are produced by *mixtures* of different wave-lengths of light and not by single wave-lengths. To obtain a stimulus that has only one wave-length, one can pass a beam of ordinary mixed light (*e.g.,* sunlight) through a glass prism. The various rays, in traveling through the prism, become separated, bent out of their paths by different amounts, for the rays of long-wave light are bent less than those of short-wave light. If the beam, after being thus sifted, is allowed to stimulate the eye, the observer sees a band of rich colors of many different hues.

This band, the spectrum, contains an orderly series of hues ranging from red through orange, yellow, yellow-green, green, green-blue and blue to violet. Red corresponds to the longest waves, violet to the shortest. These spectral colors are the most saturated that one can get from any sort of light.

The spectrum shows us, then, that *single wave-length stimulation produces a highly saturated color whose hue depends on the length of the waves.*

So much for the origin of the spectrum. Consider now its appearance. The band is red at one of its edges. As we pass away from this extreme red, the hue of the spectrum grows constantly more yellowish and less reddish. Finally we reach a yellow which is nothing but yellow, with no trace of red left in it. At this point the hue begins to change in a new direction, the direction of green. We pass through yellows which continually grow more greenish, until eventually we arrive at a green which is nothing but green and devoid of any yellowishness whatsoever. Here again a new direction of hue change begins —a change from green towards blue. At blue there is a new turning point, where the hue goes away from blue back in the direction of red again.

The spectrum ends with a violet, which is a blue that is only slightly reddish; but the spectrum does not contain all possible hues. There are secondary hues intermediate between blue and red which are still more reddish than the extreme spectral violet. These are the purples and carmines. Such hues are not produced by any single wave-length, but always require a mixture of wave-lengths; they can be obtained, *e.g.*, by mixing lights from opposite ends of the spectrum. Adding these colors to those of the spectrum, we can pass from blue through violet, purple and carmine back again to red, our starting point. The extreme red of the spectrum is, to be strictly accurate, a slightly yellowish red. The true primary red, like the purples and carmines, lies outside the spectrum.

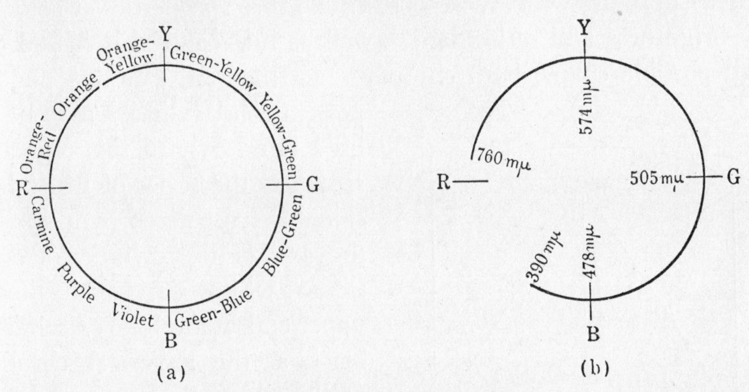

FIG. 84. PSYCHOLOGICAL COLOR CIRCLE.

(*a*) *R, Y, G* and *B* represent the four primary hues.

(*b*) Relationship of the series of spectral colors to the psychological color circle. The wave-lengths of the spectral limits and of the three spectral primary hues are indicated in the diagram.

Thus the total series of hues, a sequence that comes back to its starting point, can be symbolized by a closed geometrical figure, such as a circle (Fig. 84, *a*).

In this series the four *primary hues* represent four turning points, or places where the hue change takes on a new direction. These are (1) a yellow which is neither reddish nor greenish, (2) a green which is neither yellowish nor bluish, (3) a blue which is neither greenish nor reddish, and (4) a red which is neither bluish nor yellowish (Fig. 84). In order to do justice to these 'turning points,' a square rather than a circle is sometimes used to represent the hue series, with the four primary hues placed at the corners.

All the secondary hues between the primaries are called intermediate hues. It ought to be noticed that, whereas there are intermediates between *R* and *Y*, *Y* and *G*, *G* and *B*, and *B* and *R*, there exist no such colors as a 'reddish green' or a 'yellowish blue.' In short, primaries that are adjacent on the hue circle have intermediates, but those that stand opposite do not. This fact is very important for theories about the physiology of vision.

The color solid. Suppose we wish to construct a geometrical figure which will represent all three properties of color —brightness and saturation as well as hue—and will include all possible colors, both chromatic and neutral. For this purpose, a solid cylinder may be used (Fig. 85). In this representation the series of neutral colors is symbolized by a line, the axis of the cylinder. Extreme white stands at the upper end of the line, extreme black at the lower. A chromatic color is represented by a point outside the axis. The greater the distance of this point from the axis, the greater the saturation of the color. The height of a point, measured perpendicularly from the base of the cylinder, represents the brightness of the color. Hue varies circumferentially around the axis.

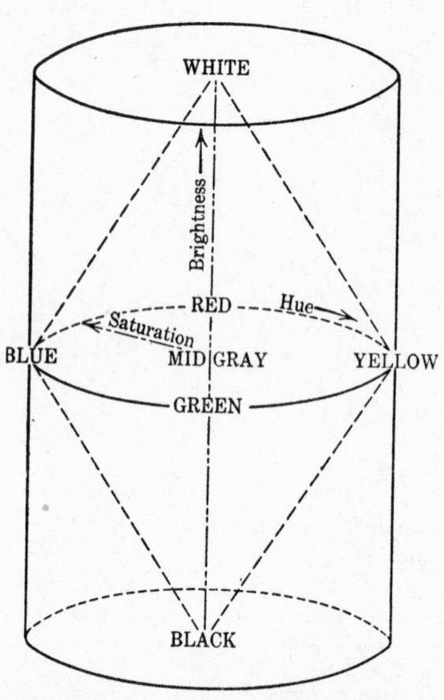

Fig. 85. Psychological Color Solid. The solid is drawn sometimes as a cylinder and sometimes as a double cone. After L. T. Troland, *The principles of psychophysiology*, 1929, I, 251; by permission of D. Van Nostrand Co.

A line drawn parallel to the axis at any place in the cylinder represents a simple brightness series—a series of colors with the same hue and saturation, differing only in brightness. A line beginning at the axis and drawn perpendicularly to it, at any place, stands for a series of colors which, having the same brightness and hue, yet differ in saturation—a simple saturation series. A circle of any size, drawn concentric to the axis, indicates a simple hue series, constant in brightness and saturation.

It so happens that very bright and very dark colors are always low in saturation. The richest colors are always colors of intermediate brightness. If we wish to take account of this fact, in a rough way, we can substitute for the cylinder a solid figure which tapers towards either end, such as the *double cone* shown in Fig. 85. All colors are to be thought of as lying within the boundaries of this cone.

STIMULI TO COLORS

Colors and simple stimuli. Let us now study, more thoroughly than we have done so far, the relationships of colors to the light-waves acting on the eye.

Light-waves may differ from each other in *wave-length* and in *energy*—just as waves on a surface of water may be either long swells or short ripples, and may be either weak waves or strong waves. One must make a clear distinction between the *energy* of the light-waves (which the physicist can define and measure without making any reference to human vision) and the *brightness* that a human being may see when the waves act on his eye. Energy is physical, brightness is psychological. Although there are, furthermore, certain relationships between quantity of energy and level of brightness, there is by no means a perfect correspondence between the two.

Light-waves are one—but only one—example of a kind of wave that is called electromagnetic. They are electromagnetic waves of exceedingly short wave-length. The wave-lengths of light are usually measured in terms of a unit called the millimicron (abbreviated mμ), which is equal to one-millionth of a millimeter. The longest waves (at the extreme red end of the spectrum) are about 760 mμ in length; the shortest (at the extreme violet end) are about 390 mμ in length. Under exceptional conditions, *i.e.,* when the energy of the waves is especially great, the spectrum is broadened; the range of waves that may, under extreme conditions, have an effect on human vision extends from 800 to 365 mμ.

There exists a great variety of *invisible* electromagnetic waves longer than 800 mμ—for example, the waves of radiant heat and the waves used in radio broadcasting. There are also invisible waves shorter than 365 mμ, among them the ultraviolet radiations and the X-rays. The length of the longest waves known to the physicist is about 30 million million mμ, and that of the shortest is about 0.0001 mμ. Even though all these waves are alike in kind and different merely in length, the receptors in the human eye are so constituted that they respond only to a tiny range of these wave-lengths.

The light stimulating the eye may contain waves that are all of the same length, or it may contain a mixture of wave-lengths. Mixed stimulation varies in two ways: in the wave-lengths it contains, and in the energy going along with each individual wave-length. Thus there is possible a vast variety of different kinds of stimulation.

Now we may inquire concerning the relationships existent between the brightness, hue and saturation that we see and the properties of the physical stimulus which are responsible for our seeing.

When the light is all of the same wave-length, there is, as we already know, a relation between *hue* of color and *wave-length* of stimulus. Wave-lengths ranging from 760 to 390 mμ give us a spectrum including an orderly series of hues that form almost, but not quite, a complete hue circle. The relation of the hue circle to the wave-length limits of the spectrum is shown in Fig. 84, *b*. This figure also indicates the wave-lengths of the three spectral stimuli that furnish primary hues—the primary yellow, green and blue.

A second important fact already familiar to us is that single wave-lengths furnish colors of high *saturation*.

About *brightness*, the following principle holds: For any particular wave-length, if the *energy* of the waves is increased or decreased, the *brightness* of the spectral color increases or decreases also.

It is not correct to say, however, that the brightness of a spectral color depends upon energy alone. It happens that the different wave-lengths of light have different brightness-producing powers. For the wave-lengths toward the middle of the spectrum, a given amount of energy furnishes more brightness than for wave-lengths toward the red and violet ends.

So much for single wave-lengths. The case of a stimulus which is a *mixture* of wave-lengths will be understood after we have gained insight into the following general problem.

Stimulus mixture. If we mix together any two stimuli which produce different colors, what principles determine the color of the mixture?

Fig. 86 illustrates a scheme for the experimental study of stimulus mixture. S_1 and S_2 are two differently colored areas. They may be, for instance, two areas of spectral light, each of a different wave-length, or they may be two areas of colored paper. A glass plate P is so placed that the light rays from S_1 are reflected into the observer's eye, striking the same area of the retina as the direct rays from S_2. Or, one can superpose spots of differently colored light from two projection lanterns upon a screen.

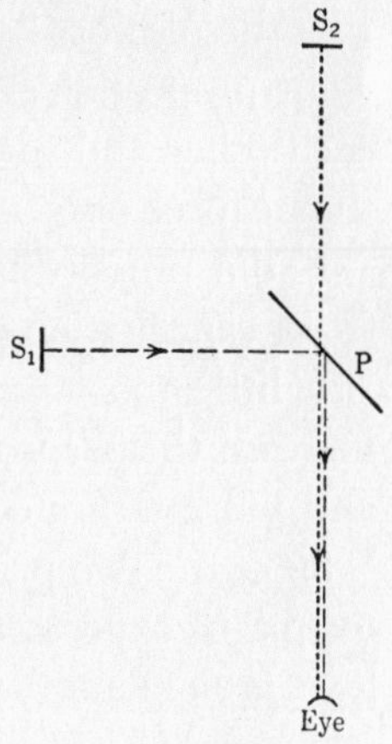

FIG. 86. SCHEME FOR EXPERIMENTATION ON THE MIXTURE OF STIMULI.

The glass plate P reflects the light rays from S_1 into the observer's eye; the rays from S_2 pass directly through the glass and enter the eye in the same direction.

A convenient method for use with colored papers is the method of rotating disks. A disk made up of two differently colored sectors is rotated at such high speed that its surface looks perfectly uniform and shows no flicker. In this method the two kinds of reflected light do not actually strike the same area of the retina at the same time, but in very rapid alternation; the effect for perception, however, is like that of a true light-mixture.

The mixture of *pigments* or paints, since it does not furnish a simple additive mixture of light-rays, is unsuited for our experiments. There are, as we shall see later, complicating physical factors that enter into such a mixture.

Experiments show that brightnesses add together in a very simple manner. The brightness of a color produced by mixing stimuli depends only on the brightnesses of the individual colors, regardless of their hues or saturations. For example, if we mix a yellow with an equally bright blue, we obtain the same brightness that would be produced by mixing the yellow with an equally bright red, green or white.

The first important fact for us to learn about hue and saturation is the existence of *complementary hues.* Primary yellow and primary blue are one pair of complementary hues. If we mix these colors by the method of rotating disks, and have the right proportion between the sectors, the two hues will *cancel* each other and give a neutral gray. Any pair of hues that can thus cancel or neutralize each other is called complementary.

If the proportion of yellow to blue is a little too high for exact cancellation, we obtain a weakly saturated yellow; if it is a little too low, we obtain a weakly saturated blue. If we increase the disproportion, this yellow or blue becomes more and more saturated.

Since the two primaries, yellow and blue, are complementary, we might expect that the other pair, red and green, would also be complementary; but that is not true. The complementary to primary red is a bluish green; the complementary to primary green is a bluish red. It follows that primary red and primary green, when mixed with each other in the right proportions, give a weakly saturated yellow.

For *every* hue there is some complementary hue. Let us refer back to the psychological hue circle (Fig. 84, *a*). *Y* and *B*, which stand opposite on the circle, are complementary. Now let us change the figure so that *R* stands opposite not to *G* but to its complementary, a bluish green; and so that *G* stands opposite to its complementary, a bluish red. We then have the circle that is shown in Fig. 87. *Any pair of hues which are opposite to each other in Fig. 87 are complementary.*

About any such pair of hues we can say what was said above regarding primary yellow and blue: If the hues are mixed in the right ratio of brightness and saturation, they cancel each other. If they are mixed in any other ratio, the resulting color has the hue of the stronger component, in reduced saturation.

Let us now agree to use Fig. 87 as a representation, not only of the hues, but also of the *saturations* of colors. The point *N*, the center of the circle, stands for the zero point of saturation (a neutral color). Distance from the center represents degree of saturation, whereas the rim of the circle signifies a series of highly saturated hues, all equal in saturation. (Compare the color cone, Fig. 85.)

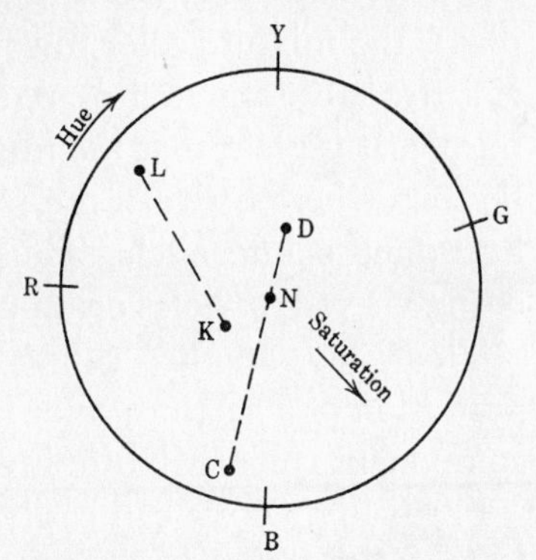

FIG. 87. FACTS OF STIMULUS MIXTURE.

R, *Y*, *G* and *B* stand for the four psychological primaries. *N* is a neutral color (gray). *C* (strong violet) and *D* (weak greenish yellow) are complementaries, and their mixtures lie on the line *CND*. *L* (strong orange) and *K* (weak purple) are not complementaries and their mixtures (purples, reds, oranges) lie on the line *KL*.

Let us choose any pair of opposite or complementary hues. Each of these colors will be represented in our figure by a point, the location of which will depend upon the saturation of the color. The point will be near the rim if the color is strongly saturated (like *C* in Fig. 87), or near the center if the color is weakly saturated (like *D* in Fig. 87). If we draw a straight line connecting the two points, this line will be a diameter of the circle—or part of a diameter, like the line *CD* in our figure.

We can now state our rule for complementary hues in the following way: *The color produced by mixing C and D lies somewhere on the line CD.* Its exact position on this line depends on the relative brightnesses of *C* and *D*. Given the proper brightness relation, it will lie at *N*. So much for complementary hues.

The next point to observe is that *exactly the same sort of rule applies to hues that are not complementary*. Take two colors, such as *K* and *L*, having any hues and saturations whatever. Draw *KL*. Then *the hues and saturations of all possible mixtures of the two are represented by all the various points in KL.*

The location of the mixture color will depend on how *bright* the one color is in relation to the other. Increasing the relative brightness of *K* displaces the mixture color along the line in the direction of *K*; increasing the relative brightness of *L* displaces the mixture color towards *L*. The color *K*, in our figure, is a strongly saturated orange, the color *L* a weakly saturated purple. It is plain that the hue of the mixture color will always lie somewhere between the position of *K*'s hue and that of *L*'s hue on the hue circle. Thus, the mixture color may be an orange, a red, a violet or a purple.

Then, too, another general principle is now obvious: The saturation of a mixture color is less than the saturation of either component color. Mixture involves a loss of saturation.

From Fig. 87 we can easily deduce the following important law: All the hues in the entire hue circle can be obtained by mixing only *three* properly chosen stimuli, in various proportions. Take, for instance, three stimuli which individually furnish the primary hues *R*, *G* and *B*. Notice that the complete hue circle can be divided into three arcs: the arc *RYG*, the arc *GB* and the arc *BR*. Now, by mixing our first two stimuli in various proportions of energy, we can produce all the hues on the chord *R*(*Y*)*G*. Mixtures of the second two stimuli furnish all the hues on the chord *GB*. Finally, by mixing the first and third stimuli, we can obtain all the hues on the chord *BR*.

If we mix all three stimuli in a certain proportion, a gray or white will result. Mixtures of all three stimuli in other proportions will yield chromatic colors of relatively low saturation.

Of course there are a great many different ways of dividing the hue circle into three sections. Therefore there are many different possibilities for choosing the set of three stimuli. The student can easily see, however, that the three hues must be rather far apart on the hue circle if the mixture colors are to have good saturation.

Mixture of pigments. The mixture of pigments gives different results from the mixture of lights.

A pigment consists of small particles having the property of absorbing light of certain wave-lengths, and reflecting light of other wave-lengths. If, for instance, sunlight falls on a yellow pigment, the short waves, corresponding to the color blue, are mostly absorbed. In the reflected light, then, there will be a mixture of many wave-lengths whose net effect is to produce a yellow hue. A blue pigment reflects mostly the short waves, corresponding to blue, as compared with the other waves.

What happens if particles of yellow pigment are mixed with the blue particles? Very little blue can be reflected by the mixture, because the yellow particles will absorb it. Also the blue particles will absorb most of the yellow that is reflected by the yellow particles. The light reflected by the mixture will as a consequence be that light which *neither* pigment absorbs. And it happens that the net effect of this light is to produce a *green* color, since both pigments reflect some green light and neither absorbs it.

BRIGHTNESS

Brightness in relation to wave-length. The brightness produced by light of a single wave-length depends, we recall, upon the energy of the waves and also upon their length. Different wave-lengths have different 'brightness-producing power.' This condition is implied by the very fact that light of wave-length greater than 800 or less than 365 mμ is invisible to us. No matter how great the energy of such waves, they produce no brightness at all—that is to say, the *sensitivity* of the eye to waves of these lengths is zero.

Not only does the eye fail to respond to all waves, but it is also more sensitive to some of the waves lying within its limits than to others. In its unequal sensitivity to different waves the eye may be compared to a photographic film; the film, however, is especially sensitive to blue, violet and ultra-violet and is scarcely affected by red light, whereas the retina is affected by red and especially sensitive to yellow and green. Among the insects there are certain species having retinas that resemble film in their sensitivity to ultra-violet light.

The panchromatic films are specially treated to make their sensitivity more like that of the human eye. In photographs made with ordinary films, red and orange objects appear unnaturally dark; when panchromatic films are used, objects of all hues are reproduced in their natural brightnesses. In the early days of motion pictures, before panchromatic films came into use, the actors had to paint their faces very grotesquely in order to produce a natural effect on the screen.

The comparative sensitivity of the human eye to different wave-lengths is determined in the following way. First, one prepares a standard stimulus, let us say a square of white light, that has some fixed brightness. Alongside this white square one has a square of spectral light of some chosen wave-length. A radiometer or some similar instrument is provided for measuring the energy of the spectral light, the energy being varied until the spectral light produces exactly the same brightness as the standard white. The value of this energy is then measured.

The lower the energy, the higher, of course, is the brightness-producing power of the spectral light—or the greater is the sensitivity of the eye to that light. If one spectral light requires only half as much energy as another, we say that the eye is twice as sensitive to the first light as it is to the second. In general: If E is the amount of energy required for the match, the sensitivity is $1/E$. The relative sensitivity of the eye to the different spectral wave-lengths can be represented by a *sensitivity curve*, in which $1/E$ is plotted against wave-length.

In our discussion of the eye and its structure, we encountered the fact that the retina has two kinds of receptors, the rods and the cones, different in function as well as in structure. Now we meet an example of the difference between them: the sensitivity curve of the rods is not the same as that of the cones.

The center of the retina, it will be recalled, contains only cones. Outside this area there is a mixture of rods and cones, with the rods becoming more and more numerous towards the edges of the retina.

Consider now the sensitivity curve of the *cones*, that is to say, the curve that is obtained when the stimulus falls on the central area. This curve has the form shown by the full-line graph in Fig. 88. The cones are most sensitive at 554 mμ, a light towards the middle of the spectrum which gives a greenish yellow hue. At wave-lengths differing more and more from

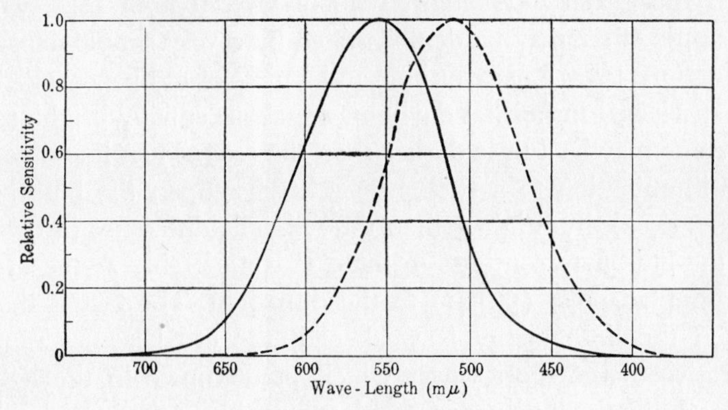

FIG. 88. SENSITIVITY CURVES.

Full-line graph = sensitivity curve of the cones (according to the standard data adopted by the International Commission on Illumination, 1931). Dashed-line graph = sensitivity curve of the rods. Data from Hecht and Williams.

554 mμ, the cones are less and less sensitive, and at the limits the sensitivity drops to zero.

How is the sensitivity curve of the *rods* to be obtained? As we shall see later, *only the rods respond when the light striking the retina is very weak*. By using a weak stimulus that is off the center of the retina, we can, therefore, measure the sensitivity of the rods. We then find that the sensitivity curve has the form shown by the dashed-line graph in Fig. 88. The data for this curve were secured by measuring the energies required to make the various spectral stimuli match the low brightness furnished by a surface of luminous paint.

Though the curve as a whole has much the same shape as before, it is shifted in the direction of the shorter wave-lengths. The place of maximum sensitivity is no longer in the greenish yellow, but in the yellowish green part of the spectrum, at about 511 mμ. The eye has become relatively more sensitive to the short wave-lengths in the blue and violet regions; at the same time it has become relatively less sensitive to the long wave-lengths in the red and orange part of the spectrum.

Thus, when the illumination changes from strong to weak, objects of different hues change in their comparative brightnesses. This brightness change is called the *Purkinje effect*, after the Czech physiologist who discovered it in 1825. The Purkinje effect may be demonstrated by a very simple experiment. One takes a piece of blue and a piece of red paper which, when viewed in normal daylight, are about equally bright (or the blue may be a little darker than the red). Then he reduces the illumination to a twilight level, whereupon the blue becomes decidedly brighter than the red. The difference in favor of the blue may continue to increase considerably as the eyes become 'adapted' (p. 541) to the dim light. The fact is that, when the light-energy is weakened, the eye becomes more sensitive to the short waves which predominate in the light reflected by the blue paper, and less sensitive to the long waves which are predominantly reflected by the red paper.

One can also observe the Purkinje effect by watching the appearance of a varicolored carpet, or of the flowers in a garden, as twilight advances.

In such experiments one notices another striking change in addition to the change in the relative brightnesses. As the illumination is reduced, the colors become less and less *saturated*, until at the very lowest illuminations they lose their saturation completely. Instead of a blue and a red object, for example, one now sees a light gray and a dark gray. In other words, at the lowest energies of light all colors become *neutral*: the eye is 'totally color-blind.' These two parallel phenomena, the Purkinje effect and the loss of saturation of colors, are, as we shall learn later, intimately connected.

In the central rod-free area of the retina the Purkinje effect does not occur. To obtain a rough verification of this fact, one may repeat the above experiment with blue and red objects of very small size, taking care to look directly at the objects, so that their retinal images stimulate the central region only. One then finds that the relative brightnesses of the blue and red are the same in weak as in strong light.

Dark-adaptation and the self-light. When we pass suddenly from bright sunlight into a very dimly illuminated room, we can see nothing for a time until our eyes become *adapted* to the faint light. Gradually the retinas become increasingly *sensitive*; they acquire the ability to respond to quantities of energy which, at the first moment, were too small to stimulate them. This increase of sensitivity continues for half an hour or more—very rapidly at first, and then more slowly.

If, after having become thoroughly adapted to darkness or to dim light, we return to bright daylight, our eyes are now too sensitive for adequate vision under the new conditions, and we experience an annoying glare. Quickly, however, the sensitivity of the eyes diminishes, and the state of 'dark-adaptation' is replaced by one of 'light-adaptation.' Thus the brightness resulting from a given stimulus is not determined simply by the light itself, but depends also upon the state of the retina.

As a matter of fact, we experience *brightness* even when there are no physical light-waves striking the retina. When we go into a completely dark room, our whole visual field appears as a uniform dim expanse of gray. This gray is the so-called *self-light*, which represents an activity going on in the physiological mechanism of vision when there is no external stimulation of the eye. The faintest visible object furnishes a brightness that is just barely higher than that of the self-light.

The least strength of stimulus that will suffice to make a surface visible may be called the *light-threshold*. When we are light-adapted, this threshold is high; if we then become thoroughly dark-adapted, the threshold sinks to 1/10,000 or even a smaller fraction of its original value.

In our discussion of brightness in relation to wave-length,

we noted that very dim lights act only on the *rods*, not on the *cones.* Stating the same fact in different words, we may say that the rods have a high capacity for dark-adaptation, the cones a low capacity. There is, as a matter of fact, very little dark-adaptation in the central area of the retina containing cones alone. If we test the eye with a very small stimulus which is carefully confined to this central area, we find that the threshold decreases through adaptation to only about 1/100 of its initial value.

If the rods, but not the cones, are able to respond to very dim light, it ought to follow that exceedingly faint objects which are invisible in direct vision can be seen with the peripheral retina. To prove that this is indeed true is very easy. Look, for example, at a very faint star at night. When one tries to observe the star, he discovers that there is an involuntary tendency to look a little to one side, instead of fixating it directly. Make an effort to look at the star directly, and it disappears from view. In this situation the center of the retina is no longer the region of best vision, and the fixation of the eye automatically adjusts itself to the changed conditions.

RODS AND CONES

The duplicity theory. The idea that the rods and cones differ in function is called the *duplicity theory.*

That the peripheral retina has pronounced dark-adaptation as compared with the slight adaptation of the central rod-free area is the first outstanding piece of evidence in support of this theory. A second is the fact that the Purkinje effect appears only in the periphery, where there is a mixture of rods and cones, and not in the central area. That is to say, at high energies of light the response of the periphery to the various wavelengths is like that of the central cones; at low energies the response of the periphery is strikingly different from that of the central cones. Herein lies a suggestion that the Purkinje effect is a shift from cone-vision to rod-vision—a shift which can occur only in the parts of the retina containing both kinds of receptors. There is also a third fact in support of the theory—namely, that in very dim light no hues are seen, only neutral colors. This fact leads us to infer that the rods are *totally color-blind*, and that chromatic vision depends upon the cones alone.

The facts of normal human vision make the duplicity theory seem plausible enough; but there are in addition facts of animal vision and of abnormal human vision that strengthen it greatly. Vertebrates of nocturnal habits, it has been found by anatomists, have very few cones in the retina, whereas vertebrates active only in daylight possess very few rods. There are, moreover, a few human beings who are totally color-blind even in bright daylight. In the most common form of this defect the Purkinje effect is absent; the sensitivity curve has its peak at about 511 mμ at all levels of illumination. Often the central retina is completely blind. On the assumption that the cones are absent or fail to function, these cases fit in neatly enough with the duplicity theory.

There are also certain persons who are congenitally 'night-blind,' or lacking in the normal power of adaptation to dim light. In these persons also the Purkinje effect is absent. The sensitivity curve has its maximum at about 554 mμ. This defect is easily explained as an absence of active rods.

Photochemistry of the retina. Light-waves act on a photographic film by causing chemical change in the materials with which it is coated—a so-called *photochemical reaction*. There are strong reasons for believing that the response of the rods and cones is a process of this same type.

The rods contain a bluish red pigment, the *visual purple*, which bleaches when it is exposed to light, but which gradually regains its color when kept in the dark. Light causes a chemical change in this pigment; in darkness an opposite chemical change restores the original substance.

Dark-adaptation, it has been shown, depends on the visual purple. The more of this purple material the rods contain, the more sensitive are they to light; the more of the bleached substance they contain, the less their sensitivity. Our gradual adaptation to darkness is the result of the slow regeneration of the visual purple.

The sensitivity of the rods to various *wave-lengths* of light—the dashed-line curve in Fig. 88—can also be explained in chemical terms. The visual purple, like any other colored pigment, has stronger absorbing power for some waves than for others. If light is to cause any chemical effect in the visual purple, it has to be absorbed by it. The rods, therefore, are unequally sensitive to the different kinds of spectral light.

No one has yet discovered any light-sensitive chemical in the cones. Doubtless the cones contain such a substance, or a number of substances, but in dilute form. Doubtless also the sensitivity of the cones to different wave-lengths—the full-line graph in Fig. 88—deserves the same kind of explanation that holds good for the rods.

ADAPTATION AND INTERACTION

Light-adaptation and chromatic adaptation. Light-adaptation is the converse of dark-adaptation. Light, acting upon the eye, reduces its sensitivity; the stronger the light, the greater the loss of sensitivity.

Suppose one looks steadily, for a period of a few minutes, at a small bright area on a dark ground. As time goes on and the retina responds less and less vigorously to the stimulating light, the area will appear less and less bright. Such a loss of sensitivity becomes obvious if at some nearby place in the dark ground one suddenly introduces a comparison stimulus, exactly like that which is being fixated. This new stimulus, acting on a retinal region which has not been desensitized by strong light, looks brighter than the fixated stimulus.

Since under the ordinary conditions of vision the eyes are constantly moving, no part of the retina has time to become much adapted to any stimulus. Complete adaptation is seldom reached except under artificial conditions of steady fixation.

If a *chromatic* stimulus acts continuously on the eye, its color decreases, not only in brightness, but also in saturation.

A color which is not, at the outset, too highly saturated or too bright loses its saturation completely after a few minutes of adaptation and appears gray. With very saturated and very bright stimuli, chromatic adaptation does not reach zero saturation; and, when the eyes are moving, the loss of saturation is relatively slight.

After-images. Let the student look steadily at Fig. 89 for about 40 sec., with unwavering fixation on some particular point in the figure, and then suddenly transfer his gaze to a blank sheet of white paper. On the paper will appear a *negative after-image*, an illusory figure which is like the original stimulus in form, but with its brightness relations reversed. As in a photographic negative, the original blacks will be replaced by whites, and the whites by blacks.

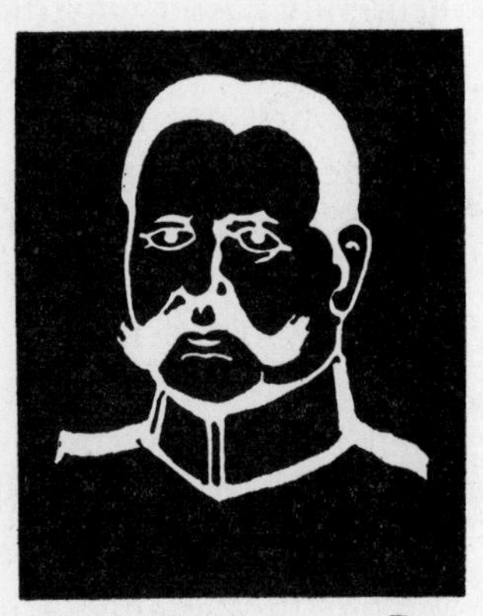

FIG. 89. FIGURE FOR THE DEMONSTRATION OF THE NEGATIVE AFTER-IMAGE.
After A. Noll, *Psychol. Forsch.*, 1926, 8, 7.

Given the facts of light-adaptation, it is easy enough to understand why this after-image appears. While the figure was being fixated, certain parts of the retina were exposed to the strong stimulus provided by the white patches in the figure. We should expect these retinal areas to become less sensitive to light than the neighboring areas on which the black patches formed their retinal images. With continuing fixation this inequality of sensitivity would become more and more pronounced. What ought to happen when uniform white paper is substituted for the original figure? The light reflected by the paper should call out a strong response from the more sensitive, a weak response from the less sensitive retinal areas. In other words, we should expect a pattern like the figure, but with opposite brightness relations, to appear on the paper.

There is a similar phenomenon for colors. If one stares for a long time at a chromatic color and then looks at a uniform white surface, the after-image tends to have a hue that is *complementary* to the original color. Thus, a yellow color gives a blue after-image, a purple color gives a yellowish green after-image, and so on.

For theories about the physiology of chromatic vision the facts of chromatic adaptation and of the complementary after-image following chromatic adaptation are especially important. Why, with adaptation, do chromatic colors tend towards neutrality? And why should it be that, after being adapted to one color, we see a new color having a hue that would neutralize the first one if mixed with it on a rotating disk?

Different theories explain these phenomena differently. There is one theory, that of Young and Helmholtz, which applies to chromatic adaptation and complementary images the same sort of interpretation that was given above for light-adaptation and black-white images. We shall see later how the Young-Helmholtz theory goes about explaining these facts.

Besides after-images that are 'negative' in brightness and complementary in hue, there are other after-images which resemble the original stimulus in brightness (*positive after-images*) and in hue (*homochromatic after-images*). A glowing match, for example, whirled about in the dark, is followed by a positive after-image in the shape of a long bright streak. Positive and homochromatic after-images are due to the persistence of a state of excitation in the retina, with the result that impulses continue to be discharged in the optic nerve after the removal of the stimulus.

Contrast and summation. The color we see at a given place in our field of vision depends not only upon the stimulation that is acting at the corresponding place on the retina, but also upon the stimulation that is acting in *neighboring regions.*

Brightness contrast is one example of this principle. The brightness of a surface is lowered by increasing the brightness of its surroundings, raised by darkening its surroundings. Thus, when a small area of moderate light-intensity looks white on a dark ground, the brightening of its surroundings may change the brightness of the area all the way from white to black. Strong contrast effects are obtained only when the small area and its surroundings are in the same plane. An object standing out in front of a bright or dark wall is comparatively unaffected by the wall. An object whose contours are blurred, furthermore, receives more contrast effect than one with sharp contours.

There is also a *chromatic contrast.* A small area of gray paper, when placed on a background of rich blue paper, looks slightly yellowish. On a red background, the gray becomes bluish green. If the gray and its background are about equally bright, the effect is strongest. It is also greatly enhanced by covering the colors with a sheet of tissue paper.

In general, any chromatic color tends to arouse the *complementary* color in its neighborhood. Thus neighboring neutral colors acquire a tinge of the complementary hue, and neighboring chromatic colors are changed in hue. The more saturated a color, the stronger is its influence on neighboring colors. Contrast is a phenomenon which artists must continually take into account in their choice of colors for painting. The first person to write about the phenomenon, as a matter of fact, was an artist, Leonardo da Vinci.

The French scientist Chevreul tells the following anecdote. A manufacturer was sent some colored textiles—red, violet and blue—with the request that they be ornamented with black patterns. When the goods were returned, however, the customer complained that the patterns were not black, that those stamped on the red stuffs were greenish, on the violet stuffs greenish yellow and on the blue stuffs yellowish. Chevreul then took a sample of the goods and covered the cloth with white paper, in such a way as to expose only the pattern; thereupon it became immediately evident that the pattern was indeed truly black. The effects which had caused the customer's complaint were entirely due to contrast. In such cases the remedy is to add to the black a tinge of color like that of the background, making it just strong enough to cancel the complementary tinge that is caused by contrast.

The facts of contrast imply that the physiological system underlying vision is not simply a group of independent local parts corresponding to the different parts of our visual field; they signify, on the contrary, that the parts of the system can interact with each other. Although the physiological nature of this contrast interaction is unknown, there is evidence to indicate that the interaction occurs not in the retina, but in the brain.

One line of evidence comes from experiments on 'binocular contrast,' that is to say, on the interaction of two colors, one of which is seen by one eye and the other by the opposite eye. Here no interaction can take place except in the brain. According to certain experiments, the contrast effects obtained in this fashion are just as strong as when both stimuli are seen by the same eye. The implication is that the interaction underlying contrast is wholly confined to the brain, and that the retina plays no part in it. That such interaction occurs, moreover, in the cortex rather than in the lower centers of the brain is indicated by still further data. For instance, there is a report of a patient who, having a cortical injury, displayed almost a complete loss of contrast phenomena.

In the so-called phenomena of *summation* we have to do with a sort of interaction quite different from contrast. It has been found, in experiments on the light-threshold, that the visibility of a small, weakly illuminated area depends on the *size* of the area, and not merely on the strength of the light. Thus, a very minute area may be invisible, whereas a somewhat larger area which receives the same illumination may be easily perceptible. In other words, the visibility of a stimulus depends on the *number of receptors* that it stimulates.

This phenomenon, called *brightness summation*, is to be explained in the following manner. The retina, it will be recalled, not only contains neurons for the conduction of nerve impulses towards the brain, but also contains lateral neurons which connect one part of the retina with another (Fig. 83). Such interconnecting pathways, typical of nervous centers rather than of sense organs, are found in no sense organ except the eye. It has been shown experimentally that these retinal interconnections play a part in brightness summation. By means of the lateral neurons a response set up at any point in the retina can reinforce the responses at neighboring points.

Besides brightness summation, there is also a *chromatic summation*. The saturation of a small area of chromatic color increases as its size is increased. Conversely, hues turn into grays when the stimulus area is made small enough.

In summation and contrast we have two different types of interaction, each of which has definite biological advantages. Summation, of course, helps in the perception of small and weak stimuli; whereas contrast tends to sharpen the contours of objects and to accentuate their differences of brightness and color. Without contrast our vision would always be blurred. Even the best human eye is a poor optical instrument; a point of light is not accurately focused upon a single retinal cone, but is dispersed over a retinal area that includes about 40 cones. This blurred retinal image is bright in the center and dim towards the edges. By virtue of the physiological mechanism of contrast, however, we see a fairly sharp point; the bright part of the spot darkens the dim part and erases it from our field of vision.

Black. Black is a peculiar color. Popularly, black is regarded as corresponding to the absence of stimulation; but the 'self-light' which we experience in the absence of any external stimulation is grayish and not black. Black may, however, be produced as an *after-effect* of strong stimulation (an after-image, p. 545). Thus, when we pass from strong light into a dark room, our visual field appears black rather than gray during the first few moments.

Black may also be produced by *contrast*. An unlighted area which is *surrounded* by an area of strong light may appear, through the action of contrast, in a brightness which is much lower than that of the self-light. Even a lighted area may look black, if its surroundings are sufficiently bright.

In both these cases, black results from the *indirect action of intense stimulation*, rather than from the simple absence of stimulation.

Many of the blacks that we see in everyday life—the black of a fountain pen, or of a pair of shoes—are surface-colors, the colors of objects. In the perception of these blacks, a new principle comes into play—the principle that our perception separates object-color and illumination, that, when illumination is changed, we see the change *as* a change in the illumination rather than in the illuminated object. Whether an object shall appear white, gray or black depends not only upon how much light it sends into the eye, but also upon how strong this light is *in relation to the prevailing illumination of the visual field*. For the same illumination, those objects that give our eyes a comparatively strong stimulus appear white, those that furnish a medium stimulus look gray and those yielding a comparatively weak stimulus look black. If the illumination is changed, the same objects continue to look white, gray and black; for the *relations* between the strengths of light that they reflect are still the same as before.

To sum up: black may be produced by way of after-image, by way of contrast or by virtue of the fact that object-color in perception depends upon a relationship and not upon the mere strength of retinal stimulation.

The color *brown* also deserves a special word of comment. By adding a tinge of red, orange or yellow to a dark gray or black, a brown color can be produced. Curiously enough, the mixture color is so different in quality from a bright, saturated red, orange or yellow that it seems fitting to give it a new name. In the same fashion, if one adds a tinge of green to a dark gray or black, one obtains a quality that seems different from a bright, saturated green—a color to which we apply the special name of *olive-green*.

PERIPHERAL VISION

Peripheral vision is less distinct than vision with the central retina (p. 522). The periphery also differs from the center in that it has a more primitive type of *chromatic vision.*

Under ordinary conditions, these differences between direct and indirect vision do not impress us. The eye is in constant motion. Since different parts of the visual field are viewed in quick succession with the central retina, the total effect for perception is that of a field which is fairly distinct throughout its whole extent, each color possessing the color in which it appeared to central vision. If, however, one keeps the eye steadily directed at some given point and meanwhile carefully observes the color of an object lying above, below or to one side of the fixation point, one becomes aware of the peculiarities of peripheral vision.

When a stimulus is moved from the center towards the extreme periphery, its color decreases continually in *saturation.* Stimuli of moderate intensity, such as are furnished by colored papers, lose their saturation completely in the extreme periphery and appear *neutral.*

For most colors, this loss of saturation is accompanied by a change of *hue.* As a stimulus passes away from the center, its color tends very quickly to lose any *reddishness* or *greenishness* which it originally possessed, while any *yellowishness* or *bluishness* which originally belonged to it is retained for a time. Thus, an orange changes towards yellow before it finally becomes gray, and a purple changes towards blue.

In general, when we pass from central towards extreme peripheral vision, two tendencies show themselves: a tendency for all hues except yellow and blue to disappear first, and then a tendency for chromatic colors, including even yellow and blue, to degenerate finally at the extreme periphery into neutral colors.

These tendencies are most evident when the test colors are weak in saturation and in brightness. A weakly saturated, dark red, for example, turns into yellow at a small distance from the center of vision, and, if this distance is increased only a little more, this yellow turns into a dark gray. But a strongly saturated, very bright red can be seen as a red even in the extreme periphery. Thus, the partial color blindness of the middle periphery, as well as the total color blindness of the extreme periphery, are not absolute, but represent diminished sensitivity.

The greater the distance from the center of the retina, the more the rods outnumber the cones. It might be thought that the loss of saturation in the periphery could be attributed to this fact. The rods, however, play a significant role only when the light striking the retina is very weak indeed, whereas the loss of saturation occurs even with intense lights. Evidently, then, chromatic vision for the peripheral cones is different from that for the central cones. In the cones at the edge of the retina this difference reaches its extreme.

COLOR BLINDNESS

Color blindness, which may be either congenital or acquired, may also be either total or partial. A totally color-blind person is one who lacks hue discrimination completely. A partially color-blind person can discriminate hues but often fails to distinguish between stimuli which appear unlike to the normal person.

Congenital total color blindness is rare; there are fewer than 100 cases on record. Congenital *partial* color blindness, on the contrary, is common—displayed by about one man in 30 and about one woman in 1000. Its most frequent variety is often called 'red-green blindness,' because persons with this defect characteristically fail to distinguish between the hues of objects which, for the normal person, are colored red and green.

It is a curious fact that, although red-green blindness is so common, the earliest case on record dates only as far back as 1777. According to Huddart, who reported the case, the subject (an English shoemaker) declared that "he had reason to believe other persons saw something in objects which he could not see; that their language seemed to mark qualities with confidence and precision which he could only guess at with hesitation, and frequently with error. . . . He observed also, that when young, other children could discern cherries on a tree by some pretended difference of color, though he could only distinguish them from the leaves by their difference of size and shape. He observed also, that by means of this difference of color, they could see the cherries at a greater distance than he could, though he could see other objects at as great a distance as they; that is, where the sight was not assisted by the color." In 1794 the great chemist John Dalton aroused interest in the abnormality by publishing a description of his own case.

How do colors appear to the red-green blind? There is only one way in which any data bearing on this question can be obtained, and that is to study the rare cases in which there is color blindness in one eye and normal chromatic vision in the other. Such studies show that in the world of the color blind there are only two hues, *yellow* and *blue*, in different degrees of saturation. The long-wave parts of the spectrum appear yellow, the short-wave parts appear blue.

In spite of their defect color-blind persons often name colors correctly. They hear a color called red which to them may appear as a very dark yellow, and they associate the name and the shade together. Color-naming tests, therefore, are not reliable indicators of color blindness. There is a widely used test, the Holmgren wool test, which requires the subject to sort colored yarns according to hue. A more reliable and more delicate test is that of Ishihara. This test consists of a series of charts, in each of which a colored pattern appears on a background of another color. For example, there may be a red number on a green ground, easily distinguishable to the normal eye, but impossible for the red-green blind to read because for them there is nothing to set the number off against its ground.

There are many occupations to which color blindness is a barrier or in which it is a serious disadvantage: medicine, chemistry, painting, the trade of the weaver, upholsterer, tailor, milliner or florist, the navy, the railway, the post office and so on. For many practical considerations, however, color blindness is so slight a handicap that it is entirely possible for a color-blind person to go through life without ever learning of his defect.

There are two distinct types of congenital red-green blindness, called *protanopia* and *deuteranopia*. The protanopes, or persons having the first type of defect, are abnormal in their perception of brightness as well as in that of hue. They are extremely insensitive to red light; a piece of saturated red paper looks black to them, and the spectrum appears shorter than to the normal person. The deuteranopes, on the other hand, have normal brightness vision.

The laws of stimulus mixture for both protanopes and deuteranopes are different from those applying to normal persons. For a color-blind individual of either type, any light in the spectrum can be exactly matched by a suitable mixture of *two* lights, one from the long-wave end and the other from the short-wave end of the spectrum. For this reason partially color-blind persons, both protanopes and deuteranopes, are sometimes called *dichromats*; whereas normal persons, who require three lights to match the whole spectrum, are called *trichromats*. The protanopes and deuteranopes differ from each other in the relative amounts of long-wave and short-wave light which they use in making any such match.

If we compare the color discrimination of the red-green blind with that of normal persons, we find both a certain unlikeness and a certain likeness. On the one hand, the color-blind person is often unable to distinguish between stimuli which have different colors for the normal person. On the other hand, any stimuli which look exactly *alike* to the normal person also look exactly alike to both protanopes and deuteranopes. Thus, although the protanopes and deuteranopes often reject each other's color matches, they both accept any color match made by a normal observer. These facts suggest that red-green blindness represents, in some sense, a simplification of normal vision, rather than a totally different type of perception. In protanopia and deuteranopia we evidently have two different kinds of simplified color systems.

Color blindness can be *acquired*. Acquired color blindness is caused by injury or disease of the retina or the other nerve structures concerned with vision; one of its most common causes is the excessive use of tobacco.

Acquired color blindness may be either total or partial, though often there is a gradual progression from the partial to the total form. It is an especially interesting and theoretically important fact that in this progression the vision of the central retina continually becomes more and more like the vision of the normal periphery. Red-green vision weakens before yellow-blue vision. Furthermore, the color-blindness, like that of the normal periphery, is not absolute; bright and saturated colors can be seen when dark and unsaturated colors cannot.

THEORY OF CHROMATIC VISION

The Young-Helmholtz theory. We come now to the problem of the physiological basis of chromatic vision. To explain chromatic vision is a much more difficult task than to explain the mere seeing of brightness. We can refer the brightness of a stimulus to the intensity of its chemical effect on the cones and rods. But it is not so obvious what is the difference between a chromatic and a neutral color, or between two hues, in terms of processes in the retinal cones.

One must always remember that the stimulation of the retina is only the first step in the whole visual process. The retina sends impulses along nerve paths to the brain, and then physiological effects are aroused in the brain itself. That the brightness of a stimulus corresponds to the number of impulses per second that travel from the retina along the optic nerve, we already know (see pp. 507f.). But what is there in these optic-nerve impulses to correspond to saturation and hue?

At first thought, one would be tempted to say: Different kinds of light must produce chemical effects on the cones that differ, not only in intensity, but in some sort of *qualitative* fashion; then these differences of quality must somehow be telegraphed along the optic nerve. Such a theory, however, is contrary to the findings of modern physiology, according to which all nerve impulses are alike in kind. How are we to find our way out of this dilemma?

We can do so by assuming that there exist in the retina a number of different types of cone, which differ in their sensitivities to the various wave-lengths of light. Each kind of cone sends impulses along its own special pathways to a special place in the visual region of the brain, setting up a kind of brain process that is characteristic of that particular place. The color that we see depends, not upon any special *quality* of the cone response, but simply upon *which* cones are responding.

The next question is: How many types of cone must such a theory assume? At first one might be inclined to say that there must be a different type for each of the four primary hues. It might also seem that perhaps there should be still other cones to represent neutral color. There is, however, an old and famous theory which attempts to meet the issue by assuming only *three* types of cones. This theory was proposed by the great German scientist Hermann von Helmholtz in 1852, following a basic idea outlined by the English scientist Thomas Young in 1801; and it is still in favor at the present time.

The Young-Helmholtz theory emphasizes especially a law of *stimulus mixture*: that by mixing only *three* stimuli, which individually appear red, green and blue, one can produce a chromatic color of any desired hue, or a white or gray. Because this law holds, the theory assumes that there are three types of cones; we may call them the R-cones, G-cones and B-cones. The R-cones, if they were stimulated in isolation from the other two, would give us the experience of a red hue. Likewise the G-cones and B-cones, when stimulated alone, would make us see green and blue, respectively. If the R-cones were stimulated together with the B-cones, we should see a red-blue; whereas combined activity of the G-cones and B-cones would give a green-blue.

The theory assumes that when R-cones and G-cones function

at the same time, a peculiar thing happens. The 'red' process and the 'green' process in the brain do not produce a mere intermediate, a reddish green, but rather a new color, *yellow*—a color which is just as different from red or green as they are from each other. This happens when the excitement of the

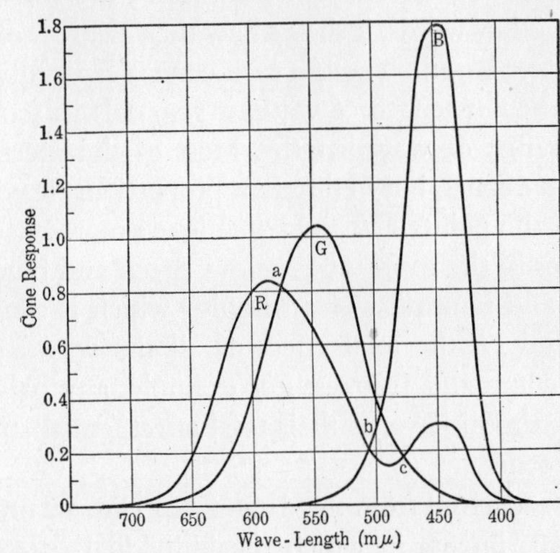

FIG. 90. *R, G* AND *B* CURVES OF THE YOUNG-HELMHOLTZ THEORY.

These curves represent the stimulus-mixture relationships for the normal observer (the 1931 standard observer of the International Commission on Illumination), and were constructed with the aid of Deane B. Judd. The primary stimuli to which these curves refer have been chosen so that the following criteria are satisfied: (1) the crossing points *a*, *b* and *c* correspond to the three psychological primaries of the spectrum—the primary yellow, green and blue—for the average observer (according to Westphal); (2) the *G* and *B* curves represent the stimulus-mixture relationships for one type of partially color-blind observer (the protanope); (3) the *R* and *B* curves represent the stimulus-mixture relationships for a second type of partially color-blind observer (the deuteranope).

R-cones and G-cones is equal; when it is unequal, we see reddish or greenish yellow.

The theory says further than when *all three* types of cones are excited together, and in equal degrees, we see a *neutral* rather than a chromatic color. (Hence yellow and blue are complementary.) Once more a combination of activities produces a new and unique effect.

Most stimuli, according to this theory, act not on a single kind of cone but on all three kinds at once. Provided the three excitements are not exactly equal, the color produced is chromatic. Its hue depends upon which cone, or which pair of cones, responds most strongly to the light-waves. Its saturation depends upon how far the three responses depart from exact equality.

Figure 90 shows the sensitivity curves of the three types of cones, or, in other words, it shows how their degrees of response vary with wave-length. Though each cone is especially sensitive to some particular length of wave, it responds in some degree to a wide range of wave-lengths. Most of the spectral lights excite all three cones, but in different proportions. It will readily be seen that the points *a*, *b* and *c* in Fig. 90 represent the three primary hues in the spectrum—yellow, green and blue.

The hue and saturation of a stimulus which is a *mixture* of waves depend on the total effect of all the waves upon the R-cones, G-cones and B-cones. For example, any pair of complementary stimuli have, as their total effect, equal stimulation of all three cones.

Figure 90 is derived from the data of experiments on stimulus mixture—experiments in which the individual spectral lights were matched, one by one, with a mixture of red, green and blue lights. In computing the curves the relative amounts of the three lights that are needed for a match are taken as indices of the three cone-responses.

Applications of the Young-Helmholtz theory. The Young-Helmholtz theory offers a simple explanation for the fact that chromatic colors, when continuously fixated, tend to become neutral (*chromatic adaptation*). Most stimuli excite all three cones; neutral stimuli excite them all three equally, and chromatic stimuli excite them unequally. When with continued fixation the cones lose sensitivity, the response of the more strongly excited cones diminishes faster than that of the less strongly excited ones. This loss makes the three excitations become more nearly equal; hence the seen color approaches white or gray. A primary green stimulus, for instance, arouses a strong G-response, together with equal weak responses of the

R-cones and B-cones. With adaptation, the G-response suffers a relatively large loss, the R-response and the B-response a relatively small loss. As a result, the G-response predominates over the others less than it did at the outset, and the color loses saturation.

This hypothesis also explains why, after we have become adapted to a color, we see an *after-image* of complementary color upon turning our eyes to a white surface. Take, for instance, the case where one has become adapted to primary green. The G-cones have suffered the greatest loss of sensitivity. Normally a white surface stimulates all three types of cone equally; but now the more sensitive R and B will be stimulated more than the insensitive G. Consequently the color that is seen is a bluish red, the color complementary to green.

The Young-Helmholtz theory has attempted to explain *partial color blindness* on the assumption that persons with this defect lack one of the three types of cone—the protanopes the R-cones, and the deuteranopes the G-cones. This interpretation, as a matter of fact, fits the data of stimulus mixture for both protanopes and deuteranopes with remarkable exactness. Unfortunately, however, it is inconsistent with the fact that both protanopes and deuteranopes have yellow-blue vision. The theory would predict that the color-world of the protanopes should consist of greens and blues, whereas that of the deuteranopes should consist of reds and blues. It is curious that the theory fits one group of facts so well and yet fails with the other group.

Inadequacies of the Young-Helmholtz theory. The Young-Helmholtz theory not only has difficulty with the facts of congenital color blindness, but it also has no satisfactory explanation for the phenomena of peripheral vision, and the very similar phenomena of acquired color blindness. All these facts, taken together, show, first, that yellow-blue vision is, in a way, more fundamental than red-green vision, and, secondly, that brightness vision is more fundamental than chromatic vision. Blue and yellow survive the loss of red and green, whereas brightness survives the disappearance of all hues. These facts are difficult to reconcile with the idea that neutral color depends on a combination of red, green and blue responses, and that yellow depends on a combination of red and green responses.

The Young-Helmholtz theory also offers no satisfactory explanation of contrast. It must be remembered, however, that this theory is primarily a theory about the retinal cones; it cannot be considered as a complete theory of vision, for the latter must take into account the nervous system as well as the retina. Especially is this obvious when we recall that injury or disease of the optic nerve or brain can cause an acquired color blindness, and that the phenomena of contrast probably depend on the brain and not on the retina at all. A complete theory will undoubtedly have to be very complex.

REFERENCES

1. Graham, C. H. Vision: some neural correlations. *A handbook of general experimental psychology.* Worcester, Mass.: Clark University Press, 1934. Pp. 829-879.
2. Hecht, S. Vision: the nature of the photoreceptor process. *A handbook of general experimental psychology.* Worcester, Mass.: Clark University Press, 1934. Pp. 704-828.
3. Helmholtz, H. L. F. von. *Treatise on physiological optics* (translated from the third German edition). Rochester, N. Y.: The Optical Society of America, 1924-1925. 3 vols.
4. Ladd-Franklin, C. *Colour and colour theories.* New York: Harcourt, Brace, 1929.
5. Parsons, J. H. *An introduction to the study of colour vision.* (2nd ed.) Cambridge: Cambridge University Press, 1924.
6. Troland, L. T. Vision: visual phenomena and their stimulus correlations. *A handbook of general experimental psychology.* Worcester, Mass.: Clark University Press, 1934. Pp. 653-703.
7. Troland, L. T. *The principles of psychophysiology.* New York: D. Van Nostrand, 1930. II, 51-205.

Chapter 18

AUDITION

An understanding of the sense of hearing involves a knowledge of the physics of the stimulus, the structure and operation of the receptor and the nature of the phenomena which arise when the receptor is stimulated. In this chapter, therefore, we shall begin with a consideration of the physical nature of sound and the anatomy and physiology of the ear, and then turn our attention to the various phenomena of hearing. The final division of the chapter on auditory theory is an attempt to coordinate our knowledge of the various phases of the process of hearing.

THE PHYSICAL NATURE OF SOUND

Simple harmonic motion. Many objects, when energy is applied to them in an appropriate way, are set into a state of vibratory movement. A bell when struck, or a violin string when bowed, will present a long series of back-and-forth movements, continuing until the imparted energy is exhausted.

If the body is vibrating in air, as is usual, a part of the energy will be transmitted from the moving surfaces to the air particles in the vicinity. And further, through a series of collisions between the air particles themselves, the vibration will be conducted outward as waves of sound to all parts of the surrounding air.

One type of vibratory movement is of fundamental importance. This is *simple harmonic motion*, the simplest kind of vibration known. Not many bodies give this kind of vibration exactly, but many approximate it. The most familiar acoustic

---

This chapter was written by E. G. Wever of Princeton University.

instrument that gives simple harmonic motion in nearly pure form is the tuning-fork.

The simple pendulum also executes simple harmonic motion, though it is too slow in its movements to produce sound. The slowness of the movements is, however, an advantage to their study, for it permits direct visual examination of them. If a pendulum bob, as in Fig. 91, is displaced from its position of rest and then released, it will swing regularly over a definite path. Each to-and-fro movement, from L to R and back again to L, constitutes one complete vibration, or one *cycle*. The time required for one cycle is the *period* of the vibration; the reciprocal of this, the number of cycles in one second, is the *frequency*. The distance LM, the maximum displacement from the position of rest, is the *amplitude* of the vibration. It will be noted that, as the pendulum uses up the energy originally imparted to it, the amplitude gradually diminishes, but the period remains constant. The same is true of all such vibrating

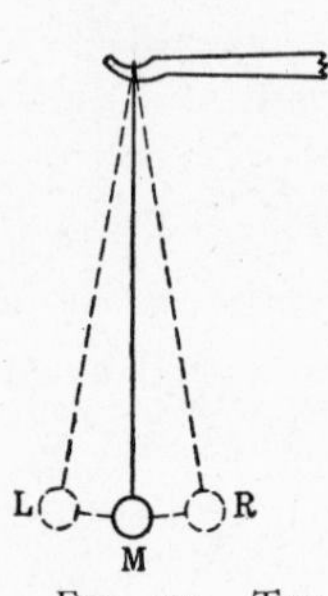

Fig. 91. The Simple Pendulum.

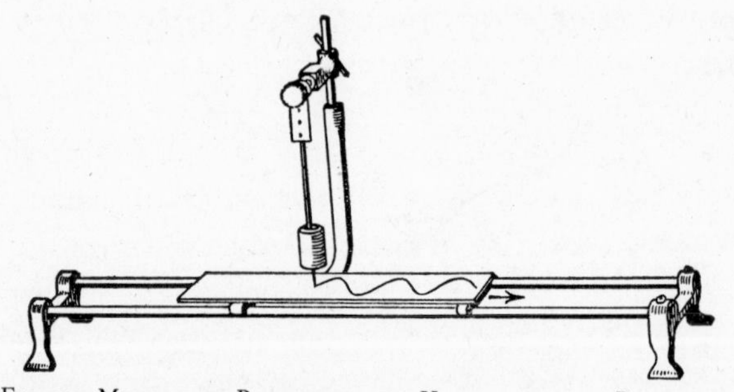
Fig. 92. Method of Recording the Vibrations of a Pendulum.
The smoked glass plate is drawn from left to right while the pendulum is swinging to and fro.

bodies, and can easily be observed in the tuning-fork, whose tone retains its particular quality while its vibrations die away in strength.

The details of vibratory motion are conveniently studied in a graphic record. Such a record for the movements of a pendulum may be obtained by the method illustrated in Fig. 92. A smoked-glass plate is drawn uniformly to the right, while a pendulum fitted with a marking point is moving back and forth. The result is that the back-and-forth motions are drawn

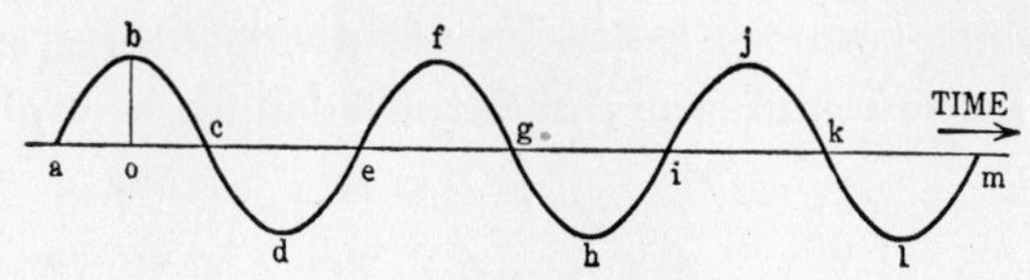

FIG. 93. A SINE CURVE.

The curve is drawn as vertical displacements from the time line *am*. One cycle is the portion *abcde*, or *bcdef*, or any similarly recurrent portion regardless of the starting point. The distance *ob* is the amplitude. The time elapsing from *a* to *e* is one period.

out in an undulating curve, known mathematically as a *sine curve*. Such a curve is shown in Fig. 93.

Simple harmonic motion has an elementary relation to uniform circular motion. If we observe the point *P* in Fig. 94, which is considered as moving uniformly in the circular path indicated by the arrow, and measure from time to time the vertical distances *PO* from the point to a fixed horizontal line *XX′*, these distances will vary in the form of a sine curve. This relation is easily observed in the driving mechanism of a locomotive. The driving wheel executes regular circular motion, while the driving rod moves back and forth in simple harmonic motion.

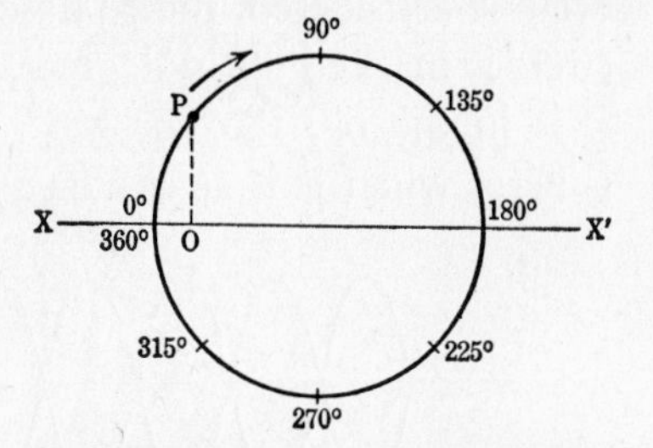

FIG. 94. THE RELATION BETWEEN CIRCULAR AND HARMONIC MOTION.

As *P* moves uniformly around the circle, the displacement *PO* changes harmonically.

Relations of waves. It is sometimes necessary to state the position of a vibrating body exactly, as when, for example, we wish to indicate the point on its swing that a pendulum bob occupies at a particular instant. For such a purpose we require a system of measurement by which positions within any period of a vibration can be designated. The direct relation between harmonic and circular motion makes it convenient to transfer to harmonic motion the familiar system of circular measurement. We divide the circle into 360°, by which we can indicate any position. Likewise, we divide the period of vibratory motion into 360°, and thus designate any position.

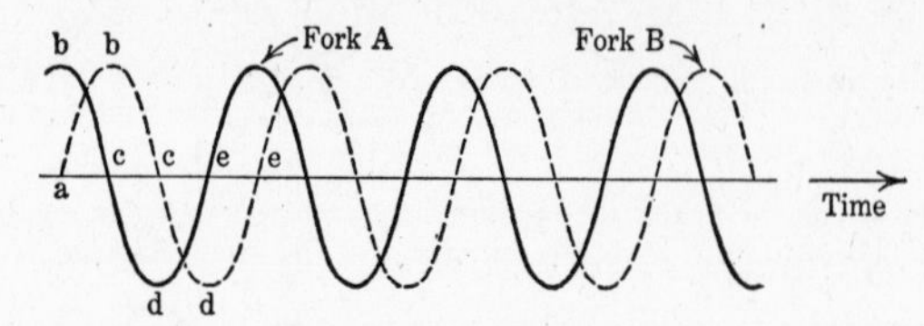

Fig. 95. The 90° Phase Relation.

Fork *A* leads fork *B* in phase by 90°, because at any instant of time shown in the figure the phase of the wave for *A* is a quarter of a wave-length ahead of the phase of the wave for *B*.

This positional feature of vibration we call the *phase*, and the relation between two different vibrations when position in the cycle is considered, their phase relation. In Fig. 94, where the circle is marked off in degrees, it may be seen that, when point *P* is in the 0°, 180° or 360° positions, the displacement *PO* is zero, when it is at 90° or 270° the displacement is a maxi-

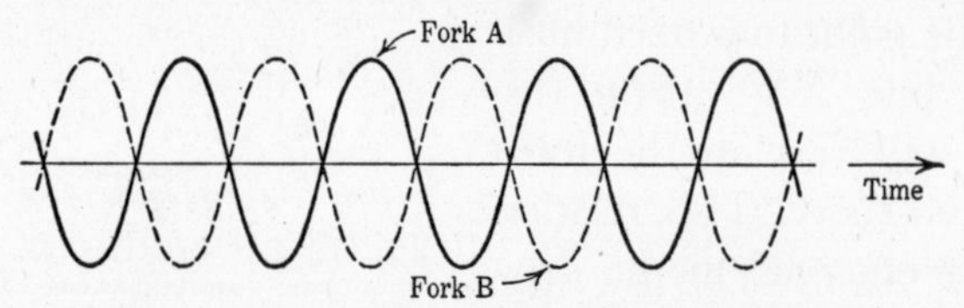

Fig. 96. The Opposite or 180° Phase Relation.

mum and at other points the displacement is of intermediate value. If we refer now to Fig. 93, we find that point *a* corresponds to the zero phase position, point *b* to the 90° phase position and so on. The point *e* has the same phase as *a* and, in general, corresponding points of different cycles have identical phase positions.

Two vibrations otherwise similar may differ in phase; thus

if we strike two identical tuning-forks, one slightly before the other, we obtain movements as in Fig. 95, where corresponding points in the waves are lettered similarly. It will be observed that fork *B* is in the *a* or zero-phase position when fork *A* has advanced to the *b* or 90°-position, that when an instant later *A* is at *c* (180°), *B* is at *b* (90°), and so on. Since at every moment during the progression of the waves the movements of fork *A* are ahead of those of *B* by 90°, we say that fork *A* leads in phase by 90°. It is the same thing to say that fork *B* lags in phase by 90°.

If the two forks are struck exactly simultaneously, their movements will be in phase; there will be no phase difference. If fork *B* is struck just half a period later than *A*, the phase difference will be 180°, which is called contrary or opposite phase. This last condition of contrary phase, in which the two movements are precisely opposite at all times, is shown in Fig. 96. Two vibrations may have any phase relation between exact agreement and complete opposition.

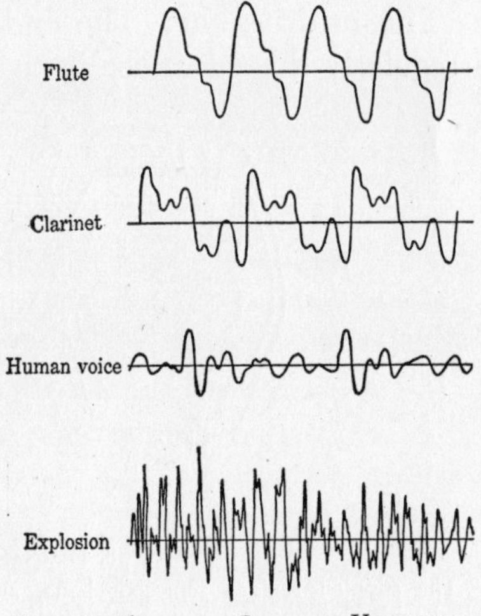

FIG. 97. TYPES OF COMPLEX VIBRATION. From D. C. Miller, *The science of musical sounds,* 1926; reprinted by permission of the Macmillan Co.

Most vibratory movements, far from being so simple as those of the tuning-fork and pendulum, have forms of various complexity. Several types of complex vibration are shown in Fig. 97. The first three curves represent the waves of a flute, a clarinet and the singing voice; the fourth represents the explosion of a sky-rocket. Of these the first three are periodic, since the wave form is repeated at least several times; the last is aperiodic, with no exact repetitions. We shall study later the relation between wave form and auditory experience.

ANATOMY AND PHYSIOLOGY OF THE EAR

The ear may be considered anatomically as divided into outer ear, middle ear and inner ear. The outer ear includes the visible portions—an expanded flap called the *auricle* or *pinna*, and a short tube, the external auditory canal. In man the auricle has so unimportant a function that it may be lost without appreciable impairment of hearing. The auditory canal, the path of entrance of aerial waves, leads internally to the *eardrum*, which forms the boundary of the middle ear.

The middle ear. The middle ear is contained within an irregularly shaped cavity in the temporal bone. The cavity is

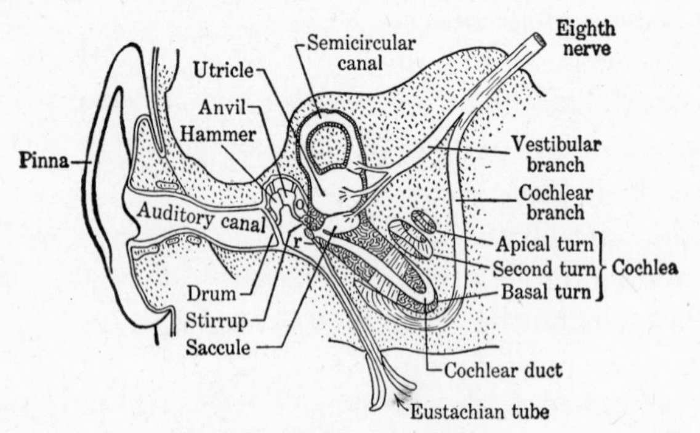

FIG. 98. DIAGRAM OF THE EAR.

The stippled regions represent bone, and the shaded portions indicate cavities filled with perilymph. *r*, round window. *o*, oval window. After Czermak.

filled with air, conveyed by the *Eustachian tube* which enters from the throat. Although the Eustachian tube is normally closed, it opens during the act of swallowing to permit an adjustment between the pressure of the air within the middle ear and that of the atmosphere.

A chain of three small bones, the *auditory ossicles*, leads across the cavity of the middle ear from the drum to a small oval-shaped membrane, the *oval window*, which closes an opening in the inner wall of the cavity. The first ossicle, the *hammer*, is attached to the inside surface of the drum; the third, the *stirrup*, nearly covers the oval window to which it is attached; the middle ossicle, the *anvil*, connects the other two. A number of ligaments hold the ossicular chain together and keep it suspended in the cavity of the middle ear; two of these ligaments are attached to muscles whose contractions control the tensions of the drum and ossicles.

When sound waves enter the auditory canal and strike upon the eardrum, they set it in motion, thereby moving the arm of the hammer which is attached to the drum. The movements are transmitted through the anvil to the stirrup and finally to the fluid content of the inner ear by way of the oval window against which the stirrup rests.

Because it acts as a kind of mechanical transformer, the middle-ear system is of considerable importance in determining the sensitivity of the ear as a receiver of air vibrations. Vibratory energy is not readily transferred directly from a light medium like the air to a denser medium like the fluid of the inner ear, but through the middle-ear system the transfer is greatly facilitated. The transformer action occurs in two ways. First, the eardrum is about twenty times larger than the oval window, which gives a corresponding increase in pressure. Second, the ossicles are arranged in the form of a lever system with a reduction ratio of 1.5 to 1, and therefore give an increase of pressure of 1.5 times. Together these two effects produce an increase of pressure of 20 x 1.5 or 30 times, and hence a very efficient transmission of the sound energy.

The apparatus of the middle ear does not, however, act as a perfect mechanical system, especially when the sounds are loud. The reason lies partly in the peculiar properties of the eardrum, which does not respond equally well to all sounds, and partly in the nature of the joints of the ossicles. Since these joints have a small amount of looseness or 'play' in them, they allow a degree of discrepancy between the drum movements and the movements impressed upon the stirrup. The situation may be compared to that in a simple lever system where the arms of the lever are subject to a small amount of bending. These effects, which cause the movements of the fluid of the inner ear to depart from a strict proportionality to the air waves, constitute middle-ear distortion and contribute to the production of a number of peculiar auditory phenomena, which will be described later.

The inner ear. The inner ear is contained in the bony labyrinth, a space of complex form hollowed out in the deeper portion of the temporal bone. Three divisions of the labyrinth are recognized: the *vestibule, cochlea* and *semicircular canals.*

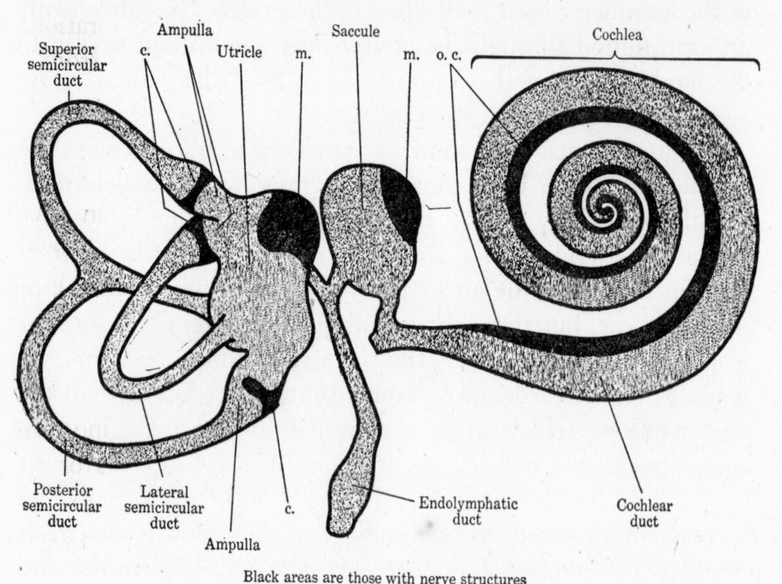

Fig. 99. Diagram of the Membranous Labyrinth.

The cavities of these parts contain a fluid, the *perilymph*, in which lies a complex system of membranous sacs, the *membranous labyrinth.* Of the several parts of the membranous labyrinth, only the cochlea has to do with hearing. The semicircular ducts and the vestibular organs (the utricle and saccule) are concerned with bodily equilibrium.

The *cochlear duct* is a spiral-shaped tube lying to one side of the spiral bony canal of the cochlea. Like other parts of the membranous labyrinth, it contains a fluid, the *endolymph*, which is distinct from the perilymph outside the duct. As seen in cross-section in Fig. 100, the cochlear duct is of triangular form, and lies between two larger tubes, the *vestibular canal* and the *tympanic canal*, from which it is separated by membranes. The vestibular and tympanic canals extend to the basal end of the cochlea at the vestibule, where each communicates with the cavity of the middle ear through a perforation in the lateral wall of the vestibule; these perforations are the *oval* and *round windows*. The first, the oval window, opening as it does from the end of the vestibular canal, bears the membrane

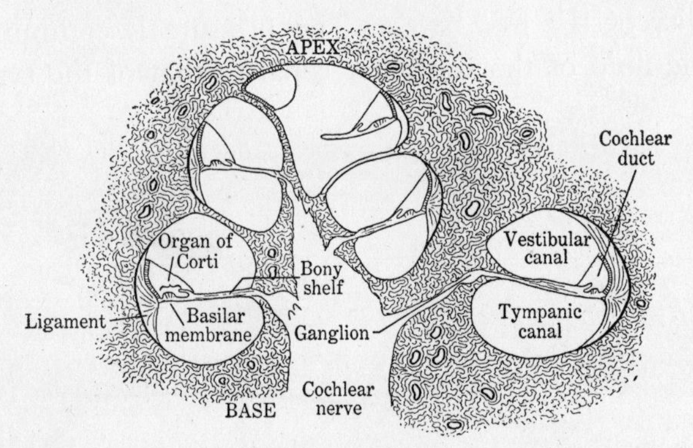

FIG. 100. THE COCHLEA IN MID-SECTION.
The section passes through the axis of the spiral, and cuts across the canals in five places.

to which the base of the stirrup is attached. The second, the round window, which opens from the end of the tympanic canal, is also covered by a thin membrane.

The *basilar membrane*, situated between the vestibular canal and cochlear duct on the one hand and the tympanic canal on the other, is attached to a bony shelf on the inner wall and to a ligament on the outer wall.

Upon the basilar membrane and within the cochlear duct lies the *organ of Corti*, a complex structure bearing *hair cells*—the auditory receptor cells. These cells contain the dendrites of nerve fibers that run inward through tunnels within the bony core around which the cochlear canals are wound, and that finally come together to form the cochlear division of the eighth cranial nerve. A fold of fibrous tissue, the *tectorial membrane*, extends from the bony shelf into the cochlear duct and over the ends of the hair cells.

When the stirrup is momentarily forced inward in its response to a sound wave, it exerts pressure upon the perilymph of the vestibular canal. As the perilymph is practically incompressible and the cavities in which it is contained are enclosed by bone except at the oval and round windows, the pressure exerted at the oval window can be relieved only by the outward bulging of the membrane at the round window into the cavity of the middle ear. The pressure is communicated from the fluid of the vestibular canal to that of the tympanic

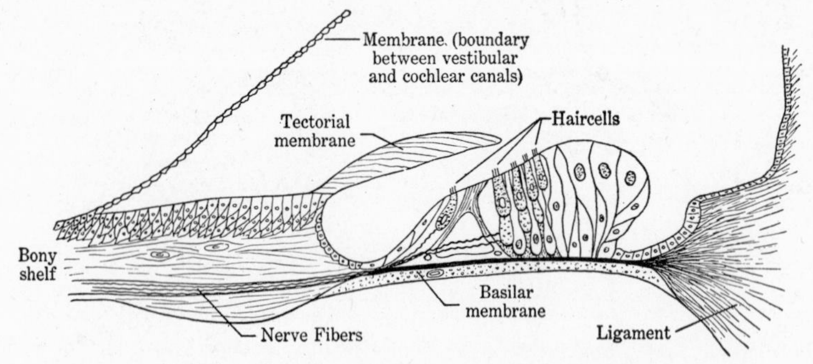

FIG. 101. SECTION THROUGH THE ORGAN OF CORTI.
See Fig. 100 for orientation of this section.

canal through the basilar membrane, depressing this membrane in the process. When, an instant later, the stirrup is moved outward under the influence of the sound, the fluid pressures are reversed, the basilar membrane is moved upward and the membrane of the round window is moved inward. As the basilar membrane moves, the hair cells of the organ of Corti are stimulated, and they in turn excite impulses in the nerve fibers by which they are supplied.

SENSITIVITY OF THE EAR

Discrimination of frequency. The sound frequencies that can be perceived by the ear lie between a lower limit of about 20 cycles per second and an upper limit of about 20,000 cycles. Not only do these limits vary in different individuals, but they may be greatly modified by disease. The upper limit

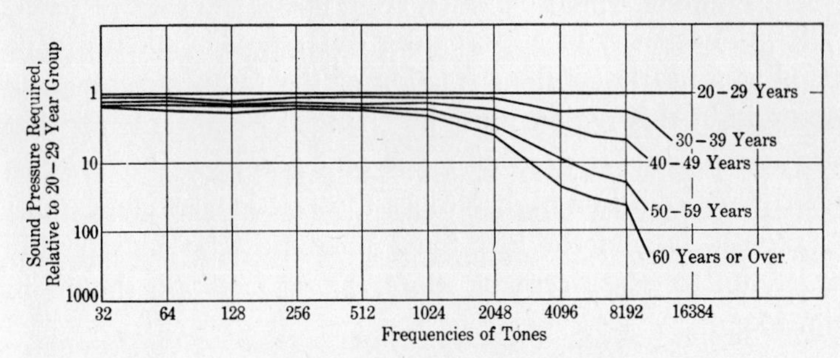

FIG. 102. RELATION BETWEEN AGE AND AUDITORY ACUITY.

Five age groups were examined under similar conditions. The curves show the averaged results, with the youngest (20-29 year) group as the base or 'normal' line. For tones above about 1024 cycles per sec. the older groups require a sound pressure many times larger than the 'normal,' and they fail completely to hear the extremely high tones. Data from C. C. Bunch and T. S. Raiford, *Arch. otolaryng.*, 1913, 13, 423-434.

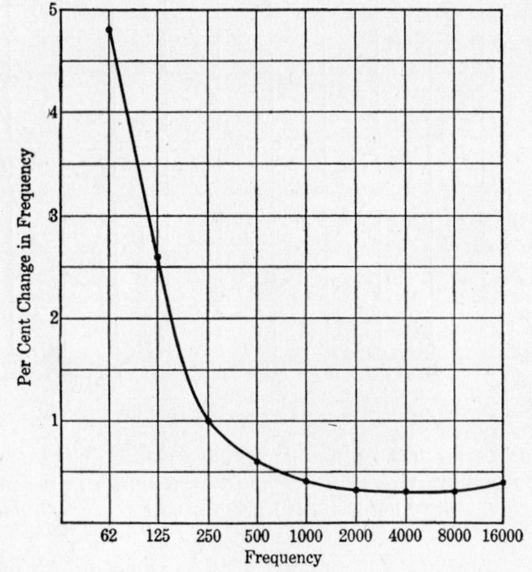

FIG. 103. PITCH DISCRIMINATION.

At low frequencies, the ability to distinguish pitch is considerably poorer than at frequencies above 1000 cycles per sec. Each tone is 40 decibels above threshold. Data from E. G. Shower and R. Biddulph, *J. acoust. Soc.*, 1931, 3, 284.

varies likewise with age; in young persons it may be a little above the value stated, whereas with persons above 25 years it usually decreases progressively, as shown in Fig. 102.

Within the audible range of frequencies there is considerable variation in the ability to distinguish one pitch from another. For the middle region of tones, from about 500 cycles to 4000 cycles, the capacity of appreciating differences of pitch can be stated as a nearly constant fraction of the frequency. A given tone within this region must be changed by an amount that for most persons is 3/10 of 1 per cent before a difference in pitch is noticed. For higher tones the fractional change must be slightly larger; for low tones they must be considerably larger, up to 4 per cent or more. These facts are shown in Fig. 103.

Discrimination of intensity. In its intensitive sensitivity, the ear also varies, both as regards the limits of intensity to

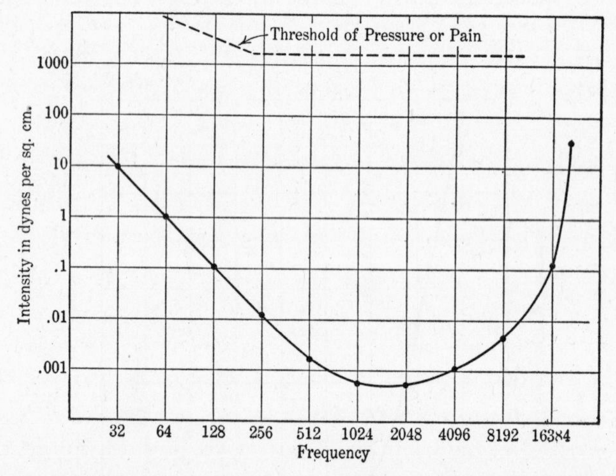

FIG. 104. AUDIOMETER CURVES, SHOWING THE SENSITIVITY OF THE NORMAL EAR. The lower curve represents the lower intensitive threshold; the upper curve indicates the upper intensitive threshold. The intensity is shown as the pressure exerted upon the eardrum, measured in dynes per sq. cm. After R. L. Wegel, *Ann. Otol.*, 1932, 41, 770.

which it will respond and the changes of intensity that can be appreciated. If tests are made to determine for a great number of frequencies the least energy of sound that can be perceived, the results will give an audiometric curve such as the lower curve of Fig. 104. Because this curve represents the average of several individuals, it is smoother than the curve for a single ear. It is evident that the ear is most sensitive in the middle range of 800 cycles to 4000 cycles, and that its sensitivity drops off rapidly for higher, and somewhat more slowly for lower frequencies.

Not only is there a lower limit of sensitivity of the ear (lower intensive threshold), but for practical purposes there is an upper limit also, because, as the intensity of any sound is raised, a point is finally reached where there is stimulation of pain receptors located in the middle ear or elsewhere. For low frequencies, up to about 1000 cycles, pressure and kinesthetic endings also are excited. The intensities where pain and other qualities enter may be taken, for practical purposes, as the upper intensive threshold, for, though the ear doubtless will operate above these intensities, the true limits cannot be investigated without risk of damage. The upper curve of Fig. 104 shows the general location of the upper intensive threshold. Between this curve and the lower curve of the same figure we have the useful range of auditory experiences. That the range of intensities is particularly great for the middle frequencies is evident. For a 1500-cycle tone, the variation of pressures from bare audibility to the maximum that may safely be applied to the ear is more than a millionfold.

The ability to distinguish differences of intensity varies both with the frequency of the tones and with their level of intensity. For faint tones sensitivity is poor, as also for tones near the limits of the frequency scale. Loud tones of the middle range have a relative difference threshold of nearly constant value; to produce a noticeable alteration in loudness such sounds must undergo a pressure change of 9 per cent. Figure 81 on page 512 shows how the relative difference threshold for intensity varies with intensive level.

Measurement of pitch and loudness. The essential constancy, within the limits shown, of the relative difference thresholds for pitch and intensity makes it convenient when dealing with either of these characteristics to use logarithmic rather than linear scales of measurement. Logarithmic scales for frequency were used in Figs. 102, 103 and 104, in which equal steps represent successive octaves. Another logarithmic scale for frequency is found in the tempered scale of modern music, where successive notes, representing semitone steps or intervals, differ in frequency by the constant ratio of 1:1.06 ($1:\sqrt[12]{2}$).

Logarithmic scales of intensity have also been used in Figs. 102 and 104. In both figures a given step represents a tenfold change of pressure. A logarithmic scale of intensity in common use is the *decibel* scale, in which each successive unit represents an energy increase of 26 per cent over that preceding. It should be noted that this scale expresses a relation between quantities, and not their absolute values. Thus, to say that one sound is 20 decibels greater in intensity than another does not state their energies, but implies merely the ratio of these energies. In any given case the number of decibels between two tones is equal to ten times the logarithm of the ratio of the energies of the two tones.

We may of course select a standard energy, and reckon the intensity in decibels above or below this as a base. A useful base is the threshold energy of the sound under consideration. Thus we may say that, from distances of 6 ft. or so, the loudness of the rustle of leaves is about 10 decibels, of average speech from 40 to 60 decibels and of a loud shout from 80 to 90 decibels, all measured from the threshold of audibility.

We may also measure in decibels the amount that a sound is changed in loudness by various disturbing noises, using as a base in this instance the loudness of the sound under conditions of quiet. Thus it is found that the noises of the average business office have a disturbing effect on speech of 30 decibels. In a noisy office the disturbing effect may amount to 40 decibels, while in the New York City subway it is 60 decibels and in a boiler factory it may be as great as 80 decibels. By comparing these values with those given above for speech, we discover that, whereas in a noisy office understanding will be considerably reduced, in the subway and boiler factory ordinary speech will be inaudible—even a loud shout perceived so faintly as to be largely incomprehensible.

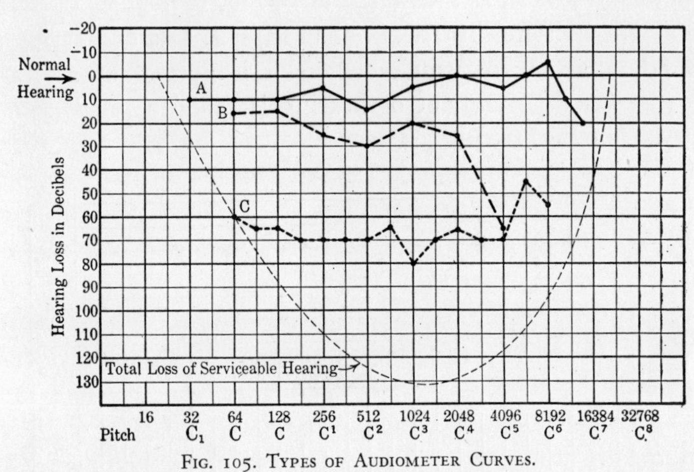

FIG. 105. TYPES OF AUDIOMETER CURVES.

A, practically normal hearing, except that the upper limit is slightly curtailed. *B,* a case of high-tone deafness. *C,* a case of general deafness of serious degree. Data from S. R. Guild, S. J. Crowe, C. C. Bunch and L. M. Polvogt, *Acta oto-laryng.,* 1931, 15, 292-301.

Defects in hearing. In many persons, as a result of diseases affecting essential portions of the auditory mechanism or its nervous connections, sensitivity is impaired in greater or less degree. The impairment takes many forms. In some persons, when the cochlea or auditory nerve is damaged, the deafness is total. In others, as shown in curve *C* of Fig. 105, the ear still functions, but all tones to be heard must be of considerable strength, far above that required by the normal ear. In many instances sensitivity is normal or nearly so for some frequencies, but reduced or lacking for others, as in curve *B* of Fig. 105, which illustrates *high-tone deafness.* Occasionally persons are found whose sensitivity is normal or practically so for most tones, but who have a *tonal gap,* a restricted region of frequencies within which tones are heard only if their intensities are raised to an extraordinary height. Such a case is shown in *D* of Fig. 106. As in the case illustrated, a tonal gap is usually restricted to the region of 4096 cycles. Though such gaps are fairly common in men, they are rare in women. Usually in the course of time they expand to form general high-tone deafness, as illustrated in *B*, Fig. 105. Their cause is unknown. In some instances, all hearing is lost except for a limited range of frequencies where it is normal or at least fairly good; this remnant of hearing is called a *tonal island* (curve *E* of Fig. 106).

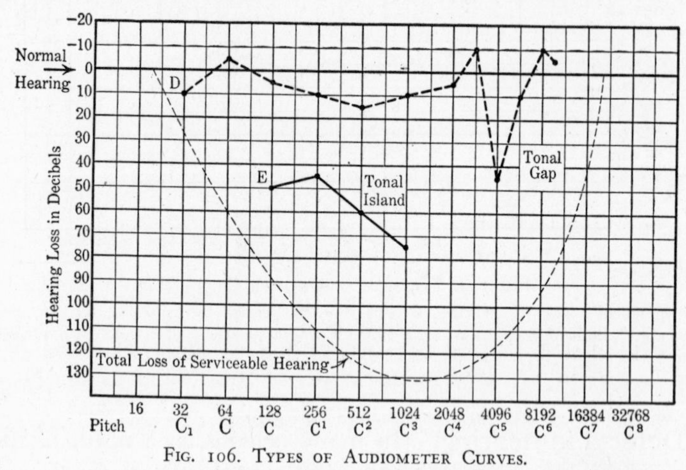

FIG. 106. TYPES OF AUDIOMETER CURVES.

D, a case of nearly normal hearing, except for a partial gap in the region of 4096 cycles. *E*, a tonal island extending from 128 cycles to 1024 cycles. Data from the same source as those of Fig. 105.

Many persons who are deaf to sounds conducted to the ear in the usual way, by the passage of aerial vibrations through the external auditory canal, are nevertheless able to hear when the sounds are applied directly to the bones of the head. Often a person who cannot perceive the vibrations of a tuning-fork as it is held near the ear may nevertheless hear them when the foot of the fork is pressed against the side of the skull or held between the teeth. The vibrations, conducted in this way directly through the bones of the skull to the inner ear, thus circumvent obstructions in the auditory canal or middle ear. When deafness exists for air-conducted but not for bone-conducted sounds, it is a sign that the essential tissues of the inner ear are functioning and that the defect lies in the conductive system of outer and middle ears. When, on the other hand, sensitivity is low for air and bone conduction alike, it is probable that the defect is of the inner ear itself or its nervous connections.

By wearing a mechanical device that amplifies the sound waves before they are presented to the ear, the partially deaf may often compensate for their defect. One such device is the ear trumpet; another is a kind of portable telephone system. For persons with good bone conduction, best results are usually obtained from an instrument which applies the vibrations to the mastoid bone just behind the ear.

PHENOMENA OF HEARING

Auditory experiences present a number of fundamental characteristics or attributes. Of these the most prominent are *pitch*, *loudness* and *complexity* (see pp. 500f.).

Pitch. From low to high, or deep to shrill, tones vary continuously in pitch, as illustrated by the rising and falling note of the siren. In this instrument the sound is made by directing a jet of air against a revolving disk which bears around its periphery a row of holes. As the disk moves, the holes permit the escape of air in separate puffs, the rate of which depends upon the number of holes and the rate of revolution of the disk. When the disk moves faster and the puffs increase in rate, the pitch becomes higher. Thus it is shown that pitch varies with the frequency of sound waves, that slow frequencies give rise to low-pitched sounds and rapid frequencies to high-pitched sounds.

But sound frequency is not the sole determinant of pitch. It changes also, in variable degree, with intensity. Tones of low frequency are lowered in pitch when the intensity is increased, and there is some evidence that tones of high frequency are raised in pitch. For example, a tone of 400 cycles at high intensity may seem equal in pitch to a weaker tone of 390 cycles.

Finally, pitch is a function of sound composition. Tones have definite pitch; noises, on the contrary, are essentially lacking in this characteristic. Many sounds, of course, are intermediate between tones and noises, possessing the qualities of both. Such sounds as the roll of thunder, the howling of the wind and the hiss of a steam jet present both tonal and noisy features. Harsh and irregular though they be, it is easy to recognize a characteristic pitch difference among them.

Loudness. A characteristic of tones and noises alike is loudness. Varying from the faintest whisper to the deafening thunder-clap, it depends upon both the energy and the frequency of sound waves. For a tone of a given frequency, the loudness varies with the energy in a fairly regular manner. But if sound energy is kept constant while frequency is varied, the tones will not appear equally loud, for the sensitivity of the ear varies greatly with frequency in a manner closely resembling the curve for the lower intensitive threshold in Fig. 104.

Since the sensitivity of the ear is in part a function of frequency, it follows that the loudness of a complex of several tones or of noises does not depend in any simple way upon the total energy in the waves, but rather varies with the manner in which the energy is distributed among the various frequencies present.

Complexity. In respect of the attribute of complexity, sounds vary all the way from the simplest, clearest tone to the most bewildering noise. Simple or pure tones are rare in ordinary experience, for even the tuning-fork gives a complex tone unless care is taken to strike it gently. Musical instruments produce tones of various degrees of complexity, ranging from the simple tone of the flute to the harsh jangle of the cymbals. Noises, often complex to the point of confusion, are typically not steady but continually changing in loudness and composition.

An examination of the sound waves which produce the above series of experiences shows that the pure tone arises from a sound wave of simple sine form and that, as the wave form departs more and more from this elementary type, the experience becomes increasingly complex. In Fig. 97 were shown the waves typical of the flute, the clarinet, the voice and the explosion of a sky-rocket.

ANALYSIS AND DISTORTION

Analysis. It is one of the fundamental laws of physical acoustics that any complex periodic wave may be regarded as the sum of a series of simple harmonic motions of suitable amplitudes and phase relations, whose frequencies are in the ratios of the simple numbers 1, 2, 3, 4, 5, etc. This is Fourier's law.

The first member of the series, bearing the ratio number 1, is called the *fundamental*; the remaining members are *overtones.* The first overtone, with the ratio number 2, has a frequency twice that of the fundamental; the second overtone, with the ratio number 3, has a frequency three times that of the fundamental and so on. Thus, for example, a complex sound may be considered as made up of a fundamental frequency of, let us say, 100 cycles per sec., and overtones of 200, 300, 400 cycles, and the like.

Any member of the series of frequencies may vary in amplitude or in phase, or may be absent (zero amplitude). The resolution of a complex vibration into the series stated by Fourier's law, with a determination of the component frequencies, amplitudes and phases, may be accomplished by mathematical methods, or, less laboriously, by a mechanical apparatus called a harmonic analyzer.

The ear itself, however, is capable of analyzing complex vibrations—an analysis of the same general type as that performed by mathematical or mechanical methods. On listening to a complex tone we are able, especially after training, to 'hear out' the fundamental and several of its overtones. The fact that by ear we are able to resolve a complex tone into components that conform approximately to Fourier's series is known as *Ohm's law* of hearing.

In the sounds produced by many musical instruments, the largest amount of the total energy is in the fundamental, and most of the remainder in the first few overtones. For any given instrument the form of distribution of the energy is usually fairly definite, as it depends in a measure upon distinctive mechanical features. It varies, in short, with the method of producing the vibrations. For example, distinctive forms are found in the piano, where strings are struck, and in the clarinet, where air is blown across a reed. The form varies too with the type of resonator, and is different, for example, in the piano, which has a sounding-board, and in the trombone, which has a variable tube of particular form. Since, owing to differences of material and workmanship, mechanical features vary somewhat among instruments of given design, the distribution of energy among the components of the sounds will vary for particular instruments. Thus we have the difference between a good instrument and a poor one. Finally, also, the distribution will vary with the method of playing, such distinctions marking off the master from the mediocre performer.

The particular distribution of energy that is regarded as acceptable for an instrument or a player is determined by musical conventions, the standards of which have varied over the course of musical development. During comparisons of instruments or performers, the fundamental note is usually kept constant, so that any differences which appear can be ascribed to the overtones and their relative amplitudes and phases. The subjective differences arising from variations of the overtones under these conditions are called differences in *timbre*. Thus we speak of the difference in timbre between a clarinet and a violin, or between one voice and another. We readily recognize a familiar instrument or singer by the timbre of the sounds produced.

The approximate character of auditory analysis is due to the peculiarities of the ear and its nervous connections, among which are the limited range of sensitivity, the different sensitivity to various sound frequencies and the distortion to which sound vibrations are subject in the middle ear and elsewhere.

Distortion. A system for the reception and transmission of vibratory movements will often fail to represent exactly the energies acting upon it. Under some conditions, in fact, all known forms of acoustic apparatus show distortion in their operations. The ear is no exception.

Two forms of distortion are to be distinguished: *frequency distortion* and *amplitude distortion.*

Frequency distortion occurs in so far as a system fails to respond equally well to all frequencies. The ear is subject to this type of distortion, for its range is limited and even within this range sensitivity varies greatly. Hence, if complex sounds are impressed upon it, the ear alters the form of wave by emphasizing components of the middle frequencies, and minimizing or even excluding components of low and high frequencies.

Since sensitivity varies somewhat in different persons, it follows that complex sounds, such as the sounds of speech, may appear different to them. Ordinarily, of course, we have no way of appreciating these differences; but, to persons who suffer sudden impairments of sensitivity in a part of the auditory range, the new pattern of distortion becomes immediately apparent. Such persons complain of the strangeness of sounds and of difficulty in interpreting them. In time, if their sensitivity changes no further, they may become adjusted to the altered pattern of distortion.

Ordinary adjustments to distortion patterns are strikingly demonstrated if a person listens to his own voice recorded on a high-fidelity phonographic recorder. The quality is wholly strange and unfamiliar. Usually when we speak the sounds are heard in large part through bone conduction, a situation which gives a pattern of distortion characteristically different from the air conduction by which the phonographic record is made.

The second form of distortion is a failure in the exact reproduction of sound amplitude. When sounds are faint, or only moderately strong, the ear represents them with fair fidelity, but let them become intense and the distortion is great. A tone that is physically simple seems pure so long as it is no more than about 40 decibels above threshold; raised above that level it seems more and more complex. Experienced persons can analyze the effect of a strong sine wave into a fundamental tone and its series of overtones, in the manner expressed by Ohm's law. The degree of distortion of a single tone can be formulated by the extent to which energy is transformed from the fundamental frequency into the various overtone frequencies. When two or more tones are simultaneously present, the distortion takes more complicated forms.

Distortion in the ear probably enters at various levels. Middle-ear distortion, already mentioned, has been ascribed to peculiarities of the drum and ossicles. It is also likely that additional distortion occurs in the inner ear and in the processes by which nerve impulses are set up and communicated through the auditory tracts.

BEATS, COMBINATION TONES AND MASKING

When two tones are conducted simultaneously to the same ear, one of three phenomena may result. If the two tones differ but little in frequency and are somewhere near the same intensity, there occur peculiar variations in the loudness of the sound, known as *beats*. If the frequency difference of the tones is increased, with tones both of which are fairly loud, a third tone, called a *combination tone*, is heard in addition to the two primary tones. But if one of the tones is considerably stronger than the other, it *masks* or obscures the other tone, and we hear only the stronger.

Beats. Two tones identical in frequency produce no beats, and the combination of the tones differs from either of the tones alone only in loudness. The loudness, which in a given case depends upon the phase relation of the tones, may vary anywhere from a maximum equal to the sum of the two intensities when the tones are in phase, to a minimum representing the difference of the two intensities when the tones are in contrary phase. If the two tones are of equal intensity, the intensity at phase agreement is doubled, giving a loudness 3 decibels above that of either tone, whereas at phase opposition the two waves cancel and the result is silence. Intermediate phase relations give intermediate intensities.

When the tones differ slightly in frequency, the phase relations change periodically, and beats occur at a rate that is directly a function of the frequency difference. If the frequency difference is 1, as with the tones 1000 and 1001 cycles per sec., there must be during 1 sec. a change from phase agreement to contrary phase and back again to agreement—which means

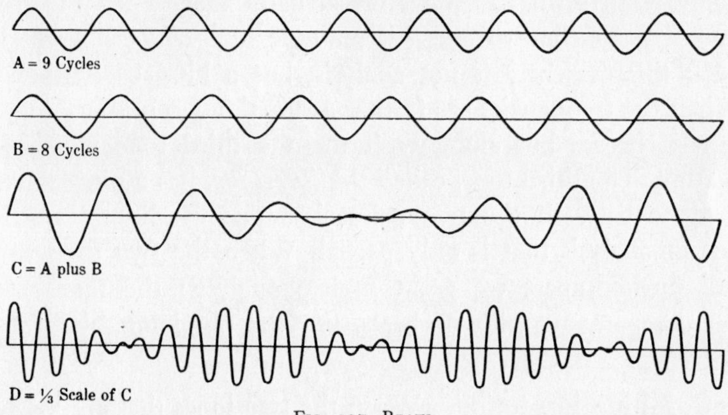

FIG. 107. BEATS.

Two tones, *A* and *B*, of adjacent frequencies in the ratio 9:8 combine to form *C*, a wave-form of periodically changing amplitude. *D* is the same as *C* pressed together to show the 'beat-pattern' better. If these tones had frequencies of 90 and 80 cycles per sec., then there would be 10 beats per sec., and curves *A*, *B* and *C* would be 0.1 sec. long, and curve *D* 0.3 sec. long.

that the intensity changes from maximum to minimum and back again to maximum. Should the frequency difference be greater, then this variation of intensity must occur correspondingly more often during each second. The combination of two tones of adjacent frequency gives a wave of varying amplitude, illustrated in Fig. 107.

As the frequency difference of the tones is increased, the experience changes from a slow waxing and waning of the sound to a rather unpleasant 'pounding,' in which changes of intensity within each beat are no longer perceptible but each beat is a distinct impulse. With further increase of the frequency difference the experience first passes into a stage of prominent roughness, and then fades and finally disappears. The point of disappearance of the beats varies with the region of the scale from which the primary tones are chosen; with high tones, beats as fast as 250 per sec. can be heard, but with low tones the limit is lower.

The appearance of beats between two tones of adjacent frequencies reveals a limitation of the ear's capacity of analysis. If analysis were perfect, we should hear the two tones separately, with no beats. What we actually hear, when the frequencies are close together, is a single tone of varying loudness; this evidently is not analysis, but a kind of synthesis. When the frequencies are farther apart, the two primary tones can be heard, but along with them a third tone which is beating. The third tone, called the *intertone*, has a pitch intermediate between the two primaries. The condition here is one of analysis that is only partial. When the two tones are still farther apart we get complete analysis; the tones are heard separately, with no beats. For the physiological theory of beats, see p. 598.

Combination tones. When the two tones that are led to the ear are fairly strong, and have a frequency difference of about 50 cycles or more, one or more tones may be heard in addition to the primary pair. The most prominent of such tones is a *difference tone*, which has a frequency equal to the difference in frequency of the primaries. Under good conditions, when the primaries are loud, there can also be heard a *summation tone*, whose frequency is the sum of the frequencies of the primary tones. Thus, for example, the tones 700 and 1200 cycles may produce a difference tone of 500 and a summation tone of 1900 cycles. Although, if the primary tones contain strong overtones, there may be other combination tones, these usually are so faint as to escape notice.

The appearance of combination tones is a further indication that the ear as a whole is not a perfect analyzing mechanism. New frequencies appear subjectively which would not be revealed in a physical analysis of the sound waves entering the ear. The most reasonable explanation of this phenomenon is that the new frequencies arise through distortion in the middle or inner ear.

Masking. In the event that the two tones that are led to the same ear differ considerably in intensity, the weaker is

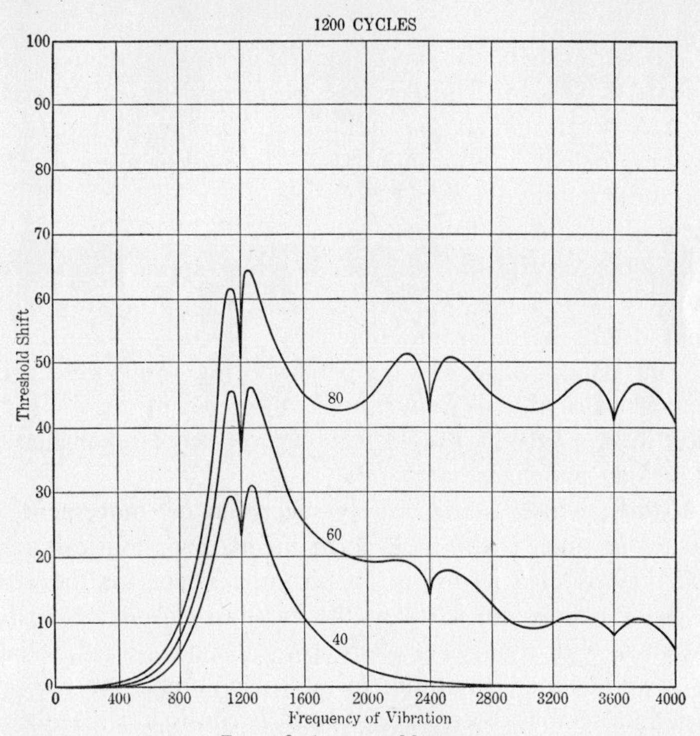

FIG. 108. AUDITORY MASKING.

Three curves are given to show the masking effects of a 1200-cycle tone at intensities of 40, 60 and 80 decibels above threshold. Modified from R. L. Wegel and C. E. Lane, *Phys. Rev.*, 1924, 23, 271.

masked and only the stronger is heard. Unless the tones are so near as to lose their identity in the production of strong beats, masking is greater for tones close together in frequency. For ordinary tones which contain overtones the effect is greater for frequencies above the masking tone than for frequencies below it. The masking effect of a 1200-cycle tone is presented in Fig. 108. The curves show how high above their normal thresholds the various neighboring tones must be raised in order to be perceived in the presence of a masking tone, at three different intensities, 40, 60 and 80 decibels. For the physiological theory of masking, see pp. 598f.

NATURE OF MUSICAL SOUNDS

Music consists of the use of sounds in complex patterns for esthetic expression. The patterns are formed by variations in *pitch, loudness* and *timbre*, according to accepted standards of rhythm, melody and harmony. Even in a given musical tradition these standards are not fixed; they vary greatly for different peoples and in different ages.

In some very primitive music, *rhythm* appears almost exclusively as the form of expression. The sounds, usually noises from drums or other instruments of percussion, are woven into intricate patterns of a temporal and intensitive kind. This element of rhythm is found in all music, but in our own it is used in a relatively simple way owing to its subordination to melody and harmony.

Melody, which is the orderly succession or 'movement' of pitches in time, is the basic form in our own musical tradition. Probably in its origin an accompaniment for the voice in poetic expression, it still is the medium of song. Note follows note with changes of pitch upward or downward, usually in a well-defined rhythmic form. In a number of respects, melody resembles poetry and speech. It consists of a sequence of sounds arranged in phrases and measures, and it expresses a unitary theme. The constituent tones—like the syllables of speech, of little significance in themselves—form through their relations with others in the melodic sequence a meaningful pattern.

Harmony, which is the use of many sounds in simultaneous combination, is a more recent acquisition. It springs from the discovery that pleasing variety is achieved when a number of voices and instruments use different pitches together instead of singing or playing in unison.

The use of pitch in musical patterns led to the development of a great many instruments of various ranges and timbres. Some of these, like the trombone and violin, are capable of producing any pitch within their scope; but most, like the organ, piano and horns, produce only certain fixed pitches. This latter limitation has contributed to one of the outstanding characteristics of our music, the use of only a limited number of tones chosen from the audible range. These particular tones are represented by the notes of a musical scale.

It must be pointed out that the notes of a musical scale represent no absolute frequencies of sound, but rather a set of tones whose frequency ratios are fixed. So long as the frequency ratios remain constant, the intervals between the notes will be sensibly the same, even though the absolute values of the frequencies may vary over a considerable range. In other words, music is concerned fundamentally with relative rather than absolute pitch. It is a familiar fact that a melody sung or played at different regions of the scale may still be recognized as the same. The melodic relations, and also the harmonic characters, of a piece of music are not altered by changes of scale position.

Relative pitch ability, or the capacity to appreciate the intervals between notes when they are heard or when they are presented visually in musical notation, is common to persons of musical accomplishment. Readily acquired through practice, it may reach limits of high accuracy. Singing from memory or from printed music naturally depends upon this ability. But *absolute pitch* ability, or the capacity to identify a given isolated note either by stating its frequency or its musical name in reference to a standard system of tuning, is rare even among practiced musicians, and when it does exist it is not very accurate. Although persons with musical training can judge relative intervals with an accuracy better than one-fifth of a semitone, most persons even after special practice are unable to make judgments of absolute pitch within less than about 3 semitones. A few especially gifted individuals have greater absolute pitch ability than that just described, but usually their accomplishment is limited to a given instrument with which they are familiar, and thus probably dependent upon the peculiarities of the several notes as regards timbre and loudness as well as pitch.

AUDITORY LOCALIZATION

The cues that are involved in the localization of sounds may be divided into two classes: primary or binaural cues, which depend upon differences of stimulation of the two ears; and secondary cues, which are not significantly different for the two ears.

Binaural cues. A difference in the stimulation of the two ears, within the proper limits, results in the perception of a single sound displaced to the right or left of the median plane. For simple tones, this difference in stimulation may be one of *intensity* or of *phase*, or a combination of the two. For complex tones and noises, the difference may be of *intensity, time, complexity* or possibly of *phase*, or a combination of these.

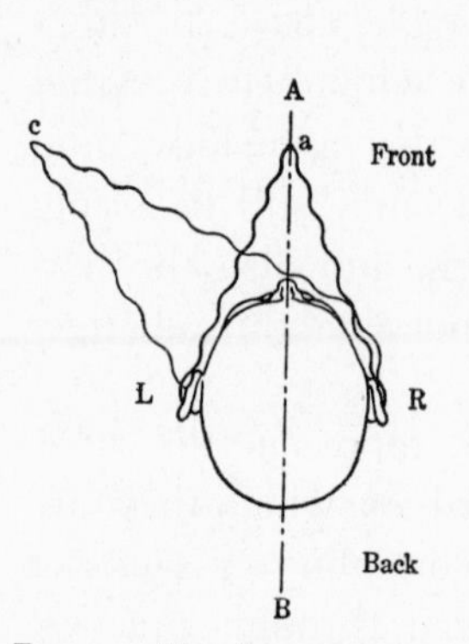

FIG. 109. THE LOCALIZATION OF SOUNDS.

A sound at *a* will stimulate the left and right ears equally; but a sound at *c* will stimulate the left ear (1) sooner, (2) more strongly, and (3) in different phase.

The direction of the displacement of the sound depends upon which ear is favored by the binaural difference in stimulation, and the amount of displacement depends upon the magnitude of this difference.

If the source of sound is in the median plane, as at point *a* in Fig. 109, or anywhere on the plane that may be drawn through *AB* perpendicular to the paper, then it is equidistant from the two ears, and, barring any intervening object, must stimulate the two ears in precisely the same manner. If, however, the source is moved to point *c*, it will stimulate the two ears differently. (1) Because it is nearer to *L*, it will stimulate that ear sooner. (2) For the same reason, and also because *R* is somewhat in a sound 'shadow' cast by the head, it will stimulate *L* more strongly. (3) Further, because of the difference in distances *cL* and *cR*, there will be a difference in phase, except for those few tones for which the difference in distance equals some integral number of wave-lengths. The phase difference will vary for different tones, because it depends upon the relation between wave-length and the difference in distance.

Under normal conditions of stimulation these three cues operate concurrently; but under experimental conditions they may be controlled individually and separately studied. The best methods for such control involve the use of electrical apparatus. Separate telephone receivers are placed over the ears, and to these are conducted oscillating electrical currents whose magnitude, phase and time of incidence may be changed at will.

If time and phase are kept constant, and the sounds at the two ears are varied in intensity, it is found that a shift of the apparent source of sound from the median plane begins to appear when the intensity in one ear is 3 to 5 decibels greater than that at the other. As the ratio of intensity is further increased, the sound seems to move toward the side of greater intensity, until eventually it appears to be directly opposite the favored ear.

When the intensity is kept constant, the localization of tones varies with the phase. The sound is localized in the median plane so long as the tones at the two ears agree in phase. If the phase is made to lead in one ear, however, the sound seems to be shifted toward that side. The lateral shift becomes maximal for a phase difference of nearly 180°. At exactly 180° the phase is equivalent for the two ears, and localization is median or uncertain. A phase lead of more than 180° is the same as a lagging phase, when localization shifts to the opposite side.

The change of localization with phase is most easily illustrated by applying a given tone to one ear, and to the other ear a tone of the same intensity but of slightly different frequency. Though the difference in frequency may be so small as to be imperceptible, the physical effect is to give a periodic variation of phase relations. The situation is one that would give beats if both tones were led to the same ear; but here, with the tones in separate ears, beats do not occur. The fused sound, though maintaining a steady intensity, seems to shift back and forth between right and left sides of the observer. This binaural shift from right to left and back again occurs at a rate that is numerically equal to the difference in frequency of the tones.

For simple tones, time differences are inherently related to phase differences; but for noises, priority may be considered independently. If intensity is kept constant, and the binaural sounds varied in time of incidence, a shift of localization begins to appear when the priority at one ear exceeds 30 microseconds (30 millionths of 1 sec.). As the time difference increases, the apparent source moves farther from the median plane toward the ear where the stimulation is prior, until finally it is directly opposite that ear for a time difference of 630 microseconds. There is no change of localization for further increases of priority up to 2000 microseconds; for this and greater values, however, the two sounds no longer fuse into one, but are heard separately, one on one side and then one on the other.

Noises, we discover, are much easier to localize than simple tones, a fact due perhaps to a difference in the complexity of the sounds at the two ears. It happens that sounds of low frequency, with their relatively great wave-lengths, do not maintain straight paths after passing obstacles, but readily bend around them. The head does not, therefore, give an appreciable sound shadow for low tones, and a source on the extreme left will stimulate the right ear nearly as strongly as the left. At 256 cycles per sec. the screening effect of the head is less than 0.5 decibel, and is therefore negligible. At 512 and 1024 cycles the screening effect reaches 3 and 5 decibels respectively, enough to be significant, whereas for still higher tones it becomes increasingly important. Hence it follows that, if the source is out of the median plane, sounds which are made up of both low and high frequencies will not appear at the same degree of complexity at the two ears. The ear toward the source will receive the waves in their true complex form, while the ear that is away from the source, and in the head's shadow, will receive the sound with the high frequencies considerably weakened. This difference in complexity is probably appreciated in terms of localization.

Because there is little screening action of the head at low frequencies, differences of intensity are much less significant for low than for high tones. A difference of phase, on the other hand, is particularly important for low tones. Its effect grows progressively less for high frequencies until it becomes of little value beyond about 1500 cycles per sec. For complex tones and noises which contain high frequencies, a difference in intensity operates in much the same way as for high tones. Phase differences, however, will usually be ambiguous as a cue to the localization of complex tones, since the phase relation varies for the different components of the wave. Time differences are very important in the localization of noises. Differences of complexity are naturally effective only for complex tones.

That there are considerable differences in the cues available for the localization of various kinds of sound is evident. For low tones, the binaural differences are chiefly of phase, and to a slight degree of intensity. For high tones the differences are chiefly of intensity. For complex tones and noises there may be differences of intensity, time and complexity. These differences in available cues are reflected in the relative ease of localizing different types of sound. High tones are localized only with difficulty, low tones somewhat more readily and noises with comparative ease. Consider, for example, the relative difficulty of localizing a cricket's chirp, the whistle of a locomotive and the sound of a person's voice.

Secondary cues. The binaural cues, we have seen, are effective only in determining the angle of a source of sound to the right or left of the plane drawn between the two ears. These cues give no aid in determining the position up and down, or front and back, nor do they determine the distance from the observer.

Our actual judgments of localization are more definite than mere angular direction to the right or left only because additional, secondary cues enter into their formation. These cues are in part auditory and would include the absolute loudness, the timbre and the temporal pattern of the sounds, and changes in the character of the sounds in correlation with movements of the head or body. Though cues like absolute loudness and timbre are particularly useful in judging the *distance* of a source of sound, obviously they are adequate only for sounds that are known and in a familiar setting. In addition to the secondary auditory cues there are extra-auditory cues—the visual perception of objects suspected of being possible sources of sound, or our knowledge of those things in the environment which are reasonable sources of the sounds that we hear.

AUDITORY THEORY

We have already seen (pp. 567, 570) how the action of sound vibrations on the ear extends to the stimulation of the hair cells of the organ of Corti. Now we shall attempt to follow in further detail the process of excitation in the cochlea, and to inquire into the nature of the responses set up in the fibers of the auditory nerve.

The phenomena of hearing, as we know, depend upon three dimensions of the stimulus: frequency, intensity and complexity. How these dimensions are represented in the actions of the cochlea and auditory nerve is what we need now to know. The problem is limited by the fact that the variations possible for a bundle of fibers like the auditory nerve are but two: (1) the location of the fibers activated by a given stimulus and (2) the rates of impulses in these fibers.

Representation of frequency. Two suggestions have been made for the representation of frequency. One, known as the *place hypothesis*, is that every tone within the audible range affects a particular region of the cochlea, and hence excites a particular group of nerve fibers. The other, known as the *frequency hypothesis*, is that the frequency of the stimulus is preserved not only in the movements of mechanical structures in the cochlea but also in the rates of impulses in the auditory nerve.

The *place hypothesis* is best known in its formulation by Helmholtz in his resonance theory. According to this theory, different transverse fibers of the basilar membrane vary in mechanical properties so as to give a progressive tuning from low to high, like that of the strings of the piano. This tuning would cause a certain region of the membrane to respond most actively to some particular frequency, the resonant frequency, just as in the piano certain strings will be set into sympathetic vibration if, with the dampers raised, a given note is sung. Since the action of the basilar membrane at any given place would excite the particular nerve fibers that supply that region, such action would thereby lead to the hearing of a tone of a given pitch.

Several lines of evidence must be considered in relation to the place hypothesis. Because the basilar membrane varies in width from base to apex, the fibers which extend transversely from the bony shelf on the one side to the ligament on the other are about six times as long near the apex as they are near the base. Moreover, the ligament is larger near the base, and presumably exerts more tension there than near the apex. Finally, the masses of cells lying on the membrane and weighting it are smaller near the base and larger toward the apex. It is argued that these three factors operate so as to produce a continuous gradation of response properties from base to apex; the transmission of high-frequency vibrations from oval to round window involves the basal regions of the membrane, whereas the transmission of low frequencies involves the apical regions.

More direct evidence has been sought in experiments in which animals have been exposed for a long time to an intense tone. After such stimulation examination of the cochlea by histological and other methods has often revealed changes in the structure of the organ of Corti. Some investigators have reported specific changes in the basal region of the cochlea after exposure to high tones; others have observed more widespread experimentally induced changes. The effects of low tones are less certain.

The experiments just mentioned are restricted to animals, but evidence of a comparable kind is gradually being accumulated for human beings. Such data are obtained from the histological study of the inner ears of persons whose hearing has been tested and whose temporal bones have become available after death. The results show a relationship between deafness and local degenerations within the cochlea. In a significant number of subjects with high-tone deafness, regions of degeneration are found in the basal part of the organ of Corti, and also in the nerve fibers supplying this region. When deafness is general, the degenerations are more widespread.

This evidence is in agreement in indicating that the basal portions of the cochlea are involved in the hearing of high tones. The relationship between stimulus frequency and anatomical region is not highly specific, since a given tone may involve a fairly broad band of the basilar membrane, containing many transverse fibers. The evidence is not so clear, however, for the action of low frequencies; probably they involve larger bands. The very low frequencies, indeed, may affect practically the whole extent of the membrane.

The *frequency hypothesis* is supported by two main lines of evidence. The phenomenon of phase localization seems to indicate that, for low tones at least, the phase relations of tones presented to the two ears are somehow preserved in the nervous action. The phase relations would be preserved most strictly, and at the same time most simply, if the entire waveform could be preserved in the nerve transmission process. Since, however, a nerve fiber acts with only discrete impulses and cannot reproduce an undulating wave, this preservation of wave-form cannot occur in any simple manner. The facts of phase localization indicate merely that there exists some fairly definite relation between the number of waves in the stimulus and the number of nerve impulses.

Direct evidence of a correlation between the frequency of the sound and the frequency of nerve impulses is obtained from experiments on animals, in which an electrode is placed on the auditory nerve or its connections in the central nervous system, and the nerve impulses are studied during stimulation of the ear by sound. It is found that, for low and intermediate tones, impulses passing along the auditory nerve represent accurately the frequency of the sound waves.

This fact, that low and intermediate frequencies are represented in the action of the cochlear nerve, does not mean necessarily that individual fibers of the nerve operate at correspondingly high rates. Nerve fibers are limited in their actions, for after a given impulse they require a period of recovery, the refractory period, before they are again stimulable. The lengths of this period in mammalian nerves are too great to permit, in a given fiber, the continuous passage of impulses at a rate higher than a few hundreds per second (see pp. 232f.).

A way around this limitation is provided by the *volley* principle. A number of nerve fibers, each responding at a relatively slow rate, may cooperate to establish a more rapid rate, just as a drummer, by using two drumsticks, can beat a tattoo of double the rate of each stick. At very slow frequencies, each fiber may of course respond at every wave of the stimulus, but as the frequency becomes higher the fibers respond at every second wave, or every third, and so on. Different fibers, since their rates of recovery differ slightly, and because the strength of stimulation varies over the region of the basilar membrane involved, become out of step with one another. That is to say, they come into the total discharge of impulses at different times, and if there are enough fibers there can be several impulses for each wave of the stimulus. Although many of the fibers are out of step with one another, they are all in synchronism with the waves of the stimulus. Hence the total of their impulses represents with a high degree of faithfulness the frequency of the sound.

The principle is illustrated in Fig. 110. The upper part of this figure shows a curve that represents a tone in which the time of the wave-length is so much shorter than the refractory

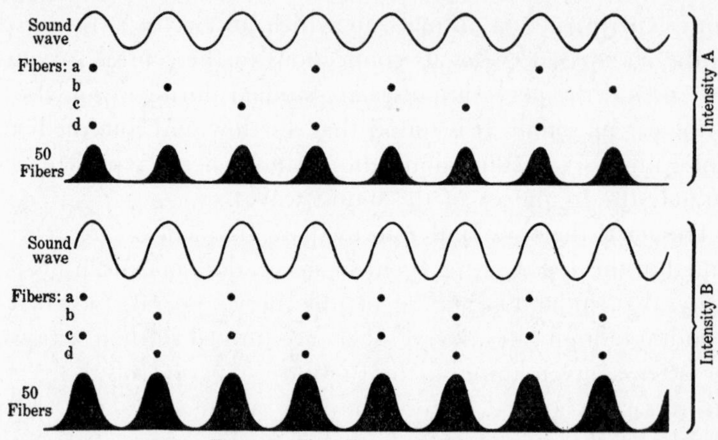

FIG. 110. THE VOLLEY PRINCIPLE.

Each nerve fiber is shown as responding at a frequency less than that of its sound wave, but in synchronism with the wave. In the upper part of the figure, the fibers respond at every third wave; in the lower part, where the sound intensity is greater, they respond at every second wave. A large number of fibers gives a total response indicated by the series of black hillocks, which reproduces both the frequency and the intensity of the original sound. When the intensity is raised, the hillocks are higher, since the total number of nerve impulses is greater, but the synchronism with the sound waves is unaltered. The fibers would get out of step with each other, discharging as shown, some in one volley and some in another, because they would vary somewhat one from another in refractory period. Modified from E. G. Wever and C. W. Bray, *Psychol. Rev.*, 1930, 37, 378.

period of the auditory nerve fibers that any single fiber can be discharged only at every third wave. The dots in the figure indicate the times of 'firing' of four fibers, *a, b, c* and *d*. Below the dots the black hillocks represent the total effect of fifty fibers being discharged, a third of them in each volley for each wave. Thus the total impulse in the nerve tract (which consists of many fibers) has the frequency of the original stimulus, even though that frequency is too rapid to be carried by any one fiber.

The lower half of Fig. 110 shows what would happen for a louder tone of the same frequency. Since the amplitude of the stimulus would be greater, the fibers could be excited earlier in their relative refractory periods, so that they could be discharged, as the figure supposes, every other time instead of every third time (see Fig. 78, p. 507). Fibers *a* and *c* would go off together, and similarly *b* and *d*. Thus half of the total number of fibers, instead of a third, would contribute to every volley, and the total effect—the height of the black hillocks at the bottom—would be greater, while the frequency remained the same.

In general it appears that, within limits that are not yet completely defined, the evidence validates both the place and the frequency hypotheses. The two principles seem to be complementary, in that low tones are mainly represented by frequency, and high tones by place.

Representation of intensity. As the intensity of a stimulus is increased, the movements of the basilar membrane increase both in amplitude and in extent. The result is the stronger stimulation of the sensory endings in the region first concerned and, in addition, the stimulation of more endings both in that region and on either side, owing to the greater spread of movement. In the individual nerve fibers the effect of stronger stimulation is to increase the rate of impulses, since with stronger stimulation a fiber can respond earlier in its refractory period. This change in the rate of 'firing' of the fibers does not impair the synchronism with the sound waves. It simply means that a given fiber enters the volleys more often, as we have just seen in the explanation of Fig. 110.

This type of explanation of loudness is in accord with what we already know of sensory intensity in general (see pp. 506-508).

Representation of complexity. In so far as the ear obeys Ohm's law, we can formulate the representation of complex sounds simply as an elaboration of that of single frequencies. Their representation will be the total pattern of actions of the various simple tones of which they are composed. The analysis of complex tones is said to be facilitated by the distribution of the different components over the linear extent of the basilar membrane, and by the consequent involvement of different groups of nerve fibers.

Relation to auditory phenomena. As Ohm's law is not followed exactly by the ear, we have such phenomena as beats, combination tones and masking. Beats may be accounted for in part by the fact that the response of the basilar membrane to single frequencies is not highly specific, and that adjacent frequencies involve somewhat overlapping regions.

We can suppose, for example, that a tone of 1000 cycles produces up-and-down movements of the segment of basilar membrane *A* of Fig. 111, whereas a tone of 1010 cycles produces movements of segment *B*. A small segment, *S*, is involved in both movements. The amplitude of movement of this common segment will vary periodically, for, when *A* and *B* are moving in the same direction, the displacement will be a maximum, and when they are moving in opposite directions, the displacement will be a minimum. The changes from maximum to minimum displacements for this common segment will occur at a rate that is equal to the difference in frequency of the two tones, for just so often will the phase changes occur. It will be seen further that the more separated the frequencies are, the less will be the overlapping, and the more prominent the primary regions *A* and *B*. With nearly complete overlapping, *A* and *B* lose their identity, and the primary tones are not heard. On the other hand, with slight overlapping, *A* and *B* are analyzed out, and the beating intertone fades into insignificance.

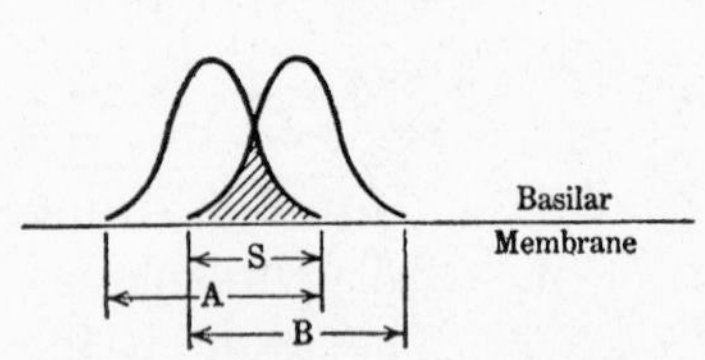

FIG. 111. THE ORIGIN OF BEATS.
Two sound frequencies, 1000 cycles and 1010 cycles, are represented as affecting adjoining regions of the basilar membrane, *A* and *B*. A common segment, *S*, is involved in both movements.

An explanation of masking likewise involves the assumption of overlapping regions of the basilar membrane. If the overlapping is considerable and one tone is much the stronger, it will stimulate most of the nerve endings in that region and will leave few or none available for the other frequency. The weaker tone then is masked.

Marked changes of sensitivity, such as high-tone deafness and tonal gaps, are explainable as due to local disturbances of the mechanical system or its nervous connections. Finally, as already suggested, the localization of low tones in terms of phase can be accounted for on a basis of the fairly accurate time relations between the waves of the stimulus and the impulses that are transmitted by the auditory nerve.

REFERENCES

1. Beatty, R. T. *Hearing in man and animals.* London: G. Bell, 1932.
2. Fletcher, Harvey. *Speech and hearing.* New York: D. Van Nostrand, 1929.
3. M'Kendrick, J. G., and Gray, A. A. The ear. In E. A. Shäfer, *Textbook of physiology.* Edinburgh: Y. J. Pentland, 1900. Vol. II, pp. 1149-1205.
4. Miller, D. C. *The science of musical sounds.* New York: Macmillan, 1926.
5. Stevens, S. S., and Davis, H. *Hearing, its psychology and physiology.* New York: John Wiley, 1938.
6. Wever, E. G. The physiology of hearing: the nature of response in the cochlea. *Physiol. Rev.,* 1933, 13, 400-425.
7. Wever, E. G., and Bray, C. W. The nature of acoustic response: the relation between sound frequency and frequency of impulses in the auditory nerve. *J. exper. Psychol.,* 1930, 13, 373-387.
8. Wilkinson, G., and Gray, A. A. *The mechanism of the cochlea.* New York: Macmillan, 1924.
9. Wood, A. B. *A textbook of sound.* New York: Macmillan, 1932.

Chapter 19

SMELL, TASTE AND SOMESTHESIS

Besides sight and hearing man is endowed with other senses —*smell, taste* and *somesthesis.* This last term is used to cover touch and all the other bodily senses of the skin, the underlying tissues and the internal organs. About these three classes of sensation we know less than about sight and hearing, and indeed they are in many ways less important.

Certainly smell and taste ordinarily play but minor roles in human affairs. Yet man has a great capacity for olfactory discrimination; it has been said that he could make as much practical use of smell as does the dog, were it not for the fact that, in the course of evolution, he has assumed the erect posture and got his head away from the ground, where most of the smells lie. Nor is it certain that man's capacity to taste is poorer than the fish's. These senses have not degenerated. All that has happened is that human civilization has furnished man with so much important visual and auditory stuff for his mind's occupation that he has no time or interest for going around smelling and tasting. Sight and hearing are distance senses. They enable man to extend the scope of his attention far beyond the range of smell, taste and somesthesis, which are thus not so much 'lower' senses as they are 'nearer' senses. They are limited always to the immediate environment.

The somesthetic senses include the four primary qualities of *pressure, pain, warmth* and *cold* that arise in the skin and in the deep tissues and organs, and also such complex perceptions as hunger and dizziness. These senses are obviously of

In this chapter the editors reprint, with minor changes, the principal portions of the chapter on taste and smell by M. J. Zigler and of the chapter on somesthesis by K. M. Dallenbach, as they appeared in Boring, Langfeld and Weld, *Psychology: a factual textbook,* 1935.

fundamental importance for the conduct of the organism, for without them a man could not stand or walk or eat or feel hungry or feel jubilant or know enough to take his hand off a hot stove. Somesthesis is also the oldest sense, the direct descendant of the amoeba's capacity to respond to contact. All animals have somesthesis. No animal in disease or injury can lose all capacity for bodily sensation and live.

SMELL

Stimulation. The sense organ for smell is an aggregation of *olfactory cells* in the uppermost recess of the nasal cavity. These cells are the receptors. They are spindle-shaped, their central ends continuous with the afferent nerve fibers (Fig. 112). The region which contains them is about 600 sq. mm. in area. Because the main current of the breath does not reach these olfactory cells, which are stimulated only by eddy currents that arise from the principal stream, sniffing increases their sensitivity greatly.

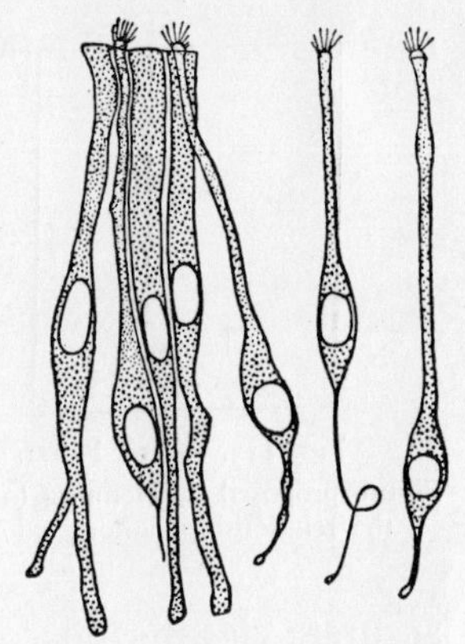

FIG. 112. OLFACTORY CELLS, TOGETHER WITH SOME SUPPORTING CELLS.

From the olfactory regions of the nose. After Von Brunn, from G. H. Parker, *Smell, taste, and allied senses in the vertebrates;* by permission of J. B. Lippincott Co.

It has been estimated that there are about 60,000 different odorous substances, but the chief effect of many of these is tactual or gustatory. Perhaps there are not more than fifty substances for which the particles diffused in the air have no sensory effect other than the stimulation of the olfactory receptors. The total list of stimuli would contain many organic and inorganic compounds. Although most chemical elements are odorless, chlorine, bromine and iodine have smells. The large group of organic compounds which are derivatives from benzene contain so many odorous substances that the class has been called 'aromatic.'

Odorous substances liberate molecular particles into the air, either by evaporation or by chemical change. The particles, spread about by gaseous diffusion, are the true stimulus to smell. Odorous liquids in direct contact with the olfactory region, as when the nose is completely filled with Eau de Cologne with the head inverted, do not arouse smell.

Quality. We have names for the sensory qualities of colors, tastes, tones and tactual impressions: *green, bitter, F-sharp, pain.* There is, however, no such vocabulary for smell. Odors are named only by the objects that give rise to them. The following objects may mean either a thing or the odor of the thing: cinnamon, cloves, fish, rose, onion, camphor, sulphur, cologne, dog, stable, garden, wharf, bakery, orchard. Even such general classificatory names as *flowery* and *fruity* are derived from classes of objects which have such odors.

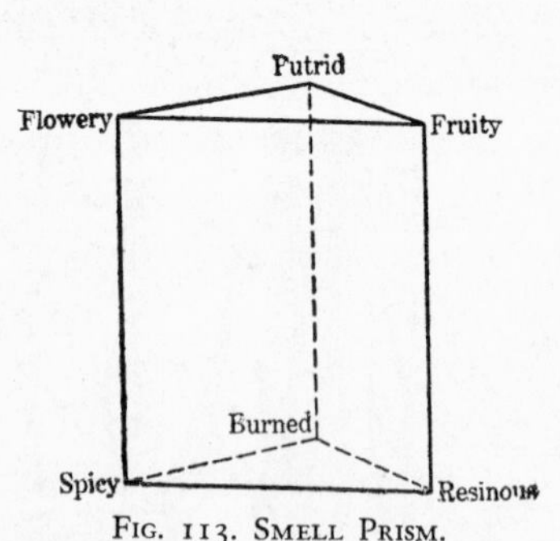

FIG. 113. SMELL PRISM.
Figure proposed by Henning to show the relationships among odors.

The world provides a great diversity of olfactory experiences, and there has never been an accurate classification of them or a perfectly correct system of relations among them. The triangular prism of Fig. 113 is, however, a great convenience in the designation of odors. The figure establishes six primary classes of odors: *flowery, fruity, spicy, resinous, putrid* and *burned*. Odors of intermediate qualities lie on the edges or in the surfaces of the prism, being thereby established in relation to two or three or four of the primary classes. Thus the smell of arbor vitae is flowery-fruity-spicy-resinous, and the odor of onion is mostly putrid, but also somewhat flowery, burned and spicy. In general, putrid and burned odors tend to be unpleasant, the odors of the other four classes pleasant, but the rule has innumerable exceptions. Some people like garlic and some dislike nutmeg.

One reason why casual experience does not yield insight into the qualitative relationships of odors is that most olfactory stimuli arouse tactual or gustatory qualities, or both, in addition to their odors. Chloroform tastes sweet, and ether tastes bitter. Menthol is cool in the nostril; vinegar produces a 'penetrating' tactual quality. A person anesthetic to smell can identify coffee by its 'prickle' and illuminating gas by its taste.

Laws of smell. The mixture of two odorous substances gives rise to a perceived *fusion*, which by attention can be analyzed into its two components—some mixtures quite easily, and others only with difficulty. Although the intimate fusions sometimes closely resemble the odors that come from single unmixed stimuli, they are never quite the same. A mixture of pure red and pure yellow lights, to be sure, can give a color identical with the color from pure orange light, but the analogous case in smell is never fully realized.

Some mixtures show intensitive *compensation*. The resultant odor is much weaker than either of the odors of its separate components. When the antagonistic components are weak, compensation is most effective. It is, for all that, never complete; it is not possible for two perceptible stimuli to mix so as to give an odorless resultant. The effective use of perfumes to combat the odors of the body, in the days when frequent bathing was less common than it is now, depended upon partial compensation. Both components persisted, but in a weak fusion.

Olfactory *adaptation* takes place fairly rapidly and may become complete in a few minutes. The time depends upon the nature and intensity of the stimulus. Measured times for complete adaptation to camphor, for example, vary between 5 and 7 min.; to balsam, between 3 and 4 min.

How adaptation is dependent upon the stimulus substance and its intensity is shown in Fig. 114. Intensity is computed in olfacties. The degree of adaptation is measured by the threshold, *i.e.*, the average minimal intensity of stimulus necessary to elicit the odor. The curves of the figure show that the threshold increases as adaptation continues, that adaptation is more rapid for benzoin than for rubber and that adaptation is more rapid with either substance for the greater stimulus intensity.

Adaptation is *selective.* Sensitivity, which is reduced most for the stimulus to which adaptation has been taking place, may at the same time be somewhat reduced for other stimuli as well, and yet not at all for still others. Thus adaptation to camphor results in diminished sensitivity to cologne, clove and ether. Adaptation to ammonium sulphide reduces the effectiveness of hydrogen sulphide and bromine, but not of oils and coumarin.

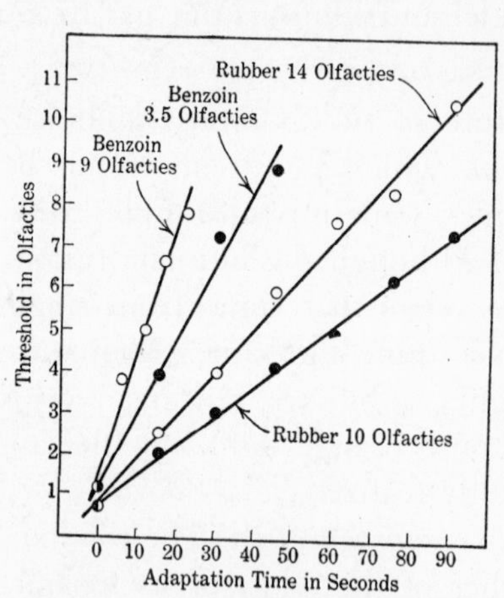

FIG. 114. OLFACTORY ADAPTATION CURVES.

Increasing adaptation is measured by the increase of the olfactory threshold (in olfacties). Adaptation is shown to be faster for benzoin than for rubber, and also with each substance it is faster for the more intense stimulus (as indicated in olfacties). After Zwaardemaker.

Adaptation shows *modulation,* that is to say, the qualities of some odorous substances change as adaptation goes on. Thus at high intensities ionone resembles cedarwood, but in the course of adaptation it becomes less intense and changes to a quality like violet. Modulation sometimes has a disastrous effect with cheap perfumes, which shift from a flowery odor toward the putrid as stimulation continues. Though pronounced with some stimuli, modulation is slight for others and even non-existent for still others.

Recovery after complete adaptation seldom requires more than 5 min. The rate of recovery depends upon the time of adaptation and the intensity of the stimulus.

That adaptation plays an important role in everyday life is evident. Man is very sensitive to odor, and some of the unpleasant odors, as of foul matter, are warnings useful in the preservation of health. The warning once given, however, adaptation takes place rapidly. Adaptation is consequently a great advantage to garbage collectors and the workers in cheese factories, for unpleasant olfactory substances often have to be lived with. When, on the other hand, the environment changes and the stimulus disappears, there is rapid recovery, with the result that a new stimulus or the recurrence of the old is again as effective as before.

To some substances the olfactory organ is very sensitive, as we have already seen in connection with the threshold for mercaptan (see p. 515), but substances differ greatly from one another in effectiveness. Moreover, the threshold is increased about fourfold when the observer is required to say exactly what odor it is that he perceives. Ordinarily he is required to report only whether he perceives some odor or no odor.

TASTE

Stimulation. Taste is served by specialized spindle-shaped receptors, the *taste-cells.* These cells, which bear hair-like processes on their outer ends, are assembled in groups of from two to twelve to form *taste-buds* (Fig. 115). Each taste-bud has at its outer end a small opening, the *taste-pore*, through which stimulus substances in solution can penetrate to affect the receptors.

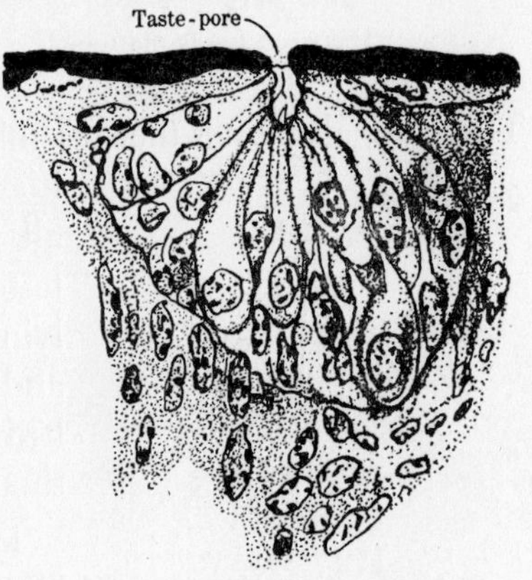

FIG. 115. DIAGRAMMATIC VIEW OF A TASTE-BUD, SHOWING A NUMBER OF TASTE-CELLS GROUPED TOGETHER TO FORM THE TASTE-BUD.

The taste-pore is the opening through which the sapid stimulus reaches the taste-cells. After Kolmer.

Taste-buds are flask-shaped, about 0.06 mm. long and 0.04 mm. in diameter. They are scattered irregularly on the surfaces of the oral cavity: on the tongue, the epiglottis, the larynx and the parts of the throat. Since children have many more of these organs, especially on the tongue and throat, than do adults, presumably therefore they have more reason for crowding their mouths with pleasant-tasting food.

The stimuli to taste are solutions of certain chemically effective substances that enter the taste-bud through the taste-pore. Typical stimuli for the four primary qualities are as follows:

For sour	hydrochloric acid
For saline	common salt
For bitter	quinine
For sweet	cane sugar

Quality. *Sour, saline, bitter* and *sweet* are the four primary qualities of taste. There are also intermediate qualities, the relationships among which have been represented by a tetrahedron, as in Fig. 116. The following are examples of sapid substances that give rise to qualities intermediate between the six pairs of primaries, *i.e.,* qualities that would be placed on each of the six edges of the tetrahedron:

Between saline and sour	carbonate of soda
Between saline and bitter	potassium bromide
Between saline and sweet	alkali
Between sweet and bitter	acetone
Between sweet and sour	acetate of lead
Between bitter and sour	potassium sulphate

There are also tastes that resemble three different primary qualities in varying degrees and even all four of the primaries. Such tastes would be represented as lying respectively in the surfaces and in the interior of the tetrahedron, which must therefore be thought of as a solid figure.

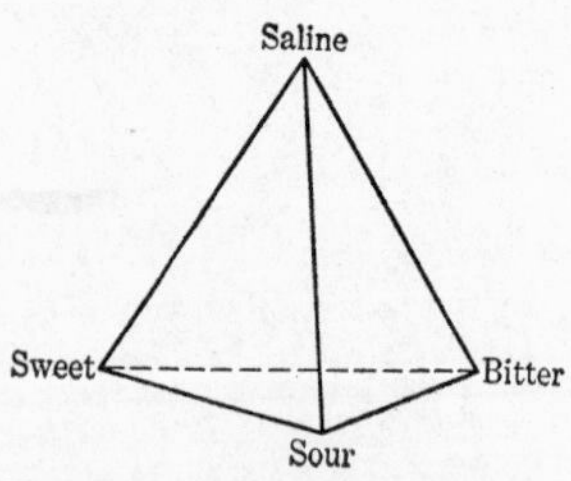

FIG. 116. TASTE TETRAHEDRON.
A figure proposed by Henning to show the relationships of the various gustatory qualities to the four primary tastes. The figure must presumably be regarded as a solid.

These four primaries and their intermediates do not furnish nearly so rich a variety of tastes as a common knowledge of gastronomic esthetics might lead one to expect. Food owes its rich diversity not merely to taste, but also to touch and smell. A careful observer can sometimes distinguish between the gustatory, olfactory and tactual components of a 'taste' complex; but anyone who wishes can by the simple expedient of closing his nostrils demonstrate the role of smell in the flavor of food. When smell is excluded, claret tastes like vinegar, and beef tea resembles a weak solution of salt. Even so, the beef tea may still be distinguished from a saline solution, because its greasiness adds a tactual component that identifies it.

Laws of taste. When the stimuli to different taste qualities are mixed, the resultant perception is a *fusion* in which the components can be distinguished, sometimes with ease and sometimes only with difficulty. Mixtures that involve bitter are usually more easily analyzed than those that do not. The taste of sweet chocolate (sweet-bitter) is a fusion, though not so intimate a fusion as the taste of weak lemonade (sour-sweet) or of a 'marguerite' (a confection on a salt cracker, hence salt-sweet). Salads present a great variety of gustatory fusions. All these gastronomic delicacies, it must be noted, involve touch, temperature and smell as well as taste.

There is mutual *compensation* in the mixtures of stimuli for sour, saline and sweet; in other words, the components in the fusion are perceived as less intense than each would be alone. Bitter, however, appears not to enter into these compensatory relations. Compensation is greater for weak stimuli. Thus, for example, lemonade is less sour and also less sweet because the acid and sugar weaken each other's effects, this mutual diminution being greatest in weak lemonade. Compensation is never total, as it may be with complementary colors.

Adaptation to taste, which occurs fairly rapidly, may be complete in from one to three minutes, depending upon the strength of the stimulus. Since it occurs independently for the four primary tastes, adaptation to one does not affect sensitivity to another. As a matter of fact, recovery from gustatory adaptation is so rapid that sensitivity does not long remain diminished even for the same quality. Ordinarily adaptation is not noticed because in the savoring of food the periods of stimulation are short and the times for recovery between stimulations much more than ample.

As with color and brightness, taste adaptation seems, in some cases at least, to lead to *successive contrast.* Everyone knows that a plum may be too sour after candy, but quite sweet after grapefruit.

Sensitivity varies slightly in different regions of the oral cavity. The general rule is that the tip of the tongue is most sensitive to sugar, the back of the tongue to quinine sulphate and the edges of the tongue to hydrochloric acid. Sensitivity to salt is approximately the same in all regions of the tongue.

This lingual topography is said to find its consequences in certain facial expressions. There is, for instance, the 'complete pout,' in which the lips are opened and protruded and the throat becomes thickened because the base of the tongue is lowered. The resulting expression is one of distaste. Functionally it is this attitude that an infant takes in getting an unpleasant bitter substance out of his mouth. The base of the tongue, most sensitive to bitter, is lowered so that it gets minimal stimulation, while the lips are arranged as in spitting something out of the mouth. There is also the 'sweet mouth,' that may perhaps have some relation to the smile. In it the lips are held tightly together and drawn slightly in, and the tip of the tongue, most sensitive to sweet, presses forward—altogether an attitude that would yield the maximum of the pleasant sweet stimulation.

CUTANEOUS PRESSURE

Pressure is the commonest of the four tactual qualities. The tactual apprehension of the nature of external objects depends far more upon the pressure quality than upon warmth, cold or pain.

Stimulation. Pressure is aroused by a deformation of the skin. Such deformation may be either positive or negative; that is to say, the end-organs of pressure respond to a pull as well as to a push. For example, if we pull a tuft of hair gently, or a thread glued to the skin, we find that the same quality is experienced as though we had depressed the skin. Any stimulus, in short, that gives rise to sufficient deformation of the skin will arouse a quality of pressure.

On the other hand, the occurrence of deformation is not alone sufficient to explain stimulation. For example, if a hand is placed in a bucket of water, or a finger is dipped into a bowl of mercury, pressure is not sensed over the immersed areas, where the positive deformation occurs, but only at the points of emergence. Again, if the skin is drawn into a glass tube or jar by means of a vacuum, pressure will be sensed, not over the entire area where the negative deformation occurs, but only along the edges. Since sensations occur only at points on the skin where differences in stimulus intensities obtain, the conclusion seems inescapable that the receptors are excited, not by the physical pressure itself, but by differences or gradients in pressure.

This theory of the *pressure gradient* accords with all the known facts. The skin is composed principally of water, which is incompressible; consequently, if a force is applied to the skin, the physical pressure extends in all directions. This pressure, greatest at the point of contact, diminishes rapidly as the distance increases vertically into the skin or laterally along its surface. Thus a steep gradient is correlated with a strong stimulus, a gentle gradient with a weak stimulus.

When the skin is explored with a very small stimulus, like the end of a hair pressed down against the skin, the pressure sensation is sometimes elicited and sometimes not, and it is possible to make maps of these more sensitive spots (see Figs. 117 and 118). This punctiform distribution of sensitivity is due doubtless to the fact that the nerve endings for pressure are necessarily distributed in a punctiform manner. On the other hand, the number of spots found depends upon the area stimulated and the effectiveness of the stimulus, for a stronger stimulus deforms the skin more than a weak stimulus and its effect is felt at a greater distance.

The number and distribution of the *pressure spots* vary

greatly for different areas of the body, as well as for the intensity and size of stimulus. When weak punctiform stimuli are used, the sensitive spots on the hairy regions of the body, comprising about 95 per cent of the skin surface, are found to the 'windward' of the obliquely emerging hairs (Fig. 117). On the hairless regions, like the palms of the hands and the soles of the feet, there are also definite points or spots of maxi-

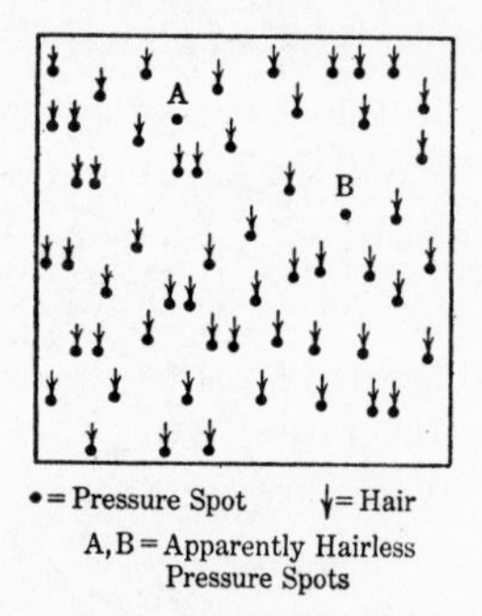

FIG. 117. MAP OF PRESSURE SPOTS AND HAIRS ON VOLAR SIDE OF MIDDLE FOREARM.
After Strughold.

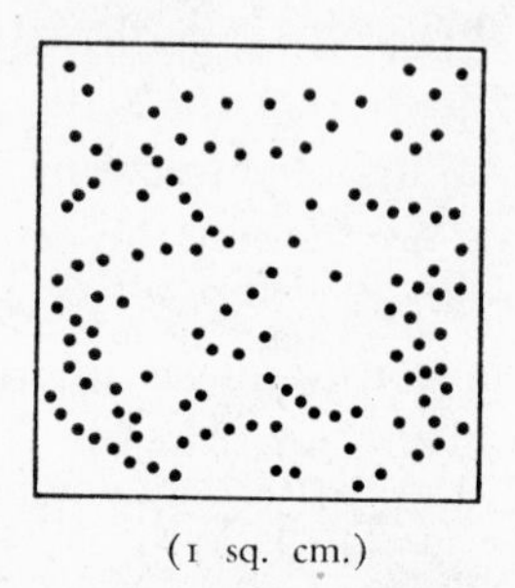

(1 sq. cm.)

FIG. 118. MAP OF PRESSURE SPOTS FROM HAIRLESS REGION BETWEEN THUMB AND INDEX FINGER.
After Goldscheider.

mal sensitivity (Fig. 118) which yield qualities similar to those derived from the hair regions.

Some parts of the skin—*e.g.,* finger tips, lips and scalp—are highly sensitive, with more than 100 pressure spots per sq. cm. Other areas—*e.g.,* the conjunctiva of the eye and parts of the mouth cavity—are insensitive to cutaneous pressure. Between these extremes may be ranged the remaining areas of the body as the figures for the following sample areas show.

Region	*No.*	*Region*	*No.*	*Region*	*No.*
Back	26	Elbow	12	Upper leg	14
Breast	22	Forearm	16	Lower leg	6
Upper arm	9	Back of hand	28	Top of foot	24
		Ball of thumb	135		

The close topographical relationship which obtains between the hairs of the skin and the pressure spots, together with histological findings to the effect that the hair bulbs are supplied with higly specialized nerve endings (Fig. 120), leads to the conclusion that the hair follicles are end-organs of pres-

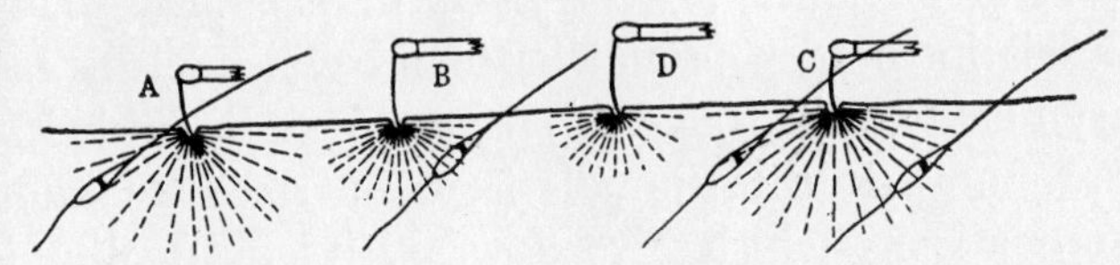

FIG. 119. THE EFFECT OF STIMULI OF DIFFERENT INTENSITIES WHEN APPLIED TO DIFFERENT SPOTS OF THE SKIN.

The stimuli are hairs which are pressed against the skin. The longer and finer the stimulus-hair, the less the pressure.

sure in the hairy regions of the body. For the hairless regions Meissner's corpuscles (Fig. 121) are generally assumed to

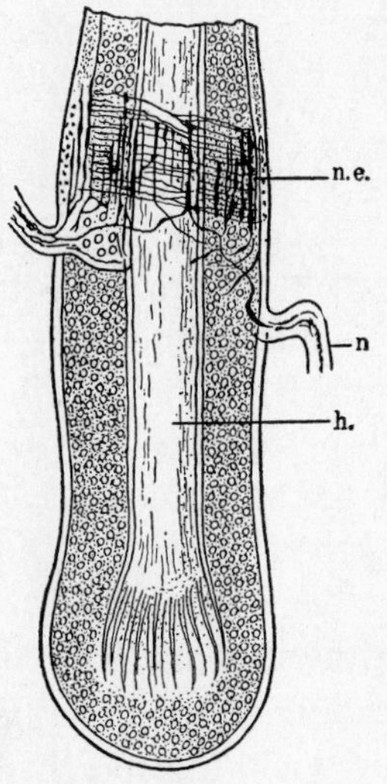

FIG. 120. THE SPECIFIC NERVE ENDINGS IN THE HAIR BULB.

n.e. = nerve endings, *n* = nerve, *h* = hair. After Böhm.

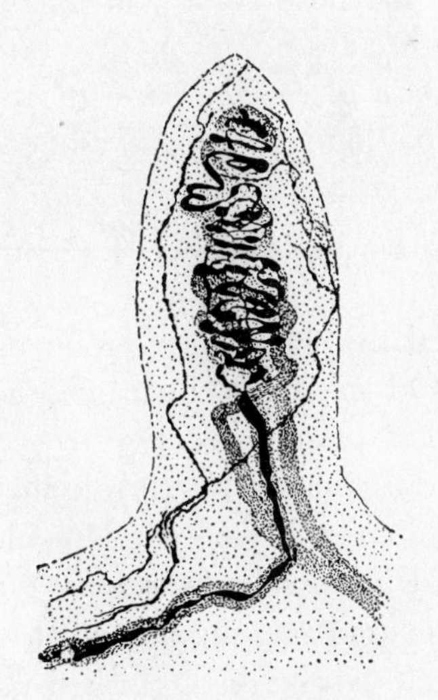

FIG. 121. MEISSNER CORPUSCLE. After Simonelli.

function as end-organs. They are the only specialized end-organs in the hairless regions occurring in sufficient numbers to be correlated with the pressure spots.

Quality. The qualities of pressure vary for different spots and for different stimulus intensities. If the hair of the skin is moved slightly or if the smoothly shaved skin is gently brushed with floss or a feather, a weak *tickle* may be aroused. If the stimulus is intense, spots will be found which yield a solid, pressury quality, called *neutral pressure* to distinguish it from other pressures. If the stimulus is of intermediate intensity, there occur spots which give a weak, bright quality intermediate between tickle and neutral pressure—a quality called *contact.*

Adaptation. With weak stimuli the phenomenon of adaptation is readily observed. Then the pressure experience declines rapidly in intensity and disappears, although it sometimes recurs at the removal of the stimulus. Complete adaptation may also occur with intense stimuli. Instances from everyday life are numerous; we do not perceive the pressure of our clothes, glasses, rings, etc. All that seems to be necessary for adaptation is prolonged and constant stimulation.

Perception of vibration. The surface of the body is very sensitive to vibration. Rates up to 2600 per sec. may be perceived as vibration and not as continuous pressure. The differential threshold is less than one-tenth, which is to say that a deaf observer can, by touch and with practice, readily discriminate a difference between 500 and 550 vibrations per sec. or the difference between middle C and the D above it. By feeling the diaphragm of a telephone receiver deaf persons can be aided in perceiving speech, especially when this 'vibro-tactile' aid is used as a supplement to lip-reading. Gross differences in vowels can be distinguished tactually when the speech sounds are applied to the skin. Although this capacity is sometimes called the "vibration sense," it is proper to regard it, not as a separate sense, but as a special function of the pressure sense; and, since sensitivity to vibration is only slightly diminished by cutaneous anesthesia, it is supposed that the pressure organs for it lie, at least to a large extent, beneath the skin.

CUTANEOUS PAIN

Pain, once regarded as a common sensation produced by excessive stimulation of any sensory nerve or end-organ, is now known to be a separate sense with its own qualities and specific sense organs. With few exceptions, pain is aroused in all tissues and organs of the body. For the present, however, we shall limit the discussion to cutaneous pain.

Stimulation. Cutaneous pain is aroused by various classes of stimuli: mechanical (sharp as well as dull points), thermal (extremes of physical heat), electrical and chemical. Any stimulus, in short, that is intense enough to injure the free nerve endings in the skin will arouse pain.

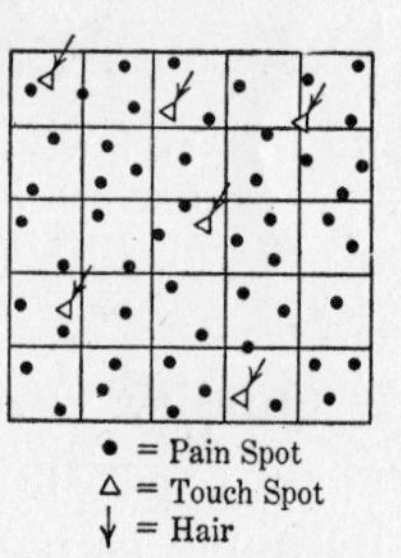

FIG. 122. MAP OF PAIN AND PRESSURE SPOTS AND OF HAIRS. ¼ sq. cm. on volar side of forearm. After Strughold.

The *pain spots* are much more numerous than the pressure spots. In Fig. 122 the ratio is about 7 : 1. The distribution of the pain spots is haphazard and unrelated to that of the pressure spots or the hairs, whereas the frequency of distribution varies considerably in different parts of the body. A few regions are insensitive to pain, like the insides of the cheeks opposite the second lower molars; other areas vary widely in the number of pain spots found within them. Although their average number per square centimeter of body surface is estimated at about 175, this value is actually of little significance because the skin is everywhere sensitive to prick if the stimulus is strong enough. The evidence from the spots nevertheless indicates that the receptors for pain must be more numerous than the receptors for pressure.

The free nerve endings in the epidermis, shown in Fig. 123, are identified by most investigators as the *receptors* that function in the arousal of cutaneous pain. The evidence, though indirect, is fairly conclusive. The free endings are the only nerve structure in the epidermis; and they alone are found in sufficient numbers to account for the number of pain spots. They are, moreover, the only structures found in areas which are exclusively sensitive to pain—*e.g.,* the cornea—and they are absent from areas that are completely insensitive to pain—*e.g.,* the mucous membrane of the cheeks. Further evidence for the correlation between pain and the free nerve endings is obtained from the use of local anesthetics. If, for example, an oleic acid solution of cocain, which acts only on the superficial nerve endings, is rubbed into the skin, only the sense of pain is lost, while sensitivity to pressure, to warmth and to cold remains unimpaired.

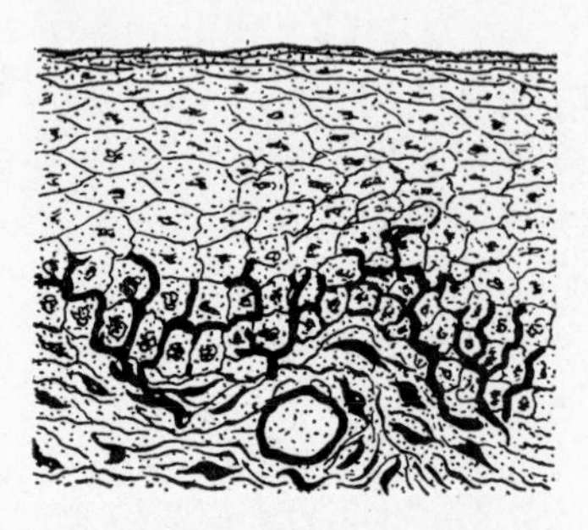

FIG. 123. FREE NERVE ENDINGS IN THE EPIDERMIS. After Kadanoff.

Quality. Language is particularly rich in terms descriptive of the experiences of pain: achy, beating, biting, boring, bright, burning, clear, cutting, dark, digging, dragging, drawing, dull, fluttering, gnawing, hard, heavy, itchy, nipping, palpitating, penetrating, piercing, pinching, pressing, pricking, quick, quivering, radiating, raking, savage, sharp, smarting, squeezing, stabbing, sticking, stinging, tearing, thrilling, throbbing, thrusting, tugging, twitching, ugly, vicious. Most of these terms, however, characterize (1) the temporal course of the experience—*e.g.,* palpitating, throbbing; (2) its spatial distribution—*e.g.,* penetrating, radiating; (3) its fusion or integration with pressure—*e.g.,* heavy, pressing; or (4) its affective coloring—*e.g.,* savage, ugly. Only a few of the terms are purely qualitative, *viz.,* achy, bright, clear, dull, itchy, pricking and quick.

Any of the qualities of pain may be either pleasant or unpleasant according to circumstances. The itch of a healing wound, the prick of spice upon the tongue or the clear pain of a loose tooth which a child wiggles and pries with its tongue is pleasant. In other situations the same qualities may be indifferent or unpleasant.

Time relations. The rise and fall of pain, from the application until after the removal of the stimulus, are slow and gradual. Although the times vary considerably, they tend, nevertheless, to be longer for pain than for any other sense. Instances illustrating the slow rise of pain are common in everyday life. If one stubs a toe, pressure is sensed appreciably earlier than pain; if one touches a burning hot object, pressure and temperature experiences come first before the pain. Experiments merely make these observations more precise. Cutaneous pain rises in from 0.03 to 1.00 sec. The disappearance of pain is usually even slower than its rise.

Recent experiments show that pain undergoes *adaptation.* If the stimulus is of unvarying intensity, complete adaptation can be reached. The painful stimuli of everyday life, however, are seldom constant. The time of adaptation varies considerably (from 6 sec. to about 12 min.) with the observer, with the nature of the stimulus (mechanical, thermal, etc.) and with the spot stimulated.

CUTANEOUS COLD AND WARMTH

Though cold and warmth are qualitatively as dissimilar as any two senses, we nevertheless consider them together here because both are aroused by thermal stimuli.

Stimulation. The direct stimulus for cold and warmth is a change in the temperature of the receptors and not the outside molecular and radiant energies known physically as heat. Thus, a given temperature may, according to circumstances, be cold, indifferent, warm or hot. Moreover, only a small range of the intensities of physical heat—that extending from about —10° to +70°C.—gives rise to temperature experiences.

Temperatures below and above this narrow range usually evoke only pain; those falling within it tend to evoke cold or warmth or nothing at all, accordingly as they affect the temperature of the skin and the heat flow which normally passes outward from it. As long as the outward flow of heat, which is maintained by the blood, is normal and constant, cold or warmth is not aroused—in other words, we are indifferent as regards temperature. If, however, the heat flow is increased and the temperature of the skin falls, cold is evoked; if the outward flow is decreased below the normal, or if it is reversed so that the flow is inward and the temperature of the receptor rises, warmth is evoked.

The temperature of the skin at the point of indifference is known as *physiological zero*. The value of this constant varies in different parts of the body. It also varies in the same part of the body at different times and with such factors as one's health, activities, surroundings and mental state. When a normal and healthy person is resting or moving quietly in a room at 20° to 22°C., physiological zero is about 37°C. under his tongue, 35° on the normally clothed parts of his body, 33° on his hands and face and about 26° on the earlobes in which the blood flows sluggishly. That the physiological zero varies markedly in different parts of the body is quickly demonstrated by grasping an earlobe between thumb and fingers. The lobe is cold to the fingers, and the fingers are warm to the lobe, although each region by itself is thermally neutral.

If the skin is touched with objects differing in specific heat and thermal conductivity (*e.g.*, wool, cotton, cork, wood, oil, silk, metal, glass) but having the same temperature—let us say that of the room (22°C.)—they are not neutral, like the air of the room. Some of them are warm (wool, cotton), others cold (metal, glass), whereas still others are first cool, then indifferent and then mildly warm (wood, oil, silk, cork). The reason wool is warm is that, although it conducts heat as poorly as air, it checks the flow of heat from the part of the skin covered, the result being that the temperature of the skin and of the underlying receptors rises. Metal, on the other hand, is cold because it conducts heat much better than air, and thus draws more heat from the skin, so that the temperature of the skin and of its receptors falls.

Cold spots, normally stimulated by temperatures below physiological zero, are also stimulated by certain temperatures above it. For example, though a cold spot, in a region of the skin whose physiological zero is 33°C., gives no response to temperatures ranging from 34° to 43°, to temperatures above about 43° it responds with a distinct and intense experience of cold. This response is called *paradoxical cold*, since it seems paradoxical that a warm object should arouse cold.

The *cold* and *warm spots* are found, with moderately strong stimuli, over practically the entire surface of the body. They differ greatly from each other, however, in number and distribution. The cold spots, which have a characteristic distribu-

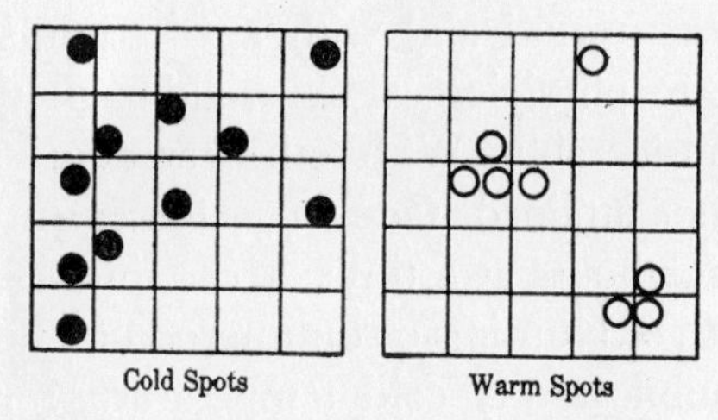

FIG. 124. SEPARATE MAPS, BY PUNCTIFORM THERMAL EXPLORATION, OF AN AREA ON THE UPPER ARM.
Area = 1 sq. cm.

tion shown in Fig. 124, are more or less uniformly scattered over the skin. The warm spots, on the contrary, vary considerably in number and distribution with the method of localization.

Quality. Besides cold and warmth a third quality should be added to our list. A unique quality resembling a stinging pressure, it is aroused by the simultaneous stimulation of cold and warm spots. It is easily demonstrated when the hand rests upon a series of parallel metal tubes and warm water is run through the even tubes and cold water through the odd tubes. Then one feels this new quality, mixed in with the warmth and cold. When a warm spot is stimulated with warmth and an adjacent cold spot with cold, one gets the new sensation alone. This quality has been called *heat*, because it is similar to the experience got from a warm areal stimulus that stimulates the warm spots normally and their adjacent cold spots paradoxically.

Time relations. Cold, like pressure, rises rapidly after the application of the stimulus and comes quickly to its full intensity; warmth, like pain, rises slowly and comes only gradually to full intensity. These latent periods, however, vary in different parts of the body; they are short where the skin is thin, and long where the skin is thick. The difference in the latent periods of cold and warmth is responsible for the momentary flash of cold when one passes one's hand rapidly through hot water or steps under a hot shower.

Complete *adaptation*, or thermal indifference, can be realized with punctiform stimuli and with areal stimuli having temperatures close to physiological zero, although the adaptation time varies considerably. With other areal stimuli complete adaptation is not attained. One may, for example, have cold hands or feet for hours at a time. A certain degree of adaptation in the sense of blunting or dulling occurs, however, rather rapidly. The unpleasantly cold temperature, for example, of the first plunge in a pool is quickly blunted if the swimmer persists; though it may never reach thermal indifference, it very soon becomes less intense and it may, as experience bears frequent witness, become pleasantly cool.

KINESTHESIS

The sensitive motor apparatus of the body—the muscles, tendons, ligaments, bones, cartilages and membranes of the joints—furnishes a mass of sensation which is called *kinesthesis*, because it forms the basis for the perception of bodily movement. It is also referred to as *proprioception*, and it provides the necessary afferent impulses which enable the organism to adjust its movements accurately (see pp. 227, 257f.). Since it is now known that kinesthesis derives from stimulation in *muscles*, *tendons* and *joints*, we shall take up these three sources successively.

Muscles. Mild stimuli, like weights and weak electrical currents, arouse muscular pressures characterized as dull, dead and diffuse, whereas strong stimuli, like heavy weights, strong electrical currents and penetration of sharp points, arouse muscular qualities called *dull pressure*, *dull pain* and *ache*.

The muscles are abundantly supplied with sensory nerves and receptors. Free nerve endings terminate between the muscle fibers, and muscle spindles (Fig. 125) lie within the connective tissue surrounding bundles of muscle fibers. It is probable, from what is known of the distribution of these structures, that the muscle spindles mediate dull pressure, whereas the free nerve endings, at different intensities of stimulation, mediate dull pain and ache.

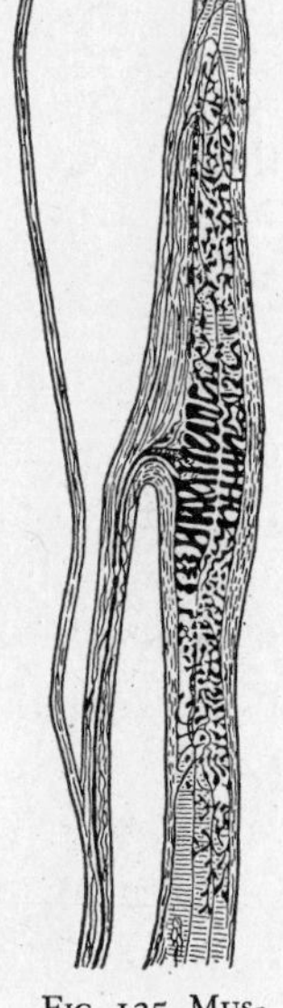

FIG. 125. MUSCLE SPINDLE. After Ruffini.

Tendons. The tendons cannot be stimulated independently. All we can do is to see what there is in kinesthesis that is not already attributed to the skin and the muscles. Thus we find *strain*, which, as the intensity of stimulation is increased, gives way first to *dull pain* and then to *ache*. These qualities may be observed, once they are identified, whenever we actively and vigorously exert ourselves (wrestling, lifting a heavy weight) or even better when we passively sustain a heavy weight.

Except at their junctions with the muscle, the tendons are sparsely supplied with receptors. Those which they have include free nerve endings and tendon spindles.

Joints. Movement of the elbow, knee and other joints ordinarily does not present any new quality. When, however, we use a joint that is rarely moved independently (*e.g.*, the first joint of the index finger), or when we move one in an unusual direction or manner (*e.g.*, the sidewise movement of the wrist with fingers extended), or when we increase the pressure upon the articular surfaces (*e.g.*, by moving a finger while it is strongly pressed into its socket), a soft, smooth pressure quality is evoked. This is called *smooth pressure* to distinguish it from the other qualities of pressure.

Smooth pressure is particularly clear when the fingers are placed in the position shown in Fig. 126. The forefinger is clinched, the other fingers extended and the first joint of the forefinger, which is pendant, is moved slowly back and forth. The pressure is clearest when the observer has his eyes closed and the movement is passive—when, in other words, the finger is manipulated by another person. Qualities from muscles are then entirely lacking, whereas those from the skin are minimal.

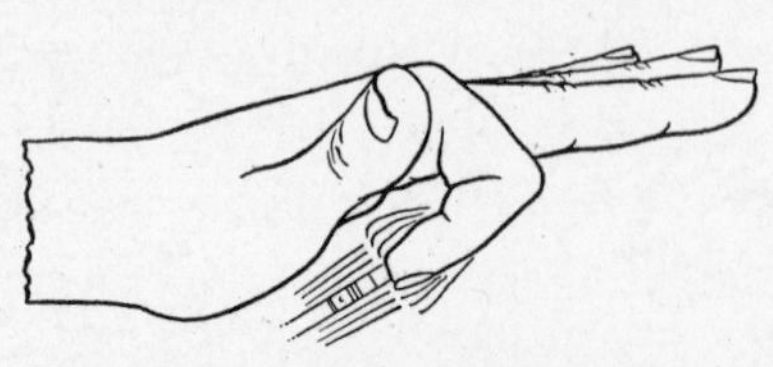

Fig. 126. Procedure for Eliciting the Quality of Smooth Pressure.

INTERNAL SENSIBILITY

Mucous membrane. When the alimentary tract and its orifices are explored by methods similar to those employed for the skin, no new qualities are found excepting, of course, taste and smell. The marginal zones of the orifices, which are highly sensitive, yield all the qualities with which we are familiar: pressure, pain, cold and warmth. Some cavities are insensitive. Others, such as the buccal and nasal cavities, respond to stimulation, much like the skin.

Punctiform stimulation is not feasible for exploring the alimentary tract. Special methods and devices must be used: stomach tubes having electrical heating coils, elastic balloons or electrodes attached to their inserted ends.

Except for the intestines, which cannot be reached experimentally, the entire alimentary tract yields pressure when its walls are distended by the inflated balloon; increased distention gives pain. Pain is also evoked by extremes of temperature or in some places by certain chemical stimuli.

The esophagus and the stomach yield also diffuse and faint experiences of cold, warmth and heat, which presumably derive from the mucous membrane. Hunger, thirst and nausea cannot be obtained through experimental stimulation of the alimentary tract; they are not simple qualities, but, as we have seen (pp. 505f.), complex perceptual experiences.

Internal organs. Our knowledge of the nature and origin of the experiences from the internal organs and tissues and of the part they play in our behavior and conscious life is meager, because of the vague and indefinite character of the experiences themselves, and because of the inaccessibility of the tissues involved. What we know of them comes from various sources—surgery, physiology, pathology, psychology—and much of it is conflicting as well as fragmentary and incomplete.

Evidence from surgery is the most precise—and probably the most misleading. When the abdominal or thoracic cavities are opened under local anesthetics, which affect only the skin and the underlying connective tissue, it is found that the internal organs—lungs, heart, esophagus, stomach, intestines, liver, kidney, etc.—are apparently insensitive. They may be burned, cooled, cut, crushed, torn, without yielding experience of any kind. The serous membranes, on the contrary—peritoneum, pericardium, pleura—yield pain; and the peritoneum and diaphragm seem also to respond with pressure.

The insensitivity of the internal organs appears from other points of view, however, to be an artifact. All the internal organs are abundantly supplied with afferent nerves. There is no *a priori* reason for questioning their sensitivity. Their failure to respond to such stimuli as the knife, the forceps, the cautery, may be due, not to their normal lack of sensitivity, but to the effects of the anesthetic, of the exposure or of the surgical shock or to the ineffectiveness of external attack. It seems reasonable, moreover, to suppose that the stimuli most capable of exciting these afferent nerves should be the natural processes inherent in the organs.

SENSIBILITY OF THE SEMICIRCULAR CANALS

The labyrinth of each internal ear is made up of three parts: (1) the cochlea with its organ of Corti (see pp. 568-570), (2) the semicircular canals with their cristae and (3) the saccule and utricle of the vestibule with their maculae (see Fig. 99, p. 568). We are now concerned only with the second. These are the most inaccessible tissues and organs that we have thus far considered.

Stimulation. For the non-acoustical organs of the labyrinth the normal stimulus is a change in the position of the head or a change in the acceleration or direction of the movement of the head, either circular or rectilinear. Circular movement probably affects the *cristae* of the *semicircular canals* (see below); rectilinear movement and change in position of the head probably act upon the *vestibular* organs—the *maculae* of the *utricle* and *saccule* (Fig. 99).

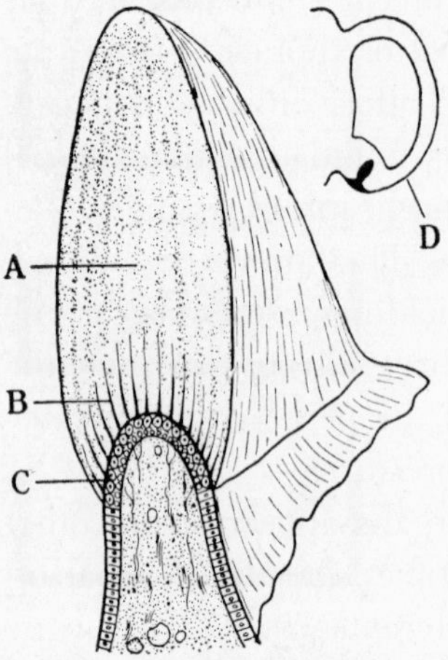

FIG. 127. CROSS SECTION OF CRISTA.

A = gelatinous mass (cupula). *B* = hair tuft. *C* = hair cell. *D* = diagram showing position of crista in ampulla of semicircular canals. Adapted from Schaffer.

The receptors in the *semicircular canals* may also be stimulated directly in a number of other ways: (*a*) electrically, by passing current through the mastoid regions of the head; (*b*) thermally, by irrigating the external ear with hot or cold water. When the eardrum is missing, it is possible to induce stimulation (*c*) mechanically by pressing or pricking the canals with dull or sharp points and (*d*) chemically by applying certain drugs to them. They, or the nerve centers upon which they act, may be stimulated (*e*) indirectly or reflexly by excitations from the eyes and stomach, and by the indirect action of drugs. This indirect effect may result when one is looking down from great heights, or looking at the rotating walls of a room (the 'haunted swing' of many amusement parks) or looking at stationary walls while one is himself rotating. Again, an upset stomach—as in extreme nausea—or the action of certain drugs, like alcohol, may have the same effect.

The semicircular canals, three in each ear, lie approximately at right angles to one another in the three planes of space. At one end of every canal there is a swelling, an *ampulla*, containing a transverse membrane called the *crista* (Fig. 127). This membrane is the functional organ of this part of the inner ear. It is a high, narrow, rounded prominence in the ampulla. The membrane contains hair cells, the hair tufts of which are imbedded in a gelatinous mass called the *cupula.*

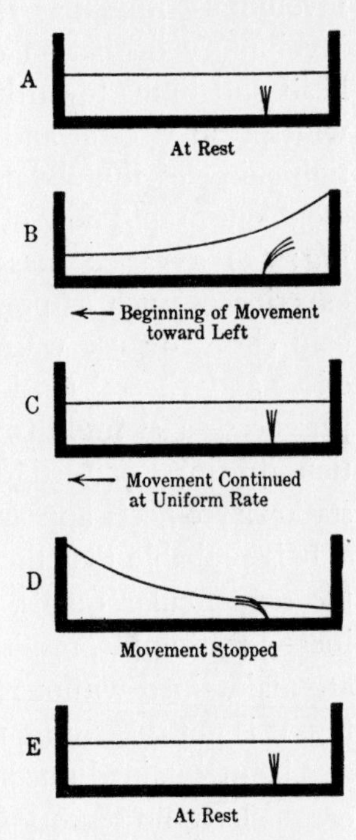

Fig. 128. Diagram Illustrating the Hydrodynamical Principles of the Semicircular Canals.

According to the generally accepted theory, the nerve endings in the ampullae are stimulated hydromechanically by the flow or pressure of the endolymph which fills the semicircular canals. When the head is turned, the endolymph, because of its inertia, does not immediately follow the walls of the canals. It lags behind, and the amount of the lag or the force exerted upon the cupula depends upon the rate of change in the speed of the stimulus. The physical principles involved are illustrated in Fig. 128, in which a pan, water and a tuft of hairs are substituted for a canal, endolymph and cupula. When the system is at rest, as at *A*, the water and hair tuft are at equilibrium. If now the pan is moved to the left, as at *B*, the water will at first lag behind and bend the hair tuft toward the right. But then, if the movement is continuous and regular, it will gradually take up the movement, with the result that water and hair tuft will return to an equilibrium, as at *C*. If a change is made in the rate of movement, or if the movement is suddenly interrupted, as at *D*, the water will rush forward, because of its inertia, and incline the tuft of hairs to the left. In either case, whether the rate is changed or the movement stopped, equilibrium will soon again be established, as at *E*.

Effects of stimulation. The following effects are obtained from the stimulation of the semicircular canals: (1) involuntary muscular reactions, such as nystagmus (a rapid, involuntary oscillation of the eyes), and adjustments of the head and limbs toward the maintenance of equilibrium; (2) widespread visceral and autonomic changes, among them the tightening of the abdominal walls, reversed peristalsis in the esophagus, rapid flow of saliva, excessive perspiring and blushing; (3) a varied mass of kinesthetic, cutaneous and other experiences, such as pressures around the neck, face and eyes, cold chills, diffuse warmths, bad tastes, hints of disagreeable odors and visceral tensions; and (4) numerous perceptual experiences—a swimming sensation, perceptions of bodily rotation, dizziness or vertigo, nausea and visual illusions in which stationary objects appear to move and float in space.

It is probable that there are no unique sensory qualities for the semicircular canals. Other highly organized motor activities—for example, respiration and the pulsations of the heart—are maintained without the arousal of specific conscious qualities. It is not surprising, therefore, that bodily equilibrium may also be maintained unconsciously. The point of view that these organs have no sensory function but are merely afferent reflex mechanisms is strengthened by the fact that the vestibular nerve, which carries their impulses, has no path to the cerebral cortex. Some of its central branches run to the vestibular nuclei in the medulla, from which there is no known tract to the thalamus; others go without interruption to the cerebellum.

The effects of stimulation of the semicircular canals appear with positive or negative changes in the *acceleration* of rotation of the head and disappear when the speed remains *constant*.

Prolonged stimulation of the semicircular canals leads slowly, or not at all, to complete *adaptation*. What is a mere matter of seconds in the skin is at least a matter of minutes or hours in the canals. Some people become adapted to the motion and churning of a boat, for example, in a short time; others may 'feel' the effects for as long a time as they are on the boat, and still others for hours afterward.

Periodic stimulation, on the other hand, may radically alter the experiences aroused by the semicircular canals. The intensity and complexity of the responses associated with the canals may be reduced and the various components gradually drop out. Thus people whose occupations or professions occasion repeated stimulation of the canals—sailors, dancers, whirling dervishes, acrobats and stunt flyers—do not experience the effects which are normal to other persons.

The *after-effects* of stimulation of the canals are as complex and varied as the primary effects. If the canals are stimulated by way of rotation, for example, almost all the phenomena aroused continue unabated after the speed of rotation is decreased or the rotation is stopped. The most striking of these phenomena is the illusion of *reversed rotation*. When the objective movement is slowed or stopped, the observer perceives himself to be spinning around in the opposite direction. If the rotation or the swimming sensation circles clockwise during the objective movement, it will appear to circle counterclockwise when the speed of rotation is diminished. This phenomenon has been called the negative after-sensation of movement, but it is clear that it is a perception that depends directly upon stimulation in the normal manner. It results from a change in the acceleration of the objective movement, the kind of change that always affects the receptors in the canals.

REFERENCES

Smell and Taste

1. CROZIER, W. J. Chemoreception. *A handbook of general experimental psychology.* Worcester, Mass.: Clark University Press, 1934. Pp. 987-1036.
2. PARKER, G. H. *Smell, taste, and allied senses in the vertebrates.* Philadelphia: J. B. Lippincott, 1922.
3. VON SKRAMLIK, E. *Handbuch der Physiologie der niederen Sinne: Die Physiologie des Geruchs- und Geschmackssinnes.* Berlin: W. Junk, 1926.

Somesthesis

4. CANNON, W. B. Hunger and thirst. *A handbook of general experimental psychology.* Worcester, Mass.: Clark University Press, 1934. Pp. 247-263.
5. DUSSER DE BARENNE, J. G. The labyrinthine and postural mechanisms. *A handbook of general experimental psychology.* Worcester, Mass.: Clark University Press, 1934. Pp. 204-246.
6. LUCIANI, L. *Human physiology.* London: Macmillan, 1917. Vol. 4. Cutaneous sensibility, pp. 1-55; Sensibility of the internal organs, pp. 57-125.
7. NAFE, J. P. The pressure, pain and temperature senses. *A handbook of general experimental psychology.* Worcester, Mass.: Clark University Press, 1934. Pp. 1037-1087.

See also BORING, LANGFELD and WELD, *Psychology: a factual textbook,* 1935, 140-187, where the exposition is less condensed.

Chapter 20

THE NATURE OF MAN

Da capo. That is the sign that should stand here at the end of this book, as at the end of a passage of music. In Chapter 1 a theme was announced which has since been developed and extended. Let the reader now return to the book's beginning, and end with a recapitulation of that theme. As a preface Chapter 1 was merely a promise about the nature of psychology. Now, as a summary, its phrases will quicken with new and richer meanings. The reader will know at last what was meant by that preliminary sketch of psychology as a description of man adjusting himself to his environment and his environment to himself. In returning to Chapter 1 he will build out of his own new knowledge at once a broader and a more discerning comprehension of that initial statement. So now let him repeat.

INDEX